Our
MODERN BANKING
and
MONETARY SYSTEM

by

ROLLIN G. THOMAS
Professor of Economics
Purdue University

THIRD EDITION

16735

Englewood Cliffs, N. J.
PRENTICE-HALL, INC.
1957

PRENTICE-HALL ECONOMICS SERIES

PRINTED IN THE UNITED STATES OF AMERICA

64404

To
The Memory of My
MOTHER AND FATHER

Preface

In our changing world much that is written about economic institutions and problems has a way of becoming outmoded all too quickly. Institutional structures and practices change constantly and new problems emerge to supplant them or to take their places beside the old. From time to time, therefore, a book on banking and monetary systems must be reexamined and its contents reappraised.

This third edition, like its predecessors, is designed to achieve two fundamental purposes: First, to describe the nature and operations of our money and banking systems; second, to apply modern monetary and banking theory to present-day domestic and international problems. Although the principal objectives have not changed, the contents have been altered appreciably. A considerable amount of material appearing in earlier editions, but no longer of vital importance in understanding today's problems, has been eliminated. Furthermore, by combining and relocating chapters, some previous duplication has been avoided and, it is hoped, a more effective arrangement achieved. Finally, the chapters dealing with the determinants of the supply of money and the demand for money, and those on the relationships existing among money, the level of income, prices, and employment have been rewritten. This rewriting was done to eliminate outmoded doctrine and to retain only the analysis needed to deal with current monetary problems, especially those associated with attempts to use monetary and fiscal policy to promote economic stability and growth. All this has had the incidental effect of reducing the book to more manageable proportions.

The formidable size of the field of money and banking creates a serious problem of selection and organization. The division of the book into nine major parts may aid in the choice of materials that best satisfy the particular aims of the user.

Parts I to IV provide the institutional background for the study of central bank and monetary theory and the problems related to them. They are designed to accomplish three things: First, to describe the nature of money, the various monetary standards with their good and bad features, and the emergence of our present system; second, to show the place of commercial banks and their money-creating powers in a free economy through a study of how banks acquire and protect deposits, collect checks, maintain reserves, and carry on their loan and investment operations; third, to show the development of our banking system, including the Federal Reserve Banks, and provide an opportunity to compare it with the systems of Canada and England.

Parts V and VI apply present-day monetary theory to the problem of explaining the supply of money and its demand, and the resulting effect upon the level of income, output, and prices. In so doing, they explore the reasons for inequality of planned saving and planned investment, the multiplying effects of such inequality upon income, and the possibility of influencing the income flow through monetary policy.

Part VII explores the matter of appropriate goals of policy and the significance of both central bank monetary policy and government fiscal policy in the pursuit of such goals.

Part VIII deals with the problems of foreign exchange rates and international price relationships as they affect the maintenance of balance-of-payments equilibrium both in a free exchange market and under exchange controls.

Part IX examines the problems of the restoration of domestic stability and international multilateral trade with currency convertibility after the upheavals arising from war.

A large part of the material that appears in this book is drawn from the body of common knowledge in the field of money and banking, and its origin cannot be credited to any particular source. However, in some instances material has been quoted or reproduced from other publications. My debt to the publishers of such material for their generous permission to reprint it in the present volume is gratefully acknowledged.

ROLLIN G. THOMAS

Contents

V

PRICE CHANGES AND THE DETERMINANTS OF THE
VOLUME OF MONEY

VI

THE DEMAND FOR MONEY, INCOME, THE PRICE LEVEL

VII

APPLICATIONS OF MONETARY AND FISCAL POLICY

VIII

INTERNATIONAL MONETARY RELATIONSHIPS

IX
POSTWAR MONETARY PROBLEMS

I____

MONEY AND MONETARY SYSTEMS

The Role of Money in Our Economic System

Money has always been recognized as an essential tool in a specialized economic society. Nevertheless, in the past, economists often relegated it to a secondary place in their discussions. To be sure, money's humble and basic functions, that of providing a standard of value and a medium of exchange, were noted, and economists regularly paid their respects to money's sterling if pedestrian virtues before they moved on to the more absorbing questions of equilibrium price and income distribution. Consequently their concern with money was limited mainly to an examination of the necessary characteristics of good money and the forces operating to determine its purchasing power.

The real significance of money in the modern world. A brief look at the world of today indicates clearly that money can no longer be thought of as the drab, utilitarian handmaiden of economic society. Instead it stands forth as a kind of genie with tremendous, all-pervading powers over economic good and evil. By newspaper and radio we are constantly reminded of monetary problems. Inflation and deflation, currency stabilization and reform demand our attention. One cannot escape some knowledge of the intimate relationship between economic recovery in the postwar world and the "dollar shortage" of Britain and Western Europe. The fate of governments can be seen hanging in the balance as they struggle for a statisfactory solution to their acute monetary problems.

What is to be the future of gold in the world's monetary affairs? Can we expect an eventual return to an international gold standard?

Ought we to work toward such a goal or is gold outmoded? Ought the American dollar be made freely convertible into gold coin for everyone to see, hold, and use as he sees fit? Have we found a way to harmonize public debt management with sound monetary policy? These questions and many others arising in the postwar world have their roots in the powerful influence of money on the behavior of economic society. Small wonder that money and its problems have become a central theme in economic discussions! Nothing is more evident than the need for a sound knowledge of money if one is to understand the world in which we live.

One may well ask why money and monetary problems play such a vital part and wield such power in the economic affairs of mankind. The answer is found in the dynamic, restless, changing nature of economic society. The rate of economic activity ebbs and flows, old commodities disappear and are replaced by new, a growing population must be absorbed, and new resources and inventions must be exploited. Moreover, the fighting and financing of wars creates both desolation and economic maladjustments. Society's adaptation to these changes involves actions based largely on decisions and calculations made in monetary terms, actions accompanied by and largely accomplished by monetary expenditures. The movements of the business cycle are closely bound up with monetary phenomena. Monetary changes both contribute to and are influenced by changes in the level of business and employment. Most plans for reducing the severity of cyclical fluctuations involve attempts to influence and control the money supply and the volume of money spending.

The Meaning of Money

Before attacking the complex monetary problems of a modern society it is best to arm oneself with a thorough understanding of the fundamental nature of money and its functions, and the general framework of the monetary system, which includes, as an integral part, the banking system. Only then is one equipped with the essential tools for attacking contemporary monetary problems. Therefore, we necessarily must apply ourselves to the mastery of a good many undramatic details concerned with our money and banking system. To understand the requirements of good money one must first discover the meaning of the term.

What is money? Money is something that is readily and generally accepted by the public in payment for the sale of goods, services, and other valuable assets, and for the payment of debts. This ready and general acceptability may arise from legal tender laws and from convenience and habit of use. Necessarily one's willingness to accept money in exchange for other valuable assets arises essentially from confidence that it will in turn be readily accepted by others. The stock of such money held by the public in immediately spendable form constitutes the money supply and includes the following types:

1. Government issues of currency and coin.
2. Bank note currency issues.
3. Checking accounts or "deposit currency."

Such money, held by the general public, is regularly used for purchases and sales and for paying debts. Government currency issues and bank note currency are now clothed with legal tender powers and so bear the blessing of government recognition of their status as effective money. Checking accounts in banks are not endowed with the advantages of legal tender powers. Consequently they acquire general acceptance solely from their convenience and the confidence in the validity and collectibility of the checks through which claims to checking accounts are transferred from one holder to another. The fact that checking account currency can be used only by persons able to give satisfactory evidence of the collectibility of the issued checks does not prevent it from being counted as money. Actually many more business transactions are settled by the issue of checks against bank demand deposits than by the payment of paper currency and coin.

The money supply, as we have used the term, does not include gold, currency, coin, or checking accounts held by the banks themselves as reserves against their liabilities. Such holdings are not held by the general public and consequently are not part of the public's supply of money. Likewise, currency, coin, and checking account deposits held by the Federal Government are not a part of the public's money supply.

Other asset holdings — "near money." All of the money supply is held by someone. Between exchanges it acts as a store of value for its holders. Being immediately spendable, money is the most liquid of all assets that a person can hold. Of course, money is but one of many forms in which a person can store up values. He can hold land, merchandise, corporate stocks, and various kinds of corporate bonds. He also may hold savings bonds, savings and loan company shares, and savings deposits in banks. One thing, however, distinguishes these other forms of assets from a person's holdings of money. They must normally be converted into money before they can be freely exchanged for other things. Clearly some of these assets are more easily converted into spendable money than are others. Land, merchandise, and most securities must be sold, and, when the markets are weak, their liquidity may sometimes be relatively poor. In contrast, savings deposits (and other time deposits) of banks may be converted into money within a relatively short time. Likewise, one may, in good times, readily "cash" one's savings and loan shares, and United States Savings Bonds, outstanding 60 days, will be redeemed by the Treasury on demand. Highly liquid assets such as these are sometimes called *near money* because they are readily convertible into money without loss. In many respects they relieve the burden from the money supply in that they help to satisfy some of the liquidity requirements of the public.

The Functions of Money

Money is commonly said to perform a number of different functions. These functions, though separated for purposes of classification and consideration, are intimately interrelated. They include:

1. Money as a standard of value.
2. Money as a medium of exchange.
3. Money as a store of value.
4. Money as a standard of deferred payment.

Money as a standard of value. In an exchange society, some standard is needed by which things to be exchanged may be evaluated. The pricing of things in terms of some common denominator can hardly be avoided if accurate and easy comparison of values is to be made. In the United States the standard of value is the dollar.

Money is of maximum usefulness as a standard for comparing values when its own value is reasonably stable in terms of the general mass of things to be exchanged. We are quite properly accustomed to think of the standard units of weights and measures as constant. It is easy to fall into the error of looking upon our standard of value as constant also. But the lack of stability in our standard of value cannot escape our notice when we observe the changes that occur in the general level of prices. For example, the 38 per cent fall in average wholesale prices between 1929 and February 1933 involved a rise in the purchasing power of the dollar of about 60 per cent. On the other hand, when wholesale prices rose by more than 129 per cent between 1939 and 1951 the dollar's buying power over commodities at wholesale fell about 56 per cent.

It sometimes happens that money may act as the standard of value without actually becoming the medium of exchange. In primitive societies, for example, cattle were sometimes used as a standard of value but were not necessarily used as a medium of exchange. Among some American Indians the beaver skin was the unit of value and was the basis for fixing the exchange ratio between goods exchanged on a barter basis.[1] In the use of modern currencies, too, the money unit frequently does not enter directly into certain exchange transactions. This fact is true not only in the barter transactions in which farmers' wives trade eggs for groceries at the local store, and in credit transactions such as those in which the share-cropper purchases supplies and later pays in crops, but also in the elaborate clearing transactions on the security exchanges where only small residual amounts are settled in cash. Nevertheless it is difficult, in a modern money-using economy, to divorce money as the standard of value from money as the medium of exchange. Both must be described in terms of the legal monetary unit, that is, the dollar, the pound, the franc, the mark, and so forth. The monetary unit is the country's standard of value. But until it is embodied in the form of spendable money which is measured against goods in the market place, the standard of value has little meaning. This fact is readily seen in the case of inconvertible paper currencies where the only value that money can have is established by its being offered in exchange for goods and services.[2]

Money as the medium of exchange. Acting as a medium of

[1] Cf. Laughlin, J. L., *New Exposition of Money, Credit, and Prices,* Vol. I, University of Chicago Press, 1931, pp. 12-14.

[2] When a currency is convertible into a given quantity of gold, the gold unit is sometimes looked upon as the standard of value. This practice, however, appears to confuse the *standard monetary unit,* gold, with the standard of value which is the monetary unit in any form. Thus, the *dollar* is our standard of value and has continued to be so regardless of its convertibility status since 1932. But the *standard monetary unit* in 1932 was the gold dollar weighing 25.8 grains, nine-tenths fine. From April 1933 until January 1934 it was inconvertible. Since January 1934 it has been convertible for industrial and export purposes into 15 5/21 grains of nine-tenths fine gold.

exhange is a second function of money. It is not enough that there be a basis for comparing the value of things to be exchanged. If the troublesome problem of the "double coincidence of wants" is to be avoided, some readily acceptable thing must be available as a go-between to bring about a smooth and effective exchange of goods. Some form of money, therefore, must be called into use to act as the intermediary. The media of exchange may include both standard money itself and its various paper and credit substitutes.

The importance of money as a medium of exchange involves much more than conveniently overcoming the awkwardness of barter. The impact of money upon the economic world is vastly greater than this. Money incomes become a primary consideration in the lives of men. The public's vast money income, which may be spent first one way and then another to suit the buyers' fancies, enables consumers to record their choices in the market and exert a powerful influence on the character of goods produced and the success or decline of individual firms and industries. Without money, consumers of goods obviously would find shifting from one type of goods to another much more difficult, if indeed it would be possible at all to any substantial extent. This fact has a profound effect upon the behavior of our dynamic industrial society. Moreover, not only are incomes and expenditures calculated in terms of money but also most business calculations are reduced to monetary terms.

To satisfy the requirements for a good medium of exchange money must above all be generally acceptable to the public. Such acceptability is enhanced by ease of identification, convenience in handling, and legal tender qualities endowed by law. Custom or habit of use of a given form of money also strongly supports its acceptability. Finally, if money is to be readily taken in exchange for other things, it must be free from the threat of complete collapse in purchasing power. The precious metals, silver and gold, and money convertible into them, historically have made up a large part of the acceptable money supply. Consequently, some have believed that only "commodity money" of this kind can actually become acceptable to the public. But modern experience with inconvertible paper currencies indicates that such money, properly limited in supply, can become entirely acceptable to the public within the country of its issue. To be sure, it is not difficult to cite examples of over-issued paper currencies that so collapsed in value that they were refused by the public, who turned to barter instead.

For a money to be a truly satisfactory medium of exchange more is needed than general acceptability alone. In addition it ought to possess a high degree of stability in purchasing power. Money may be sufficiently stable in value to retain its general acceptance by the public and yet be unstable enough to make it perform badly as a medium of exchange. Let us see why this is so. Whenever money is increasing in value, or prices are falling, the public is encouraged to hoard its money and postpone expenditures. The result is a decline in output and employment and a still further decline in prices. Thus, falling prices may tend, in themselves, to develop into a cumulative downward movement of employment and prices. On the other hand, when money is losing value, or prices are rising, the public may hasten its spending to escape rising prices. As a result of such an increased rate of spending the upswing in prices may become cumulative and create additional inflationary pressure upon the economy.

We have all had the experience of spending our money hastily (and perhaps unwisely) to escape rising prices, and of postponing purchases in anticipation of lower prices. Every income receiver, whether laborer, a salaried worker, a capitalist, or an active business enterprise, has need for money as a store of value. This need exists primarily because of the impossibility of synchronizing exactly all income and expenditure. For the economic system to operate properly, money should adequately perform this function of storing up values. This means that money should have sufficient stability of value to permit its being held without either enriching or impoverishing its holders in the process. Only in such a case is money able to perform its work as the medium of exchange without in so doing inducing changes in economic activity.

Money as a store of value. Because of the importance of hoarding and dishoarding of cash as a source of economic instability, the use of money as a *store of value* needs special emphasis. We have already seen how changes in the value of money affects its efficiency as a medium of exchange by inducing the public to change the rate of spending money. But the matter is broader than this. Whenever profit prospects decline, businessmen tend to reduce their rate of investment in capital goods, and, in some cases, disinvest by converting inventories into cash. Moreover, savers may conclude that the risks of investing in securities have so increased that it is wiser, for the time being, to keep savings in cash form. Thus, a decline in business profit prospects may cause an increased accumulation of cash hoards in the hands of current savers and businessmen, an evidence of an increase in the public's "liquidity preferences" (desire for liquid cash assets rather than securities and capital goods). In other words, the demand for money as a *store of value* has risen.

Because of the changes in the public's desire for holding cash, a good monetary system should accommodate itself to these changing demands. Particularly it should be capable of expanding the money supply sufficiently in bad times to meet the increased demand for cash hoards without drawing the life blood out of the economic system. Actually, however, our money supply, largely created out of bank credit, tends to move in just the opposite direction. When business is poor and cash hoarding is increasing, bank credit tends to decline, and with it the supply of money. Plans for correcting this difficulty loom large in some programs for monetary reform.

Money as the standard of deferred payments. A fourth basic function of money, closely related to the three previously mentioned, is that of acting as a standard or unit of account for contractual credit transactions. Purchases of goods in modern economic society are commonly made with the use of credit, extended either directly by the seller or indirectly by the loan of money. Payment must eventually involve the use of money. To use a common phrase, money is the "standard of deferred payment." Not only credit transactions but all contracts involving future payments are framed in terms of money. Stability of value in terms of other economic goods is also required for the proper fulfillment of this monetary function. In truth, money's function as a standard of deferred payments provides a more exacting demand for stability of value than that arising from its other functions. For example, to behave properly as a medium of exchange, money needs sufficient stability of purchasing power to offer no obvious short-run inducements to postpone or to hasten normal money expenditures. But even very moderate changes in the value of money over long periods of time must be prevented if money is to meet the test of a good standard of deferred payments, for mild instability in the value of money over long periods leads to unjust enrichment and impoverishment of debtors and creditors.

Economic Disturbances Arising from the Use of Money

The upswings and downswings in economic activity involve changes in the amount of money expenditures. Depression and unemployment arise from the failure of money expenditure to equal the costs of current output as represented by current money incomes. Expansion and booms arise from money expenditures in excess of the pre-existing level of money incomes. Such shifts in expenditures can only come about as a result of the use of money. This may readily be understood by contrasting the behavior of a money-using economy with that of one in which exchange is on the basis of barter.

Under a simple barter system, however inconvenient, exchange of goods for goods would be directly under the control of specialized producers concerned. Unless a producer were willing to extend credit or make a gift, parting with his goods by barter would require that he take another's goods in return. Only a change in the traders' desires for each other's goods would interfere with the normal exchange process. Under such circumstances one may truly say that goods are exchanged for goods and, therefore, the production of goods by one person creates a demand for other goods.

A fall in expenditure and the use of money. But as we have seen, the situation is quite different when money is in use. When goods and services are exchanged for money, the money may be held until a suitable object of expenditure appears. This in itself need cause no trouble in the normal process of exchanging goods and services so long as no extraordinary reason appears for postponing the spending process. But at times these extraordinary reasons for holding money do appear, with disturbing results to the functioning of the economic system. For instance, some who receive money income normally devote a substantial part of that income to the purchase of capital goods or claims to capital goods in the form of securities. This is true both of private investors and of corporations which withhold income from stockholders for direct reinvestment in the firm. But let circumstances arise which reduce the apparent desirability of purchasing capital goods out of current income and there may result a drastic reduction in money spent.

Closely related to this postponement of investment of savings in capital goods is the actual disinvestment which occurs once prices begin to fall and profit prospects dim. As goods are sold, business firms may postpone the replenishment of inventories and replacement of depreciated equipment. The buyers of durable consumers' goods also readily postpone purchases whenever prices and employment prospects worsen. The paralyzing effect of such cash hoarding upon industry and employment is readily observed during periods of business depression. As we shall see later, the depressing effect of cash hoarding upon income and employment may sometimes be worsened by the reduction in the quantity of money brought about when banks require borrowers to repay their loans.

Increases in expenditures and the use of money. The use of money is likewise associated with increases in expenditures which induce an upward change in income, employment, and prices. Unlike the trader operating under barter, buyers in a money economy are not limited in their expenditures to the income arising out of current output. Instead they may draw upon both old cash hoards and upon an expanded quantity of money created by credit extended by commercial banks.

The problem raised by the failure of the volume of money to correspond to the need for it. The effective operation of a money economy may be impaired because there is not the "right" quantity of money. In general, the right quantity of money is that which fits neatly into the monetary job at hand and encourages sound economic growth and progress. Unfortunately there is no easy and simple test of such a money supply. One test, commonly suggested, is a quantity of money that insures a stable price level. Another is a money supply that promotes full employment. These two suggested goals are not necessarily in entire harmony.

Regardless of the test selected for determining the right money supply, the chances are strong that no actual money system will satisfy the requirements. For example, gold standard countries in the past were constantly exposed to the possibility of a rise or fall in the world price level due to the failure of the gold supply to increase at the appropriate rate corresponding to the growth of monetary requirements. Thus, a lagging gold supply tended to induce long-run falling prices, while an excessive supply of gold promoted rising price levels. The enthusiasm for managed paper currencies so often expressed since 1933 arises from the recognition of the difficulty of managing the gold standard.

The problem of having the "right" supply of money is further complicated by the fact that in monetary systems such as ours the media of exchange consist largely of bank notes and bank deposits subject to check. Such forms of money are at times subject to substantial short-run variations in volume, arising from changes in the willingness and ability of banks to extend credit by expanding loans and investments, and from changes in the desire and ability of businessmen, other individuals, and government agencies to borrow. The price levels of both gold standard and managed paper standard countries are exposed to the varying influences that determine the quantity of bank credit.

Some economic effects of windfall gains and losses arising from changing price levels. Some of the evil effects of changing price levels arise from the tendency for falling prices to cause windfall business losses and a shrinkage in the volume of spending for durable goods. The depressing effect of falling prices upon business activity is accentuated by the stickiness of some production costs (wages, interest payments, and so forth) which encourages businessmen to reduce output whenever possible rather than to continue to operate at lower prices.[3]

Rising prices likewise bring disturbances. Profits tend to become excessive when prices are rising and thus create an unreal but glowing sense of prosperity in the minds of businessmen. This optimism occurs largely because of the stickiness of wage and interest costs, which lag behind commodity prices on the upswing as well as on the downswing. The resulting windfall profits enjoyed by business are a temptation to overconfidence. Poor managers, their errors concealed by the profits of rising prices, gain and retain control over a large number of business enterprises and prove a source of difficulty later on when their wholesale failures follow a reversal of the price trend. But even more important, from the standpoint of stable business, is the fact that windfall profits either deceive good businessmen in respect to future prospects, or tempt them beyond their strength of resistance to expand the scale of their operations in order to obtain a lion's share of profits. Thus the

---

[3] This fact is especially true when competition is limited by the use of brands or by the existence of a few large-scale producers in the field.

competitive spirit, bolstered by the optimism from windfall profits, tends to lead to a rate of expansion of capital equipment greater than that called for by basic economic conditions and greater than can be continuously maintained. The inevitable reversal that follows such an excessive rate of expansion is an important cause of depression. This conclusion must not be taken to mean that money is the root of all cyclical evil in our economic world. But it cannot be denied that monetary phenomena in the form of changing prices not only permit and accompany cyclical disturbances but also to a considerable degree contribute to them. Historically speaking, the growth of recurrent periods of prosperity and depression parallels the growth in importance of the use of money.

Finally, changes in the price level cause serious shifts in the distribution of income. Rising prices impoverish persons with fixed incomes. At the same time, debtors find their burdens lightened while business profits expand because of "sticky" costs of production. Falling prices, on the other hand, benefit the receivers of fixed incomes, whereas debtors and businessmen tend to be injured.

The disturbances in the flow and distribution of the national income arising from changing price levels indicate the importance of minimizing such price level changes. They suggest the need to avoid, so far as possible, monetary changes that generate and contribute to movements of the price level. They also suggest the importance of using monetary controls to counteract price level movements that originate from nonmonetary cyclical forces.

Questions for Study

1. The specific monetary problems that command public attention vary from time to time. Name some of the most urgent monetary questions of the present time.

2. Why are economic changes closely associated with changes in money expenditures?

3. What is money? What makes up the money supply held by the public?

4. What assets can a person hold that may be called "near money"? In what ways are these assets similar to money? In what ways do they differ?

5. What is the standard of value in the United States?

6. "To be a good medium of exchange money must have general acceptability." What characteristics are needed for acceptability?

7. How is stability of value related to the proper functioning of money as a medium of exchange?

8. What is the meaning of "liquidity preferences"? When do they tend to increase? How should an ideal money react to changes in liquidity preferences?

9. Why is a money economy more exposed to fluctuations in output and employment than a barter economy would be?

10. What is the "right" quantity of money? How effectively is the right quantity of money provided by the gold standard? By bank created currency?

11. What are "windfall profits"? "Windfall losses"? How do they arise and how do they affect the functioning of the economy?

2

The Nature of Money

A brief examination of the origins of money will help one understand the nature of modern money systems and the reasons for their development. Modern capitalistic society developed under the benign influence of gold and silver money. But these metals did not acquire their monetary status suddenly or by providential intervention in the economic affairs of mankind. Rather, their use as money came as a gradual development, the roots of which extend back to antiquity. After 1931, most currencies of the world lost their convertibility into gold and became "nominal," or "fiat," paper currencies.

The Origins of Money

Because money plays such a vital part in economic processes, it seems certain that some use of money was a prerequisite to the emergence of the modern type of economic society. That it did in fact precede the appearance of modern capitalism is of course well known, for money in various forms goes back many centuries. Adam Smith, in his *Wealth of Nations,* suggested that money originated in the rational effort of man to meet the necessity of finding some medium of exchange. This view probably places undue stress upon the idea of a rational establishment of monetary systems. A more satisfactory view of the origins of money may be obtained by examining the primitive money of both ancient and modern times.

Primitive trade and the use of money. A well-developed money could hardly have preceded the appearance of trade. Some writers suggest that trade, developing upon the foundation of property ownership, first may have taken a unilateral form through the plunderings of conquest and the making of gifts. Resistance to the former and encouragement to the latter may have been the source of the appearance of bilateral exchange or barter. The desire to trade with foreigners who could furnish strange and unusual commodities must have provided important incentives to barter for peoples living in a simple and largely self-sufficient fashion.[1] Barter required methods of measuring both amounts and values. In addition to counting, units of weight were introduced. The carat, it is said, originated from the kernel of the carob bean, while the English troy grain was derived from the weight of a grain of barley. A primitive way of establishing values was to compare the size of things to be exchanged. Strings of cowrie shells called *dewarra* were exchanged, length for length, with fish. More significant in the development of money, however, was the appearance of standards of comparison in the form of some well-known and valuable thing. In warm or temperate climates, for example, the cow or ox was commonly used as a standard of value. The use of numerous other commodities may be mentioned. In the interior of Africa, the slave was used as a standard, with a value of five oxen, one hundred pieces of cloth, or a double-barrelled gun; a string of glass beads was worth a gourd bottle of water, a measure of milk, or an armful of hay.[2]

Primitive forms of money. The basic requirement of a medium of exchange is such popular esteem as to provide general acceptability by the trading public. Things in common demand, whether articles of necessity or ornaments, frequently acquired the status of money. In addition to the ox or the cow, people living in colder areas used as money such articles as furs, skins, and blankets. Salt, weapons, and utensils of various sorts were also used. Hoes and knives are said to have been used as money by the Chinese, and later, through the slow process of evolution, miniature copies of these articles, lacking any utility as commodities, circulated as pure money. Primitive fishermen sometimes used fishhooks, which, like the Chinese hoes and knives, gradually lost their original value as commodities and shifted into the category of pure money with only the symbolic shape remaining. The early appearance of orna-

---

[1] Cf. Helfferich, Karl, *Money*, New York, Adelphi Co. (Greenberg), 1927, Vol. I, pp. 3-7.

[2] Helfferich, *op. cit.*, p. 9.

ments in the role of money is illustrated by the cowrie shells, which from ancient down to modern times have been held in high esteem as money among primitive folk. Of this type was the American Indian's wampum, consisting of belts and necklaces of black and white polished shells. Feathers, heads of red-headed woodpeckers, as well as strings of polished shells, served as money among California Indians. In Iceland, dried fish, and in North America, beaver skins, tobacco, and rice were at one time used as media of exchange.[3]

The use of metals. The precious metals seem to have acquired monetary functions, among peoples who knew them, almost as early as did other commodities. The "talent," a gold unit weighing about 130 grains troy and worth one ox, is referred to in the Homeric poems of about the eighth century B.C.[4] Among the less valuable metals copper and silver, and later iron and tin, found use as money. The metals were exchanged not only in the form of implements, utensils, and ornaments, but also in bars, wires, cylinders, and balls. Although these metals possessed monetary functions, they were themselves evaluated at first by weight or measure. Gold dust was sometimes measured by the length of a quill container, and weighing was a common method of evaluating it. Sometimes bars or rings of precious metals were marked at regular intervals to facilitate dividing them into smaller units. It was not until relatively late years that coinage was developed as an aid to the identification of the weight and fineness of precious metals. Although there may have been earlier attempts at private coinage by merchants and goldsmiths who stamped their mark upon metals, it is believed that state coinage began in Lydia about 660 B.C.[5]

The superiority of the precious metals. The monetary triumph of the precious metals was due to their superiority in monetary uses. This superiority over other commodities can be readily seen by calling to mind the requirement of a good money. Good money must be relatively stable in value and be generally accept-

---

[3] For more complete accounts of primitive forms of money, see J. Laurence Laughlin's *Money, Credit, and Prices,* Vol. I., and Kemmerer's *Money,* New York, The Macmillan Co., 1936, Chapter I. For the original source of much information given by other writers, see W. Ridgway's *The Origin of Metallic Currency and Weight Standards,* 1892.

[4] Laughlin, *op. cit.,* p. 19.

[5] Laughlin, *op. cit.,* pp. 53-54. Chapter II contains a detailed account of the early use of metallic money.

able. To a very marked degree, the precious metals fulfill these requirements better than other commodities. Since gold, among all the metals, became the monetary choice of very nearly the whole world, let us see to what extent it is deserving.

Stability of value of gold. There are several reasons for the wide acceptance that gold achieved as the monetary metal of modern times. First, its immense durability has led to the accumulation of a tremendous stock of gold, little affected by the variations in gold output from year to year. This stability of quantity has had a favorable effect upon the stability of the value of gold, an obvious advantage. In addition, gold's freedom from deterioration gives it great superiority over most other commodities.

Second, because gold is widely admired for its ornamental and prestige uses, it falls into the luxury class. When general prices rise because gold is overabundant, the relative cheapness of things fashioned out of gold leads to a marked increase in their popularity. Hence a larger fraction of newly mined gold is diverted to industrial uses and away from monetary use. In a similar manner, a rise in general prices reduces the real cost of hoarding gold and encourages the flow of gold away from the monetary systems and into idle hoards. Clearly, the substantial absorption of gold by these non-monetary uses has helped stabilize the value of gold in the face of overabundant gold production. Conversely, when gold mining lags, falling general prices have caused the industrial use and the hoarding of gold to shrink, leaving a larger fraction of the reduced gold output for monetary use.

Third, a rise in the value of gold, indicated by falling prices, stimulates gold production while a rising price level, indicating a falling value of gold, causes the output of gold to shrink.[6]

Other attributes of gold. Gold has the added advantage of (1) embodying a relatively high value in a small compass; (2) being readily divided, coined, and melted; and (3) being easily identified and of uniform quality.

In modern times gold has the further advantage of having acquired social acceptance as money. The fact that it has been the customary monetary standard over many years in a large measure explains the esteem that it commands as money. Today, gold

---

[6] Cf. Edie, Lionel D., *Money, Bank Credit and Prices,* New York, Harper & Bros. 1928, pp. 256-257.

retains its monetary value largely because of its customary acceptance as money rather than because of its value for industrial uses.

In these days of paper money and bank credit substitutes for gold, some of the characteristics mentioned as contributing to the acceptability of gold have lost much of their significance. These substitutes have all the qualities of convenience in handling and use that can be claimed for gold itself, and are in fact superior to gold for domestic use. Even when inconvertible into gold, paper money may remain readily acceptable in the issuing country because it may possess legal tender power and because of habit of use.

Coinage of Money

The advent of coinage marked a very important step in the development of money, for with it money achieved a distinctive place among other goods. When made into the form of coin, money ceased to be merely a convenient commodity for comparing and storing values. The coin itself, bearing the stamp or mark of the State that issued it, came to be the important thing rather than the bullion content. This admiration for the coin itself frequently goes so far that the coin may circulate at a value considerably in excess of its bullion value. The fact that it is money, approved by the State and in customary use, is sufficient to maintain its acceptance at face value within its own country.

Free coinage. In the past, free coinage of the standard monetary metal was a normal characteristic of currency systems. Under free coinage, the money metal or metals may be brought to the mints and converted into standard coins without limit. In the United States before 1933, one could bring to the mint standard gold bullion (nine-tenths fine) and have it converted into coin without any expense save the delay involved in the process. If gold in other than standard bullion form was presented to the mint, a *brassage* charge was made to cover the expense of converting the metal into standard bullion.[7] Sometimes the State charged more than the actual cost of minting the coins. As a result the State made a profit called *seigniorage*. The coins so minted had a face value somewhat above their bullion value. The free coinage

---

[7] The term *brassage* is used to describe any mint charge not designed to yield a profit to the State.

of standard metals is normally accompanied by the right to exchange coin for bullion or the right to convert coin into bullion by melting. It follows, therefore, that the coin value and the value of the bullion content of coins can never be separated by more than the cost of conversion from one form to the other. It is through the free interconvertibility of coin and bullion that the value of money is tied up with the value of the metal itself.

Limited coinage. Although standard money metal may be freely coined, other metals may be converted into coins only at the option of the State. For example, subsidiary silver coins, silver dollars, and token five- and one-cent pieces are coined by the Treasury in such amounts as public convenience or public policy seem to warrant. Since there is no privilege of free coinage in such a case, these coins are the result of what is known as "limited coinage." Such coins normally bear a heavy seigniorage charge, or to put it another way, their face value is considerably greater than the value of the metal they contain. Coins issued under the limited coinage principle, therefore, derive their value from the fact that they are directly or indirectly convertible into standard money. In reality they are a form of promissory note written on metal discs instead of being engraved on paper.

Free conversion without free coinage. After World War I, countries wishing to return to the gold standard economized their limited supply by abandoning the coinage of gold. Instead, they provided that bullion might be freely converted into currency or bank credits by sale to the central bank. Those wishing gold bullion for export or industrial purposes could purchase it at a fixed price from the central bank. In this way gold coin was not allowed in common circulation, yet free conversion from money into bullion and bullion into money was provided. Though technically different from free coinage, the result was similar in that the value of paper currency and the equivalent amount of bullion were always substantially the same. The practice of converting gold bullion into money by Treasury purchase began in the United States in 1934.

Inconvertible Paper Money

In the past, standard money has normally consisted of some form of metal. Although both gold and silver were often standard money metals, the modern practice steadily moved in the direction of gold alone. Standard money, however, need not necessarily be metal at all, but sometimes may be inconvertible paper currency.

The inauguration of the use of inconvertible paper money in a country is generally accompanied by a promise of the issuer, whether the State or a note-issuing bank, that the paper will some day be redeemed in standard metal money. This fact has led some observers to conclude that inconvertible paper money derives its acceptability and its value from the expectation of redemption in standard metal at some future date. According to this view, the value of pure paper money must fluctuate in direct proportion to changes in the possibility of future redemption. This view also denies that pure paper money, in itself, can have value independent of its theoretical metal worth. This explanation of the value of inconvertible paper money was understandable at a time when the metallic standard was the rule and inconvertible paper was the exception that was to be eliminated as soon as possible. But today, in the light of modern monetary experiences with inconvertible paper currencies, it is difficult to hold that pure paper money can have no value in and of itself.

One may say, therefore, that inconvertible paper money sometimes may achieve the distinction of being "standard" or the "last word" in a country's monetary system. Its acceptability is derived not only from habit of use developed before conversion privileges were abandoned, but also from legislative fiat or legal tender qualities. Sometimes a sheer lack of any available substitute currency plays its part in compelling people to use inconvertible paper.

Two basic types of inconvertible paper money. Inconvertible paper money may take either of two forms: (1) government issue; or (2) bank note.[8]

1. Governments have frequently been forced to meet their necessary expenditures by the issue of paper promises to pay metal money. The occasion for such issues has most frequently been

---

[8] Many excellent accounts of historical experience with inconvertible paper are available. For compact, competent summaries of the work in this field, see J. Laurence Laughlin's *Money, Credit, and Prices*, Vol. II, Chapters III-XI, and Edwin W. Kemmerer's *Money*, Chapters X-XIII. W. C. Mitchell's familiar *History of the Greenbacks*, 1903, is an authoritative work on the experiences with the United States notes.

war, when needed expenditures tend to outstrip tax income. Direct resort to the printing press by financially distressed governments has not been unknown in American history. The Revolutionary War was the occasion for paper money issues (bills of credit) by both the individual colonies and the Continental Congress. The outbreak of the Civil War was the signal for the issue of inconvertible greenbacks.

2. Both in the past and in modern times, inconvertible paper money, with most if not all of the attributes of standard money, often has originated in the form of bank notes. In England, 1797–1821, the currency mainly consisted of inconvertible Bank of England notes, and today, in practically all countries of the world (with the exception of the U. S.), standard money consists of inconvertible promises of the central banks.

Different Types of Money and Their Place in Contemporary Monetary Systems

In any modern monetary structure there are a number of components that make up the whole. To avoid confusion let us examine each of the parts of our monetary system and see in what way it fits into the whole monetary picture. In doing this we must keep in mind that money proper, directly available for public spending, consists only of the media of exchange held by the public itself. Such money excludes gold and gold certificates, which are held by the Treasury and by the Federal Reserve Banks. It also excludes central bank deposits and interbank deposits, which comprise part of the mechanism of the system but are not in the public's hands.

Standard Money and Other Treasury Issues

Standard money. Standard money is the monetary unit recognized by the State as the ultimate basic standard of value. It is the unit of ultimate convertibility for all other forms of money. Direct or indirect convertibility into standard money assures a uniform value for all kinds of money. Standard money is normally designated as "standard" by law, although at times the formal legal standard may be suspended in practice through administrative action. For instance, Congress defines the United States dollar as a unit containing a given weight of nine-tenths fine gold. Such a unit, whether coined or uncoined bullion, is presumably the ultimate standard. But there have been times when in fact the gold dollar ceased to be the operating standard monetary unit. During the Civil War and extending down to 1879, the inconvertible United States note or greenback was the last word or the ultimate standard, since ordinary forms of money in circulation (bank notes and deposits) could not be converted into gold. Likewise, from April 1933 to the end of January 1934 paper money was not tied to the gold dollar and it depreciated in terms of gold. Under those conditions the gold dollar was no longer the real standard.

This variation in the standard monetary unit, in respect to both its gold content and its vacillation between convertibility into monetary metal and inconvertibility, provides an illustration of the distinction between the monetary unit of the dollar, in which monetary obligations are expressed, and standard money, the equivalent of which can be used in making payments. For example, the dollar is the monetary unit in terms of which are stated various sorts of economic obligations. The satisfaction of these obligations requires the payment of dollars. But the particular *thing* that constitutes the *dollar* is subject to change.[9] Thus, the dollar as a unit for expressing economic obligations remains unchanged, but the particular standard money in which payment may be made is subject to change at the will of the Government. Standard money, therefore, is the ultimate means of payment for obligations expressed in terms of the unit of account.

The relation of the State to standard money. Standard money in the modern sense requires the sanction of the State. This sanction normally would carry with it legal tender power. But when the standard money is uncoined gold bullion, as it sometimes is in modern monetary systems, it has little need to be made legal tender. Rather, legal tender powers are conferred upon paper currencies, with the standard acting as the ultimate redemption unit for all the currencies of lesser status. When the ultimately obtainable currency is itself inconvertible paper, the distinction between legal

---

[9] J. M. Keynes distinguished between money as a "unit of account" and money that may be used in making payments. He likened this distinction to that between the King of England, a continuous institution, and the particular ruler on the throne at any given time. The latter is subject to change at the will of the State, but the former enjoys continuity of existence. See his *Treatise on Money*, New York, Harcourt, Brace & Co., 1930, Vol. I, p. 4.

tender currency and standard money is wiped out, since for all practical purposes any legal tender currency is standard. In modern society the sanction of the State is often a very powerful force in making standard money acceptable. So important is this sanction that some persons hold to the view that money derives its value from the State's stamp of approval.

Representative money. Under the old gold standard, which permitted individuals to obtain gold coins, the standard gold pieces frequently were in actual circulation. The small size and ease of abrasion of gold coins, however, discouraged their circulation. Before 1933, gold certificates, claim checks to gold held by the Treasury, commonly circulated in place of gold coin. Gold certificates are, therefore, called *representative money,* for they stand in the place of the standard gold. Today it has become the practice to use other forms of currency for actual payments, leaving gold certificates in the Federal Reserve Banks to act as a reserve or the ultimate redemption basis for nonstandard money.

Other government issues. Not only does the government regulate and control the issuing of standard money of a country but also it normally issues other types of money that do not qualify as standard. Government notes in currency form, redeemable in standard money, are sometimes issued. Our greenbacks are examples of such currency. Governments also purchase and coin silver and other metals, and the resulting coins, although not standard, are part of the money supply.

Standard money and the media of exchange. Neither gold nor its representatives, gold certificates, are a part of the public's supply of spendable money. Instead, monetary gold itself is held by the Treasury, while gold certificates issued against the gold are held as legal reserve by the Federal Reserve Banks. However, other currency issued by the Treasury, such as silver certificates, silver dollars, and other coins, is for the most part in general circulation and is a part of the public's money supply. The only exception is the currency held by banks as "till money" reserves. Such currency cannot be counted as a part of the supply of the media of exchange.

Contemporary Forms of Money: Bank Money

The major part of our media of exchange consists not of currency issued by the government but of *bank notes* and *bank checking accounts.* Such note and deposit currency may be designated *bank money* to differentiate it from money issued by the government.

Central bank credit as money. Bank money falls into two classes: (1) the notes and deposits of the central banks (in our case the Federal Reserve Banks); and (2) checking accounts of commercial banks. Most countries now have central banks that enjoy the privilege of note issue and hold the deposits of commercial banks. These deposits are looked upon as "cash reserves" by the commercial banks and are freely transferred among the banks in payment of debts owed to each other. Furthermore, these deposits in the central bank may be drawn out in cash (central bank notes), to meet the public's changing demands for currency. Commercial banks quite rightly look upon the notes and deposits of the central bank as acceptable "money." Such central obligations, therefore, comprise what might be called *secondary* standard money, since all obligations of commercial banks to each other and to the general public may in practice be liquidated by the payment of central bank notes or deposits and need not involve the use of the *ultimate* standard itself. The central bank, in turn, holds the gold certificates that represent the standard gold money as a reserve or basis for the support of its note and deposit liabilities.

Commercial bank credit money. Commercial banks today have little if any note-issuing power. Nevertheless, by making loans and investments, they can create a large volume of bank money in the form of *demand deposits subject to check,* based upon a relatively small volume of cash reserves. These cash reserves, as we have just observed, are mainly in the form of central bank obligations. Commercial bank money, then, consists of checking accounts; and borrowers receive the proceeds of their loans in this form of promises to pay currency, rather than in currency itself. So long as banks command public confidence, their promises are readily acceptable and are actually superior to currency in respect to convenience in transfer and freedom from theft. Most commercial transactions are settled by the payment of such bank money or checking accounts. Therefore, commercial bank money may be said to be our principal medium of exchange.

The Supply of Money

We have seen how money falls into three main categories forming a kind of hierarchy. At the top is standard money, the "last word," so to speak, in the family of monies. Second, comes central bank or secondary standard money, comprised of the IOU's of the central bank in the form of notes and deposits. This money is convertible into standard money proper, except in those cases in which the central bank note has become the "last word" in its own right with no conversion into any standard government issued money. Finally, there is commercial bank money, comprised of checking accounts of banks.

At this early stage of our study of money matters we are not equipped to look very deeply into the determinants of the supply of these different forms of money. Yet it is desirable to take a quick preliminary look.

The quantity of standard money. The quantity of standard money, when it is not convertible into gold, is determined by the action and policy of the government or, when central bank notes have become standard, by the action and policy of the central bank. In such a case it is entirely possible for standard money to be issued with such wisdom and restraint as to provide the country with the correct monetary base needed for economic stability and growth. It is this possibility that provides the case for independent, managed paper currencies. However, inconvertible paper money may be created by the government, or by the central bank at the behest of the government, in times of fiscal difficulties. In such times the amount of standard money may reflect the financial ineptitude and irresponsibility of the Treasury rather than the sound judgment of those with monetary authority. The very real danger of an over-expanded money under these circumstances provides the case for a standard money based upon some scarce and valuable thing such as gold.

When standard money is gold, the quantity available to the monetary system of any one country is limited by (1) the world's total quantity of monetary gold that has been assembled out of the output of gold over many years; and (2) the share of that total gold supply that the given country has acquired by excessive exports of goods and services and by borrowing abroad. Clearly there is something to be said for these powerful limits upon the standard money supply. Convertibility of all currencies into standard gold provides genuine protection against the more extreme forms of currency inflation.

The supply of central bank money. Let us next look briefly at the supply of central bank or secondary standard money. So long as gold is the ultimate standard, central bank IOU's (notes and deposits) are convertible into gold, and, therefore, gold reserves or their equivalent must be carried by the central bank if it is to maintain gold convertibility. Also, the law governing the central bank may set some minimum limit to its gold reserves. For example, the Federal Reserve Banks are legally required to have gold certificate reserves equal to at least 25 per cent of their note and deposit liabilities. We can see, therefore, that the available supply of standard money held by the central banks, and the customary or legal reserve requirements, set a maximum limit to the supply of central bank money that can be created. But quite generally central banks limit their creation of notes and deposits to some amount believed to be in the public interest, leaving a cushion of unused standard money reserves. Within the limits set by gold reserve requirements, central banks are free to expand their own notes and deposits according to their credit policy. By buying Government securities and by lending to commercial banks asking for accommodation, central banks may expand the supply of secondary standard money in the form of their notes and deposits. Should this expansion ultimately lead to such an increase in the public's money supply that rising prices occur, exports of the country tend to shrink and imports tend to rise so that the country owes gold to other countries. Converting its notes and deposits into gold for export may so reduce the gold reserves of the central bank that it has to check its expansion of notes and deposits. It is clear that the necessity for a central bank to hold enough gold reserves to insure convertibility of its currency provides a definite limit to its money-creating activities. But when the currency is inconvertible and the notes of the central bank are themselves standard money, only the conscience of the central banker, embodied in "credit policy," produces a limit to the quantity of central bank or secondary standard money.

The determinants of the supply of checking account money. Commercial banks must always be prepared to pay in currency for checks drawn against them. Consequently they must carry an amount of reserves in cash, or deposited with the central bank, sufficient to meet this requirement. Because most checks drawn against a bank are in fact offset by an equal amount of checks deposited, the banks succeed in maintaining the convertibility of their checks into currency with relatively small amounts of reserve cash. This necessity for carrying cash reserves, generally established by law as a certain fraction of the banks' checking accounts, fixes a definite limit to the amount of checking accounts that the banks can support. Therefore it sets a limit to the loans and investments that result in the creation of checking account money.

The supply of cash reserves of the commercial banks depends (1) upon the quantity of standard money;[10] and (2) upon the quantity of central bank credit money. The latter reflects the credit policy of the central banks and provides the means for monetary management in a modern economy.

Within the limits set by their available reserves, commercial banks are prone to push their creation of checking account money to the limit. This tendency arises because private bankers do not like to pass up an opportunity to earn interest on loans and investments. The appearance of any excess reserves above normal and legal requirements is likely to be followed by an expansion of bank loans and investments, and by an equal expansion of checking account currency. This statement requires one qualification. Unless business conditions are sufficiently favorable, borrowers of acceptable credit standing may not put in an appearance. In such a case, no expansion of checking account money from that source will take place. However, if securities of high grade, which are acceptable to the banks, are available for purchase in the markets, the banks tend strongly to utilize their excess reserves by investing in such securities.

To sum up, the quantity of standard money in a country is determined, when the gold standard is in operation, by the power of that country to attract and hold gold. Inconvertible paper standard money has no such limit, its quantity being determined by the policy (or lack of one) of the Treasury or the central bank in issuing inconvertible paper currency. Under the gold standard central bank credit policy dictates the supply of central bank notes and deposits within the limit of gold reserve requirements. The supply

---

[10] Any increase in the standard money supply results in an increase in commercial bank reserves. For example, gold importers either deposit gold in their banks or sell gold to the Treasury or to the central bank, and receive in payment checks on the central bank which they deposit in the commercial banks.

of checking account currency is limited by (1) the supply of available reserves, which is in turn dependent upon the supply of standard and central bank money; and (2) the existence of suitable loan and investment opportunities for the commercial banks.

The Monetary Structure of the United States

Let us now look at each of the three broad monetary categories and determine the direct contribution of each to the total supply of the public's spendable money. This can best be done by constructing a table showing for each category the total amount and the part of that total going to make up the supply of money held by the public.

TABLE 1

Monetary Liabilities of the Treasury, the Federal Reserve Banks, and Commercial Banks and the Contribution of Each to Money Held by the Public, February 29, 1956

	Total	Held by Banks and in Circulation
1. Monetary issues of the Treasury:		
a) Gold certificates	$21,045,000,000	
1) In the Federal Reserve Banks	21,011,000,000	
2) In banks and in circulation	34,000,000	$ 34,000,000
b) Treasury currency	5,012,000,000	
1) In the Treasury	68,000,000	
2) In the Federal Reserve Banks	443,000,000	
3) In banks and in circulation	4,501,000,000	4,501,000,000
2. Monetary liabilities of the Federal Reserve Banks:		
a) Federal Reserve notes	27,186,000,000	
1) Held by the Treasury	71,000,000	
2) Held by Federal Reserve Banks	1,487,000,000	
3) Held by banks and in circulation	25,628,000,000	25,628,000,000
b) Federal Reserve deposits	19,650,000,000	
1) Held by banks	18,428,000,000	18,428,000,000
2) Held by U.S. Treasury	553,000,000	
3) Held by others	669,000,000	

3. Monetary liabilities of
commercial banks:

Total demand deposits 123,360,000,000
a) U.S. Treasury 3,610,000,000
b) Interbank 14,150,000,000   14,150,000,000
c) Other 105,600,000,000   105,600,000,000

Total monetary liabilities held by
banks and in circulation $168,341,000,000
Less: Deposits held by banks in the
Federal Reserve Banks ..$18,428,000,000
Deposits in other banks 14,150,000,000
Currency and coin in banks 2,929,000,000
35,507,000,000

Total money held by the public $132,834,000,000

Questions for Study

1. Why did the emergence of modern capitalism depend upon the existence of a system of money?

2. What does primitive money tell us about:
    a) The manner in which money came into use?
    b) The importance of commodity usefulness in money?
    c) The emergence of pure money forms having little value as commodities?

3. Why have ornamental objects been used as money?

4. What reasons can you give for the superiority of gold and silver as money?

5. When gold mining expands and the supply of gold becomes excessive, prices rise. What is the effect of such a rise in prices upon:
    a) The use of gold in industry?
    b) The hoarding of gold?

6. How can you account for the universal willingness of countries that use inconvertible paper currencies to accept gold in settlement of trade balances?

7. When free coinage of gold exists in a country's monetary system what significant results arise? Do the same results appear as a result of the present practice in the United States?

8. What is limited coinage? How does it usually result in seigniorage?

9. What are the two origins of inconvertible paper money?

10. Why does the public often accept and use inconvertible paper money?

11. What is the proper test for determining the standard money of a country?

12. Does convertibility into standard money determine the value of money in common use?

13. Was the standard monetary unit of the United States changed in 1934 when the gold content of the dollar was reduced?

14. What are the forms of money that are created by:
   a) Central banks?
   b) Commercial banks?

15. Why exclude time deposits from money?

16. What determines a country's supply of standard money when it consists of:
   a) Inconvertible central bank notes?
   b) Gold?

3

Monetary Standards

A country's monetary standard is adopted by the authority of the State as a measure of value. The monetary standard, therefore, is synonymous with standard money, which we have already studied. A country's monetary system consists of its supply of standard money plus all the paper and credit substitutes tied to and convertible into standard money. Involved in the operation and maintenance of the monetary system is the whole government mechanism established to regulate the creation of money, and the banking system responsible for the issue of bank notes and the creation of checking account money.

The Meaning of Monetary Standards

It is customary to describe the monetary system of a country in terms of its standard money. Thus, when the standard monetary unit is gold, the country is said to have a *gold standard system,* or more simply is said to be "on the gold standard." If the standard monetary unit is defined in terms of both gold and silver, the system is one of *bimetallism.*[1] When a country's currency is not redeemable in either gold or silver, it is said to have an *inconvertible paper money system,* or a nominal currency.

Importance of the type of monetary system. The nature of a country's money system has a double significance. First, there is the question of its suitability for domestic requirements. Monetary systems are basically national in nature, since they are established and maintained by the governments of each country. There is no prerogative of sovereignty more jealously guarded than that of regulating the monetary system. It is to be expected, therefore, that monetary systems of all countries tend to be governed by inter-

33

nal needs. Yet, because countries must also be concerned about trade with other nations, the international aspects of currency management cannot be disregarded. A suitable monetary system should therefore satisfy both domestic requirements and the necessities of international trade. As we shall see a little later in this chapter, no single type of monetary standard entirely satisfies both domestic and international requirements.

Early Monetary Standards

The development of monetary systems providing standard coins of uniform value was the result of long and trying experience. Early attempts at coinage often resulted in the appearance of a number of separate, independent types of money, each with its own subdivisions. This situation resulted from the assimilation of the coins and coinage practices of neighboring trading states, from irregular minting, and from abrasion and clipping.[1] Gradually it became possible for central governments, by preventing debasement, to bring different coins of the same metal into a fixed relation to each other. But even this improvement left a parallel standard of two independent currencies, one of silver and the other of gold. With price calculations and debts made in either of the two currencies, the situation left much to be desired. A standard, uniform currency was still lacking.

Bimetallism

The next step in the development of currencies was to devise a system in which standard coins of a given value might be minted out of both gold and silver. In this way not only would gold and silver coins circulate side by side, but they would also be interchangeable. Thus, a debt calling for the payment of a given number of dollars could be discharged by the payment of either silver or gold. Both metals were given the right of free and unlimited coinage into standard monetary units. Such a system was called *bimetallism*.

But certain difficulties always tended to arise under bimetal-

---

[1] A detailed account of the chaotic condition of early currencies can be found in Helfferich, Karl, *Money*, New York, Adelphi Co. (Greenberg), 1927, Vol. I, pp. 34-50.

lism. Its adoption required a decision as to the appropriate weight that should be given to each type of coin. Since both were to have the same nominal value and each was to be freely coined, it was necessary that the relative size of coins of the two metals bear a close relationship to their relative value as bullion. The mint ratio was the relative quantities of the two metals required at the mint to make a standard monetary unit. Thus, a mint ratio of 16:1 meant that the silver dollar required an amount of silver 16 times the amount of gold in the gold dollar, and was chosen because it was thought to correspond to the relative bullion values of the two metals. But new discoveries of the metals caused marked disturbances in the relative values. When silver discoveries reduced the bullion value of silver, the silver dollar no longer contained as much bullion value as did the gold dollar. On the other hand, when gold discoveries reduced the value of gold as compared to silver, the bullion value of the gold dollar became less than that of the silver dollar. Such a situation invited the action of "Gresham's Law" and led to the displacement of the dearer metal by the cheaper metal in the monetary system of the country. A similar disturbing result occurred when other bimetallic countries had mint ratios that differed from those of the country concerned. These foreign mint ratios affected the domestic "market" ratio.

Gresham's Law. In its simple form, the monetary principle known as "Gresham's Law" is this: "Bad or overvalued money tends to drive out of circulation good or undervalued money." A fuller and somewhat more correct statement is that, given a sufficient supply of bad or overvalued standard money with the characteristic of general acceptability, the good or undervalued standard money may be displaced by the lighter or overvalued money. Bad money or overvalued money is that which contains less bullion value for a stated face value than the good or undervalued money.[2]

Under bimetallism, Gresham's Law begins to operate whenever the market ratio of silver to gold shifts away from the mint ratio.

[2] Sir Thomas Gresham is said to have used this principle in explaining to Queen Elizabeth why the new fullweight coins did not remain in circulation in the face of old, underweight, clipped coin. For a statement of the origin of the use of Gresham's name in connection with this long-known principle, see Laughlin, J. L., *New Exposition of Money, Credit, and Prices,* University of Chicago Press, 1931, Vol. I, pp. 51-52.

For example, if the mint ratio and the market ratio were both 16:1, both gold and silver coins would circulate. But if silver production should expand enough to make silver cheaper than before, as compared to gold, and to make the market ratio change to 17:1, it would become profitable to convert gold coin into bullion and to exchange it in the market for silver at 17:1. Out of the seventeen parts of silver thus obtained, sixteen parts could be made into silver coins to replace the gold coins melted, and one part silver would be left as a profit on the transaction. So long as the market ratio remained sufficiently different from the mint ratio to make such a profit possible, the process of displacing gold coins with silver would continue. If the shift in relative silver and gold values represented a world-wide change, the gold coins of an individual country acting alone on the bimetallic standard would almost certainly be displaced by silver without causing a corrective change in the market ratio. If increased gold output lowered the relative value of gold as compared to silver so that the market ratio became 15:1, the reverse of what we have just described would occur. Gold, being the cheaper money, would displace the dearer silver coins, which would be melted up and sold as bullion.

Experience has shown that it is difficult for a single country to maintain its mint ratio equal to the market ratio. The latter fluctuates with changes in production and in the nonmonetary demand, whereas mint ratios, once established, are unlikely to be changed with any frequency. Attempts to establish and maintain bimetallism, therefore, have generally resulted in an alternating standard, with first one and then the other of the two metals making up the currency.

Claims made for bimetallism. Because bimetallism developed naturally out of the need for gold and silver currency of a uniform value, little reason arose to justify its original appearance. After its abandonment,[3] however, repeated efforts were made to re-estab-

---

[3] England closed its mints to the free coinage of silver in 1798, although the gold standard was not established by statute until 1816. The United States was on the bimetallic standard from 1792 until 1873. The Latin Monetary Union, composed of Italy, Belgium, France, and Switzerland maintained bimetallism until 1878. Cf. Hawtrey, R. G., *Currency and Credit*, New York, Longmans, Green, 1928, Chapter XVI. Also see Laughlin, J. L., *History of Bimetallism in the United States*, 1888, pp. 146-160.

lish bimetallism. Such efforts were supported vigorously by its advocates with appropriate arguments.

Efforts to restore bimetallism coincided with periods of economic depression and falling value of silver. The reasons are easy to understand. First, if cheap silver bullion could be converted into standard coin at the old statutory price, silver producers would obviously benefit. Second, the agrarian debtor groups, especially hard hit by falling prices characteristic of depressions, desired the free coinage of silver in the belief that it would result in an expanded quantity of money and higher prices. Support for bimetallism sometimes arose from quite a different quarter. When silver became cheaper the value of silver standard currencies (of which there were a few) also became cheaper in terms of gold standard currencies. Persons interested in exporting to those countries found that a cheapening of silver increased their difficulties, and therefore they supported a return to bimetallism.

Besides the support, obviously partisan, of the groups that felt their interests were directly involved, bimetallism found theoretical support of a more sophisticated kind. It was argued that the operation of Gresham's Law introduced a "compensatory action." Whenever one metal became cheaper, its flow into the monetary system would raise its bullion value. At the same time, the expulsion of the dearer metal would reduce its bullion value. Two beneficial consequences might therefore be expected: (1) The two metals would in fact both remain in circulation, although in varying proportions; (2) the aggregate stock of money would tend to be more stable than one comprised of a single metal. It was agreed that these benefits would be realized only if bimetallism were established on a wide scale—preferably on an international basis.

Although bimetallism has been officially dead for many years, the impact of its past still has been felt in later monetary discussions. As we shall see in the next chapter, the ghost of bimetallism repeatedly appeared in our monetary history after 1873, the year of its official demise.

The Gold Standard

In contrast to bimetallism, which involves the free coinage of two standard money metals—silver and gold—the gold standard provides only for the use of gold as the basic money metal.

Thus, under the gold standard, the standard monetary unit is a given fixed quantity of gold. Paper money and bank credit substitutes for the standard money are maintained at par by being convertible into gold. Free coinage of gold, in its broader sense, is a necessary characteristic of the gold standard. This means that gold bullion can readily be converted into standard money, and conversely, that standard money can be converted into gold bullion. This conversion must be at a fixed price so that the value of a given amount of gold bullion and the value of standard money are equal. Therefore, essential characteristics of the gold standard include:

1. The unlimited right to convert gold bullion into money.
2. The right to convert money, both currency and coin, into gold bullion for industrial uses.
3. The right to export gold for conversion into foreign currencies.

When gold standard countries maintain free convertibility of gold into money and money into gold, and allow gold to move freely from one country to another, the rates of exchange among the several countries are stabilized close to the "gold parities" (the relative gold contents of their standard monetary units). This result is of genuine importance to international trade.

The gold coin standard. Several modifications of the gold standard were introduced after World War I. These modifications may best be visualized by beginning with a description of the old-fashioned type of gold standard, which, for purposes of contrast, may be called the *gold coin standard*.

Under the gold coin standard, gold coins of a certain weight and fineness are the standard monetary units. Thus, the gold dollar containing 25.8 grains of nine-tenths fine gold was the standard monetary unit of the United States prior to January 31, 1934. Standard gold bullion (.900 fine) could be brought to the mint in unlimited quantities and be converted without charge into coin. At the same time, the mint would receive gold coin in lots of $5,000 or more and give out gold bars in exchange.[4] The British

---

[4] The gold dollar itself was not coined after 1890, except in limited amounts for commemorative purposes. Because of its small size, the gold dollar was inconvenient and was superseded by the silver dollar and silver certificate. The most common gold coin was the double-eagle, or $20 piece. In addition, there were the eagle, or $10 piece; the half-eagle, or $5 piece; and the quarter-eagle, or $2.50 piece. Coinage of the $2.50 piece was discontinued in 1930. *Annual Report of the Director of the Mint*, 1932, p. 87.

sovereign, or pound sterling, contained 123.27447 grains of gold eleven-twelfths fine.[5] Before World War I, the French franc contained 4.97806 grains of gold nine-tenths fine. Under the gold coin standard, other forms of currency were convertible into standard gold coins that anyone was privileged to hoard, spend, export, or melt, as he saw fit.

The gold coin standard, therefore, provided for the unlimited conversion of bullion into standard gold coin, the conversion of gold coin into bullion, and the right of private citizens to convert other currencies into gold, and export or use either gold coin or bullion without restrictions save those against mutilation.

The gold bullion standard. At the outbreak of World War I in 1914, England, along with other belligerents, put an embargo on the export of gold and thus effectively abandoned the gold standard. When the gold standard was re-established in May 1925, the Bank of England was required to redeem its notes, not in gold coin, but in gold bullion in amounts of not less than 400 ounces. At the same time the Bank bought gold bullion at the established price, paying for it in current paper or credit pounds. No restriction was placed upon the right of private citizens to hold or use gold bullion. It might be hoarded, used in the arts, or exported. The only essential difference between the gold bullion standard and the gold coin standard is that the former provides no gold coin for hand-to-hand circulation. Since a substantial volume of gold was in circulation before 1914, the gold bullion standard resulted in some economy in the monetary use of gold. The currency that replaced coin in circulation was not backed by a full 100 per cent gold reserve. France, like England, adopted the gold bullion standard when it resumed gold payments in 1928. The bullion feature was optional with the Bank of France, which could convert its notes into either bullion or coin as it chose.

The U. S. limited gold bullion standard. In 1934, when the gold content of the U. S. dollar was reduced, gold coin was with-

---

[5] The Bank of England sold gold (eleven-twelfths fine) at the statutory price of £3 17s. 10½d. per ounce. The English mint would coin, without charge, one ounce troy of gold bullion into £3 17s. 10½d. For the convenience of holders, the Bank of England bought gold bullion at £3 17s. 9d. per ounce (under the act of 1844). The difference of 1½d. between this and the price at the mint represented an interest charge for the advance by the Bank. Cf. Laughlin, *Money, Credit, and Prices,* Vol. I, p. 80.

drawn from circulation and melted into bars, and further gold coinage was banned. Since that time the Treasury has purchased gold from licensed holders at $35 per fine ounce minus a handling charge of one-fourth of 1 per cent and a small charge for assaying and testing. In payment the seller gets Treasury drafts payable in some form of bank credit. In this way gold bullion can be freely converted into deposit currency. Unlike the British gold bullion standard of 1925-1931, gold bullion may not be freely purchased. Nevertheless, money may be converted into gold for industrial uses and for export. First, special licensees may buy gold for industrial use at $35 per fine ounce plus one-fourth of 1 per cent for handling. Second, through the Federal Reserve Bank of New York, the Treasury exports gold to foreign central banks and treasuries in order to procure foreign exchange needed to settle trade balances and other debts.

Because gold bullion may readily be converted into dollars at a fixed price, and the holders of dollars may obtain gold needed for industry and export, our monetary system can be described as the gold standard. This is true in spite of the following definite departures from the traditional forms of the gold standard:

1. The individual can obtain neither gold coin nor gold bullion for private hoarding.
2. Neither individuals nor banks can convert money into gold for *private* export.
3. The purchase and sale of gold by the Treasury is not mandatory but is carried out at the discretion of the Secretary of the Treasury.

The purchase and sale of gold bullion at a fixed price necessarily results in tying the value of the dollar to the industrial value of its gold content. Also, so long as gold is available for export at the fixed price, the dollar, in terms of foreign currencies, must necessarily be worth as much as the value of a dollar's worth of gold in terms of those currencies. Thus, the basic essentials of the gold standard are satisfied. It is not important, from the standpoint of the gold standard, that individuals are denied the right to obtain gold for hoarding or that gold coin is not available for domestic circulation.

We are on somewhat shakier ground in respect to point 3 raised above. The fact that the necessary minimum requirements for a gold standard are satisfied by *optional* practices of the Treasury raises a suspicion that our gold standard position is at best a bit uncertain. But in view of the fact that the Treasury has continued to buy and sell gold at the fixed price of $35 per ounce for more than twenty years, we are justified in concluding that the dollar is in fact a gold standard currency. It might be preferable if Congress would eliminate the uncertainty concerning future Treasury actions by *requiring* that gold be freely bought and sold at the statutory price.

The Gold Exchange Standard

Gold standard countries customarily maintain domestic supplies of gold to insure the ready convertibility of their currencies. Such gold normally is held by the central bank or, as in the United States, by the Treasury, which issues gold certificates for the central bank to hold. Furthermore, before the coinage of gold was stopped, gold coins (and gold certificates) found their way into hand-to-hand circulation.

Because of the importance of gold as a means for settling international debts, the privilege of converting domestic currency into gold for export is a more significant gold standard requirement than is the right to obtain gold for industrial use. Consequently, on occasion, countries with few gold reserves have sought for an economical way to tie the value of their domestic currency to the value of gold standard currencies in the outside world. This has been accomplished by establishing funds on deposit in banks in gold standard countries and selling drafts (or checks) on such deposits at a fixed price to holders of domestic currency who wish to make payments abroad. This effectively establishes foreign exchange rate stability between the domestic currency and foreign gold standard currencies. This arrangement is known as the *gold exchange standard*.

The principle of the gold exchange standard is a simple one. In its early form, it was designed to permit silver standard countries to enjoy the advantage of having their currencies so tied to the international gold standard as to provide fixed rates of exchange while retaining the traditional or customary silver currency for domestic use. Without some device for maintaining fixed exchange rates on gold standard countries, silver-using countries were in the awkward position of seeing the value of their currencies in terms of gold currencies fluctuate with the changes in the gold value of silver bullion on the world's bullion markets. This fluctuation was unimportant so long as international bimetallism, even on a limited scale, helped to maintain a fairly stable ratio between the market value of the two metals. It became more acute during the last quarter of the nineteenth century, when silver began to drop sharply in value. A shift to a complete gold standard by such countries would have been both unduly expensive and in conflict with the monetary habits of the people. The gold exchange standard was the answer to the problem.

For convenience, the gold exchange standard systems may be divided into two classes. The first, typified by the original Philippine system, was automatic or nearly automatic in its operation under established rules. The second, represented by the European systems of the 1920's, was the managed type operated under the discretionary control of central banks.

The Philippine gold exchange standard. The automatic type of gold exchange standard may be easily understood by examining the system organized for the Philippine Islands in 1903.[6] The uncoined gold peso, worth fifty cents in United States currency, was made the standard monetary unit. Local currency consisted of the silver peso, made light enough to insure against melting, and Philippine Treasury certificates redeemable in silver pesos.

To maintain the parity of the silver peso with the theoretical gold peso ($.50), the Philippine Government maintained a Gold Standard Fund, part of which was held in Manila in pesos and part deposited in a New York bank. The Insular Treasurer was required to sell drafts on the gold standard fund in New York at the rate of two pesos to one dollar. The New York depositary bank in turn was required to sell drafts on the Philippine Treasury Fund in Manila at the same rates.

Philippine importers obtained foreign exchange by giving pesos to the Insular Treasurer for the purchase of drafts on the New York fund. These pesos were held in the Manila fund. Philippine imports, therefore, caused both a decline in the New York fund drawn against and a shrinkage of Philippine domestic currency in circula-

---

6 For a complete account of the Philippine gold exchange standard, see E. W. Kemmerer's authoritative work, *Modern Currency Reforms,* New York, The Macmillan Company, 1916, Chapters V-IX.

tion. Philippine exporters, on the other hand, offered foreign exchange drafts for sale to the Insular Treasurer in exchange for pesos. Exports, therefore, tended both to replenish the fund in New York and expand the circulation of domestic currency. So long as exports and imports were equal in value, the domestic circulation and the New York fund remained unchanged. When exports were in excess of imports, more pesos flowed out of the Treasury fund into the Philippine monetary system, tending to raise the level of internal prices and to restore equality of imports and exports. In case the Manila fund became exhausted by excessive exports, more silver could be bought out of the increased New York fund and coined into pesos, or Treasury certificates could be issued against the New York funds. On the other hand, an excess of imports caused a decrease in the volume of circulating currency. This in turn tended to reduce the internal price structure, reduce imports, and stimulate exports. Thus the system tended to work automatically under the established rules. Only when the government made the mistake of depositing part of the Manila fund in the Manila banks, and thus failed to withhold from circulation the pesos paid in by importers, did trouble arise.[7]

When the dollar was devalued in 1934, the Philippine gold peso was abandoned and the peso was made redeemable only in $.50 worth of New York exchange. It thus formally became a "dollar exchange" rather than a gold exchange standard.[8]

After World War II, the Philippine monetary system was modified by the abandonment of the old regulations designed to tie the peso automatically to the United States dollar. A new central bank was established with the duty of maintaining the external value of the peso at $.50.[9] The central bank, in the interest of promoting the domestic rehabilitation of the Philippines through the encouragement of full employment, did not impose adequate domestic currency restraint when its dollar reserves became impaired. In consequence it has been compelled to institute a system of exchange control to ration out its insufficient supply of dollars to preferred importers.

---

[7] *Hearings Before the Committee on Banking and Currency*, U. S. Senate, S3486, "Philippine Currency Reserves," February 27 and March 5, 1936.

[8] This change was accomplished by legal enactment on March 16, 1935.

[9] Cf. "The Philippine Central Bank Act," *Federal Reserve Bulletin*, August 1948.

Other countries before 1914 made use of the gold exchange standard. The most important example was India, which through administrative order, adopted a *de facto* gold exchange standard.[10] The Indian currency, consisting of small coins, silver rupees, and government issued notes, was convertible into sterling drafts drawn on London.

Managed gold exchange standards of the 1920's. As a step in the re-establishment of a world gold standard after World War I, the gold exchange standard was adopted by a number of countries. One marked difference existed between the systems developed during the 1920's and the old Philippine type. The latter was designed to operate automatically to maintain an equality between imports and exports. In contrast, the systems established in the 1920's were adjuncts of the central banks of the respective countries and were under central bank management and control. When the responsibility for converting the domestic currency into foreign gold standard currencies is placed upon the central bank, its credit policy must be guided primarily by the state of its foreign exchange reserves. A dangerous decline of such reserves, like the loss of gold under the regular gold standard, is the signal for a tighter domestic credit policy, a reduction in the money supply, and a reduction in the internal price level. Should the central bank fail to act to restrain credit, the ultimate result will be the abandonment of the free convertibility of currency into exchange on the gold standard country.

Reasons for the use of the gold exchange standards in the 1920's. The exchange rate confusion that accompanied the inflationary period after World War I made urgent the restoration of monetary and exchange stability. Consequently, the return to the gold standard became the common goal of monetary policy. The gold exchange standard offered the main advantages of the full gold standard. The convertibility of the domestic currency into drafts on

---

[10] The Indian mints were closed to the free coinage of silver in 1893. After 1898, the Calcutta government sold sterling drafts for rupees at 15²⁹⁄₃₂d. per rupee and sold rupee drafts in London at not over 16⅛d. per rupee. Because of the great demand for Indian exports during World War I, the price of rupee drafts and the silver comprising the rupee rose to over 22d. and India was in effect on a free silver standard again. After 1924 the exchange value of the rupee was maintained at 18d., and when England abandoned gold in 1931 the rupee became a sterling exchange standard. See *Report of the Royal Commission on Indian Currency and Finance*, 1926, Vol. I, p. 1.

full gold standard countries insured both stable exchange rates and the appropriate limits on internal currency expansion. In addition, the gold exchange standard promised some substantial economies for the country concerned. First, like the British gold bullion standard, it insured against the waste of gold in domestic circulation. Second, it lowered the cost of obtaining and carrying gold reserves. Some countries, preparing to restore gold convertibility, were compelled to borrow funds in other gold standard countries. This was more easily arranged when the funds were left on deposit with the lender, for this left the lender's gold reserves undisturbed. In addition, such funds often earned interest when deposited in banks or invested in the short-term money market of foreign countries.

Besides the advantages directly accruing to the gold exchange standard country itself, there was a widely held belief that the system provided an advantageous way to economize the world's gold reserves. This economy arose out of the double use of the gold reserves of the depositary country. For example, when a foreign central bank carried $100,000,000 of its reserve funds in New York City, three possibilities existed. First, if it carried the fund deposited in the Federal Reserve Bank of New York, gold reserves amounting to 35 per cent of the deposit (under the requirements of that time), or $35,000,000, were tied up. Second, if the fund were deposited in a big commercial bank, gold reserves of only $4,550,000 were required. Finally, if the funds were invested in the short-term money market no gold at all was tied up in the United States banking system. The question of economy of gold had a considerable appeal during the 1920's when some doubt arose as to the adequacy of the world's gold supply to support the existing price level.

Objections to the gold exchange standard. The gold exchange standard, when adopted by a relatively small country, proved to be a successful device for maintaining stable exchange relationships with full gold standard currencies. But the widespread use of the system in Europe during the 1920's revealed a number of unfortunate features.

First, there were undesirable results in the depositary country holding the reserve funds of foreign central banks. Whenever too high an internal price level induced an excess of imports, a tighter credit and monetary policy was needed. But, because gold exchange standard countries allowed their claims to accumulate instead of withdrawing them in gold, the depositary country was under little compulsion to impose internal credit restraint.

Even more objectionable was the threat to the solvency of the depositary country arising from the accumulation of sizable amounts of foreign-owned short-term funds. These funds exposed the monetary and banking system of the depositary country to the hazard of entirely unpredictable gold drains. Any loss of confidence in the safety of foreign-held reserves precipitates their withdrawal. The experience of 1931-1932, when different money markets of the world were subjected to extremely heavy pressure of this sort, is ample evidence of this risk. It was pressure from this source that forced England off the gold standard in September, 1931.

In addition to the risks imposed on the depositary country, the gold exchange standard country itself is exposed to the danger that its foreign-held reserves may be partially lost by the suspension of gold payments by the depositary country. This risk is well illustrated by the sharp losses of the Bank of France on its London balances when England suspended gold payments in 1931 and the pound depreciated sharply in terms of gold.

Paper money exchange standards of the 1930's. When England abandoned the gold standard in 1931, a number of other countries having close commercial ties with her took similar action. Because of their trade relations with England, they soon found it advantageous to maintain a fairly fixed exchange ratio between their own currencies and the pound sterling. They elected, therefore, to tie their currencies to the depreciated paper pound rather than to try to cling to the gold standard. The central banks of these countries maintained reserves in the form of London balances. The procedure was almost identical with that under the postwar gold exchange standard, except that their currency was maintained at a fixed relation with, and was convertible into, paper pounds instead of a gold standard currency. Further, unlike the gold exchange standard, the parities maintained with sterling were not rigidly fixed but were allowed to shift somewhat as national interest seemed to dictate. England and the countries that tied their currencies to the pound were popularly known as the *Sterling Area*. Chart 1 shows the relation of the currencies of some of these countries to the pound. It clearly shows that the tie-up with sterling

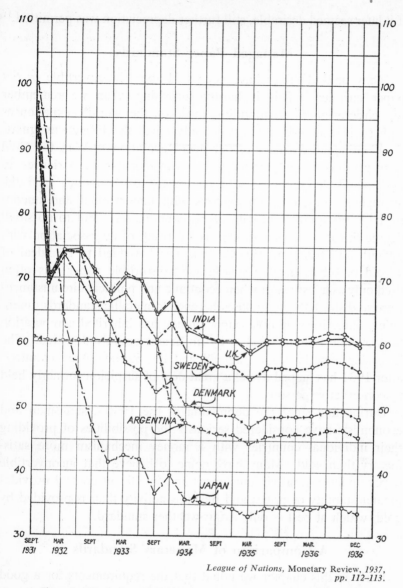

League of Nations, Monetary Review, *1937,*
pp. 112–113.

Chart 1. Deviation of Exchange Rates of Representative Sterling-Area Countries Away from Gold Parities of 1929. 1929 Gold Parity = 100.

was at best a loose one. In general, countries not under British control allowed their currencies to depreciate somewhat more than did the pound before beginning their stabilizing efforts. Moreover, if it later seemed desirable, still further depreciation was permitted.[11]

Managed Paper Standards

Many unkind things have been said about inconvertible or *fiat* paper currency. This is hardly surprising when we remember the circumstances surrounding most of the world's experiences with such standards. One need only recall the French assignats, the Continental currency of our own Revolutionary War, the Civil War greenbacks, and modern postwar monetary experiences to understand the skeptical attitude toward paper money. To the average person, it is synonymous with uncontrolled and uncontrollable price inflation, with all its connotations. But to no small degree this unsavory reputation is the result of an association with difficult and troublous times. In a world wedded to the ideal of a gold or other metallic standard, inconvertible paper was often used only as a last resort when economic and political circumstances were so distorted as to make adherence to metallic standards untenable. Thus, inconvertible paper money has inherited a reputation in economic thinking that is by no means entirely deserved. The favorable experience of England and the Sterling Area countries after 1931 has helped dispel a great deal of suspicion formerly held by conservative persons.

During and since the depression of the 1930's, statesmen and economists have considered seriously the possibilities of providing their individual countries with a money mechanism more satisfactory than gold. Many have come to believe that inconvertible paper under normal circumstances and intelligent control provides greater stability of prices and business activity than is provided by gold, which at best is only a fair-weather standard.

A Comparison of Monetary Standards

Early in this chapter we noted that the requirements for a good monetary standard were so exacting that no single type of money could be expected to be entirely satisfactory. Domestic require-

---

[11] For more detailed information as to the actual rates of exchange between the pound and other Sterling Area currencies, see the League of Nations, *Monetary Review, 1936-37*, 1937, pp. 19-22. Thirteen countries were listed as being in the Sterling Area. They were: Sweden, Finland, Denmark, Norway, New Zealand, Portugal, Japan, South Africa, Siam, India, Australia, Estonia, and Argentina.

ments call for (1) a money of sufficient stability in value to prevent economic disturbances arising from purely monetary causes; and (2) a money that permits domestic fiscal and monetary action to resist depression and unemployment. In contrast, a monetary system externally should lend itself to the promotion of international trade and international lending. This is needed if a country is to join with the rest of the world in the enjoyment of the bounties of international specialization and exchange. To what extent, then, do the several types of money standards fulfill the requirements?

Bimetallism may be dismissed from consideration on the grounds that it is unlikely to be a serious candidate for adoption as the monetary standard. Gold, on the other hand, is still strongly favored, as witness our own adherence to gold. Although a casualty of the two World Wars and the Great Depression of the 1930's, gold still commands respect and even affection in certain circles. What, then, are its main virtues and its limitations?

The advantages of the gold standard. It should be clearly understood that the gold standard of the United States, a golden island in a world sea of paper currencies, cannot, in itself, convey many of the blessings usually associated with the world gold standard. Our gold reserves are so immense that reserve requirements do not provide restraint on the quantity of domestic currency and credit. And, because other currencies are not freely convertible into gold, there is no automatic assurance of stable exchange rates between the dollar and the currencies of other countries.

What advantages might be gained if some form of gold standard were re-established through the world? First, when all currencies are convertible into gold at a fixed rate and with the right of free export of gold, the gold reserves of the world, limited by the slow and arduous process of gold mining, provide a top limit to the overall world supply of currency and credit. This limit grows out of the necessity, both legal and customary, of carrying substantial amounts of gold reserves to insure gold convertibility. Second, each individual country is compelled to exercise restraint in its issue of currency and credit. Failure to practice adequate restraint results in a country's getting "out of step" with the rest of the world. When this occurs, currency expansion within the country permits and encourages such a rise in its internal price level that it checks its exports, stimulates its imports, and induces an outflow of gold to the outside world. To maintain convertibility of the currency into gold a country must allow and even impose restraints sufficient to maintain its domestic price level at the point where imports and exports are in balance.

A third advantage of a world gold standard rests in its effect on international rates of exchange. Because of the free convertibility of world currencies into exportable gold, rates of exchange between gold standard currencies are stabilized. They cannot vary from their relative gold parities by more than the cost of converting currency into gold and shipping it to the other country. For example, should the British pound contain the same amount of gold as $2.80 the exchange rate (the price of one currency in terms of the other) could not differ much from £1 = $2.80.

Weaknesses of the gold standard. The shiny merits of a world gold standard are somewhat dimmed in actual experience. First, although gold fixes an over-all limitation of the quantity of money in the gold standard world, and provides protection from the vagaries of uncontrolled paper currencies, it is quite incapable of assuring the world that the money supply will expand at a rate needed to assure stable prices. In fact, history demonstrates that world gold currencies have been subject to substantial long-run changes in value.

Second, the pressure of a world gold standard to restrain individual countries from excessive monetary expansion becomes inoperative at the very time of greatest need. The greatest threat to currency stability is war. But when war breaks out, a first step taken by belligerents is to throw off the binding shackles of gold convertibility, for it is unthinkable that the prosecution of war should be hindered by the adherence to gold.

Finally, the stable exchange rates of the international gold standard exact a serious price. The necessity for keeping "in step" with the outside world compels each country to allow its price level to adjust to the changes in the outside world. Inflation abroad will inexorably dump gold into the noninflated country until its prices rise. More serious is the effect of a foreign depression. Should one country try to fend off the spread of depression by domestic monetary expansion, it finds that adherence to gold convertibility is a serious handicap. Any monetary and fiscal steps that it may undertake to maintain domestic prices and employment tend to shrink exports, encourage imports, and generate a gold drain out of the country's monetary system. There is danger that eventually the loss of gold reserves will compel either the abandonment of the policy of stabilization at home or the abandonment of gold convertibility.

The advantages of inconvertible paper standards. The international gold standard offers the twin advantages of setting limits on monetary expansion and providing an international currency with stable rates of exchange between individual countries. The price exacted is the lack of freedom for individual countries to regulate their own price levels and monetary supply in the interest of domestic stabilization. In sharp contrast, the claims that can be made for inconvertible paper currencies are just the opposite. Such currencies permit individual countries to regulate their monetary supplies in the interest of domestic stabilization. But this freedom to control their domestic currency, in turn, removes the limiting influence of gold convertibility and the stability of exchange rates related to such convertibility.

The issuance of inconvertible paper money has sometimes been so unrestrained that it has become the source of extreme inflation. Yet there are reasons to believe that a responsible government ought to be able to avail itself of the benefits of managed paper currency without succumbing to the flagrant evil of inflation.[12]

The objections to inconvertible paper currencies. The objections to inconvertible paper standard currencies are easy to understand. First, there is the possibility of excessive issue and consequent inflation, with the well-recognized evil results. There is always the chance that the moral fortitude of the monetary authorities will prove inadequate to resist inflationary pressure. Second, an independent paper currency that insulates the domestic price level from changes in prices and business in the outside world will lead to instability of foreign exchange rates. It is pretty well agreed that exchange rate instability hinders foreign trade and foreign lending and tends to be made worse by its invitation to speculative activity.

---

[12] The favorable experience of England during the 1930's strengthened the belief in the possibility of combining restraint with monetary management of inconvertible currencies. Yet one cannot be too optimistic about the resistance of managed currencies to overexpansion. Cf. Robertson, D. H., *Money,* New York, Pitman Publishing Corporation, 1948, p. 147.

The reasons for exchange rate instability with managed inconvertible paper currencies may be readily understood. Let us suppose a threat of depression, originating abroad, induces a country to take energetic monetary and fiscal measures to prevent domestic deflation and unemployment. If, as a result, domestic prices are held at their existing level while foreign price levels fall, the country concerned will find it increasingly hard to sell to the lower priced countries abroad and increasingly easy to purchase from them. In other words, an "unfavorable" balance of payments with the outside world will inevitably appear. Under the international gold standard, an unfavorable balance will cause a drain of gold and will impose a fall in the domestic price level to the point at which the necessary import and export balance is restored. This result, of course, defeats attempts at monetary management.

It is the merit of inconvertible paper currencies that under similar circumstances domestic prices need not be forced down. But, because a country must eventually pay for its imports by exporting, something must be done to increase exports and check imports without reducing the domestic price level. This can be accomplished by a fall in the *foreign exchange value of the domestic currency*. To use a simple example, assume that, at the beginning, trade between England and the Western World (represented by the United States) is in balance. The price level index in both the United States and England is 100, and the rate of exchange is £1 = $4.00. Now let us assume that depression forces the price level of the United States and the rest of the outside world to fall by 25 per cent to an index of 75. At the same time prices in England are maintained at 100. If the exchange value of the British pound in terms of dollars should drop by 25 per cent, the effect on British trade would be about the same as if the British price level were forced down 25 per cent. Actually, the natural forces of the foreign exchange market tend to bring about this cheapening of the pound needed to restrain imports, expand exports, and restore balance in foreign trade. The beauty of managed inconvertible paper currency, of course, is that by allowing the exchange value of a currency to slide downward it is possible to resist domestic price deflation and the resultant aggravation of unemployment in the face of depression in the outside world.

Since World War II many countries have used managed paper

currencies as a tool to promote domestic employment and economic expansion. At the same time they have tried to avoid the trouble of flexible and changing exchange rates by establishing and maintaining "official" exchange rates at some fixed point. Whenever the degree of monetary expansion and inflation in one of these countries exceeds that of the outside world, its exports fall, its imports expand, and it finds itself in trouble. But neither the deflationary correctives of the gold standard nor the fall in the foreign exchange value of the currency is allowed to take place. Consequently, other steps must be taken to reduce imports and, where possible, to expand exports. Quotas, tariffs, and rationing of scarce foreign exchange are invoked to reduce imports. Subsidies and bilateral trade agreements may be used to encourage exports.

This brief review of some of the good and bad features of the different types of monetary standards reveals clearly that there is no single, easy answer to the quest for the "best" monetary standard. The whole question of the problems associated with the use of gold and inconvertible paper money standard currencies will be examined in more detail in Chapter 36.

Questions for Study

1. A country's monetary standard must be judged by its suitability both for domestic use and international trade. Why is this so?

2. Can you explain why Gresham's law came into operation so often under bimetallism?

3. What theoretical arguments have been raised in favor of bimetallism?

4. What minimum requirements should be fulfilled if a country is to be on the gold standard? To what extent does the United States' system qualify? Do you agree with those who hold that the gold standard requires that individuals be given the right to have gold coins?

5. Why was the gold bullion standard adopted by England in 1925?

6. What difference does it make that the United States is on a gold standard? What difference would it make if the rest of the industrialized world were also on gold?

7. In order for a world gold standard to be workable and tolerable, disturbances in trade and price levels must be held to small proportions. Why?

8. Before World War II the Phillippine gold exchange standard was automatic in its operation. Why was this so?

9. What essential difference is introduced when central bank management of such a system is substituted for automatic regulation?

10. Examine Chart 1 and compare the behavior of the Sterling Area countries with the situation under the gold exchange standard.

11. Why are managed paper currencies so often looked upon with suspicion? Why have they become popular among persons who wish to introduce monetary management in a country in order to promote full employment?

12. What benefits would you expect from a world-wide adoption of the gold standard? Why are inconvertible paper currency standards more attractive than gold when a country wishes to avoid price deflation arising from foreign depression?

4

The Monetary System of the United States

Our present day monetary system can best be understood against a background of its historical development. Limits of time and space permit but the briefest outline of the earlier episodes of our monetary history, but the depression of the 1930's brought changes of such magnitude and significance as to merit more detailed examination.

The United States Monetary System Before 1933

After the Revolutionary War the newly founded United States became heir to a miscellaneous collection of currencies. These currencies included the paper money issues of the Continental Congress and of the individual states, and also English, French, Portuguese, and Spanish coin. To simplify and bring order to the currency, Congress chartered the Bank of the United States in 1791 and gave it note-issuing powers. Also, a year later, Congress established a bimetallic monetary system with the silver and the gold dollar as the official monetary unit.

The dollar, 1792-1834. The new American dollar contained 24.75 grains of fine gold or 371.25 grains of fine silver. Thus, the mint ratio between the two metals was 15 : 1 and was chosen in the belief that it corresponded to the market ratio. However, because of the powerful influence of the French monetary system, which had a mint ratio of about 15.5 : 1, the world market ratio between gold and silver was close to 15.5 : 1. Consequently the silver dollar was overvalued, or too light, and, in keeping with Gresham's Law, became the sole standard money in circulation.

55

Because there was very little domestic producton of gold or silver, the new currency system was largely dependent upon silver from the West Indies. But the silver so acquired was largely drained away by the unfavorable balance of trade with England, leaving the domestic silver supply inadequate for the expanding needs of the growing country. As a consequence there was a constant clamor for bank note currency to fill the needs.

The silver currency was in a disorganized and unsatisfactory condition. The new American silver dollars were somewhat lighter than the Spanish silver dollars then in common use, and, although the law stated that the two were to be of equal value, the Spanish dollars actually commanded a premium. The bright, shiny, newly minted American dollars, in spite of their light weight, found ready acceptance in the West Indies, and a profitable business of exchanging new American dollars for the tarnished but heavier Spanish dollars developed there. Spanish dollars were brought to the United States, melted, and recoined at the mint into lighter American dollars. The United States Mint was thus actively minting silver dollars, but the supply of coins in the country did not show any corresponding increase. To stop the needless expense, the coinage of silver dollars was suspended in 1805 and no more were coined until after 1834. The coinage of silver half-dollars was continued, however, with substantially the same results as those that attended the coinage of silver dollars.[1]

Bimetallism, 1834-1861. In 1834 the coinage laws were changed to make the gold eagle (ten-dollar piece) contain 232 grains of fine gold instead of 247.5 grains; the silver dollar was left unchanged with 371.25 grains of fine silver. This made the mint ratio 16:1. The market ratio in the meantime stood at 15.7:1. The result was the gradual replacement of silver by gold coins. In 1837, further changes in the coinage laws provided that both gold and silver coin should be minted from bullion nine-tenths fine. Two-tenths of a grain of fine gold was added to the gold eagle. The gold dollar then contained 25.8 grains of nine-tenths fine gold

---

[1] Laughlin, J. L., *History of Bimetallism in the United States,* 1888, pp. 52–54. At President Jefferson's direction, James Madison, then Secretary of State, wrote a letter to the Director of the Mint ordering the cessation of the coinage of silver dollars. Although the letter was dated May 1, 1806, other evidence indicates that coinage of the dollar was actually suspended in 1805. Cf. Watson, David K., *History of American Coinage,* 1899, pp 74–75.

and the silver dollar contained 412.5 grains of nine-tenths fine silver.[2]

The discovery of gold in California, Australia, and Russia pushed the output of gold to unprecedented heights, and gold became cheaper in relation to silver. By 1853 the market ratio had become 15.4:1 and the pressure to melt silver coins increased. Although badly needed for small change, small silver coins could not be kept in circulation. To remedy this, subsidiary silver coins were reduced in weight by 6.91 per cent. The total weight of one dollar's worth of subsidiary silver coins was thus reduced from 412.5 grains to 384 grains. This placed subsidiary silver coins definitely in the position of token money, with a face value above their bullion value. At the same time the right of free coinage of subsidiary silver was withdrawn and its legal tender powers limited.[3]

The greenback period of 1861-1879. The outbreak of the Civil War put heavy pressure on the Treasury. Reluctance to increase taxes and the initial difficulties in borrowing led Congress to authorize the issue of legal tender United States notes. During 1862 and early 1863 about $450,000,000 of these notes, known as "greenbacks," were issued. They were from the beginning inconvertible into gold and consequently sold at varying discounts in terms of gold.[4]

Both subsidiary silver and gold disappeared from circulation during the greenback depreciation period. It was 1877 before the paper currency had risen in value to the point where it was no longer profitable to melt the debased subsidiary silver, and silver change again appeared in circulation.[5] The redemption of greenbacks in gold began in 1879.

The greenbacks were the source of much political controversy. The conservatives urged that they be retired at the earliest possible moment until their parity with gold was restored. Others, anxious to expand the money supply in order to remedy the depression of 1873-1879, proposed that the issue be increased. In 1878 the quantity was finally frozen at $346,681,000, the present figure.

---

[2] Laughlin, *op. cit.* pp. 70–74. Previous to this, silver coins had been eight-tenths fine and gold coins were eleven-twelfths fine.

[3] *Ibid.* pp. 79–85.

[4] Cf. Kemmerer, Edwin W., *Money,* New York, The Macmillan Co. 1935, Chapter XII.

[5] Laughlin, *op. cit.,* pp. 90–91.

Being legal tender, greenbacks could be used to pay all debts except those made expressly payable in gold or silver coin. Consequently it became the common practice to insure against the contingency of receiving debt payment in depreciated currency by including a "gold clause" in all bonds. This clause expressly required payment "in gold coin of the United States of the present standard weight and fineness." Such clauses remained in common use until abrogated by Congressional action in 1933.

The end of bimetallism. When the coinage laws were revised in 1873 the privilege of converting silver bullion into standard silver dollars was omitted and the United States currency was put on a monometallic basis. This action passed unnoticed at the time, for since 1834 silver had been too valuable for profitable coinage. Very soon, however, the question of the free coinage of silver became a political issue of first magnitude. Silver became cheaper under the double impact of great silver discoveries in the West and the closing of European mints to free coinage. By 1876 the market ratio of gold to silver reached 17.75:1, making it profitable again to coin the old silver dollar. Silver miners demanding free silver were joined by the agricultural debtor group that hoped for relief from the pressure of falling prices by an expansion of the supply of silver currency. In spite of great pressure, bimetallism was not restored. Instead, compromises resulted that involved the purchase of silver by the Treasury.

The Silver Purchase Acts of 1878 and 1890. The Bland-Allison Act of 1878 required the Treasury to make monthly purchases of between $2,000,000 and $4,000,000 worth of silver. It was supplanted by the Sherman Silver Purchase Act of 1890 (in force until 1893), which increased the mandatory purchases to 4½ million fine ounces of silver per month. These acts added $576,-166,000 of silver currency (silver dollars and certificates) to the country's monetary supply.

The gold standard, 1879-1933. The Resumption Act of January 14, 1875, provided that the convertibility of legal tender greenbacks into gold should begin on January 1, 1879. From that time until 1933, with the exception of World War I (when gold exports were limited), gold was the standard money of the country. This was true in spite of both the attempts to restore bimetallism and the silver purchase acts mentioned above.

The Abandonment of Gold, 1933

The depression of the 1930's resulted in many changes both in the monetary structure of the United States and in that of the world at large. Under the impact of economic collapse old and established systems broke down. One of the most significant victims was the gold standard and the international network of currencies and trade associated with it.

The bank holiday. As the depression worsened during the years 1930-1932, banks were caught between the falling value and liquidity of their loans and security investments and the rising pressure of deposit withdrawals. Losses of deposits that arose out of economic readjustment during the depression were augmented by "runs" that developed as bank failures increased and public confidence in bank solvency declined. The cumulative increase in failures among banks finally led to the closing of all banks on March 6, 1933, by a Presidential order declaring a general banking holiday. Later in the month, banks that were certified as being solvent were permitted to reopen.

During those bitter days of bank and business failure, price deflation, and economic distress that preceded the bank holiday, the United States clung steadfastly to the gold standard. Not until after the New Deal Administration assumed office on March 4, 1933, pledged to take effective steps to relieve the depression and to restore prosperity, did changes in the monetary structure make their appearance.

The retreat from gold convertibility. The bank holiday accomplished its purpose of stopping depositors' runs and the hoarding of cash. When the banks were reopened and currency was again freely available, banks were not allowed to pay out gold; all gold payments and gold exports were put under Treasury regulation.

On April 5, 1933, a Presidential order required that all gold and gold certificates held by banks and by the public be turned in to the Federal Reserve Banks. This action, while concentrating gold in the hands of the central banking system, did not constitute an abandonment of the gold standard, since banks were allowed to carry on normal foreign exchange transactions and were allowed freely to obtain gold for export.

On April 20, however, a new Presidential order repudiated the existing practice of permitting gold export and definitely banned both the export of gold and its earmarking for foreign account.[6] From this time until the devaluation of the dollar early in 1934, the United States dollar was not convertible into gold and, consequently, it depreciated in value in terms of the European Gold Bloc currencies.

Two reasons lay behind the abandonment of gold convertibility of the dollar in 1933. First, it removed the threat of gold loss as a possible check to domestic price and output expansion. Second, there was the possibility that the depreciation of the dollar in terms of foreign currencies might encourage United States exports and thus help domestic economic recovery. The example of England and the rest of the Sterling Area countries that experienced a substantial improvement following the abandonment of gold in 1931 strengthened the case for the abandonment of gold convertibility here.

The Devaluation of the Dollar

After the reopening of the banks and the abandonment of gold convertibility, business and prices sharply improved during the second quarter of 1933. However, new signs of weakness appeared in early autumn. Farm prices and industrial output fell decidedly from the July peak. The Administration's efforts to raise prices and employment seemed to be bogging down and some new stimulus was needed.

Authority to reduce the gold content of the dollar. The price and monetary theories of Professor George F. Warren had already captured the imagination of many who sought relief from low prices. Warren held that "by reducing the weight of gold in the dollar any desired price level can be established." [7] There was support for reducing the gold value of the dollar in other circles also. The advantages of currency depreciation as a stimulant to exports began to appear attractive in the light of the economic recovery in the Sterling Area, noted above, after its abandonment of gold and the depreciation of its currencies. Consequently those who favored the attempt to stimulate export trade by currency

---

6 Earmarked gold is generally held by the Federal Reserve Bank of New York for the benefit of a foreign owner and is not a part of the United States' gold stock.

7 Warren, George F., and Pearson, Frank A., *Prices*, New York, John Wiley and Son, 1933, p. 371.

exchange depreciation joined in favoring the reduction in the gold content of the dollar.

The Thomas Amendment, or "Inflation Rider," of the Agricultural Adjustment Act of May 12, 1933, reflected the influence of the pressure for devaluation. Among other things it authorized, but did not require, the President to reduce the weight of the gold dollar to not less than 50 per cent of its existing weight.[8]

The President did not see fit to exercise his power to reduce the gold content of the dollar under the authority of the Thomas Amendment. Instead, he ordered the Reconstruction Finance Corporation, a government agency established in 1932 to give financial aid to distressed banks and other institutions, to purchase gold at prices above the statutory price of $20.67 per fine ounce. This action tended to reduce the value of the dollar in terms of gold. Gradually the RFC pushed up its buying price for gold until, by the end of 1933, it reached $34.00 per ounce.

The Gold Reserve Act of 1934. In January 1934 the Administration determined to try out-and-out devaluation of the dollar in its attempt to raise prices. It sponsored a new law, the Gold Reserve Act of 1934, which amended the Thomas Amendment to the Agricultural Adjustment Act of 1933, to *require* that the President reduce the gold content of the dollar to some point

---

[8] Other provisions of the Thomas Amendment were:

1. The President and the Secretary of the Treasury might encourage the Federal Reserve Banks to purchase an additional $3,000,000,000 of United States obligations without incurring any penalty for possible reserve deficiency.

2. The President might direct the Treasury to issue up to $3,000,000,000 in currency (greenbacks). This privilege, never exercised, was removed by Congressional action June 12, 1945.

3. The President might establish bimetallism. This power expired unused on June 30, 1943.

4. For a six-month period the President might accept up to $200,000,000 in foreign silver on inter-governmental debts.

5. All coins and currency issued under the authority of the United States were made full legal tender. A Congressional Joint Resolution on June 5, 1933, specified that Federal Reserve notes, Federal Reserve bank notes, and national bank notes should be included as legal tender.

Only two immediate changes resulted from the passage of the Thomas Amendment: (1) The legal tender provision corrected the anomalous situation created by the regulations making it illegal to hold gold or gold certificates. (2) A small amount of silver was received from abroad on war debt payments. No other discretionary powers were exercised until January 31, 1934, when the President devalued the dollar under the authority of the Thomas Amendment as amended by the Gold Reserve Act of 1934.

between 50 and 60 per cent of its old gold content.[9] In addition, the Act provided that: [10]

1. A stabilization fund of $2,000,000,000 be established out of the profits of the devaluation of the dollar. This fund might be used by the Secretary of the Treasury to deal in gold, foreign exchange, and other instruments of credit, and was to have an existence of two years. Subsequently its life was extended indefinitely by Congressional action. In 1945 the Treasury was directed to use $1.8 billions from the fund to pay the United States' subscription to the International Monetary Fund.

2. All gold coin and bullion should become the property of the Treasury; all gold coinage should become prohibited and any existing coin melted into bars.

3. Gold certificates should take the place of gold as reserves of the Federal Reserve Banks.

4. The Treasury should regulate and control all dealings in gold for industrial purposes and for export. Moreover, it was authorized to buy and sell gold at such prices and in such amounts as was deemed to be in the public interest.

On January 31 the President, by proclamation, fixed the gold content of the dollar at $15\frac{5}{21}$ grains of $\frac{9}{10}$ fine gold. The new dollar therefore was given a gold content equal to 59.06 per cent of its old gold content; and, in terms of the new gold dollar, the price of gold was fixed at $35 per fine ounce. The gold dollar will remain at its present size unless Congress authorizes changes at some time in the future.

The Return to the Gold Standard

Immediately following the devaluation of the dollar on January 31, 1934, and the fixing of the price of gold at $35 per fine ounce, the Treasury began to buy gold freely from licensed holders [11] at $35 per ounce less one-fourth of 1 per cent handling charge. It also undertook to sell gold to licensed industrial users at $35. Furthermore, it agreed to export gold to foreign central banks or governments in order to maintain the foreign exchange value of the dollar at the new gold parity.

---

[9] The law originally allowed the President to shift the gold content within the prescribed limits at any time for a period of two years, plus one additional year should emergency conditions appear to require it. Congress subsequently extended the time limit. The authority expired without further devaluation on June 30, 1943.

[10] For the text of the Gold Reserve Act of 1934, see the *Federal Reserve Bulletin,* February 1934.

[11] The license requirement prevents illegal hoarders of old gold coin from selling their gold at the new price of $35 per ounce.

Despite the provisions of the Gold Reserve Act, which permit the Treasury to buy and sell gold at any price "most advantageous to the public interest," the door has been effectively closed to future changes in the price of gold by administrative act. The Bretton Woods Agreements Act of July 31, 1945, authorizing membership of the United States in the International Monetary Fund, states that there shall be no change in the gold value of the dollar without Congressional action. Moreover, under the rules of the Fund, gold may be purchased and sold at a price that is not more than one-fourth of 1 per cent away from gold parity, and members of the Fund must *purchase* gold at par from the Fund upon request. Apparently the Treasury is not required to *sell* gold if such actions appear to the Secretary as being not in the public interest. Congressional action will be required to make the sale of gold at $35 per fine ounce mandatory for the Treasury. However, after over twenty years, the practice of selling gold at its statutory price is unlikely to be abandoned.

The repeal of the gold clause in contracts. With the withdrawal of the right of private citizens to possess gold or gold certificates, an anomalous situation arose in connection with the provision, commonly appearing in debt contracts, that payment was to be made in dollars containing 25.8 grains of .900 fine gold. The existence of such provisions is explained by the experience of creditors in the paper money period following the Civil War, when ordinary debts incurred before the suspension of gold payments were discharged by the payment of the inconvertible and depreciated paper currency, whereas debts expressly payable in coined dollars could be satisfied only by payment in such dollars.[12]

To meet this situation, Congress passed a Joint Resolution approved by the President on June 5, 1933, declaring that contracts to pay obligations in gold or in any particular kind of coin or currency, or in an amount in money of the United States measured thereby, to be against public policy. All obligations were therefore to be discharged by the payment, dollar for dollar, in any legal tender money, that is, any coin or currency of the United States. The constitutionality of this resolution was contested in the Federal courts, and a final decision was given by the United States Supreme Court on February 18, 1935. In these cases two issues

---

[12] For a good summary of the Legal Tender Cases of this period, see Kemmerer, Edwin W., *Money*, New York, The Macmillan Co., 1935, pp. 260–268.

were presented. Two cases represented attempts of creditors to collect the equivalent of the old gold dollars in terms of the smaller new dollar from a private debtor. A third case arose out of the attempt of a holder of $10,000 in Liberty bonds to collect $16,931.25 from the Treasury in new gold dollars when the bonds were due. In the case of the actions brought to collect the equivalent of old gold dollars from private debtors, the Court held that, since Congress has the right to regulate the currency, the exercise of such a right could not be fettered or obstructed by limitations placed in private contracts. It therefore refused the plaintiffs a remedy. In the action against the United States Government itself, the Court held that Congress did not have the power to abrogate existing contractual obligations of the government. Therefore, it held that the plaintiff had a cause of action for breach of contract. But, because the plaintiff was unable to demonstrate that the devaluation of the dollar had actually caused him any loss, he was unable to recover.[13]

On August 27, 1935, Congress passed a resolution withdrawing the right of an individual to sue the United States on the gold clause in its securities. This shut off the possibility of troublesome litigation based upon damage arising from devaluation of the dollar.

Gold Inflow After Devaluation

Before the devaluation of the dollar on January 31, 1934, the monetary gold supply of the United States was of modest proportions. At that time, the world supply of monetary gold was roughly 12 billion dollars, of which the United States held about one-third. By 1940, the situation had markedly changed. Measured in terms of the new, smaller gold dollar, the supply of monetary gold in the United States had risen to $22.2 billions. This total amounted to roughly three-quarters of the world's total supply of monetary gold and was a new high point in gold holdings for the United States. In a period of seven years, our gold supply increased $18.2 billions.

Causes of the increase in the gold stock. The $18.2 billion increase in our stock of gold came from three main sources. These were: (1) gold profit from devaluating or reducing the gold content of the dollar; (2) scrap gold and domestic mining; and (3)

---

[13] For a discussion of this decision, see Hart, Henry M., "The Gold Clause," *Harvard Business Review*, May 1935.

imports. The relative importance of each of these sources may be observed in Table 2 below.

TABLE 2

Sources of Increases in the Gold Supply of the United States, 1934-1940
(In billions of dollars)

Profits from devaluation of the dollar		2.8
Domestic production, scrap, etc.		1.1
Imports resulting from:		
Repatriation of American-owned foreign funds	2.0	
Excess of exports over imports	3.3	
Foreign-owned capital seeking investment and security in the United States	9.0	
		14.3
Total		18.2

It is worth noting that not all of the increase in the gold stock found its way into the money system. For example, the profit from the devaluation of the dollar was absorbed in large measure by the establishment of the $2 billion stabilization fund. In addition, $600 million was used to retire United States bonds used as security for the issue of national bank notes. To accomplish this, gold certificates were deposited with the Federal Reserve Banks and Federal Reserve notes were issued to replace retired national bank notes, with no increase in bank reserves. Even so, the inflow of gold raised bank reserves to unprecedented heights, with member banks in possession of reserves in excess of legal requirements to an amount of over $6.9 billion, in October 1940. This excess was, of course, absorbed later by the wartime expansion of credit.

Silver After 1933

Before 1934 the silver currency issues of the United States came from two sources. First, subsidiary silver coins, along with five- and one-cent pieces, were regularly coined by the Mint to meet the fractional currency needs of the country. Such silver coinage involved the purchase of silver bullion in the market and its conversion into fifty-cent, twenty-five-cent, and ten-cent pieces. The process, like the coinage of five- and one-cent pieces, produced a seigniorage, or a profit, for the Mint, since the metals cost much less than the face value of the resulting coins. The second source of silver money before 1934 was the limited coinage of silver dollars that occurred under the Silver Purchase Acts of 1878 and 1890-1893.

During the depression of the 1930's, the silver money supply of the country increased greatly. The basic reason for this increase was the same as that which resulted in the Silver Purchase Acts of 1878 and 1890. The low price of silver in 1933-1934 stimulated the agitation on the part of the silver producers that something be done to raise its value. These efforts were directed at (1) an increase in silver's international market value; and (2) a subsidy for the domestic production of silver through government purchase of domestic silver at an artificially high price. As in earlier times, the efforts of the silver producers were enthusiastically supported by advocates of monetary inflation as a remedy for depression.

To make their arguments more palatable, the advocates of special measures for silver appealed for public support on the following general grounds:

1. An increase in the value of silver would increase the purchasing power of something over one-half of the world's population represented as being dependent upon the price of silver. It was alleged that this would greatly aid American export trade and promote recovery.

2. Adding silver to the metallic money supply would greatly broaden the metallic base and offset the inadequacy of the gold supply.

3. It would furnish a means of controlled inflation.

The Silver Purchase Act of 1934. The effects of the activities of the Silver Bloc were first seen in the Thomas Amendment, mentioned earlier, which authorized the President to establish bimetallism with the free coinage of silver. Actually, the President did not establish bimetallism. Consequently the Silver Bloc adopted other tactics.

Yielding to the combined pressure of inflationist Congressmen and those representing the silver-producing states, Congress passed the Silver Purchase Act of 1934. This Act declared it to be the policy of the United States to increase the proportion of silver to gold in the country's monetary stocks, with the objective of "having and maintaining" one-fourth of the monetary value of such stocks in silver. To this end, the Secretary of the Treasury was directed to purchase silver, at home or abroad, at a price not to exceed its monetary value of $1.29 per fine ounce. Further, existing stocks of silver in the United States were to be bought at a price of not over 50 cents per ounce. Silver certificates were to be issued against purchased silver to the amount of its cost, and such certificates were made full legal tender and redeemable in silver dollars. Under the original law, the Treasury could not *sell* any silver so purchased unless and until its market value reached $1.29 cents per fine ounce or the monetary value of the stocks of silver in the monetary system exceeded 25 per cent of the monetary value of the combined stocks of silver and gold.

Three distinct actions were taken under the mandate of the Silver Purchase Act of 1934. First, the Treasury required holders of domestic silver stocks to turn in their silver to the Treasury at a price of 50 cents per ounce. Second, the Treasury embarked upon a policy of buying foreign silver at the going market price. Third, under Executive Orders of the President, and later in obedience to specific instructions of Congress, the Treasury bought domestically mined silver at special prices.

The purchase of foreign silver. Following the direction of the law, the Treasury proceeded to purchase silver from foreign markets. The result, for a time, was a substantial increase in the open market price of silver. In 1933, before Treasury buying influenced the market, silver sold at a low of 24.8 cents per fine ounce in the New York bullion market. Thereafter, until the Treasury ceased all purchases of foreign silver in May 1942, the open market price fluctuations largely reflected the degree of vigor with which the Treasury pursued its purchase policy. The effects may best be seen in Table 3.

As may readily be seen, the silver purchases resulted in but modest

TABLE 3

Highest, Lowest, and Average Price per Fine Ounce of Silver
in New York City*
(In cents)

Year	Highest Price	Lowest Price	Average Price
1933	43.3	24.8	34.9
1934	56.0	42.0	48.2
1935	81.3	50.0	64.5
1936	50.0	45.0	45.3
1937	47.0	45.0	45.1
1938	45.0	43.0	43.5
1939	43.0	35.0	39.3
1940	35.9	35.0	35.0
1941	35.4	35.0	35.0
1942	45.0	35.4	38.6

* *Annual Reports of the Director of the Mint.*

improvement in the long-run price of silver. There was, however, an unexpected result that deserves attention. Advocates of the silver purchase plan believed that trade relations with the Orient would be improved by an increase in the world price of silver. Actually, the opposite result appeared. The sharp increase in the price of silver in 1934 and 1935 so increased the exchange value of Chinese silver currency that it destroyed China's export trade and consequently further reduced China's ability to purchase imports. Furthermore, the high price of silver, resulting from Treasury purchases, led traders and speculators to buy Chinese silver currency for export to the United States. The resulting drain upon the Chinese silver reserves was so great that in 1935 China abandoned the silver standard and adopted instead the gold exchange standard.

The effect on domestic silver. From the standpoint of the Silver Bloc, the domestic effects of Treasury purchases of silver were gratifying. This was especially true because both by Presidential order and, later, by Congressional action the purchase price of domestic mined silver was generally considerably higher than the price paid for silver from other sources. Foreign silver purchases terminated in 1942; but the Treasury has continued to offer to buy domestic silver. After World War II ended, the Silver Bloc increased its demands that the price of silver be raised. Its first goal was a price of $1.29, corresponding to the "statutory value" of silver for the purpose of coining silver dollars or for backing silver certificates. In July 1946 a compromise was reached which provided that domestic silver should be bought and sold by the Treasury at 90.5 cents per ounce. Because the world market price of silver generally has been below this price, most of the domestic silver production has gone to the Treasury.

The various prices paid by the Treasury for domestic mined silver since 1933 is shown in Table 4.

TABLE 4
Prices Paid by the U.S. Treasury for Domestic Mined Silver*
(In cents)

Period	Price
Dec. 21, 1933, to April 9, 1935	64.64
April 10, 1935, to April 23, 1935	71.11
April 24, 1935, to Dec. 31, 1937	77.57
Jan. 1, 1938, to June 30, 1939	64.64
July 1, 1939, to Dec. 31, 1946	71.11
Since Jan. 1, 1947	90.50

* Annual Report of the Director of the Mint.

The sale of silver by the Treasury. The Silver Purchase Act of 1934 provided that silver might be sold whenever the market price was above $1.29 per fine ounce or when silver made up one-fourth of the total monetary gold and silver stocks of the country. Neither of these contingencies has so far occurred. Hence during the war, when the need for silver for industrial and other uses expanded greatly, the silver in the Treasury acquired under the Silver Purchase Act of 1934 could not be sold. Several expedients were therefore used to meet the need. First, newly mined domestic silver was diverted from the Treasury by the simple method of fixing the OPA ceiling price a bit above the Treasury price. Second, free silver held by the Treasury (not needed as security for outstanding silver certificates) and, later, silver held as backing for silver certificates was "lend-leased" by the Treasury for use as "bus bars," or electrical conductors, in defense plants. This released copper for critical war use. Third, under special legislation, known as the Green Act, in 1943 the Treasury was authorized to sell free silver for industrial uses under priorities issued by the War Production Board.

From its free silver supply the Treasury also lend-leased 410,814,-344 ounces of fine silver to foreign governments during the war.[14]

Summary of the Treasury silver transactions. Some of the results of the silver purchase policy are revealed in summary form in the tables below.

TABLE 5
Treasury Silver Purchases During the Fiscal Years 1934-1955*
(In fine ounces)

Silver taken on foreign debts (1933)	22,734,824
Nationalized silver (1935-1938)	113,032,916
Foreign silver (1934-1942)	2,045,231,408
New mined domestic silver (1933-1955)	831,067,900
Total	3,012,067,048

* *Annual Report of the Director of the Mint,* fiscal year ended June 30, 1953, p. 35, and the *Treasury Bulletin,* September 1955. These figures do not include purchase of "ordinary" silver derived from multilated silver coin, miscellaneous silver recoveries from melting, refining, and coining, and silver contained in gold deposited with the mint.

---

[14] This silver was to be returned in from five to seven years after the termination of the war emergency. The emergency terminated officially with the signing of the peace treaty with Japan on April 28, 1952. Consequently the dates for the return of the lend-leased silver by foreign governments are April 28, 1957, and April 28, 1959. Belgium returned 261,333 fine ounces, the full amount of its borrowings, before July 1, 1948. This information was furnished by the Director of the Mint.

TABLE 6

Disposition of Silver Acquired Under the Silver Purchase Act for the Fiscal Years 1934-1955*

(In fine ounces)

Lend-leased to foreign governments	410,814,344
Sold to war industries, Green Act (at 71.11 cents)	167,380,240
Sold under the Act of July 31, 1946 (at 90.5 cents)	1,647,605
Processed into U.S. coin	688,118,274
Monetized as security for silver certificates	1,642,539,337
Total	2,910,499,800

* *Annual Report of the Director of the Mint,* fiscal year ended June 30, 1953, pp. 35–39, and the *Treasury Bulletin,* September 1955. The figures do not include disposition made of "ordinary" silver derived from mutilated silver coin, miscellaneous silver recoveries from melting, refining, and coining, and silver contained in gold deposited with the Mint.

Seigniorage from silver purchases. One ounce of fine silver, when "monetized"—that is, converted into silver dollars or set aside in bullion form as security for silver certificates—becomes worth $1.29. When used for minting subsidiary coins, which contain 6.9 per cent less metal than is contained in the silver dollar, a fine ounce of silver becomes $1.38. The price paid for silver by the Treasury is much less than its monetized value. For example, between 1933 and 1955 the Treasury issued over $2.1 billion of silver certificates against 1,642,539,337 ounces of silver. In so doing it realized a seigniorage, or profit, of $1,153,300,000.[15]

Results of the purchases of silver on the relative proportion of silver to gold. The avowed purpose of the Silver Purchase Act of 1934 was to make silver at least one-fourth of the total metal monetary stock of the country, or its market price $1.29 per ounce. It is of interest to see the extent to which the original purposes of the Act have been realized. When the law was passed in 1934, the ratio of monetized silver to the combined stock of silver and gold was 9.6 per cent. In 1955, after the monetization of over 2 billion ounces of silver, the ratio was 15.3 per cent. So far as the price of silver is concerned, the special price for domestic silver, determined by Congress, is only 90.5 cents. The free market price for silver has generally been considerably lower. Thus we see that neither of the goals of the Act have been reached. In the meantime, the Treasury limits its silver purchases to that mined domestically.

---

15 *Treasury Bulletin,* September 1955, p. 53.

The economic effects of our silver purchase policy. From the very beginning there was no real justification for our silver purchase policy. It was not needed to overcome any shortage in the money supply, and its results were merely a boon to silver traders and a subsidy to domestic producers. Today, with purchases limited to domestic silver alone, at the price of 90.5 cents per ounce as fixed by Congress, only the readily acknowledged subsidy element remains.

When purchased silver is "monetized," that is, used as a basis for the issue of silver certificates, the value of the bullion into which the silver certificates are convertible is considerably less than the face value of the certificates. Consequently all of our silver-based currency is essentially token in nature. There seems to be no good reason for subsidizing the production of silver for use as token money. Even though the Treasury may not feel a direct burden from the silver purchase, the silver subsidy makes it a party to the diversion of economic resources into unproductive uses. If, in place of silver certificates, the Treasury or the Federal Reserve Banks were to issue paper currency of small denominations, a real economy would be realized. The cost of printing the currency itself would of course be unchanged. But the resources now involved in the production of domestic silver would be put to productive use. Silver now put into sterile "reserves" would be available for normal general uses. Or, if the mining of silver were to be discouraged by the sale of silver at world prices, the resources of the industry would be diverted to more needed productive areas.

The Over-all Effects of Our Gold and Silver Policies Since 1933

The monetary changes since 1933 have been the object of much criticism. Without in any way attempting to evaluate such criticism let us tie together some of the practical consequences of the changes and actions which we have been examining.

The effects of our gold policy. Although the dollar was reduced in gold content, the devaluation itself did not directly increase the monetary supply, since the profit from devaluation was used to establish the stabilization fund and to retire outstanding national bank notes. Indirectly, however, devaluation ultimately resulted in an increase in the monetary gold stock by increasing the dollar value of the large volume of gold that was imported during the 1930's. Contrary to some popular opinion, devaluation of the dollar was not responsible for the increase in prices that occurred in the 1940-1951 period. To be sure, the gold base of our currency was larger, dollar-wise, when we entered the war than it would have been without devaluation. But the expansion of credit arising from war and postwar finance would undoubtedly have occurred upon a somewhat smaller gold reserve base if devaluation had not taken place.

As the law now stands, the Treasury is not compelled to buy or sell gold freely at the statutory price. Nevertheless, that fact does not prevent its actions in this respect from constituting a *de facto* gold standard. The Treasury has consistently bought and sold gold at $35 per ounce since 1934. The further fact that gold cannot be obtained for private hoarding does not invalidate the conclusion that we are in fact a gold standard country.

It would doubtless be useful to remove the shadow of doubt that hangs over the *de facto* gold standard by a clear-cut Congressional action to *require* that the Treasury should buy gold freely at $35 per ounce and sell it freely at the same price for industrial and export purposes. It is not necessary, in order to have a gold standard, that domestic holders of money be given the privilege of hoarding gold coins or bullion. However, with our present ample supply of gold and the strong position of the dollar in international circles, there seems to be very little reason for continuing to refuse to convert currency into gold for domestic holders.

The effects of our silver policy. So far as silver is concerned, it should be clearly understood that the Treasury purchase of domestic silver does not mean that silver is a standard money metal or that we have bimetallism. Instead, before 1956, virtually all of the domestic silver production was absorbed, at a somewhat excessive price, into the token money supply of the country. This process was wasteful in so far as cheaper metals or paper currency could take the place of silver. Furthermore, the subsidy involved for silver producers was difficult to defend. The rise in the market price of silver above 90.5 cents per ounce prevents this useless absorption of domestic silver.

Silver is coined on a limited basis only. It provides part of the money needed for hand-to-hand circulation and has a value equal to that of all other money, since it may be used interchangeably with all other kinds of money. There seems to be no danger that the modest accumulations have diluted the gold monetary base in such a way as to endanger gold convertibility of the currency.

Questions for Study

1. Explain why American dollars in circulation before 1834 were silver. Why were they gold after that time?

2. Why were the subsidiary silver coins reduced in silver content in 1853?

3. What was the standard money of the country in 1861-1879? How did the gold clauses in long-term debt contracts arise out of this period?

4. In 1873 a currency change was made that later was denounced by politicians as the "Crime of '73." What was it?

5. What changes occured in silver that resulted in the Bland-Allison Act of 1878 and the Sherman Silver Purchase Act of 1890?

6. Why, apparently, did the New Deal Administration abandon the gold convertibility of the dollar in 1933? What was the result on the foreign exchange value of the dollar in terms of foreign gold currencies?

7. What were the main inflationary provisions of the Thomas Amendment of the Agricultural Adjustment Act of 1933?

8. Why was the dollar devalued in January 1934? Why did the act of devaluation not result in any immediate increase in the supply of money?

9. To what extent can it be said that the United States is on a gold standard?

10. What were the main reasons for the great inflow of gold in the period 1934-1941?

11. What was the Silver Purchase Act of 1934? Whom did it benefit?

12. Does the subsidy to the silver miners cost the Treasury anything? What objections can you give to its continuance?

II___

BANKS AND THEIR OPERATIONS

II

5

The Banker's Place in Economic Society

We have already learned something of the importance of bank credit or "bank money" in the modern monetary system. Most of our supply of money in common use by the general public takes the form of bank notes and bank deposits. It is necessary, therefore, that we now make a careful examination of the mechanism, the operations, and the principles of banking. This will provide the background needed for the later analysis of the theory of money and prices and an exploration of modern monetary problems.

Financial Institutions

Banks as financial institutions. A brief look at the broader field of financial institutions will help us to understand better the unique functions of the commercial banks. A financial institution provides the means for making funds, in the form of money and claims to money, available to individual, business, and government borrowers who wish to expand their purchases beyond the limits of their own resources.

The capital requirements of modern industry greatly exceed the resources of those responsible for the immediate management of productive activities. Rare indeed is the firm that has not at some time depended upon capital funds supplied by outsiders. Financial institutions, in one way or another, are involved in the process of getting these additional funds into users' hands. This function is useful not only to the immediate parties involved, but also to the economy as a whole. When properly carried out, the extension of credit by financial institutions increases the available supply of capital goods and the effectiveness of their distribution.

77

Types of financial institutions. The stock market, using the term in its widest sense, is one important type of financial institution. Through its operations, funds of speculators and investors are put into the hands of corporations whose stock is being offered for sale. It facilitates the exchange of funds intended for permanent investment and certificates of stock representing ownership.

Investment bankers, bond houses, security companies, and underwriting syndicates act as intermediaries between persons needing capital funds and the investors. By purchasing securities with funds at their command, the investment bankers are able to seek out potential investors and induce them in turn to purchase securities. Somewhat akin to the activities of investment bankers are those of the different varieties of investment trusts, which issue their obligations to investors and use the proceeds for the purchase of securities. The trust departments of banks and trust companies also perform the functions of financial middlemen. Life insurance companies, accumulating reserves through their use of straight-line premium payments and endowment policies, constitute another special form of financial institution. Bill brokers and commercial paper houses, although less in the public eye, are also important cogs in the financial machinery.

Savings banks and savings and loan associations. A function similar to that of other financial institutions described above is performed by savings banks and savings and loan associations. Both gather in the thrift accounts of the modest savers and make them available to the loan market. The savings bank promises to return the money deposited on due notice (normally waived) and invests the funds in conservative securities, mortgage loans, or other suitable earning assets. The depositor benefits from the security derived from the expert diversification of loans and investments provided by the savings bank and by the protection arising from the bank's capital. Any loss on the bank's loans or investments falls on the bank's capital and surplus which acts as a guaranty fund against losses by depositors. Often depositors get additional protection in the form of deposit insurance.

The savings and loan associations receive deposits of savings for the purchase of shares in the associations. The saver thus becomes a part owner of the association and as such has no absolute contract right to withdraw his deposited funds. Instead, he has the right to request that the savings and loan association repurchase his shares. This it will normally do so long as new incoming funds are sufficient to meet the requested withdrawals. Most of the funds of the savings and loan associations are lent out on real estate mortgages to finance the purchase of houses. All Federally chartered and some state chartered savings and loan associations are insured against insolvency to the amount of $10,000 per individual account by the Federal Savings and Loan Insurance Corporation.

Both the savings banks and the savings and loan associations encourage thrift by providing a convenient way to assemble small sums and by paying interest. The relatively high liquidity (ease of converting into money) of both savings deposits and savings and loan association shares puts them, along with U. S. Savings Bonds, in the class of "near money." They are not, however, a part of the immediately spendable money held by the public.

The Commercial Bank

Commercial banks receive deposits payable on demand and subject to check. The essential difference between the commercial bank and the savings bank is in the nature of their deposits. Commercial bank checking accounts are a part of the money supply. Savings deposits, in contrast, are *not* money, although their liquidity justifies their being classified as "near money." Because of this difference it is important that we give special attention to the commercial banks. This difference between savings bank and commercial bank functions is often blurred by the fact that, except in New England and some other eastern states, savings banking and commercial banking are generally carried on together by a single bank organization.

The commercial banks. Commercial banks specialize in satisfying the short-term (rather than long-term) credit needs of business. Consequently they are financial institutions of the highest importance. Their ability and willingness to make loans for relatively short periods enables businessmen to adapt the scale of their operations to the changing requirements of a dynamic world. Furthermore, there is another significant characteristic of the commercial banks. All financial institutions except commercial banks merely mobilize and transfer funds provided by savers who have set aside part of their income for investment. In contrast, the lending of commercial banks is not based upon accumulated money savings. Instead, in substance, these banks *create* checking account money which they lend. Consequently, commercial bank loans cause an equal expansion in the supply of money. This unique distinction of commercial banks may be understood more easily if we examine briefly the sources of funds offered in the market by various types of financial institutions.

Loan funds not originating in commercial banks. Investment bankers, investment trusts, life insurance companies, savings and loan associations, and savings banks have one basic source of funds which they lend in the market. That source is the savings which are accumulated out of current incomes. These savings are funds withdrawn from the current flow of income and returned again to that flow by passing through the hands of the financial institutions. Practically speaking, the flow of money funds, though detoured through the financial institutions, continues without interruption so long as the process proceeds normally and regularly. The process does not in any way increase the supply and flow of money so long as savings are the only source of borrowed funds. Nor does the process *reduce* the supply and flow of money except as savings banks and savings and loan associations hold back part of the money received from savers as a cash reserve to insure the payment of deposits on short notice.

The source of funds lent by commercial banks. To a very limited extent, the owners' capital invested in a commercial bank provides a part of the bank's loan funds, but most of the funds lent by commercial banks have a different origin. They are not derived from accumulated capital funds of the owners or from savings seeking investment, but are created by the banks in the process of lending. How this takes place can best be seen by looking first into the origin of reasons for bank checking accounts.

From the standpoint of both safety and convenience, one may best keep one's supply of money on deposit in a checking account of a solvent bank. Consequently, anyone who comes into possession of cash in excess of his immediate needs, receives claims to standard money through gold imports, or obtains claims against the central bank in the form of notes or checks drawn against it, normally will exchange these types of money for credit on his checking account. Such a depositor is unlike the savings bank depositor in that he has no intention of using such accounts as a means of investment for savings. Rather, he has merely exchanged a less convenient form of money for the more convenient checking account. This practice results not only in an increase of commercial bank deposit liabilities but also leads to a corresponding increase in their cash reserve assets as well. The money brought in for deposit in commercial banks as a whole originates in three main sources:

1. Any increase in the country's standard money supply tends to increase the quantity of checking accounts. For example, a private gold importer who sells gold to the Treasury receives in payment the Treasury's check drawn against its balance in the Federal Reserve Bank. This check, payable at the Federal Reserve Bank, is deposited by the gold importer in a commercial bank. The bank that receives the check on deposit receives credit at the Reserve Bank on its reserve account.

2. Any decline in the need for money in circulation results in the deposit of cash in the commercial banks.

3. Whenever the Federal Reserve Banks create central bank money by purchase of government securities from private investors, insurance companies, and other nonbank investors, they pay for their purchases with cashiers' checks on themselves. These checks are normally deposited by the security sellers in checking accounts of commercial banks. This correspondingly increases the cash reserves of the commercial banks.

In each of the above three cases the increase of "bank money," or checking accounts and cash reserves, occurs without any sense of saving on the part of the depositors. They are merely shifting their money holdings into a more convenient form. Moreover, the increase occurs without any extension of credit by the commercial banks in the form of loans and investments.

Fractional reserves. Each deposit of the kind we have been considering brings to the bank an equal amount of cash reserve. For each dollar of checking account liability taken on by the bank it has a dollar of cash reserve. Now, 100 per cent reserves against bank checking accounts is an unnecessary luxury. Because the public is willing to hold and use checking accounts instead of currency, banks can maintain a volume of checking accounts several times as large as their cash reserves. When depositors write checks, the receivers of these checks also will almost certainly be depositors in banks. Hence, the writing of checks on the ordinary bank deposit does not cause the total volume of demand deposits to shrink. Of course, if a bank had but a single depositor, any checks written would certainly cause a shrinkage of that bank's deposits and an increase in the deposits of other banks. But the typical bank with a large number of depositors finds that, on the average, it will receive checks on other banks to an amount substantially equal to funds drawn out by its depositors. Hence, the net amount of cash reserves that such a bank must carry to meet the demands of its depositors is only a modest fraction of its total deposits.

If for some reason or other cash reserves of banks had to be kept equal to the deposits, banking would be unremunerative and depositors would have to hire the banker to care for their accounts by paying more service charges. Fortunately for both the banker and the depositor, fractional cash reserves are entirely adequate to meet the net amount of deposit withdrawals at any normal time.

Loans and investments as an origin of checking account money. Because fractional reserves in cash are adequate to insure payment of checking account liabilities, commercial banks can lend or invest that part of their cash that exceeds their reserve needs. For example, if a bank receives $1 million on deposit from gold imports and needs to keep 20 per cent, or $200,000, as cash reserve, it can lend or invest the remaining $800,000. When this is done the money supply has been increased by the amount of $800,000, for the original depositors of the $1,000,000 continue to possess that amount in checking account money while at the same time the new borrowers have $800,000.

When banks lend (or invest), the borrowers receive their funds either in the form of cash or in checking account credit. Normally, borrowed funds will be spent promptly and will be deposited in other banks by the receivers. When banks buy securities, the sellers normally will deposit the funds received in other banks. Consequently, the lending (or investing) bank tends to lose cash to other banks to the amount of its new loans and other banks' cash, and demand deposits increase by a like amount. These other banks, needing, let us say, cash reserves of 20 per cent, will have thus received cash in excess of their reserve requirements and will be in a position to lend the excess. The important thing to note here is that each added loan (or investment) made by a commercial bank creates additional checking account money in the banking system.

The total limit to this process of creating new checking account money by expanding commercial bank loans and investments is set by (1) the fractional cash reserves that banks must carry; and (2) the supply of such cash reserves available. If reserve requirements are 20 per cent, the banks can lend and expand checking accounts only to the point at which the existing cash reserve is 20 per cent of deposits. Beyond this point banks cannot go without further additions to their cash reserve supply. It is proper to point out again that this discussion of the manner in which loans lead to deposit expansion does not mean that individual banks can lend more than their own excess cash without danger of loss of cash to other banks. This subject will be more fully discussed in Chapter 19. It is sufficient for our purpose here to recognize the basic fact that the commercial banks *as a system* can and do, by lending and by purchasing securities, expand the quantity of demand deposits to a point at which their actual cash is but some fraction of their total deposits.

Commercial banks "monetize" borrowers' debts. It is well to consider for a moment the real results of the action by commercial banks in creating "money" by expanding checking accounts through the loan process. First, what the commercial banks actually do is to "monetize," or convert into acceptable checking account form, the credit obligations of borrowers. A borrower of good credit standing can be thought of as the possessor of *potential* purchasing power. In fact, he may be able on some occasions to exchange his promissory note directly for commodities that he wishes to purchase. Generally, however, the seller is able and willing to make such an exchange only if the buyer's note is "bankable"; that is, if it can be sold to a bank in exchange for checking accounts. Therefore the borrower who can go directly to the bank and exchange his own note for the much more acceptable checking account in the bank has bettered his position substantially. He has traded his own note for the more highly acceptable demand promises-to-pay of the bank in checking account form. For this service the borrower is willing to pay the bank interest, for he is now in position to purchase productive capital resources in exactly the same way as would a man who had borrowed from the savings bank funds deposited there by voluntary savers. The earnings of the bank, of course, must be applied to meet the considerable expense of operating the checking account service and the cost of assuming the risk of loss on the individual borrower's note. Any remainder goes to the banker as profit.

It is necessary to point out that the banks can and often do destroy part of the supply of checking accounts previously created by their loan expansion. For example, when a borrower repays a loan, he does so by accumulating a sufficient balance in his checking account to enable him to give the banker a check in payment. When the check is drawn, the bank returns the canceled note to the borrower and the borrower's checking account is reduced by the amount of the repayment. Whenever the bank refrains from making a new loan to replace the one repaid, the supply of checking account money is reduced.

Commercial banks, as we have seen, are in the position of being able to expand the supply of funds available to borrowers so long as there is an adequate supply of excess reserve cash. This means that opportunities for borrowing available to businessmen are not tied down to the "thrift" accumulations of income receivers, but instead are mainly limited by the available cash reserves of banks and their minimum reserve requirements. Thus, if the commercial banks hold $1,000,000,000 in free excess cash reserves and are required to carry 20 per cent cash reserves against demand deposits, bank loans can be increased by $5,000,000,000 [1] regardless of the volume of voluntary savings out of income. This power of the commercial banks to lend newly created money in checking account form without regard to the rate of saving out of income is a matter of great economic importance.

The Economic Functions of Commercial Banks

The economic functions of commercial banks fall into three main categories. First is the operation of a system of clearing and collecting checks, which makes possible the use of checking accounts as a part of the country's media of exchange. The mechanism involved in performing this function will be examined more fully in a later chapter. Second is the function involving the creation of checking account money through the process of lending and investing. It is through this function that commercial

---

[1] This disregards the possible accompanying increase in requirements for money in circulation, which would drain away part of the original free reserves and leave somewhat less to provide the basis for loan and deposit expansion.

banks influence the accumulation of capital goods or real savings. Third is the function of directing the distribution of funds and current working capital among the users of capital in the business world.

Let us now examine some of the effects of the expansion of money by commercial banks as they "monetize" the credit of individuals and firms. Assuming that the banks possess excess cash reserves, they can expand their loans and their deposits to the appropriate multiple of such excess reserves. Whenever businessmen of good credit standing wish to expand their real capital resources, they may borrow either from the savings banks or from the commercial banks. The lending ability of the savings banks is limited strictly to the funds deposited with them by voluntary savers. Not so the commercial banks, however. The latter are able to create new money in the form of new checking accounts lent to borrowers. This power of the commercial banks has great economic significance, for commercial bank loan expansion frees the rate of investment in capital goods from the plodding pace set by voluntary saving and permits it, on occasion, to bound rapidly ahead. It follows, of course, that when the expansion of bank credit stops, as it eventually must when the excess cash reserves of the banks are exhausted, the rate of investment is rudely reduced. Furthermore, when banks *reduce* the level of their loans, the subsequent fall in the quantity of checking accounts tends to reduce real investment.

Commercial bank credit and capital formation. How does commercial bank credit expansion bring about an increase in real investment or the accumulation of real capital goods? It is clear that the creation of new checking accounts does not in itself contain a magic that creates a corresponding amount of new capital goods. Somewhere in the economy someone must produce more than he consumes in order that this expansion may come about. In other words, there must be *real saving* by someone before an expansion in capital goods can occur. The question is how this real saving does come about. The answer can best be found by following through the sequence of events set in motion when banks grant borrowers loans. Armed with what is essentially *new money,* borrowers set out to buy supplies and equipment they need to expand their business operations. Whenever the capital goods industries whose products are wanted are operating at less than full capacity, as frequently happens during depressions, such purchasing by the business borrowers leads to an increase in industrial output. From this increase the borrowers obtain their capital goods. The expansion of bank credit, therefore, has had the benevolent result of making possible an increased supply of productive equipment out of what otherwise might have been mere idle time. In this case consumption need not decline at all. On the contrary, the improved employment in the capital goods trades will lead to more activity in industries producing consumers' goods. It should be evident, then, that bank credit expansion may be decidedly beneficial in time of business depression and unemployment.

The situation is different when bank credit expansion continues, as it often does, after the industrial system reaches full employment. In such a case it is no longer possible to obtain the additional capital goods out of expanding output. Instead, someone must actually curtail consumption so that borrowers' desires for supplies and equipment may be satisfied. Under these conditions, borrowers' spending can only raise the prices of capital goods and the prices of labor and materials out of which they are made. Consequently the costs of consumers' goods must rise, since their makers must compete for labor and materials with those who produce capital goods. Consumers whose incomes as yet are unchanged find themselves compelled to reduce the volume of their purchases in order to pay the higher prices of consumers' goods. These consumers, therefore, have been compelled to reduce their consumption so that the supply of capital goods can expand. Such unwilling reduction of consumption is called *forced saving*.

The same net results described above tend to occur when the banks lend to the government. During World War II the banks purchased government obligations to the amount of $75.8 billion. This amount exceeded the growth of time deposits by about $56 billion and caused a corresponding increase in the supply of checking accounts belonging to the public and to the Treasury. This expansion of credit caused results similar to those which arise from the expansion of bank credit for business purposes. At first the added purchasing power received by the government from the banks was instrumental in bringing about a vast expansion in employment and production, and greatly aided our reaching the production goals necessary for the prosecution of the war. Later, as the possibilities for further expansion in production dimmed, the main effect of the continued credit expansion was to relieve the Treasury of the troublesome need of raising taxes to meet the desired expenditures. However, while the war continued, the new money so created was not allowed to raise prices. Instead, price controls were coupled with rationing to reduce consumer spending.

The distribution of capital through the action of commercial banks. Commercial banks, in making loans to business, play an important part in the control over the distribution of existing capital. In self-protection it is necessary that bankers seek to make loans to the *best* borrowers, who are, of course, those who will pay the best rates of interest compatible with good security and who are, therefore, firms or persons in position to utilize borrowed funds most profitably and effectively. Thus the banker is instrumental in getting capital into good hands. In this respect, however, the commercial banker is in a position no different from that of other lenders. But in making *short-term* loans he plays a somewhat different role.

The commercial bank as a short-term lender. A very sizable part of commercial loans made by banks is intended to care for the short-term capital needs of business. Quite irrespective of changes in the total volume of commercial bank loans and deposits, the loanable funds are shifted from one borrower to another as needs arise. It is apparent that this shift is of immediate advantage to businessmen, who are thereby enabled to operate with a smaller volume of capital funds, either owned or borrowed at long term, since they can borrow short-term funds to care for seasonal and irregular needs. Thus, the commercial bank may be said to economize in the use of capital funds by enabling businessmen to dovetail their short-term capital needs.

The peculiar service performed by the commercial bank arises from its power to introduce *flexibility* into the capital equipment of businessmen. It is a well-known fact that the economic system is in a constant state of flux. Demand for the products of different firms and industries is continuously varying, both with seasonal changes, which are partially predictable, and with the quite unpredictable changes in agricultural output, styles, popular tastes, and costs of production. In order for these changing demands to be met, capital funds must be shifted from industries with declining demand to those with an increasing demand. Such shifts, if predictable, might take place easily without resort to short-term loans. But even seasonal changes can by no means be accurately forecast. Variations in crops, temperatures, and length of seasons make for changing and uncertain seasonal requirements. Likewise, variations arising from the dynamic, growing nature of economic life introduce a large unpredictable element into the capital requirements of industries and individual firms.

Let us examine the situation that would arise in the face of these unpredictable changes in capital needs in a society not provided with short-term loan facilities. Let us assume that there has been a decline in the demand for the services of fruit canners, owing to a fruit shortage, and an increase in the demand for the services of dealers in and processors of grain, arising from a large grain crop. Under these circumstances, the canners will reduce their scale of operations, and in so doing increase their hoards of cash capital. With no access to short-term loans, the grain dealers and processors would be confronted with the task of expanding their purchases of grain, labor, and supplies within a short period of time, with only the cash capital which they estimated as sufficient for an ordinary and smaller supply. (We may properly assume that they would not be able to increase their cash capital to meet the emergency by borrowing in the long-term capital market.) The results could only be a disastrous depression of the market price of grain owing to a *shortage of money* in the hands of grain buyers and processors. This fall in price would be quite unrelated to the basic supply and demand situation in the grain market.

In contrast, what happens in a situation like that described above when there are commercial banks making short-term loans? If commercial banks have loaned to the canners, the slump in canning will permit the canners to reduce their borrowings at the banks, which in turn can advance funds to the grain interests. As a result, there will be much less effect on the total volume of funds in consumers' hands (since reduced spending by canners is offset by increased buying in the grain market). Short-term loans are essential to an easy, smooth adjustment to meet such conditions. If there were no commercial banks with power to make short-term loans and to expand credit, business enterprise would suffer from a straitjacket of capital rigidity that would greatly impair its effectiveness.

Similarly, the development of a new or growing industry, a common occurrence in a dynamic society, is greatly facilitated by the existence of an elastic short-term loan market provided by commercial banks. The commercial banks enable one industry to relinquish part of its capital funds and another to gain it with a minimum of disturbance. Even when a growing industry needs capital from the long-term market, the short-term loans of the commercial banks (whether or not they result in forced saving) hasten the process by advancing funds to security underwriters and others in the security market.

Some evils of commercial bank credit. We have considered the ease with which commercial banks can provide investment funds for business enterprise and other borrowers without waiting for the voluntary saving of income receivers. The genuine advantage of flexibility, which commercial bank loans give to economic society, cannot be denied. Yet this flexibility is obtained at a price. Indeed, in the minds of some the price is thought to be so high as to outweigh the advantages.

The price of bank credit flexibility and elasticity is found in the tendency for fluctuations in bank credit to go to extremes. In other words, bank credit sometimes seems to have a "perverse" elasticity. This perversity of bank credit relates to its part in business fluctuations, or the business cycle. For example, during periods of recovery from depressions, it is essential that some expansion in credit occur in order that employment may increase and full utilization of our economic system may be realized. But there is no automatic brake applied to credit expansion when full employment is reached. Rather, the general optimism of businessmen and bankers, stimulated by improved profits, is likely to lead to inflationary credit expansion, which is but a prelude to depression. Thus, elastic bank credit may become a menace rather than a friend to economic well-being. Furthermore, bank credit that expands readily can also contract. Once the tide of prosperity has changed and business depression appears, businessmen reduce their borrowings and frightened bankers require liquidation of loans regardless of the wishes of the businessmen. Hence we find that the depression is aggravated by bank credit contraction. This tendency to overexpansion and overcontraction of money by the banking system has led some students to suggest that the flexibility associated with fractional reserves be abandoned altogether by the adoption of a 100 per cent reserve requirement for commercial banks.

Questions for Study

1. Can you name the main types of financial institutions and explain, in general, their economic function and significance?

2. What is the source of loan funds made available by savings banks, savings and loan associations, and insurance companies? To what extent do commercial banks lend funds derived out of savings?

3. Why can bankers get along on cash reserves that are but a fraction of their deposit liabilities?

4. Can you distinguish between the commercial bank deposits that arise out of the deposit of money and those that are created out of loan and investment operations of the banks?

5. What is meant by the expression that banks "monetize borrowers' debts"? When is this of advantage to the economy?

6. The monetary function of commercial banks involves the creation of "bank money" through loan and investment expansion.

   a) How can the expansion of loans to business lead to an increase in capital goods available for business use when (1) there is less than full employment? (2) full employment exists?

   b) How did the purchase of government securities by banks during the war affect the supply of money? The level of output?

   c) How does this assist business to adjust to changing conditions?

   d) How may this lead to perverse elasticity in the money supply?

7. A savings bank receives $10,000 on deposit, sets aside $500 as cash reserve, and invests the remaining $9,500 in an FHA real estate mortgage:

   a) Has the supply of money been increased, decreased, or left unchanged by the transaction?

   b) Has the transaction helped in the accumulation of real capital goods in the form of a house?

_____6

Credit and Credit Instruments

The nature of credit. In a general sense, credit is based on confidence in the debtor's ability to make a money payment at some future time. Its existence involves a creditor, who extends credit, and a debtor, to whom the credit is extended. Basically, the reason for credit is found in the need or desire of individuals and business firms to obtain economic goods ahead of their ability or desire to pay. Merchants are called upon to extend trade credit to buyers, and banks and other lending institutions extend credit to borrowers who wish to obtain cash with which to make purchases.

Financial institutions and credit instruments. The stock market, investment bankers underwriting stock issues, and, to some extent, investment trusts are mainly engaged in converting savings into investment in corporate shares. In this case, credit instruments are not involved, since the savers of funds acquire equity or ownership claims instead of extending credit. But most financial institutions deal to a large extent in some form of credit instruments or evidences of debt.

Credit instruments, debt, and the supply of money. Any formally acknowledged debt creates some kind of credit instrument. Because borrowers wish to use borrowed funds for a period of time, the credit instruments generally are made payable at some future time.

We have seen how banks take borrowers' notes and give in exchange either bank notes or checking account credit. When this occurs the debts of the borrowers are monetized by the banks' issue of their own *demand obligations,* or promises to pay. In this way the good credit standing of the borrowers enables them to

91

trade their promissory notes for the highly acceptable demand promises (notes and checking accounts) of the banks. Not only are the borrowers' debts thus the basis for the bank-created money, but also the newly created bank note and checking account money is itself a form of debt.

Of course, not all debts are used as a basis for the creation of money. As we already know, the investment of savings results in no expansion of money, even though savers who obtain savings deposits and savings bonds may look upon their holdings as a form of "near money." Only those debts that are taken by commercial banks and central banks as a basis for bank notes and checking accounts are instrumental in causing a monetary increase.

Except for standard gold bullion, all types of money appear to be instruments of debts payable on demand. This is true of the several kinds of currency issued by the Treasury. Gold certificates, for example, are promises to pay gold. United States notes (greenbacks) are likewise a form of the Treasury's promise to pay. Other issues, such as silver certificates, silver dollars, subsidiary silver, and minor coin, actually being token money, are in substance a kind of promise of the Treasury to redeem in standard money.

Secondary standard or central bank money, in the form of notes and deposits of the Federal Reserve Banks, are not only the debts of the banks that create them but also are backed by assets which in turn are in the form of debts.

Finally, checking accounts, or bank demand deposits, are debts of the commercial banks. Like central bank money, they too are supported by bank assets that are in turn someone else's debts. This relationship between debt, in the form of credit instruments, and the money supply will become clearer as we study the balance sheet position of both the commercial and the central banks in a later chapter.

The bank and credit instruments. The banker's stock in trade consists largely of *negotiable* credit instruments. The deposits he receives consist mainly of checks, drafts, and paper currency, all of which are negotiable in form. Only specie and minor coin are not negotiable in form, yet they too have some of the characteristics of bearer demand negotiable credit instruments.

When the banker receives a deposit, he may create a negotiable credit instrument directly if he gives the depositor a negotiable certificate of deposit, or indirectly if he enters the amount on the depositor's pass book so as to entitle him to draw checks. Checking accounts, used as substitutes for currency, are transferable by the use of another form of negotiable credit instrument, the bank check. Central banks, in contrast to ordinary commercial banks, create credit instruments in yet another form. Not only can they create deposit credit but they can also create negotiable instruments in the form of bank notes. These notes have the advantage of being directly transferable from person to person without the necessity of writing checks. Moreover, because of their form and appearance, they are readily accepted without regard to the credit standing and identity of the person offering them. In modern banking systems, they are legal tender.

The promissory notes and bills of exchange that banks take from borrowers, and the securities they purchase, are in the form of negotiable credit instruments. It is evident, therefore, that the rules governing credit instruments, and particularly those instruments that are negotiable in form, are of great practical importance both to banks and to those who deal with them. We shall examine the nature of negotiable credit instruments and the rules governing them in some detail.

What is a negotiable credit instrument? To be negotiable, the credit instrument must be in a tangible form physically transferable from one holder to another. Hence the requirement that it must be a *written* promise or order to pay money signed by the person who originates it. (Thus, a charge account cannot be a negotiable instrument.) Furthermore, it must contain "words of negotiability" that indicate clearly the intent of the parties that it be negotiable. Generally words of negotiability are "pay to the order of" or "pay to bearer," although the word "negotiable" is sufficient. Also a negotiable instrument must be payable in a "certain sum of money." A promissory note promising to deliver grain or other commodities would not qualify as a negotiable instrument. In addition, the promise or the order to pay money must be clear and without conditions. For instance, a promise to pay $100 on the election of a certain man to public office would be conditioned upon the outcome of the election, and so could not be a negotiable instrument.

Negotiable instruments fall naturally into two classes. The first is the negotiable promissory note, which is simply the *promise* of the maker of the note to pay a sum of money to the order of another on demand or at a certain future date. The second type of negotiable instrument is the bill of exchange. The bill of exchange is in the form of an *order* to pay money addressed to (drawn on) a debtor by a creditor. For example, a trade bill is an order drawn by the seller of merchandise upon the buyer. If the buyer is to be given credit, the bill will be payable at the proper future date. The seller will, in that case, present the bill of exchange to the buyer, who "accepts" by putting his name on it. This signature binds the acceptor to pay the bill of exchange and makes the bill a *trade acceptance.* Under certain circumstances, time drafts or bills of exchange are drawn against banks, which "accept," by signing, and thus create *bankers' acceptances.*

Finally, a very common form of bill of exchange exists in the ordinary bank check. Here the depositor, a creditor of the bank, orders payment to some specified person or payee. Also, banks themselves draw bills of exchange against deposits carried with their city correspondents. These bills are commonly referred to as "drafts." Except for bank checks and drafts, the use of bills of exchange in American domestic business is rather limited. The trade bill does not have widespread use in settling domestic transactions because of the prevalence of the practice of extending credit by selling on open account. In foreign trade, on the other hand, bills of exchange are very commonly drawn by sellers on buyers, or on the buyers' banks, as a means of obtaining payment for goods and services sold abroad.

Importance of negotiability. What difference does it make whether or not a credit instrument is negotiable? The answer is simply this: A person who receives a *non*negotiable credit instrument by purchase or assignment, obtains, like any ordinary assignee, only those rights to collect which the previous owner or the assignor had. If the title of the transferor of a nonnegotiable instrument was faulty in any particular, the title received by the transferee or assignee is equally faulty. For example, if the payee (the person named to receive payment) of a nonnegotiable instrument cannot enforce it because he obtained it from the maker by fraud, the person who receives the instrument, or any subsequent holder, cannot collect it for the same reason. This resembles the effect of the assignment of an open account, which the assignor cannot collect because of some defense. The assignee, too, cannot collect.

But if a *negotiable* credit instrument is taken by a person who is a *holder in due course*, it can often be collected even though the original payee or holder could not collect it. This superior position of the holder in due course arises apparently from the fact that the courts are eager to facilitate the use of credit instruments. Their acceptability is considerably enhanced by the protection afforded the holder in due course.

A holder in due course is one who has taken an instrument: (1) that is complete and regular upon its face; (2) before it became overdue, and without notice of any previous dishonor; (3) in good faith and for value; and (4) with no notice of any infirmity in the instrument or defect in the title of the person negotiating it.

Advantages of a holder in due course. Let us see the nature of the advantage that the law gives the innocent holder in due course. The law classifies defenses against the payment of credit instruments into two types. The first are called *absolute* defenses because, when proved, they defeat *any* holder's attempt to enforce payment from the person nominally obligated to pay. Absolute defenses defeat even the claims of that specially favored person, the holder in due course. Such defenses include: (1) forgery of the maker's name or forgery of the payee's endorsement of an instrument payable to his order; (2) lack of legal capacity of the maker or obligor to contract, whether because of infancy (under 21 years) or insanity; (3) lack of delivery of an incompleted instrument. In the last case, should a person sign a note or check and lose it before completely filling in the blanks (date, payee, or amount) a finder cannot complete the instrument and make it enforceable against the one who signed it.

Of more importance to us here, however, are the advantages accruing to the holder in due course because of his freedom from the second type of defenses. These defenses are called *personal* because they apply only to persons who are immediate parties to the instrument and who, therefore, are aware of the objections or defenses to its payment. Such personal defenses include: (1) fraud; (2) lack of delivery; (3) lack of consideration; (4) wrongful filling out of an incompleted instrument; (5) conditional delivery when the condition has not been fulfilled; (6) illegality; and (7) duress. For example, if a seller of merchandise misrepresents its quality and so induces the buyer to give him a negotiable promissory note, the fraud practiced on the buyer is a defense against paying the seller. But, because fraud is only a personal defense, if the seller negotiates the note to the bank, which takes it in good faith for value, unaware of the fraud, the bank *can* collect. Similarly, when the maker of a promissory note has not yet intentionally delivered it to the payee, the latter could not collect it even though he found it or otherwise improperly came into possession. An innocent holder, however, could collect. Again, the obligor on a negotiable instrument need not pay the person to whom he gave it, should it later appear that he received nothing of value in return; that is, there was lack of consideration. But the holder in due course can collect if the instrument comes into his hands. Finally, should a negotiable instrument be delivered to the payee with date, amount, or payee's name left blank, the payee is authorized to fill in the blanks *correctly*. Should he, for example, fill in an amount in excess of what is correct, he cannot collect. But the holder in due course can collect if it is negotiated to him.

Material alteration. A material alteration of a negotiable instrument may consist of changes in: (1) the date; (2) the sum payable; (3) the time or place of payment; (4) the number or the relations of the parties; and (5) the medium or currency in which payment is to be made. It may also consist of the addition of a place of payment where none is specified, or any other change altering the effect of the instrument.

Probably material alteration most commonly takes the form of raising the amount to be paid. When this or any other material alteration is made by a person holding the instrument, such a holder cannot collect anything and, so far as he is concerned, the instrument is discharged. But a special concession is made to an innocent holder to whom it may be negotiated, for he may collect it according to its terms *before* alteration.

Transfer of title. There are various ways in which a holder in due course can acquire the title to a negotiable instrument. If the instrument is payable to the order of the payee, two steps are required: First, the payee must give an "order" by endorsing the instrument; second, the instrument must be delivered physically.

If either of these steps is lacking, no title passes. On the other hand, should the instrument be payable to *bearer,* any holder, whether he owns it or not, can transfer title to the holder in due course by mere delivery alone. For example, should an instrument payable to bearer become lost, a finder would have no right to collect it. But he may pass the title with full right to collect to an innocent holder who is unaware that the instrument was lost and had been found by a person with no title.

Whether an instrument is payable to order or not, it is customary for anyone receiving it from a previous holder, to require that holder to endorse it. This permits the holder in due course to come back to the endorser and hold him liable in case the instrument cannot be collected. Persons who receive negotiable instruments from previous holders necessarily depend on their endorsements for assurance of payment. It is for this reason that endorsement is required on instruments payable to bearer.

Endorsement. There are four common types of endorsement, of which the first is *endorsement in blank.* This consists of the mere signature of the endorser, and passes title with delivery. In addition to passing title, the endorser warrants: (1) that the instrument is genuine and in all respects what it purports to be; (2) that he has good title to it; (3) that all prior parties had capacity to contract; and (4) that the instrument at the time of his endorsement is valid and subsisting. Further, he promises that the instrument will be paid if properly presented when due. If the instrument is dishonored and proper notice is given of the fact, the endorser must pay it. After an instrument has been endorsed in blank, it becomes a bearer instrument, negotiable by mere delivery. A second type is the *restrictive endorsement.* This consists of the endorser's signature, accompanied by some expression that prohibits the further negotiation of the instrument. For example, an instrument endorsed "for collection" is restrictively endorsed. The person taking an instrument so endorsed is presumed to have been aware of it and holds the instrument as the agent of the endorser; any proceeds realized are held in trust for the endorser. Thus, a person taking an instrument bearing a restrictive endorsement cannot become a holder in due course. A third type is the *special endorsement,* specifying the person to whose order the instrument is to be payable. Its further negotiation requires the endorsement of that person. In case he fails to endorse, the holder is entitled to the endorsement needed to pass title. The special endorsement gives protection in case of loss of the instrument in the mails. Finally, the *qualified endorsement* (without recourse) transfers title and warrants the paper's genuineness, but eliminates the guaranty of payment by the endorser.

Liability of endorsers. As noted above, endorsers ordinarily bind themselves to two things: First, they warrant *unconditionally* that the instrument is genuine (not forged), that the obligor and all previous endorsers are legally capable of making binding contracts, and that there is a good title to convey to the endorsee. Thus, should the final holder of a negotiable instrument be unable to collect because of forgery, for example, or lack of capacity to contract, he can demand that the endorser assume the loss. The second undertaking of those who endorse in the ordinary manner (not restrictively or without recourse) is that the instrument *will be paid*. In other words, such endorsers guarantee payment. But the guaranty is *conditional* only. To bind the endorsers on their guaranty the holder must present the instrument to the obligor for payment. This presentment must be in the proper manner and place and at the proper time. This requires that a time instrument be presented on the day it is due; otherwise the endorser is free of liability. If the instrument is payable on demand, it must be presented within a reasonable time. This stipulation is interpreted to mean that the last holders of bank checks and other demand bills of exchange must present them, or start their collection, within the next business day after receiving them. Otherwise the endorser is freed from his liability as guarantor of payment. Thus a holder in due course of a check may protect himself by starting presentment, either by turning the instrument over to his bank or by other means, within the next business day after its receipt. In case of dishonor, notice must be sent to each endorser against whom the holder desires recourse. Notice of dishonor may be either in writing or oral, and given in any terms sufficient to identify the instrument and indicate that it has been dishonored. Notice of dishonor must be started so as to reach the party notified within the next business day if the parties live in the same place. Where the parties to the notice reside in different places, notice of dishonor must be deposited in the post office in time to go by mail the next business day, or, if there is no mail at a convenient hour on that day, by the next mail thereafter. If notice is not sent by mail, it must arrive within the time at which notice properly sent by mail would have arrived. Whenever notice is properly addressed and deposited in the post office (or box), the sender has given sufficient notice, even if the notice never actually arrives. A party receiving notice of dishonor has, after its receipt, the same length of time as the original holder for notifying and binding antecedent parties. Notice of dishonor may be waived by the endorser.

A dishonored bill of exchange drawn or payable in another state (that is, a foreign bill) must be "protested"; otherwise the drawer and endorsers will be discharged. The protest must be annexed to the bill or contain a copy thereof and be under the hand and seal of a notary. It must contain the time, place, and fact of presentment and be sent as notice of dishonor to parties to be held. Endorsers sometimes mark checks "no protest" to indicate that they waive the requirement of proper presentment and formal notice of dishonor. This procedure means that they will unconditionally assume their liability as guarantors. Such a waiver has the advantage of avoiding the costs of the formal protest, which are attached to the check as returned to the endorser.

The depositor and the bank. When a depositor draws checks on his bank he promises that they will be paid. Even though a holder delays unreasonably, the depositor is duty bound to maintain an adequate balance out of which to pay outstanding checks. In other words, delay in presentment of checks does not discharge the drawer except in one special circumstance. Should delay in presentment beyond the next business day after issue result in the check not being paid because of the failure of the bank on which it is drawn, the drawer is excused from liability to the extent of his loss.

Drawers of checks frequently try to protect themselves and the bank by making a notation on the face to the effect that the check will not be honored by the bank after a certain number of days time. This has the effect of a "stop-payment" order but does not relieve the depositor of his obligation to pay the check eventually.

Sometimes depositors carelessly draw checks in such a way as to make it easy to insert additional figures or words. This carelessness invites alteration by unscrupulous holders. The courts, therefore, frequently rule that when a bank has paid a check in ignorance of the alteration, which the depositor's carelessness made easy, the bank should not suffer the loss, but instead is entitled to charge the amount to the depositor. For this reason, drawers of checks and other instruments ought to use care in filling up all unused spaces.

Questions for Study

1. Why can one properly say that our money is generally a form of debt?

2. Can you distinguish between a promissory note and a bill of exchange?

3. How can you tell whether or not a note or bill is negotiable? Why is it important to know?

4. What is a trade acceptance? A banker's acceptance?

5. What must a person be prepared to show in order to qualify as a holder in due course of a negotiable instrument?

6. What is the advantage of establishing the fact that one is a holder in due course?

7. Distinguish between (a) the absolute defenses and (b) the personal defenses to the payment of a negotiable instrument.

8. What is a material alteration? What is its effect on the right to collect of the one who alters the instrument? How is the innocent holder affected?

9. Name the four types of endorsement of negotiable instruments. What is the effect of each?

10. What is the difference between an endorser's "warranty" and his "guaranty" of a negotiable instrument? Under what conditions may the two liabilities become separated?

11. What must a holder of a negotiable instrument show in order to hold endorsers upon their guaranty?

12. What is the effect of "no protest" stamped upon the face of a check by a payee living in another state?

7

The Commercial Bank

By lending and investing, commercial banks create the main part of our supply of money. To understand this process of money creation and the banks' part in the extension of credit, we need to become familiar with both the structure and the operations of the commercial banks. As a first step in this direction, we shall examine the essential elements of the individual bank as revealed by the simple balance sheet. Later we shall try to catch an over-all view of the whole banking system by looking at a combined and somewhat more detailed balance sheet for all commercial banks.

The Balance Sheet of the Individual Bank

The evolution of a commercial bank's balance sheet throws a good deal of light upon the basic process of credit expansion and money creation. Therefore, let us look at the process of organizing and opening a bank, examine a simple statement of assets and liabilities of the bank as first organized, and trace through the results of its expanding activities.

Organization and opening of a bank. Banks organized under the banking laws of a state are called *state banks,* and those organized under the Federal laws are called *national banks.* The type of charter preferred depends somewhat upon the kind of banking in which the organizers expect to engage. For example, if a non-stock mutual savings bank is to be organized, it must be done under state laws. Also, if a bank wishes to engage extensively in lending on real estate security, the opportunities are frequently greater under state than under Federal law. Likewise, capital requirements are sometimes less rigid under state law, and the supervision of state banks has frequently been less strict.

To obtain a charter to start a new bank, application must be made to the proper authority. Applications for national bank charters go to the Comptroller of the Currency, who is in charge of organizing and regulating national banks. For state charters, application must be made to the state banking department. Such applications for charters are now more than mere formalities, and properly so. At least five prospective shareholders must sign the application for a national bank charter. They should not be "promoters" in the professional sense of the word, for to receive favorable consideration the application must reflect a *local* demand for the banking accommodation that the proposed bank will provide.

Before approval is granted, the proposed organization is scrutinized to make certain that the organizers are competent and trustworthy. Moreover, the existing banking facilities and practices must be taken into account in order to evaluate the community need and the probability of success of the proposed bank. Today the organizers will desire that the bank become a member of the Federal Deposit Insurance System, and therefore the proposed bank must be approved for deposit insurance by the Federal Deposit Insurance Corporation.

When approval to organize is received, the stockholders' subscriptions to the bank stock must be obtained and the capital paid in.

The balance sheet of the individual bank. Let us assume that all the requirements have been fulfilled for organizing a new small national bank. Its common stock has a total par value of $50,000, but because such stock must now be sold at a 20 per cent premium,[1] the bank has actually received $60,000 from the stockholders. Of this amount $50,000 has been spent on a building and some equipment, $1,800 invested in stock of the Federal Reserve Bank,[2] and $8,200 kept as cash. The bank's balance sheet, or statement of assets and liabilities, now stands as follows:

Assets		Liabilities	
Cash reserves	$ 8,200	Capital stock	$50,000
Stock in Federal Reserve Bank	1,800	Surplus, paid-in	10,000
Build. & equip.	50,000		
Total assets	$60,000	Total liabilities	$60,000

[1] To step up the stockholders' capital contributions above the minimum capital stock requirements, the law requires a paid-in surplus of 20 per cent when national banks are organized.

[2] National banks must belong to the Federal Reserve System and must buy stock in the Federal Reserve Bank of their district to the amount of 3 per cent of their own capital and surplus.

Our bank is now ready to receive deposits. Friends and relatives of the organizers are prevailed upon to bring in for deposit $1,000,-000 in the form of checks on other banks. When these checks are collected our bank's balance sheet reads:

Assets		Liabilities		
Cash reserves	$1,008,200	Demand deposits		$1,000,000
Stock in Federal		Capital stock .	$50,000	
Reserve Bank	1,800	Surplus, paid-in	10,000	
Build. & equip.	50,000			
		Total capital account ..		60,000
Total assets	$1,060,000	Total liabilities		$1,060,000

Our bank's successful campaign for deposits has obviously depleted the cash reserves and the deposits of other banks by $1,000,-000. This loss of cash reserves, equal to the loss of deposits, will put a squeeze on the reserve position of the other banks.

We shall assume that the cash reserve which our bank must carry against its demand deposits is 20 per cent. Consequently, to provide adequate cash to support its new $1,000,000 in deposits, the bank needs only $200,000 in cash reserve. The remainder, along with the $8,200 left from the stockholders' contribution, can be lent or invested in securities. The loan fund of the bank, equal to its excess cash reserves, is therefore $808,200. Let us next assume that the bank lends $400,000, purchases $400,000 of U.S. securities, and invests $8,200 in other securities. Normally, the proceeds of the bank's loans will be paid out by the borrowers to persons and firms that are customers of other banks. Also, sellers of bonds purchased by the bank will normally be customers of other banks. In consequence, the loans and investments of our bank will cause a rise in its earning assets by $808,200 and a drop in its cash reserve by a similar amount. On the other hand the cash reserves and the deposits of other banks will increase by $808,200. Our bank's balance sheet now reads as follows:

Assets		Liabilities		
Cash reserves	$ 200,000	Demand deposits		$1,000,000
Loans	400,000			
U.S. securities	400,000	Capital stock .	$50,000	
Stock in Federal		Surplus, paid-in	10,000	
Reserve Bank	1,800			
Other securities	8,200			
Build. & equip.	50,000	Total capital account ..		60,000
Total assets	$1,060,000	Total liabilities		$1,060,000

To be realistic we must now assume that our bank, like its fellow commercial banks, establishes a savings department and receives on deposit $50,000 in savings accounts. These deposits are made either (1) by bringing in cash; or (2) by depositing checks drawn against other banks. The immediate result will be an increase in cash reserves of our bank by $50,000 and in savings deposits by a like sum. The new savings accounts require some cash reserve, 5 per cent let us assume, so that $2,500 of the $50,000 in cash received through savings deposits must be impounded as reserve. This leaves $47,500 in free cash that may be lent out. When this money has been lent the balance sheet of our bank will look like this:

Assets		Liabilities	
Cash reserves	$ 202,500	Demand deposits	$1,000,000
Loans	447,500	Time deposits,	
U.S. securities	400,000	savings accounts	50,000
Stock in Federal		Capital stock . $50,000	
Reserve Bank	1,800	Surplus, paid-in 10,000	
Other securities	8,200		
Build. & equip.	50,000	Total capital account ..	60,000
Total assets	$1,110,000	Total liabilities	$1,110,000

Let us now carry our bank one step further. After some months of operation the bank finds that it has paid all of its expenses and has $5,000 left, out of its interest earnings. Assuming that there has been no change in the amount of deposits, this gain of $5,000 will appear as an increase in assets by this amount. The banker, being thrifty, has invested the $5,000 in other securities. On the liability side of the balance sheet the accruing profit must be shown as an addition to the capital accounts, or net worth. Therefore $5,000 will be put in a new item among the capital accounts, namely, "undivided profits." The balance sheet now reads:

Assets		Liabilities	
Cash reserves	$ 202,500	Demand deposits	$1,000,000
Loans	447,500	Time deposits, savings	
U.S. securities	400,000	accounts	50,000
Stock in Federal		Capital stock . $50,000	
Reserve Bank	1,800	Surplus, paid-in 10,000	
Other securities	13,200	Undivided	
Build. & equip.	50,000	profits 5,000	
		Total capital accounts ..	65,000
Total assets	$1,115,000	Total liabilities	$1,115,000

The place of the new bank in the banking system. So far as the banking system is concerned, the appearance of our new bank has merely compelled the other bankers to share with the newcomer the pre-existing supply of cash reserves and the loans and deposits supported thereby. The new bank did not cause any addition to the supply of reserve funds nor did it enable the banking system to make any net additions to its loans and deposits. It was able to make loans only by taking away from the other banks some of the pre-existing deposits. This fact explains the intensity of the interbank competition for deposits which so frequently arises.

The Banking System — A Combined Balance Sheet

Some sense of the magnitude of the credit and money-creating operations of our commercial banking system is provided by a combined balance sheet for the insured commercial banks. These banks, with 99 per cent of the total deposits of all commercial banks, constitute the significant portion of the commercial bank system. The combined balance sheet (Table 7) reveals details not shown on the simple statement that we previously examined. For example, it reveals the different varieties of cash or its equivalent carried by the banks. Besides "till money," or currency and coin, bank cash reserves include deposits in the Federal Reserve Banks (by member banks) and deposits in other banks (city correspondents) carried by member and nonmember banks alike. The latter deposits are a convenience for the depositing bank not only because they provide a ready means for making payments to other banks, but also for the services that the city correspondent stands ready to perform in return for the deposit. The combined balance sheet also reveals something of the magnitude of the "float" of uncollected checks received on deposit but not yet deducted from the account of the drawers.

Most significant of all, the combined balance sheet of the commercial banks gives us a picture of the magnitude of the checking account money that the banks have created in exchange for cash, debts of borrowers, and securities. It also shows why, with our mixed type of banks (savings and commercial), total loans and investments cannot be taken as a measure of the money-creating activities of the commercial banks. Savings and other time deposits bring into the banks existing money which is lent and invested by the banks. Consequently, loan and investments in part reflect the time deposits of banks. Though "near money," these deposits are not money itself. Only loans and investments made by banks in excess of those based on funds received from time deposits can properly be looked upon as a source of increase in money.

TABLE 7
Assets and Liabilities of Insured Commercial Banks, April 11, 1955
(In thousands of dollars)

Assets

Cash, due from banks and cash items:

Cash in vault	$ 2,682,964	
Collection items	9,764,803	
With Federal Reserve Bank	17,940,586	
With other domestic banks	10,273,975	
With foreign banks	102,498	
Total cash and due from banks		$ 40,764,826
Securities:		
U.S. Government obligations	62,453,893	
Obligations of state and local governments	12,582,949	
Other securities	3,914,590	
Total securities		78,951,432
Loans—gross total	76,054,690	
Less valuation reserves	1,124,095	
Net total loans		74,930,595
Miscellaneous assets:		
Customers' liability for acceptances	440,311	
Bank premises, etc.	1,602,278	
Other assets	876,392	
Total miscellaneous assets		2,918,981
Total assets		$197,565,834

Liabilities

Deposits:

Individuals and firms:

Demand	$98,885,201	
Time	45,257,057	
U.S. Treasury	5,439,032	
States and local governments	12,612,398	
Banks	14,836,893	
Certified checks, etc.	3,143,472	
Total deposits		$180,174,053

Money borrowed	137,666	
Acceptances outstanding	461,609	
Other liabilities	2,185,091	
		2,784,366

Total liabilities, excluding capital accounts	182,958,419

Capital accounts:		
Capital stock	4,457,269	
Surplus	6,976,016	
Undivided profits	2,724,922	
Reserves for contingencies	449,208	
Total capital accounts		14,607,415

Total liabilities and capital accounts	$197,565,834

Management and Control of Banks

The management of a bank is vested in its board of directors and the officers appointed by the board.

The bank directors. The boards of directors of national banks may consist of not less than five nor more than twenty-five directors. In their election stockholders have the privilege of cumulative voting. The directors must be citizens of the United States, and three-fourths of the board members must have resided in the State, Territory, or District, or within 50 miles of the bank's head office, for at least one year before election, and must continue such residence during their term of office. They are sworn to administer the affairs of the bank diligently and honestly.

Bank directors are chosen both for their business experience and skill and for their value in attracting important customers' accounts. The intelligent businessman, holding a responsible position in trade or industry, makes a valuable member of a bank's board of directors. His knowledge and experience enable him to contribute wise counsel to the bank management. Furthermore, his position as director may be expected to attract the accounts of other businessmen.

It sometimes happens, however, that directors, chosen largely for their prestige value, fail to understand clearly the nature of the responsibilities they have assumed. In such cases their attention to the bank's affairs may be purely perfunctory, leaving the actual control of bank policies and operations in the hands of the officers. Such an attitude may matter little when officers are honest and competent and times are good. But sometimes incompetency and dishonesty, preventable by diligence on the part of the directors, lead the bank to ruin. Even honest and competent officers need and are entitled to receive the wise counsel of the directors. Directors who fail to take an active and constructive part in determination of the banking policies are failing in their duties and may incur a serious penalty for such negligence. The law requires that directors exercise ordinary care and prudence in the administration of the bank's affairs. Although they may entrust the actual operations to duly authorized officers, they must exercise reasonable supervision and cannot hide behind the shield of ignorance when ignorance is the result of gross inattention. If the courts find that a director's neglect has been responsible for the bank's loss, they hold him liable.

The directors of member banks may be removed from office by the Board of Governors of the Federal Reserve System on proof that they have been guilty of violation of the banking laws or have knowingly permitted the continuance of unsound or unsafe practices by the officers.

Public supervision and bank management. Bank managers are not entirely free to determine their policies as they may choose. Banks are among the most regulated of our economic institutions and the banker's policies must be set up within the framework of the regulations imposed by public authority. These regulations are primarily aimed at safeguarding the banks and maintaining a sound banking system.

The foundation for bank regulation is found in the banking laws under which the banks operate. National banks must conform to both the National Banking Act and the provisions of the Federal Reserve Act. State banks similarly are controlled by the laws of their respective states and, if they are members of the Federal Reserve System, by the Federal Reserve Act also. We shall have occasion later in our study to take note of these laws as they apply to particular banking operations. Out of these laws that regulate banking there necessarily arise supervisory boards and examiners charged with the duty of enforcing compliance. It follows that these regulatory and supervisory bodies play a significant part in bank management. They impose rules of banking conduct consistent with the banking laws and, by examination and reports, attempt to compel observance of these rules. Unhappily for the banker, there is a good deal of duplication in the efforts of the banking supervisors, and individual banks often find themselves making reports to and being examined by two or more supervisory authorities.

Questions for Study

1. Can you explain a preference that an organizer of a bank might have for state or national bank charters?

2. What requirements exist to aid in insuring that newly formed banks are needed and will be properly operated?

3. Why are newly organized national banks now required to pay in a surplus equal to 20 per cent of their capital?

4. What is the main source of loan funds of a newly organized bank? Why does the new bank's expansion reduce the lending capacity of other banks?

5. What determines the amount of loan funds that a bank acquires out of $100,000 in deposits attracted away from neighboring banks?

6. When a bank receives $10,000 in savings deposits:
   a) What is the effect upon its supply of loan funds?
   b) When this money is received on deposit and then relent, what is the result of the whole transaction upon (1) the public's supply of money? (2) the supply of "near money"?

7. When the bank realizes earnings of $4,000 over a period of time, how will those earnings be recorded in its balance sheet?

8. What are the duties of bank directors? If they act in good faith in trusting the bank's operations to the officers, are they legally responsible to depositors and stockholders in case of losses arising from the officers' negligent and illegal practices?

9. Refer to the combined balance sheet for insured banks shown in Table 7. Arrange the following items to form a bank balance sheet: Loans $749,300; time deposits $452,570; due to banks $148,360; certified checks outstanding $31,430; cash in vault $26,820; U.S. securities $624,530; surplus $69,760; reserves for contingencies $4,490; other securities $164,960; deposits with the Federal Reserve Bank $179,-400; demand deposits $1,169,360; collection items $97,640; other liabilities $27,840; due from other banks $103,750; other assets $29,-180; undivided profits $27,770; capital stock $44,000. Total assets and total liabilities are $1,975,580.

10. Show the immediate effect of each of the following transactions on the bank's balance sheet. Indicate the amount of change in individual balance sheet items. Remember that the balance sheet must balance.
   a) The bank notifies its city correspondent to purchase the fol-

lowing in the market and charge the price against its deposit
with the city correspondent:

1) $10,000 face value of open market paper (bearer notes
of a well-known finance company) having 4 months
maturity, discounted at 3 per cent per annum.

2) $50,000 face value 3¼ per cent U.S. bonds at 102.

b) The bank extends a $10,000 loan to one of its customers for
6 months, at 4 per cent interest, with the privilege of renewal for another 6 months on the payment of interest.

c) The bank receives on deposit: $3,000 in checks on other
banks, $4,000 in checks on itself, $1,000 in currency.

d) Customer A, with a balance of $400, drew a check for $500
payable to B. The bank honors the check by crediting B's
account for $500.

e) The bank sells a $10,000 Treasury bill nearing maturity for
$9,998.

f) Because a borrower appears to be unable to pay a $1,000
note the bank writes it off.

g) The directors declare a 3 per cent dividend on the stock
and pay it with cashiers' checks.

_____8

Bank Deposits and Their Protection

We have already observed the manner in which a new individual bank is able to gain a foothold and establish itself in the banking world. One thing stands out clearly: For the bank to expand, it is necessary that it first acquire deposits. This it can do only by taking them away from its banking neighbors. Although the banking system as a whole is able to expand the total loans and demand deposits on the basis of new reserves, the individual bank has no such option. For, when the single bank makes a loan, it must have cash available to meet that amount of cash withdrawal. The loans of one bank lead to the expansion of cash and deposits of other banks.

So far as the individual bank is concerned, the quantity of bank deposits is fixed, and its only hope for taking part in profitable loan and investment activities is to acquire deposits from other banks. This is the reason for the active and sometimes destructive competition among banks for deposits.

Kinds of Deposits

Some types of deposits are more profitable for banks to hold than others. For example, the cash reserve required both by law and by operating necessity differs with the kind of deposit. In general, time deposits require the carrying of a lower percentage of cash as reserves than do demand deposits. Thus a time deposit of a given number of dollars provides a greater volume of loan funds than does a demand deposit of the same amount. Moreover, the operating cost of handling time deposits is smaller. Consequently, banks can afford to pay interest on time deposits, whereas they not only legally cannot pay interest on demand deposits, but sometimes make service charges on unprofitable checking accounts.

Time vs. demand deposits. Bank deposits are differentiated into *time* and *demand* categories for a number of important reasons:

1. Demand deposits make up a very significant part of the money supply, whereas time deposits are not money.

2. Legal reserve requirements against demand deposits are higher than are those against time deposits.

3. Time deposits, particularily those made up of thrift or savings accounts, are less subject to irregular withdrawal than are demand deposits. Consequently, the investments and loans based on funds arising from time deposits often differ from other bank loans and investments.

The definition of time and demand deposits for member banks, as stated by the Board of Governors of the Federal Reserve System, makes clear the distinction between the two types:

1. Demand deposits are all deposits not classified as time deposits.

2. Time deposits fall into three classes:

(a) The time certificate of deposit, issued by the bank to the depositor and payable in not less than thirty days after its issue or upon at least thirty days' written notice. Business firms and individuals use time certificates to earn interest on funds that are not seasonally employed.

(b) Time deposits, open account, that differ from time certificates in that they permit accumulations of current deposits. They also may not be withdrawn until maturity or until the expiration of a required thirty-day notice period. They include Christmas and vacation savings clubs.

(c) Savings deposits. These must be evidenced by a pass book, or other written receipt or agreement, and consist of funds deposited to the credit of individuals (except partnerships operating for profit) or nonprofit organizations. Banks must have the right to require at least thirty days' written notice of withdrawal of such deposits. Payment is made only upon the presentment of the pass book or directly to the depositor himself.

The withdrawal of time deposits. To prevent the evasion of the rule against paying interest on demand deposits, some restraint is needed on the withdrawal of time deposits. Otherwise some deposits, actually demand in nature, might masquerade as time deposits in order to earn interest. Consequently, the law prohibits Federal Reserve member banks from paying time certificates and time deposits, open account, before they are due (at maturity or after the expiration of the required period of notice), except in accordance with rules laid down by the Board of Governors. It also prohibits any member bank from paying any savings account without notice unless *all* savings accounts of that bank are similarly payable. However, banks need not require any notice on savings accounts before withdrawal, since savings accounts are genuine thrift accounts and are not likely to represent demand deposits in disguise. The Board of Governors now permits member banks to pay out time deposits before maturity if the depositor, in a written application, shows that the payment is necessary to prevent great hardship in meeting an emergency. Banks may also lend on unmatured time deposits at rates of interest not less than 2 per cent above the rate paid on the deposit. The Federal Deposit Insurance Corporation enforces similar regulations on nonmember insured banks.

Kinds of depositors. The holders of deposits in commercial banks may be classified into four main groups:

1. Holders of business and personal accounts. These accounts include both time and demand deposits (checking accounts). In the latter category are included certified checks and cashiers' checks.

2. The United States Government, with deposits mainly payable on demand. These deposits, originating during wars, are now mainly used to receive the current governmental revenues that arise from employer withholdings of income and social security taxes, certain excise taxes, and quarterly receipts of corporate and personal income tax payments. These accumulations are left on deposit with qualified depositaries until needed for disbursement by the Treasury. From time to time, in anticipation of expenditures, the Treasury makes calls on these accounts for transfer to the Treasury account at the Federal Reserve Banks. The purpose of these accounts is to minimize the disturbances to bank reserve positions when Treasury receipts exceed expenditures.[1]

3. State, county, and municipal governments, with accounts mainly in demand deposit form.

4. Banks with funds deposited in city correspondent banks. These accounts are known as interbank deposits or bankers' balances. They are of great value to the depositing bank because they:

a) Provide the bank owning them with working cash reserves.

b) Enable the bank to provide customers with drafts payable in large cities.

---

[1] Cooke, Helen J. and Straus, Kathleen N., "Treasury Tax and Loan Accounts at Commercial Banks," *The Treasury and the Money Market,* Federal Reserve Bank of New York, May 1954.

c) Facilitate the collection of checks.

d) Facilitate making loans and investments in the city money markets.

Chart 2 provides a visual measure of the relative importance of deposits held by the different classes of depositors.

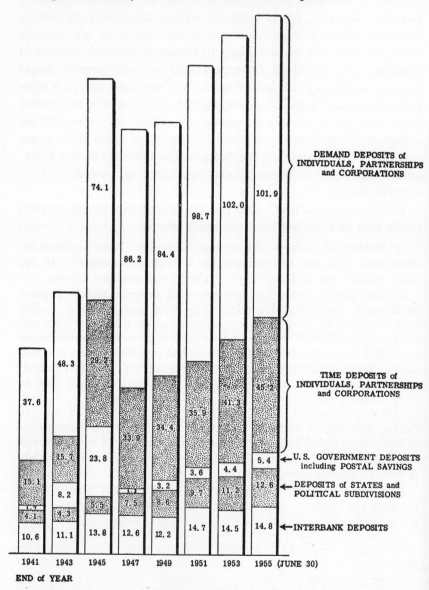

Chart 2. Deposits of Insured Commercial Banks by Classes of Banks (in billions of dollars).

Methods of Acquiring Deposits

Competitive methods. The banker has a number of methods by which he may seek to attract deposits. He may erect an imposing building whose entrance is flanked by marble pillars, symbols of strength. Where legally permitted he may seek new customers by establishing branches in newly developed shopping centers and in residential areas. He may expand the free services and conveniences available to his customers. He may advertise, in a restrained and dignified manner, on billboards and in newspapers. He may organize a "new business department" whose function is to make contacts with new customers. He may persuade the stockholders to elect a prominent business executive to the board of directors in order that all or part of the deposits of the executive's firm may be captured. Finally, he may compete with other bankers for deposits in a more direct way by offering higher rates of interest on deposits. This last form of competition has been especially important. A good many depositors are influenced by the interest payments and respond favorably to offers of higher returns. Therefore, when one bank offers higher interest to depositors, other banks are forced to do likewise. There always seems to be excess capacity in any given bank for absorbing and utilizing additional deposits. Therefore, to some degree, banking is exposed to the danger of cutthroat competition. There exists a powerful temptation to try to attract added deposits by offering higher interest rates. This practice tends to reduce banking profits and encourages the banker to seek increased earnings by making less conservative and more remunerative loans and investments. If all bankers could be trusted to refuse to make unsafe loans under the stress of competition and profit seeking, unlimited competition for deposits among bankers might have no dire results. What borrowers would pay for well-secured loans and the banker's necessary profit margin would tend to fix the limit on interest payments to depositors.

In actual practice, however, not all bankers can be trusted to watch competition cut into profits without taking some unwise action to prevent it. There seem always to be some potential borrowers who will promise to pay higher interest on loans in order to finance untried and hazardous ventures. The banker, seeking greater earnings to compensate for high interest paid on deposits, may turn to these more speculative loans and investments. But, because of circumstances or short-sightedness, he is unlikely to increase his earnings margin enough to compensate for the greater risks involved. The evil consequences of such action are concealed during periods of prosperity, but depression reveals them. Experience has repeatedly shown the fatal results of such competition. To guard against excessive competition for deposits, clearinghouse associations have sponsored agreements among their members regulating competitive practices. Particularly, they have attempted to control the charges made by banks for services rendered to customers and the payment of interest on deposits. The Banking Acts of 1933 and 1935 recognized the need for regulation of competitive interest payments by prohibiting all insured banks from payment of interest on demand deposits and by providing for the setting of maximum rates of interest paid on time deposits.

Prohibition of interest payments on demand deposits. In earlier times, banks often paid interest on the average demand deposit balances of their more important customers. Especially was this the practice of city correspondent banks as they bid for the deposit balances of country banks. The legal prohibition of interest on demand deposits seems to have been aimed at holding in check excessive competition of this kind among city banks and to discourage the accumulation of country bank funds in the hands of city correspondent banks.

Although interest can no longer be paid on demand deposits, banks are free to compete in other ways. Free services are legitimate bait to offer depositors, even though they involve expense to the bank. In boundary-line cases, supervisory authorities must rule on the question of whether or not a given practice constitutes in fact the payment of interest. Banks may absorb incidental out-of-pocket expenses incurred for the depositor. But, in the case of banks belonging to the Federal Reserve System, the absorption of costs of over $2 per month for any one deposit is ruled to be a payment of interest.

Regulation of interest on time deposits. Time deposits are subject to two limitations as to interest payments. First, member banks may pay no more (but may, of course, pay less) interest than that prescribed by the Board of Governors. Second, they may pay no more than the maximum rate permitted to state banks and trust companies. Under the 1935 banking act, the Board of Directors of the Federal Deposit Insurance Corporation is empowered and directed to put into force regulations on the payment of interest by nonmember insured banks. The maximum rates of interest that nonmember insured banks may pay on time deposits have been made the same as those for member banks. The maximum rates on time deposits fixed for member banks are shown in Table 8.

TABLE 8

Maximum Rates of Interest on Time Deposits of Member Banks, in Effect Since Jan. 1, 1936

(As Set by the Board of Governors of the Federal Reserve System)

Savings deposits	2½ %
Postal savings	2½
Other time deposits payable in:	
6 mo. or more	2½
90 days to 6 mo.	2
Less than 90 days	1

In some states, the state banking authorities have fixed maximum rates of interest payable on time deposits at figures lower than those set by the Board of Governors. In such states, the lower state figures become the maximum that can be paid by all member banks.[2]

Making the individual account pay its way. Although banks no longer may pay interest on demand deposits, they commonly perform many services designed to attract customers. The customer's checking account is likely to involve a considerable expense to the bank. Even without the frills of special services the handling of checks written by the depositor, the collection of deposited checks drawn on other banks, and the keeping of records all require expensive supplies and equipment and the services of skilled bookkeepers.

Before the depression of the 1930's, many bankers were inclined to view the size and activity of individual accounts with a good deal of tolerance. Because, in general, bank operations were profitable, a careful consideration of costs and earnings seemed unnecessary. But the depression and its losses brought a sharp awareness of the need to increase revenues and to cut costs. It became imperative for the banker to know whether or not a deposit justified itself and,

---

[2] For a careful survey of the problem of regulation of interest paid on deposits, see Watkins, L. L., "Commercial Banking Reform in the United States," *Michigan Business Studies*, Vol. VIII, No. 5, Part 2, 1938.

if it did not, what to do about it. Today most banks attempt to measure the costs of carrying accounts, and levy service charges against those that do not pay their way.

To evaluate the desirability of a customer's account the banker needs to know what the account costs to handle and how much earning power it brings to the bank. To calculate the cost of an account to the bank some estimate must be made of the unit cost of each operation performed by the bank in connection with the account. Thus, the bank needs to know the cost involved in paying checks drawn by the depositor and the cost of collecting checks on other banks brought in for deposit. A cost analysis of the several operations involved has been the practice of some banks. More frequently, however, the banker seizes upon the results of some other bank's cost study and applies these cost figures to his own bank. Often he appears to follow some rule-of-thumb estimates or hunches as to costs. In any event, some unit cost estimates are applied to the items that have moved through the depositor's account, and the combined results constitute the costs of handling the account for the month concerned.

To find the earning power of an account, the bank subtracts the required reserves from the average collected balance (funds deposited less any float of uncollected checks), and multiplies the remainder by the average rate of interest earned by the bank on its loans and investments. A comparison of the estimated costs charged against the account with the estimated contribution to the bank's earnings provides the basis for the service charge levied against the account.

Not all accounts are analyzed in detail. Most banks, in fact, seem to prefer a simpler method for levying service charges, with an earnings allowance based on the *minimum* rather than the average balance. The schedule of service charges given on the following page is more or less typical of common practices.

Some banks provide the small depositor with checking account privileges by selling him a special checkbook containing a limited number of checks. The price is supposed to cover the bank's costs of handling the account and yield a small profit. This is a simple way to levy service charges on small accounts.[3]

---

[3] There is apparently no standard practice for charging for these special checks. Such charges range from 2 to 10 cents each, with 5 cents and 10 cents

---

Schedule of Service Charges on Checking Accounts

A. ACTIVITY CHARGES

Maintenance charge per month $0.50
First ten items .... Free
Per item charge for next 200 items 0.04
Items in excess of 210—per item 0.02

The term "item" includes all checks charged and all deposits credited to the depositor's account, as well as all checks on other banks that are accepted for deposit or that are cashed. The charge for issuing drafts and out-of-pocket expenses will also be added to the "item" account. Carryover credit from one month cannot be used to offset charges of a subsequent month. A service charge of less than 10c will not be debited on any account.

B. ANALYSIS ALLOWANCE

We will allow a credit of 10 cents for each $100 of the minimum balance for the month with a minimum allowance of 10 cents.

C. STUDENT ACCOUNTS

Student accounts are regarded as temporary and will be subject to a charge of $1.00 when the account is opened.

The importance of service charges to banks may be seen in the fact that in 1955 they constituted 5.1 per cent of gross earnings, 16 per cent of profits before taxes, and about 2 per cent on the invested capital of member banks. The importance of these contributions to the banks' earnings is enhanced by the fact that their collection requires only a very small added cost to the banks.

Protection of Depositors — The Capital Accounts

The bank's capital. The capital invested by the bank's stockholders is a kind of guaranty fund protecting depositors from losses arising from bad loans and investments. The invested capital, or capital fund, of a bank consists of the capital stock, surplus, and undivided profits, plus contingency reserves. So long as the bank's loans and investments do not shrink by an amount greater than the invested capital, depositors cannot lose. The invested capital, therefore, must be adequate to protect depositors against a

---

being the most common charge. Cf. "Survey of Service Charge Trends, a Study of 2406 Country Banks," *Banking,* April, 1950, p. 36. See also *Business Conditions,* Federal Reserve Bank of Chicago, October 1955, pp. 12–14, for a description of the sale of these special check books to depositors for use with household accounts.

depreciation of the bank's assets arising from business depression, errors of judgment by the banker, or any other cause.

What constitutes an adequate amount of invested capital is difficult to determine. On the face of things it would appear that adequacy of capital should be measured in relation to the volume of deposits. Thus the proper criterion would be the capital-deposit ratio. As a matter of fact, supervisory authorities have generally emphasized this ratio as a proper guide to bank regulation. During the 1930's the Federal Deposit Insurance Corporation attempted to establish a rule that insured banks should have a ratio of net sound capital to deposit liabilities of at least 1:10. Thirteen states also established statutory requirements for minimum capital-deposit ratios at 1:10.[4] Before 1929, few banks would have had any trouble conforming to this rule. At present, however, the case is somewhat different. Bank deposits increased tremendously as a result of the war. At the end of 1955 the capital accounts of insured commercial banks were but 7.8 per cent of deposits.

Now clearly there is nothing sacred about the 1:10 ratio. Like many rules of thumb, it seems to have been adopted because of convenience in calculation. There has developed, therefore, considerable opposition to the blind adherence to the rule. It is quite properly held that the size of necessary capital funds is more closely related to the type of assets than to the volume of deposits. Were a bank to carry all its assets in cash, there would obviously be no need for capital to protect depositors. Likewise, when a bank's earning assets consist mainly of government securities, there is need for but little owner's equity to provide adequate protection to depositors. There have been proposals that, instead of a fixed capital-deposit ratio rule, a standard be set up based upon the class of assets held by the banks. Thus, against deposits represented by cash and highly liquid and safe bonds, or open market paper, the required capital ratio would be lower than against deposits backed by more hazardous and speculative assets. The

---

[4] The Indiana law permits the Department of Financial Institutions to require an increase in capital or a decrease in deposits if the net sound capital for the preceding year is less than 10 per cent of the bank's average daily deposits. Such action may not be taken if the bank's cash plus United States Government securities (direct and guaranteed) amount to 50 per cent of the total deposits. Cf. Robinson, R. I., "Capital-Deposit Ratio in Banking Supervision," *Journal of Political Economy*, February 1941.

effect of applying a capital-risk asset standard rather than a capital-deposit standard may be readily seen. On December 31, 1955, the total loans and investments of insured commercial banks were $159.6 billion. Of this total, $60.8 billion were U.S. Government obligations. Deducting government securities from the total on the assumption that they involved no credit risk, there remained $98.8 billion of risk assets. The ratio of invested capital of $15.0 billion to the $98.8 billion of risk assets was 15.1 per cent. This cushion of owners' equity is much more adequate than one is led to expect by the 7.8 per cent capital-deposit ratio of that time.

The adequacy of capital accounts is in no way assured by legislation governing national banks. The law merely provides for a minimum capital of from $50,000 to $200,000, depending on the size of the city in which the bank is located at the time of organization. The main pressure on banks to increase their capital accounts is the desire to carry an amount that seems appropriate to the banker, and the wish to be free from criticism of supervisory authorities. Before 1937, bank stock generally carried "double liability." This meant that stockholders of banks that failed might be called upon to pay to the receiver an amount of money equal to the par value of the stock in order to meet the claims of depositors. To encourage the sale of new stock during the depression of the 1930's, double liability provisions applying to national banks were removed and have since been eliminated from most state bank stock as well.[5]

Protection of Depositors — Federal Deposit Insurance

Bank failures have been a serious source of loss to American bank depositors. Between 1921 and March 1933 over 16,000 banks permanently closed their doors and caused inconvenience and loss to the holders of over $9 billion of deposits. Failures result not only in direct loss to depositors of the banks concerned, but also they create great and disastrous disturbances in the whole economy. For when banks fail, solvent banks must attempt to protect themselves against possible runs. This they do by improving their liquidity,

---

[5] Only Minnesota and Arizona retain full double liability on bank stock. In Arkansas, Oregon, and South Dakota, double liability applies only to stock issued before a given date. Colorado has triple liability on certain old shares. *Banking,* May 1953, p. 80.

or cash position. But this involves a reduction of their loans and investments. To reduce loans causes great distress among businessmen, forces sales of merchandise at times when commodity markets are already demoralized, and increases business failures. To liquidate investments during a liquidity crisis merely induces further collapse and chaos in the security markets. The cumulative ruin brought on by such actions was well illustrated by the collapse of banks and of business activity that culminated in the banking holiday of March 1933.

The public interest in the protection of depositors. One can readily understand the urgency behind the search for remedies for bank failures. Such remedies are neither easy to discover nor to apply. Bank failures arise from a wide number of causes. Except in periods of serious business depression, failures may normally be blamed on the ineptitude, the negligence, and the dishonesty of the bankers themselves. Therefore, in nondepression times, remedies ought to strike at the root cause of bad management. Attempts to improve bank management must mainly center around strengthening legal restraints and improving public supervision.

Bank failures become an even greater public issue when depression strikes and failures become much more numerous. At such times good banks are dragged down along with the bad in the general panic of depositors. Here a remedy is needed that goes beyond the improvement of management of the individual bank. The remedy generally called for is some form of deposit insurance. If effective, such insurance will reduce panic, stop runs, and enable banks to meet demands made on them in an orderly fashion. Thus they will be free from the pressure to liquidate their loans and investments, and the cumulative effects of market demoralization will be lessened. In addition, there is of course the more immediate advantage of protecting the deposit holdings of individuals and firms from becoming frozen or lost as a result of bank failure.

Deposit insurance, early plans. The earliest attempt to guarantee or insure bank liabilities occurred in 1829 when the State of New York set up the Safety Fund System of banks. It was only partially successsful, for it found its funds inadequate to pay both the note and deposit liabilities of the members that failed.[6] Modern

---

[6] For a description of state insurance systems designed to protect bank creditors in the 1829–1858 period, see the *Annual Report of the Federal Deposit Insurance Corporation*, 1952, pp. 59–65.

experience with guaranty of deposits followed the panic of 1907. The year 1908 saw the inauguration of a compulsory system of bank deposit guaranty in the state of Oklahoma, followed by guaranty legislation in seven other states; thus eight states tried a system of guaranty in some form or other. The results of these experiments were such as to dampen the enthusiasm of people who had previously advocated the plan. In times of good business and up to the depression beginning in 1920, they worked well; but bank failures became so numerous during and after this depression that in every case the burden became too great and the systems collapsed.[7]

Federal Deposit Insurance. The first nationwide system of deposit insurance was established under the provision of the Banking Act of 1933. The separate enactment of the Federal Deposit Insurance Act of September 21, 1950, provides the present legal framework for the system.

The significant features of the present insurance system may be summarized as follows:

1. Each depositor in an insured bank is protected up to the amount of $10,000 (after deducting offsets for debts which he may owe the bank). To determine the amount owed to any depositor by the bank, all deposits in the bank maintained "in the same capacity and the same right for his benefit either in his own name or in the name of others," except trust funds, are combined.

2. The Federal Deposit Insurance Corporation, a government corporation, maintains a corps of examiners who regularly examine insured nonmember state banks and who may, at the option of the FDIC, examine Federal Reserve member banks.

3. All banks belonging to the Federal Reserve System must be insured. Should insurance privileges be withdrawn for persistent violation of law or of sound banking practices, a state member bank loses its membership and a national bank must give up its charter. Deposit insurance privileges are not limited to commercial banks but are also extended to mutual savings banks. Over 200 mutual savings banks, holding three-fourths of all mutual savings bank deposits, are insured under this privilege.

4. Any nonmember bank may terminate its insured status upon ninety days' notice. A bank that persists in unsound and illegal practices may, after a hearing, be suspended from insured status. In such a case, all depositors must be notified of the fact by the bank, and existing

---

[7] For an account and criticism of the state guaranty systems, see *The Guaranty of Bank Deposits,* Economic Policy Commission of the American Bankers Association, 1933. Also see the *Annual Report of the Federal Deposit Insurance Corporation,* 1952, pp. 66–72.

deposits continue to be insured for two years with the bank liable for
regular premium assessments. New or additional deposited funds are
not insured.

5. Insured banks are assessed semi-annually an amount equal to 1/24
of 1 per cent of their assessment base. This base is the bank's total
deposit liabilities less uncollected checks.

Since 1950 the assessment burden has been reduced as compared
to earlier years. At the end of each year the FDIC calculates its
total cost of operations, including administration expenses, net additions to reserves, and insurance losses. When the assessments for
the year are more than the costs, 40 per cent of the "net assessment
income," as the surplus income is called, is transferred to the FDIC's
surplus account. The remaining 60 per cent is applied to the
assessment for the following year.

Procedure of the FDIC in case of bank insolvency. The
Federal Deposit Insurance Corporation is appointed receiver of all
failed national banks and *accepts* appointment as receiver of failed
insured state banks when such receivership is tendered by state
supervisory authorities under the state law.

As soon as possible after failure of an insured bank, the Corporation makes available to each depositor the amount of the insured
deposits, either by transferring it to another insured bank in the
same community, by depositing it in a new national bank with a
temporary organization if public interest so requires, or by direct
payment to depositors.

The Corporation is subrogated to the rights of the insured depositors of the closed banks to the extent that it is entitled to receive
the same dividends from the proceeds of liquidation of assets as
would have been payable to the depositor on a claim for the insured
deposit. The depositor retains his claim for any uninsured portion
of his deposit. The Corporation, therefore, is in the position only
of a general rather than a preferred creditor.

The FDIC is authorized to do more than to pay insured deposits
and preside over the liquidation of the failed insured banks for
which it has been appointed receiver. To facilitate the liquidation
of failed insured banks it may purchase the banks' assets and may
make loans on the security of such assets. Furthermore, whenever
the Board of Directors of the FDIC believes that the risk of loss
to the Corporation will be reduced by merging an insured bank

threatened with failure with a sound insured bank, the Corporation is authorized to make loans upon or purchase the assets of the bank to such an amount that the sound bank will be protected in taking over the liabilities of the other. This power has been extensively used and few insured banks have been placed in receivership since 1944. Finally, if it seems desirable, the FDIC may lend funds to threatened banks to assist their return to solvency.

Protection offered by the FDIC. In 1950 the amount of insurance coverage was raised from $5,000 to $10,000 for each individual account. The following year, 1951, the Corporation made a special study of the extent of insurance coverage under the new $10,000 limit. Some of the results of this study are shown in Table 9.

TABLE 9

Extent of Insurance Coverage Under the $10,000 Limit*

	Number of banks	% of accounts fully protected	% of volume of deposits Insured	% of volume of deposits Not insured
All insured banks	13,652	98.5	54.3	45.7
Banks with deposits of:				
$ 250,000 or less	49	99.6	95.0	5.0
$ 250,000 to $ 1,000,000	2300	99.3	89.5	10.5
$ 1,000,000 to $ 5,000,000	7463	98.9	81.6	18.4
$ 5,000,000 to $ 25,000,000	3035	98.7	71.0	29.0
$ 25,000,000 to $ 100,000,000	564	98.5	59.7	40.1
$100,000,000 to $ 500,000,000	201	98.3	50.0	50.0
$500,000,000 to $2,500,000,000	37	97.4	34.1	65.9
Over $2,500,000,000	3	98.4	36.6	63.4

* *Annual Report of the Federal Deposit Insurance Corporation,* 1951, pp. 61, 63.

During the period 1934-1954, 424 insured banks were either placed in receivership for liquidation or helped to merge with solvent banks. These banks had 1,392,793 depositors, whose deposits amounted to $540,672,000. Depositor losses, all from receiverships, were but $1,952,000.

The experience of the FDIC. Since the Federal Deposit Insurance Corporation was started in 1934 conditions have been most favorable for bank survival. In general, the banks that were admitted to insurance had proved their stability by surviving the bank holiday of 1933. Moreover, from that time on, business conditions, in spite of cyclical setbacks, tended to improve over the years. The expansion of the war years provided bankers with an abundance of nonrisk assets and high earnings. Consequently the number of failures has been lower than for any similar period in our history, and the ability of the FDIC to stand the strain of serious depression has not been tested.

During the period 1934-1954, the Corporation's income exceeded its expenditures by over $1,542,700,000, an amount now available as a deposit insurance fund. In addition, the Corporation has the authority to borrow up to $3 billion from the United States Treasury should an emergency require it. During this period the FDIC stepped in to aid in the liquidation or merger of 424 banks that were in difficulties. Of these, 245 banks, with deposits of $109 million, were placed in receivership and 179 banks, with deposits of $450 million, were absorbed by other banks. For the banks placed in receivership the FDIC paid out $87 million to depositors. Of this amount $72 million was recovered with a loss of 16 per cent on the amount disbursed. To aid in the merger of banks, the Corporation paid out $241 million, recovered $234 million, for an estimated loss of 2.1 per cent of the amount disbursed. This superior experience with the banks absorbed is due to the advantage of early action in salvaging banks in difficulties rather than waiting for failure to become complete. For the depositor the merger method has the added advantage of providing complete 100 per cent coverage of deposits regardless of size, since the deposit liabilities are taken over intact by a solvent bank.

At the end of 1955, total deposits of insured banks were $212.2 billion and insured deposits were $116.3 billion. The deposit insurance fund at this time was $1.6 billion. This made the ratio of the deposit insurance fund to *total* deposits of insured banks .77 per cent and the ratio to *insured* deposits 1.41 per cent. Before 1950, all assessment income not used up by expenses and losses was accumulated as surplus and provided a substantial annual addition to the funds available to the Corporation. Changes in the law, largely because of pressure from bankers for a reduction in assessments, resulted in the present rule that only 40 per cent of the "net assessment income" (assessment income minus all current expenses) is to be accumulated by the Corporation as surplus. The remaining 60 per cent is credited against next year's assessments. As a consequence, the rate of accumulation is now sharply reduced in comparison with past years. The results of the operation of the old and the new rule may readily be seen in Table 10.

TABLE 10

Federal Deposit Insurance Corporation Income, Expenses, and Additions to Surplus for 1949 and 1955*

(In millions of dollars)

	1949	1955
Income from assessments	$119.8	$151.4
Less expenses, losses, and additions to reserves	6.5	9.2
Net assessment income	113.3	142.2
Credited against next year's assessment .	0.0	85.3
Net assessment income to surplus	113.3	56.9
Interest on invested funds	25.5	39.2
Total carried to surplus	138.8	96.1

* *Annual Report of the Federal Deposit Insurance Corporation,* 1949, 1955.

There is no sound actuarial basis for determining the losses that the FDIC might be called upon to meet in time of acute depression. Therefore it is impossible to judge the adequacy of the deposit insurance fund. There are some favorable considerations. First, so long as confidence in its ability remains unimpaired, the very existence of the FDIC tends to reduce the hazard of runs which have caused so many bank failures in the past. Second, the FDIC can draw upon the Treasury to the amount of $3 billion if necessary. Coupled with this is the strong probability of added governmental assistance should the FDIC find itself in serious trouble. Third, the present policy of promoting mergers of banks threatened with failures, and the power of the FDIC to make loans to banks in difficulties where mergers are not possible and the bank's preservation is needed, tend to prevent the development of such disastrous situations as we have known in the past. Finally, the banks themselves are basically in a stronger position than ever before in respect to liquidity. Their substantial holdings of U.S. short-term securities provide sources of liquidity never before available to our commercial banks.

Consequences of the $10,000 limit on insurance coverage.
The limited insurance coverage provided by the FDIC was expected
to accomplish two things. First, it would give protection to the small
depositor who is neither capable of protecting himself by selecting
sound banks nor of withstanding the losses incident to bank failure.
Second, limited coverage would tend to dispose of the old bogy that
insured bankers become reckless and tend to allow bank management to deteriorate. The large bank depositor, receiving little insurance protection, would seek for and insist upon high banking standards in the banks that he patronizes. In addition, the further point
was made that limited coverage would reduce the burden of deposit
insurance to a tolerable level.

Two basic criticisms have been made of the limited insurance
coverage. First, it is properly argued that although the small depositor is well cared for, the bankers themselves are inadequately protected against the disastrous threats of silent runs by the large, uncovered depositors. Only assurance of 100 per cent coverage provides genuine protection against the threat of runs. Second, and
closely related to the first criticism, large banks paying assessments
on the whole of their deposits receive insurance protection upon
only a modest fraction. As we already know, since 1944 the FDIC
has been providing 100 per cent protection to depositors by merging unsound banks with sound banks. This practice is justified on
the grounds that it is more economical for the Corporation than
allowing unsound banks to continue to operate until liquidation
becomes necessary. The experience of the FDIC seems to indicate
that the cost of extending coverage to 100 per cent would not prove
excessive in the light of the probable advantages.

Questions for Study

1. To the individual banker the total volume of bank deposits is
fixed by forces beyond his control. Why does this explain a tendency of
banks to compete for deposits?

2. Why are banks more able to afford to pay interest on time deposits than on demand?

3. Distinguish between the nature of and the normal withdrawal
privileges of: (a) time certificates of deposit; and (b) savings deposits.
What is the significance of this distinction?

4. Can you explain why competition among banks by paying interest
on deposits tends to be dangerously cutthroat?

5. What appears to have been the main purpose of the prohibition of interest payments on demand deposits?

6. How was the conflict between the prohibition of interest payments on demand deposits and the absorption of exchange and other charges for depositors resolved?

7. What are the essential steps in a proper analysis of a depositor's account? How reliable and exact are the costs charged against the account? Are banks justified in making service charges?

8. Why is the capital-deposit ratio less significant than the capital-risk asset ratio? Why are legal requirements in respect to minimum bank capital inadequate in themselves to insure needed capital?

9. What is meant by double liability of bank stockholders? What is its present status?

10. Give some good reasons why insurance of bank deposits is good public policy.

11. What is the position of the large city banks in respect to the extent of insurance protection received in comparison to the premiums paid?

12. Where does the FDIC obtain its funds?

13. What relief was given banks from the burden of deposit insurance premiums in the amended law in 1950?

14. How has the FDIC in practice extended full 100 per cent coverage to depositors of banks that find themselves in trouble?

9

Clearing and Collection of Checks

Two basic requirements must be fulfilled if bank checking accounts are to function as money. First, some smoothly working, economical machinery must be provided to enable one bank receiving on deposit checks drawn on other banks to present these checks and receive payment. Only then can bank checks become readily acceptable instruments for transferring funds from one person to another. Second, banks must maintain sufficient reserves to enable them to pay cash for any checks drawn on them which are not offset by checks on other banks. As we already know, the amount of such cash reserves need be but a fraction of the banks' deposit liabilities. In this chapter we shall examine the first of these requirements for the effective use of bank checks as means of payment.

Clearing and Collecting Checks

Whenever the payees or the receivers of bank checks are also depositors in the bank on which the checks are drawn, collecting becomes only an internal bookkeeping transaction. But generally, because of the number of banks in operation, a large proportion of checks are deposited in other banks. Consequently, the banks receiving the checks on deposit must collect the proceeds from the drawee banks.

When checks are drawn on banks in the local community they are collected through the local clearinghouse. When they are drawn on banks in other cities, agents located in those cities must be used to make collection. In such cases the local bank carries a deposit with a city bank that agrees to act as the collecting agent.

The clearinghouse. The clearinghouse is a convenient place where the representatives of the several banks meet and exchange checks received on deposit and settle the differences owed to each other. Banks belonging to the clearinghouse form an organization called a clearinghouse association, whose affairs are governed by a clearinghouse committee. The committee, made up of influential bankers chosen by the banks, establishes rules and regulations in respect to the process of exchanging checks and settling the differences.

The committee also sometimes fixes rules of competition for the banks belonging to the association. It may establish maximum rates of interest that may be paid on time deposits, uniform charges for collecting out-of-town checks, and service charges. In the past, it also has sometimes been instrumental in having the banks of the association jointly undertake to guarantee the liabilities of one of their members whose insolvency threatened public confidence in the local banks. The committee sometimes requires periodic reports from the clearing banks and may hire a staff of examiners to watch over the practices of these banks to determine their fitness to remain associated with the clearinghouse.

The clearing mechanism. The clearing operation is itself simple in principle. Before being sent to the clearinghouse, each check must be inspected to make certain that it is properly endorsed by the payee and that it appears to be regular in every way. Further, it is endorsed with a rubber stamp bearing the date, name, clearinghouse number of the presenting bank, and some notation to the effect that payment is received through the clearinghouse. The checks are then sorted according to the bank on which they are drawn, and the amounts are totaled and recorded on a slip which is attached to each package of checks.

At the time of clearing, the messengers from each bank go to the clearinghouse and exchange the packages of checks so that each messenger comes into possession of the checks drawn on his own bank. On a specially prepared statement sheet containing the names of other clearing banks, the messenger records the amount of checks received from and delivered to each of the other clearing banks and computes the total of checks brought to and received from the clearinghouse. If the amount received exceeds the amount brought to the clearinghouse, the bank has an unfavorable balance, or is a net debtor, and must pay the difference to the clearinghouse. If the amount of checks brought exceeds the amount of checks received, the bank has a favorable balance and receives payment for the difference.

In some cities check clearing is formally carried out oftener than once a day. In any event, large banks sometimes expedite their bookkeeping by informally exchanging checks on each other at frequent intervals during the day by messenger. They then put the receipt for the checks delivered to the other bank through the clearinghouse at the next regular clearing period. In the larger cities, small banks may not wish to assume the responsibilities of clearinghouse membership or are unable to qualify. They, therefore, arrange with a clearinghouse bank to clear their checks for them.

Methods of settlement. One principle of settlement prevails. The debtor banks pay only the *net* amount of their debts to all the banks at the clearinghouse. The creditor banks receive in turn only the *net* amount due them. Thus the settlement is made with a minimum of payments. In small city clearinghouses, debtor banks commonly make settlement in acceptable drafts on city correspondent banks or on the Federal Reserve Bank of the district. In Federal Reserve Bank cities, the manager of the clearinghouse provides the Federal Reserve Bank with a certified list of clearing balances with instructions to debit the reserve balance of debtor banks and credit the reserve balances of the creditor banks on the books of the Federal Reserve Bank.

Use of the Federal Reserve collection system for out-of-town checks. Two methods are available for presenting and collecting checks drawn on out-of-town banks. The first and most common method is through the Federal Reserve Banks; the second uses correspondent banks in other cities. We shall examine first the Federal Reserve collection system.

The Board of Governors of the Federal Reserve System has arranged to have each Federal Reserve Bank collect checks for such of its member banks as desire to avail themselves of its privileges and for such nonmember state banks and trust companies as may maintain adequate balances with the reserve banks. Such nonmember state banks and trust companies are called *nonmember clearing banks.* Only checks drawn on "par banks" (banks that agree to remit the full face value of all checks presented through the mail) can be collected through the Federal Reserve Banks.

The system of check collection begins with the bank that has received out-of-town checks from its customers. Such checks must be prepared for collection in somewhat the same manner as local checks intended for the clearinghouse. They must be inspected for the endorsement of the payee and for any evidence of irregularity. They must then be stamped with the bank's endorsement. This is in the form of a special endorsement calling for payment to "any bank or banker," thus minimizing the danger of loss in case the checks should be stolen.

This work of preparing the checks for collection is done by the "transit department" in the larger, departmentalized banks. Proper record of each check is made, often on microfilm, for the bank's own use, and an identifying list is prepared to accompany the checks when they are sent in for collection.

If the collecting bank is a member or a nonmember clearing bank, the checks are sent next to the Federal Reserve Bank, where the sending bank receives deferred credit. The Federal Reserve Bank in turn endorses the checks and starts the process of collecting them from the drawee banks. Four possibilities arise at this time:

1. If the checks are drawn on banks in the city in which the Federal Reserve Bank itself is located, they will be presented directly to the drawee bank or through the local clearinghouse.

2. If the checks are drawn on member or nonmember clearing banks in other towns or cities of the district, the Federal Reserve Bank will mail the checks directly to the drawee bank and request a remittance. After the drawee bank has had an opportunity to inspect the checks for genuineness, it will remit the amount to the Federal Reserve Bank. In doing so it has a choice of: (*a*) drawing a draft on its reserve account with the Federal Reserve Bank; (*b*) sending a draft on other banks located in the Federal Reserve city; (*c*) shipping currency at the expense of the Federal Reserve Bank; or (*d*) making any other form of payment acceptable to the collecting Federal Reserve Bank. If a remittance is not promptly made, the amount will be deducted from the member's reserve account in any event; promptness in remitting is thus desirable.

3. If the checks are drawn on nonmember banks outside the Federal Reserve city, the Federal Reserve Bank may send them directly to the nonmember banks and request a remittance, or present them through a nearby member bank, which collects and remits.

4. If the checks are drawn on a bank in another Federal Reserve

district, the collecting Federal Reserve Bank sends the check to the reserve bank of the other district.[1] The check then proceeds through the ordinary collection channels of that district, and settlement is made between the Federal Reserve Banks through the Interdistrict Settlement Fund, which will be described later.

As we observed at the beginning, the original bank sending checks for collection to its Federal Reserve Bank receives deferred credit only. After collection has been completed by the reserve bank, the proceeds of the checks are credited to the member bank's legal reserve account on deposit with the Federal Reserve Bank. In order that member banks may know when checks sent to the Reserve Bank for collection will be fully available for use, each Federal Reserve Bank has set up a time schedule showing the number of days that must elapse before checks drawn upon banks located in different areas will be available for full reserve credit.

When checks payable in the Federal Reserve Bank city or drawn on a Federal Reserve Bank are received sufficiently early in the day, the Federal Reserve Bank immediately gives the sending bank full credit on its reserve account. Proceeds of other checks sent in for collection are made available at the time stated in the time schedule. In no case is the time period longer than two days after the receipt of a check by the Federal Reserve Bank.

In actual practice, a collection of checks by the Federal Reserve Banks often is delayed beyond the period stated in the published time schedule. Consequently, member banks frequently receive reserve credit for checks before they have been deducted from the reserve accounts of the banks on which they are drawn. These uncollected checks for which member banks have received premature credit are known as "Federal Reserve float," which constitutes an addition to the total reserve balances or deposits of member banks in the Federal Reserve Banks. Its importance varies with the season and the direction of check payment flow. It becomes highest, generally, before Christmas.

Member banks are not required to use the collection facilities of

---

[1] Time in collection is saved by the use of shortcuts in the routing of checks for collection. Intradistrict checks may be collected through Federal Reserve Bank branches. Also, under special arrangements, one member bank may send checks drawn on another member bank directly to the drawee bank and notify the Federal Reserve Bank. Interdistrict collection time is reduced by authorizing member banks to route checks directly to the Federal Reserve Bank of another district for credit at the sending bank's reserve bank.

their Reserve Banks. They may and often do send out-of-town checks to their city correspondents, who in turn send them to the Federal Reserve Bank for collection or collect directly from the drawee bank.

Use of the Interdistrict Settlement Fund. In the custody of the Board of Governors of the Federal Reserve System in Washington, D.C., there is an $8 billion fund carried as a book credit with the Treasury. This fund, in which each Federal Reserve Bank has a varying share, is known as the Interdistrict Settlement Fund. It was established and is replenished from time to time by the Federal Reserve Bank deposit of gold certificates or the transfer of equivalent credits on the Treasury books.

When checks drawn on banks located in other Federal Reserve districts are sent to a Federal Reserve Bank for collection, it proceeds to forward these checks to the Federal Reserve Banks of those districts. When collected, the proceeds of these checks are added to the share of the original Federal Reserve Bank on the books of the Interdistrict Settlement Fund. The amounts are deducted from the shares of the Federal Reserve Banks that carried out the collection and owe the original sending bank. Checks and similar items amounting to over three-quarters of a trillion dollars are cleared annually through the Fund.

Collection of checks without use of Federal Reserve Bank facilities. Although the Federal Reserve Banks furnish excellent facilities for the collection of checks for member and nonmember clearing banks, a substantial number of checks are collected without the use of the reserve banks. As was observed before, member banks sometimes prefer, for one reason or another, to collect through city correspondents rather than through the reserve bank. For example, a member bank in Lafayette, Indiana, might wish to send its checks drawn on Indianapolis or the surrounding area to its Indianapolis correspondent, which would be in a position to make collection through the Indianapolis clearinghouse and grant immediate credit, whereas if they were sent to the Federal Reserve Bank of Chicago for collection, the checks would not be added to the reserve credit until two days after receipt of the checks by the Chicago bank. Thus, the Lafayette bank's funds would become available two days sooner by collecting them through Indianapolis.

Frequently, member banks find it more convenient to collect

checks drawn on banks located near the reserve bank through correspondents in the reserve city. The real advantage of using a city
correspondent as a collection agency in such a case is the convenience of accumulating balances with the city correspondent by
sending checks to it for collection instead of collecting through the
reserve bank and then transferring the funds to the correspondent.
It must be remembered that member banks still find it necessary to
maintain balances with city correspondents in spite of the operations
of the Federal Reserve System. City correspondents are important
links in the process of purchasing commercial paper, bankers' acceptances, and bonds. Further, they are useful in furnishing customers with drafts on other cities, which are still frequently needed
in spite of the increased acceptability of ordinary checks. Likewise,
any connection that the smaller banks have with the foreign exchange market is through their city correspondents. Finally, country
banks call upon their city correspondent banks for miscellaneous
types of services not available from the reserve bank, including
the furnishing of credit information desired by both the bank
itself and its customers.[2]

Collection of checks by nonmember banks. The nonmember
bank, unless qualified as a clearing nonmember, has no direct access
to the clearing facilities of the reserve banks. It does have indirect
access, however, through its member bank correspondents, which
cheerfully undertake the task of collection in return for the favor
of the nonmember's deposit.

Only one form of check is denied access to the reserve bank
collection system—namely, checks on nonmember banks that refuse
to remit at par for checks presented through the mails; that is,
charge exchange. Checks drawn on these banks must be collected
through the correspondent bank system.

The nonpar bank and the exchange charge. It is important
to understand just what is involved in the *exchange charge* made by
the nonpar banks. Briefly it is this: When checks drawn on such
a bank are sent to persons or firms located in other cities, and are

---

[2] H. Parker Willis believed that this dependence of country banks upon their
city correspondents is due to the pressure exerted by the city bankers upon the
Federal Reserve Banks to prevent the latter from performing correspondent
services. He reported that at first the Federal Reserve Bank of New York offered
full correspondent services to its members but later withdrew them to avoid
antagonizing the big city banks. *The Theory and Practice of Central Banking,* New
York, Harper & Brothers, 1936, p. 92.

deposited in the banks of those cities, they are returned by mail to the drawee bank for payment. The latter, instead of remitting the sending bank the *full amount* of checks presented for payment, remits the face amount of the checks minus an exchange charge. This charge commonly amounts to one-tenth of 1 per cent of the face of the checks. In justification for this practice, the bankers claim that their contract with the depositor is to pay cash at the bank's own window. To remit to some out-of-city banker through the mails involves an added burden of carrying balances with city correspondents against which they can draw drafts in payment. For this extra trouble they make an exchange charge. Actually, however, the excuse just given is not at all a valid one. Carrying balances with city correspondents is an indispensable practice of country banks, for through such correspondents the country bank must collect out-of-town checks deposited with it by its customers. The truth is that the practice of charging exchange arises from the simple fact that it is profitable! It is profitable because the nonpar bank pays less than par on its own checks, although it is able to collect the full face amount of city-bank checks that it sends to its city correspondent for collection. In support of this contention one need but note the anguished and enraged cries of country banks when the Federal Reserve System undertook to abolish the practice of charging exchange by using agents to present checks for payment at the window of the nonpar banks. The reserve banks were compelled to give up this attempt when state legislatures hastened to come to the aid of the nonpar banks by passing laws designed to prevent their being coerced into giving up the exchange charge.[3]

The nonpar banks are of necessity small state banks located mainly in rural areas where they need not compete with banks that belong to the Federal Reserve System and pay their checks at par. The Great Depression of the 1930's saw a substantial increase in the number of nonpar banks. The excuse appears to have been the urgent need for some source of increased profits. But, since 1940, the number of banks on the nonpar list has sharply diminished. In February 1956, only 1,775 small country banks remained as nonpar banks. These banks were located in nineteen

---

[3] Exchange charges are specifically authorized by the laws of Alabama, Florida, Georgia, Louisiana, Mississippi, North Carolina, South Dakota, and Tennessee.

states. The States of Minnesota, North Dakota, South Dakota, and Missouri accounted for 660 of these banks. The remainder, with a few scattered exceptions, were located in southern states. In a few states, laws have been passed making the par payment of all checks mandatory.

It is important to distinguish between the *exchange charge* made by nonpar banks and the *collection charge* that banks make for cashing out-of-town checks for customers. The collection charge compensates the bank for advancing the money and for the trouble and delay involved in collecting the check. Should the check be drawn on a nonpar bank, the exchange charge that the drawee bank will make in paying the check is quite properly included in the collection charge.

Collection of nontransit items. The collection facilities of the Federal Reserve Banks are not limited in use solely to the collection of checks. The Federal Reserve Act permits the reserve banks to receive, for collection, maturing notes and bills of exchange. A member bank owning a note or bill of exchange payable in another city may therefore utilize the services of the reserve banks to effect its presentment and payment. If the note or bill is collectible without cost through some member bank, the reserve bank, on receipt of the proceeds, credits the full amount to the reserve account of the member sending it in for collection. If the reserve bank is compelled to pay a collection fee to the bank presenting and collecting the instrument, it credits the account of the original member for the amount, less the collection charges. Items sent to other Federal Reserve districts for collection are settled in the same general manner as interdistrict check collections.

Federal Reserve exchange. In spite of the great improvements in the ease and effectiveness of the use of personal checks for making payments, there still remain many occasions when such checks are inappropriate. In such cases remittance is made by purchasing a *bank draft,* or check drawn by one's local bank on its city correspondent. The Federal Reserve System has undertaken to provide a similar way to make acceptable remittances by the use of drafts drawn by member banks on their Federal Reserve balances. These are known as Federal Reserve Exchange Drafts, require special arrangements with the Federal Reserve Bank against which they are drawn, and have little advantage over ordinary drafts on city correspondent banks. Consequently they have had little use.

Telegraphic transfers. An additional service that the reserve banks offer to members is the right to utilize the leased wire system, maintained between the Board of Governors at Washington and the several reserve banks and branches, for the transfer of funds by wire. Any member bank may request its reserve bank to transfer to any other member bank, whether located within or outside its own district, any sum of money in multiples of $1,000.

Questions for Study

1. How do banks usually settle their adverse clearinghouse balances? Does your town have a clearinghouse? If so, how are settlements made?

2. Clearinghouse associations often exercise supervision and restraint over the clearing banks. What form do these interferences take? Why are they necessary?

3. Can you trace the process by which a check drawn on a bank located in another Federal Reserve district is presented and paid?

4. What is Federal Reserve "float"?

5. The maximum deferred availability period is now two days for checks sent in to the Federal Reserve Banks for collection. What is the effect upon total reserves of member banks of a storm that slows down transportation?

6. When will banks utilize the services of their city correspondents, rather than those of the Federal Reserve System, for collecting out-of-town checks?

7. How do banks that are not members of the Federal Reserve System get the benefits of the System's collection services?

8. What is the Interdistrict Settlement Fund? How it it used?

9. What are nonpar banks? Why do they refuse to remit at par? Why do their customers continue to patronize them?

10

The Bank's Primary Reserves

When a bank's depositors are sufficiently numerous and diversified, it may reasonably expect that funds withdrawn on any given day by one group of depositors will be offset in large measure by the new deposits of other customers. If the offsets were perfect, the cash requirements of a bank would be very small indeed. Actually, a considerable variation in the rate of new deposits and of withdrawals exists from day to day even though the general level of deposits is relatively stable.

To be prepared to meet these variations, the bank must carry *primary* reserves of cash, or its equivalent, in amounts sufficient to insure its ability to fulfill its obligations as they arise. These reserves, being but a fraction of the bank's deposits, are described in terms of percentages of deposit liabilities. Thus, when reserves are one-fifth of deposits the reserve ratio is 20 per cent.

Form of primary reserves. The primary reserves of a bank take the form of cash in the bank's own vaults and demand deposits with other banks. Banks that are members of the Federal Reserve System carry reserve balances with two kinds of banks. First, the law requires that an amount equal to a certain fractional part of the deposits be maintained with the Federal Reserve Bank. This constitutes the "legal" reserve. In addition, banks normally carry deposit balances in banks of cities with which the local community has active trade relations. These banks are called "city correspondents."

Barring some contingency which may make funds unavailable when wanted, the deposits in other banks are the equivalent of cash to the depositor bank. Further, they have advantages over vault cash. Many checks drawn by the customers are sent out of town and are presented for payment through the mails by banks in other cities. A draft drawn on a reserve balance in a bank of another city is an acceptable means of paying these checks and is cheaper than shipping cash. On the other hand, the bank receives from depositor-customers checks and drafts payable in distant cities. These checks are sent to city correspondents for collection, and the proceeds may then conveniently be credited to the sending bank's reserve account. Thus it is evident that balances carried in banks of other cities are often a more useful form of reserve than cash in the bank's own vault.

The amount of primary reserves that banks carry. The relative size of a bank's primary or cash reserves, expressed as a percentage of deposits, is determined by a number of considerations:

1. Each bank must take into account its own peculiar cash requirements. These will vary with:

(a) The number and diversity of its depositors.

(b) The special cash needs arising from the payroll requirements of customers.

(c) Peculiar, unpredictable behavior of certain large accounts.

(d) Public confidence in the bank.

(e) The readiness with which the bank can increase its cash by borrowing or liquidating part of its earning assets.

2. In uncertain, depressed times, reserve ratios of banks are often abnormally high because of a lack of suitable outlets for loans and investments.

3. Minimum reserve ratios required by law seriously influence the size of bank reserves.

Legal reserves of banks. Guided by experience, the intelligent banker will maintain such a proportion of his deposits in cash as will enable him readily to meet all demands. To carry less is to court disaster; to carry more than is reasonably necessary cuts into earnings. In the belief that individual freedom should be extended to banking, the chartering of banks in the United States in earlier days was carried on with little discrimination as to the skill and integrity of those wishing to enter the field. The resulting failures and public inconvenience have brought about universal regulation of bank operations. Because of the recognition that adequate cash reserves are necessary to insure the bank's ability to convert its deposits into cash, these regulations have included the fixing of minimum reserve requirements.

The laws establishing legal reserve requirements for banks have not had the results that were originally expected. They were intended to insure liquidity so that banks could always pay their depositors on demand. But, as the laws and regulations have been interpreted, required reserves are to be *kept* rather than used. For example, banks that are members of the Federal Reserve System are expected to maintain their average reserves at a certain required level. Should they fail to do so, any reserve deficiency is subject to a penalty amounting to 2 per cent per annum above the Federal Reserve Bank discount rate on 90-day commercial paper. Furthermore, should a member bank appear negligent in maintaining its reserves, special notification is sent to each of its directors. Should the member bank continue to disregard warnings in respect to deficiencies in reserves, the Board of Governors may institute legal proceedings to terminate the bank's membership in the Federal Reserve System. In view of all this, a bank is loath to pay out cash when by so doing it impairs its legal reserve position.

The result of this attitude toward legally required reserves is that, in practice, except for the privilege of averaging their reserves, as explained below, such reserves constitute, for the individual bank involved, little more than a possible last line of defense against emergency depositor demands. Indeed, in the past they have failed to function even in that capacity. In the days before there were Federal Reserve Banks to come to their rescue, banks periodically found themselves unable to meet depositors' demands without impairing their legal reserves. Under those circumstances they chose temporarily to suspend payments rather than reduce their reserves below the legal minimum. It follows, then, that legal reserves constitute funds that can make but limited contributions to the direct liquidity of a bank.

The contribution of required reserves to bank liquidity. In practice, legal reserves can and do make a limited contribution in helping banks to meet deposit withdrawals. First, when deposits shrink, reserve requirements shrink proportionally. Consequently, a bank having legal reserve requirements of 20 per cent, for example, can use this released required reserve to meet 20 per cent of the withdrawn deposits. The remaining 80 per cent of the lost deposits, however, must be paid out of cash resources not provided by the legal reserves. Second, as reserve requirements for Federal

Reserve member banks are now calculated, legal reserve balances in the Federal Reserve Banks may be temporarily drawn down below the minimum, provided they are later built up enough *above* the minimum to make the *average* reserve carried equal to the average requirements over the computation period of one or two weeks, depending on the location of the bank. This reduces the rigidity of earlier regulations that penalized any reserve deficiency whatever.[1]

Working reserves of banks. Because banks can depend only to a limited extent on legal reserves for meeting deposit withdrawals, they find it necessary to carry *working reserves* over and above their legally required ones. Working reserves of Federal Reserve member banks include:

1. Till money, or vault cash, carried for cashing checks, making payrolls, and to meet other local needs. The amount of such cash varies with circumstances. If the bank is remotely situated, so that considerable time is involved in obtaining additional cash from the Federal Reserve Bank or from a city correspondent, vault cash will be relatively large. The differences in the relative importance of vault cash to country banks and to big city banks may readily be seen in Table 11.

2. Deposits in other banks or balances with city correspondents. These reserve balances are especially important for country banks and to a lesser degree to reserve city banks. Some of the latter banks are located in the same city as their Federal Reserve Bank or branch and can therefore get along with relatively small cash funds. Such working reserves are almost nonexistent for the central reserve city banks of downtown Chicago and New York. To meet excessive withdrawals these banks depend mainly on converting highly liquid assets into cash, by borrowing from the Federal Reserve Banks, or borrowing from each other.

3. Banks often carry some legal reserve balances above the minimum legal requirements. These are available for use as working reserves and are known as "excess reserves."

Legal reserve requirements. All banks belonging to the Fed-

---

[1] Before the Federal Reserve Act Amendment of July 7, 1942, member banks were prohibited from making any new loans or paying any dividends so long as their reserve balance required by law was impaired. This was interpreted to mean that a deficiency *any given day* prevented additional lending. This was so even though the 2 per cent penalty was applied only on *average* deficiencies over the computation period. Cf. *Regulations of the Federal Reserve Board, Regulation D,* Series 1928, which continued in effect until the change in the law in 1942. After that time all reference to any prohibition of loans and dividends because of reserve deficiencies was eliminated. *Federal Reserve Bulletin,* March 1942, p. 202, and August 1942, p. 452.

TABLE 11

Reserves of Member Banks in Percentage of Gross Deposits
as of April 11, 1955*

	Central reserve city banks of New York	Central reserve city banks of Chicago	Reserve city banks	Country banks
Cash in vault	.60	.43	1.08	2.14
Reserves in the Federal Reserve Banks	16.32	14.82	12.68	9.37
Deposits in other banks	.15	1.43	3.45	7.78

* Compiled from the *Federal Reserve Bulletin*, September 1955.

eral Reserve System, whether state or national banks, are subject to the reserve requirements set by the Board of Governors of the Federal Reserve System under the authority of the Federal Reserve Act. Nonmember state banks must maintain reserves established by the banking authorities of their own states.[2] The reserve requirements for Federal Reserve member banks are tied to an outmoded classification of banks inherited from the days before the System was established.[3] *Country banks* are located in the small towns and cities and in outlying areas of the reserve cities. *Reserve city banks* are located in specified cities that are larger and economically more important than country areas, and in the outlying areas of New York and Chicago.[4] The downtown banks in the financial districts

---

[2] For an account of the reserve requirements of state banks not members of the Federal Reserve System, see *Monetary Policy and the Management of the Public Debt*, Part I, Joint Committee on the Economic Report, 1952, pp. 468–471. In twenty-three states banking authorities have power to change state nonmember bank reserve requirements. In nine states the changes must correspond to changes made by the Board of Governors for member banks.

[3] The old national banks were classified into three categories: (1) country banks; (2) reserve city banks, eligible to hold on deposit part of the required reserves of the country banks; and (3) central reserve city banks that were authorized to hold part of the legally required reserves of the reserve city banks. Since the reserve city and central reserve city banks held deposited funds of other banks, the law required them to have higher cash reserves than was required of country banks.

[4] Reserve cities include (1) cities, other than New York and Chicago, having Federal Reserve Banks or branches thereof; (2) cities whose member banks carry a specified fraction of interbank deposits of the country; and (3) certain other cities (previously classified as reserve cities and no longer eligible under the above rules) in which the banks request to remain reserve city banks for purposes of prestige or to qualify as holders of state bank balances under the provisions of state laws. *Federal Reserve Bulletin*, January 1948, p. 40.

of Chicago and New York are known as *central reserve city banks.* The only significance of this threefold classification lies in the fact that central reserve city banks must carry higher reserves against demand deposits than do reserve city banks, and the latter have higher reserve requirements than do the country banks. A justification for these differences might be that the big city banks, holding deposits of smaller country banks, require greater liquidity. The weakness of this point lies in the fact that legal reserves make little contribution to this liquidity.

The Federal Reserve Act fixes a minimum and a maximum limit to the percentage of required reserves for each class of member banks. The Board of Governors is required to fix the actual requirements for each class of banks within the statutory limits. By raising and lowering the required reserves, the Board of Governors can reduce or increase the excess or free reserves available to the member banks and thereby influence the volume of bank credit and the supply of effective money. Table 12 shows the range of reserve requirements for each class of banks and the actual requirements as established by the Board.

TABLE 12

Reserve Requirements for Federal Reserve Member Banks*

	On Net Demand Deposits			On Time Deposits
	Central Reserve City Banks	*Reserve City Banks*	*Country Banks*	*All Banks*
Minimum and maximum requirements set by law .	13%–26%	10%–20%	7%–14%	3%–6%
Actual requirements in effect May 1, 1956	20%	18%	12%	5%

* On August 16, 1948, as an anti-inflationary measure, Congress granted the Board of Governors temporary authority to increase reserve requirements on demand deposits by not more than 4 percentage points over the existing statutory maximum and on time deposits by not over 1½ percentage points. This authority expired on June 30, 1949.

Method of computing required reserves. Central reserve city banks and reserve city banks compute their required reserves on the basis of their average daily net deposits (as of the beginning of each business day) over a period of one week. Country banks, on the other hand, calculate their reserve requirements on a semimonthly basis. The required reserves against time deposits are calculated simply by applying the required reserve ratio to the average daily time deposits for the computation period.

Demand deposits against which reserves are to be carried are computed by deducting from gross demand deposits (1) the checks on other banks in process of clearing or collection; and (2) demand balances carried in domestic incorporated banks other than the Federal Reserve Bank. Gross demand deposits include government and individual demand deposits, deposits of other banks, and certified and cashiers' checks outstanding. The "net demand deposits" resulting from the above deductions is the base to which is applied the required reserve ratio.

To satisfy the regulations governing member bank reserve requirements it is necessary that the reserve balances carried at the Federal Reserve Bank, *averaged over the computation period* (one week for central reserve and reserve city banks and half a month for country banks), be equal to the average requirements for that period. Consequently, the banks avoid criticism and the 2 per cent penalty by making certain any deficiency appearing in the first part of the period is offset during the latter part by an appropriate excess of reserves so that the correct average can be maintained.

Methods of adjusting legal reserves. A member bank that finds its legal reserve position impaired may resort to any one of several methods for remedying the situation. The simplest and most direct way to increase reserves with the Federal Reserve Bank is to transfer working balances carried with other banks, when they can be spared. This method is readily available to country banks. A second method, used often by the big city banks, is the borrowing of legal reserves (Federal funds) from other banks having an excess supply. Another method is to dispose of readily salable assets in the open market. Short-term government obligations and bankers' acceptances are particularly adapted to this use. Finally, the member may borrow from or discount eligible paper with the Federal Reserve Bank. In the long run, as an ultimate method of improving its reserve position, the bank may scale down its loans and investments other than those mentioned above.

Borrowing Federal funds. Over a short period of time, member banks sometimes find it advantageous temporarily to purchase or borrow reserves from other members which at the moment have an excess. Both the borrowing and the lending bank may profit from this transaction. The borrowing bank may wish to increase its balance at the Federal Reserve Bank for a short period in order to bring its average actual reserves to the required level for the computation period. The lending bank, on the other hand, holds excess reserves with which it is willing to part for a short period. The rate of interest on loans of "Federal funds," as such reserves are called, generally is somewhat lower than the prevailing Federal Reserve discount rate.

The process of lending reserves may involve the issue of a cashier's check by the borrowing bank (listed in its statement as money borrowed instead of deposits). The lending bank either issues a draft on the Federal Reserve Bank to the borrowing bank or arranges for a transfer by the reserve bank of funds from its reserve balance to that of the borrowing bank.[5]

Originally, the market for Federal funds was largely concentrated in New York City. Banks there found it convenient and economical to adjust their reserve positions from day to day by borrowing and lending among themselves deposit balances at the Federal Reserve Bank. During the tightening of the money market in 1955 some of the big New York banks organized a kind of country-wide market for Federal funds by arranging with correspondent banks in other cities to report and make available for loan any excess reserves that they might have. The New York City banks act as broker to allocate such funds among banks that are short of reserves, with transfers carried out through the Federal Reserve leased wire system. This development tends to reduce the supply of excess reserves that otherwise may pile up in banks in smaller cities while reserve shortages exist elsewhere.

Criticism of present reserve requirements. The existing pattern of legal reserve requirements for banks is by no means ideal. A number of objections may properly be raised. First, the requirement that all legal reserves of member banks must be carried as deposits in the Federal Reserve Banks tends to discriminate against member banks not located near the Federal Reserve Banks. Such banks, naturally enough, find it necessary to carry considerably more cash in vault (till money) in proportion to their deposits

---

[5] For a good account of the use of Federal funds, see Hobart C. Carr's "Federal Funds," *Money Market Essays,* Federal Reserve Bank of New York, March 1952.

than do banks located in Federal Reserve Bank cities. But such cash cannot be counted as legal reserve. These banks therefore suffer in comparison with the more fortunate members located near the reserve bank. In addition, they are at a disadvantage in comparison with competing nonmember banks, which can generally count vault cash in satisfaction of their legal requirements.

Second, the objection is properly made that the threefold classification of banks (country, reserve city, and central reserve city) for the purpose of determining the size of reserve requirements is outmoded and without justification. Differences in reserve requirements should be based more on the nature of deposits than on the city in which the bank is located.

Third, it is unfair to banks which are members of the Federal Reserve System that nonmember banks are not, in most instances, subject to changes in reserve requirements imposed by the Board of Governors in the pursuit of proper credit policy.

Fourth, the Board of Governors' use of changes in reserve requirements as a means of influencing credit expansion is hampered by the existence of over 7,000 nonmember banks whose reserve requirements are outside the control of the Board. In the interest of both effectiveness and fairness to member banks the Board of Governors has proposed that its control over member bank reserve requirements should be made applicable to nonmember banks as well.

Legal reserve requirements as restraints on the volume of credit. We know that the reserve requirements imposed upon banks by law make but a modest contribution to bank liquidity. Their real significance lies in the fact that neither the individual bank nor the banking system is able to make additional loans and investments unless there is at hand a supply of unused free cash, or excess reserves. The total quantity of available bank reserves, as we know, is determined and limited by the supply of money issued by the Treasury, the credit extensions of the central bank, and by the amount of money in circulation.

With a given supply of available bank reserves, the volume of commercial bank loans and deposits is limited to some appropriate multiple of the reserve supply. Thus, if reserve requirements are 20 per cent, bank credit or loans and deposit expansion cannot go beyond the point at which deposits are five times the available reserves. But should the Board of Governors lower reserve require-ments to an average of 10 per cent, the same amount of reserves could support approximately twice as much bank credit as when requirements were 20 per cent. It is the restraining influence of legal reserve requirements that justifies the provision of the law giving the Board of Governors power to change member bank reserve requirements within specified limits.

The origin of bank reserves. The basic reserves of the whole

TABLE 13

Factors Governing the Volume of Member Bank Reserves*
(In thousands of dollars)

	July 31, 1955	Changes, July 31 to August 31	August 31, 1955
Sources of Member Bank Reserves:			
Gold stock	$21,682	——	$21,682
Treasury currency outstanding	5,003	+ 2	5,005
Federal Reserve credit	25,719	—808	24,911
Total sources of member bank reserves	$52,404	—806	$51,598
Deductions from Sources of Member Bank Reserves:			
Treasury cash holdings ...	$ 798	+ 4	$ 802
Treasury deposits with Federal Reserve Banks .	623	—230	393
Deposits of foreign and nonmember banks, etc. in Federal Reserve Banks .	829	— 59	770
Money in circulation	30,244	+ 75	30,319
Other Federal Reserve accounts (capital accounts minus bank premises and other assets, net)	910	+ 35	945
Total deductions	33,404	—175	33,229
Member Bank Reserves	$19,000	—631	$18,369

* Data from the *Federal Reserve Bulletin.* For a detailed statement of this method of explaining the volume of member bank reserves, see *Banking and Monetary Statistics*, Washington, D.C., Board of Governors of the Federal Reserve System, 1943, p. 360.

banking system are found in the member bank legal reserves which are deposited in the Federal Reserve Banks. Even nonmember bank reserves are to a large extent tied in by being deposited with city correspondent banks that are members of the Federal Reserve System. Member bank reserves, therefore, provide the foundation for the whole bank credit structure. The amount of available reserves, along with the current reserve requirements, determines the limits of commercial bank credit expansion. Therefore we need to look briefly at the origins of bank reserves and the factors that determine their quantity.

One important source of member bank reserves is the supply of standard money (gold) and other government issues of money. Whenever gold is imported and sold to the Treasury, the importer receives in payment a check upon the Treasury's account with the Federal Reserve Bank. When this check is deposited in a commercial bank and collected, the deposits and the legal reserves of the bank are increased by the amount of the gold purchased. Needing only fractional reserves for the new deposits, the excess reserves of the bank are increased. Similarly, the Treasury purchases of silver and the issue of paper and token money add to the supply of bank reserves. The second main source of bank reserves is found in the purchases of securities and in the loans of the Federal Reserve Banks. The price of the securities and the proceeds of loans to member banks appear promptly as additions to member bank reserve accounts.

The reserves provided by gold imports, Treasury currency issues, and central bank credit extension may be offset by the following developments. First, the Treasury may decide to increase its holdings of funds in cash or on deposit in the Federal Reserve Banks. Its application of current taxes to building up its account with the Reserve Banks reduces member bank reserves, since the Treasury balance is built up at the expense of member bank reserve balances. Also, any increase in currency and other cash that the Treasury may hold has the effect of reducing the supply of bank reserves. Second, there may arise a demand for more currency for hand-to-hand circulation purposes. As bank customers convert their deposits into cash, the banks must pay out an equal amount of cash reserves. Because till money supplies are small, the banks will be compelled to convert reserve balances in the Federal Reserve Banks into Federal Reserve notes. Thus the need for more money in circulation reduces the legal reserve balances of the member banks.

Finally, as a result of international transactions, foreign banks sometimes come into possession of funds that they hold as deposits in the Federal Reserve Banks. These are obtained at the expense of member bank reserves. Also, nonmember banks, carrying clearing balances with the Federal Reserve Banks, reduce in some measure the reserve funds available to member banks.

A clear summary view of the origin of member bank reserves is given in Table 13.

Questions for Study

1. What is meant by "primary" reserves? Do they include legal reserves? Do they include "working" reserves? Do they include "excess" reserves?

2. Why have legal reserve requirements been imposed on American banks?

3. Why do banks need working reserves in addition to their legal reserves? What are included in these working reserves?

4. Which class of banks carries the greatest relative amount of vault cash? Which class carries the greatest relative amount of "due from banks"?

5. How is the base calculated for computing reserve requirements for member banks?

6. Suppose that a member bank's legal reserve during the first half of the computation period shows a 10 per cent deficiency. What steps can and should it take? Why?

7. If legal reserves of banks contribute but little to bank liquidity, why must they be maintained? Why does the Board of Governors have power to regulate member bank reserve requirements?

8. What are "Federal Funds"? How are they used to avoid borrowing at the Federal Reserve Banks? In what other ways can banks adjust their reserves?

9. Examine carefully Table 13, which shows the factors that govern the volume of member bank reserves. How are member banks' reserves affected by:

   a) The purchase of imported gold by the Treasury?
   b) The Federal Reserve Bank purchase of U.S. securities?
   c) The Treasury withdrawal of tax funds from deposits in commercial banks for transfer to its account in the Federal Reserve Bank.
   d) The increase in money in circulation.
   e) The increase in Federal Reserve float?

III

BANK LOANS
AND INVESTMENTS

11

Loans Made by Banks

Bank Earning Assets

Legal reserves, vault cash, and funds deposited with city correspondent banks bring no revenue to the bank and are therefore "nonearning" bank assets. Likewise the bank's fixed assets, such as equipment, fixtures, and building, are considered as nonearning assets even though incidental revenue may be derived from rentals of office and safety deposit space. In contrast, earning assets are made up of the bank's portfolio of interest-bearing loans and investments.

The significance of bank earning assets. Bank earning assets are vital both to the banks and to the general public. To the banks they are the source of earnings. Their character and quality determine both the essential liquidity and the ultimate solvency of the bank. To the general public, bank earning assets are important because it is through them that banks make their direct contribution toward meeting the community's credit needs. Furthermore, it is through the expansion and contraction of the aggregate quantity of bank loans and investments that banks can and do bring about changes in the supply of money.

Bank Loans

Before the depression of the 1930's, loans made up the main part of commercial bank earning assets. In October 1929, the loans of member banks comprised 73 per cent of their portfolios. The depression caused bank loans to shrink, and the gold imports after 1934 greatly expanded bank reserves. Consequently, banks sought to find outlets for funds by increasing their investments in

155

government securities. The result was that by the middle of 1936 member bank loans were only 38 per cent of their earning assets. During World War II banks purchased government securities in ever increasing amounts while loans made but a modest gain. By the end of 1945 member bank loans made up but 21 per cent of their earning assets.

Some doubt arose after the war as to the ability and willingness of commercial banks to recapture their former importance in financing private business. But by 1956, commercial bank loans amounted to $82 billion and were 52 per cent of total earning assets. Thus the banks have in fact re-achieved a responsible place in the financing of the American economy. But, as compared to the days before the 1930's, business is still relatively less dependent upon bank loans.[1] The best explanation for this seems to be that during the depression and, to a much greater degree, during the war, the government borrowings from banks were very large. The expenditure of the resulting new money so expanded the money flow and the scale of economic output that business firms were able to finance an unusually large part of their needs out of profits arising from their share of the general expansion. Even so, the substantial expansion of bank loans after the war reflects the borrowing firms' need for more funds than could conveniently be obtained from new security issues and from withheld profits. Chart 3 provides a visual basis of comparison of the loans and investments of commercial banks since 1939.

Types of bank loans. Commercial banks, according to traditional theory, should be limited to making loans for short periods to provide temporary working funds to finance current business operations. Because such loans failed to meet all the needs of bank customers and because other lucrative outlets for bank funds appeared, banks quite generally have forsaken the ideal loan practices of the theorists and have embarked upon a widely varied loan program. Also, as we know, commercial banks have taken on sav-

---

[1] The ratio of commercial and agricultural loans of Federal Reserve member banks to the gross national product was about 12 per cent in 1929, and in 1955 it was only about 8 per cent. However, consumer credit financing by member banks that has developed since 1929 may properly be included along with commercial and agricultural loans as a part of the necessary financing of business. If one includes consumer credit, the ratio of member bank financing to gross national product in 1955 is over 10 per cent.

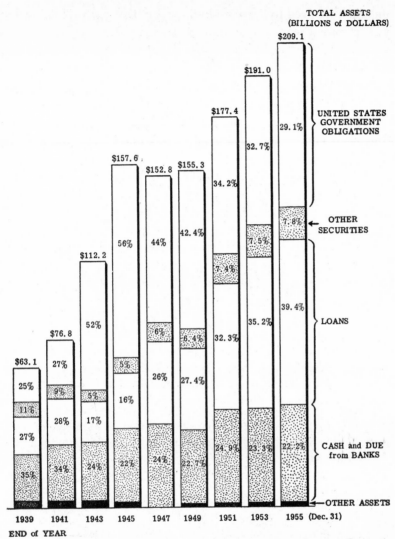

TOTAL ASSETS
(BILLIONS of DOLLARS)

Chart 3. Percentage Composition of Assets of Insured Commercial Banks.

Annual Reports of the Federal Deposit Insurance Corporation.

ings bank functions. Funds received from savings deposits quite
properly are lent for longer periods and for purposes unsuited for
commercial bank loans. As we briefly examine the various loans
of commercial banks we can readily see the extent to which modern
commercial banks have departed from traditional theory. At the

same time we need to keep in mind the fact that part of bank excursions into what seems to be unorthodox loan channels are in reality but a normal and proper use of funds received from savings depositors.

Classification of bank loans. Bank loans may be classified in several ways:

1. *The purpose of the loan.* Regularly published statements of banks divide loans into classes based upon the use made of the funds. These classes include:

(a) Loans to business—commercial and industrial.
(b) Loans to agriculture for current purposes.
(c) Loans for purchasing and carrying securities.
(d) Loans on real estate mortgages.
(e) Consumers' loans.
(f) Other loans not falling in the above categories.

The relative importance of these different classes of loans may be clearly seen in Chart 4.

2. *Loans to customers vs. loans in the open market.* Customers' loans, by far the major type, involve a direct personal relationship between the borrower and the lender. Open market loans, in contrast, are made impersonally to borrowers of sufficient credit rating to benefit from competition for their paper among lenders in the money market. Formerly, stock market loans made at the money desk of the New York Stock Exchange were true open market loans. Such loans have been discontinued. Consequently, open market borrowers today are limited to the sellers of bankers' acceptances and prime open market commercial paper. In 1955, out of business loans by member banks of $31.6 billion, $30.8 billion were to customers and only $800 million were in the open market.[2]

3. *Secured and unsecured loans.* When the lender obtains some protection over and above that afforded by the borrower's signature on the note, the loan is said to be *secured.* The security may consist of pledged securities, warehouse receipts, liens on equipment and other chattels or titles thereto, real estate mortgages, and assignments of receivables and future income from ship charters and oil runs. Sometimes the security takes the form of an accommodation endorsement or cosigner who guarantees payment. In contrast, unsecured loans give the bank a right only to sue the debtor and get a judgment against him if the note is not paid at maturity. In this case the bank take its chances along with any other general creditors seeking to collect from the defaulting debtor. Naturally, bankers like to make secured loans whenever possible, but

---

[2] "Business Loans of Member Banks," *Federal Reserve Bulletin,* April 1956.

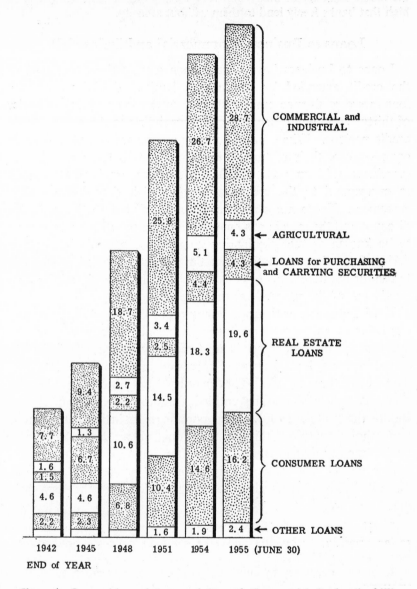

Chart 4. Composition of Loans of Insured Commercial Banks (in billions of dollars).

the credit standing of many borrowers, especially business firms, is so high that banks freely lend to them without security.

Loans to Business (Commercial and Industrial)

Loans to business have always been a very significant part of the credit extended by commercial banks. Traditionally, such loans were to finance current short-term needs and had maturities of thirty, sixty, and ninety days, corresponding to the normal trade credit periods. When trade acceptances or trade notes were in common use, their maturities ran from one to three months. If merchants sold on open account, their own credit needs tended to correspond to the credit terms on which they sold to their customers. Trade notes and acceptances offered to the bank for discount and the merchant's own single-name promissory note came to be known as "self-liquidating commercial paper." This name derives from the expectation that the money borrowed can be put to use for the purchase of goods, which can be resold, and the loan repaid out of the proceeds at the time of maturity.

Bank loans to continuous borrowers. The true self-liquidating character of the short-term loans to business depends upon the fact that the borrower's needs are temporary and seasonal. But in actual business, borrowers need borrowed funds for periods longer than one to three months. They may have but little seasonal variation and yet need and be entitled (credit-wise) to bank loans. Before the middle 1930's banks continued to insist that business loans should mature within the traditional ninety days. Yet it was perfectly clear that borrowers very often required the funds for a longer period and were relying upon the bankers to renew at maturity.[3] The excuses given for clinging closely to the very short maturities were:

1. The loan was safer because the bank might review the borrower's position frequently and take steps to collect if his position worsensed.

2. It was necessary to limit business loans to not over ninety days'

---

[3] Cf. Moultan, H. G., "Commercial Banking and Capital Formation," *Journal of Political Economy,* 1918, p. 658. In 1942 a survey revealed that 41 per cent of the total loans made during one month were renewals. Jacoby, N. H. and Saulnier, R. J., *Business Finance and Banking,* New York, National Bureau of Economic Research, 1947, p. 48.

maturity in order that they should be eligible for rediscount at the Federal Reserve Bank.

3. Examiners often criticized business loans with longer maturities by classifying them as "slow," a term of opprobrium.

The practice of limiting loan maturities to ninety days, with the understanding that renewals were to be expected, turned out to be especially unsatisfactory and dangerous to business when depression and financial crisis appeared. At such times banks refused renewals and borrowers were forced to attempt repayment at a time most disadvantageous to both businessmen and to the general economy.

The term loan. During the late 1930's, banks began a more realistic practice in respect to loan maturities. With a slack demand for loans, banks were more disposed to adjust their lending habits to the needs of borrowers. The depression had left many meritorious borrowers with inadequate supplies of continuous working capital. Many large and well-established firms wished to take advantage of the lower bank loan interest rates to refinance their outstanding bond issues. As a result, banks began to make *term loans* to business, *with maturities of from one to ten years.* Such loans, unlike the true short-term self-liquidating loan, are not expected to be repaid out of the immediate sale of current inventory. Instead, since the funds are for continuous working capital needs, the repayment must come from depreciation and net earnings. Hence the maturities must be sufficiently remote to make such repayment possible.

Two legal changes worked to encourage banks to embark upon the making of term loans: (1) An amendment to the Federal Reserve Act in 1935 removed the critical significance of thirty, sixty, and ninety-day commercial paper as a basis of obtaining funds from the Federal Reserve Banks. This amendment permits member banks to borrow on any sound assets without regard to maturity. In addition, the substantial volume of government securities held by banks at that time provided an abundant basis for member bank borrowing at the Federal Reserve Banks. (2) The rules governing the classification of bank assets by examiners were changed so as to remove the stigma of "slow" from sound paper with longer maturities. Instead, sound loans, regardless of maturities, were given a clean bill of health.

The importance of the term loans made by banks to business

borrowers may be judged by the fact that in October 1955, member banks reported outstanding term loans to the amount of $10.5 billion. These term loans comprised 34 per cent of the banks' total loans to business.[4]

Term loan agreements, especially those involving large advances to big borrowers, frequently provide that the loan be shared among a number of banks. They also frequently provide for an original maturity of from one to two years, with an option to the borrower to extend the loan for a number of additional years. The agreement may call for a maximum credit line that permits the borrower to borrow and repay according to his needs, while paying a small fee for the privilege of keeping open the unused part of the credit.

It should be recognized that the making of capital or term loans by commercial banks involves risks that are somewhat greater than those on loans made for shorter periods. To facilitate the repayment out of earnings, it is well for such loans to mature serially. Further, special protection is needed for the lender. This may take the form of warehouse receipts issued against the inventory of the borrower, mortgages on the plant, title to and liens on equipment, assignment of receivables and future income from leases, charters, and oil production, and special agreements not to mortgage or pledge any assets during the life of the loan and to maintain a minimum current ratio.

Secured Business Loans

As we saw earlier in our discussion, many bank loans are made without security. Especially is this true of loans to business borrowers. Nevertheless, a very substantial fraction of total business loans are secured. Because banks, in their published reports, do not distinguish between secured and unsecured loans to business, one must rely upon the Federal Reserve study of 1947. It revealed that, as of November 20, 1946, 61.1 per cent of the total *number* of business loans made by member banks was secured. At the same time but 43.8 per cent of the total *amount* of business loans, measured in dollars, was secured.[5] The explanation, of

---

[4] "Business Loans of Member Banks," *Federal Reserve Bulletin,* April 1956, p. 334.

[5] "Security Pledged on Member Bank Loans to Business," *Federal Reserve Bulletin,* June 1947.

course, lies in the fact that large borrowers generally enjoy sufficient credit to be able to borrow without security. Being large, though relatively fewer, such borrowers account for a larger part of the total business loans. Smaller borrowers with weaker credit stand-ing borrow less in the aggregate but account for the larger number of loans that are classified as secured.

The types of security used for member bank loans to business, as reported in the 1947 study, were:

		Per cent of total secured loans
1.	Inventories	20.6
2.	Stocks, bonds, and mortgages	18.5
3.	Plant and other real estate	16.3
4.	Equipment	12.2
5.	Endorsed and co-maker	12.2
6.	Assignment of claims	5.4
7.	Accounts receivable	3.3
8.	Oil runs	3.3
9.	Life insurance	2.6
10.	Government guarantees	2.1
11.	Other security	3.7

Loans on inventories. Inventories, or commodity collateral, stand highest in the list of securities for loans to business. Such inventory loans are mainly based upon warehouse receipts issued by public, independent warehousemen. Generally they are issued against goods stored in public warehouses, although some use is now made of field warehouse receipts issued by the warehouseman against goods stored in the borrower's own warehouse. In such cases the control over the warehouse must be transferred to the public warehouseman for the life of the loan. In addition to ware-house receipts, banks lend against order or negotiable bills of lading that call for posseession of goods in transit, and against trust receipts in which the borrower recognizes the title of the lending bank in goods released to the borrower. In this case, proceeds from the sale of the goods released under the trust receipt belong to the lending bank. Banks also make loans on the security of chattel mortgages on inventory.

The underlying commodities used as security for bank loans are of great variety. Originally they included mainly such staples as grain, cotton, wool, and meat products. With modern improvements in the art of cold storage, a vast array of commodities can be stored, and warehouse receipts against them may appear as collateral for bank loans.

A relatively new type of loan secured by borrower's inventory is that now made by banks on the basis of proved supplies of underground oil. These are appraised by the bank, and loans made are paid off out of the proceeds of oil production and sale.

Problems of commodity collateral. Commodity collateral loans present problems of marketability and value. If the underlying commodities are regularly traded in on organized exchanges, there is the advantage of assured marketability as well as opportunity to keep close check upon changes in market value. But many commodities on which warehouse receipts are issued and offered as collateral for banks are not dealt in on regular exchanges. Their marketability depends, often, upon a relatively narrow range of buyers. Under such circumstances, the lending banker must rely not only upon a wide margin of collateral but also upon the borrower's general credit standing and the probability that the collateral will in due time be turned into income. Although not so satisfactory as a loan on more staple articles, loans on the less marketable forms of commodity collateral have an obvious advantage over unsecured loans in that they give the lender a prior claim on certain specific valuable assets in case of bankruptcy. Collateral notes of all kinds ordinarily contain a power of sale in case of default or bankruptcy. Loans on warehouse receipts are preferable to loans on chattel mortgages because of the greater convenience and lack of legal procedure involved in realizing on the collateral.

Both warehouse receipts and bills of lading collateral are exposed to the risk that the borrower may not in fact have a clear title to the underlying commodities. Moreover, the warehouse receipts are no better than the financial responsibility of the warehouseman. He is responsible for reasonable care in the safekeeping of the goods, for the correctness of the description of the goods on the receipt, and for proper delivery of the goods to the holder of the warehouse receipt.

To insure honest grading and financial responsibility on the part of warehousemen of agricultural products, the Secretary of Agriculture may license warehousemen of agricultural products and require that they be satisfactorily bonded to the United States Government. Any person injured by the default of the warehouseman may sue in his own name on the bond.

Stocks, bonds, and assigned mortgages. Almost as important as commodity collateral is that comprising securities. The advantages of such collateral are several. If the securities are highly marketable, the bank has something that can be readily sold to satisfy the debt in case of default. Even when not readily marketable on organized exchanges, securities pledged on the loan give the banker definite protection by giving him prior claim against valuable assets. The borrower benefits by being able to borrow more than he otherwise might be allowed. Not only does the security improve his credit position, but also permits size of the loan to be increased if the bank has a small capital and surplus. National banks, for instance, can lend not more than 10 per cent of their capital and surplus to any one borrower unless certain collateral requirements are met. If the borrower offers collateral of U.S. Government obligations, for example, the individual loan limit becomes 25 per cent.

It should be remembered that the margin requirements placed on loans made for carrying securities do not apply to business loans secured by stocks and bonds. The reason is of course easy to see, since the banks need require no collateral at all. Margin requirements are designed to hold in check speculation in stocks on borrowed money.

Assignment of title and chattel mortgages on equipment. Many small companies are able to give necessary security for loans to purchase equipment by assigning the title or by giving a chattel mortgage to the lending bank. Similarly, they may offer mortgage liens on plant and other real estate. Such security is often used to protect the bank making term loans.

Accounts receivable. Before the depression of the 1930's, banks did not often venture into the field of lending on borrowers' accounts receivable. The depression years so impaired the credit standing of some small and medium-sized firms that they were compelled, in the absence of better collateral, to offer to assign their accounts as a basis for loans. In general, banks have not favored lending on the assignment of accounts receivable because of the added expense and trouble involved. Nevertheless, seeking for profitable loan outlets, the banks have gradually moved into this field that previously was the special province of the finance companies and discount houses.

In financing on receivables, banks advance cash to the borrowers in amounts up to 70 to 90 per cent of the face amount of the assigned accounts. Generally the debtors whose accounts are assigned are not notified and, consequently, the banks must rely on the agreement of the borrowing firm to turn over the daily check receipts received in payment of the accounts. The banks reserve their right of recourse against the borrower for ultimate payment. Interest rates charged on such loans are usually higher than on loans secured by other forms of collateral.[6]

Unsecured Business Loans

As we learned earlier, although more than one-half of all business borrowers offer some form of security, measured in dollar amounts more money is lent for business purposes without security than with it. Therefore, some of the problems relating to the making of unsecured business loans deserve separate consideration.

Open market loans. There are two types of open market paper that can be included among the unsecured loans of banks for financing business operations. The first is the banker's acceptance, an obligation of the accepting bank to pay a stated sum of money at a given future date. It is discounted by the lending bank and is an unsecured commercial loan. The second is open market commercial paper purchased by banks from commercial paper dealers. Both of these classes of paper are generally unsecured.

Trade paper. One type of unsecured loan takes the form of discounted or purchased trade paper owned by the borrower. Such paper consists of trade acceptances and promissory notes. By his indorsement the borrower assumes a contingent liability to

---

6 Cf. Saulnier, R. J. and Jacoby, N. H., *Accounts Receivable Financing,* New York, National Bureau of Economic Research, 1943. Banks also buy conditional sale paper from merchants, without recourse but reserving 10 per cent of the price to cover collection risks.

pay the instrument on notice of dishonor by the primary obligor. Trade paper thus bears two signatures and is designated *two-name* paper. The discounting bank, therefore, gets the specific promise of the buyer of goods, in addition to the indorsement of the seller-borrower. The selling and credit policies of American business are such that two-name paper of this kind is relatively scarce, most firms preferring for one reason or another to stick to the usual method of selling on open account.

Single-name paper. Finally, there is the single-name unsecured note, which looms large among bank loans. The use of single-name paper arises from the American habit of making credit sales on open account with a heavy discount offered for cash. The heavy cash discount obtainable for payment within ten days furnishes an inducement to the buyer to pay cash, if it is at all possible. If he possesses insufficient funds of his own, and his credit standing is sufficiently good, he will borrow on his unsecured note from his local banker. On the other hand, if the buyer is unable to pay cash but waits until the expiration of the full credit period to pay, the seller will obtain funds by borrowing at his bank on his unsecured notes. Thus, in either event, banks will be called upon to finance the transaction on single-name unsecured notes.

In order that a banker may make unsecured loans safely, it is essential that he have complete and accurate information as to the borrower's credit. The methods used in acquiring such information are varied. The small-town banker tends to rely upon his general acquaintance with the borrower's affairs, supplemented by specific personal inquiries. Larger banks find it impossible to rely upon haphazard credit information and develop more or less elaborate credit departments whose function it is to gather and record credit information about customers and prospective borrowers. The multiplicity of their borrowers, the greater difficulty of measuring the credit standing of complex and large-scale firms, the size of the accommodation required—all make necessary a more complete and orderly assemblage of information than could be had with less formal methods of collection. Moreover, large city banks are frequently called upon by their country correspondents to supply credit information about open market borrowers.

Borrowers' statements. Credit information of the more formal sort may be obtained from a variety of sources. There are available for banks as well as others the services of the well-known credit-rating agencies, such as Dun and Bradstreet. There is also the method of direct inquiry from the business houses that have dealings with the individual or firm whose credit standing is being examined. If the borrower has borrowed before at the bank, his record there is available. Finally, there is the direct inquiry from applicants for loans. Foremost in such an inquiry is a request for a statement of assets and liabilities (or balance sheet) and an income statement, preferably certified by a certified public accountant. Supplementing these will be specific inquiries bearing on the borrower's business affairs.

The use of the borrower's statement of assets and liabilities received impetus through the rise of credit departments. Since unsecured commercial loans are made for a relatively short period of time, the banker is vitally concerned with the relation of the borrower's current income to his liabilities. Only when his probable income shows a satisfactory margin over his liabilities, including the proposed loan, will the banker be justified in lending without security. A careful analysis of the borrower's statements will give the desired information. The items of the balance sheet of most interest to the banker are the current assets and the current liabilities.

Current Assets	*Current Liabilities*
Cash	Accounts payable
Accounts and notes receivable	Notes payable
Inventory, made up of:	Accrued interest on long-time debt
Raw materials	Any long-time debt nearing
Finished goods	maturity
Goods in process	Accrued expenses

The ratio of current assets to current liabilities, called, for convenience, the "current ratio," should show a satisfactory margin of assets over liabilities. What the margin should be in practice depends primarily upon the quality of the current assets and the degree of regularity of income and outgo. The quality of the current assets depends upon, among other things, the following conditions:

1. The general state of business, whether normal or dangerously inflated. This has a direct bearing upon both the marketability of the inventory and the ability to collect the accounts receivable.

2. The freshness of the accounts receivable. If any substantial proportion represent past-due, slow, and uncertain accounts, their value must be discounted. This may be discovered by comparing the volume of accounts receivable with the volume of sales during the normal credit period just preceding. Since some buyers take cash discounts, the accounts receivable should be less rather than more than the sales for the period.

3. The marketability of the inventory. This is indicated by comparing the present rate of inventory turnover with (1) the past experience of the company; and (2) the experience of other firms of a similar type. Furthermore, the marketability is affected by the degree to which the product is a staple, subject to a continuous demand. Not only will the banker rely upon an analysis of the borrower's statements as a means of discovering the true worth of the assets, but he must also check carefully, insofar as possible, on the accuracy of the statements themselves. This may involve an audit of the borrower's accounts either by certified public accountants or by representatives of the bank.

Although the banker relies heavily upon the current ratio of the borrower in order to assure repayment of the loan when due, he cannot afford to disregard the question of the long-time solvency of the firm as evidenced by an adequate stockholders' equity. This consideration may not appear so important in the case of short-time loans intended to tide the borrower over a seasonal peak. In such cases sufficient protection is afforded by the current assets. But the tendency among some borrowers to obtain loans for longer periods of time alters the situation. In such a case the question of the ultimate solvency of the borrower becomes a vital one, for upon it rests his ability either to pay the loan or to shift it to other banks.

The Line of Credit

In the event that the customer wishes to borrow at intervals during any given season, it is frequently more convenient both for him and for the bank to make an analysis of his credit and to establish a maximum line of credit that the bank is willing to extend. Thereafter, so long as there is no material alteration in the borrower's condition, he may borrow at any time, without investigation, up to the amount of his credit line. The line of credit imposes no legal obligation upon the bank. It is merely an expression of willingness to lend up to a certain amount if the borrower's credit standing is not impaired and if the bank is in a position to lend at the time when the customer wishes to borrow. Not only does the bank not assume any legal liability to lend, but the customer in no way obligates himself to borrow any or all of the line extended to him. But the bank incurs a moral obligation to keep open the line if the customer carefully preserves his credit standing, and it could hardly afford to violate the confidence of a valuable customer. If necessary, it may borrow funds required to care for the customer's needs. Lines of credit are extended not only to business houses but to correspondent banks as well. Nonmember banks that experience heavy seasonal drains of cash frequently resort to their city correspondent for loans. These loans may be either secured or unsecured.

Banks usually make two requirements of customers for whom they extend a credit line. First, the customer may be expected to clean up his loans at least once a year. This is designed to indicate that the borrower is obtaining funds to care for a seasonal peak in his business. After the need is past, he will pay off his loans. The bank's loans are, therefore, self-liquidating in character. The continuous borrowers, however, can conform to this rule only by borrowing elsewhere in order to pay off the original lending bank. Although loans of this kind are not strictly self-liquidating merely because they are paid off, the bank has the advantage of compelling the borrower to subject his affairs periodically to the scrutiny of other bankers.

A second requirement commonly made by commercial banks in extending a line of credit is that the customer shall maintain a certain fractional part of the line on deposit with the bank during the life of the credit. This rule is by no means uniformly applied. It is more commonly insisted on in the larger money centers, but is a well-established principle among practical bankers, whether or not it is actually adhered to. A variation of the same principle appears in the form of a requirement that a borrowing customer shall maintain a certain fraction of his total loans on deposit during the life of the loan. Still another variation is that any loans made may be only a certain multiple of the average deposit balances carried by the borrower during some preceding period. Some form of the average balance requirement is in common use, particularly among metropolitan bankers.[7]

---

[7] In response to a questionnaire sent the 100 largest banks in the country, 65 per cent indicated that they made the carrying of compensating balances

Bankers attempt to justify the compensating balance rule on various grounds. Basically, however, there seems to be one reason for it. Individual bankers compete for deposits in order to increase their power to lend. The compensating balance rule provides a method of inducing would-be borrowers to carry a substantial balance with the bank. In times of tight money the applicant whose "account has not been satisfactory" will be turned down in favor of the applicant who has carried a good balance at the bank. In times of easy money the rule tends to fall into disuse. In any event, it is less likely to be enforced against the better borrowers who are in a position to shop around for loan accommodations.

Bankers' Acceptances

In addition to making loans, banks sometimes assist in the process of credit extension by guaranteeing the credit of merchants through the use of bankers' acceptances. Bankers' acceptances, as we have already seen, are negotiable drafts drawn against a bank, payable at some future date and "accepted" by the drawee bank on presentment. This acceptance has the effect of binding the acceptor to pay the draft when due. When the accepting bank is well known and of good credit standing in the community, its acceptance is considered prime paper and is much sought after by banks for use as secondary reserve and by other institutions desiring a highly liquid and sound investment.

The use of bankers' acceptances. An acceptance of a well-known bank can be discounted in the money market at a low rate of interest. The owner of a banker's acceptance, therefore, can convert it into cash on favorable terms. When a bank places its signature upon a bill drawn against it and thus "accepts" it, the effect is to bind the bank to pay the instrument at maturity. For this act the bank receives a commission of perhaps 1 or 1½ per cent

---

a requirement for obtaining a line of credit. The amount of the required balance varied from 10 to 20 per cent. Most banks apparently do not attempt to enforce such requirements against borrowers of term loans. Actually, the application of the rule varies greatly among banks and somewhat among different line-of-credit borrowers in the same bank. Gallot, F. P., "Why Compensating Balances?" *Bulletin of the Robert Morris Associates, Supplement,* June 1954. Also see "Credit Lines and Minimum Balance Requirements," *Federal Reserve Bulletin,* June 1956, for information in respect to lines of credit and required balances revealed in the System's survey of commercial and industrial bank loans on October 5, 1955.

per annum. The commission must be sufficient to compensate the bank for its trouble and risk, and yield a modest profit. But it need not include any interest charge since the acceptance does not involve a loan. The loan funds derived from the acceptance come from the bank or other investor who purchases or discounts the acceptance.

Bankers' acceptances are used for:

(1) Financing imports and exports.
(2) Financing trade between foreign countries.
(3) Financing goods in storage.

The method of using them in financing foreign trade will be explained later in Chapter 29, which deals with foreign exchange. Acceptances to finance goods in storage must be based upon "readily marketable staples" and must be secured at the time of acceptance by warehouse receipts or other documents of title.

A person or firm having such readily marketable staples in storage may arrange with an accepting bank to accept a time draft drawn against it, secured by documents of title representing the stored goods. The documents may be held or released by the accepting bank, and the drawer of the accepted draft discounts it in the acceptance market.

The accepting bank earns its commission for accepting the bill, and the businessman borrower obtains his funds at the relatively low rate of discount commanded by a good banker's acceptance. The advantage of borrowing by the use of a banker's acceptance lies in the possibility of getting funds more cheaply than by paying the ordinary customers' rate at the borrower's own bank.

Roundabout extension of credit by the accepting bank creates on the liability side of the statement the item "acceptances outstanding." Since the offsetting protection for the liability consists solely of "customers' liability," it follows that the extension of acceptance credit involves just as careful scrutiny of the ability of the borrower to repay as does a straight loan. To prevent the abuse of such credits by American banks, the Federal Reserve Act carefully limits and regulates the acceptance powers of member banks.[8]

---

[8] In Regulation C, the Board of Governors of the Federal Reserve System sets the rules under which "accepting" member banks must operate. These

The magnitude of American bankers' acceptance business and the kinds of financing done by acceptances may be seen in Chart 5.

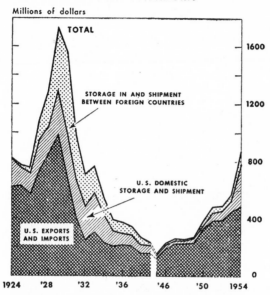

DOLLAR ACCEPTANCES OUTSTANDING

Millions of dollars

TOTAL

STORAGE IN AND SHIPMENT BETWEEN FOREIGN COUNTRIES

U. S. DOMESTIC STORAGE AND SHIPMENT

U. S. EXPORTS AND IMPORTS

1600

1200

800

400

0

1924   '28   '32   '36   '46   '50   1954

NOTE.—Year-end figures. Acceptances based on U. S. exports and imports include dollar exchange acceptances.

"Bankers' Acceptance Financing in the United States," Federal Reserve Bulletin, *May 1955, p. 483.*

Chart 5. Bankers' Acceptance Financing.

Questions for Study

1. Which of the assets listed in the bank's balance sheet are "earning assets"?

2. Before 1930 what was the relative importance of loans in banks' portfolios? Why did this proportion change in the 1930's? In the 1940's? What is the present trend of the proportion of loans in banks' portfolios?

---

include: (1) A maturity limit of six months. (2) A quantitative limit of 50 per cent of a bank's capital and surplus, with the provision that the Board may grant permission for a bank's acceptances to rise to 100 per cent of its capital and surplus. (3) Upon approval of the Board of Governors a bank may accept three-month drafts drawn on it by Latin-American banks to finance seasonal exports of the United States to Latin American countries.

   3. Can you identify each cf the following terms?
         Customer loans.
         Open market paper.
         Self-liquidating commercial loans.
         Term loans.
         Secured loans.
         Line of credit.
   4. Why has the "term loan" assumed such an important place?
   5. Name four important types of commodity collateral offered to banks as collateral for business loans.
   6. Why are securities offered as collateral for loans to business?
   7. What are open market commercial loans?
   8. How can a banker justify lending to business without collateral security?
   9. What must an applicant for a line of credit be prepared to show if he is to receive favorable consideration?
   10. What are bankers' acceptances? Who provides the funds made available through their use?

12

Nonbusiness Loans
of Commercial Banks

Business loans (industrial and commercial) comprise about 40 per cent of all loans made by commercial banks and are therefore the most important single class of bank loans. Yet to understand the place of the commercial banks in the field of credit one must know something about the other types of loans constituting the remaining 60 per cent of the total. In addition, some knowledge of the bank investment portfolio is needed to get a full picture of the bank assets that provide the basis for our money supply.

Agricultural loans. Farmers, like businessmen, need short-term credit for seasonal and irregular needs. Normally they depend on trade credit and bank loans. However, there exist added sources of short-term credit for farmers in the government sponsored and subsidized Production Credit System and in the disaster, emergency, and subsistence loans of the Farm Home Administration operating under the Department of Agriculture. These government sponsored sources of agricultural credit provide approximately one-fourth of the total non-real estate farm loans made by lending institutions, and commercial banks provide nearly three-fourths.[1]

Farmers also need medium-term credit to finance nonseasonal capital needs involved in the purchase of equipment and breeding stock. Apparently banks dealing with farmers have been less inclined to make loans for extended terms than have city banks dealing

---

[1] Excluding loans held or guaranteed by the Commodity Credit Corporation for the support of farm prices. Cf. *Agricultural Finance Review,* U. S. Department of Agriculture, Washington, D.C., November 1955.

with business. The predominant practice is to make agricultural loans with maturities of six months or less. Such maturities, while suited to meet the strictly seasonal needs of the farmer, are wholly inadequate to meet his medium-term credit requirements.

Banks, however, have not altogether disregarded the long-term credit needs of farmers. A study of commercial bank agricultural loans in 1947 showed that about 6 per cent of the total amount was made with maturities of from one to five years.[2] Furthermore, about 10 per cent of the total agricultural loans was payable on demand. Such loans were doubtless intended to be repaid at the borrowers' convenience over moderately long periods. Altogether, in 1947 at least, about 16 per cent of bank agricultural loans were of maturities suited for financing medium-term needs. This compares rather unfavorably with banks' medium-term loans to business, which at about the same time amounted to over one-third of total business loans. It is likely that farmers are still dependent, even more than are some business borrowers, upon the renewal of short-term loans to meet medium-term needs.

About one-third of bank agricultural loans are unsecured. The remainder are secured by claims on livestock, equipment, and crops, and by endorsement. Most loans are small in size; over 60 per cent were for less than $500 and 80 per cent for less than $1,000 in 1947. But 20 per cent of the farmers, who borrowed over $1,000 each, accounted for over 70 per cent of the total agricultural loans.

Consumer loans of commercial banks. For many years finance companies and small loan companies have successfully operated in the field of consumer loans. Commercial banks, however, are late-comers in the field. Before 1931, they made little effort to enter the field of consumer financing because of the risk, the stigma commonly attached to that type of loan, and the extra trouble involved. Instead, they preferred to confine their lending to the larger commercial borrowers from whom there generally was an ample demand for loans. Only indirectly did the bankers assist in consumer financing through their loans to the finance companies.

The depression of the 1930's, with its sharp decline in the demand for commercial loans, caused bankers to seek other outlets

---

2 Allen, P. T. and Smith, T., "Commercial Bank Loans to Farmers," *Federal Reserve Bulletin,* October 1947, p. 1220.

for their funds. Consequently, they began to establish Personal Loan Departments and entered the field of consumer financing.[3] Their ventures into this field take the form both of purchasing installment paper from retailers and finance companies and making direct installment loans and single-payment loans to consumers. In addition, modernization loans made under Title I of the FHA are considered consumer loans.

Commercial bank experience in the field of consumer credit has been favorable. By 1956, commercial bank consumer credit was $12.7 billion in amount, or 17 per cent of total loans. The relative importance of the different types of consumer credit granted by banks may be seen in Table 14.

TABLE 14

Consumer Loans of Commercial Banks
as of February 1956*

Retail automobile installment paper $5,135,000,000
Other retail installment paper 2,099,000,000
Repair and modernization loans (FHA Title I) 1,245,000,000
Personal installment loans 1,919,000,000
Single payment consumer loans 2,387,000,000

* From reports on consumer credit, *Federal Reserve Bulletin,* April 1956.

Real estate loans by banks. The mere fact that a borrower has given a real estate mortgage to secure a loan does not necessarily create a real estate loan. For example, a loan made to a business firm on a medium-term basis to provide working capital may be secured with a mortgage on the firm's real estate. The loan, however, is for business purposes and is not classed as a real estate loan. Real estate loans include loans made to finance the purchase of land, preferably improved, and to finance the construction of buildings or the making of other improvements upon the land. Real estate loans should be made on such a basis that the value of the real estate will sufficiently exceed the amount of the loan as to insure the repayment through liquidation and sale, should the borrower's income prove inadequate to enable him to make payment.

---

[3] It has been estimated that between 80 and 90 per cent of the commercial banks have established consumer credit departments. *Time Sales Financing,* April 1954.

At the end of 1955, real estate loans of insured commercial banks were: [4]

On farm land ....$	1,278,753,000
On residential property:	
Insured by FHA	4,506,346,000
Insured by Veterans Administration	3,670,740,000
Not insured	7,538,257,000
On other properties	3,773,179,000
Total ....$	20,767,275,000

Loans on residential property far outweigh real estate loans of other types.

In addition to holding real estate mortgages for investment, commercial banks often contribute funds for the mortgage loan market in other ways. First, they make short-term loans to mortgage bankers to provide funds needed to carry mortgages until they can be placed with permanent holders. Second, the banks sometimes "warehouse" mortgages for insurance companies, that is, they purchase and hold mortgages for a limited time, with a repurchase agreement by the insurance company at the end of the stated period. This arrangement permits the insurance company to accumulate funds needed to hold the mortgages permanently. Sometimes mortgage bankers who have originated mortgage loans find the insurance companies and other regular purchasers lacking in funds. They therefore must postpone the taking over of mortgages for a time. The mortgage banker may carry the mortgages awaiting final placement by warehousing them with commercial banks.[5]

All commercial banks may now make real estate loans. Central reserve city banks (in the financial centers of New York City and Chicago) are but little involved in such lending, but loans on real estate have a prominent place in the portfolio of other banks. Although state chartered banks have long been permitted to lend on real estate security, national banks were late entering the field. However, since 1955 they have been allowed to make loans for periods of up to ten years and to 66⅔ per cent of the appraised value of improved property, provided that 100 per cent of the loan is amortized (paid off gradually at stated intervals) by maturity. Real estate

---

[4] *Preliminary Report,* The Federal Deposit Insurance Corporation, April 2, 1956.
[5] *The Wall Street Journal,* November 30, 1955.

loans of national banks may also include loans insured by the FHA, loans guaranteed by the Veterans Administration, and ordinary uninsured loans that mature within five years and are for not over 50 per cent of the appraised value of the property.

To prevent excessive involvement in unliquid loans on real estate, except for veterans' guaranteed loans, national banks may not make such loans in total amount to exceed 60 per cent of their time deposits or 100 per cent of their capital and surplus, whichever is the greater.

Security Loans

In contrast to small city banks that lend mainly to business, agriculture, consumers, and to people who want to finance real estate, large city banks, especially those of New York and Chicago, actively engage in lending to the money market. Essentially, such loans are for the purpose of financing the trading and carrying of securities and other financial paper of various kinds. These loans, known as security loans, are based upon the pledge of financial paper of various kinds ranging from stocks and bonds and short-term obligations of corporate enterprises to bankers' acceptances, obligations of state and local government, and the obligations of the United States Government.

Security loans are made to three major classes of borrowers. These are:

1. Brokers, who execute customers' orders to buy and sell securities and borrow from banks to finance customers' margin trading. Their income is derived primarily from brokerage fees, although they may profit from the spread between the interest they charge customers and the rate at which they borrow at banks.

2. Dealers in securities, who buy, hold, and sell securities. Their income is mainly derived from the spread between their buying and selling price, although they may gain something by the difference between cost of borrowed money and the yield on the securities held. Dealers operate mainly in the field of outstanding securities, providing a market for sellers of securities and a supply for those who wish to buy. Dealers acting as underwriters sometimes purchase and carry new security issues. This occurs in the case of investment bankers who are carrying unsold underwritten securities of commercial enterprises and local governmental bodies, and dealers who buy new issues of the

Treasury. In either case, funds for carrying the security inventories are largely obtained through borrowing at banks.

3. Customers of banks. These include individuals who borrow from their banks to finance their security purchases and holdings. Security loans of this kind are classified as loans to "others." Also, brokers borrow from their banks to finance their "own position," that is, securities purchased and held on their own account rather than to finance their customers.

In their published statements, banks report separately security loans to (1) brokers and dealers; and (2) others. The dividing line between brokers and dealers is blurred by the fact that brokers borrow to finance both the purchases of their customers and their own trading. In trading for themselves they resemble dealers. Furthermore, a given firm may act as a broker for customers, dealing for them on the stock exchange and in the over-the-counter market, while at the same time it acts as a dealer in securities.

Loans to brokers. Brokers, as we noted above, borrow for two separate reasons. First, as brokers they not only *buy* and *sell* securities for customers but also undertake to finance the carrying of securities for customers that wish to trade on a margin. In margin trading the customer pays part of the purchase price of securities out of his own funds and borrows the remainder from his broker. The margin is represented by the excess value of securities held in the customer's account over the customer's indebtedness to the broker. Thus, if securities in the account are worth $10,000 and the customer owes $5,000, his margin is 50 per cent. The minimum amount of such margins that customers are required to maintain with their brokers is set by the Board of Governors of the Federal Reserve System in order that it may exercise control over the amount of securities that may be purchased and carried on borrowed money. Margin requirements apply to money borrowed from brokers to finance the purchase of "listed" securities. Regulation T, issued by the Board, applies to credit extended by the broker to his customers.

To finance their customers' trading, brokers must borrow from banks. Such bank loans to brokers are not subject to regulation as to margin requirements, since the advances to customers are already under the restraints of Regulation T. However, when banks lend funds to brokers to finance the holding of securities for the brokers' own accounts the case is different. Such loans, when made on "listed stocks," are subject to Regulation U of the Board of Governors, which fixes maximum loan values for stocks offered as collateral for loans by banks to finance the carrying of listed stocks.[6]

Bank loans to brokers may be made on time or on call. Call loans may technically be called for repayment by the bank, but call loans to brokers tend now to be looked upon as a demand loan to customers with an indefinite maturity that enables the borrowers to repay at their own convenience.

Before the stock market collapse in 1929, security loans, mainly made to finance security trading on the New York Stock Exchange, reached enormous proportions. Brokers' loans rose to about $9 billion. For many years before the collapse of 1929, the New York call loan market provided the outlet for excess funds for both commercial banks and other lenders. Call loans, made to customers, through money brokers, and at the money desk at the Exchange, were used by banks to adjust their reserve position and keep fully loaned up. Whenever lending banks needed funds, they called in their loans without hesitation, especially their loans to noncustomers. The consequent ebb and flow of excess funds into and out of the stock market tended to create sharp changes in interest rates and serious disturbances to security prices and trading. But the easy money conditions during the depression and the years after, coupled with regulations on security trading, lowered call money rates to the point where brokers and dealers have been able to satisfy their loan requirements at favorable rates at their own banks. Consequently the call loan desk on the Exchange was abolished because of disuse.

Loans to dealers in securities. Security dealers stand ready to buy and sell securities at their quoted prices. Thus they make a market for the securities in which they deal. Their profit is derived mainly from the difference between their buying and selling price, and, because of vigorous competition, the spread is generally narrow. The survival and earnings of dealers, therefore, depend upon adroit trading, based on skill in making market judgments, and upon

---

[6] Listed stocks are those listed on national security exchanges registered with the Securities and Exchange Commission. Cf. Miller, S. L., "Financing Security Brokers and Dealers," *Money Market Essays,* Federal Reserve Bank of New York, March 1952.

a large volume of business. Dealers, therefore, rely heavily upon borrowed money, which they obtain primarily from the commercial banks of New York and Chicago.

Some dealers are more specialized than others and may concentrate their operations in certain types of corporate obligations, state and local government securities, or securities of the United States Government. Because of the magnitude of the marketable Federal debt (over $160 billion in 1956) dealers in U.S. Government securities have acquired a key position in the money market. Consequently, to understand the operations of the money market, including the practices of the commercial banks, it is necessary that we give some special attention to these dealers in Government securities.

Dealers in U.S. Government Securities

The market in U.S. Government securities is maintained by the trading activities of a relatively small group of specialized dealers. These dealers, with head offices in New York and Chicago, maintain branches in all other principal cities of the country. The head office and the branches are connected by telephone and teletype services so that each dealer is in continuous communication with all important cities. Moreover, dealers maintain, through private wires, telephone connection with each other.

The bulk of the trading in Government securities of all types is carried on through this network of dealers in the over-the-counter market, that is, not through the auctions of the New York Stock Exchange. Whenever a bank, a corporate treasurer, an insurance company, the managers of pension funds, or individuals wish to purchase or sell Government securities, orders placed with security companies or brokers are passed on and executed through the dealers.

Each dealer stands ready to purchase Government securities offered for sale at prices that he considers appropriate in the light of market conditions at the moment the transaction is made. The deal is made by negotiation between the seller and the dealer and is carried out by telephone communication. Similarly, when brokers or others have received orders to purchase Government securities, the purchase is made from the dealers at prices arrived at by negotiation. Because of the close communication maintained among dealers, the market is very sensitive to changes in money market conditions. Prices of securities are subject to constant change under the impact of sales and purchases.

Financing the dealer in Government securities. In some few instances "dealers" are large commercial banks in New York and Chicago. For them, of course, no special problem of financing arises. However, the nonbank dealers, carrying substantial inventories of securities, must borrow heavily on that inventory. The primary source of nonbank dealer funds is the big commercial banks of New York and Chicago. Here dealers commonly borrow on call. Because the quality of collateral offered is high, such loans can normally be had at very favorable rates. Dealers are also able, at times, to borrow from other sources. Banks in other cities, corporate treasurers, and other large holders of funds temporarily idle sometimes lend to the dealers.

Banks also make advances to dealers for short intervals of time through what are known as "repurchase agreements." In this case a bank purchases the securities at the going market price and the dealer agrees to repurchase them on or before a given date, paying the price received plus an amount equivalent to an interest charge on a loan for the elapsed time. This method of providing funds to dealers has the advantage of enabling a bank to provide funds to one dealer in amounts greater than would be permitted on a straight loan, since legal limits on the size of loans to one borrower do not apply.

The key position of Government security dealers in the money market. Banks in the important money centers that make call loans to dealers look upon these loans on Government securities as an ideal outlet for excess funds available for very short periods. Consequently, these loans are used to adjust banks' reserve positions in much the same manner that call loans on the stock Exchange were used before 1930. When a bank finds itself short of reserves, it calls the loans to dealers. The dealers, in turn, must either find accommodations from other lenders or dispose of some of their security holdings. Thus they are in a very exposed position in respect to changes in money market conditions. Whenever the reserve position of the banks in New York or Chicago becomes tight, loans to dealers are called. Furthermore, banks also tend to dispose of some of their highly liquid short-term securities, mainly Treasury bills. Such action depresses the market price of such securities. Thus, part of the burden of the stringency of the commercial banks is passed on to the dealers.

To protect themselves in the face of money market stringency, the dealers may do a number of things. First, they may attempt to borrow short-term funds from nonbank lenders. Second, through their branches in other parts of the country, they may seek to sell Treasury bills to banks and other investors in areas where funds are plentiful. If the reserve shortage is localized in New York City the discovery of buyers for bills in Houston, San Francisco, or Omaha will ease the situation. For example, through the telephone communication network maintained by the dealers, Treasury bills may be sold to a bank in San Francisco. The proceeds of the sale can then be transferred to New York City for the benefit of the seller by way of the Federal Reserve leased wire system. In this way a San Francisco surplus of bank reserves (called Federal funds because they consist of deposits in the Federal Reserve Banks) is made available to ease the situation in New York City. Incidentally, the delivery of Treasury bills to the buyers in San Francisco can be arranged through the Federal Reserve System. Dealers may surrender to the Federal Reserve Bank of New York the Treasury bills sold to San Francisco buyers. Thereupon the Federal Reserve Bank of San Francisco will deliver duplicate Treasury bills to the buyers in San Francisco.

At times Government security dealers have access to another source of funds at the Federal Reserve Bank of New York. Whenever the tightness in the money market threatens to reach an undesirable level, the Federal Reserve Bank of New York may notify the dealers that they may sell Treasury bills to the Bank at the current market price, under an agreement to repurchase within a fifteen-day period. A dealer taking advantage of this privilege is expected to repurchase the bills within the stated time at the same price plus an amount equal to interest for the period. The interest charge is generally equal to the Federal Reserve discount rate. This privilege of turning to the Federal Reserve Bank of New York for assistance is not a continuous one but is made available at the option of the Bank.

Legal Regulation Affecting Bank Loans

Because competition among banks and the self-interest among bankers cannot be relied on to insure safe lending policies, the legislatures of the various states, as well as Congress, have provided regulations governing bank loans. There are several reasons for this. First, excessive competition once caused the banker to pay high rates of interest on deposits, which in turn stimulated the making of dangerous but high-interest-bearing loans and investments. Second, our unit banking system has brought more personal contact between customer and banker than is likely to exist in the larger and more impersonally managed branch banks of other countries. Hence there is greater danger of granting personal favors to friends, whether warranted or not. Third, our American banking traditions and methods have developed along the lines of American business. The banker is a businessman, and as such normally sees no reason why the funds of the bank should not be at his disposal. In other words, a well-defined professional attitude among American bankers has sometimes been lacking.

For various reasons, then, it has seemed necessary to attempt control from the outside. The effort is frequently of little effect because of evasion, and because to some extent control has been misguided. It is next to impossible to supervise the banks in such a manner as to prevent violations of the law, as is evidenced by the not infrequent discovery of violations that have been going on for years before bank failures. Moreover, when violations are discovered, the examiners and supervisory authorities sometimes fail to take adequate and prompt measures to terminate them. Yet, it must be said that the great majority of bankers attempt to obey the law and that the legal regulations seriously influence the make-up of bank portfolios.

Limits on loans to one borrower. Perhaps the most common form of regulation of bank loans deals with the size of the loans that a bank is permitted to make to any one borrower. The purpose of such regulation is in part, at least, to insure some degree of diversification among the bank's loans. When enforced, it tends to give diversification as to individual borrowers, although it quite obviously fails to insure diversification among industries or territories, which is of almost equal importance. Further, it is sometimes said that the rules limiting the size of individual loans are designed to insure that the lending capacity of banks is not monopolized by a few borrowers but is made available for the community at large. Whatever the purpose behind such regulations, they are universally found in American banking laws.

The limitations placed upon the loans of banks to one individual or firm may best be illustrated by the National Banking Act. A national bank may lend to any one borrower (including, in the case of partnerships, the obligations of any partner, and, in the case of corporations, all subsidiaries in which the corporation has a controlling interest) not more than 10 per cent of its capital and surplus. To this limitation there have been grafted exceptions which ease the burden of the 10 per cent rule. Excepted altogether are all forms of commercial paper (notes, acceptances, and the like) endorsed by the borrower and offered for discount at the bank. In addition, the rule is modified to permit added amounts to be lent to one borrower when he pledges certain types of collateral. For example, when a borrower pledges U.S. Government obligations as collateral, the bank may lend as much as 25 per cent of its capital and surplus. These exceptions have been added to the basic 10 per cent rule to improve the relative competitive position of national banks. State banks quite generally have somewhat more lenient limits.

The 10 per cent rule makes difficult the position of the small bank, which may be unable to hold the business of the large firms of its community. The existence of the rule, however, encourages banks to expand their capital accounts and, at times, has been a factor in inducing the merger of banks.

Loans on a bank's own stock. National banks, like state banks, are prohibited from making loans on the security of their own shares of stock. Were this not the rule, there would be the constant danger that stockholders might borrow from the bank the equity they are supposed to have contributed for the protection of the depositors. Such a result would be similar to the effects of the common practice in the early days of banking when stockholders paid for their stock subscription with their promissory notes.

Loans to executive officers. Because officers of banks appeared to have borrowed excessively from their banks during and after the stock market boom of 1928-1929, the Federal Reserve Act was amended to fix a $2,500 maximum limit on the amount that an executive officer of a member bank can borrow from his own bank. Furthermore, whenever an officer of a member bank borrows from any other bank he must make a written report of such borrowings to his board of directors.

Classification of loans by examiners. Bank examiners must check on the observance of the law and regulations set up by the supervisory authorities. They also have the duty of checking on the quality of the loan portfolio. They tend to follow a uniform practice of classifying loans into four groups: [7]

1. Loans whose repayment appears *assured,* regardless of original maturity, and hence free from criticism.

2. *Substandard* loans, involving a substantial and unreasonable risk, and requiring special attention by the bank.

3. Loans whose collection is considered *doubtful.* Fifty per cent of such loans must be written off in calculating the bank's net sound capital.

4. Uncollectible loans that must be entirely written off as a *loss.*

The legal regulations governing the loan activities of banks are supplemented by numerous administrative regulations. The responsibility for enforcement rests upon the bank examiners and the supervisory authorities under whose direction they work. Regulations sometimes appear excessively severe and at other times too lax. And, even though compliance by bankers is sometimes less than perfect, one cannot doubt that banking practices and bank development have been profoundly influenced by the controls imposed upon them.

Questions for Study

1. How important to farmers are the agricultural loans made by banks? To what extent do these loans appear to provide middle-term capital for farmers?

---

[7] Cf. *Federal Reserve Bulletin,* July 1949, pp. 776–777. This classification has the merit of substituting "substandard" for "slow," which appeared in earlier examiners' reports and was subject to criticism. Examiners tended to classify as "slow" not only loans on which borrowers had been forced to ask for renewal but also any business loan with an original maturity of over ninety days.

2. Why have commercial banks entered the field of consumer financing?

3. If a bank lends $100 to a consumer who is to repay $106 in 12 monthly installments, about what is the actual interest cost as a per cent of the average amount of money the borrower has during the year?

4. To what extent do you think bank consumer credit acts as a substitute for commercial borrowing by business?

5. Before 1936 most real estate mortgage loans of banks were for from one to five years with no provision for amortization in monthly installments. What do you think is gained by present day longer-term amortized housing loans in the way of (a) protection for the borrower and (b) protection for the bank?

6. What is meant by "mortgage warehousing"?

7. Who are the important borrowers on security loans?

8. What are margin requirements? To which security loans by banks do they apply?

9. Open market call loans to brokers are no longer made by banks. Consequently brokers loans are no longer relied upon to adjust big city bank reserve positions. What loans today have partially taken over that function?

10. How does a nonbank dealer in U.S. securities finance his security inventory? Why are such dealers so exposed to pressure when the money market gets tight or lacks reserves?

11. What are repurchase agreements? Why are they made?

12. What reasons can you give for the heavy regulations put upon American banks?

13. What is the 10 per cent rule applying to bank loans?

Bank Investments

Bank investments comprise over one-half of the total earning assets of commercial banks. This means that investments, mainly government obligations, provide the asset base for over half of our checking account money supply. It also indicates the substantial dependence of banks upon the revenue derived from their security holdings. A picture of the general nature of commercial bank investments appears in Table 15.

TABLE 15

Investments of Insured Commercial Banks
June 30, 1955*

1. Obligations of the U.S. Government:

   Treasury bills (3 mo.) ....$ 3,001,321,000
   Treasury certificates of
       indebtedness (9 to 12 mo.)   1,667,331,000
   Treasury notes (3 to 5 yrs.) 16,504,965,000
   U.S. bonds maturing in 5
       years or less 10,634,538,000
   Other U.S. bonds 30,645,738,000

   Total U.S. Government obligations $62,453,893,000

2. Other securities:

   Obligations of States and
       subdivisions thereof $12,572,949,000
   Other bonds   3,501,906,000
   Federal Reserve Bank stock   295,075,000
   Other corporate stock   117,609,000

   Total other securities $16,497,539,000

3. Total securities $78,951,432,000

* From *Report No. 43, Assets, Liabilities, and Capital Accounts, Commercial and Mutual Savings Banks,* Federal Deposit Insurance Corporation, Washington, D. C., June 30, 1955.

Why banks invest in securities. Banks invest in securities for two reasons. First they depend upon certain investments for liquidity. Second, they are seeking to enhance their earnings. After liquidity needs are satisfied local borrowers have a first claim on the banker's credit. In the rather remote past, bank investments, along with open market loans, were often mainly an outlet for funds not absorbed by the bank's own customers. Even so, bankers generally maintained a suitable inventory of securities considered appropriate for the investment of funds brought to the bank by savings and other time depositors.

The great depression of the 1930's brought a dramatic shift in the place of bank investments. No longer were they merely the outlet for excess loan funds. Instead they became a major segment of the banks' portfolios of earning assets. Moreover, with the depression came a drop in the supply of open market paper and call loans previously relied on as a source of liquidity, and banks turned to short-term Government securities for their main form of liquid secondary reserves.

The rise of bank investments in the 1930's was both encouraged and made possible by the appearance of government deficit financing. During the depression years, and later on a greatly augmented scale during the war, the government actively sought bank credit accommodation. It was the depression and wartime government demand for funds that wrought the overwhelming shift in the importance of bank investments.

The stabilizing influence of bank investments upon the volume of money. The rising importance of United States securities among the earning assets of commercial banks has had a stabilizing influence upon the supply of bank-created money. This arises from the fact that in times of depression banks replace shrinking loans with such securities, and dispose of these securities to obtain funds for expanding loans in times of prosperity. Consequently, the perverse changes in bank-created money that tend to accompany business fluctuations are to a considerable degree avoided. This does not mean, of course, that money arising out of the purchase of securities will be pushed into the income stream so as to replace entirely the money withdrawn by loan reductions. Money in the hands of the sellers of securities bought by the banks must await new investment before it can bolster the income flow. But it does serve the very useful purpose of helping to satisfy the public's growing demand for liquidity, which accompanies depression.

Legal regulation of bank investments. The law governing the investments of national banks and the regulations of the Comptroller of the Currency based thereon apply also to the investments of state bank members of the Federal Reserve System. State banks also must obey any regulations of their own state banking authorities whenever they are more restrictive than the rules governing national banks. A brief summary of the investment regulations applicable to Federal Reserve member banks will provide a representative example of all such regulations.

In general, member banks are not allowed to:

1. Underwrite new corporate security issues.
2. Purchase corporate stocks.
3. Invest in the obligations of any one issuer an amount greater than 10 per cent of the bank's capital and surplus.

To these general prohibitions there are some exceptions:

1. The 10 per cent limit does not apply to bank purchases of obligations of:
   a) The U.S. Government.
   b) Any State or political subdivision thereof.
   c) Federal Land Banks, Federal Home Loan Banks, and the Federal Housing Administration when guaranteed by the United States Government.
2. Banks may invest in corporate stock of:
   a) The Federal Reserve Banks, as required for membership.
   b) Corporations conducting a safe-deposit business. (Not more than 15 per cent of the bank's capital and surplus.)
   c) An affiliate solely engaged in holding the banking premises. Without permission from the Comptroller of the Currency or the Board of Governors this cannot amount to more than 100 per cent of the bank's capital.
   d) Certain affiliates, such as foreign banking corporations and national agricultural credit associations, in which national banks are allowed to invest up to 10 per cent of their capital and surplus.

On the positive side, member banks are permitted to purchase and hold on their own account obligations classified as "investment securities." The Comptroller of the Currency has issued regulations defining investment securities. In general they must be marketable with reasonable promptness at a fair price, and must not be "distinctly or predominantly speculative" or in default.[1]

Valuation of investment portfolios. Before and during the early stages of the depression of the 1930's, examiners customarily required banks to follow the time-honored accounting rule for inventory valuation, "cost or market, whichever is the lower." The sharp decline in market value of all securities, both good and bad, during the liquidity crisis of 1930-1933 threatened the solvency of banks holding sound securities, because of the necessity of writing them off to market value. The recognition of this problem led to the making of a new rule. As it now stands the rule provides that examiners shall classify all securities owned by banks into four groups:

Group I consists of securities in which "the investment characteristics are not distinctly or predominantly speculative." This group includes rated securities falling into the four highest rating grades (for example, Aaa, Aa, A, Baa, according to one method) and unrated securities of equivalent value.

Group II consists of securities in which the "investment characteristics are distinctly or predominantly speculative." This class includes securities, not in default, rated below the four highest grades or their equivalent in unrated securities.

Group III consists of securities (bonds) in default.

Group IV consists of corporate stocks.

Securities in Group I are to be evaluated at cost, with neither appreciation nor depreciation shown on the examiner's reports. Moreover, appreciation and depreciation of such securities will be disregarded in computing a bank's net sound capital. Thus, so long as a bank's securities remain within the classification of investment securities, no question of inventory losses need arise unless an actual loss is realized through sale.

Securities in Group II are valued at their market price, and 50 per cent of any net depreciation so calculated must be deducted in computing the bank's net sound capital.

---

[1] The basic regulation covering this appears in the *Federal Reserve Bulletin,* July 1938. Since that time the Comptroller has specifically mentioned the obligations of the International Bank as eligible for purchase as investment securities, and Congress has similarly specified the obligations of the Central Bank for Cooperatives. The statement "not distinctly or predominantly speculative" permits banks to purchase securities that fall within the first four upper classifications of most security rating agencies.

Net depreciation in securities classified in Groups III and IV must promptly be written off as losses. Such securities must be carried at market value.

Premiums paid when securities are purchased must be amortized so as to be written off at maturity.

Until losses have been written off and adequate reserves established, profits from the sale of securities may not be used for any other purpose.

The latest regulations governing the evaluation of securities relieves the banks of the danger of loss due to a fall in capital value of high-grade bonds so long as they are not actually liquidated in the market. To the extent that the long-term investments are protected by an adequate margin of short-maturing securities not subject to capital loss with changes in interest rates, the banks are now in no danger of suffering any serious loss from the purchase of long-term securities. This point is especially important now when securities (largely governments) comprise such a large fraction of bank earning assets. The distribution of maturities of securities held by the banks, therefore, takes on considerable significance.

Risks of bank investments. Like any extension of credit, a bank's investment portfolio presents certain risks. These risks are of two sorts. First, there is the credit risk arising from the default, threatened or actual, on the part of the issuer of the security. The market's estimate of this risk is reflected in the market price and, as we observed earlier, banks are required to write off only one-half of the loss in market value of any speculative obligations held, so long as default has not actually occurred. The second risk related to the investment portfolio results from the effect of changes in the market rate of interest upon the price of high-grade bonds. An increase in the market rate of interest reflects the insistence of lenders on a higher annual yield. When buying old, outstanding securities bearing a fixed rate of return, investors can realize this higher yield only by paying a lower price for the security itself. When investors take the contrary view and are willing, if necessary, to take a lower yield, they bid the price of securities up.

The changes in the price of securities that accompany changes in the market rate of interest may readily be observed in the data appearing in Table 16.

TABLE 16

Changes in Prices of Long-term, High-grade Bonds, with Accompanying Yields*

	U.S. Government Bonds (15 years or more)		Municipal High-grade Bonds	
	Price	Yield	Price	Yield
1948 (Average) ...	100.84	2.44%	125.3	2.40%
1950 (January) ...	104.16	2.20	131.4	2.08
1953 (June)	91.56	3.09	115.2	2.99
1954 (April)	100.36	2.47	123.9	2.47
1956 (March)	94.88	2.90	120.3	—

* From data appearing in the *Federal Reserve Bulletin*.

Banks need take no "paper loss" from the decline in market price of investment securities that they hold. All they need do to avoid loss, therefore, is to continue to hold them until maturity, when they will presumably be paid at par. Only if they sell while the market price is low will they suffer any actual loss from a rise in interest rates. Consequently, to avoid the necessity of selling securities in a falling market, banks need only carry a sufficient cushion of short-maturing paper that may readily be liquidated without noticeable loss. Banks now fortify themselves against cash drains by carrying U.S. Treasury bills (3 mo.) and U.S. Treasury certificates of indebtedness (9-12 mo.). Also, Treasury notes (3–5 yr.), as they approach maturity, can be liquidated without loss. The extent of the banks' protection against the possible necessity of selling long-term bonds at a loss in a falling market is shown in the following figures:

Government Securities Held by Commercial Banks January 31, 1956.*

Maturing within 1 year .... $ 6.7 billion
Maturing within 1 to 5 years .... 21.9 billion

* *Federal Reserve Bulletin*, April 1956, p. 373.

Altogether, of the Government securities held by banks, amounting to over $52 billion, about 13 per cent had a maturity of less than one year.

Bank Earnings from Loans and Investments

Table 17 shows the rate of earnings on loans and on investments and the contribution of each to the total earnings of insured commercial banks.

TABLE 17

Earnings of Insured Commercial Banks on Loans and Investments*

	Rate of Earnings		Percentage of Total Earnings Received	
	Loans	Investments	Loans	Investments
1943.........	3.85%	1.52%	36.0	43.9
1944.........	3.44	1.49	31.5	49.2
1945.........	3.09	1.46	29.2	52.3
1946.........	3.43	1.56	33.2	48.7
1947.........	3.79	1.60	41.3	40.6
1948.........	4.04	1.64	47.0	35.1
1949.........	4.22	1.68	48.9	33.7
1950.........	4.34	1.66	51.0	31.5
1951.........	4.45	1.71	55.	28.0
1952.........	4.64	1.84	56.4	27.9
1953.........	4.84	2.01	57.5	27.4
1954.........	4.79	2.01	56.5	27.6
1955.........	4.88	2.10	57.9	26.4

* *Annual Report of the Federal Deposit Insurance Corporation,* 1952, p. 116, and 1953, p. 108, and *Preliminary Release,* May 14, 1956.

Three things stand out clearly in Table 17. First is the downtrend of the rate of earnings on both loans and investments during the war and the gradual rise thereafter. This reflects the cheap money policy of the war period and a modest retreat from it beginning in 1948. Second, investments consistently yield a lower rate than loans. This reflects the overwhelming proportion of Government securities, a large part of which were of short maturity. Third, during the war and the first year thereafter, security investments in spite of their lower yield greatly outstripped loans as a source of bank earnings. Since 1947 the growth of bank loans, with their superior earning rates, and the reduction of U.S. security holdings has pushed total earnings from loans far above those from investments.

The figures in Table 17 are, of course, averages for all insured banks. The behavior of individual banks generally differs substantially. Small banks generally obtain a larger part of their earnings from loans than do the larger banks. This is due both to the more modest security investment of small banks and to the higher rate of interest charged on loans in comparison with large banks.[2]

Questions for Study

1. In view of the important place of government securities among bank earning assets, if the Treasury were to embark upon a program of retiring the bank-held debt, what would be the consequences upon:

  a) The reserve position of the banks?

  b) The supply of money?

  c) The quality of bank assets and bank solvency?

2. Can you account for the marked increase in the relative importance of Government securities during the 1930's? The 1940's?

3. The rules governing Federal Reserve member bank investments are those established by the Comptroller of the Currency for national banks.

  a) What are the rights of member banks in respect to the kinds of securities that they may purchase and hold?

  b) To what limited extent may they purchase stocks?

  c) If a bank's security holdings fall in market price, what will be the effect upon the "net sound capital" as calculated under the examiners' regulations?

4. What two risks confront a banker in respect to his investment portfolio?

5. What are the four groups into which security investments of banks are classified? What method of valuation applies to each?

6. Why must bankers carry a substantial volume of short-term securities these days? Would this have been so necessary in earlier years, when security holdings were less important?

7. In general, do banks obtain a higher rate of return on loans or on investments? How do you account for the difference?

---

[2] For example, in 1954, interest earned on loans by banks with deposits of $1,000,000 or less was 6.20 per cent. Big banks with deposits of over $500,000,000 earned but 4.03 per cent. *Annual Report of the Federal Deposit Insurance Corporation,* 1954, p. 149.

14

The Bank's Portfolio

Requirements of a bank's portfolio. We have considered the various forms that a bank's earning assets may take. These earning assets, as they actually exist in any given bank, make up its portfolio. The portfolio must be arranged with three distinct considerations in mind: (1) liquidity; (2) solvency; and (3) earnings. Without liquidity, the bank cannot operate and meet depositors' demands. Without solvency, it must ultimately fail, with subsequent losses realized by the stockholders and probably by the depositors. Finally, without earnings, the banking operations cannot be carried on by private enterprise.

It is apparent that these three essential requirements placed upon the bank portfolio are not altogether in harmony. True, liquidity implies short-run solvency, to say the least, but it varies inversely with the earning power of assets. Likewise, it is possible to achieve ultimate solvency without liquidity, as is illustrated by the well-secured real estate loan. Finally, earnings are sometimes sought at the expense of both liquidity and solvency. It is evident that earnings, essential as they are, must at all times be made secondary to the requisite liquidity and the solvency of the bank. This must not be construed to mean that bankers should never make a loan or an investment that is less sound than the maximum humanly possible. Such an attitude would be too rigorous for business, which cannot provide absolute security for its borrowing. But any margin of speculation in the portfolio should be amply covered by the stockholders' equity.

Obviously, liquidity is the first consideration in organizing the portfolio. Without adequate provision for this, the bank faces certain extinction when the pressure of deposit withdrawals is met. But to maintain excessive liquidity is to sacrifice earnings. It is clear that a bank should carry liquid assets in amount sufficient to meet: (1) the seasonal demands of depositors, which can be forecast in the light of experience; and (2) the cyclical variations in deposits, taking measures to increase the liquidity of the portfolio during times of boom or excessive prosperity. A bank's cash or primary reserve and its "secondary" reserve are relied upon to provide liquidity. After the necessary liquidity has been provided, the remainder of the bank's portfolio may be arranged with an eye to solvency and earnings only. Naturally, the particular kind of assets used will depend to a large extent upon the type available.

Secondary Reserves

Relation of primary to secondary reserves. The primary reserves of a bank consist of cash on hand and demand deposits in other banks, which are equivalent to cash. The relation of these reserves to the bank's deposits has already been considered in Chapter 10.

The primary reserves of banks, whether required by law or carried by the banker by his own choice, must meet the immediate net withdrawals of deposits as they develop from day to day. Because such cash reserves are normally meant to meet only immediate needs, it is necessary that banks be prepared to convert some of their earning assets into cash whenever the cash reserves fall below the level dictated by sound judgment or the law. Seasonal and irregular changes in depositors' and local borrowers' requirements may put heavy pressure on a bank's cash position. To meet this, the bank must carry excessive reserves in the slack season (obviously an uneconomical procedure), be prepared to borrow, or carry highly liquid earning assets that can be readily disposed of *without loss*. Such assets are called *secondary reserves*.

Banks commonly depend upon all three of the above mentioned sources to enable them to meet their liquidity needs. County banks depend to a considerable degree upon cash reserves in excess of legal requirements to meet part of their irregular cash drains. Part of such reserves may be carried as working reserves on deposit with city correspondents. By using these, the country banks shift the burden of obtaining cash to the city banks. The city banks, especially those in the central money markets, tend to keep themselves "loaned up" to the maximum limit. They depend upon borrowing from other city banks or at the Federal Reserve Banks whenever a reserve shortage appears likely to be temporary. They dispose of part of their secondary reserve when the shortage of cash promises to be for a longer period.

Why, one may ask, are secondary reserves needed? Member banks may borrow at the Federal Reserve Banks and nonmember banks may borrow from their city correspondent banks. Banks can and do borrow to tide themselves over periods of cash shortage rather than dispose of their secondary reserve assets. There are a number of good reasons, however, why banks should maintain a substantial quantity of secondary reserves even though they have recourse to borrowing. In the first place, banks prefer not to become exposed to the possibility of having to borrow continuously in order to care for the needs of their local customers. Although deposits are a form of debt, they are quite different in the minds of both the banker and the examiners from "bills payable," which must be paid or renewed when due. Renewals of loans from the Federal Reserve Banks and from city correspondents may prove difficult. Perhaps an equally important reason for not wanting to depend upon borrowing is the fact that there is a common rule that, except for borrowings at the Federal Reserve Bank, banks cannot become indebted by an amount in excess of their own capital stock. Banks, therefore, have a genuine need for a cushion of liquid assets of which they may dispose whenever a shortage of cash proves to be more than temporary.

A second reason for the need for secondary reserves is found in the Federal Reserve "taboo on continuous borrowing." This taboo reduces the attractiveness of member bank borrowing for more than temporary purposes. It is fortified by the knowledge that the Federal Reserve Banks, while ready to assist in emergency or seasonal needs, are entirely capable of refusing to renew advances to member banks when they mature.

Size of secondary reserves. The relative size of a bank's secondary reserve depends upon a variety of circumstances. Primarily, the nature of the bank's business, the diversification of deposits, and the seasonal variations in cash requirements all determine the volume of highly liquid assets required by any individual bank. The correct amount can be discovered only through experience. In addition to the minimum requirements indicated by experience, the conservative banker must necessarily allow for unusual, unpredictable needs. Local or general depression in business often tends to set up a heavy adverse trade balance for a given area, which then experiences heavy drains of cash out of the banks located therein. A loss of confidence in banks, growing out of business and bank failures, may also create trouble. Since such needs are more likely to arise at the culmination of periods of prosperity or boom, it would seem desirable that particular care be taken to maintain a high proportion of liquid assets at such times.

One sound suggestion for estimating the needed volume of secondary reserves is based upon the expected behavior of both the bank's deposits and its local loans. Thus, when experience indicates that deposits will shrink at the same time that the demands of local borrowers increase, the shrinkage of deposits plus the increase in local loans gives the probable cash loss during the period. In the unlikely event that local loans decline while deposits fall off, the repayment of loans provides funds to meet the deposit shrinkage. In estimating probable needs for secondary reserves, local loans should be included for the reason that local borrowers must be accommodated if the bank is to maintain its position in the community, and loans, when spent by borrowers, tend to induce a loss of cash to other banks.[1] In computing the cash drain to be expected from deposit withdrawals, an offset allowance can be made for the accompanying decline in required reserves, which releases cash.

Composition of secondary reserves. Before the present-day abundance of short-term Treasury obligations, banks were dependent mainly upon three types of assets for secondary reserves. These were: (1) open market commercial paper, available in varying sizes and maturities to fit the needs of individual banks; (2) bankers' acceptances, of high quality and readily convertible into cash at

---

[1] Hartzel, Elmer, "The Measurement of a Bank's Secondary and Investment Reserves," *Journal of Business*, October 1934, p. 344.

maturity or by sale to the Federal Reserve Banks before maturity; and (3) call loans on the New York Stock Exchange. Today none of these three is an important source of bank liquidity. Open market paper and bankers' acceptances are entirely inadequate in quantity to be of any significant benefit. Stock Exchange security loans are no longer used by banks to provide outlets for surplus funds.[2] Consequently, bank secondary reserves today are predominantly composed of short-maturing Treasury obligations. These Treasury obligations can be converted into cash by being allowed to "run off" at maturity, that is, paid by the Treasury, or by sale to other banks and investors. In addition they may be used as collateral for loans from the Federal Reserve Bank. Because of the large holdings of short-term Treasury obligations, the American banks since the war have been in a more liquid position than at any time in their history. Consequently they are much better fortified than ever before to withstand the shock of a severe depression. Without such assets available for secondary reserves, the liquidity problems of the banks would indeed be serious.[3]

Arrangement and Composition of Earning Assets

The first requirement for a proper arrangement of bank earning assets is provision for a suitable amount of short-term, highly liquid assets that qualify for secondary reserve use. After this, within the limits set by legal regulations and by availability, the banker may follow his own conscience in the arrangement and proportions of his earning assets. His preferences will normally lean toward his customers' loans. Such loans not only provide strong and valuable bonds with the business community but also, on the average, tend to yield a higher level of earnings than do investments. Yet the banker may find that high-grade investments, in the form of long-term U.S. Treasury obligations and tax-exempt obligations of States

---

[2] New York City banks make some use of call loans to dealers in U. S. Government securities as a means of adjusting their reserve position.

[3] The holdings of these short-maturing obligations for secondary reserves provide, for a price, protection against the possibility of losses from forced liquidation of other bank assets. Highly liquid assets normally earn less than do the less liquid assets. Secondary reserves are a kind of insurance against uncertainty and risk of losses from liquidation of other assets. The premium for this insurance is the reduction in earnings from carrying secondary reserves.

and the subdivisions thereof, compare very favorably with loans in the light of the former's low risk and low administrative costs. Also, as we know, during wars or other emergencies requiring sizable borrowings by the Treasury, pressures of one sort or another are put upon banks to increase their "preference" for Government issues. The large volume of reserves now available to the banking system inevitably tends to permit and encourage banks to carry investments beyond the point needed for secondary reserve purposes. In consequence, the banks are confronted with the necessity for making marginal decisions between more loans or more long-time investments.

The actual decision between loans and investments cannot be reached by any simple rule. The proportion of each will reflect (1) the urgency of the demand for accommodation (as in the case when a Treasury deficit requires recourse to banks); (2) the current availability of suitable loans and securities appropriate for investment; (3) the profit margin from each; and (4) the individual preferences of the bankers. At the end of World War II the belief was sometimes expressed that bankers were so satisfied with the profitable and effortless process of carrying Government securities that they no longer could be counted on to make loans to finance business when the need again arose. As we know now, this opinion proved unfounded. Bank loan portfolios expanded substantially in response to the postwar demand for loans.

Types of bank loans. Quite naturally the loans of a particular bank reflect the nature of the community it serves. Security loans are highly concentrated in the financial centers; agricultural loans are made mainly by country banks. Among city banks we find a wide array of loans to business and industry. In the smaller cities real estate loans are important, but they are of little importance in the big banks of Chicago and New York.

Irrespective of the particular types of loans made, bankers establish some credit standard by which to judge the loan applications of particular borrowers. Unless a loan appears to be sufficiently sound it will not be made. Although the banker must strike a balance between perfect security and practical business, he will not feel justified in making a loan without reasonable certainty that it is sound and can be paid at maturity. These loan standards, while in themselves stable, result in considerable variation in bankers' willingness to lend. For example, when times are good, business profits high, and the feel of prosperity is in the air, the bankers' opinions of prospective and actual borrowers are favorable and tend to be revised upward. Loans tend to be favored even at the expense of existing investment holdings, if the latter can be disposed of without excessive losses. On the other hand, when times are bad and profit prospects worsen, bank loans become more hazardous and bankers tend to scrutinize more carefully the credit position of loan applicants. Consequently, banks tend to reduce their lending at such times. This is the main source of the frequently expressed belief that bank credit is "perversely elastic," or tends to move in directions contrary to the best interests of economic stability.

Bankers' attitudes toward loan applicants are also affected by the degree of "tightness" or "easiness" in the money market. When reserves are scarce, banks must either borrow or sell some of their liquid assets in order to obtain funds to expand loans. Both borrowing and parting with secondary reserves reduce somewhat the attractiveness of expanding loans and induce bankers to ration out their limited loan funds to the most worthy applicants. The result is some tightening of loan standards as a way of selecting the borrowers who will be accommodated. Conversely, easy money and abundant reserves tend to cause the bankers to lend to borrowers who would be refused loan accommodation if money were tight.

The investment portfolio. In addition to short-term Treasury obligations held for secondary reserve purposes, bankers must determine the size and composition of their investment portfolios. So far as the total amount of investments is concerned, bankers may merely decide to invest the residual funds left after caring for sound loan requirements. Or they may try to maintain some balanced ratio between loan accounts and investments. As for type, some bankers prefer to limit themselves mainly to the purchase of Treaury obligations, with their absence of credit risk. Others, seeking tax-exempt returns, invest also in obligations of States and their political subdivisions. Some seek better investment returns by the purchase of bonds of private corporations. Decisions as to the distribution of investments among the various types must rest with the managers of banks and cannot be determined by any given rule.

Even though a bank may have established what is considered an adequate secondary reserve, it may still find it desirable temporarily to invest newly received funds in short-term Treasury obligations. This enables the bank to obtain modest earnings while awaiting the final or longer term use of the funds involved. Loan portfolios cannot be expanded immediately, for time is required to process applications. Also, should the bank intend to invest funds in long-term securities, some delay may be involved in making decisions and executing orders. Even more important, perhaps, is the possibility that the banker believes that interest rates are about to rise and cause bond prices to fall. In such a case it is desirable to purchase short-term securities while awaiting anticipated changes in interest rates. If bankers' convictions that interest rates are about to rise are strong enough, long-term securities may be sold and replaced with short terms in order to be in a position to repurchase long-term obligations after they have become cheaper.

Just as the accumulation of new reserve funds causes banks to step up their short-term holdings, so a shrinkage of reserves induces a reverse action. The disposal of secondary reserve assets, however, tends to set in motion the gradual and orderly readjustment of the general portfolio so that the desired balance between liquid and general earning assets is restored.

The Self-Liquidating Commercial Paper Theory of Bank Assets

Banking theory of the past heavily favored the view that bank earning assets should be limited to short-term self-liquidating commercial paper or to loans made to finance the short-time current working capital needs of commerce and industry.[4] These loans were held to be more appropriate for banks with demand liabilities, because of both liquidity and security. This theory held that commercial banks should avoid making advances to industry to provide fixed capital, but should leave such loans to other financial agencies without demand obligations (such as savings banks, investment trusts, and the bond market in general).

---

4 For example, see Willis, H. Parker, Chapman, John M., and Robey, Ralph W., *Contemporary Banking,* New York, Harper & Bros., 1933, p. 437.

In spite of this theory, American banks generally have in practice departed from the exclusive holding of self-liquidating commercial paper. One need but examine the growing importance of securities among bank earning assets to discover this fact. Also, loans on real estate and loans to security dealers, investors, and speculators are for the most part used for fixed capital rather than for temporary working capital purposes. Since this is the trend, it is of little use to bewail the departure from the standards of classical bank theory. We are confronted with an actual situation that appears, with some notable exceptions, to work fairly well in practice.

Let us examine self-liquidating commercial paper and observe its similarities to and differences from other forms of bank loans. Self-liquidating commercial paper arises in connection with a loan to a borrower who uses the proceeds to increase his working capital. This new working capital, in the normal course of events, will be transformed into salable goods or services that will return to the borrower the funds with which to pay the loan. If the period of the loan is long enough to enable the borrowed capital to make the cycle—from money, to working capital, to salable goods, and back to money again—the loan may properly be called self-liquidating. If the period of the loan is too short, it is not self-liquidating. It follows from the above definition that a loan whose proceeds are to be used by the borrower to acquire fixed capital goods might be self-liquidating if the loan were to run for a period of time sufficient for the capital goods to earn back the interest and principal of the loan.

The continuous borrower's paper. Some question may arise concerning the self-liquidating character of short-time loans made to firms engaging in continuous operations with very little seasonal variation. If they borrow at banks, they tend to borrow constantly. Should their paper be considered self-liquidating in the face of the fact that their borrowing tends to be continuous? From a strictly logical viewpoint, such paper can hardly be considered self-liquidating for the reason that the borrowing firm is not automatically able to retire the loan at its maturity. To require that the borrower pay the loan at maturity would involve either a reduction in the volume of working capital (obviously not normally desired) or a recourse to borrowing at other banks. Strictly speaking, it is possible for such a borrower to repay the loan if he has an adequate excess of current assets over current liabliities and is willing to reduce to some extent the scale of his operations. One might, therefore, say that this loan is self-liquidating. But it differs from loans made to supply working funds needed to carry the borrower over a seasonal peak, since such loans can be repaid at maturity without embarrassment to the borrower.

Shiftable vs. self-liquidating loans. A self-liquidating loan, as we have seen, is one that will normally be repaid out of the receipts resulting from the use to which the funds are put. A loan that is not self-liquidating, on the other hand, gives rise to no chain of events which will naturally and normally return funds to the borrower within the life of the loan. This fact can best be illustrated by two examples. Suppose, first, that a person borrows a sum from a bank for thirty days to finance a transaction which cannot be completed within six months. The ability of the borrower to repay his loan in thirty days rests solely upon his ability to increase his income by some method unrelated to this transaction or to borrow elsewhere to replace the first loan. Let us take a second case. Suppose a person obtains a thirty-day loan at a bank for the purpose of buying securities. At the end of thirty days, the borrower's ability to repay rests upon: (1) his ability to borrow elsewhere; or (2) his ability to sell his securities to some other party who perhaps borrows elsewhere. Thus it is clear that the liquidity of loans that are not self-liquidating depends entirely upon the success with which the loan can be shifted to some other bank. The same reasoning naturally applies to the outright security holdings of banks. Those with a ready market can be easily sold to other banks or to borrowers at other banks.

To what extent are self-liquidating commercial loans similar to loans that acquire liquidity only through shiftability? In practice, some of the best forms of so-called self-liquidating paper acquire their liquidity through shiftability. This is true of that part of the commercial loans of the country which represents continuous working capital of the borrowers. Liquidity of open market paper is often achieved (1) by the flotation of new issues; and (2) by the utilization of bank credit lines; and the annual "cleanup" demanded of commercial borrowers frequently involves a mere shifting of loans to other banks. To the extent that this is true, what seems to be self-liquidating paper turns out to be merely shiftable. The continuous operation of the borrower under these circumstances does not permit the liquidation of a sufficient amount of the firm's working capital actually to pay off the bank loans. As we already have learned, many business short-term loans are commonly renewed. The "annual liquidation" requirement often made by banks to "line of credit" borrowers is frequently cared for by borrowing elsewhere, either directly from another bank or indirectly through the commercial paper market.

What of the short-time loans to businessmen, which are actually self-liquidating? What is the source of their liquidity? Simply this: The borrower will have something to sell before the loan matures. In the ordinary course of business events, the goods can be sold and the loan repaid out of the proceeds. But what determines whether or not the goods can actually be sold? Assuming that they are staple goods, readily marketable, they can be sold at a reasonable price provided that the normal buyers are able to obtain funds, loans let us say, in the ordinary manner to which they are accustomed. Stating it in another way, the self-liquidating character of a good commercial loan depends upon the continuation of the willingness of other banks to extend loans to the buyers of the goods produced by the original borrower. All of this is, of course, a matter of shiftability again. Fundamentally, then, both types of loans depend for their liquidity upon the continuation of the willingess of the banking system as a whole to maintain a given general level of loans and investments.

One thing should be clearly evident from the above discussion. Regardless of the nature of credit extended by commercial banks, it is entirely impossible to expect the whole banking system to possess any large degree of liquidity. Whether loans are self-liquidating or merely shiftable, in the final analysis the liquidity of any particular bank's assets depends basically upon the continued willingess of the other parts of the banking system to lend or invest freely. To some extent, of course, commercial banks may shift the burden of providing liquidity upon the central bank. But any wholesale attempt on the part of the banking system to liquidate its loans and investments must necessarily fail.

The alleged advantages of self-liquidating commercial

paper. Three general arguments have been advanced in favor of self-liquidating commercial loans as bank assets:

1. They automatically provide banks with liquidity through loan repayment.
2. They are sounder and safer for banks to make than are "capital" loans with remote maturities.
3. They automatically respond to the needs of trade, rising as production expands and declining as production declines. Consequently they provide a kind of neutral base for the creation of bank money, which cannot overexpand. They therefore afford a sound protection against inflation.

In contrast to self-liquidating commercial loans, loans of other types, such as loans on real estate or loans to business to finance longer-term capital needs, are characterized by remote maturities and hence are not liquid; and, along with security loans, they result in the creation of money based on long-term credit that is not accompanied by a corresponding increase in the flow of goods for immediate sale. Even worse, in the eyes of the advocates of self-liquidating commercial loans, are bank investments. Such investments result in "monetizing" long-term debts and therefore are looked upon as especially undesirable. The self-liquidating commercial paper theory purports to provide an automatic means for insuring bank liquidity and soundness, and, in addition, a quantity of bank-created money that is noninflationary and satisfies the needs of trade. If the quality of bank assets is correct, the quantity of bank credit need not cause concern. This theory, as we shall see later, was embodied in the Federal Reserve Act in 1913 and still has no little influence in our central bank credit policy.

Actual banking practice, as we have already seen, has departed widely from the theory just considered. Judging by our bank failure record, our banking practices have not proved entirely satisfactory. It is proper to ask, therefore, to what extent would strict adherence to the self-liquidating commercial paper theory by the banks improve bank liquidity and solvency? To what extent would such practice insure us against inflation and resulting economic collapse?

For liquidity purposes banks carry secondary reserves that may readily be sold (or shifted) to other banks or investors. They do this because they recognize the first and leading fallacy among the claims of the self-liquidating theory advocates. Customers' loans to finance current business are *not* a safe and reliable source of bank liquidity because: First, a bank's need for increased cash is almost certain to coincide with the time when customers' borrowings are high. Obviously the bank cannot reduce its loans to customers in order to improve its liquidity at such a time if it is to perform its normal credit functions in the community. Second, during money market crises, which sometimes accompany depressions, customers' self-liquidating loans become uncollectible and are therefore useless from a liquidity standpoint. In contrast, high-grade, shiftable assets of short maturity provide the individual bank with a certain source of funds to meet its individual needs. It also provides the best assurance possible, however modest that may be, of being able to obtain cash during general emergencies. Even during crises, purchasers for high-grade short-maturing assets often appear. We must conclude, therefore, that the claim of superior liquidity in self-liquidating commercial paper is not true.

Next, what of the question of soundness? There is no denying the fact that short-term loans to business have the advantage of requiring a shorter range forecast of the borrowers' credit position than do longer-term capital loans. Yet banks often suffer losses on what are essentially self-liquidating commercial loans. Longer-term capital loans naturally require careful attention to collateral security. But term loans, carefully made, and real estate mortgage loans, with adequate excess of value over the loan or with FHA or government insurance, need not create a special hazard to bank solvency. Similarly, careful attention to collateral makes security loans relatively safe for banks to make.

Finally, what of the contention that limiting commercial bank assets to self-liquidating commercial loans provides the community with the right quantity of bank-created money? Even here the theory is unreliable. In prosperous times, business borrowers, offering what appears to be self-liquidating paper, seek to expand their inventories and working forces. As full employment is approached, such borrowings increase the money supply faster than output can be expanded, and price inflation results. As prices rise, the legitimate needs for business loans also rise, with a resulting spiral of inflationary consequences.

One must conclude that the claims of the advocates of the self-liquidating commercial paper theory of bank assets are of doubtful validity. Neither bank liquidity nor solvency are dependent upon adherence to it. Protection of the economy from inflationary over-expansion or deflationary contraction requires more than the automatic variations in the money supply arising out of the application of the rules of self-liquidating paper. Rather, it requires a monetary policy based upon quantitative criteria, difficult as that may be to achieve.

Questions for Study

1. Why is adequate liquidity a first requirement in arranging a bank's portfolio? Why does the banker, nevertheless, wish to avoid excessive and unnecessary liquidity?

2. What is meant by a bank's "secondary reserve"?

3. What is the rule recommended by Hartzel for calculating the proper size of a bank's secondary reserves? Why does he take *local* loans into consideration?

4. Why are long-term high-grade bonds inappropriate for use as secondary reserve?

5. Why does paper eligible for rediscount not fit the requirements for secondary reserves?

6. On what, in fact, do banks mainly depend for liquidity today?

7. What is a self-liquidating loan? A shiftable loan? Are other assets shiftable?

8. Are the following self-liquidating, shiftable, or neither?
   a) Three-month loans to business to purchase seasonal inventory.
   b) Call loans to dealers in U. S. securities.
   c) Three-month loans to a business having a satisfactory current ratio but which tends to borrow continuously.
   d) U. S. Treasury bills.
   e) Term loans to business.
   f) A ten-year real estate loan.

9. What differences and what points of similarity exist between the liquidity characteristics of shiftable and self-liquidating bank assets?

10. Why is it said that the banking system *as a whole* cannot achieve a high degree of liquidity?

11. What is the basis for the contention that self-liquidating commercial paper loans are noninflationary? To what extent is it valid?

12. Why do self-liquidating commercial paper loans not provide assurance of protection against the danger of inflationary expansion of bank credit?

IV——

BANKING SYSTEMS

15

The Development of
American Commercial Banks

American commercial banks fall into two main categories: state chartered banks and Federally chartered national banks. Regulations governing both types of banks and the customary practices of bank managements are deeply grounded in banking experience. It will help us understand better the present-day banking system if we take a glance at some of the outstanding banking events and developments of earlier years. In this chapter, therefore, we shall first briefly examine some of the historical background of today's banking system.

Banking Before the Civil War

Early America, like all new and vigorous countries with many resources to exploit, was capital hungry. Savings accumulated all too slowly. Specie was scarce, as were money lenders, so quite naturally there existed a demand for banks, for bank note expansion provided an effective way to get trade capital and natural resources into the hands of enterprisers.

Land banking vs. commercial banking. During the first half of the eighteenth century most of the American colonies established "land banks." These were operated by the colonial governments and issued provincial paper money as loans on various kinds of land and improved real estate. Low land values and excessive paper money issues resulted in substantial depreciation of this currency in terms of specie.[1]

---

[1] Thayer, Theodore, "Land Bank Systems in the American Colonies," *Journal of Economic History*, Spring, 1953.

Even in the days before charters were issued to banking corporations, a division between land banking and commercial banking
appeared among the private banks. As early as 1741 a land bank,
organized in Boston, issued circulating notes against land and mortgages. These notes were payable, without interest, after twenty
years. The bank, highly popular with the general public but vio-
lently opposed by the conservative elements of the community, was
outlawed by act of Parliament the following year.

In 1733 and again in 1740, groups of merchants and traders of
Boston organized private banks to discount short-term commercial
notes and issue private bills of credit. These bills acquired a popularity and value much greater than that of the Colonial bills, for
they were paid off punctually in specie. These private merchant
bankers were the forerunners of the commercial banks of later times.

One of the most sought after and readily available types of property in early America was land. Speculators, eager to buy government land, clamored for banks to provide the money. It was quite
natural that banks were chartered for this purpose and that the
loans made by such banks were tinged with personal favoritism
and politics, and characterized in many cases by a gross absence of
security. In addition to banks organized to lend on land, state
governments sometimes organized banks to finance such internal
improvement ventures as turnpikes, canals, railroads, and bridges.
These various note-issuing banks were especially vulnerable to
collapse and failure, both because of the open-handed and reckless
manner in which many were operated and because of the inherent
instability of land values, which comprised the basic security for
their loans. Moreover, the excessive quantities of cheap money
created by these banks periodically supported speculative booms,
which later collapsed.

In contrast to the banks that issued notes against land were
those that confined their activities to making short-term loans to
commercial houses. The currency issued by the latter type of banks
proved much more sound, and the banks themselves were able, in
the long run, to command public confidence. It was this fact
which helped to establish the rule, accepted among banking theorists if not by the general public, that note-issuing and deposit-
creating banks should avoid loans on land and other fixed proper-

ties and confine their lending to merchants and other businessmen for short-term purposes. In spite of the attractions of sound commercial banking, agricultural interests, with their needs for long-term credit on reasonable terms, have never believed that it adequately meets their requirements. Consequently, we find that rural banks have frequently, and to their sorrow, become deeply involved in long-term agricultural credit based on land.

Problem of incorporation. There was considerable dispute in the fifty years preceding the Civil War as to the propriety of confining banking privileges to incorporated banking firms. In general, banks of deposit were permitted to operate privately, but banks with the right to issue notes were required to incorporate, although private banks frequently issued notes in spite of the efforts of the law and the incorporated banks to prevent them from doing so.

The first incorporated commercial bank appears to have been the Bank of North America, established in Philadelphia by Robert Morris in 1782. It financed the short-term needs of merchants and was soundly operated. By the year 1836, the number of banks organized under state charters had reached about seven hundred. Their note issues made up a large fraction of the total currency of the country.[2]

The importance of note issue. Before the Civil War, bank notes furnished the major part of the nonspecie currency of the country. Outside the cities particularly was this the case. The use of checks drawn against demand deposits is feasible only when individuals using them have confidence in the credit standing and honesty of each other and when facilities are available to accomplish prompt presentment. Naturally, at a time when transportation and communication were but poorly developed, the use of engraved notes of banks payable to the bearer was superior in most cases to the use of checks.

It was not until after the Civil War that deposits became substantially larger than bank notes. This can readily be seen in Chart 6. It is not surprising, therefore, that the banking legislation of the times placed a good deal of emphasis upon regulation of the note-issuing powers.

---

[2] Board of Governors of the Federal Reserve System, *Banking Studies*, 1941, pp. 6, 8.

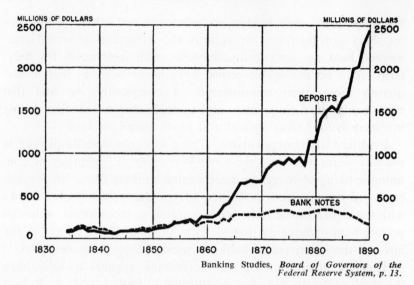

Banking Studies, *Board of Governors of the Federal Reserve System*, p. 13.

Chart 6. Bank Notes and Deposits.

Evils of bank note currency. The characteristic of bank notes that makes them adaptable to the economic circumstances of pioneer societies is also a source of weakness, as the experiences of the early banks indicate. Even in the absence of any effective means for presentment and redemption, bank notes could be issued and kept in circulation, since they bore the appearance of money itself. Redemption was made difficult by the fact that banks were deliberately set up in remote and inaccessible places, far from the centers of trade. The notes were then loaned by agents in other districts. In the West such banks earned the title of "wildcat banks," because of the penchant of their organizers to locate deep in the woods, out of reach of such disagreeable persons as brokers and agents of other banks who were bent upon presentment of bank notes for specie. Not only were bankers prone to set up their banks in inaccessible places, but they also put many obstacles in the way of payment to persistent collectors who actually discovered the den of the "wildcatter." A favorite practice was to pay out small change, a process making for prolonged periods of delay and embarrassing transportation problems. Moreover, public sentiment favored the bankers by condoning the ingenious practices developed to avoid redemption.[3] This situation opened the

---

[3] Dewey, Davis R., *State Banking Before the Civil War*, N. M. C., 1910, p. 74.

way to abuses. A bank that was able to keep a large volume of its notes in circulation could expand its loans by this amount. Indeed, some bankers even exchanged bank notes for property. Under such circumstances it was easy for banks to issue an excessive quantity of notes that could not be redeemed in specie if occasion demanded. The banker, lulled into repose by his success in avoiding redemption, often maintained an entirely inadequate specie reserve. Furthermore, there was a strong temptation to issue bank notes against purely speculative ventures, thus feeding the fires of speculative fevers and causing subsequent collapse and disaster.

The result of all this malpractice was widespread confusion and uncertainty in currency matters. Some bankers, through sound operations and prompt redemption, kept their notes circulating at par with specie. Others all too frequently failed to follow the example of the sound banks and found their currency accepted at varying discounts.

The situation was further disturbed by the fact that counterfeiting of bank notes became popular. The multitude of issues made the practice easy. The West and South, particularly, suffered from the currency troubles. All merchants kept bank note reporters at hand in order to determine the value, if any, of currency presented in the course of trade. Not only were as many as 5,400 counterfeit notes catalogued in one bank note reporter, but also genuine notes were acceptable at varying discounts, depending upon the possibilities and costs of redemption.[4]

The problem of bank note redemption. There is only one certain way to insure that bank note currency will not depreciate in value below that of its specie or standard money equivalent. That way is regularly and continuously to present notes to the issuing bank for redemption. This has the effect of restraining the note issue of any particular bank to the point at which its receipts of specie and notes of other banks will in general be equal to the volume of its own notes that are received by other banks and presented

---

[4] White, Horace, *Money and Banking,* Boston, Ginn & Co., 1896, pp. 405-406. A conductor on an early Indiana railroad, in 1857, reported to the company officers that "on account of meeting with so much broken and uncurrent money these days I am often obliged to take a due bill . . . or put the passenger off the train or carry him for nothing." Hargrave, Frank F., *A Pioneer Indiana Railroad* (published privately), 1932.

for redemption. Only in this way can there be assurance against an excessive quantity of notes and careless loan policies. Three outstanding examples arose before the Civil War wherein redemption of note issues was imposed upon the banks. The first and second of these were the result of the actions of the First and the Second Banks of the United States. The third was the result of the creation of a bank note redemption system for the New England banks by the Suffolk Bank of Boston in 1825.[5] The First and Second Banks of the United States were of such significance as to deserve a brief consideration here.

The First Bank of the United States. Even a brief discussion of early banking history of the United States cannot omit reference to the two banks of this period which were chartered by the Federal Government. The First Bank of the United States was established in 1791, with its main office in Philadelphia and branches in New York, Boston, Baltimore, Washington, Norfolk, Charleston, Savannah, and New Orleans. It issued a limited volume of bank notes, acted as fiscal agent for the government, and served to restrain excessive note issue of state banks, which were becoming numerous, by forcing them to redeem their notes in specie. This it could do by rejecting notes which were not convertible and by making such notes nonacceptable by the Treasury, for which the Bank was fiscal agent. Unfortunately, upon the expiration of its charter in 1811, the friends of the Bank were unable to overcome the political opposition of those who feared the growth of money monopoly and the extension of the power of the central government. Much was made of the fact that British capitalists owned over two-thirds of its capital. This argument was particularly telling in view of the strained diplomatic relations then existing with England. The charter was not renewed, and the only uniform, sound bank note currency capable of wide circulation in the country at that time was lost, along with a powerful and effective aid to government financial operations. The country was left to face the financing of the War of 1812 with only the unreliable state-chartered banks to support it.

The number of state banks increased from 88 to 208 in the four

---

[5] For a discussion of the Suffolk Bank, see Root, L. Carroll, *Sound Currency,* June 1, 1895, pp. 277-279.

years from 1811 to 1815, while their note issues increased from
$23,000,000 to $110,000,000. In 1814 most of the banks outside
New England suspended all pretense of redemption of notes in
specie, and the currency system of the country was badly demoralized. It was the opinion of Secretary Gallatin that much of this
could have been avoided had the First Bank of the United States
continued to function[6]. The suspension of specie payments by the
state banks sadly embarrassed the government, which was unable
to transfer what funds it possessed in the form of bank deposits
from one district to another to meet varying needs.[7]

The Second Bank of the United States. The chaotic condition
of the banking system led many to favor a new bank, similar to
the First Bank of the United States, and on April 10, 1816, a bill
was approved by President Madison granting a charter for the
Second Bank of the United States. During its first two years the
Bank was the victim of mismanagement, but beginning with 1819,
under the new and conservative management of Mr. Langdon
Cheves, it assumed its place as an effective, conservative bank and
fiscal agent for the government. Through its branches it forced
specie redemption upon the state banks. Bank notes deposited
with it by customers or received from the Treasury as governmental revenues were presented for redemption. Banks that refused to redeem their notes found them rejected and not acceptable
for payments to the Treasury.

The action of the Bank in exerting pressure upon state banks
to maintain their notes at par provoked the hatred of banks of the
West and South, which had been the worst offenders against sound
banking. Depression brought distress to debtors, who were easily
persuaded that the Second Bank of the United States was causing
all their troubles by curbing the activities of the state banks.
When the time of the expiration of the old charter arrived, the
Bank was embroiled in a political quarrel with President Jackson,
and a renewal of its charter by the Federal Government became
impossible. The Bank therefore disposed of its branches, obtained a charter from the state of Pennsylvania in February 1836,

---

[6] Hepburn, A. Barton, *A History of Currency in the United States,* 1915, p. 90.
[7] White, Horace, *Money and Banking,* 1896, p. 272.

and for some time continued to operate. After difficulties in the panic of 1837, it finally closed in 1841.[8]

The free banking system. The state of New York inaugurated a plan that was destined to color the banking practices of the United States when it adopted the "free banking system" in 1838. This came as a reaction against the banking monopoly created by specially chartered banks.

Free banking involved two principles. First, banking was to be made a "free trade," open to all without discrimination or favoritism. Second, banks were to issue notes only against the security of proper collateral sufficient to insure ultimate redemption. It was incumbent upon the state, therefore, to lay down the rules under which banks might be organized and notes issued.

At first, the free banking system worked badly in New York. The comptroller was authorized to issue circulating notes to any association organizing itself as a bank and depositing with him the obligations of the United States or any individual state, or real estate mortgage bonds. Twenty-nine free banks failed during the first five years, with substantial losses to note holders, who received payment of only 74 cents on the dollar. To correct the evil of depreciation in the value of securities pledged for the protection of bank notes, amendments were made in the law to permit only the use of bonds of the United States and the state of New York, and qualified mortgages.

The free banking system proved popular. Ohio adopted it in 1845, Illinois in 1851, Indiana in 1852, and Wisconsin in 1853. Free banks were for the most part primarily interested in the issuance of notes. Since the system was designed to insure the safety of bank note holders, it is not surprising that little, if any, provision was made for regulating banks except in regard to note issue. Because of the acceptance of low-grade securities as collateral for the notes, even protection for noteholders was not achieved. The outbreak of the Civil War found many of the free banks in Illinois owners of obligations of Southern states, which rapidly fell in value.

---

[8] Hepburn, *op. cit.* For a thorough account of the history of the Second Bank of the United States, see Smith, Walter B., *The Economic Aspects of the Second Bank of the United States,* Cambridge, Harvard University Press, 1953.

The free banking experience left its indelible mark on the banking system of the times. Commercial banking is now uniformly "free" in the sense that banks are incorporated under the general banking laws without special legislative grants of charters. Furthermore, bank note issue became uniformly based upon the free banking principle of deposit of collateral security with some public authority. In addition, a lesson was learned in respect to the quality of collateral used. With the inauguration of the national banking system, national bank notes were issued only against the deposit of U.S. bonds with the Treasury of the United States. Today, Federal Reserve notes are based upon special collateral deposited with a representative of the Board of Governors of the Federal Reserve System.

Three outstanding problems bearing on sound banking practice and note issue appeared in the years before the Civil War. First, as we have already seen, was the all too common lack of facilities for imposing upon the banks the responsibility for the redemption of their notes. Second, it was a common practice among early banks to operate without what would now be called "sound capital." Laws governing incorporated banks were notoriously loose in this respect. Although nominal capital was normally high, wide latitude existed in respect to amounts to be actually paid in. Frequently only a small amount of specie was contributed by stockholders, for it was considered entirely proper that stockholders should give their promissory notes in payment of their stock subscriptions. It was confidently expected that profits realized from the bank's operation would enable stockholders to retire their notes shortly. Equally dangerous was the common practice of allowing stockholders to borrow on the pledge of their bank stock. The proceeds of loans of this kind might be used either to complete installments due on the stock subscription, or for business ventures. It is evident that such a capital structure was inadequate to give proper support to the bank liabilities when difficulties arose. The lessons learned in the early period were applied to national banks and to the modern state banks. Quite uniformly, laws governing the organization of banks now require cash payment of stock subscriptions. They also prohibit banks from making loans on the security of their own stock.

Finally, an outstanding difficulty that arose among early banks was the inadequacy of specie or legal tender money reserves. To a considerable extent this inadequacy arose from lack of adequate means of presenting notes for redemption. Success in avoiding redemption led many banks to pay little heed to the need for cash reserve. As a result, there was little limit to the amount of notes that banks could issue and lend save the statutory limit commonly set at an amount equal to the bank's capital. But such capital, as already noted, failed generally to bring in much specie and frequently was largely fictional. With the creation of the national banking system this difficulty of inadequate cash reserves was rigorously attacked. Reserve requirements were set by law for banks of various classes. Originally these requirements applied to both note issues and deposit liabilities. Some early state banks also were required to carry definite amounts of cash reserves. New York at first required the free banks to carry 12½ per cent reserves against outstanding notes, a requirement removed in 1844. Beginning in 1842, Louisiana banks were required to carry reserves equal to one-third of their combined note and deposit liabilities, and the remainder of their notes and deposits might be represented only by short-term notes of not over three months. By 1858, Massachusetts adopted a reserve requirement of 15 per cent against bank notes and deposits. Gradually the practice of requiring reserves against liabilities increased until all state banks as well as national banks now have such requirements.

Examples of good banking during period. Generally speaking, the banks in New England and in the East were soundly operated. Even in that part of the country noted for wildcatting, the period was not without its examples of good banking. Both South Carolina and Indiana operated state-owned banks with singular success. Each bank had the right of note issue without any collateral requirement; each operated branches; and each was blessed with sound management. The Bank of the State of South Carolina was founded in 1812 and was finally liquidated in 1870 after many years of useful existence. The State Bank of Indiana was established in 1834 and operated as a state-owned institution for 25 years, when its business was absorbed by a newly organized but privately owned bank of the same name, which itself operated successfully until 1866, when the tax on state bank note issues caused it to liquidate. There were also privately owned banks that stood out in bold relief against the general mass of low-grade banking of the times. One of these was the State Bank of Ohio, which maintained 36 branches and was a model of excellence. Also, the requirements of the Louisiana banking law of 1842 were models of good commercial banking practice. Banks operating under it successfully weathered the crisis of 1857, which took a heavy toll among weaker banks.[9]

The National Banking System

Congressional provisions for a national currency. As early as 1861 it was proposed that United States bonds should be made available to support the issue of a sound and uniform currency. It was hoped that such a scheme would have the double advantage of stimulating the government bond market and of furnishing the country with a currency secured by the obligations of the government. The War made it imperative that the government should be able to obtain necessary funds; at the same time it was important that the disadvantages of an uncertain currency be avoided if possible.[10] Nevertheless, it was not until March 3, 1863, that there was passed "An act to provide a National currency, secured by a Pledge of United States Stocks, and to provide for the Circulation and Redemption thereof." This act was the legal beginning of the national banking system. That the main interest of Congress in passing this act was centered upon the currency question is evident from the title. The following year (June 3, 1864), the original law was repealed and a new law enacted, incorporating some changes that appeared, in the light of previous experiences, to be desirable. This law, like its predecessor, prescribed in minute detail the requirements pertaining to note issue, but little attention was given to the discount and deposit functions of the national banks.

Administration of the new National Banking Act was placed in the hands of an official known as the Comptroller of the Currency.

---

[9] Board of Governors of the Federal Reserve System, *Banking Studies,* 1941, p. 11.

[10] Davis, Andrew M., *The Origin of the National Banking System,* N.M.C., 1910, pp. 36–37.

The Comptroller is appointed by the President and operates under the general direction of the Secretary of the Treasury. His duties are many and his authority is wide. It is to him that applicants for national banking charters must go, and the decision to grant or withhold a charter turns upon the Comptroller's opinion of the applicants' fitness and the community's banking needs as well as on technical compliance with rules governing organizations. It is the Comptroller who maintains a corps of examiners responsible for the annual examination of each national bank. It is he who requires periodic reports of the condition of national banks and under the law sets forth operating regulations. Until the creation of the Federal Deposit Insurance Corporation, in 1934, a representative of the Comptroller, as receiver, presided over the last rites of defunct national banks. All in all, the Comptroller has been and is a powerful figure in our banking system.

Intent on creating a sound banking structure, Congress established rigid capital requirements for the new national banks. Minimum capital requirements varied according to the population of the city in which the bank was organized. These requirements were:

$ 50,000 in cities of not over 6,000 inhabitants
$100,000 in cities of from 6,000 to 50,000 inhabitants
$200,000 in cities of over 50,000 in habitants.

At least one-half of a bank's subscribed capital was to be paid in before starting business, with the remainder to be paid within five months. Moreover, taking warning from past evils, Congress forbade banks to lend on their own stocks. To encourage growth of owners' equity, national banks were originally required to apply one-tenth of their net profits to the accumulation of a surplus until the latter amounted to 20 per cent of the capital. Today the minimum capital requirements are the same as given above, but with two exceptions. First, banks newly organized, and not merely converting from state to national charters, must now sell their stocks at a premium so as to create a paid-up surplus of at least 20 per cent of the capital before beginning business. Second, all national banks must now devote at least 10 per cent of their net profits to surplus accumulation until the surplus account equals the capital stock. Double liability was attached to national bank stock and remained until 1937. It is evident that the national banking system achieved a much more substantial capital structure than existed for many banks in the earlier period.

National bank notes. Until 1917, national banks were required to purchase and hold a certain minimum amount of United States Government securities. These securities were given what was called the circulation privilege and provided the foundation for the issue of national bank note currency. When these bonds were deposited with the United States Treasurer the banks received national bank notes that they could lend and pay out into circulation. To make doubly certain that the notes were secure against depreciation, the law originally provided that the national banks carry lawful money reserves for the purpose of redeeming their notes, and, in addition, the Comptroller of the Currency was duty bound to redeem them in Washington.

Bonds issued by the United States Government during and after World War I could not be used as collateral for the issue of national bank notes. Consequently, as the earlier issues of government bonds were paid off, only a limited amount of eligible bonds was available for note issue. However, during the banking troubles of 1931-1932, to permit the issue of additional quantities of national bank notes for circulation, additional bond collateral was made available. For a three-year period national bank notes could be issued against any U.S. bonds bearing less than 3⅛ per cent interest. This privilege expired in 1935. Furthermore, using funds arising out of the profits from the devaluation of the dollar, the Treasury, in 1935, paid off and retired all of the remaining bonds eligible for use as national bank note collateral. Consequently, the notes are being retired from circulation as they are worn out. The Treasury, holding cash funds instead of bonds as collateral, assumes the obligation of redeeming and retiring national bank notes as worn ones are turned in. By 1956, listed as a part of Treasury currency, only $66 million remained in circulation.

Reserve requirements of national banks. The National Banking Act provided that national banks should carry certain specified reserves in cash or its equivalent against deposit and note liabilities. After 1874, when the acceptability of national bank notes was so firmly established that there was little demand for their redemption, reserve requirements against outstanding notes were abandoned, leaving the requirements to apply only to deposits.

For reserve requirement purposes national banks were divided into the familiar categories of "central reserve city banks," "reserve city banks," and "country banks." Central reserve city banks were eligible to hold on deposit one-half of the required reserves of the banks located in "reserve cities." The latter, in turn, might hold on deposit three-fifths of the required reserves of the country banks. Two significant results stemmed from these reserve regulations. First, they gave banks legal encouragement to deposit their reserve funds with their city correspondent banks. Because at that time the city correspondent banks competed for bankers' balances by paying interest, any excess funds that accumulated in the hands of the country banks and the reserve city banks tended to find their way to the big central reserve city banks, mainly those in New York City. New York City banks had special powers of attraction because the stock market generally provided loan outlets for funds received from the banks in the interior. The second consequence of the national bank reserve requirements was the adoption of the same classification of cities by the Federal Reserve Act for establishing reserve requirements for members of the Federal Reserve System.

The growth and development of national banks. At first the response to the new national banking law was disappointing. Existing state banks preferred to retain their state charters with their note-issuing privileges. Congress, therefore, passed an act on March 3, 1865, that levied a 10 per cent tax on any bank or individual paying out or using state bank notes. This effectively abolished note issue by state banks. The law also encouraged state banks to switch to national charters by permitting them, as national banks, to retain existing branches. National banks were normally not allowed to establish branches. Thus encouraged, national bank chartering increased at a rapid rate, and soon national banks became much more numerous than state banks.

The ascendency of the national banking system was not to last. Beginning about 1885 there developed such an interest in chartering state banks that they soon outstripped the national banks in numbers. By 1920, there were about 21,000 state-chartered banks as compared to about 8,000 national banks. Although, on the average, state banks have always been smaller than national banks, the aggregate resources of the state banks were at that time larger than those of the national banks. The reasons for this sharp ascendency of the state banks were:

1. The decline in importance of bank note issue with the growth in the use of checks. This reduced the earlier disadvantage of the state banks in having no power of note issue.

2. The legislative and other pressure against private, unincorporated banks which generally acquired state charters when incorporating.

3. The emergence of a demand for large and profitable types of banking business that national banks either could not accept because of legal restrictions or were unable to compete for effectively. The national banks at that time were not allowed to lend on real estate, operate trust departments, or engage in bond underwriting. Because of high uniform reserve requirements against all deposits, national banks could not compete for savings accounts with state banks, which enjoyed special low reserve requirements against time deposits.

Some of the competitive handicaps under which the national banks labored were removed or reduced with the enactment of the Federal Reserve Act. Special low reserves were allowed against time deposits, and national banks were authorized to enter the trust company field. Gradually the powers of national banks to lend on improved real estate were expanded. The rigors of the rule that loans to one individual could not exceed 10 per cent of the bank's capital were relaxed and, since 1937, double liability on national bank stock has been ended. National banks, therefore, have gained in comparison with state banks, both because of an improved competitive position and because they better withstood the bank failures of the years since 1920. Today, although the state banks still heavily outnumber national banks by about 9,000 to 4,800, they now hold something less than 45 per cent of all commercial bank resources.

Some weaknesses of the national banking system before 1913. The national banking system successfully met the problem of establishing a sound and uniform currency. National bank notes, backed by government bonds and the pledge of redemption by the United States Government, could hardly have been excelled for security. Moreover, the national banks themselves were a very substantial addition to the banking facilities of the country, particularly in the West and South, where banking had been chaotic. They furnished the backbone of the development of a commercial banking system on the discount and deposit basis at a time when deposit banking was becoming a more important function of American banking than note issue.

Seasonal variations in business. Nevertheless, there were some definite weaknesses in the financial and banking structure which the national banking system failed to meet successfully. These weaknesses grew out of the seasonal character of American business activity and the tendency of banks to deposit surplus cash funds with city correspondents who undertook to pay interest and return the funds on demand.

The pronounced seasonal factors in the American economy before World War I arose largely from the relatively great significance of agriculture in the total economy. Banks in the agricultural areas, and other banks as well, experienced marked seasonal changes in their need for currency and reserve cash. During the winter and summer months currency demands slackened. Under those circumstances banks in the interior parts of the country gathered together their accumulations of excess legal tender money and sent them to New York City for deposit at interest in the Wall Street banks. The Wall Street banks, in turn, used these incoming supplies of reserve cash to expand their loans to stock market speculators. The country banks profited from the arrangement to the extent of the interest earned on what would otherwise have been idle funds. The Wall Street banks profited by lending, largely on call, on the New York Stock Exchange. At such times, given a promising psychological basis, the speculative market would happily absorb the loans made available by the action of the country bankers, and a boom in stock prices and stock trading would develop. From the bankers' standpoint the arrangement appeared favorable, since no loan funds were compelled to stand idle.

However, the whole arrangement frequently terminated abruptly and with a rude shock to all concerned. When seasonal needs for currency in the country areas returned, the banks in the interior wished to withdraw their funds deposited with the Wall Street banks. At times when the stock market had not become overextended, the New York banks were able to call their loans in sufficient amounts to provide themselves with cash reserves in excess of legal requirements. This could be achieved if borrowers could find investors willing to take the securities off their hands at prices equal to the amounts owed the banks. This would reverse the process that took place when incoming money allowed the New York banks to expand their loans and deposits. Loan repayments reduced the banks' deposits and created excess reserves for return to the country banks. In times of excessive speculation, when stock prices were pushed so high as to cause a genuine fear of future values, the speculator-borrower found himself with no market for his securities. The lower prices fell, the more general became the refusal of others to buy stock. There followed an acute panic in security prices, a situation that has often preceded a major depression in business.

Panic in the stock market, induced by the pressure for loan liquidation, prevented banks from reducing their loans and deposits. Consequently, they found themselves with no excess reserve cash to return to the country banks. At such times the Wall Street banks had to choose between (1) sending cash back to the country banks and allowing their own cash reserves to fall below the legal limit; or (2) refusing to honor country bank demands for cash on the excuse that legal reserves must at all times be maintained at the required level. Generally they followed the latter course. The result was a general suspension of cash payments by banks all along the line, with paralyzing effects upon the country's economic life. At such times the banks themselves were unable to ease the stringency by issuing more national bank notes because they normally maintained in circulation all that they could issue on their bond holdings.

The need for a central bank. The bankers made attempts to ease the credit situation just described by devising forms of private money acceptable among the banks of a given city. These were known as "clearinghouse loan certificates." Their use enabled banks to settle adverse clearinghouse balances with neighboring banks without giving up jealously guarded cash reserves. Also, the Treasury came to the rescue at times by putting cash into the banking system, by redeeming outstanding bonds, and by making special deposits of Treasury-held cash in national banks.

The real need was for a central bank that had the power to issue notes and was willing and able to hold sufficient amounts of excess cash reserves to insure its ability to aid the commercial banks in time of need. It was not until 1913, however, that Congress passed the act that authorized the setting up of the Federal Reserve Banks.

Growth of Concentration Among Commercial Banks

Paralleling the growth of large-scale business enterprise is the development of large-scale banking. In part, this development has been the natural result of the expansion of individual banks as they have shared in the industrial and commercial development of growing cities; in part, it has been the outcome of combinations effected sometimes to satisfy the desire for power, sometimes to combat actual or threatened failure. To no small degree it has come from attempts to secure the real and fancied advantages of size.

Large-scale banking. Concentration in banking control takes a number of forms. First is the emergence of gigantic unit banks, some maintaining a single banking office. Such banks, located in the financial centers of the big cities, have become big both by natural growth and by merger. Second are branch banks that acquire size by lateral expansion into territory surrounding the parent or home office. Third are the combinations of banks tied together through the ownership of stock by holding companies. Such combinations are commonly referred to as *group banking*. Holding-company groups frequently contain both unit and branch banks. Finally, there is that informal type of concentration of control called *chain banking,* which involves common stock ownership and interlocking directorates without holding-company intervention.

The reasons for combinations. No single cause has been responsible for bank mergers. The practice of the FDIC of inducing the merger of unsound with sound banks as a means of avoiding receivership was used by bankers long before its use was introduced by the FDIC. Consequently, many of today's banks owe their size, in part, to their absorption of the weaker banks in their communities. Such a procedure generally makes it possible to expand both deposits and earning assets on advantageous terms, since it is unneccessary to pay any "going value" premium and the absorption may be accomplished with little if any increase in the bank's invested capital. Sometimes such mergers were facilitated by a clearinghouse guarantee against loss should assets taken over prove inadequate to offset the deposit liabilities acquired from the failing bank.

A second reason for mergers has doubtless been the prestige that attaches to larger institutions. Moreover, there is the added attraction of the possible and probable increased monetary rewards afforded the executive officers who survive the merger.

Finally, the reason generally advanced to stockholders who are asked to vote approval of a proposed merger is the expectation of increased earnings on invested capital.

The movement toward consolidation or merger among banks has taken a spurt upward since 1950. Five hundred ninety-eight bank mergers or consolidations were reported for the five-year period 1950-1954, and eighty-one more during the first four months of 1955.[11] Mergers have involved both the absorption of small banks by larger ones and the joining of large institutions. Reasons for this situation appear to vary all the way from the favorable prices at which smaller banks may be purchased to the desire of larger banks to acquire new banking outlets in suburban areas.

The Board of Governors' authority to enforce the Clayton Act's prohibition of the purchase of bank stock when the effect is substantially to lessen competition, is not applicable to the case of mergers among banks. However, along with the Federal Deposit Insurance Corporation and the Comptroller of the Currency, it does have jurisdiction in approving mergers in cases in which the result is a reduction in the aggregate invested capital.

The holding company. The holding company has been used by bankers to serve two purposes. The first and by far the more laudable is that of unifying the management and control of several banks. The second and less desirable purpose is that of tying up nonbanking corporations with banks. A combination of these two uses has often appeared in a case in which a group of banks and a number of nonbanking affiliates are tied together. The sponsors of holding companies prefer to call this type of combination

---

[11] *Federal Reserve Bulletin*, June 1955, p. 642.

group banking, reserving the title of *chain banking* for combinations tied together in other ways.

Bank holding companies become owners of a controlling interest in the shares of affiliated banks either through outright purchase or through an exchange of stock. The banks remain separate corporations, but their affairs are brought under the control of the holding company, which elects the management. It is not necessary, of course, that the holding company own over one-half of the shares of a bank in order for it to exercise control over the affairs of the bank. Even a modest fraction of ownership will often place the holding company in the position of being the largest stockholder and clothe it with the authority associated with that position. The holding company itself is frequently affiliated through common stock ownership with a large city bank, whose officers dominate the policies of the group.

Advantages claimed for holding-company banking. The sponsors of group banking claim that stockholders of banks which join a group enjoy definite advantages, such as the following:

1. The individual bank may participate in loans to large borrowers who would look elsewhere for accommodation if the group did not exist.

2. Working reserves can be concentrated in the hands of one city correspondent, normally a member of the group. Thus, less idle funds will be required in the hands of city correspondents. The acting correspondent for the group stands ready to give aid when needed.

3. Operating economies may be expected from improvements in management. Supplies may be purchased in larger amounts. Advertising becomes more economical. The cost of insurance and bonding of employees can be reduced.

4. The stock of the holding company is often of more value than that of the operating bank, since it has greater diversification of risk behind it, is a larger issue commanding the interest of a wider market, and enjoys the higher earnings derived from the expected economies.

Objections to holding-company banking. With intelligent and honest management, holding-company banking may be decidedly more desirable than unit banking. Certain vital criticisms, however, can be made:

1. Examination of chains and groups is difficult, since the banks may be spread over a wide area and may be under the control of several separate state authorities in addition to national bank examiners. Under such a situation juggling of funds and assets may be overlooked.

2. The banks may be mismanaged and exploited for the benefit of those in control. This danger was demonstrated in the case of certain failures during the banking crisis of 1932-1933. Banks lent heavily to officers to finance speculation in the stock of the holding company. Unit banks were compelled to pay unwarranted dividends in the face of operating losses to enable the holding company to maintain its dividend policies. Holding companies borrowed from the banks which they owned to finance speculative dealings. The subsidiaries of holding companies in one case included not merely banks but corporations owning office buildings, a chain of hotels, a coal mine, residential and business properties, a produce market, and a security company.

3. When the group becomes so large that it overshadows the independent banks of its area, there arises a real danger that banking competition will be unduly restrained. This was the situation in the case of the Transamerica Corporation of California, which was reported, at the end of 1948, to control 40 per cent of the banking offices and 38 per cent of the commercial bank deposits in the five states of Arizona, California, Nevada, Oregon, and Washington. In the state of California, alone, it controlled about 50 per cent of the total banking offices.[12]

Branch banking. The contrast between holding-company banking and branch banking is that a branch system is one single bank incorporated under a single charter, answerable to a single supervisory authority, all the branches of which are subject to direct central control. The branches are merely devices whereby it is possible to extend banking contracts into areas beyond the reach of the home office. Branch banking may, of course, be tied up with holding-company control.

In the United States, branch banking can exist only within the confines of individual states,[13] and to a large extent is limited to the home city and the immediately surrounding territory. The limited nature of American branch banking may be seen in the data given in Table 18.

Advantages of branch banking. The advantages of branch banking may be enumerated as follows:

1. The larger banking unit resulting can better handle the requirements of the large customers.

2. The smaller communities enjoy the advantage of the service of

---

12 Cf. *Federal Reserve Bulletin,* April 1952, pp. 384–387.

13 Except in two cases where national banks have a total of four out-of-state branches. Apparently these were acquired by merger. *Federal Reserve Bulletin,* May 1954, p. 536.

TABLE 18

Commercial Banks Maintaining Branches, December 31, 1955*

	Number	
	Banks	Branches
Total for the United States	1,659	6,710
National banks	543	3,196
State member banks	304	1,916
Insured nonmember banks	790	1,563
Noninsured banks	22	35

Location of Branches

In head office city	3,048
In head office county but outside home city	1,986
In contiguous counties	913
In noncontiguous counties	1,093

* *Federal Reserve Bulletin*, April 1956, p. 399.

more powerful and presumably sounder banks. The assets of the whole branch bank system are behind each branch, in contrast to the situation in group and chain banking, where no legal responsibility attaches to one part of the system for the other units in case of difficulty.

3. More convenient banking facilities are possible. The population per banking office is considerably greater in unit banking than in branch banking cities.

4. Branch banks can command better managerial skill. Branch managers can be carefully trained and supervised, with greater opportunity for promotion for those of most promise.

5. When branch bank operations extend over a wide geographical area, they resist the shock of depressions more successfully than do unit banks, both because of the greater opportunity for diversification of loan risk and because of the industrial and geographical diversification of deposits so necessary if forced liquidation of loans and bank failure are to be avoided in areas suffering adverse trade balances during depression.

6. Branch banks increase the mobility of capital and make for greater uniformity of interest rate throughout the area served.

Objections to branch banking. The objections raised to branch banking naturally are voiced by the unit banker, who visualizes himself swallowed up in a branch banking development:

1. Branch bankers are likely to require collateral on all loans and refuse to lend on the character of the borrower, perhaps retarding local economic development. This objection is hardly valid, since even a branch banker is interested in the business development of the bank's locality. Moreover, a more careful loan policy than that of many unit banks is desirable.

2. Funds are withdrawn from rural areas and are placed in cities. In answer to this, it has been shown that Canadian city borrowers complain that the reverse is true, with city funds transferred to rural districts in response to the higher interest rates there.[14]

3. Red tape and delay arise from the lack of authority of managers and the necessity for referring loans to the main office. But it is estimated that over 95 per cent of the loans of Canadian branch banks are handled without delay by the branch managers and by the use of the telephone. Branch managers may lend up to a fixed limit or reject loans without reference to the main office.[15]

4. Managers are not properly sympathetic with local needs.

5. Branch managers are shifted too frequently to be of the best service to the community served.

6. Too much concentration in the control of banking operations will arise. Furthermore, mismanagement on a large scale can arise more easily with branch than with unit banking.

The objections just mentioned are hardly sufficient to constitute a serious criticism of branch banking. Certain broader problems exist, however. Branch banks operating solely within the home city are hardly more than handy devices for attracting business to the parent. They offer only part of the genuinely important characteristics of branch banking What, then, should be the territorial limits of branch banking? Should it be confined to trade areas, or should it be permitted to extend throughout the country? Should it be confined within individual states? The wider the area, the greater become the opportunities for diversification, but at the same time managerial and supervisory problems increase. If it be agreed that the present restrictions on branch banking should be relaxed, under what conditions should banks be permitted to organize branches?

Obviously, great care is required if powerful branch banks are not to be allowed to put unfair pressure upon unit banks. Ex-

---

[14] Cartinhour, G. T., *Branch, Group, and Chain Banking,* New York, The Macmillan Company, 1931, Chap. XX.

[15] *Ibid.*

cessive competition by branch banks with the unit banks might be quite as undesirable as between unit banks themselves. Finally, the supervision of large branch banking systems presents a problem. If the number of branches is large, it is impracticable to examine all at the same time. The head office may be required to furnish a consolidated balance sheet when examined, and the largest branches and the head office may be examined at the same time.

Chain banking. A wide variety of interbanking relations falls under the general head of "chain banking." Control in such chains arises out of various degrees of common stock ownership, ranging all the way from identical ownership represented by trusteeing stock of one bank for the benefit of the stockholders of another to the loose, informal control arising from interlocking directorates.

Chains of banks develop both in rural districts and in cities. Sometimes they arise from the purchase of stock in banks in other locations as a means of extending the banking power of some individual or group of individuals. Rarely are they the result of attempts to restrain competition. Frequently they arise from the efforts of large city banks to attach to themselves a collection of banking satellites. Often this has been accomplished when an officer in a large bank invests in the stock of a smaller one and assumes an important place on its board of directors. Smaller banks, themselves, are frequently interrelated by complex interlocking directorates and common officers.

The benefits of chain banking are slight. As in the case of holding-company control, gains may be had through concentration of reserves and uniform management, or operating economies may arise through the purchase of supplies and services. On the other hand, chain banks are especially susceptible to mismanagement and exploitation. The failures experienced by chains of banks have been so numerous that sponsors of the modern holding-company plan insist upon differentiating their type as "group banking" in contrast to "chain banking."

Regulation of Branch, Group, and Chain Banking

Governmental regulation of branch, group, and chain banking takes the form of (1) permission or prohibition; and (2) special investigation and control.

Legal status of branch banking. The law now permits national banks to establish branches in states where branch banking is expressly permitted. The following restrictions apply, however:

1. National banks are subject to the same territorial limits as are the state banks. Wherever state banks are limited to city- or county-wide branches, national banks are similarly limited.

2. Approval of the Comptroller of the Currency must be obtained.

3. National banks with out-of-town branches must have a minimum capital amounting to the aggregate total capital stock that would be required to establish a national bank at each of the various places where its offices are located. They must also have as much capital and surplus as would be required of state banks under similar circumstances.

In 1951, 18 states (counting the District of Columbia) specifically permitted state-wide branch banking, 17 specifically permitted limited-area branch banking, 10 states prohibited branches, and 4 had no law dealing with the subject.[16] In all states, banks wishing to establish branches must obtain the permission of supervisory authorities. In general, branches outside the home city may be established where there is no existing bank, or, if other banks operate in the same community, upon the purchase of an existing bank, or by obtaining the consent of the other banks.

Under existing legislation there is no possibility of the establishment of anything like a broad system of branch banking in the United States. Only an extension to national banks of the right to engage in interstate branch banking seems likely to accomplish this purpose. The distinct superiority of branch over chain and holding-company banking, which often acquire an interstate character, make such legislation highly desirable.

Regulation of group banking. There are two ways in which holding-company groups are subject to regulation. The first is

---

[16] *Compilation of Federal and State Laws Relating to Branch Banking Within the United States,* Board of Governors of the Federal Reserve System, July 1, 1951. States permitting state-wide branch banking are: Arizona, California, Connecticut, Delaware, District of Columbia, Idaho, Maine, Maryland, Nevada, North Carolina, Oregon, Rhode Island, South Carolina, South Dakota, Utah, Vermont, Virginia, and Washington. States permitting limited-area branch banking are: Alabama, Arkansas, Georgia, Indiana, Iowa, Louisiana, Massachusetts, Michigan, Mississippi, Montana, New Jersey, New Mexico, New York North Dakota, Ohio, Pennsylvania, Tennessee. Those prohibiting branch banking are: Colorado, Florida, Illinois, Kansas, Minnesota, Missouri, Nebraska, Texas, West Virginia, and Wisconsin.

through the provisions of Section 7 of the Clayton Antitrust Act. This makes illegal the holding companies that substantially lessen competition or result in monopoly in interstate commerce. Should it be established that a given holding company is covered by the law, the Board of Governors would be responsible for the enforcement of suitable orders to correct the situation. The Board vainly sought to compel the dissolution of the Transamerica Corporation in a protracted series of hearings that culminated by the Board's order that the Transamerica Corporation divest itself of the stock of forty-seven banks. The order, however, was set aside by the Federal Courts.[17]

Bank holding companies also come under the regulations established by the banking acts of 1933 and 1935 and the Bank Holding Company Act of 1956. These regulations involve (1) the requirement that to vote shares of member bank stock bank holding companies must first obtain a "voting permit" from the Board of Governors; and (2) limitations on the creation and operation of bank holding companies. To obtain a voting permit a holding company must submit to examination of its affairs and accumulate a suitable reserve to enable it to meet its liabilities as a bank stockholder. The Holding Company Act of 1956 defines a "bank holding company" as any company that controls the voting power over 25 per cent of the voting shares of each of two or more banks, or in any manner controls the election of a majority of the directors of two or more banks. Any company, whether engaged in banking or other forms of business, in which the bank holding company controls 25 per cent or more of the voting shares, or controls the election of a majority of the directors, is known as a "subsidiary." To give the Board of Governors of the Federal Reserve System control over the expansion of bank holding companies, the law requires that prior approval by the Board must be obtained for (1) acts that result in the establishment of a bank holding company; and (2) any future acquisitions by bank holding companies of voting shares of banks if the result is to give control over 5 per cent of

---

[17] For the findings of the Board of Governors and its order to the Trans-America Corporation, see the *Federal Reserve Bulletin*, April 1952, pp. 368–398. For the subsequent court actions resulting in the dismissal of the order, see the *Bulletin*, August 1953, pp. 836–841, and December 1953, p. 1329.

such shares. Likewise, prior approval of the Board is required before the purchase of the assets of a bank by a bank holding company or for a merger of bank holding companies. In granting or withholding approval of such actions the Board consults with the bank supervisory agencies and must take into account the financial history, prospects, and management of the banks and holding companies concerned, as well as the needs of the communities served and the probable effect upon sound banking and the preservation of competition. The Board's decisions are subject to review by the Federal Court.[18]

Yet another restraint is placed by the new act upon the extension of holding-company banking in the requirement that bank holding companies may not acquire any voting shares or interest in banks located outside the holding company's home state unless the laws of the state in which such banks are located specifically authorize such purchase by out-of-state holding companies.

To cope with the danger that nonbanking subsidiaries of bank holding companies may borrow from banking subsidiaries, the law provides that bank holding companies, within a limited time, must divest themselves of ownership of voting shares of all nonbanking subsidiaries. Exception is made for subsidiaries holding properties used by subsidiary banks or whose business is incidental to carrying on banking business. In addition, it is made illegal for any bank to purchase the securities of or make loans to a holding company of which it is a subsidiary or to any other subsidiary.

Chain bank regulation. Chain banking, being informal and involving stock ownership in banks by one or a number of individuals, with common officers and directors, is less exposed to special regulatory control. However, the Clayton Act provides that no private banker, director, officer, or employee of any member bank shall at the same time be a director, officer, or employee of any other bank, state or national, except that: (1) the Board of Governors may grant a permit in the case of one other bank; and (2) restrictions do not apply to banks 90 per cent of whose stock is owned by the United States, banks in liquidation, foreign banking corporations, banks 50 per cent of whose stock is owned by the stockholders of another member bank, banks not located in the

---

[18] *Federal Reserve Bulletin,* May 1956, pp. 444-449 and August 1956, p. 835.

same town or city (or a contiguous one), and banks not engaged in the same class of business.

Questions for Study

1. Why, in the early days, was there so much popular enthusiasm for bank loans based on land?

2. Why did the early commercial loan banks succeed so much better than the land banks?

3. Why did early banking laws pay so much attention to the note-issuing function?

4. Where did wildcat banks get their name? Why were their note issues so often in default?

5. What forward step toward sound bank note issue was taken by the Suffolk Bank?

6. In what manner could and did the First and the Second Bank of the United States impose restraint upon the issue of state bank notes?

7. What principles incorporated in the early state free banking systems were later found in the national banking system and in the Federal Reserve Banks?

8. What was the main accomplishment of the national banking system? What were its limitations?

9. What part did each of the following play in the development of periodic banking crises before 1914?
   a) Seasonal variations in business.
   b) The bond security requirements for national bank notes.
   c) The attraction of the Wall Street banks for the excess reserves of country banks.
   d) Legal reserve requirements.
   e) The absence of a central bank.

10. What steps were taken to ease the pre-1913 crises: (a) by the Treasury; (b) by the clearinghouses?

11. Explain why American banks have expanded through mergers.

12. What are the main characteristics of each of the following methods of concentrating banking control: (a) Holding-company or group banking. (b) Chain banking. (c) Branch banking.

13. Why is holding-company control over banking sometimes better than chain banking?

14. In what ways is trade-area branch banking likely to be superior to holding-company banking? Chain banking? Our present type of branch banking?

15. Why has there been concern about holding-company banking of the kind illustrated by the Transamerica Corporation?

_____16

The Federal Reserve Banks

During its first forty years the national banking system was plagued by periodic crises and breakdowns. The commercial banks, it will be recalled, had the habit of sending seasonal excess cash accumulations to Wall Street to become the foundation for increased speculative loans on the Stock exchange. In more critical years the country banks found these funds unavailable when needed during the busy season, because of the impossibility of forcing a sufficient reduction of stock market loans on an overextended market. At such times there was no refuge to be had in an increase in the currency. The country's supply, consisting of United States notes, silver and gold certificates, coins, and national bank notes, was entirely inelastic in any short-run sense. Obviously, there was need for a central bank capable of expanding the currency to meet the country's varying cash needs. A central bank is a place of refuge— a "lender of last resort" for the money market. As such it necessarily must carry sufficient reserves of cash to enable it to advance funds to relieve monetary stringencies when they arise. If, as generally is the case, the central bank can issue its own notes for use as currency, its ability to meet the currency needs of the money market is considerably enhanced.

After the banking crisis of 1907, Congress created the National Monetary Commission to investigate the problems of money and banking reform. The results of its studies furnish a voluminous source of historical information on banking experiences before 1910. It was the Commission's recommendation that a central bank be established. In 1913, Congress passed the Federal Reserve Act calling for a *regional* system of central banks under the general supervision of a Federal Reserve Board, the predecessor of the present Board of Governors of the Federal Reserve System. The regional system of twelve banks, rather than a central bank with branches, was chosen to allay the fear of domination by the "Money Trust" of Wall Street.

The Function of Central Banks

Central banks are creators of "central bank money" in the form of their own notes and deposits. Such money is available to commercial banks (1) to satisfy legal reserve requirements; and (2) to provide the funds needed by individual banks to meet obligations to other banks and to customers wanting cash or currency for general circulation.

Originally, central banks were solely concerned with their position of "lenders of last resort." Their purpose was to provide currency and reserves needed by the banks as they met the varying needs of the economic community. Put another way, the central bank was expected, by discounting commercial paper and making loans, to provide funds needed "to facilitate trade and commerce" and to insure that banks had adequate funds to enable them to finance the legitimate short-term credit needs of business. If it accomplished this it had discharged its obligation as a central bank. This essentially was the view of the founders of the Federal Reserve System.[1]

The ability of the central bank to create new reserves and new currency for the commercial banks carries with it grave responsibilities. The capacity to create money and bank reserves, or to withhold their creation, gives the central bank power to permit business overexpansion and boom, or to impose, through tight credit policy, deflationary pressure upon the economy. Consequently central bank functions have been recognized as extending beyond that of a mere lender of last resort, important as that is. The modern view is that, in addition to providing seasonal and emergency sources of cash for member banks, central banks also must exercise their

---

[1] The Federal Reserve Act is headed: "An Act to provide for the establishment of Federal reserve banks, to furnish an elastic currency, to afford means of rediscounting commercial paper, to establish a more effective supervision of banking in the United States, and for other purposes."

reserve and currency-creating powers in such a manner as to contribute to price stability and economic growth. This view goes far beyond the original injunction in the Federal Reserve Act that the System was created to provide an elastic currency by the rediscount of commercial paper. With the trend away from automatic convertibility of currencies into gold and toward the direction of monetary management, it has become much more necessary and desirable that the Federal Reserve policy include a goal of promoting economic stability and growth.

The actual functions performed by the Federal Reserve System fall naturally into two categories. The first involves the System's responsibility for making available and controlling the volume of cash reserve funds of the commercial banks. In this category lies the responsibility for (1) the liquidity of individual commercial banks, that is, the availability of cash to meet irregular cash needs; (2) the elasticity of currency and credit needed to meet seasonal and other requirements of the economic system; and (3) such control of the volume of reserve cash as may best promote economic stability and employment. The primary functions of any central bank fall into this category. These are the functions that necessitate the development and application of what is called *central bank credit policy,* consideration of which must be postponed until later.

The second category of functions of the Federal Reserve System includes the performance of numerous tasks essential both to the smooth and proper working of the commercial banking system and to the convenience of the United States Treasury. In spite of their routine and ministerial character, these tasks or functions are highly important. But they seldom involve the considerations of high policy that characterize the exercise of the control over credit. Included in this second category is the task of operating the Federal Reserve check collection system and wire transfer service, which we have already examined. In addition, there are vital functions performed for the Treasury as its fiscal agent. In this capacity the Federal Reserve Banks collect and hold on deposit for the Treasury billions of dollars worth of checks each year received from taxpayers and other sources of government revenue. They also pay government checks and bond coupons. In addition, the Federal Reserve Banks act as intermediaries between the Treasury and the money market when the Treasury wishes to issue securities, and they may, within limits, lend directly to the Treasury.

The Federal Reserve System and the availability of bank reserves. As was indicated above, one of the primary functions of the Federal Reserve System is to provide additional cash reserve funds needed by the commercial banks. The need for such additional cash by individual banks arises from their losses of cash incident to their normal banking operations. If such individual banks are to be able to function normally and properly, they need a "lender of last resort" to which they may confidently turn whenever seasonal and irregular losses of cash cause an impairment of required reserves. The commercial banks as a whole system require additional cash reserves because of seasonal and other developments that bring increased currency and reserve requirements.

The Federal Reserve Banks are required by law to maintain gold certificate reserves equal to not less than 25 per cent of their note and deposit liabilities. Consequently, in order that they may be able to extend credit and increase the quantity of their deposits and notes as they are needed by the commercial banks and the money market, they must maintain an adequate quantity of gold certificate reserves above the legal minimum requirements. To perform their central banking function they must, therefore, scrupulously avoid seeking to make full use of their lending and investing capacity. In this respect, unlike private commercial banks, the Federal Reserve Banks must remain divorced from the goal of maximum profits. Instead, they must extend credit only in the light of the over-all public need. Good public policy, not profits, must be their goal.

Member banks carry their cash reserves mainly in the form of deposits in the Federal Reserve Banks (legal reserves) and Federal Reserve notes.[2] Before 1933 the banks sometimes held and paid out into circulation standard money in the form of gold coin and gold certificates. This they are no longer allowed to do. Additions to the monetary gold supply, therefore, now appear as gold certificate reserves in the Federal Reserve Banks, where they act as a reserve base for Federal Reserve deposits and notes. Obviously this

---

[2] Other currency issued by the Treasury appears also in the tills of banks. This includes United States notes (greenbacks), silver and silver certificates, and minor coin.

"economizes" the use of gold and increases the amount of bank reserves and currency that can be created by the Federal Reserve Banks.

The general structure of the Federal Reserve System. The foundation upon which the Federal Reserve System rests is the member banks. All national banks and the more important state-chartered banks are members of the system. The member banks purchase stock in and therefore own the Federal Reserve Banks of their own district. The country is divided into twelve districts, each designed to include an important trading area and to be of sufficient size for each Federal Reserve Bank, when originally organized, to have a subscribed capital equal to the required minimum of $4,000,-000. The map on page 246 shows the district boundaries and the location of the individual Federal Reserve Banks and their branches.

Technically, each of the twelve Federal Reserve Banks acts as a central bank for its own district. It carries the deposited reserves of its member banks and it lends them cash reserves when more are needed. In actual practice, however, the Federal Reserve System as a whole should be thought of as comprising a central bank for the whole country. Through the unifying influence of the Board of Governors of the Federal Reserve System and the Open Market Committee, whose specific functions will be considered later, the policies and activities of the twelve individual reserve banks are closely tied together. In many ways their operations resemble those of a single central bank with twelve branches. Therefore, as a point of departure in the study of central banking in the United States, we shall examine the combined asset and liability statements of all of the Federal Reserve Banks.

Federal Reserve Bank Management

Each Federal Reserve Bank has a nine-man board of directors, six of whom are elected by the member banks and the remaining three appointed by the Board of Governors of the Federal Reserve System in Washington, D.C. Of the three so appointed, one is called the Federal Reserve Agent and is chairman of the Bank's board of directors. The chief administrative officer is the President, chosen by the board of directors for a five-year term and subject to the approval of the Board of Governors.

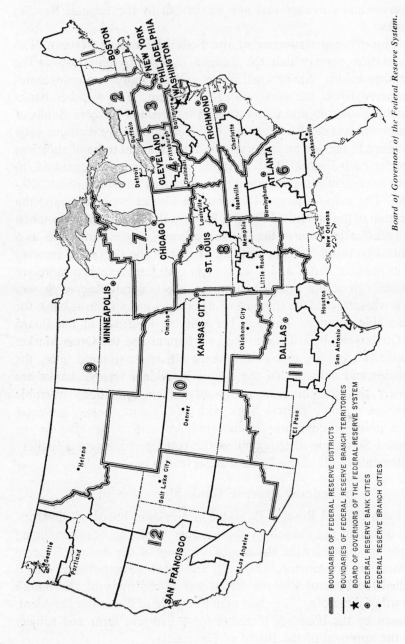

Board of Governors of the Federal Reserve System.

Chart 7. Boundaries of Federal Reserve Districts and Their Branch Territories.

Although each Federal Reserve Bank is directly administered by its own board of directors and by its president and other officers appointed by the board, the individual bank is not an independent agency so far as matters of policy are concerned. It will be remembered that the chairman, known as the Agent, along with two other members of the board of directors, is chosen by the Board of Governors in Washington, D.C. He is the Board of Governors' official representative in all deliberations dealing with the affairs of the bank.

The chief executive body of the Federal Reserve System is the Board of Governors. It is made up of seven members, appointed by the President and approved by the Senate, "with due regard to a fair representation of the financial, agricultural, and commercial interests of the country." Appointments are for fourteen-year terms so arranged that only one will expire during any two-year period. After they have served a full fourteen-year term, members of the Board may not be reappointed. Moreover, they may not resign before the end of their terms and accept any position with a member bank within two years. Two members of the Board are appointed Chairman and Vice-chairman, respectively, for four-year periods.

Powers of the Board. Some of the regulatory powers of the Board of Governors have already been noted. It regulates margin requirements, maximum interest on time deposits, and member bank required reserves. It has other significant powers over the operations of the Federal Reserve System. These include, among others:

1. Approval of the discount rate fixed by each Federal Reserve Bank.
2. Examination of the affairs of both member banks and the Federal Reserve Banks, and the publication of weekly statements of the condition of each of the latter.
3. The suspension of reserve requirements for member banks and the Federal Reserve Banks for limited periods in times of emergency, and the application of certain statutory penalties against reserve deficiencies of the Federal Reserve Banks.
4. The suspension or removal of officers and directors of the Federal Reserve Banks for cause; and the removal of officers and directors of any member bank which continues to violate the law or engage in unsound banking practices after being warned.
5. The establishment of regulations that interpret the application of the Federal Reserve Act.

The Open Market Committee. The credit extended by the Federal Reserve Banks through their open market operations now makes up the major share of all Reserve Bank credit. In earlier years each Federal Reserve Bank bought and sold securities in the open market more or less to suit itself. Since 1935, however, the open market operations of the Reserve Banks have been under the control of the Open Market Committee. This committee is composed of the seven members of the Board of Governors plus five representatives of the Federal Reserve Banks. These five include the President of the Federal Reserve Bank of New York and four others chosen from the presidents and first vice-presidents of the other Federal Reserve Banks.

The Open Market Committee, meeting frequently during the year, establishes broad policies as to when and in what general direction the Federal Reserve Banks shall deal in Government securities. The actual execution of these broad policies is entrusted to the Federal Reserve Bank of New York, which, under the direction of the Committee, acts as agent for the System. The Bank appoints one of its vice-presidents as manager to administer the open market joint account.

The Federal Reserve Banks

An examination of the combined balance sheet of the Federal Reserve Banks shown in Table 19 will help to introduce us to the nature of their structure and general characteristics.

Cash assets. The cash assets of the Federal Reserve Banks contain one main item, gold certificates, and a quantitatively less important item, "other cash." Gold certificate holdings rise whenever the Treasury deposits certificates issued against newly purchased gold. They decline whenever individuals, through their member banks, purchase gold for industrial use from the Treasury or the Treasury releases gold for export.[3]

---

[3] The domestic users of gold offer checks on member banks in payment for gold purchased from the Treasury. The Treasury pays out the gold and "buys back" for retirement an equal amount of gold certificates from the Federal Reserve Bank. The final result is that the individual purchaser of gold has given up claims against the member bank, the latter finds its reserve balance (deposit) with the Federal Reserve Bank reduced, and the Federal Reserve Bank has lost the same amount in gold certificate reserves. A similar result occurs when gold is exported.

TABLE 19

Statement of Condition of All Federal Reserve Banks, March 31, 1956*
(In millions of dollars)

Assets		*Liabilities*	
Gold certificate reserve ..	21,036.1	Federal Reserve notes ...	26,097.5
Federal Reserve notes of		Deposits:	
other banks	288.7	Member bank reserve	
Other cash	392.0	accounts .. 18,799.5	
Discounts and advances:		U.S. Treasury 534.2	
Secured by U.S. Gov't		Foreign 354.5	
securities	843.6	Other 622.7	
Other	28.0	Total deposits	20,310.9
Industrial loans	.6	Deferred availability cash	
Acceptances bought out-		items	3,158.5
right	14.9	Other liabilities and ac-	
U.S. Government securi-		crued dividends	17.6
ties:			
Bought outright	23,587.3	Total liabilities	49,584.5
Held under repurchase		Capital Accounts:	
agreement	48.4	Capital paid in 310.0	
Uncollected cash items ...	4,396.4	Surplus (Sec. 7) 693.6	
Bank premises	64.3	Surplus (Sec. 13b) 27.5	
Other assets	121.5	Other capital	
		accounts 206.2	
		Total capital accounts	1,227.3
		Total liabilities and capital	
Total assets	50,821.8	accounts	50,821.8

Ratio of gold certificate reserves to deposit and note liabilities = 45.3%.
Total Federal Reserve notes outstanding (issued to
  banks) $27,028,277,000
Collateral held against notes outstanding:
  Gold certificates $11,413,000,000
  Eligible paper 150,000,000
  U.S. Gov't securities 17,035,000,000

  Total collateral $28,598,023,000

* Federal Reserve Bulletin.

"Other cash" consists of various kinds of other Treasury issues, including United States notes, silver currency, silver certificates, and minor coin. Whenever the Treasury issues new silver certificates or new coin, "other cash" of the Federal Reserve Banks tends to rise. Variations in this item normally reflect changes in circulation requirements. Whenever a particular member bank finds its tills oversupplied with currency and coin, it ships the surplus to the Federal Reserve bank for deposit on its reserve account. Outflows of coin and small paper currency into circulation reverses the process. Whenever a member bank sends cash funds to its Federal Reserve Bank for deposit, all except Federal Reserve notes becomes "other cash" among the Federal Reserve Bank assets.[4]

Earning assets. Federal Reserve Banks hold three types of earning assets. The first, discounts and advances, arises from loans to member banks,[5] and from the purchase of bankers' acceptances in the open market. This class of earning assets is relatively small in comparison with the holdings of Government securities. A second class of earning asset is the insignificant item of industrial loans or direct loans to industry made by the Federal Reserve Banks under authority granted during the Depression. The third and quantitatively most important class of earning assets is United States Government securities. These were purchased in large amounts during World War II to provide banks with reserves and currency needed to meet the requirements of the times. After the war, securities were purchased to provide a support to the price of Government obligations. Now, the holdings of Government securities, mainly short-term, reflect current Federal Reserve credit policies.

Federal Reserve Bank earning assets are mainly significant in that they measure the contribution of the Federal Reserve Banks to the supply of member bank reserves and the country's currency. Incidentally, the earning assets provide the necessary income out of which the operating expenses of the System are met and the dividends on Federal Reserve Bank stock are paid.

The remainder of the Federal Reserve Bank assets are (1) uncollected cash items; (2) bank premises; and (3) "other assets." Uncollected cash items consist of checks received for collection from member banks. When first received they become "deferred availability credit" for member banks, an item appearing on the liability

---

[4] When a member sends in Federal Reserve notes for deposit they are either retired directly, if they are the notes of that particular bank, or they are carried as "notes of other Federal Reserve Banks." Formerly Federal Reserve notes issued by other banks had to be returned to the issuing bank for redemption. This provision was removed by the Act of July 19, 1954.

[5] Nonmember banks may also borrow from the Federal Reserve Banks on the security of U.S. obligations with special permission of the Board of Governors. This privilege is now rarely used.

side of the Federal Reserve balance sheet. Presumably, as these checks are collected by being charged against the reserve balances of member banks required to pay them, an equal amount of deferred availability credit is transferred into full reserve credit for the banks that sent them in for collection. Because member banks need to know when checks sent in for collection are made available for legal reserve purposes, the Federal Reserve Banks grant full reserve credit for deferred availability items after the expiration of a stated time after their receipt. Sometimes banks receive full reserve credit for items that have not yet actually been collected and deducted from other banks' reserves. The difference, known as Federal Reserve "float," represents a form of Federal Reserve credit extended to member banks, and increases by that amount the total reserve accounts of member banks. The item "bank premises" needs no explanation. "Other assets" include such things as premiums on securities and accrued interest.

Federal Reserve Bank obligations. The outstanding liabilities of the reserve banks are deposits and notes. These obligations originate in the same manner as do those of ordinary banks—namely, from the deposit of cash and the making of loans. Further, they resemble the deposit and note obligations of ordinary banks in another way: to the owners of such obligations they are the equivalent of cash.

It thus happens that the cash resources of ordinary banks are made up mainly of the obligations of the reserve banks; to a lesser extent, silver certificates, United States notes, and coin constitute a part of the currency held by banks. In general, variations in the cash resources of member banks and currency in hand-to-hand circulation consistently reflect variations in the obligations of the reserve banks.

Federal Reserve notes in circulation. The largest single type of Federal Reserve Bank liability is Federal Reserve notes in circulation. Whenever a member bank finds that cash withdrawals by depositors are unduly reducing till money supplies, the member bank can obtain cash from its Federal Reserve Bank. The cash paid out to the member bank is deducted from its reserve balance. If this creates a reserve deficiency, the member bank must then take appropriate corrective steps.

Deposits of the Federal Reserve Banks. As can readily be seen by referring to the Federal Reserve Bank balance sheet in Table 19, member bank balances comprise the bulk of the deposits of the Federal Reserve Banks. The remainder consists of deposits of the United States Treasury, deposits of foreign banks, and "other deposits." The last includes clearing balances of nonmember banks and deposits of numerous governmental departments and agencies other than the Treasury.

Each member bank is required by law to carry with its Federal Reserve Bank a deposit balance equal to a certain percentage of its own deposit liabilities. Such balances are known as "legal reserves," and to avoid penalty, must be maintained at the required level by the member bank. The details in respect to required and other reserves of banks have been examined in an earlier chapter.

Federal Reserve Bank deposits, largely member bank legal reserves, originate in the following ways:

1. From the Treasury's deposit of gold certificates and other newly issued Treasury currency.
2. From the deposit of currency and coin by member banks.
3. From the expansion of credit by the Federal Reserve Banks, either by making loans to banks or by the purchase of Government securities in the open market.

The capital accounts of the Federal Reserve Banks. As with other banks, the Federal Reserve Bank capital accounts fall into three categories:

1. Paid-in capital.
2. Surplus.
3. Other capital accounts.

The paid-in capital is provided by member banks. Each member is required to subscribe to Federal Reserve Bank stock to an amount equal to 6 per cent of its own capital and surplus. Of this it pays in one-half, leaving the other half subject to call. If a member bank's capital and surplus are increased or decreased, its stock subscription is correspondingly modified. The stock bears double liability. Member banks receive only 6 per cent cumulative dividends on the par value of the paid-in stock.

The Federal Reserve Bank surplus account falls into two classes. The first (Section 7) is the earned surplus accumulated in the usual way after all expenses and dividends are paid. The second (Section

13b) represents funds contributed by the Treasury to the Federal Reserve Banks to facilitate their making of industrial loans during the 1930's. The present rate of accumulation of earned surplus is modest. Before 1933, the law provided that after the surplus accounts reached a level equal to the Banks' subscribed capital (or twice the paid-in capital), only 10 per cent of their net earnings should go to surplus and the remaining 90 per cent should go to the Treasury. In 1933, Congress put one-half of the Federal Reserve Bank surplus accounts into the capital stock of the newly formed Federal Deposit Insurance Corporation. At that time, and until the outbreak of World War II, the net earnings of the Federal Reserve Banks were extremely low. Consequently the law was modified to permit *all* net earnings to be carried to surplus without any limit.

During World War II the situation changed sharply. Federal Reserve Bank earnings from their holdings of Government securities were high, and at the end of 1947 their combined surplus accounts were larger than the subscribed capital. The Board of Governors then invoked its power to levy an interest charge on Federal Reserve notes issued against non-gold collateral. The tax is so regulated as to restore, in effect, the law governing surplus accumulations before 1933, when 90 per cent of net earnings went into the Treasury after surplus equalled the subscribed capital. This practice of the Board has been severely criticized as being an improper use of administrative action to circumvent the law as laid down by Congress. The justification for the practice was that it permitted the Board of Governors to advocate a tighter money policy, including higher interest rates on Government securities, without being exposed to the complaint that tighter money tended to enrich the Federal Reserve Banks at the expense of the Treasury.

Collateral and Reserve Requirements of the Federal Reserve Banks

Collateral requirements for Federal Reserve notes. A traditional rule, established by the free banking systems of the first half of the nineteenth century and continued under the national banking system, found its way into the Federal Reserve Act when, in 1913, it authorized the creation of the Federal Reserve System. This rule was that bank note currency should be backed by sound collateral. Such a rule was entirely understandable when private banks had the note-issuing privilege. There appears to be little if any reason for it in the case of note issues of central banks. Nevertheless, for good or ill, all Federal Reserve notes must be based upon collateral.

The original purpose for the creation of the Federal Reserve System, with its note-issuing powers, was to escape the periodic crises in the money market. Consequently, care was taken to insure an adequate supply of currency to meet the needs of business as they arose. Therefore, although the new law insisted upon collateral for note issue, it sought to avoid the awkward rigidity of the old national bank note currency by requiring as collateral something believed to reflect the current needs of business. Member banks needing currency were expected to rediscount at the Federal Reserve Banks short-term business and agricultural paper of a self-liquidating type. The Federal Reserve Banks could deposit such rediscounted paper with the Federal Reserve Agent, who is not only the chairman of the board of directors of the bank but also has custody of unissued notes received from the Board of Governors in Washington, D.C. This requirement that paper rediscounted by member banks with the Federal Reserve Banks be used as collateral was designed to insure (1) an ample supply of currency to satisfy the needs of trade; and (2) the later retirement of such currency by repayment of the commercial paper collateral as the currency needs declined.

Gradually, over the years, the collateral requirements against Federal Reserve notes were relaxed by increasing the list of assets that the Federal Reserve Banks might offer to the Agent as collateral. When member banks were given the privilege of borrowing for fifteen-day periods on the security of U.S. obligations or on paper eligible for rediscount, such member bank notes were made acceptable for use as Federal Reserve note collateral. Also, to facilitate the assembly of gold coin and certificates in the hands of the Federal Reserve Banks, gold and gold certificates were made eligible for use as collateral for notes obtained from the Agent. Finally, in the depression year of 1932 Federal Reserve Banks were allowed to offer U.S. obligations as collateral. This privilege, grudgingly granted at first on a two-year temporary basis, was finally made permanent. Its necessity became apparent in the light of the great expansion of money, mainly Federal Reserve notes, in circulation at a time when nearly all Federal Reserve bank assets were U.S. obligations and gold certificates.

Several observations may properly be made in respect to the collateral requirement.

1. It applies to notes issued by the Agent to the Federal Reserve Bank.

2. It must be equal at least to a full 100 per cent of the notes issued.

3. The Board of Governors may require additional collateral if needed.

3. There is no required proportion of specific kinds of collateral. It may consist altogether of any one kind of collateral or any proportion of the various types, at the convenience of the bank.

4. There no longer appears to be any good reason, either in theory or practice, for maintaining the solemn fiction that collateral requirements insure that the money supply fits the needs of trade or in some way makes Federal Reserve notes safer.

5. The collateral requirement is separate and distinct from the legal reserve requirement for the Federal Reserve notes. The Federal Reserve Banks must hold 25 per cent reserves against both deposit and note liabilities. This reserve requirement applies to Federal Reserve notes only after they have been put into actual circulation by delivery to the member banks. It so happens that, in satisfying the 25 per cent reserve requirement against notes, any gold certificates deposited with the Agent may be counted as reserve.

The Board of Governors may, through the Agent, grant or reject an application of a reserve bank for Federal Reserve notes. Furthermore, it may levy an interest charge, if it sees fit, on notes issued against collateral other than gold certificates. No such charge was made by the Board until April 24, 1947, when, as we learned earlier, it announced that it was invoking its authority to charge interest on Federal Reserve notes. A charge was then made that was sufficient to result in the transfer of interest payments to the Treasury to the amount of approximately 90 per cent of the net earnings of the Federal Reserve Banks after the required 6 per cent dividends to stockholding member banks.[6]

---

[6] *Federal Reserve Bulletin*, May 1947, pp. 518–519. For a highly critical discussion of this application of the interest charge, see Spahr, Walter E., "More on Reserve Board's Illegal Distribution of Federal Reserve Banks' Earnings," *Commercial and Financial Chronicle*, September 18, 1947.

Federal Reserve Bank reserve requirements. As we know, the Federal Reserve Banks are required to carry 25 per cent gold certificate reserves against their deposit and note liabilities. Provisions of this kind have been common in the laws governing central banks, especially since World War I. Of what value are such requirements? Do they add to the security of the domestic currency? Do they insure the convertibility of the currency for purposes of maintaining its foreign exchange value? Do they serve any useful purpose in the present-day world?

Because central bank required reserves, like those of commercial banks, must be left intact, operating reserves in excess of the legal minimum must be kept on hand. The Federal Reserve Banks, for example, have quite properly tried always to maintain a substantial cushion of reserves above the minimum requirements so that they may (1) expand their credit when additional currency and bank reserves are needed; and (2) give up gold for export and for industrial uses without forcing a liquidation of domestic credit system.[7]

Required reserves for central banks appear to be useful mainly as window dressing to satisfy popular demand for high reserves and to put a top limit on the total volume of central bank credit that may be created on the basis of the existing quantity of standard money reserves. How valid and justified are these reasons? First, as to the window dressing effect, there is no doubt that public opinion as to the soundness of the currency may sometimes be influenced by the presence or absence of substantial central bank gold reserves. This psychological effect is stronger when gold convertibility is maintained than when otherwise. There is no evidence, for example, that the transfer of the gold reserves of the Bank of Canada and the Bank of England to a government agency at the outbreak of World War II caused any serious loss of confidence in the inconvertible currency issues of the banks. The second result of required minimum reserves is the limiting effect upon the volume of central bank credit. In the absence of an adequate policy of credit restraint such a limit may be desirable. In 1919-1920, after the first World

---

[7] In 1945, when the Federal Reserve credit expansion during the war had reached the point at which the gold certificate reserves had begun to approach the minimum requirements in force at that time (40 per cent against notes and 35 per cent in gold certificates and other lawful money against deposits), at the request of the Board of Governors, Congress reduced the reserve requirements to the present 25 per cent in gold certificates against both notes and deposits.

War, credit expansion and inflation in the United States, based upon freely available Federal Reserve Bank credit, created a highly unstable situation that resulted in collapse. The boom was brought to a halt, belatedly, partially because of the exhaustion of the excess reserves of the Federal Reserve Banks. However, more often than not, the limiting effect of central bank reserve requirements is of little practical value. As a protection against inflationary overexpansion they tend to appear too late. In our own case today, the excessively high gold reserves make it mandatory that credit restraint be based upon sound credit policy and not on the supply of reserves.

The legally required reserves of the Federal Reserve Banks, therefore, seem to be of little actual value. Excess reserves above the minimum requirements must be carried to insure convertibility for domestic industrial uses and for export. Insofar as any limiting force is to be had from our gold certificate supply, it lies in the changes in the size of the cushion of excess reserves above the minimum requirements.

Membership in the Federal Reserve System

When the Federal Reserve System was organized in 1914, national banks were required to become members and subscribe to stock in the Federal Reserve Banks. State banks, however, were not subject to this compulsion and at first they quite generally refrained from joining. During World War I many state banks, particularly those of the larger cities, entered the system as a matter of patriotic duty. Even so, most state banks remained outside. The number of member and nonmember banks, as of 1955, and the resources of each class, are shown in Table 20.

TABLE 20
Federal Reserve Member Banks and Nonmember Banks, June 1955

	Number of banks	*Total Resources*	*Ratio of resources of each class of bank to resources of all commercial banks*
National banks	4,744	$107,741,000,000	54%
State member banks	1,867	61,945,000,000	31%
All member banks	6,611	$169,686,000,000	85%
Nonmember banks	7,173	29,589,000,000	15%

The case for requiring state banks to become members. A number of reasons are sometimes advanced for requiring all commercial banks, both state and national, to belong to the Federal Reserve System. These reasons include the following:

1. The safety, solvency, and usefulness of banks themselves would be improved by the access to the lending power of the Federal Reserve Banks in time of temporary, seasonal, or emergency needs for funds.
2. The banking system as a whole would be strengthened by bringing all state banks under Federal Reserve supervision.
3. Uniformly applied rules for reserve requirements would strengthen the hands of the Federal Reserve authorities in the application of credit controls.

It must be admitted that these reasons for requiring all state banks to become members of the system do not have a wide appeal to the present nonmember state bankers themselves. Many state banks that have an active commercial banking business are already members. Moreover, state banks in smaller cities find their city correspondent banks willing and able to provide them with funds needed for seasonal and emergency reasons. On the positive side, state banks have specific objections to becoming members. These objections may be summarized as follows:

1. Although now less difficult than before the capital requirements were modified, some small banks find it a serious matter to attempt to satisfy the capital requirements for membership.[8]
2. Many state banks continue to charge exchange when remitting for checks presented through the mail. This privilege, an important source of revenue to some small banks, will not willingly be foregone in order to join the Federal Reserve System.
3. Reserve requirements for member banks are often higher than for nonmember banks.
4. Membership exposes a bank to a whole range of restrictions and regulations not experienced by the nonmember bank.

The actual advantage of membership to the smaller state banks is really not very great. Through their city correspondents they are able to collect their out-of-town checks and to borrow funds as needed. Furthermore, nonmember banks at times are allowed to borrow directly from the Federal Reserve Banks on the security

---

[8] In 1939, 2,389 nonmember banks had inadequate capital to qualify for membership under the old rule. *Banking Studies,* Federal Reserve System, 1941.

of United States Government obligations. It is small wonder, therefore, that they show little enthusiasm for membership.

Questions for Study

1. Why must central banks carry excess reserves if they are to be "lenders of last resort" to the money market?

2. Distinguish between the early policy aims of central banks and the goals of credit policy of modern times.

3. Distinguish between the primary function of central banks and their routine nonpolicy functions.

4. Federal Reserve Bank policy is largely divorced from profit making. Why should this be?

5. The Federal Reserve System is divided into twelve districts. In what way are the actions within these districts unified?

6. Who is the Federal Reserve Agent? What are some of the avenues of influence available to the Board of Governors over the general actions of the individual Federal Reserve Banks?

7. What are some of the important powers of the Board of Governors? What is the Open Market Committee and its duties?

8. What comprises the "other cash" assets of the Federal Reserve Banks? What causes changes in their volume?

9. Examine the statement of condition of the Federal Reserve Banks in Table 19.

    a) How important, at that time, were member bank borrowings in comparison to government securities purchased in the open market?
    b) What was the size of the Federal Reserve "float"?
    c) What was the reserve ratio? How much addition to the outstanding Federal Reserve notes and deposits could be made on the basis of the excess reserves of that time?

10. Why was a collateral requirement placed on the issue of Federal Reserve notes? Why did this requirement fail in its purpose? Why did it prove a handicap to the Banks when they sought to expand the member bank reserves by open market purchases during the depression of the early 1930's?

11. What reasons can you give for having a legal reserve requirement for Federal Reserve Banks?

12. Name some reasons for and against state bank membership in the Federal Reserve System.

17

Operations of the Federal Reserve System

If the Federal Reserve Banks made no loans or investments and merely limited their activities to holding cash deposited with them by member banks, they would exercise no influence over the credit conditions of the money market. Only when they extend credit and thereby create Federal Reserve deposits, available as legal reserves for member banks, and notes for circulation, do they affect the monetary and banking situation. In such a case they can be said to be in "contact with the money market." Such contact is genuinely effective, however, only when member banks are dependent upon Federal Reserve Bank credit for part of their required reserves.

The Federal Reserve Banks have two important and one unimportant contact with the money market. The important points of contact are: (1) purchasing and selling various kinds of securities in the open market; and (2) discounting for and lending to banks that are eligible to apply for Federal Reserve Bank accommodation. The unimportant contact referred to is the power of Federal Reserve Banks to lend directly to individuals, under certain restricted circumstances. Each of these three modes of getting Federal Reserve funds into the market will be examined in turn.

Open Market Operations

The main point of contact between the Federal Reserve Banks and the money market is through the open market transactions in Government securities. Although legally allowed to purchase and sell a number of different types of securities, the Federal Reserve Banks in practice confine their dealings to trading in Treasury obligations and bankers' acceptances.[1]

When the Federal Reserve Banks buy securities in the open market, member bank legal reserves increase by the amount of the purchases. On the other hand, the sale of securities by the Federal Reserve banks causes a reduction in member bank legal reserves by the amount of the sale. These effects of Federal Reserve open market "operations" may readily be traced by some simple examples.

How open market purchases of securities result in additions to the legal reserves of banks. First let us assume that the Federal Reserve Banks purchase $1 million worth of Government securities in the bond market and pay for them by the issue of cashiers' checks drawn against themselves. When the sellers of the securities are member banks, the proceeds of these checks are deposited to the member banks' credit as addition to their legal reserves. The results, in terms of balance sheet changes for member banks and for the Federal Reserve Banks are as follows:

MEMBER BANKS		FEDERAL RESERVE BANKS	
Assets	*Liabilities*	*Assets*	*Liabilities*
Legal reserves:	No change	U.S. securities:	Deposits (member
+ $1 million		+ $1 million	bank reserves):
U.S. securities:			+ $1 million
− $1 million			

Should the sellers of Government securities bought by the Federal Reserve Banks happen not to be member banks, the results are the same so far as member banks' reserves are concerned. For example, if the sellers are nonmember banks, insurance companies, or any other nonbank investors, again payments are made with checks collectible at the Federal Reserve Banks. This time the sellers deposit the checks for credit at member banks which in turn deposit them for credit at the Federal Reserve Banks. In the end, member banks receive new deposits and an equal amount of new legal reserves. This is shown in the following balance sheet changes.

---

[1] The Federal Reserve Banks may also legally buy and sell (1) bills of exchange eligible for discount; (2) tax anticipation obligations of State, county, and municipal governments with maturities up to six months; and (3) acceptances of the Intermediate Credit Banks and national agricultural credit corporations.

NONBANK INVESTOR		MEMBER BANKS	
Assets	*Liabilities*	*Assets*	*Liabilities*
Balances in member banks: + $1 million	No change	Legal reserves: + $1 million	Deposits: + $1 million
U.S. Securities: − $1 million			

FEDERAL RESERVE BANK	
Assets	*Liabilities*
U.S. securities: + $1 million	Deposits (member bank reserves): + $1 million

How open market sales of securities lower bank reserves. The open market sale of securities by the Federal Reserve Banks has just the opposite effect of that of purchases. When member banks purchase securities offered for sale by the Federal Reserve Banks they tender in payment their own checks drawn against their deposits (legal reserves) in the Federal Reserve Banks. The legal reserves of member banks are therefore depleted by the amount of the purchase. The result is that member banks have exchanged reserve balances for securities. When the purchasers of securities are nonbank investors, payment is made by checks on member banks. These the Federal Reserve Banks collect by deducting the amount from the drawee banks' legal reserves.

The fact that dealers in Government securities act as middlemen in the buying and selling transactions makes no difference in the ultimate results. Purchases of securities by the Federal Reserve Banks result in increases in member bank reserve accounts. Sales of securities, in turn, reduce members' reserve accounts. These results are in no way dependent upon the will or action of the member banks themselves. It is easy to see why open market operations have become such a powerful instrument for influencing the supply of banking reserves.

"Involuntary" open market operations. Before April 1955, the Federal Reserve Banks regularly posted a buying rate at which they would purchase bankers' acceptances in the open market from anyone who wished to sell. Purchases under this arrangement were known as "involuntary." The purpose was solely to maintain a market for bankers' acceptances by insuring for dealers and other holders a ready market at a fixed rate of discount. Beginning April 1955, the Federal Reserve Banks ceased to publish such buying rates. Instead, the Federal Reserve Bank of New York, under authorization of the Open Market Committee, has occasionally made purchases of acceptances from dealers, at the going market rates of discount, on both an outright and on a repurchase basis.

During the second World War, to insure an active market for Treasury bills, the Federal Reserve Banks posted a discount rate of three-eighths of 1 per cent at which they would buy Treasury bills in the open market. This was maintained during the war and after until July 1947, when the practice was terminated. While it was in effect, banks or other holders of Treasury bills were able to convert them into cash at any time.

Dealers repurchase agreements. Since 1948 the Federal Reserve Banks have, on occasion, purchased Treasury bills from non-bank dealers in Treasury obligations, with the agreement that they will be repurchased within fifteen days. These agreements allow dealers to sell bills to the Federal Reserve Banks at current prices and later repurchase them at the same price, plus interest at the Bank's discount rate for the time involved. This practice occurs when a tightening of the money market has caused banks to put pressure on dealers to repay loans used to carry security inventories. However, dealers may initiate a sale of this kind only when the Federal Reserve Bank has informed them that the "window is open" for such repurchase agreements.

Direct Advances to Banks

All banks belonging to the Federal Reserve System are entitled to look to their Federal Reserve Banks for accommodition in time of need. They may offer "eligible" paper for discount or they may offer their own notes secured by eligible paper or United States securities.

Let us now examine the effect of discounting and borrowing upon the member bank and the Federal Reserve Bank involved. First, as to the member bank, the discounting of eligible paper is a sale of promissory notes and bills of exchange by the member bank to the reserve bank. The discount of the member's own collateral note by the reserve bank is a loan. Since discounting or borrowing is made necessary by a depletion of the member's reserves, the payment of the proceeds to the member bank is normally made by adding the amount to the member's reserve account and notifying the member. If the member is in need of currency, the reserve bank may ship currency instead of giving credit on the member's reserve account.

Let us assume that the member bank offers for discount its thirty-day note for $60,000 and that the Federal Reserve discount rate on advances to member banks is 2 per cent. How will the balance sheets of the member bank and the Federal Reserve Bank be affected? The discount on $60,000 at 2 per cent for thirty days is $100. The member bank, therefore, receives $59,900 additional credit on its reserve account on deposit in the Federal Reserve Bank. A member bank liability (bills payable) will appear amounting to $60,000. The amount of the discount will come out of and be deducted from some net worth item such as undivided profits. The Federal Reserve Bank assets will be increased $60,000 in the form of "bills discounted" while its deposit liabilities will increase $59,900 and unearned discounts will rise by $100. This may be seen in the changes indicated in the partial balance sheets below.

MEMBER BANK		FEDERAL RESERVE BANK	
Assets	*Liabilities*	*Assets*	*Liabilities*
Reserves in Federal Reserve Bank: + $59,900	Bills payable & rediscounts: + $60,000 Undivided Profits: − $100	Bills discounted: + $60,000	Deposits: + $59,900 Unearned discounts: + $100

Should the bank offer eligible customers' paper for discount, the balance sheet entries would be the same, since discounted customers' paper must be endorsed and is looked upon as a form of borrowing at the Federal Reserve Bank.

The importance of member bank discounting and borrowing. In the early years of the Federal Reserve System, member banks' discounting was the major source of Federal Reserve credit. At that time open market operations were looked on only as a means of obtaining earnings rather than as a part of the mechanism for influencing the volume of credit. Only gradually did open market operations acquire the status of a full-fledged tool of credit policy. However, with the coming of the depression of the 1930's and

World War II, member bank discounting shrank into obscurity and open market operations began to overshadow borrowings by member banks as a source of reserves and currency. However, when the Federal Reserve System reasserted its power to impose anti-inflationary restraint in 1951-1952, member bank discounting again acquired a significant place in Federal Reserve operations. In December 1952, for example, discounting at one time reached $2 billion. The tight money conditions of late 1955 again pushed member bank borrowing over the billion dollar mark. Without a doubt, therefore, the privilege of discounting at the Federal Reserve Banks is still a very valuable one for member banks. Consequently, it is still important to know something of the requirements that must be met in order for member banks to get Federal Reserve Bank accommodation.

Paper eligible for discount. As we know, the original expectation was that member banks would discount customers' notes at the Federal Reserve Banks. The rules governing such discounting were rigorous and technical. Briefly, member banks can discount (endorse and sell) short-term commercial and agricultural paper to the Federal Reserve Banks. The test of eligibility rests both in the shortness of maturities (ninety-day maximum for commercial and nine-month maximum for agricultural loans) and its self-liquidating character. The latter is tested by the origin of the paper itself (trade notes and bills of exchange to finance sales of goods) or the use to which the funds are put. Loans to finance current business and agricultural operations are eligible, but notes to finance speculation or long-term capital needs cannot be discounted. These rules of eligibility, based upon the self-liquidating theory of bank credit, were designed to encourage member banks to make self-liquidating loans and to insure that Federal Reserve credit would properly reflect the needs of trade.

The rules of eligibility proved to be a weak defense against wartime inflation because of the inclusion, as eligible paper, of notes of borrowers to finance the trading in or carrying of U. S. securities. This exception to the strict rules of self-liquidating paper provided the gap through which a great volume of "war paper" found its way into the Federal Reserve Banks during World War I. Their second signal failure to meet the needs of the economy occurred during the crisis of 1930-1933. Because banks were not persuaded by the eligibility rules to stick closely to the making of self-liquidating loans, they were caught without a supply of eligible paper adequate to enable them to get the accommodation needed from the Federal Reserve Banks. Soundness of assets was not enough to qualify a member bank for help from the Federal Reserve if it failed to have eligible paper.

Experience soon indicated that the discount of customers' paper was not entirely convenient for member banks needing additional cash reserves for short periods only. Consequently, since 1916, member banks have been authorized to offer their own promissory notes, secured by eligible paper or by United States obligations, for discount at the Federal Reserve Banks. So long as banks were not heavily fortified with United States obligations, this rule did not lessen the importance of the technical rules of eligibility. It was not until the middle 1930's that eligibility rules lost most if not all of their significance.

Who may discount. One of the privileges of membership in the Federal Reserve System is the right of a bank to replenish its reserves by discounting and borrowing at the reserve bank. Ordinarily nonmember banks are denied this privilege, although in 1933 they were given a one-year emergency privilege to obtain advances from the Federal Reserve Banks, and since 1939 have on occasion been allowed to borrow there on government obligations.

Member bank borrowing on collateral notes. We have seen how, in addition to discounting eligible paper, member banks are permitted to borrow at the Federal Reserve Banks on their own collateral notes. These borrowings, on the collateral of eligible paper or U. S. securities, may be for periods of up to ninety days, although they are generally for much shorter periods. The right of member banks to borrow on their collateral notes enables banks temporarily in need of funds to build up their reserves without discounting customers' notes. Banks prefer such borrowing to discounting, since discounted paper with a definite maturity date is a less flexible means of obtaining funds than is the use of the collateral note. The greater convenience of using U. S. obligations as security for borrowings has now made that method the main reliance of banks seeking advances from the Federal Reserve Banks.

Borrowing on noneligible paper under Section 10b. Belatedly, an attempt was made in 1932 to relieve the difficulty confronting banks that had used up their supplies of eligible paper and government securities. Member banks were given the opportunity to organize into groups and borrow collectively from the Reserve Banks on noneligible paper. In 1935 the Federal Reserve Act was amended by the addition of Section 10b, which permitted Federal Reserve Bank advances to individual member banks on noneligible paper, secured to the satisfaction of the Federal Reserve Bank, for periods of up to four months. Such loans are to bear interest of not less than one-half of 1 per cent above the highest prevailing discount rate. Since the cost of this type of advance is greater than the cost of discounting or borrowing upon United States bonds or eligible paper, it will be used only in case of necessity.

The regulation of the Board of Governors specifically names the types of paper eligible as collateral for advances under this section. In explaining its choice of eligible collateral which may be used by member banks borrowing under Section 10b, the Board says: "Experience has demonstrated that the solvency of banks is better safeguarded by careful regard to the quality of the paper that they acquire than by strict observance of the form that this paper takes. Strict eligibility requirements in the past did not save the banking system from collapse. Greater emphasis on soundness and less emphasis on form is, therefore, a sound banking principle."

Federal Reserve Direct Loans to Individuals and Firms

Originally the Federal Reserve Banks were allowed to lend to and discount self-liquidating customers' paper for member banks only. During the depression of the 1930's, complaints about the inadequacy of bank loan accommodations were widespread and as a result the Federal Reserve Banks were authorized to make direct loans to borrowers other than member banks. These loans were and are made under certain specified circumstances and under the regulations of the Board of Governors of the Federal Reserve System. Briefly, direct loans are now permitted under these circumstances:

1. On authorization of the Board of Governors, a Federal Reserve Bank may discount eligible, well-secured commercial paper for firms unable to obtain adequate credit elsewhere.

2. Under regulations of the Board of Governors, the Federal Reserve Banks are allowed to make advances to individuals and firms (including banks) for periods of not over ninety days on the security of direct obligations of the United States. It is under the provisions of this law that nonmember banks are able to borrow at the Reserve Banks.

3. Section 13b, added in June 1934, provides that under the authority of the Board of Governors, Reserve Banks may make loans to established industrial or commercial firms unable to obtain necessary credit on a reasonable basis elsewhere. Such loans are for working capital purposes and may extend for a period of not over five years. The Federal Reserve Banks may also purchase or agree to purchase such obligations from any financial institution that agrees to assume at least twenty per cent of any loss that arises.

These various privileges granted to others than member banks have not, in the aggregate, played an important part in the credit operations of the Federal Reserve Banks. At times nonmember banks avail themselves of the opportunity to borrow on Government securities. Industrial loans at one time in 1934 reached a peak of about $32 million, but since have diminished in importance. In May 1956, they amounted to only $900,000.

Federal Reserve Bank direct advances to the Treasury. Because of the danger that Treasury dependence upon borrowing from the Federal Reserve Banks might become a general source of inflation, the law has consistently limited the power of the Banks to purchase securities directly from the Treasury. However, they are permitted to hold a maximum of $5 billion of such directly purchased securities. This privilege, periodically renewed, is scheduled to expire again on June 30, 1958. On occasion the Treasury finds it useful to obtain temporary funds by the sale of special certificates of indebtedness to the Federal Reserve Banks. This enables it to cover the gaps, during quarterly tax-paying months, between realized tax revenues, often delayed in processing, and expenditures for interest and cash redemption of maturing securities.

Federal Reserve Operations and Monetary Policy

We have examined each of the three avenues through which Federal Reserve credit is made available in the money market. The first, open market operations, enables the Federal Reserve Banks to take the initiative in increasing or decreasing the volume of member bank reserves. The importance of this method of influencing the availability of reserves is readily seen. It operates quickly and impersonally in the money market. The second, advances to member banks, arises at the initiative of the member banks rather than out of decisions of the Federal Reserve authorities. Because member banks are entitled to accommodation when they apply for loans at the Federal Reserve Banks, restraint or lack of it can be imposed only by varying the "cost" of member bank borrowing. This the Federal Reserve authorities can do by changing the Federal Reserve discount rates and by erecting such barriers as moral suasion against excessive member bank borrowing.

The application of monetary and credit policy involves not only the use of open market operations and discount restraints but also certain other tools, such as the changing of reserve requirements and the imposing of selective credit controls. The problems associated with the application of monetary policy will be examined in later chapters.

Questions for Study

1. What are the avenues through which the Federal Reserve Banks come into contact with the money market? When is such contact "effective"?

2. When the Federal Reserve Banks, through the Open Market Committee, purchase U. S. securities, what are the effects on the balance sheets of member banks and the Federal Reserve Banks in case the securities are purchased from (a) member banks; (b) nonbank sellers?

3. What are the results of security sales by the Federal Reserve Banks?

4. What are "involuntary" open market operations? How were they used during the war?

5. When are dealers in government securities permitted to make repurchase agreements with the Federal Reserve Bank?

6. Why were the Federal Reserve Banks given authority to make direct loans to industry?

7. When a member bank discounts at the Federal Reserve Bank, what are the results on:
   a) The member bank's legal reserve position?
   b) Its liabilities?
   c) The assets and liabilities of the Federal Reserve Bank?

8. Early expectations were that rediscounting of eligible paper would be the main reliance of member banks desiring to improve their reserve positions. Why were the rules of eligibility set up as they were? Why did it develop that the technical rules of eligibility lost most of their significance?

9. What is Section 10b? How did its introduction improve the service that the Federal Reserve Banks can perform for members?

10. Why do the Federal Reserve Banks have authority to make limited advances directly to the Treasury? Why do they not have unlimited privileges in this respect?

18

Canadian and British Banking

We can better understand our own banking system if we compare it with those of other countries. Especially is it helpful to know something about the banking structures of Canada and England, both of which have economies similar to our own and are served by banking systems that provide some interesting contrasts. A brief look at the banks of Canada will reveal how Canada has attempted to meet banking problems that in many ways resemble ours. A survey of the British banking system will aid, in some small measure, our understanding of a complex but surprisingly efficient mechanism that at one time was the financial hub of the modern world and today still provides the leadership for the large part of the trading world known as the Sterling Area.

The Canadian Banking System

The chartered banks. Nine chartered banks make up the commercial banking system of Canada.[1] Because the Canadian banking law permits the establishment of branches (both at home and

---

[1] Besides the chartered banks there are nearly eighty trust companies and loan companies, three provincial government savings banks, plus two Quebec savings banks, that receive trust funds and savings accounts. The trust companies invest trust funds under legal restrictions governing trustees. The loan companies lend on real estate and purchase government securities. Also the Industrial Development Bank, organized as a subsidiary of the Bank of Canada, is able to make longer term or capital loans to small and medium-sized businesses engaged in manufacturing, processing, refrigerating, ship building, generating and distributing electricity, and commercial air service when such businesses cannot find credit on reasonable terms elsewhere. *Canadian Almanac and Directory,* 1956, pp. 30, 69–72. For a recent description of the Canadian Banking System, see Jamieson, A. B., *Chartered Banking in Canada,* Toronto, The Ryerson Press, 1953.

abroad), and because a large minimum subscribed capital requirement of $1,000,000 has been adopted, Canada has built up a banking system consisting of a few large banks with a total of over 4,000 branches rather than a host of small unit banks such as we have in the United States. The charters issued under the Bank Act have a life of only ten years, giving occasion for a regular revision of the law at the end of every decade. This plan has the obvious advantage of bringing the banking law before the public for scrutiny at regular intervals, a practice in clear contrast with the sporadic efforts at amending the banking laws of the United States.

The size and the availability of numerous branches of the Canadian banks enable businessmen to obtain adequate accommodation from a single bank instead of compelling them to borrow from several banks, as often happens in the United States. Banks therefore become intimately acquainted with the borrower's affairs and can more safely extend him needed assistance than might otherwise be possible. Moreover, the law (Section 88) permits banks to obtain a first lien on that part of the borrower's goods which is listed as security when the loans are made. This privilege exists in the case of loans to dealers in the products of the extractive industries (agriculture, forestry, mining, and the like), loans to farmers on threshed grain, and loans to manufacturers. To protect the other creditors of businessmen who borrow from banks, loans made under Section 88 must be registered in the office of an appropriate agency in the province of the borrower. The liens of banks are superior to those of unpaid vendors whose claims were unknown to the bank when the loans were made. Claims to goods in process are not affected by a change in form, and when goods originally subject to the lien are sold, any substitute goods bought by the borrower come under the lien. If the borrower defaults on a bank loan or embarks upon a policy that displeases the banker, the latter may take possession of the goods. The arrangement is mutually advantageous to bank and borrower. The bank receives the same degree of protection as that afforded by warehouse receipts; the borrower, because of the superior security offered, can obtain more assistance from his bank than would be possible if he were not able to give the bank a preferential lien. At the same time he is allowed a flexibility in the use of his goods and in the disposal of them that would be impossible to obtain through the use of warehouse receipts.

Canadian chartered banks, in general, have confined their lending to financing the short-term credit needs of agriculture, commerce, and industry. Yet at times they have made excursions into the field of longer-term financing. In 1955 the Bank of Canada had occasion to criticize their making of "term loans" and their purchase of corporate securities as violations of Canadian banking tradition, and induced them to agree to abandon such practices. In 1956 the Bank obtained their agreement to maintain a minimum liquidity position (legal reserves, Treasury bills, and call loans) equal to 15 per cent of their demand deposits. To assist Canadian farmers, the banks are allowed to make medium-term farm improvement loans guaranteed up to 10 per cent by the government. Such loans, secured by liens on farm equipment, bear a maximum interest rate of 5 per cent. When such loans are for over $2,000, banks may take a real estate mortgage as added security.

The chartered banks are prohibited from making loans on any bank stock. Until 1954, except for farm improvement loans, they were also prohibited from lending on real estate. However, the National Housing Act of 1954 authorized the banks to make housing loans on real estate mortgages.[2] They cannot, however, make ordinary real estate loans on agricultural land.

The prohibition of loans upon real estate has undoubtedly exercised a wholesome influence upon the assets of the chartered banks, but at the same time it has prevented farmers from having access to banks for financing purchases of land and for making improvements. In another respect, however, the Canadian system has been of distinct benefit to agricultural regions. The branch banks collect deposits in the more populous areas, where funds are plentiful, and lend them in the prairie provinces, where capital is naturally scarce. The Canadian farmers in the prairie provinces obtained loans in the past at rates substantially below those paid by the farmers of the Dakotas.

Since 1954 the chartered banks can lend on the security of oil reserves in the ground, a right that reflects the growth in importance

---

[2] Cf. Atkinson, T. H., "Canadian Money Market Enlarged," *Commercial and Financial Chronicle*, June 24, 1954, Sec. 2, p. 7.

of the oil industry. Following the trend in the United States, the chartered banks are now permitted to make personal consumers' loans, both unsecured and secured by chattel mortgages or other liens on household goods and cars. Such loans are limited to 5 per cent discount on the nominal amount of the loan. When repayable over a twelve-month period, this makes the maximum simple interest on the unpaid balance amount to about 9¾ per cent.

Branch banking in Canada. Canadian banks are permitted to establish branches throughout the Dominion. Consequently, banking is highly concentrated, with nine banks and their numerous branches carrying on all of the commercial banking business. In 1954 there were over 4,000 branches and sub-agencies of chartered banks.

Although the branch banking systems of Canada have been criticized as tyrannical in loan practices, and for sending young managers into the country districts to gain experience at the expense of the communities they are supposed to serve, by and large they have proved successful. With branches spread across the provinces, they weathered the severe agricultural depression of the 1920's and the even greater collapse of the 1930's. They present a sharp contrast to the sorry experiences of American banks during the same periods. Credit for their depression-proof stability can in considerable measure be ascribed to the country-wide branch systems. As is well known, depressions shrink income of farm regions to such an extent that there is set up an "adverse balance of trade" with the industrial areas. With unit banking of the type found in the United States, agricultural banks find survival difficult and often impossible as deposits are withdrawn to enable bank customers to keep up their expenditures in the face of declining incomes. A branch system, such as that of the Canadian banks, is free from this threat since, on the average, funds lost from the country areas turn up in the branches in the industrial sections of the country. Another advantage of country-wide branch systems is the opportunity given for geographical diversification of risks.

Note issues. Before the organization of the Bank of Canada, the country's paper currency consisted of Dominion notes and the notes of the chartered banks. A modest amount of elasticity in the currency issue was introduced by the privilege of increasing the note issue of the banks by 15 per cent each autumn. In addition, the Minister of Finance was authorized to lend Dominion notes to the banks to enable them to increase the currency in circulation. This central banking function of the Minister of Finance was not properly regulated, with the result that the Dominion note issue became so excessive in the 1920's that the Dominion Government found itself unable to maintain gold redemption.[3] The Canadian Bankers' Association said in respect to the situation: "There exists no properly constituted body which can admit responsibility for the general supervision of credit or exchange in Canada."[4] In 1933 a Royal Commission, appointed to study the Canadian banking and currency situation, recommended the establishment of a central bank.

The organization of the Bank of Canada put an end to the Dominion note issue. Gradually the note issues of the chartered banks were reduced until now the Bank of Canada is the sole currency-issuing agency.

The Bank of Canada. To bring about proper control and order to the monetary system a central bank, the Bank of Canada, was established in 1935. Owned by the Dominion Government, it took over the currency-issuing function; it was authorized to make loans to the chartered banks and to the Quebec savings banks, and to purchase and sell ninety-day acceptances and the securities of the Dominion and the provincial governments. It was further permitted to deal in the short-term securities of the United Kingdom and the United States Government and to buy and sell coin and gold and silver bullion. The Bank is fiscal agent for the Dominion Government and may make short-term advances to it or to any provincial government. Holding the gold reserves for the whole Canadian banking system, the Bank of Canada originally was required to maintain gold reserves of at least 25 per cent against its notes and deposits. In 1940 this reserve requirement was eliminated and all gold was given to the Foreign Exchange Board.

---

[3] Curtis, C. A., "Credit Control in Canada," *Papers and Proceedings of the Canadian Political Science Association,* 1931, Vol. II, pp. 101–122.

[4] Quoted in the *Report of the Royal Commission on Banking and Currency in Canada,* 1933, p. 66. This Report contains a useful survey of the Canadian banking and monetary system as well as recommendations for improvements.

The bank was nationalized in 1938 in response to the parliamentary opinion that the vital sovereign function of controlling the money supply should respond to the sovereign will of the government.

Control over the money market. During the postwar years the Bank of Canada's authority over the Canadian money market was at first handicapped by the narrowness of the Treasury bill market. Treasury bills were held mainly by the chartered banks and the Bank of Canada. To support the market, the Bank of Canada informally was committed to purchase, at the issue rate, all bills offered to it by the banks. In this way banks were able to expand their cash reserves at will and without penalty, and therefore could escape the restraints arising from direct borrowing at the Bank of Canada. The Bank could not use open market sales or the discount rate to restrain monetary and credit expansion. After 1953, the Bank encouraged the development of a dealers' market in Treasury bills by offering repurchase accommodation to dealers. It encouraged the chartered banks to finance dealers on a day-to-day basis and to sell bills in the dealer market rather than directly to the Bank. Consequently, the Bank is now able to make use of open market operations to better advantage to influence the reserve position of the chartered banks.[5]

Regulation of banks. Before 1924 the Canadian banks were free from external regulation. The failure of the Home Bank in 1923 brought a demand for some sort of supervision, with the result that in 1924 an Inspector General of banks was provided for. The Inspector General is empowered to examine the chartered banks once each year and to require monthly statements of condition. Previously, a certain amount of self-regulation was imposed by a legal requirement that authorized the audit of the banks' books by representatives of the stockholders. Chartered banks now make annual reports to the Minister of Finance, giving information as to earnings, expenses, and other statistics for publication.

Reserve requirements for the chartered banks. Before 1935 the chartered banks had no legal reserve requirements. After the

[5] Neufield, E. P., *The Bank of Canada Operations, 1935–54,* Canadian Studies in Economics, No. 5, Toronto, University of Toronto Press, 1955, pp. 7, 16–35, 36–53. See also "Monetary and Banking Developments in Canada," *Monthly Review,* Federal Reserve Bank of New York, August 1956.

organization of the Bank of Canada, the chartered banks were required to carry reserves in the form of deposits and notes of the Bank of Canada to the amount of 5 per cent of their deposit liabilities. However, in 1954 the law was changed to permit the Bank of Canada to establish required reserves for chartered banks with minimum and maximum limits of 8 and 12 per cent respectively. This authority, reminiscent of that of the Board of Governors, is designed to enable the central bank to take strong action, if needed, to counteract any sudden inflationary tendencies.

The English Banking System

The English banking system has four important divisions: (1) the joint stock banks; (2) the Bank of England; (3) the accepting houses; and (4) the discount market.

The joint stock banks. The bulk of the commercial banking business is in the hands of eleven London "clearing banks," having total deposits of over £6.3 billion.[6] In 1953, these banks operated 8,894 branches. In Scotland, banking is in the hands of seven joint stock banks operating 1,763 branches.

Before 1946, except for the prohibition of the issue of notes and the requirement of an annual report or statement of condition to the Registrar of Joint Stock Companies, the joint stock banks were free from legal regulation or supervision. This freedom was in marked contrast to the American practice of close supervision and regulation by public authority. But the law that nationalized the Bank of England on March 1, 1946, also established the right of the Bank to exercise certain controls over the joint stock banks. Specifically, the Bank, when public interest requires, may request information from and make recommendations to bankers. Furthermore, it may, if authorized by the Treasury, issue directives to secure performance of its recommendations. A banker who is the object of such a directive is entitled to a hearing by the Treasury.

The deposits of the joint stock banks. The deposits of the joint stock banks comprise two classes: (1) current accounts, cor-

---

[6] *Monthly Digest of Statistics,* London, No. 113, May 1955, pp. 110–111. There were nine other English banks, with deposits at the end of 1952 of about £200 million. "British Banking Statistics," *Records and Statistics,* June 20, 1953 (discontinued after this date).

responding to our checking accounts; and (2) deposit accounts, corresponding to our time deposits. Some idea of the relative size of the deposits of English banks and the cash reserves maintained against them may be derived from Table 21.

TABLE 21
Deposits and Cash Reserves of the London Clearing Banks*
(In millions of pounds)

Years (Monthly Averages)	Total Deposits	Current Accounts	Deposit Accounts	Coin, Notes, and Balances with the Bank of England	Reserve Ratio
1944	4,153	2,765	1,388	437	10.5
1945	4,692	3,127	1,566	492	10.4
1946	5,097	3,377	1,720	523	10.2
1947	5,650	3,690	1,959	473	8.3
1948	5,913	3,850	2,062	486	8.2
1949	5,974	3,940	2,034	496	8.3
1950	6,014	3,979	2,036	497	8.3
1951	6,162	4,095	2,067	511	8.3
1952	6,083	3,961	2,122	505	8.3
1953	6,256	3,995	2,261	509	8.1
1954	6,495	4,141	2,354	528	8.1
1955	6,454	4,113	2,340	529	8.2
1956 (March)	6,164	3,941	2,223	506	8.2

* Monthly Digest of Statistics, London, June 1949, p. 121; March 1956, p. 108.

The reserve ratio shows remarkable stability, reflecting the force of custom and tradition among British banks, which, unlike American banks, are entirely free of legal reserve requirements. Moreover, a cash reserve ratio of 10 per cent against all deposits was approximately the same as the cash reserves required of American banks before increased reserves requirements were instituted after 1935 to absorb the excess reserves arising from United States gold imports. An interesting change in the reported cash reserve ratios of English banks appeared in 1947, when the reserve ratio dropped to 8.3 per cent. This change, however, represented no real change in the reserve position of the English banks. Before 1947, because the banks issued published statements on different days of the week, each bank "window dressed" its cash reserve position on the statement day by shifting some of its earning assets (money at call and at short notice) to other banks and thus acquiring, for the time being, a larger balance at the Bank of England. Thus, when banks found their cash position reduced below the customary level, it was possible for them to keep up appearances by this scheme of mutual aid. It happened, therefore, that when the Bank of England was acting to reduce bank reserves and impose credit restraint, window dressing practices enabled the banks to postpone adjustment while clinging to the appearance of maintaining their traditional reserve ratios.[7] But this came to an end with the adoption of a uniform date for issuing statements of condition by all banks.[8]

Loans and investments of joint stock banks. The portfolios of the joint stock banks are so arranged as to give a proper degree of liquidity. The most liquid of bank assets is money at call and lent at short notice (up to ten days). Such loans are made to the bill market, which we shall examine later, and to some extent to the stock exchange. Next in order of liquidity are bills of exchange and treasury bills that have been discounted. These bills derive their liquidity from the fact that they are of short maturities and may be allowed to "run off" at maturity (not replaced by new bills) in case the banks wish to increase their reserves. The investments of the banks are mainly long-term and short-term government issues. Finally, the banks advance funds to customers either in the form of overdrafts on current accounts or on ordinary loans. Table 22 shows the relative importance of the different elements of the joint stock banks' portfolio.

During the war, money at call and short notice, bills discounted, and advances to customers declined sharply. In their place appeared a new item, "treasury deposit receipts," which was a non-negotiable form of twelve-month Treasury obligation issued to banks. By the end of the war, about £2,000 million were outstanding and comprised a major item in British bank assets. They have now disappeared from the scene.

The accepting banks. The financing of foreign trade is a vital matter in such a country as England. It is not surprising, there-

---

[7] On this point see Sayers, R. S., *Modern Banking*, London, Oxford University Press, 1948, pp. 37–40.

[8] "The Changing Shape of Britain's Monetary System," *Midland Bank Review*, February 1948, p. 4

TABLE 22

Percentage Ratio of Different Types of Assets to Total Deposits of the London Clearing Banks*

Year (Monthly Averages)	Money at Call and Short Notice	Bills Discounted		Treasury Deposit Receipts	Invest- ments	Advances to Customers
		Treasury	Others			
1929	8.6%	12.7%			15.8%	55.5%
1935	7.1	13.3			30.7	38.0
1938	6.6	12.2			27.9	42.8
1944	4.3	4.1		33.3%	28.0	18.0
1947	7.9	12.7		23.1	26.0	19.6
1948	8.0	12.6		21.7	25.0	22.3
1949	8.5	15.3		16.4	25.2	24.1
1950	9.1	21.6		7.1	25.0	26.7
1951	9.2	19.9		4.0	26.4	29.6
1952	8.7	15.7	1.7	.1	32.6	30.2
1953	7.6	18.5	1.0	0.0	34.6	27.7
1954	7.0	17.2	1.3	0.0	35.7	27.8
1955	6.8	15.7	1.8	0.0	33.3	31.3
1956 (March)	7.0	16.8	2.2	0.0	32.6	30.3

* *Monthly Digest of Statistics,* London, June 1949, p. 121, and March 1956, pp. 108–109. Holdings of Treasury bills and commercial bills of exchange (trade and bankers' acceptances) were not reported separately until 1952.

fore, that special institutions to assist in this financing developed at an early date. One of the most important methods of caring for the credit needs of foreign traders is through the use of the letter of credit and the banker's acceptance. In England the issuance of letters of credit and the acceptance of drafts drawn thereunder have been concentrated mainly in the hands of accepting houses that specialize in the hazardous business of evaluating the credit standing of the applicants for letters of credit. Not only do they "accept" for domestic importers, but, in order to finance exports and the shipment of goods between foreign countries, they furnish the same service for foreign clients and foreign correspondent banks. These accepting houses receive a commission for their service, varying from 1 to 2 per cent per year, depending on risk involved and the client's credit. The joint stock banks also engage to a limited extent in the accepting business.[9]

Although the accepting banks do not engage in commercial banking, they carry on, in addition to their acceptance business, a rather extensive variety of financial operations, which have been well described by Hartley Withers in the following quotation: [10]

Other functions of the merchant firms and the accepting houses are their activity in general finance and in exchange business. Both of these functions arise out of their old business as merchants, which gave them close connection both with the governments and the business communities of foreign countries. Their connection with the governments naturally led to their providing credit facilities for them, and to their handling loans and other operations which these governments might have to conduct in the London market. Many of them act as regular agents of foreign governments, making issues of bonds on their behalf, paying their coupons, and conducting amortization and other business in connection with their loans; and their connection with the general business community inevitably led to their doing a considerable exchange business with foreign countries, financing drafts on them for the purposes of travel and the innumerable other arrangements which necessitate the transfer of credit from one country to another. It should perhaps be added that the Bank of England's court of directors is largely recruited from the ranks of the accepting firms and finance houses. . . .

The London accepting banks suffered a serious setback with the decline in international trade during the depression of the 1930's and with the appearance of government trading during the war years. Both events sharply reduced the importance of acceptances for financing foreign trade. In addition, the emergence of the dollar as the leading currency of the world has served somewhat to dim the prospects of the London accepting banks. The postwar revival of world trade and the continued strength of the Sterling Area, of which the sterling bill is the key, have helped to restore the vitality of the London acceptance business.

The discount market. The offerings of accepted bills of exchange are taken off the market by a class of specialists who are

---

[9] *Report of the Committee on Finance and Industry*, pp. 40–42. For an interesting discussion of the manner in which certain merchants of high credit standing took over the function of accepting drafts and hence were called "merchant bankers," see Withers, Hartley, *The Meaning of Money*, New York, E. P. Dutton & Co., 1916, pp. 160–161.

[10] *The English Banking System*, N. M. C. 1910, p. 57. There are now 15 of these merchant banks. They undertake, along with their other functions, to act as issuing houses for domestic issues. Cf. Macrae, Norman, *The London Capital Market*, London, Staple's Press, 1955, pp. 77–8.

known by the general term of *bill brokers*. These specialists possess a great volume of information concerning the credit of merchants and the standing of different classes of bills of exchange, data which they use to derive an income for themselves. These specialists fall into three general classes: [11] (1) the running brokers; (2) the retail dealers; and (3) the discount houses. The running brokers, who are relatively unimportant, act merely as intermediaries between the sellers of bills on the one hand, and banks and other investors on the other. They work for a commission and invest no capital of their own. The retail dealer operates in substantially the same manner as do bill brokers in the American bill market. They purchase bills and resell them at a profit, but in the meantime they must borrow funds with which to carry their portfolio of bills. The discount houses, although engaging in some retail business, are primarily engaged in buying bills and holding them until maturity. The funds to carry these bills are, for the most part, obtained by borrowing on call or short notice from banks or other lenders, and from general deposits on which interest is paid at a rate somewhat above that offered by the banks. The discount houses operate on a very narrow margin of owned capital, and their large volume of borrowed capital places them in an extremely vulnerable position in respect to the money market.[12] Whenever the banks, as a whole, find it necessary to improve their cash reserves, they do so by reducing their loans to the discount houses and other money market dealers. These in turn must obtain cash immediately, and they can do so only by discounting acceptable bills with the Bank of England or by borrowing from it on the security of bills or government securities. Thus, it is mainly through the discounting of bills for the bill brokers that the Bank of England acts as a lender of last resort for the English money market.

Since the depression years of the 1930's, discount houses have greatly expanded their portfolio holdings of Treasury short-term

---

[11] Withers, Hartley, *The Meaning of Money,* Chapter VIII. Also see the *Report of the Committee on Finance and Industry,* pp. 43–45.

[12] In 1952, nine discount houses reported capital of £28.5 million and borrowings and deposit liabilities of £969.7 million; against these were assets made up of cash of £9.8 million, bills of £701.9 million, and bonds of £208.3 million. *Records and Statistics,* June 20, 1953.

obligations. This trend was accentuated by the war and postwar expansion of Treasury bill issues. In the Treasury bill market the discount houses hold newly issued bills for a period, and, later, as the bills approach maturity, sell them to the joint stock banks and others in the money market who desire the high degree of liquidity furnished by the maturing bills. In addition to the earnings from carrying the bills, the discount houses gain by the difference between the higher rate at which they originally discount the bills and the somewhat lower rate of discount taken when they sell the maturing bills to the banks.

As a result of mergers and some retirements from the field, the number of discount houses declined from eighteen in 1941 to twelve in 1954. In the heyday of the London commercial bill as an instrument for financing world trade, the bill market—that is, the discount houses and the bill brokers—performed the significant function of policing the quality of bills appearing in the market. Unsound bills and the acceptances of overextended houses were quickly discriminated against, with the result that corrective steps had to be taken by their issuers. From long experience and careful attention to the credit standing of merchants and accepting banks, the bill brokers and discount houses were able to insure the high quality of bills entering the London money market. With the decline in importance of the commercial bills and the rise in importance of Treasury bills among the assets of the discount houses, this traditional function has to a considerable extent fallen into disuse.[13]

The Bank of England. Founded in 1694 for the purpose of making loans to the hard-pressed government, the Bank of England is closely bound up with traditions which have the force of law itself. Before March 1, 1946, it was privately owned and, except for the law governing its advances to the government and its note issue, and the requirement that a weekly statement be published, it was free to carry on banking functions in any way it desired.

Inaugurating the socialization policy of the Labor Party, the Bank of England Act of 1946 become effective on March 1.

---

[13] Cf. Higgins, Benjamin H., *Lombard Street in War and Reconstruction*, 1949, National Bureau of Economic Research, New York, pp. 84–5. Also, "British Banking Statistics," *Records and Statistics*, June 20, 1953.

Under the nationalization law, the private stockholders transferred their shares to the Treasury and received in return 3 per cent government obligations. It was arranged that the annual return on the government obligations issued in exchange for the Bank's stock should be equal to the average annual dividends paid by the Bank during the twenty-year period preceding March 31, 1945. These obligations may be redeemed by the Treasury on or after April 1966.[14]

The management of the Bank is in the hands of the Governor, a Deputy Governor, and sixteen Directors, appointed by the King. The Treasury, after consultation with the Governor of the Bank, may give such directions to the Bank as appear necessary in the public interest. The purpose of nationalization lay in the belief that economic planning, of the sort visualized in the program of socialization, required some direct control over the creation of the monetary and credit tools of the economy. The change is of little more than symbolic importance, since the Bank under private ownership was operated in the public interest and in close co-operation with the Treasury requirements.

Upon nationalization, the Bank was given specific authority, with the approval of the Treasury, to issue directives to the joint stock banks. This privilege formalizes the Bank's traditional influence over the actions of the banks and insures the conformance of the commercial banks with practices thought to be in the interest of current public policy. An example of the use of this authority occurred in 1952, when the Bank ordered the reduction of the length of the period of acceptance credits and urged that appropriate bank credit be made available to agriculture.[15]

Circulating notes of the Bank of England make up all of the currency of England and Wales, with the exception of minor token coins.[16] Seeking to prevent inflationary expansions of bank note

---

[14] *Federal Reserve Bulletin*, May 1946.

[15] *Midland Bank Review*, May 1952. These "selective" controls appear to have become firmly embodied among the instruments of credit policy. Banks have been requested to restrain consumer credit lending and advances to finance companies. *Ibid.*, May 1954, p. 5.

[16] The eight Scottish joint stock banks and certain banks in Northern Ireland have the right to issue notes backed 100 per cent by Bank of England notes and in addition a small volume of fiduciary or uncovered notes. *Report of the Committee on Finance and Industry*, p. 28.

currency, the Bank Act of 1844 required (1) a separation of the note-issuing function from banking operations of the Bank of England by the establishment of the *issue* department; and (2) that all notes issued, with a few minor exceptions, should be fully covered by gold. The resulting rigidity in the currency supply resulted in the rapid development of the use of checking accounts as a substitute money. Even so, it was periodically necessary to "suspend" the Bank Act in order to permit the additional issue of "uncovered" notes to meet the currency needs of critical times.

Today, Bank of England notes are entirely fiduciary—that is, are issued against government securities held by the issue department instead of against gold. A first main breach in the full gold cover rule came in 1928, when the Bank of England took over £260,000,000 of currency issued by the Treasury during World War I. Later, during World War II, the gold holdings of the Bank were transferred to the government Exchange Equalization Account and were replaced by government securities.

The banking department of the Bank of England obtains notes for its use by depositing gold, at times when it has gold, or government securities with the issue department. Since 1939 any gold accumulations of the United Kingdom are held by the Exchange Equalization Account.[17] Consequently, the Banking Department has no gold and can obtain none, so it must deposit government securities with the Issue Department to obtain notes for circulation.

Something of the nature of the Bank of England's affairs may be seen in the statement of condition given in Table 23. As can be seen, the deposits of the banking department are nominally divided into three classes. "Public deposits" are the funds belonging to the various branches of the British Government. Of the "other deposits," the "bankers' deposits" are the balances of the British banks, whereas "other accounts" include balances of Dominion and foreign banks, deposits of the Indian and colonial governments, and the deposits of financial houses and private customers. The assets of the banking department (right-hand side of the balance sheet) consist of: (1) government securities, including Treasury bills acquired on the initiative of the Bank; (2) discounts and

---

[17] The Account pays for gold purchases with pound balances borrowed in the London money market. In contrast, the U. S. Treasury buys gold with funds obtained from the deposit of gold certificates with the Federal Reserve Banks.

advances, which include bills brought to the Bank for discount and advances to the bill market and to the Bank's own customers; (3) bank notes issued by the issue department but not in circulation; and (4) gold and silver coin.[18]

TABLE 23

Bank of England Returns, April 11, 1956*

(In millions of pounds)

Issue Department

Notes issued:			
In circulation	1,850.1	Government debt and securities	1,871.2
In banking		Other securities	0.8
department	25.3	Gold coin, bullion, and other coin	3.4
Total	1,875.4	Total	1,875.4

Banking Department

Capital	14.5	Government securities	272.2
Rest	3.1	Discounts and advances	25.8
Deposits:		Other securities	15.3
Public deposits:		Cash reserve	27.2
Public accounts	15.9		
Treasury special	3.2		
Other deposits:			
Bankers	231.3		
Other accounts	72.5		
Total	340.5	Total	340.5

* Compiled from *The Economist*, April 14, 1956.

Although for many years the Bank of England refused to admit its responsibility as a lender of last resort in time of stress, it is now firmly committed to that practice.[19] This means that it is accessible to eligible borrowers at their option, and that it has a

---

[18] *Report of the Committee on Finance and Industry*, pp. 29–30.

[19] Like any central bank, the Bank of England can render this aid only if it is well fortified with reserves. Although its directors were reluctant to admit that the Bank of England was substantially different from other banks, there was a tacit admission of its responsibilities in the fact that its reserves were normally higher than those of other banks and that it did come to the rescue of the money market by heavy rediscounts of bills and advances in times of trouble. On this point, see Bagehot, Walter, *Lombard Street*, New York, E. P. Dutton & Co., pp. 43–44, 64, 164–172.

moral responsibility to make advances at all times of financial emergency. In this respect its duty is similar to that of the American Federal reserve banks. There is one important difference, however, between the English and the American central banking arrangements. Whereas American member banks go directly to the reserve banks for accommodation, the English joint stock banks traditionally do not; instead, they reduce their loans to the bill market, and the bill brokers and discount houses in turn go to the Bank of England. Each Thursday the Bank normally fixes a rate, known as the "Bank Rate," at which it will buy acceptable bills offered to it. Discount houses may either sell their bills outright to the Bank or borrow at the Bank. To be eligible for purchase, commercial bills should "bear at least two good British names, one of which must be the acceptor." [20] In actual practice the money market now always gets its accommodation at the Bank by borrowing against Treasury bills rather than by the discount of commercial bills.[21] This arises both from the comparative abundance of Treasury bills and from the more favorable rate on advances against such bills that has often existed. In addition, like American member banks, the London discount houses doubtless find it more convenient to borrow on Treasury bills than to discount commercial bills at the Bank.

The bank rate is effective in the British money market partially because of the custom of the "clearing banks" of varying their own interest rates so as to keep them in a certain relation to the bank rate. This relation, in general, is that: (1) traditionally the clearing banks allow interest on time deposits at a rate 2 per cent below the bank rate; (2) the rate charged on advances to customers is from ½ to 1 per cent above the bank rate; and (3) the rate charged on call money is somewhat above that paid on deposits.[22] Of course, it is entirely possible that, in times of excessive reserves,

---

[20] *Report of the Committee on Finance and Industry*, pp. 43–44. It is reported that, before the end of the 1930's, there was some direct discounting at the Bank of England by the joint stock banks, a violation of an 80-year-old tradition. Cf. Sayers, R. S., "Central Banking in the Light of Recent British and American Experience," *Quarterly Journal of Economics*, May 1949, p. 201.

[21] *Midland Bank Review*, May 1954, p. 4.

[22] *Report of the Committee on Finance and Industry*, p. 32. In September 1953, when the Bank rate was reduced to 3½ per cent, the clearing banks reduced the rate of interest paid on deposits to 1¾ per cent. *Midland Bank Review*, May 1954, p. 4.

competition for loans will force the market rate of interest below that justified by the customary relation to the bank rate. The small number of banks in the English money market and long experience with the leadership of the Bank of England strengthens the moral effect of the bank rate. When the Bank of England wishes to make its rate effective, it does so by disposing of part of its assets. This it can do by refusing to replace maturing short-term Treasury bills. Thus, "cash" is absorbed from the money market and the bill market is forced to resort to the Bank, where borrowers feel the effect of the bank rate on new advances and rediscounts.

The discount rate of the Bank of England, like that of the Federal Reserve Banks, appears to have lost much of its significance. Abandonment of convertibility of the pound and the use of exchange controls removed most of the traditional reasons for changes in the bank rate. Changes in the rate were no longer needed as a means of protecting the London money market from short-term capital withdrawals. The function of the Bank, therefore, is mainly to provide the funds needed to enable the commercial banks to meet the business requirements of the country and the requirements of the government in its pursuit of full employment. This it does mainly through the purchase of Treasury bills. However, late in 1951 and in 1952 the postwar easy money policy was reversed. The Bank's discount rate was raised from 2 per cent to 4 per cent and the money market was allowed to tighten. The previous easy money policy, followed in the interest of postwar reconstruction and full employment, had contributed to an unfavorable international situation known as the "dollar shortage." The tight money policy and the internal credit restraint at that time aided in improving the balance-of-payments situation. Therefore in Britain, as in the United States, monetary policy has re-achieved something of its old significance—a most necessary development should currency convertibility become a reality.

Questions for Study

1. What features of the laws applicable to banking in Canada tend to encourage:
   a) Large- rather than small-scale banking?
   b) Careful reappraisal of the banking laws from time to time?

c) Adequate extension of credit to farmers and manufacturers who are unable to borrow on warehouse receipts?

2. Can the chartered banks make real estate loans?

3. Why have the branch banks of Canada been of benefit to farmers? In what way are they of less assistance in financing farmers than are American banks?

4. How stable were the Canadian banks during the great depression of the 1930's? What characteristics of the Canadian banks made for their stability in the face of depression?

5. Who owns the Bank of Canada? What reason can you give for this? Do you think that the Bank of Canada's policy could differ from that adopted by the government? Should it?

6. In what way do Canadian banks have reserve requirements similar to those applied to American banks?

7. What is the form in which the British banks carry their cash reserves? How large are such reserves?

8. How do the British joint-stock banks increase their cash reserves when needed?

9. What are the "accepting banks"? What is their main function? In what way are they of service to foreign governments?

10. Where do the discount houses obtain the funds needed to carry their inventories of bills? What is their place in the Treasury bill market?

11. In what ways do Bank of England funds get into the English money market?

12. Why is the Bank Rate set by the Bank of England so important as a device for credit control?

V___

PRICE CHANGES AND THE DETERMINANTS OF THE VOLUME OF MONEY

19

Price Movements and Their Consequences

Up to this point our study has acquainted us with the nature of modern money systems and with the nature and functioning of banks and the banking systems that provide the supply of money in our world today. We are now ready to examine the relationship of money and banking to the behavior of the price level and to the level of income and employment. Therefore, we shall next look at the ways of measuring changes in price levels and some of the consequences of such changes. Then we shall study the determinants of the supply of money and the demand for money, and their relation to the determination of the price level and the level of income and employment.

A central theme in the study of monetary problems is the behavior of prices. Some method of measuring average price movements is needed both for analyzing causes and as guides in the attempt to modify and control the movement of prices. The basic monetary problem, as it relates to economic welfare, arises from the difference in the pace and magnitude of changes which occur among prices of different types. The cost of living of wage earners, wholesale prices, agricultural prices, and durable goods prices, to mention a few, show considerable divergence in their movements. Index numbers that measure particular groups of prices are, therefore, of vital importance if factual data are to be used to enlighten the study of monetary problems.

The Measurement of Price Changes

The index number as a device for measuring price movements. The index number is a device that permits the measuring of the average behavior of a number of individual prices. Its practical usefulness derives from the fact that prices have some tendency to cluster together so that a movement in the price index may be taken as indicative of a similar movement in the bulk of the particular prices that are included in the index. If a price index be made too broad and all-inclusive, so that it averages too wide a variety of prices, its movements will show but little of practical use in respect to relative movements of different types. It is this relative movement of prices that is important. Too broad an index conceals important relative movements of the several groups of prices, and for this reason has less practical value than the more specialized types of index.

The choice of prices to be measured. The use to be made of an index number must largely govern the particular group of commodities whose prices are to be measured. For example, if the need is for a measure of changes in the cost of living of workingmen, the index must be based upon such things as the retail cost of food, clothing, shelter, and fuel of the type used by such individuals. Not only will such an index contain a somewhat different list of commodities from that of an index designed to measure living costs of business and professional groups, but it will also differ for workingmen in different geographical areas. On the other hand, if the price index is designed to measure price changes most important to the profit prospects of businessmen, it must be based largely on the prices of commodities at wholesale. Such an index is fairly sensitive to cyclical change and is, therefore, of more use than cost-of-living index numbers for discovering cyclical developments. Of even greater use for discerning cyclical price changes is the special group of commodities whose prices are sensitive to cyclical changes in business. Such commodities include farm products, rubber, silk, crude petroleum, and the like. Index numbers of prices of such raw materials are, therefore, highly sensitive to cyclical change. Students of the problem of international trade, on the other hand, are concerned with the behavior of price indexes of imported and exported goods.

Numerous specialized index numbers are used to measure the changing price trends for narrow groups of commodities. Such specialized indexes are of interest both to businessmen whose economic welfare is bound up with the behavior of such prices and to students of general business fluctuations. The latter are especially interested in the relative movements of different groups of prices as they bear upon the basic economic situation. The multiplicity of such specialized index numbers of prices may be seen by examining the list currently carried by the *Federal Reserve Bulletin*. Index numbers of wholesale prices published in the *Bulletin* are compiled by the Bureau of Labor Statistics, and are constructed for separate groups of commodities and combined into a general wholesale price index based upon 2,000 separate commodities.[1]

Measuring the purchasing power of money. Both theoretical and practical difficulties are presented by any attempt to make an index number that properly measures the purchasing power of money in a broad sense.[2] Theoretically, there is the question of what, precisely, should be the prices covered by such an index. It is sometimes argued that the most significant index of the purchasing power of money is one that would include only prices of things that enter into *final consumption,* weighted in proportion to the amount of money income spent for each by the consuming public.[3] Thus, prices of capital goods, securities, real estate, goods at wholesale, and the like, would be excluded, for they do not constitute a part of the consumers' goods purchased by the public. The justification for such a view rests on the belief that greater significance attaches to changes in the buying power of the consumer's dollar than to changes in the buying power of money held by businessmen. On the other hand, a case may be made for the creation of a comprehensive index embodying the prices of everything bought or sold by the use of money. Such an index number measures the purchasing power of money *for all uses.* This is in sharp contrast to an index designed to measure only the price level of consumers' goods alone. If one is seeking a measure of the average purchasing power of money in the hands of all types

---

[1] See "Description of the Revised Wholesale Price Index," *Monthly Labor Review,* February 1952, pp. 180–187.

[2] The price index is the reciprocal of the purchasing power of money over those commodities included in the index.

[3] Cf. Keynes, J. M., *Treatise on Money,* New York, Harcourt, Brace & Co., 1930, Vol. I, pp. 54, 57–58.

of users, when spent over the whole range of purchases and settlements made with money, this comprehensive type of index is desirable.[4]

The construction of index numbers of prices. The technical method of construction of index numbers involves complex statistical processes, the details of which need not detain us here. It is appropriate, however, to mention briefly some of the outstanding problems that arise in making index numbers, for an awareness of these problems will be of help in using and interpreting index numbers as well as in understanding their limitations:

1. The selection of the general group or class of prices to be measured.

2. The choice of the particular commodities whose price movements may be taken as representative of the price movements of the general group or class.

3. The collection of data on prices of the chosen commodities.

4. The choice of a base period with the prices of which the prices of any given year or years are to be compared.

5. The calculation of a properly weighted average of prices, or index number, showing a comparison with the base.

The selection of the general group of prices for measurement by the index number will depend on the purpose for which the index is wanted. Since it would obviously be difficult to include all possible commodities, sample commodities must be chosen to represent the general group. Expediency demands that the size of the sample be kept as small as is consistent with reasonable accuracy. So far as possible, basic commodities are used, because their price fluctuations are representative of the price movements of closely related commodities. To get proper quotations on prices of commodities sold in different markets requires the choice

---

[4] Such an index of prices was once calculated by Carl Snyder. For a description of this index, see his "Measure of the General Price Level," *Review of Economic Statistics*, February 1928. The items he included in his revised index and the weight assigned to each were as follows:

Industrial commodity prices at wholesale	10	Realty values	10
Farm prices at the farm	10	Security prices	10
Retail food prices	10	Equipment and machinery prices	10
Rents	5	Hardware prices	3
Other costs of living items	10	Automobile prices	2
Transportation costs	5	Composite wages	15

of a sample from each of the several quotations. For example, the Bureau of Labor Statistics obtains its price quotations on a particular commodity from a number of sources considered representative of the whole market, and these sample prices are averaged. The large numbers of unstandardized commodities that result from brands and product differentiation present complications. This fact is illustrated by the problem of choosing representative prices of motor cars.

Collection of adequate price data is relatively easy in the case of staple commodities traded in on organized exchanges. It is difficult where trading is mainly in the form of private transactions in which higgling plays a part. Similarly, retail price data on any comprehensive basis present difficulties.

The choice of the base period. The ordinary index number is a percentage comparison of the average prices of a given year with the average prices of the base period or base year. A near base is more desirable than a remote base for several reasons. First, it is easier to visualize price variations as percentages of a near base. For example, if one wishes to follow the movements of prices during the years 1953, 1954, and 1955, an index that compares those prices with the prices of the period 1947-1949, the present base for the Bureau of Labor Statistics' wholesale price index, would be more easily comprehended than one that compares those prices with prices of the year 1926 or 1913. The advantage of such an index over one based upon 1890 is even more marked. Second, remote base years make more difficult the task of including in the index important new commodities that may not have existed in the base year, and the proper weighting of old ones. In contrast, a near base makes possible the construction of an index giving a more valid picture of recent price changes. Yet another reason for preferring a near instead of a remote base is the tendency for errors and biases, which exist in even the most carefully constructed index numbers, to be exaggerated as the base becomes more remote.

The method of construction of index numbers. An index number is useful only if it presents a reasonably true picture of the behavior of the group of prices which it represents. To furnish a correct picture, it must be properly constructed. The theory behind the proper construction of index numbers is a complex one and need not concern us here. Our purpose will be sufficiently served if we examine briefly the most common methods in actual use.

The simple arithmetical average of price relatives is one common type of price index. The manner of calculating such an index may be easily seen. Let us suppose that we first construct an index number that will show the relative changes in the price of a single commodity such as wheat, taking the average price of wheat during the year 1949 as the basis of comparison. The average price of wheat during 1955 may be compared with the average price of wheat during 1949 by calculating the percentage of the 1955 price to the price in 1949. Thus, if wheat in 1949 were $2.00 per bushel and if a similar grade of wheat in 1955 were $2.50 per bushel, the 1955 price would be 125 per cent of the 1949, or base year, price. Similar calculations for subsequent years would give a series of percentages showing the relationship of the price of wheat for each given year to the price of wheat in 1949. This series of percentages, beginning with the year 1949 as 100, comprises an index number of the price of wheat. Similar index numbers of the prices of other commodities can be constructed in the same way. The simplest method of combining these indexes of individual prices to form a general price index is to find the arithmetical average of the percentages for each year. The resulting average is then taken as the index number for the group of commodities. This is illustrated in Table 24.

TABLE 24

Index Number Based upon Price Relatives

Commodity	1949 Price	1949 Percentage Ratio to 1949 Price	1955 Price	1955 Percentage Ratio to 1949 Price
Wheat	$2.00	100	$2.50	125.0
Butter	.70	100	.60	85.5
Wool	.40	100	.30	75.0
Coal	8.00	100	10.00	125.0
		4) 400		4) 410.5

Index for 1949 prices .... 100.0   Index for 1955 prices.. 102.6

The simple arithmetical average of price relatives provides an index number which is simple to calculate and has often been used. But this type of index has certain serious defects. First, it measures imperfectly the purchasing power of money, because it fails to take into account the differences in importance of the different commodities. The price movements of each commodity have the same weight in the final average as those of every other commodity. But some commodities obviously are of more importance than others and should therefore exert more influence in the index number. A makeshift remedy for this defect may be achieved by introducing the more important commodities more than once. For example, to include both wheat and flour would increase the weight of changes in the price of wheat, for wheat and flour prices tend to move together.

A second characteristic of index numbers constructed from arithmetical averages of price relatives is their upward bias. This means that prices that move upward exert more influence in the index number than do those which move downward. The reason for this lies in the peculiar nature of percentages that may rise to unlimited heights but cannot fall more than from 100 to zero. If, therefore, compared with the base year the price of one commodity doubled, its price relative would be 200. If at the same time the price of another commodity were cut in half, its price relative would be only 50. In the final arithmetical average of the price relatives, the effect of doubling one price is much greater than the effect of cutting the other in half. But to the ordinary observer it would seem that the movement of one price canceled the other. The index number, however, would show that average prices had increased.[5]

The aggregate type of index number. In constructing its wholesale price index, the Bureau of Labor Statistics has adopted a method that furnishes a practical solution to the problems of weighting and minimizing biases. The average base period price of each of the 2,000 commodities used in this index is multiplied by the quantity of the commodity marketed during a given repre-

---

[5] To avoid this upward bias the geometric mean may be used. This mean is calculated by multiplying the price relatives together and extracting the nth root. Cf. Fisher, Irving, *The Making of Index Numbers*, New York, Houghton Mifflin Co., 1927, pp. 33–34.

sentative period. The average price for the given year for which a comparison with the base year is to be made is also multiplied by the same quantity. This gives, for each commodity, the value of the amount sold (1) at the base year price; and (2) at the given year price. The total value of all commodities at the given year price is then compared with the total value of all commodities at the base year price. The result is a percentage figure, which is the index number. To put it in another way, the index number is the percentage relationship between the values of a given bill of goods at the given year and the base year prices. This is illustrated in Table 25.

The formula for the construction of this type of index number is:

$$I = \frac{\Sigma \; p_1 \; q}{\Sigma \; p_0 \; q} \times 100$$

when p_0 is the price of each commodity in the base year,
        p_1 is the price of each commodity in the given year, and
        q is a representative quantity of each commodity.

Price Dispersion

A rise or fall in the price level results from the movement of the mass of individual prices that make up the general average. But by no means does it follow that particular or individual prices move in proportion to movements of the general price level. On

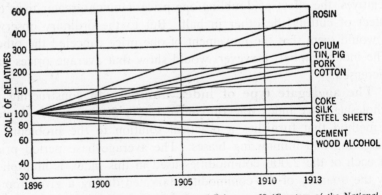

Mills, F. C., The Behavior of Prices, *p. 68 (Courtesy of the National Bureau of Economic Research, Inc.).*

Chart 8. Lines of Trend Measuring the Average Rates of Change in Individual Commodity Prices Between 1896 and 1913.

TABLE 25

Aggregate-Type Index Number

Commodity	Price		Quantity			Total Value	Price		Quantity			Total Value
			BASE YEAR						GIVEN YEAR			
Wheat	$1.00	×	400,000,000	bu.	=	$ 400,000,000	$ .95	×	400,000,000	bu.	=	$ 380,000,000
Butter	.40	×	1,500,000,000	lb.	=	600,000,000	.36	×	1,500,000,000	lb.	=	540,000,000
Wool	.14	×	400,000,000	lb.	=	56,000,000	.21	×	400,000,000	lb.	=	84,000,000
Coal	4.00	×	300,000,000	tons	=	1,200,000,000	3.24	×	300,000,000	tons	=	972,000,000

Aggregate value at base year prices .... = $2,256,000,000   Aggregate value at given year prices = $1,976,000,000

Index number, percentage of given year aggregate of
  base year aggregate   100   87.5

the contrary, some individual price movements exceed and others are less than the movement of the general average. This is true both of price movements of a long-run or secular nature and of short-run or cyclical price changes.

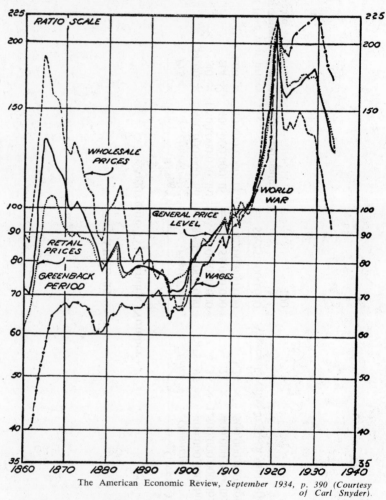

The American Economic Review, *September 1934, p. 390 (Courtesy of Carl Snyder).*

Chart 9. General Price Level in the United States, with Three Leading Components Annually from 1860. 1913 = 100.

This tendency of individual prices to scatter, called *price dispersion,* is at the root of many problems that pertain to money and prices. Especially is this true of cyclical price changes. If all prices moved together at the same time and in the same proportion, costs of production would remain in line with selling prices, and disturbances to business enterprise resulting from general price changes would be greatly reduced.

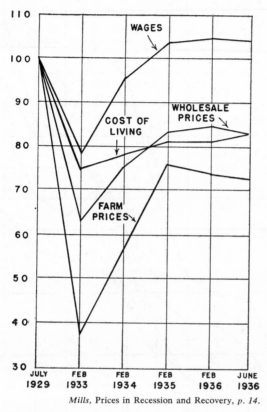

Mills, Prices in Recession and Recovery, *p. 14.*

Chart 10. Movement of Prices During Recession and Recovery.

Dispersion of individual prices. The tendency of individual prices to scatter in the face of long-run general price changes may be easily seen in Chart 8. The average annual rate of change in price of each of a selected group of commodities is shown for the period 1896-1913. This dispersion of prices, which persists over a long period of years, is mainly due to basic changes in the demand for the different commodities and in their costs of production. It is but little affected by the monetary and other forces that caused an increase in average wholesale prices from 66 to 100 (1913 = 100).[6]

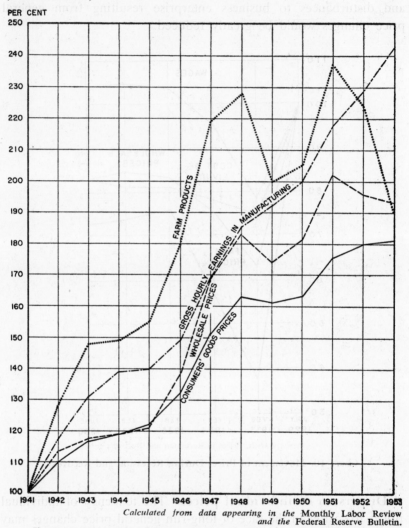

PER CENT

Calculated from data appearing in the Monthly Labor Review
and the Federal Reserve Bulletin.

Chart 11. Movement of Prices During the War and Postwar Period.

Not only is there marked long-run dispersion among the prices of individual commodities, but also groups of prices show differ-

---

[6] Cf. Mills, Frederick C., *The Behavior of Prices,* New York, National Bureau of Economic Research, 1927, pp. 65–69, for a discussion of differences in trends of individual prices.

ences in behavior. Chart 9 shows both the secular and the cyclical dispersion among wholesale prices, retail prices, general prices, and wages for the years 1860-1934. Charts 10 and 11 show the dispersion among different groups of prices during the depression and recovery period 1929-1936 and the war and postwar period 1941-1953.

Considerable interest now exists in the differences in behavior of prices of various commodities during depression and recovery. During depressions, some prices fall sharply while others show but little change. Those commodities whose prices move widely are called "sensitive," and those whose prices move but little are called "insensitive." The reason for such marked differences in behavior has been responsible for no little discussion, with which we are not directly concerned at this time.

The Effects of Changes in the Price Level

Economic disturbances provoked by changes in the general level of prices arise mainly from the failure of incomes, debts, and individual commodity prices to change proportionally. In the preceding section, we examined briefly the dispersion in movement that takes place among different types of prices. The effects of such price dispersion will next occupy our attention. These effects fall into two categories: (1) modifications in the distributions of wealth and income; and (2) the effect on business activity.

General price movements are of two general types: short-run or cyclical changes, and long-run or secular changes. Cyclical price changes are associated with the up-and-down swings of the business cycle. Such price movements are of varying magnitude, depending upon the intensity of the cycle, and contribute to the cyclical fluctuations in the level of business profits. Furthermore, during more acute cyclical changes, price fluctuations may be large enough to create violent shifts in the distribution of income, bestowing largess upon one group at the expense of others. During wartime inflation, the rise in prices is essentially cyclical in nature but more violent than the usual peacetime cyclical price increases. Long-run or secular price movements, on the other hand, are the changes in price levels over a period of time covering several cyclical movements. For example, if during a certain period of time the low point of prices in each succeeding depression and the high point in each succeeding boom tend to rise, the secular trend of prices is upward. When the secular trend of prices is downward, succeeding cyclical troughs and peaks of prices become progressively lower with the passing of time.

Effects of price changes upon income distribution between debtors and creditors. One may hardly attempt to justify the particular distribution of wealth and income that exists at any one time in economic society. But one may, nevertheless, very properly object to capricious shifts in the existing distribution induced by changes in the price level. Yet such a change does occur whenever the price level rises or falls to any appreciable extent.

It is well recognized that rising prices, for instance, tend to enrich debtors at the expense of the creditors. Because debts call for the repayment of a given number of dollars, a rise in prices almost certainly will reduce the buying power of creditors' fixed money receipts. On the other hand, unless pursued by unusually bad fortune, the debtor will find repayment easier than before because of a rise in the money value of anything he has to sell. Falling prices have just the opposite result. The fixed incomes of creditors grow in purchasing power while the luckless debtor finds his money income shrinking in the face of rigid and irreducible debts. Nor may one properly argue that the self-reversing tendencies of prices will eventually restore the losses and lead to ultimate justice. Upswings in prices, whether cyclical or secular, are not necessarily followed by equal and corresponding downswings. Furthermore, new debt structures involving new individuals and adjusted to the new price levels follow any marked changes in prices. During a period of low prices that follows an earlier high price period, new debts are created and old debts are adjusted to the lower price level. To hope that a subsequent rise in prices would correct the injustices of the falling prices would be to disregard the new injustices that rising prices would heap upon the heads of a new set of innocent creditors.

When price inflation takes extreme forms, as it did in parts of Europe after World War I, old debt structures may be almost completely extinguished. This occurred in Germany in 1921-1923, when the paper mark fell to one-trillionth of its gold value. Such results are especially damaging to small and middle-class savers holding savings bank deposits and bonds. Thrift becomes a mockery in the face of acute inflation.

On the other hand, extreme deflation, such as occurred after 1929, may be so severe as to wipe out altogether the equity of debtors in their property and to result in the transference of owner-ship to the creditors. The plight of many American farmers during the Great Depression well illustrates this fact.

The effects of price changes upon business incomes. Incomes of businessmen are residual in nature. After their contractual obligations in the way of wages, material costs, and debts are met, the remainder goes to the businessman as his share. Anything that increases or decreases the gross income of a business, without causing a proportional increase in its expenses or costs, will expand or contract, as the case may be, the size of the residual amount going to the owners. A rise or fall in the level of commodity prices tends directly to increase or decrease the gross income of business. At the same time, some costs—for instance, raw materials—will also change. But some important costs are "sticky" and respond slowly to the movement of commodity prices. Sticky costs are those controlled by custom, legal regulation, monopoly, and long-term contracts. Although by no means absolutely inflexible, these costs adjust slowly to the general commodity price situation. During rising prices, interest and principal payments on pre-existing debts are unaffected. The cost of public utility and transport services can increase only after the adjustments in rates can be wheedled out of regulatory commissions. Basic wage rates of labor tend to be adjusted belatedly to a rising price level. However, the appearance of overtime with the upswing in business activity largely offsets some lags in the adjustment of the basic scale. Furthermore, vigorous union action sometimes results in the inclusion in wage contracts of escalator clauses and rights to reopen wage negotiations in case of changes in the cost of living. Consequently there has been a material reduction in the opportunities for business gains from wage lags during inflationary periods. Still there is a substantial segment of employed workers—salaried and non-unionized—whose money incomes lag behind wholesale price changes. The gains of business arising from the lag in costs during periods of rising prices are sometimes called *windfall* profits to indicate that they are the result of the fortuitous circumstance of a rising price level instead of a reward for efficient management and meritorious anticipation of economic trends. Not only do windfall profits result in unjust enrichment of the businessman at the expense of other income getters, but also they encourage overexpansion of investment and booms.

Not all businessmen, however, are in a position to profit excessively from rising prices. This is particularly true of business enterprises whose prices or rates are subject to public control. Costs of such firms rise with rising general prices, yet rates charged for their services can be raised only when the regulating authority gives consent.

Just as rising prices with lagging costs give windfall gains, so falling prices with lagging costs result in windfall losses. Interest rates and wages are difficult to bring down, and their stickiness in times of falling commodity prices results in undeserved losses. To be sure, if invention and improved industrial technique were causing a fall in money costs that corresponds to the fall in prices, the change in prices would not be objectionable. But, as a practical matter, one can hardly expect any uncontrolled price movement to meet this exacting requirement.

The effect of changing prices on employed workers. A good many employed workers are not so situated as to benefit from overtime pay and are without union support for increased wages. Consequently they suffer a decline in real income as their salaries and wages lag behind the advancing cost of living. Moreover, even those wage earners whose hourly money wages keep up with the rising living costs often fail to participate in the increased productivity of the economy arising from technological improvements. When prices fall, lagging wage rates tend to increase labor's share in the national income. But this gain to labor depends primarily upon a gradual and moderate rather than a rapid fall in prices. Sharply falling prices destroy labor's advantage by causing a decline in business activity and employment.

Long-run price changes and business activity. The long-run price trend has been an object of deep concern to students of monetary problems. During the late 1920's, this concern led to great interest in the question of the adequacy of the world's monetary gold supply to maintain the postwar level of prices. The basis of this interest in the long-run price trend rested in the widely held belief that depressions are prolonged and exaggerated by a falling price trend, whereas shorter depressions and longer periods of prosperity characterize periods of long-run rising prices. The tangible evidence offered to support this belief is found in Table 26, which embodies the findings of Dr. Willard L. Thorp as quoted by Professor W. C. Mitchell in his study of business cycles.[7]

TABLE 26

The Relative Duration of Prosperous and Depressed Phases of Business Cycles in Periods of Rising and Falling Trends of Wholesale Prices in the United States and England

——UNITED STATES——			——ENGLAND——		
Price Trends		Years of Prosperity per Year of Depression	Price Trends		Years of Prosperity per Year of Depression
1790–1815	Prices rising . . .	2.6	1790–1815	Prices rising . . .	1.0
1815–1849	Prices falling . .	.8	1815–1849	Prices falling . .	.9
1849–1865	Prices rising . . .	2.9	1849–1873	Prices rising . . .	3.3
1865–1896	Prices falling . .	.9	1873–1896	Prices falling . .	.4
1896–1920	Prices rising . . .	3.1	1896–1920	Prices rising . . .	2.7

The moral of the data appearing in Table 26 seems to be that downward trends in prices must be avoided if depressions are to be kept at a minimum. There appear to be reasonable grounds to support the above conclusion. It is well known that falling prices are unpopular with businessmen, since they impose a reduced level of profits and, at times, losses. The stickiness of wages and interest charges contributes to the embarrassment of businessmen faced with falling prices. A scaling-down of such interest charges and wage rates can come about only by depression and unemployment. Furthermore, long-run upward price trends were generally characterized by more than normal increases in the monetary gold supply, whereas falling price trends generally have been accompa-

---

[7] *Business Cycles, The Problem and Its Setting,* New York, National Bureau of Economic Research, 1927, p. 411, quoted with the permission of the publisher.

nied by a smaller increase in the supply of gold. To the extent that prosperity was brought to an end by a shortage of bank reserves, and relief from depression was facilitated by the accumulation of a plentiful supply of reserves, rapid increases in gold available for bank reserves permitted the expansion phase of the cycle to continue longer and to hasten the termination of depression. Contrarily, slower rates of increase in gold tended to shorten the prosperous period and lead to longer depression.

Objections to the conclusion that falling price trends are undesirable. The conclusion that long-run falling prices increase the length of periods of business stagnation and are therefore highly undesirable is open to criticism on several grounds:

1. A decline in the price level need not depress business if it is accompanied by an equal reduction in costs arising from technical improvements.

2. The mere fact that prolonged periods of depression appear at the same time as falling secular price movements is no proof that depression is caused by falling prices. It may be argued with equal facility that depressions cause the declining price trend or that both are the result of some common cause and neither the cause of the other.

3. As presented by Mitchell, the evidence is biased in the direction of proving the conclusion that falling prices promote depression and rising prices promote prosperity. This bias arises from the manner in which the turning points in the secular price movements are related to cyclical movements. For example, the downward trend of English prices began with the depression of 1873 and continued irregularly until 1896. The latter year marked both the beginning of the upward trend of prices and the end of a period of depression. Thus, the period 1873-1896, constituting the period of the downward price trend, is biased in favor of depression because both the beginning and end are depression periods. The period 1896-1920 is in turn biased in the direction of prosperity. It begins in 1896 at the start of a business revival and ends in 1920 at the end of the long war and postwar boom. Periods of downward price trends include an extra period of depression, but the upward price periods include an extra period of prosperity. The choice of turning points in this manner can hardly be avoided, but such a choice inevitably provides a biased picture of the relation between price trends and the prevalence of depression.

4. The terms *prosperity* and *depression* as used by Mitchell have no very exact meaning. They cannot be defined quantitatively but are merely relative terms.[8] It follows that the existence of more or fewer

---

[8] *Business Cycles, The Problem and Its Setting*, p. 382.

months of "depression" as compared with months of "prosperity" may mean much or little, depending on the intensity of the depression and prosperity experienced.

5. The behavior of the per capita real income of the United States during periods of rising and falling trends of prices points to the conclusion that national economic welfare improved more rapidly during periods of falling prices than during the periods of rising prices. This evidence, presented in Table 27, does not prove that the rate of economic advance might not have been even more rapid during periods when prices were falling, had prices risen instead. But at least it raises serious doubts as to the validity of the widely accepted belief that downward price trends in the United States have been economically objectionable.

TABLE 27

Increase in Per Capita Real Income in the United States, 1850-1928*

Period	Price Trend	Income at Beginning	Income at End	Gain in Real Income	% Gain for Period	Average Annual % Gain for Period
1850–1860	Upward	$ 69	$ 82	$ 13	18.8	1.88
1870–1880	Downward	79	111	32	40.5	4.05
1880–1890	Downward	111	169	58	52.2	5.22
1890–1900	Irregular	169	232	63	37.2	3.72
1900–1910	Upward	232	262	30	12.9	1.29
1913–1928**	Upward and stable	368	541	173	47.0	3.13

* Data from W. I. King's *The Wealth and Income of the People of the United States,* New York, The Macmillan Co., 1917, p. 129.
** *Encyclopaedia of the Social Sciences,* Vol. XI, p. 206.

The relation of short-time price fluctuations to business activity. Short-time or cyclical fluctuations in business activity are generally accompanied by corresponding changes in the price level. High or rising prices tend to accompany prosperity, and low or falling prices characterize depressions. So closely are price fluctuations associated with changes in business activity that some regard cyclical changes in business as being essentially price phenomena. Such a view is understandable in the light of the fact that common causes lie behind both price and business fluctuations.

Any extensive examination of the causes of short-time price changes must be postponed until a later chapter. It is enough for our present purpose to suggest here that changes in the profit prospects of business tend to slow down or to speed up the tempo of business activity. Changes in business tempo are introduced by altering the rate of spending money. Through changes in the rate of spending, changes both in business activity and in the price level are brought about. If the supply of all commodities were perfectly elastic, changes in the rate of spending money and in business activity would not require changes in prices. But in fact the supply of commodities is not perfectly elastic. Changes in the rate of spending do, therefore, lead to changes in prices.

So long as cyclical fluctuations in business activity occur, it seems unlikely that cyclical price fluctuations are to be avoided. It is not at all clear, moreover, that a complete avoidance of fluctuations in business activity is either possible or desirable. In the past, periods of rapid growth in business activity have frequently accompanied a rapid exploitation of new inventions or newly found resources. Such developments, unquestionably, both quickened the whole industrial pulse of the times and left society immeasurably improved by the immense expansion of productive facilities. Without a flexible, expanding monetary supply and an upward movement of prices (either absolutely or relatively), these periods of rapid forward movements would have been unlikely if not entirely impossible. Such bursts of economic advance were probably beneficial in spite of the inevitable reactions and periods of readjustment that followed. The case for complete business and price stability is weakened by the prospect that such a goal might be obtained only at the price of stagnation and lack of progress.[9]

Although there undoubtedly are forces deeply imbedded in our economic structure that make for "appropriate" changes in output and prices, we must not become blinded to the fact that fluctuations both in business activity and in prices may become excessive. In such a case they cease to be a necessary adjunct of desirable economic change in a free money economy and become instruments of evil and destruction. Under these circumstances, the part played by price movements in inducing changes in business activity becomes important.

Disturbances to business stability arising from short-run price changes. Those price movements which facilitate fundamen-

---

[9] Cf. Robertson, D. H., *Banking Policy and the Price Level*, London, P. S. King & Son, Ltd., 1926, pp. 6–18 and 22.

tal economic changes and adjustments can be said to be desirable. Even when the process involves an expansion in the nature of a "boom," one may temper his criticism on the grounds that the boom made possible the vast and rapid expansion of the new capital equipment needed to establish some new and vital industry. Yet, by and large, most cyclical price movements cannot be justified upon such grounds, for they tend too often to exceed the bounds of economic necessity. Regardless of the originating force, once under way, such price movements tend to abandon their passive role and to become themselves active causes of economic fluctuations.

The reasons for the cumulative and self-generating nature of cyclical price movements are not difficult to understand. In the first place, let us assume that the monetary system possesses sufficient elasticity to accommodate itself to further price movements. This elasticity may come from a variation in the velocity of spending money, a variation in the quantity of money, or both. Without elasticity in the supply of money, cyclical price movements could hardly occur. A cyclical upswing in commodity prices, with lagging production costs, creates windfall business profits. Businessmen become optimistic and attempt to expand productive capacity. Bank credit is utilized to accomplish this expansion, and the rise in prices continues. But this expansion in new investment cannot continue indefinitely. Either rising costs and increased output reduce the previous optimistic expectations, or a disappearance of excess reserves in the banking system requires that credit expansion be brought to an end. The result is a reversal of the trend, a decline in the rate of new investment, falling prices, and diminished business activity.

When prices fall, lagging costs cause business to suffer windfall losses. Business expectations are made worse by the fall in prices, and activity declines. An additional unfavorable factor appears in the shape of forced credit liquidation that may be imposed upon business by the banks. This is especially likely to occur when depression leads to business and bank failures. The banks believe themselves to be acting in self-interest when they refuse loans to borrowers whose solvency is in question and when they reduce the volume of their loans in order to improve their liquidity. But such forced liquidation imposed by the banks tends to aggravate the drop in commodity prices and to make the situation of the businessman more acute.

Those who would introduce monetary control as a means of stabilizing prices and business activity believe that two benefits might be achieved. First, a stable price policy would prevent the development of powerful upswings in business activity, for it would prevent an expansion of money and prices so necessary for an upswing in business. Second, by avoiding price movements, the added cumulative effects of windfall profits and losses might be minimized.

Questions for Study

1. What does an index number tell? Why was the comprehensive index prepared by Snyder of but limited practical use?

2. Contrast the index number based upon averages of price relatives with the aggregative type used to measure U. S. wholesale prices. What are the advantages of the latter?

3. Why is price dispersion at the root of so many economic problems?

4. What is the nature of the price dispersion shown in Chart 8?

5. Examine Chart 9. How account for the long-run dispersion among wholesale prices, retail prices, and wages?

6. Examine Charts 10 and 11. Can you explain:
   a) Why different groups of prices behaved as they did?
   b) What the economic consequences of their behavior were?

8. Why don't the evil consequences of cyclical price movements cancel out? Do longer-run price movements cancel out?

9. What are windfall profits and losses? Why do they arise? Why are they objectionable?

10. Why, at the end of the 1920's, was there so much concern over the possibility of an inadequate increase in the output of gold?

11. Can you give some reasons why a long-run falling price level might not be disastrous to employment?

12. What economic results arise from cyclical movements in prices? Why do they tend to become cumulative? Self-reversing?

13. Does it appear likely that all short-run price level changes can be abolished by monetary action?

14. What are "appropriate" fluctuations? How are they related to economic growth?

20

The Supply of Money

We are now sufficiently acquainted with the nature of our monetary and banking system to enable us to take an over-all look at the monetary system and the determinants of the supply of money. The supply of money held by the public in spendable form consists of (1) net checking accounts in commercial banks; (2) notes of the central banks in actual circulation outside of banks; and (3) any currency and coin issued by the Treasury and in circulation outside of banks. This is the stuff that makes up our media of exchange and that plays such an important part in economic life.

Our money supply arises out of the actions of the Treasury, the Federal Reserve Banks, and the commercial banks. These three money-creating agencies acquire assets of various kinds and issue in payment liabilities or debts, payable on demand, that are monetary in form and readily acceptable in the discharge of debts and the making of payments. The Treasury acquires gold, silver, and other assets, and issues in payment gold certificates and Treasury currency. The Federal Reserve Banks acquire United States securities and the promissory notes of banks, and issue in payment deposit and Federal Reserve note liabilities. Commercial banks, likewise, acquire borrowers' notes and securities, and issue in payment checking account money. Thus the monetary supply in reality consists of *debts* of the money-creating agencies.

In this chapter we have two tasks. First, we shall examine in more detail than previously the process of money creation through the credit extensions of the commercial banks. Second, we shall try to draw together in orderly form the results of the actions of all

315

three factors in the money-creating process—the Treasury, the central banks, and the commercial banks.

The Money-Creating Action of Commercial Banks

The vital key to bank credit expansion is found in the basic fact that fractional cash reserves are sufficient to support the banks' deposit liabilities. To satisfy the law and to meet working reserve needs, the banker must maintain a cash reserve equal to a certain percentage of his deposits. Whenever a bank's cash reserves are greater than these minimum requirements, the banker, anxious to increase his income, tends to seek a loan or investment outlet for the excess. Thus, should a member bank's needed cash reserves be $1,000,000 when its actual reserve balance stands at $1,100,000, it can lend the $100,000 excess.

The expansion of bank credit in the banking system. Let us assume that Bank *A* holds cash reserves $100,000 above its requirements. Let us make the further assumption that bank average reserve requirements against demand deposits are 20 per cent. In the banking system, therefore, the $100,000 of excess reserves is sufficient to support additional demand deposits to the amount of $500,000 (disregarding any absorption of part of the reserves by currency-in-circulation requirements). The question is how such an increase in demand deposits may come about.

First, it must be clearly understood that Bank *A*, by itself, cannot create $500,000 in new demand deposits by lending that amount and crediting it to borrowers' checking accounts. Should it make such an attempt it would be confronted with a heavy drain of cash as soon as borrowers drew checks to utilize the proceeds of their loans, since it would be most unlikely that any sizable portion of such checks would escape being deposited in some of the 14,000 other banks of the country. In order to be prepared to pay checks drawn by new borrowers, Bank *A* must have excess cash reserves in amounts about equal to the volume of any new loans that it may make. In other words, Bank *A* is able to expand its loans by $100,000 on the basis of $100,000 excess reserves. It makes no difference whether borrowers take the proceeds of their loans in cash or in credit on their checking accounts. If the borrowers take cash, the statement of the lending bank will show an increase in loans and a corresponding decrease in cash. If the proceeds are taken in additions to checking accounts, the statement will show an increase in deposit liabilities instead of a decrease in cash until the borrowers draw checks against their borrowed funds. This may best be seen by an assumed example of Bank *A*'s increase in loans by $100,000.

Effect on Its Balance Sheet of Bank *A*'s Lending $100,000

When Proceeds are taken in Cash		*When Proceeds Are Taken In Additions to Borrower's Checking Accounts*	
Assets	*Liabilities*	*Assets*	*Liabilities*
Cash reserves:	No change	(When loan is made)	
—$100,000		Cash reserves:	Demand deposits:
Loans:		no change	+$100,000
+$100,000		Loans:	
		+$100,000	
		(When borrowers utilize funds)	
		Cash reserves:	Demand deposits:
		—$100,000	—$100,000
		(Final result of whole process)	
		Cash reserves:	Demand deposits:
		—$100,000	no change
		Loans:	
		+$100,000	

Generally, proceeds of loans to bank customers are credited to the borrower's account, but regardless of the form the loans take, the lending bank (*A*) tends to lose an amount of cash equal to the new loan. The *multiple* expansion of bank credit and checking account money on the basis of Bank *A*'s new $100,000 of excess reserve will follow this general pattern:

1. Bank *A* increases its loans or investments by the amount of $100,000. This it can do because the $100,000 is in excess of its existing reserve requirements and can be lost to other banks without embarrassment.

2. As the borrowers utilize the proceeds of the loans, either by spending cash or writing checks against the newly created deposits, they put $100,000 into the hands of other persons and firms. Those receiving funds from the borrowers are customers of other banks and therefore deposit the funds in their own banks. Consequently, the cash reserves and the deposits of these other banks, which we may designate as Banks *B,* are increased by $100,000. So far the action of

Bank *A* in lending $100,000 has resulted in the following net balance sheet changes in Banks *A* and *B*.

BANK *A*		BANKS *B*	
Assets	*Liabilities*	*Assets*	*Liabilities*
Cash reserve:	No net	Cash reserve:	Deposits:
—$100,000	change	+$100,000	+$100,000
Loans or invest-			
ments:			
+$100,000			

In the hands of Banks *B* the new deposits are mingled with other deposits and become subject to the law of large numbers so that a fractional reserve (20 per cent) will suffice. Therefore Banks *B,* with $100,000 in new deposits and $100,000 in new cash reserves, find themselves with $80,000 excess reserves.

3. Banks *B* can now lend or invest $80,000, the amount of their excess reserves. As a consequence Banks *B* will lose $80,000 to still other banks (Banks *C*) which in turn receive new deposits of $80,000 with cash reserves to match. Banks *C*, with 20 per cent reserve requirements, in turn find themselves with excess reserves of $64,000.

4. Banks *C* continue the expansion by lending their excess reserves of $64,000.

5. The process of loan and deposit expansion continues in this way until the original $100,000 of excess reserves have been absorbed as required reserve for $500,000 in new deposits.

Each loan or investment operation in the above chain of events results in (1) an increase in the earning assets of the lending or investing bank; and (2) a subsequent equivalent loss of cash to other banks which receive a corresponding increase in their deposits. Each resulting increase in deposits absorbs an appropriate fraction of the original new excess reserves with which we started. As the series of loan and deposit expansions go on, an appropriate part of the original new excess reserve with which Bank *A* started leaks away into reserve balances of other banks. When loans and deposits have reached a level that absorbs, as fractional cash reserves, all of the new reserve with which we started our illustration, the limit of multiple credit expansion has been reached.

The above illustration is perfectly accurate in its description of the theoretical aspect of the way bank credit is built up. The expansion process may and probably does in practice frequently take place in a somewhat different way. If all of the banks of the community came into possession of new reserves at the same time, it is possible that all would find themselves simultaneously making new loans and creating new deposits at a rate approximately proportional to the relative size of each bank. If this should happen, each bank would find itself gaining new deposits created by other banks at about the same rate that its own loans were tending to bring a loss of cash. To the extent that this is true, no bank would experience a loss of cash, and the expansion of loans and deposits could continue for each bank until its reserve ratio had fallen to the conventional figure. Whether or not the banks of the community expand their loans and deposits "in step," the principle of bank credit expansion is the same.

Contraction in volume of bank credit. The opposite procedure occurs when the supply of available bank reserves is reduced. Let us suppose that Bank *A* suffers a decline in its supply of legal reserves as a result of the export of gold or a sale of government securities by the Federal Reserve Bank. Assuming that the bank is "loaned up," and has no excess reserves, the loss of reserves requires that it take some action. It may, of course, borrow additional reserves at the reserve bank and thus avoid the immediate necessity of a reduction in credit. If, on the other hand, it decides to curtail its credit lines, the sequence of events will be the reverse of those of the expansion phase. Bank *A* can reduce its loans and investments by requiring its borrowers to repay their loans and by selling securities. But this process attracts an equivalent volume of cash away from the other banks in the banking system, for debtors will be unable to repay loans merely by relinquishing their claims (deposits) against Bank *A* alone. The repayment of loans to Bank *A* therefore must involve the sale of merchandise and securities to individuals and firms who are customers of other banks. Similarly, if Bank *A* sells securities to replenish its cash reserves, that process will attract cash from the reserves of other banks. The loss of cash reserves by these other banks, Banks *B*, requires them in turn to reduce their loans and investments by an amount roughly equal to their reserve shortages. This in turn attracts cash reserves from yet other banks, Banks *C*, in an ever-widening circle. With each reduction in loans and investments, deposits decline correspondingly. The progressive shrinkage of credit, therefore, must continue until the deposit structure of the banking system has fallen to the point where the reduced volume of reserves bears the appropriate relation to deposits.

Limiting factors in the money-creating action of commercial banks. There are certain definite factors that limit the creation of money by the commercial banking system. These are:

1. The quantity of unused reserves available for supporting the expansion.

2. The percentage reserve requirements against the deposit liabilities that banks must maintain. The smaller the required reserve ratio the larger is the aggregate expansion of loans and deposits that can be made.

3. The "internal drain" of bank reserves into circulation to satisfy the need for hand-to-hand currency that accompanies the increase in demand deposit money.

4. The expansion of time deposits that accompanies the increase in demand deposits and the resulting growth of money incomes. The new time deposits absorb reserve funds and so tend to limit the expansion of money.

5. The availability of satisfactory borrowers and appropriate securities to purchase.

6. The attitude of the banker and his confidence in general credit and business conditions.

Each of these limiting factors needs examination.

The supply of excess reserves available for credit expansion. Bank reserves arise mainly from four different sources. These are: (1) The Treasury's purchase of gold and its issue of other currency; (2) the expansion of Federal Reserve Bank loans and investments; (3) any return of currency from circulation; and (4) disbursement of funds carried in the Federal Reserve Banks by the Treasury. In addition to these factors affecting the absolute quantity of reserves, the quantity of *excess* reserves above existing requirements can be increased or decreased by the lowering or raising of legal reserve requirements for member banks by the Board of Governors.

The "internal drain" of cash into circulation. A limit to the maximum amount of bank loans and deposits that can be supported under existing reserve requirements by any given cash reserve is found in the so-called *internal drain* of cash into circulation which accompanies the expansion of bank loans and deposits. As bank loans and investments expand and new deposits are created, the expanding volume of demand deposits tends to be accompanied by a growth in trade, production, income, and prices. Gradually the uses for hand-to-hand currency rise through the increase of both payrolls and retail prices. If banks were free to shift their demand deposits into bank note currency form, the internal drain would not exist. But in the modern world only central banks can issue notes, and commercial banks, therefore, can obtain currency for circulation only by obtaining notes of the central bank, which

Table 28

Money in Circulation and Adjusted Demand Deposits, All Banks*

(In millions of dollars)

End of June	Adjusted Demand Deposits **	Currency Outside Banks	Percentage Ratio of Currency to Demand Deposits
1929..........	22,540	3,639	16.1
1933..........	14,411	4,761	33.0
1938..........	24,313	5,417	22.2
1939..........	27,355	6,005	21.9
1940..........	31,962	6,699	20.9
1941..........	37,317	8,204	21.9
1942..........	41,870	10,936	26.1
1943..........	56,039	15,814	28.2
1944..........	60,065	20,881	34.7
1945..........	69,053	25,097	36.3
1946..........	79,476	26,515	33.3
1947..........	82,186	26,299	31.9
1948..........	82,697	25,638	32.0
1949..........	81,877	25,266	30.8
1950..........	85,040	25,185	29.6
1951..........	88,960	25,776	28.9
1952..........	94,754	26,474	27.9
1953..........	96,898	27,369	28.2
1954..........	98,132	27,000	27.5
1955..........	103,400	26,900	26.0

* *Federal Reserve Bulletin.*
** Adjusted demand deposits consist of all demand deposits, other than interbank deposits and U.S. Government deposits, less cash items in process of collection.

are charged against the reserves that the commercial bank carries on deposit with it. Whenever there is a sharp expansion in commercial bank credit, the rising requirements for money in circulation places a much greater drain upon commercial bank reserves than does the increase in reserve requirements growing out of expanding deposits. For example, during the period of rapid credit expansion during World War II, member bank required reserves rose about $5 billion while at the same time money in circulation increased nearly $17 billion.

In addition to the loss of reserves into circulation that accompanies the expansion of bank loans and deposits, seasonal and irregular variations that occur in money in circulation affect the volume of bank reserves and, if not offset by central bank action, may create temporary changes in bank reserves and in bank capacity to make new loans.

The amount of internal drain of cash reserves into circulation varies with different conditions. Where deposits are utilized to handle dealings in securities, an expansion of deposits is accompanied by a more belated demand for currency in circulation than if an increase in demand deposits were utilized to support a commodity price expansion. Some idea of the requirements for circulation may be obtained from Table 28, which shows the money held by the public and the deposits subject to check at the end of June.

The relation of time deposits to bank credit expansion. Savings banks receive on deposit money (both in currency and in checks) representing current accumulations out of income. The desire for liquidity (convertibility into money without delay or loss) leads some savers to choose to hold their savings in this form even though the earnings are substantially lower than those from less liquid forms of investments. These accumulations of savings, represented by savings deposits both in savings banks and in the savings departments of commercial banks, have no direct expansionary result on the supply of money. After their receipt by the bank the current money deposited in the savings account is passed back again into the monetary stream by the expansion of the banks' loans and investments. The money supply, therefore, is not increased by savers' habits of accumulating their savings in savings deposit form instead of directly investing them in securities or capital goods. Instead, the active money supply is temporarily reduced during the interval between the time when savings are deposited and the time when they are lent out again. However, savings deposits, like savings and loan shares and savings bonds, increase the liquid holdings of the public and to some unmeasurable extent relieve the money supply of a part of its burden of providing liquidity.

To avoid confusion as to the consequences of the growth of time or savings deposits in commercial banks, let us briefly trace their effects.

1. Time deposits provide funds to individual banks out of which part of their loans and investments are made. Hence the individual bank is able to pay interest to induce savers to utilize savings deposits as a form of investment.

2. Not being payable by check, ownership in savings and other time deposits cannot be transferred as a means of payment. Hence their increase does not expand the quantity of money. They do, however, provide additions to the public's stock of highly liquid "near money."

3. Because commercial banks must hold legal reserves against time deposits, the time deposit growth absorbs a modest part of available reserves of the commercial banks and to that extent reduce the reserves available to support checking account deposits.

The demand for bank credit. In the foregoing analysis of bank credit expansion it was assumed that borrowers were readily available to absorb the additional loans that banks were prepared to make. In other words, there was assumed to exist an unlimited demand for any available bank credit. Obviously such an assumption is at times unwarranted. Especially is this true when depression strikes, and profit prospects fall away. On the other hand, when profit expectations improve, as they do in times of prosperity, business firms seek loans in order to expand the scale of their operations. Without attempting here to examine the intricate causes behind fluctuations in business, we may conclude that the demand for bank loans changes sharply with the business cycle. Consequently the volume of credit rises in times of prosperity and boom and falls away during depression. These changes are further accentuated by the fact that the credit position of borrowers improves with prosperity and worsens during depressions. During periods of prosperity, borrowers both have greater desire to borrow and become more eligible for credit.

Loans other than those to business also show marked cyclical variations. The demand for funds to finance speculation, construction, and consumer expenditures reflect changes in business activity, employment, and profits.

Investments of banks. When banks purchase securities they are extending credit quite as effectively as when they make loans. Hence an increase in commercial bank holdings of securities tends to cause an expansion of demand deposits. The "demand" for this form of bank credit is evidenced by the appearance in the market of securities available for bank purchase. It happens that such a demand for bank credit need not fluctuate in the same manner as does the demand for loans to private business. For example, during the 1930's, a substantial volume of securities appeared for purchase by banks. Governmental bodies, including the United States Treasury, entered the market for credit and their securities were readily purchased by the banks. The result was an expansion in bank demand deposits. One may conclude, then, that periods of governmental budgetary deficits tend strongly to lead to an expansion in the quantity of bank credit. When such deficits appear during depressions the expansion of bank credit through security purchases counteracts the shrinkage in loan credit. Of course, the most outstanding example of bank credit expansion based on bank purchase of securities occurred during World War II.

Willingness of banks to lend and invest. More than borrower demand is required for bank credit creation. Unless banks possess adequate amounts of excess cash reserves and are willing to assume the risks of lending, demand will not be translated into bank credit. But at times banks are reluctant to lend even when they possess excess reserves. When business prospects are uncertain, many would-be borrowers are unable to qualify for loans. When depression becomes severe and prices are falling, bankers will lend only to borrowers of the highest credit standing. Moreover, bankers like to be amply fortified with cash if there arises any threat of runs by depositors. At such times, even firms with good credit standing may find borrowing difficult. Clearly, then, the volume of bank credit depends in part upon the willingness of the banks to assume loan risks.

Even though suitable borrowers are not available, banks may invest in securities. Unless panic conditions create an abnormal demand for excessive cash, banks turn to investments during depressions. Unless high-grade short-term obligations are available, however, investment by banks may be slowed up by fear of capital losses induced by possible future increases in interest rates.

The monetary results of commercial bank credit expansion. When the commercial banks, as a system, expand their loans and investments, they create demand deposit or checking account money. This is true whether the expansion of loans is made possible by the appearance of new excess reserves arising from some action of the Treasury or the Federal Reserve System or by the appearance of excess reserves that result from the conversion of demand deposits and currency into time deposits by their holders. In the first case, where credit expansion is the result of the appearance of new reserves in the system, the aggregate quantity of money tends to rise. In contrast, when savers convert checking account money into time deposits and thus release reserves, bank credit expansion based on these reserves causes no *net* increase in money. The new money merely *replaces* in part that which was extinguished by being converted into time deposits.

We may readily see how bank credit expansion results in an increase in the quantity of money if we construct hypothetical balance sheets for the commercial banking system and show the changes that result from increases in total bank loans and investments under the two different circumstances just described.

Hypothetical Balance Sheets of the Commercial Banking System
(In billions of dollars)

(The example is based upon the assumption that required reserves are 20 per cent for demand deposits and 5 per cent for time deposits and that no drain of currency occurs as the expansion takes place)

Case 1.

Expansion of loans and investments on the basis of excess reserves. No time deposits.

BEFORE EXPANSION

Assets			*Liabilities*	
Cash reserves		18	Demand deposits	80
20% required	16			
Excess	2			
Loans and investments ...		64		
Other assets		6	Capital accounts	8
Total		88	Total	88

AFTER EXPANSION

Assets			*Liabilities*	
Cash reserves:		18	Demand deposits	90
20% required	18			
Excess	0			
Loans and investments ...		74	Capital accounts	8
Other Assets		6		
Total		98	Total	98

The expansion of loans and investments, made possible by the existence of $2 billion of excess reserves, amounted to $10 billion and resulted in the creation of a corresponding increase in demand deposits.

Case 2.

A switch of demand deposits to time deposits releases excess reserves and an increase in loans and investments occurs on the basis of the excess reserves. Starting with the balance sheet immediately above, assume that individuals holding demand deposit money decide to shift $10 billion of demand deposits to time deposits to earn interest. Because time deposits require but 5 per cent reserve requirements, the result is a reduction in required reserves by 15 per cent of $10 billion, or $1.5 billion. The immediate results of this shift to time deposits are shown in the following balance sheet.

Assets			*Liabilities*	
Cash reserves		18	Demand deposits	80
20% required on demand				
deposits	16.0			
5% required on time de-				
posits	.5		Time deposits	10
Excess reserves ..	1.5			
Loans and investments ...		74		
Other assets		6	Capital accounts	8
Total		98	Total	98

The banks now proceed to expand loans and investments on the basis of the excess reserves of $1.5 billion. This can go to the point where the resulting new demand deposits made available to borrowers have increased by $7.5 billion and the excess reserves have been utilized. The balance sheet for the system would then be as follows:

Assets		Liabilities	
Cash reserves	18.0	Demand deposits	87.5
Required for demand deposits	17.5	Time deposits	10.0
Required for time deposits	.5	Capital accounts	8.0
Loans and investments .	81.5		
Other assets	6.0		
Total	105.5	Total	105.5

Reference to the above balance sheets reveals that although any expansion of bank loans and investments tends to result in the creation of new demand deposit money, an expansion based upon excess reserves released by the transfer of depositors claims from demand deposit to time deposit form cannot be sufficiently large to replace entirely the demand deposits that disappeared in the transfer.

The commercial banks and the monetary equation. We are now ready to make use of what is sometimes called the "monetary equation" as it applies to the commercial banking system. This equation is based upon the ordinary balance sheet relationships. It states first:

Assets = debt liabilities plus capital accounts or net worth.

This can be shifted to read:

Assets minus capital accounts = debt liabilities.

In the case of commercial banks not all debt liabilities are monetary in form. Nonmonetary liabilities of banks include:

1. Time deposits.
2. Demand deposits held by the United States Treasury.[1]
3. Demand deposits owned by foreign banks.
4. Interbank deposits.
5. Miscellaneous liabilities in non-deposit form.

On the other hand monetary liabilities of commercial banks consist of demand deposits or checking accounts belonging to individuals,

---

[1] Treasury balances as well as foreign owned balances are not part of the public's supply of money though they are a potential source of money when spent.

business firms, and governmental bodies other than the Treasury. Applying the above classification to the monetary equation for commercial banks we have:

Assets minus capital accounts = Nonmonetary liabilities:
> Time deposits
> Interbank deposits
> Deposits of the Treasury and
> foreign banks
> Miscellaneous liabilities

plus

> Monetary liabilities—checking accounts held by individuals, business, and local governments.

Federal Reserve Banks as Creators of Money

The Federal Reserve Banks indirectly affect the supply of money by varying the reserve funds available to the commercial banks. When they discount for member banks and others, and when they buy securities in the open market, the Federal Reserve Banks create deposits that comprise legal reserves of member banks, and Federal Reserve notes that provide both till money for banks and money for circulation.

The direct consequences of Federal Reserve Bank credit expansion upon the money supply vary somewhat with the circumstances. For example, when Federal Reserve Banks discount for or lend to member banks, there results an increase in bank reserves but no increase in the money supply in the public's hands. Similar results follow the Federal Reserve purchase of securities in the open market when the sellers are banks. On the other hand, Federal Reserve purchases of securities from nonbank sellers in the open market do result in an increase in the checking account money supply as well as an increase in bank reserves. These results may readily be seen in the balance sheet changes that occur.

FEDERAL RESERVE BANKS		MEMBER BANKS	
(Results of a loan of $1000 by the Federal Reserve Bank to a Member bank.)			
Assets	*Liabilities*	*Assets*	*Liabilities*
Loans:	Deposits:	Reserves in Fed.	Bills payable:
+$1000	+$1000	Reserve Bank:	+$1000
		+$1000	

(Results of the purchase of $1000 of U.S. securities in open market when the sellers are member banks.)

Assets	Liabilities	Assets	Liabilities
U.S. securities: +$1000	Deposits: +$1000	Reserves in the Fed. Reserve Bank: +$1000 U.S. Securities: —$1000	No change

(Results of Federal Reserve Bank purchases of $1000 of U.S. securities in the open market from nonbank sellers.)

Assets	Liabilities	Assets	Liabilities
U.S. securities: +$1000	Deposits: +$1000	Reserves in the Federal Reserve Bank: +$1000	Deposits: +$1000

The monetary equation may now be applied to the Federal Reserve Banks.

Assets minus capital accounts = liabilities.

Federal Reserve Bank liabilities can be divided into nonmonetary and monetary liabilities. Nonmonetary liabilities are those that do not make up a part of the money supply. They include:

1. All deposits, whether belonging to member banks, the Treasury, or foreign banks.
2. All Federal Reserve notes held by banks and the U.S. Treasury.
3. Other non-deposit liabilities.

In contrast, monetary liabilities of the Federal Reserve Banks consist solely of Federal Reserve notes in actual circulation outside of banks. The monetary equation for the Federal Reserve Banks, therefore, may be expressed:

Assets minus capital accounts = Nonmonetary liabilities, which are deposits and notes held by banks and the Treasury, and non-deposit liabilities

plus

Monetary liabilities made up of Federal Reserve notes in circulation outside of banks.

The Treasury and the Supply of Money

The Treasury is the agency through which both standard money and the various kinds of "other issues" of Treasury currency and coin find their way into the money system.

The import of gold. When imported gold or gold from other sources is offered to the Treasury for purchase there results an increase in (1) the gold holdings of the Treasury; (2) the gold certificate holdings of the Federal Reserve Banks; (3) the deposit liabilities of the Federal Reserve Banks; (4) the legal reserves of member banks; and (5) the demand deposits of member banks. The only direct result upon the supply of money in the public's hands is the increase in checking accounts of commercial banks. Potentially, however, a manifold increase in money may arise out of the increase in excess gold certificate reserves of the Federal Reserve Banks and the increase in legal reserves of member banks. These results of the Treasury's purchases of gold may be seen in the changes that appear upon the balance sheets of the Treasury, the Federal Reserve Banks, and the commercial banks. Let us assume that $1,000,000 worth of gold is bought by the Treasury. The effects of this action may be divided into two steps. Step 1 involves the sale of gold to the Treasury by the gold importer, who receives in payment a Treasury check on its account in the Federal Reserve Bank. The importer of gold deposits the check in a bank. Should the importer be a foreign central bank it may deposit the check in the Federal Reserve Bank of New York to await the need to meet obligations in this country. In this case no change occurs in the member banks and no changes occur in the money supply until the importing central bank spends the funds acquired by the gold import. If the gold importer is a private concern it will deposit the check in a member bank and receive checking account credit. The member bank will collect the check by having the proceeds added to its reserve balance in the Federal Reserve Bank. Regardless of the importer, the ultimate result will be that just described.

Step 2 involves the Treasury's action in replenishing its working balance in the Federal Reserve Bank that was depleted by the gold purchase. To do this it issues gold certificates against the newly purchased gold, and deposits them to its credit in the Federal Reserve Bank. Thus the gold certificate reserves of the Federal

Effect on Balance Sheets of Treasury Purchase of Gold

	Treasury		Federal Reserve Banks		Member Banks	
	Assets	*Liabilities*	*Assets*	*Liabilities*	*Assets*	*Liabilities*
(Step 1)	Gold bullion: +$1,000,000	Treasury cash: +$1,000,000	No change	Treasury deposit: −$1,000,000 Member bank reserve balance: +$1,000,000	Reserves: +$1,000,000	Demand deposits: +$1,000,000
(Step 2)	No change	Gold certificates outstanding: +$1,000,000 Treasury cash: −$1,000,000	Gold certificate reserves: +$1,000,000	Treasury deposit: +$1,000,000	No change	No change
(Net final result of steps 1 and 2)	Gold bullion: +$1,000,000	Gold certificates outstanding: +$1,000,000	Gold certificate reserve: +$1,000,000	Member bank reserve balance: +$1,000,000	Reserves: +$1,000,000	Demand deposits: +$1,000,000

Reserve Bank are increased by the amount of the gold purchase, and the Treasury's balance is restored to its original position. The balance sheets on page 331 depict the effect of the Treasury purchase of gold from a private importer.

Monetary changes also result from the Treasury's issue of other forms of money. For example, Treasury issues of silver certificates, to pay for domestic silver purchases, and its issue of coin in response to circulation needs, both add to the supply of money. When first issued, such money is deposited in the Treasury's account with the Federal Reserve Banks. This increases the Federal Reserve Banks "other cash" assets. When the Treasury spends these funds, by writing checks upon its Federal Reserve Bank balance, member bank deposits and legal reserves increase in the same manner as they do when the Treasury purchases gold. The Treasury currency finds its way into the tills of commercial banks and into general circulation as banks convert legal reserve balances into needed coin and paper currency of small denominations.

Gold exports. When gold is required for export, the effect upon the money supply and the monetary mechanism is exactly the reverse of the results of gold imports. Checking account money is given up by the holder, commercial banks draw upon their balances with the Federal Reserve Banks, and the Federal Reserve Banks surrender gold certificates to the Treasury in return for the release of gold for export.

The Treasury's monetary balance sheet. The monetary balance sheet of the Treasury is comprised solely of monetary assets and liabilities which form a part of the monetary stock. It does not include funds held for fiscal purposes. Treasury monetary assets consist of:

1. The gold stock owned by the Treasury.
2. Other assets held (or presumed to have been received) as a basis for the issue of Treasury currency (silver certificates, coin, U.S. notes, Federal Reserve Bank notes, and national bank notes in process of retirement). These other assets, lumped together, are carried as Treasury currency outstanding. In actual fact such other assets can be broken down into (1) silver held in the Treasury against outstanding silver certificates; and (2) a purely fictitious "other assets" item to represent the values presumably received for the remainder of the currency outstanding.

The liability side of the Treasury's monetary balance sheet consists of:

1. Gold certificates held outside the Treasury.
2. Treasury currency issues held outside the Treasury by banks and others.
3. A net worth type of item comprised of the excess of monetary assets over the liabilities to holders of gold certificates and other Treasury currency outstanding. This is called "Treasury cash holdings." Treasury cash breaks down into (1) gold against which gold certificates have not been issued (mainly derived from the gold profits from the devaluation of the dollar in 1934, but including the $156 million gold redemption fund held against outstanding U.S. notes and Treasury notes of 1890); and (2) currency held by the Treasury.

As of June 29, 1955, the Treasury's monetary balance sheet read as follows:

Assets		*Liabilities*	
	million		*million*
Gold bullion	$21,700	Gold certificates	$21,000
Other assets*	5,000	Other currency issues held outside the Treasury	4,900
		Treasury cash holdings ...	800
Total	$26,700	Total	$26,700

* These other assets are called "Treasury currency outstanding" in the consolidated condition statement for the banking and monetary system appearing regularly in the *Federal Reserve Bulletin*.

If we apply the monetary equation to the Treasury balance sheet we find:

Assets = liabilities to outside holders of Treasury currency
plus
Treasury cash holdings

or

Assets minus Treasury cash holdings = Nonmonetary liabilities, or money issues (gold certificates and other currency) held by banks.

plus

Monetary liabilities or Treasury currency in circulation outside of banks.

The Consolidated Balance Sheet for the
Monetary System

Now that we have examined the money-creating actions of the Treasury, the Federal Reserve Banks, and the commercial banks, let us bring together into a single bundle the net results by constructing a consolidated balance sheet for all three. This makes it possible to see, in summary form, the contributions of these agencies to the supply of money.

The meaning of a consolidated balance sheet. A consolidated balance sheet is not merely the adding together of total assets and the total liabilities of the individual balance sheets involved. The purpose is to show the *net* effects of the combined statements of the items included. For example, a consolidated balance sheet of all commercial banks eliminates assets of one bank that are liabilities of other banks (interbank deposit balances are examples) to arrive at asset and liability positions of the banks as a whole. Similarly, in constructing a consolidated balance sheet for the monetary system, if assets of one part of the system are comprised of liabilities of another part, both are excluded. For example, gold certificates are liabilities of the Treasury but they are offset against the gold certificate asset holdings of the Federal Reserve Banks. Consequently they are cancelled-off against each other and neither appears in the final statement. Likewise, member bank legal reserves and till money assets are set off against Federal Reserve deposit and note liabilities and against the Treasury currency liabilities, with only net differences remaining.

The consolidated balance sheet for the monetary system. The consolidated balance sheet for the monetary system of the United States is regularly published in the *Federal Reserve Bulletin*. As compiled, it includes not only the Treasury, the Federal Reserve Banks, and the commercial banks, but savings bank and postal savings accounts as well. This inclusion of savings bank and postal savings, while raising the total figures, does not in any way distort the measure of the monetary liabilities of the system which make up the supply of money.

Table 29

Consolidated Condition Statement for Banks and the Monetary System, June 29, 1955

(In millions of dollars)

Assets			*Liabilities*		
Monetary gold			Capital accounts*	18,900	
stock	21,700		Treasury cash		
Treasury currency			holdings	800	
outstanding ...	5,000				19,700
		26,700	Nonmonetary		
Total net bank			liabilities:		
loans	91,200		Foreign bank		
			deposits	3,300	
		91,200	Treasury		
U. S. Government			deposits	5,500	
Securities held by:			Time deposits .	77,000	
Commercial &					
savings banks	71,700				85,800
Federal Reserve			Monetary		
banks	23,600		liabilities:		
Others in the			Net demand de-		
system	2,000		posits other		
			than Treasury		
		97,300	& Foreign ..	103,400	
Other securities	20,900		Currency outside		
			of banks	27,100	
					130,500
Total assets		236,000	Total liabilities		236,000

* Assets of the Federal Reserve System and other banks include only loans and investments and exclude properties and other net assets. Consequently adjustment is made in the capital account item for the omission of these assets.

The monetary equation for the whole monetary system. The monetary equation for the whole monetary system—the Treasury, the Federal Reserve Banks, and other banks—may be expressed as follows:

(1) Assets = Capital accounts + liabilities
Capital accounts + nonmonetary liabilities + monetary liabilities

Transposing, we get:

(2) Monetary liabilities = Assets − $\begin{cases} \text{Capital accounts} \\ + \\ \text{Nonmonetary liabilities} \end{cases}$

Applied to the balance sheet, this becomes (in millions of dollars):

(3) Monetary liabilities = Assets: 236,000 − $\begin{cases} \text{Capital accounts} \\ \quad \text{of banks:} \qquad\quad 18,900 \\ \text{Treasury cash:} \qquad\ \ 800 \\ \text{Nonmonetary} \\ \quad \text{liabilities:} \qquad\quad 85,800 \end{cases}$

$$= 236,000 - 105,500$$
$$= 130,500.$$

The significance of the consolidated balance sheet. The consolidated balance sheet for the monetary system is useful in bringing together the basic items concerned with the determination of the supply of money. An increase in any asset item must be accompanied by a corresponding increase in liabilities, part of which are forms of money. However, an increase in assets may be matched by an increase in nonmonetary liabilities and therefore not be a cause of a change in the monetary supply. Consequently one cannot safely attempt to understand and measure changes in the money supply by merely focusing attention upon the changes in assets.

In general, an increase in the monetary gold stock is matched by an equal increase in the money supply. Likewise, an increase in net security holdings and loans is almost certain to result in some rise in the money supply.

In attempting to relate changes in the level of total net assets to changes in the supply of money it is necessary to take into account any change in nonmonetary liabilities that has occurred during the same interval. Were it possible to say that time deposits and other nonmonetary liabilities of the banking system vary with, and in proportion to, changes in monetary liabilities (checking accounts and money in circulation), some definitive statement might be made as to the effect of changes in assets upon the supply of money. Unfortunately such a relationship cannot be shown either in the short or the long run. Consequently it is necessary to treat nonmonetary liabilities as independent variables that must be taken into account when the monetary effects of asset expansion are considered.

One must also remember that the consolidated balance sheet is merely a method of exposition whereby the relationships among the various components of the monetary system are revealed. It in no way explains the underlying causes behind changes in assets that in turn cause changes in the money supply. It reveals neither the causes of changes in the supply of monetary gold nor the causes behind the changes in Federal Reserve and other bank assets. The answers to these questions must be found in the institutional framework of the system, the policy of the central bankers, and demands for credit on the part of business, consumers, governments, and others. The latter in turn reflect the dynamic changes that constantly arise in business, and the pressures upon governmental expenditures that arise out of wars, growing population, and rising standards of living.

Questions for Study

1. Exactly what is included in the supply of money held by the public?

2. What is the normal reaction of a commercial bank that finds itself in possession of excess reserves?

3. Suppose a given Bank *A* has $100,000 in new excess reserves that arose out of Federal Reserve Bank open market security purchases, and that reserve requirements for banks are 20 per cent:

   a) How much lending can Bank *A* do on the strength of such excess reserve?

   b) What cash drains must it normally expect to arise out of its loan expansion?

   c) What will be the ultimate effect of the original $100,000 excess reserves upon the loans and deposits of the banking system as a whole?

   d) What would have been the ultimate effect if reserve requirements for the banking system were 10 per cent instead of 20 per cent?

4. What is meant by "internal drain"? Why does it limit credit expansion that can be expected on the basis of a given supply of excess reserves in the banking system?

5. Why does the growth of savings deposits in banks not constitute an increase in the money supply? In what way does this growth place a burden upon the supply of bank reserves?

6. What is the effect upon the money supply when commercial banks expand their investments in securities?

7. What is the effect upon the money supply when banks (a) expand loans and investments in an amount just equal to an increase in their time or savings deposits; (b) expand their loans and investments when there has been no growth of time or savings deposits?

8. Suppose that holders of demand deposits switch $1 million to savings deposits that require 6 per cent reserve instead of 20 per cent:

    a) What is the effect upon the reserve position of banks?

    b) Assume that the banks respond to the changes in reserves by appropriate loan and investment action. What will this be?

    c) In the end, what is the effect upon the earning assets of banks? What is the effect upon the supply of money? The supply of "near money"?

9. What is meant by the monetary equation?

10. Name (a) the nonmonetary liabilities of the Federal Reserve Banks; and (b) the monetary liabilities.

11. Trace the consequences upon the balance sheets of the Treasury, the Federal Reserve Banks, and commercial banks of the sale of gold to the Treasury by a private importer. Why do similar results arise when the Treasury issues silver certificates to pay for the purchase of domestic silver?

12. Examine the Treasury's monetary balance sheet on page 333. Are any of its assets a part of the money supply? Which of its liabilities are a part of the supply of money?

13. What is meant by a *consolidated* balance sheet? In what ways does it differ from a combined one?

14. Examine the consolidated balance sheet for the monetary system on page 335.

    a) Can you explain why monetary gold stock and Treasury currency outstanding are not a part of the money supply?

    b) What would be the immediate effect upon the money supply of each of the following changes?

        1) The spending of $100,000 of foreign bank deposits.

        2) The spending of $1,000,000 by the Treasury.

        3) A shift of $200,000 from private demand deposits to time deposits.

        4) A fall in currency in circulation.

        5) A net increase in the U.S. securities held by banks.

21

Federal Reserve Policy, Treasury Fiscal Operations, and the Volume of Money

By expanding and contracting their loans and investments central banks can expand and contract the volume of commercial bank reserves. Thus they are able to encourage and discourage commercial bank loans and investments which are based on such reserves. Because the money supply consists largely of checking accounts that result from the extension of credit by commercial banks, the central banks are in a position to exercise control over the volume of money. This control is enhanced by the fact that central banks have the exclusive power to issue bank notes for general circulation. Our Federal Reserve Banks comprise the central banking mechanism of the country. Like other central banks, Federal Reserve Banks increase and decrease the supply of currency and member bank reserves by varying their loans to member banks and by purchasing and selling securities on the open market.

The influence of the Federal Reserve System on the supply of money is shared with the Treasury. Inequality of Treasury income and expenditures, and variations in the location of Treasury funds also have a substantial effect upon the reserve position of banks and the supply of money in the public's hands. Therefore, we should investigate the manner in which the actions of both the Federal Reserve Banks and the Treasury affect the money and credit situation.

The Control of Bank Reserves by the Federal Reserve Banks

Federal Reserve Banks do not have absolute control over the cash reserves of member banks. For instance, as we already know, the import and sale of gold to the Treasury results in additions to both the deposits and reserves of member banks. Because the deposits so created require only fractional reserves, gold imports normally tend to increase the excess reserves of member banks. During the period 1934-1940, over $14 billion in gold was imported, and member bank reserves rose correspondingly. Similarly the export of gold reduces the volume of bank reserves. In addition to gold movements, changes in Treasury policy as to the portion of its funds carried in the Federal Reserve Bank and changes in the public's demands for currency in circulation affect the size of member bank reserves.

Primary and secondary bank credit expansion. A convenient distinction may be made between commercial bank loans and investments that are based on reserves not created by the central bank and those which are supported by reserves created by the central banks. The first type may be called *primary* bank credit. The second type may be called *secondary* bank credit because it is based upon reserves of "secondary standard money" created by the central bank.

A central bank's influence over the volume of *primary* bank credit is limited to (1) its authority, if any, to vary the percentage reserves that commercial banks are required to carry against their deposit liabilities; (2) its authority, if any, to establish rules limiting loans of commercial banks for certain specific purposes (selective controls); and (3) moral suasion. In contrast, central bank control over bank credit of the *secondary* type, that is, based upon reserves created by the central banks, is well established as the traditional means for applying central bank credit policy. But to exercise control by varying the available volume of bank reserves it is necessary that the central bank maintain "contact" with the money market. Only when commercial banks are actually dependent upon the central bank for necessary reserve funds can the central bank influence the market by changing the volume of reserves. Central banks attempt to maintain contact with the money market by encouraging banks to build up the general level of their loans and deposits to the point where they are obliged to rely partially upon reserve bank credit. Such contact is difficult to maintain in times of heavy gold imports such as America has experienced from time to time since 1920. The situation early in 1941 is a good case in point. In spite of the $2,184,000,000 in government securities owned by the reserve banks, they were essentially out of contact with the money market by virtue of the fact that member bank *excess* reserves were about $5,800,000,000. Had the reserve banks sold all of their securities and withdrawn completely from the money market, member bank reserves would still have been substantially in excess of requirements. In contrast, the Federal Reserve Banks, at the end of April 1956, had over $24 billion of credit outstanding. The member banks at this time had excess reserves of less than $300 million. Under these conditions, the reserve banks were clearly in a position to reduce the reserves of member banks and compel credit restriction had they wished to do so.

Methods of Control

Power to control the volume of member and nonmember bank credit. We have seen that the reserve banks are able to exercise control over the volume of bank credit through their control of secondary credit expansion, and that this necessitates maintenance of contact with the money market. There still remains the problem of the extent of their control over secondary credit expansion when this contact is maintained. Of this one thing we may be certain: Whenever the Federal Reserve Banks are providing part of the reserve funds needed by member banks, commercial bank credit expansion may be checked by the simple expedient of holding down the supply of bank reserves. This restraint is clearly within the powers of the Federal Reserve Banks, for whenever excess reserves of member banks are scarce, further credit expansion is dependent upon the creation of added reserves by the Federal Reserve Banks.

The whole question of the effectiveness of the Federal Reserve attempts at credit control is complicated by the fact that the reserve banks are essentially lenders of last resort for the whole banking system. This means that the reserve banks are expected to lend (through discounting or on collateral notes) to members who are in need of funds and apply for accommodation. This expectation arises from the normal rights of membership. It follows that it cannot be unduly restricted in the pursuit of credit policy.

The Federal Reserve Banks are obliged to provide the funds needed by the money market to meet the current needs of business and to keep the financial mechanism functioning smoothly. Consequently the Banks as well as the Board of Governors are constantly concerned with short-run considerations. But, even while they are seeking to adapt the actions of the Federal Reserve System to short-term needs, they must always be on the alert to maintain an over-all policy in harmony with the aim of promoting economic stability and growth. Whenever monetary expansion threatens to become inflationary, credit restraint is called for. But, because the Federal Reserve Banks have the obligation of lenders of last resort in the money market, they must rely, for the most part, upon *persuasion* to check the applications of bankers for accommodation, rather than using outright refusals.

Restraint through the creation of a tight money atmosphere. A number of tools or instruments of control are available to the Federal Reserve authorities for imposing restraint upon the supply of money and credit. One method alone is seldom used; instead, the authorities commonly combine several methods for the accomplishment of a given policy. Such combined methods give better results because one action supplements and fortifies the others. The particular combination chosen may vary with the circumstances. For example, a rise in the Federal Reserve discount rate is often combined with the sale of securities in the open market. Sometimes an increase in reserve requirements for member banks may be accompanied by open market operations designed to soften the impact of the change. Sometimes moral suasion and discretionary pressure upon particular borrowing member banks may be used. The important thing is that the Federal Reserve authorities may create an effective atmosphere of restraint in the money market by the appropriate use of the available instruments of credit control. To understand the actions that can be and are from time to time taken to restrain credit expansion, let us examine in a little more detail the various methods of restraint that are available for use.

The Federal Reserve discount rate as an instrument of credit control. The central bank discount rate is the traditional instrument of credit control. As lenders of last resort, the Federal Reserve Banks are under a moral obligation to provide needed reserve funds and currency to member banks. Restraint upon member bank borrowings, therefore, should take the form of an increase in the rate charged on Federal Reserve advances.

There has been considerable dispute as to whether or not the Federal Reserve Bank discount rate can in fact be raised enough, within reasonable limits, to restrain member bank borrowings. First, there is the fact that banks generally apply to the Federal Reserve Banks for accommodation to remedy a reserve deficiency. Clearly, a rise in the rate will hardly deter member bank borrowings for this purpose. Closely related is the further fact that the banker may very well look upon occasional borrowing as one of the normal general costs of the banking business. In either event, there is some question as to whether such borrowing will make a member bank willing to raise its customers' rates. Especially is this true when customers' rates are already considerably higher than the Federal Reserve discount rate, as is often the case in rural areas, and when banks are anxious not to lose valuable customers to competing banks. But a rise in the discount rate that is not passed on to the customers cannot reduce the borrowers' demands for credit accommodation. Therefore, it is often argued, a modest rise in the discount rate cannot be restrictive.

It is also urged that even though banks might increase their customers' rates because of a rise in the Federal Reserve discount rate, the resulting increase in *borrowers'* costs would be unimportant. In periods of good profit expectations, business men find the added cost arising from a rise in the cost of short-term borrowing from the banks a negligible factor in their short-run calculations of profits from current investment.

There is still another argument advanced to prove that discount rate changes by the central bank cannot be effective in imposing restraint. This argument is the entirely fallacious one that a bank cannot be discouraged from borrowing to relend to customers because it can expand its loans by some multiple of the new borrowed reserves. Were this true it would be almost impossible to raise the

Federal Reserve discount rate high enough to shut off member bank borrowing. The fallacy of this argument, of course, is that a borrowing bank *cannot* expand its own loans by an amount greater than the reserves actually borrowed. Thus, if a rate is high enough to shut off the initial borrowing of new reserves by a particular bank, it effectively shuts off multiple credit expansion.

The effectiveness of a rise in the Federal Reserve discount rate is enhanced when it is combined with the open market sale of securities by the Federal Reserve Banks. In this way member bank reserves are reduced and member banks are compelled to discount at the Federal Reserve Banks to obtain reserves. The inevitable result of this is some tightening of the money market. The reasons for the tightening effect are not hard to see. First, the added borrowing increases the burden of the higher discount rate, since banks are compelled to borrow and pay the rate. This tends to reduce the attractiveness of further loan expansion. Second, the increased discounting by member banks uses up a greater part of their "welcome" at the Reserve Banks. There exists a pretty well defined "taboo on continuous borrowing" by member banks at the Federal Reserve Banks. Because of this taboo, carefully cultivated in Federal Reserve circles, member banks generally are not likely to increase their borrowings in order to expand the level of their earning assets. There is the further threat, implied in the taboo on continuous borrowing, that the Federal Reserve Banks may apply "discretionary" pressure upon particular member banks that go too far in disregarding the rule. Federal Reserve Banks, under the law, are authorized to refuse accommodation to member banks found to be unduly extending credit for the "speculative carrying of or trading in securities, real estate, or commodities, or for any other purpose inconsistent with the maintenance of sound credit conditions." [1]

There are still other reasons for the influence of changes in the Federal Reserve discount rate upon the loans of member banks. Changes in the rate carry considerable weight in the determination of banking opinion. A rise in the rate indicates to the financial market that in the judgment of the Federal Reserve authorities a

---

[1] Federal Reserve Act, Section 4.

tightening of the market is desirable. This alone may induce a rise in customers' rates, especially among the big city banks. Second, even a moderate rate increase may be restraining when it is coupled with the threat that higher rates may follow should the initial increase prove ineffective. Especially will this prospect create doubts in the lenders' minds as to the wisdom of making longer term loan and investment commitments.[2]

Open market operations as an instrument of credit control. The sale of securities in the open market by the Federal Reserve Banks, as we have already seen, is a powerful weapon for making effective the increases in the discount rate. They thus contribute enormously to the creation of an "atmosphere of restraint" which is a necessary part of any attempt to control credit through Federal Reserve action. Because of the importance of open market operations as an implement of credit policy we need to examine the manner of their use.

In our study of the Federal Reserve Banks in earlier chapters we became familiar with the way in which open market operations cause changes in the reserve position of the member banks. Let us now look more closely at their actual applications to credit policy. Open market operations can be divided into two categories: (1) involuntary, when the initiative comes from members of the money market wishing to convert certain liquid assets into cash by sale to the Federal Reserve Banks; and (2) "voluntary" operations initiated by the Federal Reserve Banks themselves, through the Open Market Committee, for the positive purpose of achieving some policy goal.[3]

Voluntary open market operations consist of purchases and sales of Treasury obligations by the Federal Reserve Banks on the initiative of the Open Market Committee, which sets the policy and executes the transactions. These operations are directly related to carrying out credit policy. They may be used to make effective changes in the discount rate, as we saw earlier. They also are used

---

[2] Cf. Rosa, Robert V., "Interest Rates and the Central Banks," *Money, Trade, and Economic Growth,* New York, The Macmillan Company, 1951, p. 282.

[3] The use of the involuntary open market operations to maintain the market for bankers' acceptances and for the Treasury bills of World War II has already been described in Chapter 17. Involuntary open market purchases of Treasury bills ceased in 1947 and offers to purchase bankers' acceptances at posted rates were ended in 1955.

to increase and decrease the supply of legal reserves for the purpose of maintaining short-term money market stability. However, in the late 1930's, excess reserves of member banks were so large as to put the Federal Reserve Banks out of effective contact with the money market. Therefore they embarked upon the policy of trading in Treasury securities in the interest of stabilizing security prices. During the war years that followed, although Federal Reserve credit had to be increased tremendously to provide the needed funds, the easy money policy under which the war was financed forbade any attempt at open market restraint. It was not until the "accord" of March 1951 that the Treasury acquiesced to the use of Federal Reserve credit restraint as a method for checking the inflationary developments arising from the Korean War. Since that time, open market operations, along with the discount rate, have again become available as instruments of restraint.

Other restraints upon credit expansion—changes in reserve requirements. Still another weapon remains for the exercise of control over the volume of member bank credit by the reserve authorities. The Board of Governors may change the legal reserve requirements of member banks. The amount may not be less than the statutory requirements nor more than twice that amount. This authority vastly expands the power of the Board over discounting when pressure is to be exerted upon member banks. Like voluntary open market operations, it enables the Board to force members to discount. This in turn forces the member banks to face the restrictive effect of the cost of borrowing and the tradition against it. It has the advantage over open market operations that the Board can make the restrictions felt by all the member banks if necessary, whereas open market operations primarily affect banks in the financial centers.

Changes in member bank reserve requirements have some weaknesses as an instrument of credit control. When requirements are increased in order to absorb member bank excess reserves, some banks may be unfairly pinched although others may be but little affected. An increase in requirements may put an undue burden on the bank whose reserve position is already tight in order to reduce excess reserves held elsewhere in the system. Of course, this same criticism applies in some measure to open market operations. Another objection is the uncertainty to which banks would be exposed should substantial changes be made without warning and with frequency. Because changes in reserve requirements cannot be made quickly and without a good deal of public notice, they are badly adapted to regular and frequent use as instruments of credit policy. In this respect they are decidedly inferior to open market operations, which can be brought into play quickly and unostentatiously and, when desirable, can be reversed readily to meet changing conditions.

Selective credit controls. In addition to the methods of imposing general quantitative controls over bank credit that we have been considering, the Federal Reserve System has exercised certain *selective* controls. For example, the Board of Governors of the Federal Reserve System is responsible for fixing margin requirements on loans to finance the purchase and carrying of securities. Therefore, it fixes such margin requirements with an eye to regulating the amount of bank credit that can go into stock market speculation. In 1946, for instance, margin requirements were raised to 100 per cent and loans of this type were entirely shut off for a time. Such a method of control of credit tends to exercise some check on the over-all expansion of bank credit and has the merit that it permits restraint on speculative credit without limiting credit for more worthy purposes.

Another selective control device was the war-born Regulation W of the Board of Governors. This regulation dealt with all forms of credit extended to consumers. It covered charge accounts, down payments on installment purchases, the period of time for which credit could be extended, and the like. Its purpose was to hold down consumer expenditures and to assist in checking price inflation at a time when consumers' goods were scarce. The authority of the Board of Governors to regulate consumer credit has never been made a permanent part of the arsenal of weapons against inflation. Instead, it has been temporarily re-established twice since 1947. It was revived in 1948 for a short period, lapsing again in June 1949. It was again re-established in 1951-1952 during the Korean War.

Yet another form of selective control was tried during the inflation of 1951-1952. Known as Regulation X, it consisted of controls over noninsured real estate credit to finance new construction. Like consumer credit controls, this regulation fixed minimum down payments and maximum periods of amoritization. Regulations W and X proved extremely unpopular both with dealers and with their customers. With the easing of inflationary pressures in 1952 they were abandoned.

The advocacy of selective credit controls was based upon two considerations. During the war and the postwar years up to 1951, an easy money policy for financing the war and for carrying the debt at low interest rates was an accepted goal. To maintain low interest rates on the government debt, Federal Reserve Banks supported United States security prices at par or better by open market purchases. Consequently it became impossible to raise interest rates and tighten the money market for business borrowers so long as the interest rates on United States securities were held down. To many of the advocates of this easy money policy, selective controls seemed to offer a way to restrain credit expansion while maintaining low interest rates on the government debt. Moreover, support for selective credit controls has been drawn from the ranks of those who believe that low and stable long-term interest rates are a prerequisite to a program for full employment. Because wide swings in the volume of stock market credit and consumer credit are important contributors to economic instability, selective controls offer an important substitute for the traditional controls involving the availability and the cost of credit.

The effectiveness of Federal Reserve Bank restraints on credit expansion. Let us now appraise briefly the Federal Reserve powers to restrain credit. First, granted that the Federal Reserve Banks are in contact with the money market, there is little reason to question the power of the authorities to impose credit restraint through the sale of securities in the open market and a rise of the discount rate. Such action drives member banks to the discount window of the Federal Reserve Banks, where they are exposed to the combined penalties of the higher rate, the unattractive prospect of going into debt for a protracted period, and the criticism of the Federal Reserve authorities against anything that smacks of continuous borrowing. Further restraint may be imposed on all member banks by increases in reserve requirements when existing requirements are below the maximum. Tight money conditions which can thus be established by Federal Reserve action inevitably affect the money market. Interest rates rise, especially in the larger cities; but, even more important, loans become harder to get. In other words the "availability" of credit is reduced. Lenders now must choose between borrowers, and, irrespective of any lack of deterring effect from higher interest rates, some borrowers are turned away unsatisfied; and credit restraint becomes a reality.[4]

Federal Reserve credit policy as a counteraction to depression. It is quite apparent that Federal Reserve credit policy can normally be invoked to restrain an unwanted expansion of credit. This is true even though one may doubt the efficacy of the discount rate alone. But there is more question as to the ability of Federal Reserve credit policy to overcome a tendency for credit to shrink during a period of depression. Restraint, by tightening the money market, is one thing; inducing credit expansion by easing the money market is another.

Whenever a mild depression threatens to bring a decline in credit, there is reason to believe that prompt and positive Federal Reserve action may well be effective. Making new reserves available at lower costs, or at *no* cost if open market purchases are pushed far enough, may very well provide the necessary impetus to renewed expansion. For, if a recession is mild, the lowering interest rates and the general increase in availability of loan funds may bring new demands for bank credit into the market. The success of easy money credit policy must depend, in large measure, upon there being some degree of demand tension in the market awaiting the release of restraints. This makes it imperative that a positive easy money policy be adopted early in the developing stage of depression. However, once depression becomes serious, Federal Reserve credit policy is of but limited value. By lowering reserve requirements, lowering discount rates, and by making substantial purchases in the open market, the Federal Reserve Banks can certainly create an atmosphere of ease in the loan market. Such action also results in an expansion in bank deposits and excess reserves and at the same time encourages banks to expand loans and investments. The

---

[4] The question of control over the rate of investment and the flow of income by the use of monetary policy will be explored in chapter 25.

effect of the appearance of excess reserves in commercial banks during slack times will normally be an increase in bank investments. The sellers of securities bought by the bank and the Federal Reserve Banks receive additions to their money holdings in checking account form. They now hold cash instead of securities. But an expansion in investment of this cash in the form of new business inventories or construction must still await decisions to lend and invest. Consequently, even though Federal Reserve easy money policies may induce banks to maintain the level of their deposits through expansion of investments, there is little reason to expect this to have a *direct* expansionary effect upon monetary expenditure.

Because of the well recognized limitations upon the power of Federal Reserve credit policy to induce expansion of credit and spending, it has often become the habit to describe such easy money policies as merely "pushing on a string." Because of the weakness of central bank credit policy as an anti-deflation weapon, some people have tended to regard it as outmoded and have turned instead to government fiscal policy as the proper instrument for control over business activity. The strong and the weak points of fiscal policy as a means for monetary management will be studied later when we review the whole range of devices that may possibly be used to influence the value of money and the flow of money expenditure. In the meantime we need to note briefly the general relationship between the Treasury's fiscal operations and the quantity of available bank reserves.

The Relation of Treasury Fiscal Operations to the Supply of Money

In addition to the Federal Reserve System there is another important force that influences the volume of bank reserves. That force is the United States Treasury in its fiscal role of taking in, holding, and disbursing tax and other revenues. The magnitude of Treasury fiscal operations is such that their effect upon the quantity of bank reserves cannot be disregarded.

Treasury expenditures and income are never exactly equal. Sometimes tax revenue and borrowings exceed disbursements. At times the reverse is true. At all times the Treasury must carry a substantial cushion of funds to avoid embarrassment. At the end of March

1956 the Treasury's funds, carried on deposit in banks, amounted to $6.6 billion. Of this amount, $500 million was on deposit in the Federal Reserve Banks and $6.1 billion was on deposit with 11,000 approved commercial and savings banks. How, then, does the Treasury's handling of its funds affect the supply of bank reserves and, incidentally, the quantity of money?[5] To find the answer we shall need to trace through the consequences of the changes in Treasury receipts and expenditures.

Taxpayers and lenders to the Government give checks drawn on member banks (or collectible through member banks) to meet their debts to the Treasury. The Treasury may deposit these checks in its account with the Federal Reserve Banks, which then deduct the amounts from the member banks' reserve accounts. The process therefore reduces bank reserves and the public's money supply by the amount transferred to the Treasury. The effects of this operation may be seen in the balance sheet changes shown below based upon the assumption that the Treasury deposits $1 billion in tax receipts in the Federal Reserve Banks.

FEDERAL RESERVE BANKS		MEMBER BANKS	
Assets	*Liabilities*	*Assets*	*Liabilities*
No change	Treasury deposits: +$1 billion	Legal reserves: —$1 billion	Deposits: —$1 billion
	Member bank reserve balances: —$1 billion	(Assuming 20% reserve requirements, a deficiency of $800 million in member bank reserves will result.)	

Let us now suppose that the Treasury expends money by drawing checks to the amount of $2 billion on its balance in the Federal Reserve Banks. Persons receiving payment in Treasury checks deposit them at commercial banks and on the collection of these checks by the banks the proceeds are added to the legal reserves of member banks. This effect may be seen on the Federal Reserve Bank's and member banks' balance sheets.

---

[5] We are not concerned here with tracing through the effects of Treasury borrowing at the banks to finance its excess of expenditures. In such a case Treasury borrowing and spending, like private borrowing, directly increases the supply of money. This aspect of government fiscal policy, involving budgetary deficits and surpluses that directly affect the volume of money spending, will be examined in Chapter 26, which deals with economic stabilization.

FEDERAL RESERVE BANKS		MEMBER BANKS	
Assets	*Liabilities*	*Assets*	*Liabilities*
No change	Treasury deposits:	Legal reserves:	Deposits:
	—$2 billion	+$2 billion	+$2 billion
	Member bank	(Assuming 20% reserve requirements	
	reserve balances:	this results in the appearance of $1.6	
	+$2 billion	billion of excess reserves for member	
		banks.)	

Thus we see that when Treasury receipts deposited at the Federal Reserve Banks exceed expenditures, member banks' reserves tend to fall by the amount of the excess. On the other hand, when Treasury expenditures, made in checks on the Federal Reserve Banks, exceed receipts, the reserves of member banks expand. To minimize the effect of normal inequalities in Government income and expenditures, the Treasury commonly carries the bulk of its unused funds on deposit in commercial banks and from time to time transfers to the Federal Reserve Banks such amounts as are needed to maintain its working balance. The effect of such a transfer may be seen in the balance sheets below. The example is based on the assumption that the Treasury has transferred $500 million from member banks to its account at the Federal Reserve Banks.

FEDERAL RESERVE BANKS		MEMBER BANKS	
Assets	*Liabilities*	*Assets*	*Liabilities*
No change	Treasury deposits:	Legal reserves:	Deposits:
	+$500 million	—$500 million	—$500 million
	Member bank		
	reserve balances:		
	—$500 million		

We can now briefly summarize the effects of Treasury fiscal transactions on the supply of money:

1. The collection of taxes, or the sale of securities to the public, directly reduces, by the amount involved, the money supply in the public's hands.

2. The disposition of tax funds and the proceeds of borrowings determine the effect upon the reserves of banks. Whenever the Treasury deposits its receipts in the Federal Reserve Banks the reserves of member banks are reduced correspondingly. When the Treasury leaves its receipts on deposit with the member and other bank depositories, the position of the banks' reserves remains unchanged.

3. When the treasury spends money by drawing checks upon its balances in the Federal Reserve Banks (the normal method of disbursement), the money supply in the public's hands and the reserves of member banks both increase correspondingly.

Clearly, the actions of the Treasury have powerful direct and indirect influences upon the quantity of money.

Questions for Study

1. Why are the Federal Reserve Banks now in a position to exercise restraint upon the expansion of money? Why, in 1941, were they in a poor position to exercise restraint?

2. To what extent may the Federal Reserve authorities impose restraint on *primary* credit expansion?

3. What is meant by saying that the Federal Reserve Banks, as central banks, are "lenders of last resort"? Why does this create a problem when credit restraint is desired?

4. Why is the use of the Federal Reserve discount rate more appropriate than "discretionary" restraint through refusal to lend to member banks, in view of the central banks' position as lenders of last resort?

5. Give reasons sometimes advanced to support the view that the Federal Reserve discount rate changes cannot influence the volume of money and credit by inducing changes in customers' rates charged by the banks.

6. Suppose discount rate changes do induce changes in customers' rates. Why may such changes have little influence upon business demand for loans?

7. How can open market operations be used to strengthen the effect of discount rate changes? What is the "taboo on continuous borrowing" and how is it fortified by the possibility of discretionary pressure?

8. What was the effect of Federal Reserve Bank "involuntary" purchases of Treasury bills during the 1942-1947 period? What, generally, have been the purposes behind involuntary open market purchases of bills and acceptances?

9. Why are changes in reserve requirements of member banks sometimes said to be a heavy-handed method of exercising credit policy? Why are open market operations more easily adapted to changing conditions?

10. With what three kinds of "selective" controls have we had experience? Why were such controls favored by the Treasury in the years immediately following the war? Why are they believed to be

especially useful in restraining stock market speculation and consumer credit purchases?

11. Do you believe that Federal Reserve credit restraint can in fact effectively check credit and monetary expansion? What is the result of Federal Reserve credit restraint on the interest rates charged by banks? Do changes in interest rates affect the volume of bank loans? What is meant by changes in availability of credit?

12. Why may Federal Reserve credit policy sometimes prove inadequate to induce an expansion in money spending in times of severe depression?

13. What is the effect upon reserves of member banks when the Treasury:

    a) Deposits current tax receipts in commercial banks?

    b) Deposits current tax receipts in the Federal Reserve Banks?

    c) Transfers funds from its accounts in commercial banks to its account in the Federal Reserve Bank?

    d) Spends funds by drawing checks on its account in the Federal Reserve Bank?

VI____

THE DEMAND FOR MONEY, INCOME, THE PRICE LEVEL

22

The Theory of the Value of Money: The Demand for Money

The value of money is measured by what a unit of money will buy in terms of a representative assortment of economic goods. Putting it in another way, the value of money is the reciprocal of the price level, and changes in the value of money are indicated by changes in an appropriate index of prices. Indeed, it is customary to approach the study of the theory of the value of money by examining price movements and attempting to find the reasons for their occurrence. We may, therefore, visualize the problem of the value of money as the problem of explaining the behavior of the price level. The concept of the value of money is not simple. Rather, it is dependent upon *whose* money one is talking about. The money of the businessman may suffer a more rapid loss of value during a period of rising prices than may that of the consumer, whose main interests are in the cost of living instead of wholesale prices. The value of money measured by a general price index is often considerably different from that measured by an index of commodity prices at wholesale. Although one should keep in mind the limitations of any single index of prices, it is nevertheless possible to use an index such as that of wholesale prices to obtain a rough but usable measure of the changes in the value of money.

The basic problem relating to the value of money is to explain the causal forces which determine it. This necessarily involves not only an explanation of the value of money at any particular time, but also the causes of changes, both of a long- and short-time nature, which may occur.

The importance of knowing the causes that determine the price level or the value of money. Earlier economic thinking generally assumed that the level of income and employment was automatically adjusted to the available working force, other resources, and the technical knowledge of the times. In other words, the level of real output was believed to be independently determined and that changes in the price level did not affect the level of production but merely changed the money value of the real income of a country. Consequently the main importance of changing price levels was thought to rest in the inconveniences and inequities arising from changes in the distribution of income induced by unequal changes in individual prices. People now recognize that changes in the price level not only cause the inequities just mentioned but also are responsible for generating and accentuating changes in real income, output, and employment. Therefore, an understanding of the causes of price inflation and price deflation is an important tool for attacking the problem of economic instability. To the extent that changes in the quantity of money can be blamed for changes in the price level the search for economic stability requires that attention be given to the supply of money and its management.

Methods of approach. There are two basic methods of approach to the theory of the value of money. One is statistical, which seeks, so far as possible, correlations between changing economic situations that may influence the price level and changes in the price level that actually occur. Such studies may be used as a basis for formulating a theory of prices. The second method is to approach the problem by abstract reasoning. Both methods have their peculiar limitations, and dependence upon either one alone is not satisfactory. Only when both are properly combined can one have confidence in the resulting theory.

Studies of prices may proceed along two different lines. Some analyses deal essentially with long-run price movements. This approach is useful in explaining the secular or long-run trend, but contributes little to the explanation of cyclical price changes. Other studies are directed primarily to the understanding of short-run price changes. The urgent need for the latter type of study tends to make theories of long-run price change fall into relative insignificance.

The Demand for Money

The demand for money may be looked at from two points of view. The first, known as the "transactions approach," looks upon the demand for money as consisting of all the goods, services, and financial instruments offered for sale in terms of money over a given period of time. The second is the approach that stresses the public's need for cash or money balances as a store of values at some particular point of time. This latter approach involves the reasons for the public's preference for holding liquid cash or money rather than other assets that might be purchased with it. This desire for money is known as "liquidity preference." Whether the transactions approach or the liquidity-preference, cash-balance approach is used for analyzing the determinants of the value of money, the simplifying assumption is made that the supply of money is a given fixed amount. Granted this assumption, the demand for money determines its value. The results are necessarily the same whether the transactions approach or the liquidity-preference, cash-balance approach is used. Each has certain advantages in helping us come to grips with some of the problems concerning the value of money. As we shall see, neither approach provides all of the answers. Consequently it will be necessary, later, to consider factors which generate changes in the short-run money supply.

The Demand for Money — The Transactions Approach

The transactions approach to the demand for money is essentially mechanical in nature. It utilizes the same concept of demand as is used in the determination of the value of goods and securities offered for sale in the market. For example, just as the demand for any commodity is thought of as the amount of money that buyers will offer for different amounts of the thing offered for sale, so the demand for money is thought of as the commodities, services, and securities that sellers of goods will offer in exchange for money.

To illustrate the workings of the transactions theory of the demand for money let us assume that in a given community and during a given interval of time there are $1,000,000 and 1,000,000 units of goods to be sold. If all the goods are exchanged for all the dollars, each dollar is exchanged for one unit of goods; therefore the value of the dollar is one unit of goods and the price of one unit of goods is $1.00. Now, suppose that the number of dollars be increased to $2,000,000, with no change in the number of units of goods offered for sale. Two dollars will then be exchanged for each unit of goods, or the price of one unit of goods will be $2.00. From this view of the demand for money the conclusion is reached that so long as the quantity of goods and services offered for money remains unchanged, the value of money varies in an inverse proportion to its quantity and that the general level of prices varies directly in proportion to the quantity of money.

The place of velocity. Because the transactions approach deals with the exchange of things entering economic transactions against the money supply over a period of time, it follows that the money side of the picture, that is, the "supply" of money against which transactions are offered, may be more than the given stock of money. Some parts of the money supply over this period of time may and do appear more than once. The velocity of money, that is, the number of times that the average dollar appears in the market during the interval of time being considered, is a significant item in the supply. For example, to revert to our illustration above, should the stock of money be $2,000,000 and during the interval of time, one year let us say, each dollar appears on the average twenty times, the amount of money available for being "demanded" during the year is twenty times $2,000,000, or $40,000,000. If we assume that the velocity of money is stable and not subject to change by any of the considerations entering our analysis, the original assumption that the supply of money is fixed is not disturbed. In reality, changes in velocity do occur, particularly during the business cycle, and upset the original assumption of a fixed supply of money. This is true even though the stock of money itself remains unchanged.

The transactions approach, therefore, explains the price level in terms of the supply of money appearing in the market during a given interval of time, that is, the quantity of money times its velocity, and the total transactions in terms of goods, services, and securities offered for sale. Therefore, an increase in either the quantity of money or its velocity tends to raise the price level so long as the transactions remain stable. On the other hand if the quantity of money appearing in the market remains unchanged and the volume of transactions increases, the value of money will rise and the price level will fall.

One advantage of the transactions approach is that it provides the framework for statistical verification and study in the monetary field. Both the quantity of money and the velocity of its most important component, bank checking accounts, are regularly measured and published in the *Federal Reserve Bulletin*. However, this approach has the serious limitation that in making the level of transactions the sole measure of the demand for money, it provides no good explanation for changes in the velocity of money. In contrast, the cash-balance approach, based upon the demand for money to satisfy liquidity preferences of the public, offers a more revealing basis for finding the answer to the question of the demand for money.

The Demand for Money — The Liquidity-Preference, Cash-Balance Approach

The demand for money to satisfy the desire for cash purchasing power involves a very different concept from that of the transactions demand. Here the question is raised as to *why* money is wanted. The answer is that it is wanted primarily as a means for storing values in highly available or liquid form. This demand for money is commonly explained in terms of three "motives" for holding it. These are: (1) the transactions motive; (2) the precautionary motive; and (3) the speculative motive.

The transactions motive for holding money. The primary demand for money balances arises directly out of its use for carrying on the ordinary trade and business affairs of the economy. It is a basic function of a properly working medium of exchange that it should enable a person to sell his products and services today and buy other things when wanted in the future. In its capacity as a store of value, money permits one to regularize his expenditures while receiving an irregular income; to spend a regular income in an irregular manner; and to await the appearance on the market of the things specially suited to his needs. Everyone who receives an income finds it desirable and necessary to make some use of money as a store of value. The importance of such uses of money varies with the individual and his particular requirements. For example, one who receives an income at irregular and infrequent intervals must, other things being equal, feel greater need for money as a store of value than a person receiving a highly regular and frequent income. The businessman, whose success depends in part on his ability to pick up a bargain when it appears, has a greater need for cash balances than has the college professor.

Consumers, as such, mainly need money balances as a means for handling their day-to-day transactions. Each consumer must strike some point of balance at which the marginal advantage of liquid assets in the form of cash is just equal to the marginal advantage of added consumption. Both a general increase in consumer real income and in consumer goods prices increase the consumers' need for money balances.

Businessmen require money balances sufficient to enable them to carry on their enterprises efficiently. They must have enough cash to meet their bills and care for their expenditures for some certain period of time. For example, a businessman may decide that, on the average, he wants a backlog of cash-purchasing power sufficient to meet his expenditures for one month. In that case he wants liquid buying power sufficient to pay for about one-twelfth of his annual business transactions. Should the scale of his transactions increase by 50 per cent, he will require about 50 per cent more cash in order to be able to purchase or handle one-twelfth of his annual transactions. Likewise, a rise in price will tend proportionately to increase his need for cash. Changes in the structure of industry may also cause changes in the transactions demand for money. Greater vertical integration of operations under a single firm tends to reduce the monetary requirements by reducing the number of buying and selling transactions involved.

As a community becomes richer, that is, possesses a greater quantity of assets, it may become willing to increase the proportion of its assets held in liquid cash form. This is understandable in the light of the advantage and convenience of holding cash and the reduction of urgency for holding non-cash assets as they increase in supply. The result may be an increase in the demand for money that reflects the degree of richness of the community.

The precautionary motive for holding cash. In any holding of money for transactions purposes, part of the need arises from the uncertainty and irregularity of income and expenditures of the person or the business firm concerned. The extent of this desire for money growing out of transactions needs varies with individuals. Money reserves appear more important to the conservative than to the more impulsive and short-sighted. But beyond these requirements for meeting the liquidity requirements that arise out of transactions, there often appears a change in economic outlook that increases uncertainty as to future income and costs, with a resulting reduction in profit expectations. In such a case, the individual or businessman may conclude that future solvency and economic security requires that he increase the proportion of his assets that he holds in liquid money form. Thus his "demand" for money to hold will increase above the ordinary level dictated by his transactions needs. In other words, a *precautionary motive* for holding money has arisen.

Although consumers may experience such threats of insecurity as to acquire a precautionary motive for increasing their cash holdings, businessmen are even more exposed to such threats. The attitudes of businessmen are exposed to the shock of events, rumors, and opinions, and businessmen's expectations of future gains or losses are especially sensitive. For example, a businessman who normally carries money balances equal to one month's bills might decide to double his relative cash position because of an election result that he considers unfavorable to business profit prospects. Likewise, threats of war, by increasing uncertainties, tend to increase the precautionary motive for holding cash, as do hints, forecasts, and outright evidence of a decline in economic activity, prices, and profits. A rise in the precautionary motive among businessmen results in a curtailment of investment expenditures, both for expansion and for replacement. A disappearance of the precautionary motive is a signal for a resumption of investment and a reduction in the relative size of money balances.

The speculative motive for holding money. Speculation involves the pitting of one's judgment against collective judgments as revealed in the market. If one speculates for a rise in prices by purchasing ahead, he is backing his judgment that prices will go higher against the judgments of others as represented by the existing market price. If one speculates for a fall in price by selling short, one is pitting his judgment that prices will fall against the existing market opinion.

A large part of the expenditures of businessmen involve some form of investment. They spend money for merchandise and raw material, for equipment, and for expansion of capacity. An important consideration that influences businessmen is the prospect that what is purchased will rise or fall in price. Thus, if it is believed that capital goods are going to rise in price the incentive to hold back cash purchasing power intended for investment will disappear. On the other hand, should the prospect develop that capital goods are going to fall in price, there will be a strong motive for postponing the investment and for building up cash balances accordingly. The businessman has considerable leeway in his choice of investing or holding his cash. He can hoard the proceeds from current sales or he can reinvest them promptly in new merchandise inventory. He can hold depreciation funds and undistributed net earnings in cash, or he may spend them promptly on new equipment and expanded capacity. This flexibility of choice is available to him because he is not like the average consumer who is compelled to spend in order to subsist.

Individual savers and investment agencies capable of watching and evaluating the market are also influenced strongly by the speculative motive. Whenever interest rates are expected to rise, or security prices are expected to fall, there will be a prospect of gain from postponing security purchases. Therefore the demand for money balances by these individuals and firms rises sharply. Conversely, an expectation of a fall in interest rates or a rise in security prices reduces the speculative demand for money.

To use Mr. Hicks' analysis, the anticipation of gain from investment depends on the difference between the expense involved in making an investment and the expected profit or interest (including the expected gain or loss from changes in the capital value of the investment).[1]

---

[1] Hicks, J. R., "A Suggestion for Simplifying the Theory of Money", *Economica*, February 1935. Also reprinted in Lutz, F. A., and Mints, L. W., eds., *Readings in Monetary Theory*, New York, The Blakiston Co., 1951.

The changing demand for money. The demand for money by business and investing groups is subject to wide changes in response to changes in profit and price expectations. When business prospects are bad and when prices of goods and securities are expected to fall, the precautionary and speculative demands for money rise sharply. On the other hand, the appearance of good business and profit prospects and of rising prices reduce the precautionary and speculative motives for holding or demanding money. This fall in demand releases funds for spending and investment in the transactions area.

Unlike consumers, whose demand for money tends to change directly with changes in economic activity and changes in prices, the demands of business and investing groups need not rise or fall in proportion to changes in prices and business activity. The worsening of profit prospects, for example, may cause a sharp rise in the precautionary and speculative motives for holding money before any noticeable change in transactions has occurred. Similarly, during a depression, the gradual dawning of a conviction that better times and higher prices are in prospect causes a fall in the precautionary and speculative motives for holding money. Clearly, in the face of a reasonably stable transactions demand for money, the precautionary and speculative demands for money are highly variable and introduce a very unstable element into the demand for money, which inevitably tends to generate cumulative fluctuations in prices and economic activity.

How changes in the demand for money balances affect the value of money. Under any given circumstances, there is an amount of buying power that the public wishes to have available in the form of money. This buying power must be sufficient to purchase the volume of goods, services, and securities that the public feels it should be able to command with its cash balances. One may conveniently think of this aggregation of goods, services, and securities as a given fraction of the total volume of transactions for a year's time. The size of this fraction will vary with changes in the precautionary and speculative motives. How, then, do these changes in demand for money balances bring about changes in the price level?

Clearly, the desire of the public to hold money sufficient in buying power to purchase a given volume of transactions cannot directly affect the volume of available money which is assumed to be constant. Furthermore, the existing fixed amount of money is always being held by someone or other all of the time. Since this is true, the problem confronting the public that wishes to hold a given amount of buying power in the form of money is how to compel the existing supply of money to buy the required volume of goods, services, and securities. To accomplish this, the public has only one available method. To illustrate, let us suppose that the value of money is already such that the existing supply has a total purchasing power equal to one-fifteenth of the nation's annual transactions. Now if the public wishes its cash balances to equal one-twelfth of the annual transactions instead of one-fifteenth, the increase in purchasing power must be brought about by the action of individuals. The only way in which an individual can increase the buying power of his own cash holdings is to try to expand the volume of these holdings. Assuming that he will not obtain new supplies of money by borrowing, he must spend less of his money income than usual during a given period of time. But if everyone else does the same thing, the net result must be that, since the total money supply held by the public remains unchanged, the total volume of money spent is reduced. As money expenditures fall, both prices and output will fall. This reduction in spending must continue until the existing money supply will buy one-twelfth instead of one-fifteenth of total transactions.

On the other hand, a decline in the desire of the public to hold buying power in money form causes an increase in the velocity of spending. Outlays of money exceed current incomes and prices, and outputs rise until the buying power of the money stock has fallen to the required level. Under these circumstances the holders of money resemble the boy who tries to run away from his shadow; run as he may, it always remains with him. Similarly, spend as it may, the public cannot actually rid itself of the supply of money. But, like the boy, it may end up, price- and output-wise, in an entirely different place from where it started.

The cash-balance, liquidity-preference approach, therefore, holds that the value of the existing stock of money is determined by the desire of the public to store up, in the form of money balances, purchasing power over goods and securities. The value of the total supply of money must be equal to this required purchasing power. Thus, if the public requires that its money supply (which we shall assume to be 1,000,000 units) purchase 500,000 units of goods, each unit of money must be worth one-half a unit of goods. Should a rise in liquidity preferences require that the money supply purchase 1,000,000 units of goods, the value of each unit of money must double. Therefore we can conclude that with no changes in the supply of money, the value of money or the level of prices may change in response to changes in liquidity preferences. Because changes in speculative and precautionary motives for holding money change with business expectations, short-run changes in the price level may occur even though the supply of money remains stable.

Questions for Study

1. Why are changes in the value of money reciprocals of changes in the price level? Do we have an index of prices that accurately reflects changes in the value of money?

2. If full employment were expected to be normal in an economic system such as ours, what would be the basis for concern over changes in the value of money? What additional reasons actually exist for needing to know the causes of changing price levels?

3. When we use the transactions approach to the demand for money:
   a) What is the nature of "demand"?
   b) What two considerations determine the supply of money to be demanded?
   c) What serious gap appears in the analysis of causes of changes in the price level?

4. How do the "transactions" demand and the "liquidity-preference, cash-balance" demand differ?

5. What are the three "motives" for demanding money as a store of value?

6. Which of the three motives (a) is closely related to the volume of business and the price level; (b) affect business and large private investors more than the average consumer?

7. Assume that the price level (a) has risen 50 per cent; (b) is rising 10 per cent per year; (c) is falling. What will be the result in each case upon the demand for money?

8. Why may the "transactions" demand for money be greater for one individual than for another?

9. Suppose that a national election threatens to put into office persons whose attitudes toward business are believed to be unfavorable. What will happen to the demand for money?

10. Suppose, with the supply of money fixed, the liquidity-preference demand for money changes substantially. What will happen to the value of money when the demand has (a) risen? (b) fallen? How do these changes in the value of money actually come about?

11. Can you show why the liquidity-preference, cash-balance demand for money provides a much better explanation of short-term changes in the price level than does the transactions approach?

23

The Supply of Money and the Price Level

The Equations of Exchange

In the preceding chapter we considered the nature of the demand for money and some of the factors that result in changes therein. We first examined briefly the view that the demand for money consists of the "transactions" offered in the market in exchange for money. Next, and in considerably greater detail, we explored the view that money is demanded as a means of storing up liquid purchasing power over transactions, or goods, services, and securities.

In the study of the factors determining the value of money it is sometimes useful to bring them together formally into what are known as the "equations of exchange." These, called the transactions and the cash-balance equations, provide a method for calling attention to the important forces that affect the price level.

The transactions equation. The transactions equation, so named because of its common use in explaining the application of the transactions demand for money, is:

$$MV = PT.$$

M is the quantity of money,

V is the average number of times the money is spent in a year's time,

MV is the total money spent during the period,

T is the total quantity of goods, services, and financial instruments sold in the market during the year, and

P is the general or average price level of the items included in T.

The transactions equation describes the interrelationships existing among the quantity of money, its velocity, the quantity of transactions, and the level of prices over a period of time. Taken by itself it is entirely neutral. It merely states that the money spending side, MV, must equal the value of all transactions, or PT. Nevertheless it provides a useful though somewhat limited tool for bringing together the immediate factors bearing upon the price level. For example, it suggests that an increase in M or V or a decrease in T will tend to raise prices; or, a decrease in M or V or an increase in T will tend to lower prices. However, it has gained most attention from its use as a device for presenting the quantity theory of money, which we shall consider later.

The cash-balance equation. A second method of formally stating the relationship between the demand for money and its value is by the use of the "cash-balance equation." This equation is based upon the now familiar concept that the reason for demanding money is to hold purchasing power over goods, services, and other transactions. Consequently it takes a form that lends itself to a direct consideration of changes in the demand for money arising from changing liquidity preferences to the public. This equation is:

$$M = PKT.$$

M is the quantity of money,
T is the annual transactions,
K is the fraction of the annual transactions that the public
   requires purchasing power over in money form, and
P is the price level.

Thus, with the supply of money constant, a rise in either K or T, or both, will reduce prices; or, a shrinkage of K or T will raise prices. We know that K, the fraction of total annual transactions over which the public wants to hold purchasing power, is subject to sharp and rapid changes with changing expectations of businessmen and investors. Because the equation calls direct attention to this through the use of K (the fraction of T which the public wants its money to buy), it is somewhat more helpful as a tool for exploring the causes of short-run changes in prices than is the transaction equation. In the latter, changes in liquidity preferences must be inferred from changes in velocity. Unlike the transactions equation, which deals with the events over a period of time, the cash-balance equation expresses the relationships existing among the supply of money, the quantity of money, and the demand for money at a given point of time.

The Effects of Changes in the Quantity of Money

It is not enough to seek the answer to the question of how the value of money is determined when the quantity is fixed. We need to know also the probable consequences of a change in supply. It is an important characteristic of our society that changes in the supply of money constantly occur as a result of changes in the supply of monetary gold, changes in Treasury currency issues, changes in the Federal Reserve Bank credit, and changes in the loans and investments of commercial banks. Moreover, in its exercise of monetary policy the Federal Reserve System *imposes* changes in the supply of money. Consequently it is of great importance to be able to anticipate the probable results of changes in money.

The quantity theory of money. The quantity theory of money seeks to provide an answer to the question just raised. In effect it states that: (1) with other things remaining unchanged, a change in the quantity of money will result in proportional changes in the price level; and (2) in fact, in the face of changes in the quantity of money, other things do indeed remain equal; that is, changes in the demand for money are independent of changes in the quantity of money. This point of view is frequently developed with the aid of the equation $MV = PT$. Using this, the quantity theory holds that changes in M cannot cause changes in V, since V is determined by public convenience in the use of money, and also cannot cause changes in T, since T is determined by the output capacity, technology, and industrial organization of the country. Therefore it follows that changes in M must result in proportional changes in P.

The quantity theory, therefore, rests upon the assumptions that (1) the total quantity of money spent during a given period of time varies directly and proportionately with the quantity of money; and (2) that changes in the amount of money spent will not affect the volume of transactions and must therefore cause a proportionate change in the price level.

In support of the first proposition, that the money spending (MV) will vary in proportion to the quantity of money, the quantity theory makes one or the other of two additional significant assumptions. The first, associated with what is sometimes called the "naive" quantity theory, is that any increase in money must automatically be spent because its holders have nothing else to do with it. But this assumption, that an increase in money must automatically result in an increase in money spending (MV), seems to require further examination. The observed facts are that new money added to the total supply often gets into the hands of banks and investors, who are most unlikely to spend it. Consequently the "naive" theory has generally been replaced by a more sophisticated view to the effect that the holders of the increased supply of money seek investment outlets by reducing the rate of interest. As a result, borrowing by business expands and spending of the new money takes place in the purchase of capital goods.

The obvious weakness of the assumptions of the quantity theory, that spending varies in proportion to changes in the supply of money, arises from the well-known short-run instability in the demand for money. The quantity theory position that money spending varies with the quantity of money is clearly untenable in the short run. In actual fact, changes in the supply of money may result in (1) a direct increase in consumer spending; (2) an increase in investment spending for goods and services as lower interest rates or better profit expectations induce business to borrow and spend; or (3) a piling up of the new money in unused hoards to satisfy the liquidity preferences of the holders.

The second basic assumption of the quantity theory is that changes in money spending will not change the volume of transactions and, therefore, must cause a corresponding change in the level of prices. Regardless of the possible validity of this assumption in the long run, it is clearly unrealistic in the short run. We know, for example, that within the span of the business cycle, the volume of output, employment, and total transactions may change substantially with changes in the level of money spending.

Because the quantity theory assumes that money spending must vary with the amount of money, and that the level of transactions is not affected by changes in money spending, it is entirely unable to give a satisfactory answer to the question of what short-run results may be expected from a change in the supply of money.

The long-run applications of the quantity theory. We can readily understand why the modern economist, concerned with the urgent short-run problems of economic and monetary stability, has rejected the quantity theory as a tool for grappling with short-run monetary and economic problems. Does it necessarily follow that the theory has *no* useful application to the problems of the present-day world? To best understand the quantity theory and the appropriate area for its use, one must remember that it was the product of the economic thinking of a time when concern was mainly directed at problems of long-run equilibrium. Full employment was assumed to be the normal state of affairs, with temporary fluctuations of a cyclical nature occurring about that norm. Consequently, economists, who were not particularly concerned with cyclical phenomena, looked at the long-run rather than at the short-run effects of changes in the supply of money. Not being concerned with cyclical effects, they sought answers to the questions of the causes for such long-run changes in the price level as the decline in prices during the period 1873-1896 and the rise from 1896 to 1920. For this purpose the quantity theory was admirably suited. It revealed what might be expected to occur should the supply of money increase faster or more slowly than the increase in transactions and output. If money increases faster than transactions, prices will rise. When money fails to grow as fast as transactions, prices will fall. Nor did it put an undue strain upon credulity to hold that, in the long run, changes in the quantity of money would not affect its velocity. The quantity theory, therefore, though discredited as a short-run analytical device, has provided the only satisfactory tool for coming to grips with the problem of long-run changes in the level of prices.

Applying the principles of the quantity theory, then, we may conclude that if the total output of the economy continues in the future to maintain its present rate of growth of about 4 per cent per year, inducing a similar growth in transactions requiring the use or the holding of money, the maintenance of stable prices appears to call for an average annual rate of increase in the quantity of money of about 4 per cent. This conclusion would, of course, have to be modified somewhat should there develop some long-run changes in liquidity preferences that lead to long-run changes in the velocity of money. In contrast, a failure of the money supply to match the rate of growth in transactions associated with the growth of output will tend to result in long-run price deflation. Similarly, should the supply of money increase faster than the growth in output, inflation of prices will result.

Even though the rate of increase in money kept pace with the secular growth in output and transactions, there would still be reasons to suppose that short-run changes in velocity or liquidity preferences would induce short-run price instability from time to time. However, some interesting attempts have been made to establish by statistical comparisons that an increase in the money supply that matched the rate of growth might provide short-run as well as long-run price level stability. These attempts have taken the form of comparing cyclical changes in the velocity of money and the volume of transactions. To the extent that these changes occur with approximately the same timing and magnitude they tend to cancel each other out and make possible the conclusion that even cyclical changes in prices are actually the result of changes in the quantity of money. In such a case, stabilizing the supply of money to correspond to the rate of growth of the economy might well provide short-run as well as long-run stability in prices.[1]

Short-run effects of changes in the supply of money. The short-run effect of an increase in the supply of money upon the level of prices depends upon the changes in spending and in production that are generated by the monetary increase. If the new money is not spent, there can be no direct effect upon either prices or production. If the new money is spent but results in an increase in production, prices are but little affected. Whether or not new money will be spent depends upon the circumstances of its creation and the persons who hold it.

---

[1] Cf. Snyder, Carl "The Problem of Monetary and Economic Stability," *The Quarterly Journal of Economics,* February 1935. Also Cf. Clark Warburton's belief that if the volume of bank reserves is allowed to increase at a rate corresponding to the rate of economic growth, the dangers of depression and inflation would be largely avoided. Remarks at the meeting of the Committee on Economic Policy, Chamber of Commerce of the United States, Washington, D. C. February 27, 1953.

Let us assume that before new money is created the money supply is in equilibrium with the demand, and the existing stock satisfies the transactions, the speculative, and the precautionary demands for liquidity. An increase in the supply of money results in an excess quantity, that is, more than is needed to satisfy demand at the existing level of output, prices, and liquidity preferences. What will become of the additional new money? There are a number of possibilities. First, as held by the quantity theory, it may be spent directly in the market for goods, and generate output and price changes. Second, if it is in the hands of investors, it may be spent for securities — driving security prices up and interest rates down. The lower interest rates may induce business firms to issue new securities which are exchanged for the new money. The result will be an increase in spending on capital goods by business. This too conforms to the quantity theory. Third, if the new money is in the hands of investors who purchase securities with it, the rise in security prices and the fall in interest rates may not sufficiently encourage new business investment to utilize the money. In that case eventually the interest rates must fall enough to cause a sufficient rise in the investors' speculative motives as to induce them to hold the idle cash. There results, then, no corresponding increase in the quantity of spending.

We may more readily see these various possibilities by taking four different examples of a monetary increase and tracing through the possible results. These four are: (1) An increase in money that results from Federal Reserve open market purchases of Government securities from nonbank sellers. (2) The utilization of excess reserves by commercial banks to purchase securities. (3) The disbursement of funds borrowed from banks by the Treasury for unemployment benefits. (4) Business and consumer borrowing at commercial banks. Let us examine each of these examples of monetary increase and trace the possible consequences of each.

1. When the Federal Reserve Banks buy securities from nonbank sellers both member bank reserves and private checking accounts are increased. This new checking account money is held by the investors who sold the securities. What are the chances that this new money will find its way into the spending stream? First, it is highly unlikely that investment funds so released will be spent on consumption. But, the money being in excess of the current cash requirements, the holders will

purchase securities in the market. This action will raise the price of securities and lower the rate of interest on new business borrowing. If business is willing to borrow (issue new securities) at the new lower interest rates, the new money finds itself in the hands of business firms that will spend it. If, however, business is depressed and does not wish to borrow, the new money is merely spent on old securities until their yields fall to the point at which investors prefer to hold the new money rather than attempt further to convert it into securities. In other words, the speculative demand for money, arising from the expectations of higher rates of interest at a later time, absorbs the new money without effect upon the volume of spending.

However, if the investment in new securities should take place and business borrowers spend the money for capital expansion, the effect on prices is uncertain. If employment is slack, the new money may stimulate an increase in output with very little effect felt on prices. On the other hand, if there is full employment at the time the results will be mainly in the form of higher prices.

2. When the increase in the supply of money comes about by an increase in commercial bank purchases of securities the results are identical with the case just considered. The increase in money will affect the volume of spending only if interest rate reductions and availability of funds induce business borrowing and spending.

3. When the Treasury creates new money by borrowing and disbursing unemployment benefits the likelihood is high that the new money will be spent by the recipients. Even so, the full and final effect is uncertain. Should business profit expectations be low, the new money may shortly find its way into the idle balances of businessmen with unsatisfied precautionary and speculative liquidity preferences. On the other hand, if profit expectations are good, the new money will be passed on or spent by merchants to refill their inventories. If unemployment is such as to permit output expansion, there will be little effect on prices.

4. Finally, new money created by private borrowing at banks is very likely to be spent. If business is reasonably optimistic, spending will go on, creating increased output, higher prices, or both, depending upon employment conditions.

Questions for Study

1. In the transactions equation $MV = PT$, what is the demand for money? What is the demand for money in the cash-balance equation $M = PKT$?

2. What does the transactions equation actually say? What does the cash-balance equation say? In what sense are they different? How are they alike?

3. Assume that the quantity of money increases due to some action on the part of the Federal Reserve Banks.

    a) What results does the "naive" form of the quantity theory of money tell us to expect? Why?

    b) What results does the more "sophisticated" versions of the quantity theory lead one to expect?

    c) Under what circumstances may the results expected from the quantity theory analysis not materialize? Why may business borrowing fail to respond to a moderate fall in the rate of interest?

    d) Why may the decline in the rate of interest induced by an increase in the quantity of money be stopped before it reaches a low level?

4. Why is the quantity theory useful for explaining long-run or secular changes in the level of prices? Does it provide any guide to proper monetary policy aimed at long-run price stabilization?

5. What is the nature of attempts to apply the quantity theory to short-run price level changes by relating short-term changes in V to those in T?

6. If an increase in the quantity of money should generate a proportional increase in the rate of money spending (MV), why are the effects upon the level of prices uncertain?

24

Changes in Money, Income, and the Price Level

Money Supply and the Income Level

We have been studying the demand for money and the possible effects of changes in its supply upon the price level of total transactions. Now, as we know, transactions include a conglomerate mass made up of services, goods sold at retail or wholesale or in primary raw material form, and such other things as land and securities. Consequently, explanations of changes in the price level of *total transactions,* reflecting interbusiness sales and speculation in securities, land, and commodities, are not entirely satisfactory as explanations of changes in the price level of the current *real* output.

To avoid some of the shortcomings involved in explanations of the value of money in terms of the price level of all transactions, one may relate the money supply to the prices of *final products* or *real income* provided by the economic system. This can be done by the use of the equation:

$$MV_i = PR = NI.$$

M is the quantity of money,
V_i is the *income* velocity of money, that is, the number of times per year that the average dollar makes the circuit from income to income again,
R is the volume of real output of final products in goods and services,
P is the price level of the real output, and
PR is the money value of the output and equals money income (NI).

In this equation the money value of final products for a given period of time, *PR*, is equal to the money spent on income, MV_i, for the same period. One may conclude that since $MV_i=PR$, any change in the money side of the equation must result in a corresponding change in the money value of the output, *PR*. Thus changes in either *M* or in V_i must be reflected in the volume of the final output, the price level of that output, or both. From this one may further conclude that to the extent that income velocity (V_i) is stable the level of *PR* must reflect changes in the quantity of money. Were it possible to show that income velocity is cyclically stable, one could say that the level of money income changes with changes in the quantity of money. This, of course, would not be the same as saying that *M* determines *P*, since short-run changes in income accompany output changes as well as changes in the price level.

As attractive as the idea of a stable income velocity may be, the cold facts do not support it. Not only has income velocity been unstable cyclically, but also it has shown a tendency to long-run changes.[1] Therefore a simple reliance upon the hope that the level of money income will vary in proportion to changes in the amount of money is unwarranted. Nevertheless, the concept of the income velocity of money is a useful one. It provides a direct way for relating the quantity of money to the money value of the final output instead of depending upon the roundabout relationship involved in the cash-balance or the transactions approach.

What Determines the Amount of Money Spending on Final Products?

The central goal of monetary study is to discover (1) the determinants of changes in money spending; and (2) the effects of those changes on the level of output and prices. The answer to the question of the determinants of changes in money spending must be sought in terms of the causes affecting the quantity of money and its income velocity of circulation.

We already have a partial understanding of the causes of the quantity of money. The quantity of money is the result of the

---

[1] From 1909 to 1929, the income velocity of money in the United States showed remarkable stability, fluctuating closely around 3 per year, from highs of 3.25 in 1909 and 1923 and 3.29 in 1926, to a low of 2.76 in 1921. It fell off during the depression of the 1930's and during World War II and reached lows of 1.86 in 1932 and 1.68 in 1946. Since 1950 it has fluctuated in the neighborhood of 2.4.

monetary actions of the Treasury and the loan and investment actions of the banks. The velocity of money, whether for total transactions or in the income sense, is explained in terms of the public's demand for money to hold purchasing power over other things, that is, the transactions, the precautionary, and the speculative motives. The answer to the question of the effect of a change in money spending on prices and output depends on the circumstances. Should money spending fall off, prices of such things as agricultural commodities are likely to fall, since little short-run contraction of supply can be expected. On the other hand, in the case of many industrial products, a decline in spending will result in a fall in output rather than in prices when imperfect or monopolistic competition makes reductions in output advantageous. For example, a short-run decline in money spending will be more likely to result in a reduction in automobile output than in automobile prices. On the other hand, when spending increases, prices of goods that have an inelastic supply are likely to increase. This is true in the case of most farm products. But increased spending on industrial products will mainly result in increased output so long as there exists unused capacity. Clearly, the short-run effects of changes in the level of money spending upon prices can only be anticipated in the light of the supply elasticity of the different products.

Changes in the Level of Money Spending

Because the level of money incomes and the output that represents such incomes are directly related to the spending of money for the final products of the economy, we must discover, if we can, the manner in which the level of such money spending (MV_i) is determined. Specifically, we need to discover why short-run changes in the quantity of bank-created money and changes in the public's demand for money actually come about. This can only be discovered by examining the causes of expenditures.

There are three basic sources of money expenditures: (1) consumption; (2) investment in capital goods; and (3) government. Let us explore each of these and discover so far as possible what determines its magnitude.

Consumption expenditures. The largest single type of expenditures are those of consumers. Consumption expenditures depend primarily upon, and are limited by, the current level of personal incomes. They may also be augmented by borrowing. Furthermore, the level of consumption expenditures is affected by the public's attitude toward saving. Whenever, for any reason, it decides to consume a larger fraction of its current income and save a smaller fraction thereof, consumption expenditures rise. Conversely, with a given level of income, should the public decide to save a larger fraction, consumption expenditures fall. Thus we see that any change in the public's saving habits, sometimes called the average propensity to save, will alter the level of consumption expenditures. Regardless of any tendency toward long-run stability in the average propensity to save that may appear, experience shows that in the short run the public's pattern of spending and saving habits are subject to considerable variations. Consequently, changes in consumption expenditures, arising from changes in the public's average propensity to save, have sometimes been important sources of income instability.

The volume of investment expenditures; profit expectations. The second major component of money expenditures is investment. "Investment" consists of the spending of money for the purchase of new capital goods. These capital goods may be of a durable sort (tools, equipment, or buildings) or may be short-lived (merchandise and raw materials). Any investment, therefore, causes a flow of money income into the hands of the owners of the factors of production used in making capital goods.

Entrepreneurs will invest in capital goods only when they anticipate that their actions will result in some gain. The decisions to invest rest upon two basic considerations. First, what profits, in the way of net yield over depreciation and operating costs, can be expected from the investment? Second, what are the costs of obtaining the use of the capital, that is, the rate of interest in the market, and the difficulties of obtaining funds?

The profit or net income that is expected from a new investment outlay depends upon a number of things.[2] First, the magnitude

---

[2] Keynes called the expected profit from added investment the "marginal efficiency of capital," by which he meant the "relation between the prospective yield of a marginal capital asset and its supply price or replacement cost." This may be roughly described as the rate of interest at which the present values of the series of expected annuities throughout the life of the capital good would just equal the cost of the capital good.

of the income expected from a given investment, as well as the length of time that the income will continue, will depend in part upon the absolute efficiency of the capital good and its durability or its expected life. Thus, inventions of more efficient tools and machines and new lay-outs requiring new capital expenditures increase the expectation of profits from marginal or new investment. Likewise, invention of new products creates new and profitable outlets for investments. This is important because the incentive to invest is related primarily to the expected profit from *new* investment. Second, profits from new investment reflect the operation of the law of variable proportions or diminishing productivity. Consequently, when capital is relatively scarce in comparsion with other factors of production, profits from investment tend to be high. Third, profits expected from new investment — and hence, investment decisions — are affected by the movement of prices. Rising prices that are expected to continue for a time tend to increase profit expectations because costs generally lag behind the price changes. On the other hand, falling prices, with lagging costs, diminish and for a time may cause a complete disappearance of prospects of net earnings from new capital investment. Particularly sensitive to price changes is the incentive to invest in inventories. Because profit expectations reflect expected changes in consumer demand and in prices, the high consumer incomes and expenditures that characterize periods of prosperity encourage investment.

The cost of new investment. The second basic consideration affecting the incentive to invest is the cost of obtaining funds — that is, the rate of interest. Whether paid to the purchaser of securities or to the entrepreneur himself for the use of his own funds, the interest rate constitutes a cost of making new investments that must be deducted from the expected net yield on the capital in order to determine whether or not that investment is likely to be worthwhile. Clearly, new investment will not be pushed beyond the point at which the expected marginal yield is no more than the interest cost. Actually, because of the high degree of uncertainty attached to profit expectations, businessmen normally insist upon a wide margin of expected profit over the interest cost of obtaining investment funds. Consequently it is unlikely that changes in the market rate of interest are very significant in determining investment decisions, except in the case of industries involving large quantities of long-life capital investments. In other cases, as we shall see later, the decisions to invest are more likely to be affected by the changing opportunity to obtain funds, rather than by changes in the interest cost itself.

The scope of the term "investment." Investment is the spending of money to obtain new capital goods. This spending of money may take two directions. First, the term "investment" is often limited to money expenditures for net additions to the capital supply. Second, a great deal of money is expended by business for replacing capital equipment that has become obsolete and worn out. For the purpose of examining the determinants of total expenditures in the economy it is best to fix our attention upon the *total* investments, or the sum of investment for net additions and replacements. Total investment, or gross investment, therefore, will be our main concern here.

Government expenditures. In the days of modest government activity, when taxes were approximately equal to expenditures, it was not particularly important to give consideration to the role of governments in the total expenditure picture. Today, when government expenditures, Federal and others, absorb over one-fifth of the gross national product, the case is different.

The magnitude of government expenditures is, in general, determined by considerations other than the profit expectations that govern private investment. Public policy, translated into action, determines the amount of government spending. Unlike investment decisions of private investors, government expenditures are unlikely to change markedly with changes in business expectations.[3] Instead they respond to such things as threats to national security and the needs of the public for services provided only by the government.

Because of the essentially noncyclical behavior of normal government expenditure, we shall at first omit consideration of it in our search for the economic determinants of short-run changes in income, output, and prices.

---

[3] To be sure, local government units often feel able and obliged to embark upon the building of schools and the making of other local improvements in times of prosperity, when funds can more readily be raised and public support enlisted.

The Sources of Funds for Expenditure

The flow of money income depends upon the flow of money expenditures; and changes in money income, accompanied by changes in output, employment, and prices, arise because of changes in expenditures. Our next question is to inquire how and why expenditures change.

Money expenditures can be made with funds arising from three sources. First, in the ordinary course of events the income currently received is available for current spending. Although lags exist between receipt of income and the time for convenient expenditure, under ordinary conditions these will even out so that, in a sense, the equivalent of today's money income is available for expenditure tomorrow. Whenever current expenditures are equal to the current income that precedes it, no more and no less, the flow of money income continues at a stable level. But should current money expeditures for some reason rise above the pre-existing income, the level of income rises. Also, should current money expenditures fall below the income from which the funds expended were derived, the result is bound to be a decline in the money income flow by the amount of the deficiency.

How does it happen that expenditures can rise and fall without a previous rise or fall in incomes? The answer may readily be seen by assuming that the events of the economic world take place in a series of very short intervals, so that the income of one period or "day" cannot be spent until the next period or "day." Thus, yesterday's expenditures create yesterday's income which can be spent today. Today's expenditures create today's income that can be spent tomorrow. Thus it may readily be seen that tomorrow's expenditures may be (1) the same as today's income; (2) less than today's income; or (3) greater than today's income. It can be *less than* today's income by the simple expedient of "hoarding," or not spending a part of today's income. It can *exceed* today's income either by dishoarding or using funds accumulated and not spent at some earlier period, or by borrowing newly created funds from commercial banks.[4]

---

[4] This device of using successive periods is presented by D. H. Robertson in his article "Saving and Hoarding," which first appeared in the *Economic Journal*, September 1933 and is reprinted in his *Essays in Monetary Theory*, London, P. S. King & Son, Ltd., 1940.

Saving and Investment

To keep our example simple we shall for the time being ignore the role of government receipts and expenditures and fix our attention upon the private sector of the economy. Here private households and businesses receive incomes and make expenditures. The total income flowing to private income receivers and to business during a given period represents the end value of the total goods and services produced and sold. If the flow of income and expenditures is divided into separate "days," as suggested above, yesterday's income, arising from yesterday's expenditures, can today either be spent or not spent. If it is spent it continues to appear again as income. If it is not spent, and consequently does not continue in the income stream, income falls.

The total income comes into the hands of private income receivers or households in the form of wages, rents, interest, and dividends on corporate stock, and into the hands of business firms as funds for the replacement of capital goods used up in the process of production (depreciation), and as corporate profits and other income not distributed to stockholders. The personal income receivers may spend all of their incomes on current consumption or they may save a part. Because business firms do not consume undistributed profits, one can say that undistributed business profits plus depreciation allowances set aside from current receipts are "saved," that is, they are not spent on consumption. Because there are but two kinds of spending in the private sector of the economy, consumption and investment, and since consumption spending automatically accounts for the expenditure of income that is not saved, a discrepancy between yesterday's income and today's expenditure can only arise in the saving and investment areas.[5] Therefore, whenever the savings out of yesterday's income are not absorbed or spent on today's investment, total money expenditures are less than yesterday's income, and the level of income falls. When today's investment spending is greater than savings out of yesterday's income, total expenditures and income rise. When today's investment spending is exactly equal to savings out of yesterday's income, total ex-

---

[5] We may assume that any particular consumers who borrow to expand consumption beyond their current income are merely reducing the net volume of saving.

penditures equal yesterday's income and the income flow continues stable.

Charts 12 and 13 illustrate the process by which inequality of savings and investment results in changes in money spending and in the income level. The time is divided into periods, the

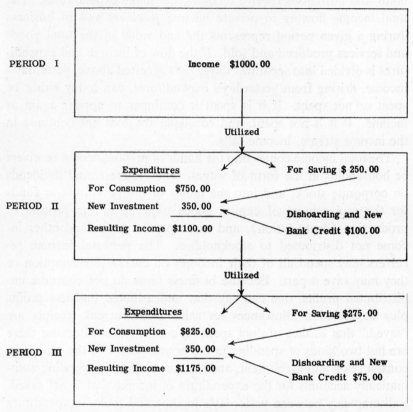

PERIOD I   Income $1000.00

                                    Utilized

                    Expenditures   For Saving $ 250.00
                For Consumption $750.00
PERIOD II   New Investment   350.00
                                                Dishoarding and New
                Resulting Income $1100.00   Bank Credit $100.00

                                    Utilized

                    Expenditures   For Saving $275.00
                For Consumption $825.00
PERIOD III   New Investment   350.00
                                                Dishoarding and New
                Resulting Income $1175.00   Bank Credit $75.00

Chart 12. When Investment Exceeds Saving and Money Income Rises. (Assuming investment in each period as $350 and saving as 25 per cent of income.)

equivalent of our "days," in which the income of each is derived from the combined spending on consumption and investment.

Planned vs. Unplanned Savings and Investments

Our preceding discussion of savings and investments showed how inequality of the two generates changes in the level of income. Based upon the period analysis, today's expenditures determining today's income may be the same as, more than, or less than yesterday's income. As the terms are used in this connection, savings and investments are sometimes described as being "planned." This is to distinguish them from what are sometimes known as "unplanned" savings and investments.

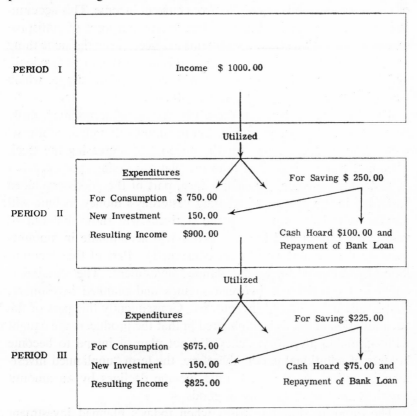

Chart 13. When Saving Exceeds Investment and Money Income Falls. (Assuming investment in each period as $150 and saving as approximately 25 per cent of income.)

Unplanned savings and investments. When one tries to observe what is actually happening to savings and investments by taking statistical measurements of the two, the rather surprising fact emerges that they appear always to be equal. This is true whether income is rising, falling, or remaining stable. Does this mean that our analysis based upon their inequality is faulty? The answer is clearly no. When statistical measures are applied to the income data for a given period it inevitably appears that (omitting governmental transactions) total income minus consumption expenditures equals savings, while, at the same time, total income (in values of real output) minus consumption equals the accumulation of unconsumed goods remaining from current income. This accumulation is counted as investment. Hence, for purposes of statistical measurement, savings and investments are necessarily the same thing and therefore equal. How, then, may this use of the terms "savings" and "investments" be harmonized with our previous usage, which we called "planned savings and investments"?

The discrepancy between these two usages of terms may easily be resolved by a simple example. Let us suppose that planned investment—money spent today for the purpose of increasing the stock of capital goods—is smaller than the planned savings provided out of yesterday's income. In such a case, part of the goods produced yesterday in the process of creating yesterday's money income will remain unsold. Consequently the statistics will show that out of yesterday's output and income, goods will accumulate in amounts equal to the amount saved (not consumed). Part of this accumulation is accounted for by the planned investment. The remainder, equal to the difference between savings and planned investment, simply pile up as unsold inventories. Consequently this part of the accumulation of goods is unplanned in that the producers are caught with unsalable inventory. They did not plan or intend to become holders of additional goods; therefore, the term "unplanned investment" applies. At the same time income declines by an amount equal to the cost of the unsold goods.

The opposite situation arises when today's planned investment expenditures exceed yesterday's supply of planned savings. In this case businessmen either draw upon idle cash, their own or that of others, or borrow newly created money from the commercial banks. Only in this way can investment expenditures exceed the savings. But as these expenditures are made they immediately become a part of the cash balances held by the general public. Such increased cash holdings are a kind of unplanned savings in the hands of the current holders of money. Added to the planned savings that preceded the investment, the sum must equal the total investment.

The Role of Government in the Determination of Income

So far in our analysis of the determinants of changes in income we have confined our attention to the effect of inequalities in planned savings and investments. It is now time to broaden our point of view somewhat to bring in the role of government.

Government expenditures make up a substantial part of the total income-producing expenditures of the economy. Likewise, government tax revenues constitute an equally important deduction from the income available for consumption and for investment uses. Therefore we need to combine the effects upon income resulting from government taxes and expenditures with those caused by planned savings and investments.

There are two main avenues of withdrawals from the flow of money income. These are (1) taxes; (2) planned saving. On the other hand there are two main channels through which these withdrawn funds find their way back into the income stream. These are (1) government expenditures; (2) planned investment. Therefore it becomes necessary to expand our earlier proposition that inequality in planned savings and investment generate income changes, and substitute the statement that whenever combined planned savings and taxes are unequal to combined investment and government expenditures, changes in income will result. Should, for example, a rise in saving or an increase in taxes reduce consumption expenditures without a corresponding rise in investment and government spending, income must fall. On the other hand, should a fall in planned savings or a fall in taxes cause an increase in consumption expenditures without correspondingly reducing planned investment and government expenditures, incomes will rise.

We have seen how the income flow is shifted upward or downward by an inequality between savings, plus taxes, and investment, plus government expenditures. Although we know the *direction* of the changes in income that will be induced by a given difference between these two important magnitudes, as yet we have no clue to the *amount* of the changes that will be generated. This is true whether the inequality is momentary, arising in a single instance during one income period, or is the result of a shift in the level of these magnitudes. To discover the factors that determine the amount of income changes to be expected, we must turn to the concept of the multiplier.

The Multiplier

The "multiplier" refers to the relation between the expenditure of a given amount of money and the amount of money income generated by that expenditure. The operation of the multiplier may most easily be understood by assuming at the start that the economy is in balance, with the rate of investment plus government expenditures just equal to the rate of saving and taxation. Under these conditions let us now inject a "lump" of additional money expenditures, either through private investment or government spending, and observe the results on the flow of money income. In order for this new lump of expenditures to be made, business or the government, as the case may be, must get the money to spend. There are two sources that may be tapped. First, funds may be withdrawn from idle cash balances accumulated in the past. In the case of business these accumulations may consist of business savings, depreciation allowances, and cash obtained by past inventory reductions. In the case of government they consist of unexpended tax revenues from the past. Moreover, both business and government may borrow past cash accumulations held by individuals and institutions awaiting favorable loan outlets. The second source of funds for the new expenditures is an expansion of money through borrowing at commercial banks. It is clear that the new lump of expenditure, the consequences of which we propose to trace, must bring into active income circulation either money previously "hoarded" or newly created bank credit money. It will simplify our discussion to refer to this money used for expanded expenditure as *new* money. It is new money so far as the existing active income circulation is concerned.

The expansion of income. New income arises directly out of the additional lump of expenditure that we are considering. For example, if the new expenditure is $1,000,000, the persons and firms hired to furnish the goods and services purchased will receive $1,000,000 in new income. But this income is not the end result, for, as we have already learned, the income of one period, when spent, provides the basis for the income of the period to follow.

Therefore, the subsequent spending of the first round of income generates income for the next round.

Let us first assume that the receivers of income generated by the new lump of spending spend *all* of their additional income on consumption and save nothing. In such a case the income flow would be permanently increased by the injection of the new lump of spending. The amount of the increase, measured in terms of *annual income flow,* would then be determined by the income velocity of the money newly injected into the income circuit. To refer to our illustration again, the $1,000,000 lump of increased spending would increase the annual income flow by $1,000,000 multiplied by the income velocity of money. If income velocity were 2.5 per year, the annual flow of income would be increased by $1,000,000 times 2.5, or $2,500,000. So long as the receivers of this $2,500,000 additional annual income continued to spend it all on consumption, and the income velocity of money continued to be 2.5, the annual flow of income would continue to be $2,500,000 higher than when we started.

Unfortunately this happy result cannot in fact be expected. The reason lies in the unreality of our assumption that all new income is spent on consumption.

Savings as "leakages" arising out of increased income. Let us now make the more realistic assumption that instead of all additional income being spent on consumption, part of it will be saved by the receivers. These savings, involving the withholdings of cash from the newly generated income stream, consist first of the personal savings of individuals. These savings may be held as money or as deposits in savings banks, or they may be invested in securities, used to pay premiums on life insurance, or used to retire debts. In any event, they constitute a net reduction in the new income flow that we are considering and will not re-enter the income stream without new additional investment spending. Second, savings include the net earnings of corporations that are not distributed to stockholders.[6] These savings, then, are not deductions from the increased income flow generated by the original lump of added

---

[6] Corporation depreciation fund accumulations can be disregarded on the grounds that business maintains its capital intact by regularly replacing worn out plants and equipment. When it fails to do so, the cash accumulated represents disinvestment.

expenditure. Because we are tracing only the direct consequences of the added expenditure upon the income flow, we cannot take for granted that these savings will automatically be reinstated into the income stream by new added investment. Instead, the important point is that if the flow of income is to be maintained, *additional* investment spending must take place to utilize the savings arising out of the increased income. Whether or not new increased investment will actually be induced by the improved profit prospects arising from increased income depends upon the existing state of business expectations. If expectations are bright, induced investment will appear readily; if gloomy, induced investment may not occur.[7]

Saving arising out of new income, then, is an important source of leakage that limits the expansion of income generated by a given increase in spending. It is important, therefore, to know something of the fraction of marginal increments of income that will be saved. This fraction, called the "marginal propensity to save," may be studied historically and the results used as a basis for forecasting future behavior. Because habitual living standards constitute a first claim upon one's income, it seems probable that a rise in income will lead to increased saving and a drop in income will reduce it. It is sometimes held that short-run changes in income are likely to result in more than proportional short-run changes in saving. The fact of the matter is that the marginal propensity to save actually shows a good deal of short-run or cyclical instability. Therefore, attempts to predict the effects of short-run income changes upon savings are likely to prove unreliable. This is unfortunate because it lessens the usefulness of the multiplier concept as a tool for quantitative predictions concerning the income effect that can be expected to follow a given increase in expenditure.

Other leakages. Besides increased savings there are other traps that catch and absorb the new money as it proceeds on its appointed income-creating rounds. One of these is the tendency for a rising level of income to attract an increased amount of imports. This

---

[7] D. H. Robertson suggests that the very appearance of new savings, arising out of expanding income, will stimulate investment by enabling business firms to use their own accumulated savings to increase investment without increasing indebtedness. Cf. his "Thoughts on Meeting Some Important Persons," *Quarterly Journal of Economics,* May 1954, p. 189.

causes some of the new money to fall into the hands of foreign banks representing the foreign sellers, and effectively removes it from the income stream. Also, as incomes rise there is an automatic tendency for tax revenues also to rise. Increased tax receipts not matched by increased governmental expenditures absorb into Treasury balances part of the new money responsible for the rise in income.

The effect of leakages on income flow. What, then, are the effects of these leakages of money out of the income stream through increased savings, imports, and taxes? Clearly, as part of the money in the new income stream is sidetracked into cash hoards of savers, foreign bankers, or the Treasury, the flow of income must inevitably decline in each succeeding round. Eventually all of the new cash put into the income stream by the initial lump of spending will have leaked away into idle cash balances, and its power to generate additional income will have disappeared. The total amount of new income that will be generated will depend upon the size of the leakages. Thus, should the leakage average one-third, we know that by the time the new income has amounted to three times the initial input or lump of spending, the original new money involved will have all leaked away into idle balances.

The length of time before the leakage becomes complete is of course considerable, for the total resulting income is the sum of a descending series of amounts. If the leakage is ⅓, the new income generated by spending a new dollar will be $1.00 + $.66⅔ + $.44⅑ + . . . ultimately reaching a total of $3.00. In this case the multiplier is 3, because one new dollar spent will generate $3.00 in income before the leakages absorb it. Should the leakage be ¼ instead of ⅓, the multiplying effect of added spending would be 4, since a new dollar put into active circulation by a lump of expenditure will not disappear into idle cash balances until an additional $4.00 worth of income has been generated. In this case the new income generated by the dollar of new spending would be $1.00 + $.75 + $.56¼ + . . . or a total of $4.00. Thus we see that the multiplier is the reciprocal of the rate of leakage.

The multiplier effect applied to a succession of lumps of new spending. The same analysis can be applied to a series of lumps of new spending or to an addition to the *rate* of spending.

Let us again start with the assumption that the existing rates of saving and taxation are equal to existing rates of investment and government expenditures. When the rate of investment and government expenditures is increased it can be financed only by drawing upon past accumulations of money balances and new money created by commercial bank credit expansion. Each lump of new, increased spending generates a declining series of new income payments. As the *series* of new lumps of expenditure are continued, the total flow of income will rise to that point at which the leakages from the rising income flow just equal the new money being injected by the new spending. If the new spending inputs of money are at the rate of $1,000,000 per month, and the leakages are ⅓, then the level of income can rise by $3,000,000 per month. At that point the leakages equal the monthly inputs of money from the increased rate of investment and government spending, and the expansion of income from that increased level of spending has reached its limit. If the leakages are ¼, the limit is four times the new money inputs, or $4,000,000 per month. Should the leakages be as small as ⅟₁₀, the multiplier is 10 and the income flow could rise by $10,000,000 per month before leakages would nullify the money put into circulation by the new $1,000,000 monthly spending rate.

The application of the multiplier to changes in the rate of investment and government spending may be seen in Chart 14. For purposes of simplicity it may be assumed that the existing level of

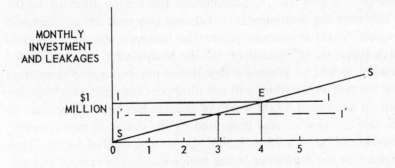

Chart 14. The Multiplying Effect of a Rate of Investment of $1 Million per Month when Leakages Are ¼ and the Multiplier is 4.

investment and government spending is equal to the existing level of savings and taxes, and that the level of income is in equilibrium. Zero on the chart, therefore, represents the point of departure for *new* investment and government spending and the *new* increase in level of income and resulting leakages that are generated by that spending. An increase in investment and government spending of $1 million per month is indicated on the chart by the horizontal line *I—I*. At the start, since no savings or tax payments are directly generated by the *new* investment and government spending, such new additions to spending are in excess of savings and tax leakages, and income, measured along the horizontal axis, begins to increase. The increase in income continues so long as the added rate of investment and government spending ($1 million per month) is greater than the new leakages. Leakages are assumed to be ¼ and are represented on the chart by the rising line *S—S*. These leakages will become $1 million per month when income has been increased by $4 million per month (marked *E* on the chart). When that level of increased income has been reached the multiplier effect is complete.

Now let us suppose that, after income has increased by $4 million per month, the rate of investment and government spending declines by $¼ million per month to a level only $¾ million above the original starting point. This reduced rate of investment and government spending is indicated on the chart by the horizontal line *I'—I'*. An examination of the chart reveals that when investment and government spending are reduced, the increased level of income of $4 million per month cannot be maintained. At that level of income, leakages are $1 million per month, but the new investment and government spending tending to absorb them and put them back into the income stream is only $¾ million. Income must therefore decline to the point at which leakages are only $¾ million. Since the rate of leakage is ¼, the income level must decline to $3 million per month above the original starting point. Then, again, leakages are equal to investment and government spending, and income will be stabilized. Thus we see that just as an increased rate of investment and government spending generates new income until the resulting leakages absorb all of the "new" money put into active circulation, so a reduction in the rate of investment and government spending from an existing level generates a fall in income. This fall must continue until income has reached the point at which the leakages are equal to the new lowered rate of investment and government spending. The multiplier, therefore, works both ways. It must be noted that this analysis is for the purpose of discovering the direct income effects to be expected from a change in the level of investment and government spending. It disregards the possible favorable or unfavorable effects of the resulting income changes upon business expectations, which in turn may induce further changes in investment.

The multiplier and other sources of expenditure changes. We have considered the multiplier as it works to generate changes in income when changes occur in the rate of expenditures for private investment and by government. However, one should remember that the multiplier effect arises from any changes in total expenditure regardless of the origin of such changes. For example, should the rate of investment and government expenditures remain fixed but a decline in net saving or a reduction in taxes lead to increased consumption expenditures, the multiplying effect upon income will appear. Similarly, when a "favorable" international balance of payments results in a net increase in total domestic expenditures, a multiplying effect upon income results.

The significance of the multiplier concept. It is important to know something about the multiplying effects of new expenditures if one is to judge their probable effects on the level of income and employment. For example, if expenditures on investment are expected to be $1 billion per month higher than before, the multiplier establishes the ultimate effect of that increase upon the level of income. But, though the multiplier concept is useful for explaining the nature of the response of income to new expenditure, it does not in fact provide a precise measure of response that may be expected. There are several reasons for this. First, the full response of income to a new series of input expenditures is realized only after the expiration of a considerable number of income periods, since the rate of expansion of income is limited by the income velocity of the newly expended money. Second, it is impossible to make a reliable estimate of the size of the leakages (and hence the size of the multiplier) at a particular time. To calculate the multiplier one must know (1) the public's marginal propensity to save, that is, the fraction of any marginal or added income that will be saved and not spent; (2) the marginal propensity to import, that is, the fraction of additional income that the public will spend on imports; and (3) the marginal or added taxes that must be paid on the increased income. In the short run, the magnitude of these leakages is uncertain. Finally, when business prospects are bad, the ultimate multiplier effect of new expenditure may be reduced by an entirely different and unpredictable leakage in the way of *disinvestment* by business.

Disinvestment leakages. When unsatisfied liquidity preferences exist, any attempt to measure the income expanding potential of a given increase in expenditures is fraught with added uncertainty. For example, should the level of government expenditures be increased with the aim of increasing the income flow in a period of depression, the application of the multiplier may be woefully inadequate to indicate the income results that can be expected. With business depressed and price and profit expectations low after the new money has been spent by those who first received it, there is a fair chance that most of the money will be swallowed up by business cash hoards as business disinvests its inventory and allows capital equipment to wear out without replacement. In this situation the multiplier, even if the leakages from saving, imports, and taxes could be accurately forecast, can give no certain measure of the probable results of the increased government expenditures upon income.

The multiplier and the price level. The merit of the multiplier concept is in the fact that it provides a tool for making estimates of the increases and decreases in the level of income that may be expected from changes in the level of investment and government spending. However, it provides no direct clue to the effect of the rising or falling income upon prices. In case the multiplier is working to expand income, one can only say that the effect will be (1) an increase in output whenever there is slack in employment; and (2) some increase in prices whenever expansion in output involves increasing costs or when full employment limits are reached. Likewise, falling income may either induce a fall in output or, when output restriction is difficult, falling prices.

Contributions of the Income Approach

The income approach to the problem of money and its value accomplishes a number of things. First, it reveals the relationship between the money spent on final output (MV_i) to the money value of that final output (PR) and to total income. In so doing it avoids the difficulties raised by the transactions and cash-balance approaches as applied to total transactions and their prices. Second, the income approach focuses attention upon and reveals the essential basis for *changes* in the level of total spending and income. These changes, we found, are grounded upon circumstances that make total current savings plus taxes unequal to total current investment plus governmental spending. Thus we find the basis for changes in MV_i that generate changes in the level of income. Third, through the use of the multiplier concept we discover the conditions that determine the magnitude of changes in MV_i and in the income level resulting from a given increase or decrease in spending. The magnitude of these changes was found to depend upon the size of the leakages that are associated with changes in the level of income. The larger the fraction of marginal leakages, the smaller the multiplying effect. The multiplier, therefore, provides a tool for estimating the income changes that may be expected to arise from changes in spending for consumption, investment, or government purposes. Because of the highly variable nature of the short-run marginal propensity to save and to import, and the uncertain leakages that may arise from business disinvestment during bad times, the multiplier cannot be predicted with much accuracy during the course of the business cycle.

Nevertheless, the multiplier concept is of great value in helping one understand the basic nature of the problem of maintaining the income level needed for full employment and economic growth. Its usefulness in this respect is enhanced by the fact that the long-run relationships of leakages to income are considerably more stable than those of the short run.

Finally, although the income approach explains how changes in expenditures generate short-run changes in total money spending and income, it does not provide any direct answer to the question of the short-run changes in the value of money or changes in the price level. Instead, it can only reveal the direction that changes in money income take and the limits to the magnitude of these changes. Before the effects on prices can be discovered, the changes in money income and spending must be measured against the output capacity and employment level.

The income approach, valuable as it is, still does not provide the answer to *why* changes in consumption, investment, and government expenditures occur. Consumption expenditures, reflecting changes in net saving, may arise out of changed consumer expectations as to future income, changes in the urgency for expenditure because of an abnormal rate of previous consumption expenditure, and changes in corporate dividend policy. Government expenditures reflect public policy and, though they have important economic consequences, they do not arise directly out of economic developments. Private investment, however, is intimately tied up with and influenced by economic conditions. Business expectations play a dominant part in the determination to invest. The analysis of the causes underlying these expectations, though outlined briefly in our earlier discussion of investment incentives, must be left to the specialized study of the business cycle. However, we need to examine the effect of changes in the money supply upon the rate of investment. This we shall attempt to do in the next chapter.

Questions for Study

1. Why does the demand for money (either the transactions or the cash-balance approach) not provide an entirely satisfactory solution to the determination of the price level of current real output?

2. What is the *income* velocity of money? How does it differ from the *transactions* velocity of the equation $MV = PT$?

3. What factors determine the income velocity of money?

4. What may be said to be the central goals of monetary study?

5. Can one confidently state what the effect upon prices will be from changes in the rate of money expenditure? Why?

6. What are the three basic types of expenditure?

7. Can you name three reasons why the marginal profit expectations on new investment may be high?

8. In addition to favorable marginal profit expectations, what other considerations help to determine the volume of investment?

9. What is involved in *gross* investment? Under what circumstances may the reinvestment of funds arising from depreciation allowances be postponed?

10. What are the three sources of funds available for money expenditures?

11. How can investment expenditures be (a) more than, (b) less than funds provided by planned savings? What tends to happen to the level of income in each case?

12. How can "planned" investment be less than "planned" saving when at the same time "unplanned investment" and "unplanned saving" are equal?

13. What effect upon income results when government expenditures are (a) greater than taxes? (b) less than taxes?

14. What is the *multiplier?* What are the several kinds of "leakages"? How do leakages determine the size of the multiplier? How will the following developments affect the size of the multiplier: (a) An increase in thrift. (b) A decline in income taxes.

15. Suppose that the rate of expenditures is increased by $1,000,000 per month and leakages are 1/5. What will be the result upon the level of income?

16. Why is it difficult to estimate the multiplier effect to be expected from a given increase in investment or government expenditure?

VII

APPLICATIONS OF MONETARY AND FISCAL POLICY

_____25

The Interest Rate,
Availability of Funds,
Investment, and Income

In the preceding chapter we traced the manner in which changes in the level of expenditures are generated with resulting changes in the level of income, prices, and output. We saw that whenever investment plus government expenditures exceed saving plus taxes, the flow of income increases. Whenever investment plus government expenditures falls below saving plus taxes, income falls. Because the level of taxation and of government expenditures is determined by public policy, they do not constitute a self-generating source of business and income fluctuations. Therefore, in seeking the causes of economic and price level instability one may well concentrate attention upon the inequality of saving and investment. For, as we know, failure of these two to be equal is a primary cause of economic fluctuations.

The Reason for Inequality of Planned Saving
and Investment

Up to now we have made only general reference to the reasons for inequality of planned saving and investment. Investment responds to changes in profit expectations and to changes in the cost and availability of funds. Savings reflect the income level and the current propensity to save part of that income. But why are these two not brought into equality by the rate of interest? To find the answer to this question one must explore more deeply into the nature of the supply of and the demand for funds available for investment.

Gross savings. Gross savings of the economy consist of personal savings, undistributed corporate profits, and capital depletion allowances of business. These savings are represented by money temporarily shunted out of the income stream, and, assuming that government revenue and expenditure are in balance, its return normally depends upon a corresponding amount of investment spending on new capital goods.

Except for capital depletion allowances of business, the long-run pattern of savings is undoubtedly somewhat influenced by the expected interest return, with higher expected returns tending to encourage and lower rates tending to discourage marginal savings. However, in the short run none of the three major sources of savings is likely to be significantly affected by changes in the rate of interest. Rather, they mainly reflect changes in the level of income and changes in consumer expectations. Consequently the level or rate of savings in the short run is pretty much independent of changes in the interest rate. Since this is so, interest rate adjustments cannot equalize saving and investment by changing the rate of saving.

Gross investment. Gross investment involves money expenditures on the production of capital goods. These take the form of new construction, equipment, and inventory. Gross investment acts to absorb gross savings and return them to the income stream. Investment will occur only when businessmen expect that marginal *additions* to their capital supply will bring added revenues that clearly exceed the interest costs of obtaining and using the required funds.[1] Therefore, it is reasonable to suppose that the rate of interest, as a cost of obtaining funds, should have some effect upon

---

[1] This is clearly so when investment funds are borrowed. It is equally true of investment decisions when they are financed by the issue of stock, since a high price for new stock sold in the market means that buyers accept a low yield in the form of claims on the average earnings of the firm. The relation of the going rate of interest to the investment of corporate savings and capital depreciation allowance accumulations is somewhat more obscure. Here too, however, through the existence of alternate outlets for funds through the money market, the going rate of interest constitutes an "opportunity cost" that must be overcome by expected earnings from the investment of such savings in new plant and equipment.

the rate of investment. A high rate of interest should discourage and a low rate of interest should encourage investment.

The demand for investment funds. The expectations of profits from new investment are exposed to the workings of the law of diminishing returns. With a given state of technology the expansion of investment in capital goods tends to increase the proportion of capital input in the combination of productive factors. The result must eventually be that the added capital inputs will cause smaller and smaller additions to the total product, that is, they suffer from the workings of the law of diminishing marginal productivity. Therefore, without corresponding increases in the labor force and in natural resources, additional capital inputs from investment must yield smaller and smaller marginal profit expectations. On the assumption that business investment decisions are made on the basis of marginal profit expectations and the interest cost of obtaining funds, one can express the demand for investment funds by the ordinary down-sloping demand curves shown in Chart 15.

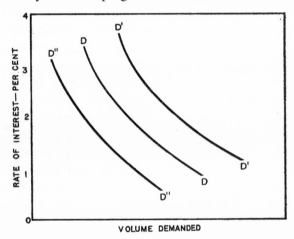

Chart 15. The Demand for Investment Funds.

A second characteristic of the demand for investment funds is its highly changeable nature. New inventions, discoveries of new natural resources, or a sharp increase in the rate of growth of population increases expectations of profit from new investment and pushes the demand curve for investment funds to the right. Thus *D'D'* indicates an increase in the attractiveness of new investment.

But of even greater importance are changes in marginal profit expectations arising from changes in price level or from any other current happening that is considered favorable or unfavorable to business. Signs of economic trouble that increase uncertainty and weaken profit expectations cause a shift of the demand curve to the left ($D''D''$).

The rate of interest and the equality of saving and investment. The volume of saving responds to changes in income and in the propensity to consume. In the short run at least it probably does not respond readily to changes in the rate of interest. Consequently, for any given level of income, one may assume that saving is independent of the rate of interest, and that a lower rate does not appreciably reduce saving. However, the rate of investment does respond somewhat to changes in the cost of obtaining investment funds, that is, to changes in the interest rate. There remains the task of discovering how the rate of interest is determined and why it may fail to equalize investment and saving.

To simplify our approach to this problem let us assume, first, that current saving is the only source of investment funds, and, second, that current savers will part with their savings at *any rate of interest that investors will pay*. With these assumptions in mind, let us now set up an example in which saving is at the rate of $100 million per day. This rate reflects the level of income, consumers' spending propensities, and corporate savings and bookkeeping practices. The market for investment funds, then, may be represented by the supply and demand curves shown in Chart 16. Because savings, at the rate of $100 million per day, are assumed to be offered in the loan market regardless of the rate of interest, the market rate of interest

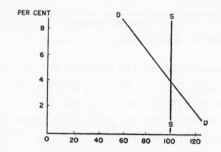

Chart 16. Loan Funds (in millions of dollars).

will be 4 per cent if investment exactly equals savings at $100 million per day. Under these assumed conditions the rate of interest equalizes current saving and investment. But neither of our simplifying assumptions, in respect to sources of investment funds, is necessarily true in all situations. Therefore, we must examine them further.

When interest rates are reasonably high and economic and credit conditions stable, it may very well be true that savers will accept the going market rate of interest and put all of their funds at the disposal of the market, as was assumed in the example above. But there are circumstances in which this may decidedly not be true. First, the act of investigating and making a loan involves trouble and expense for the lender. Unless the expected yield or rate of interest to be received is sufficient to more than compensate for this, the saver would be better off simply keeping his savings as idle cash hoards. Second, lending for private investment uses inevitably involves risks. Such risks, reflecting the uncertainty of investment prospects, must be compensated for by the expected interest returns. Adverse changes in business outlook may cause increased uncertainty in the mind of the lender and lead to an increase in his "precautionary" motive for holding cash. Only a suitable increase in the interest return will overcome this and persuade the saver to accept the risks involved in exchanging his cash for securities. Finally, whenever past experience in the capital market causes savers or their institutional stand-ins (savings banks, insurance companies, and the like) to believe that existing rates of interest are too low and that opportunity to lend at higher and more favorable rates will arise in the not too distant future, the "speculative" motive for holding cash asserts itself and some savings will not be lent in the market until interest rates actually become higher, or until the speculative motive subsides.

We can readily see, therefore, that current savings may not all be lent in the market regardless of the rate of interest. Instead, savers sometimes have "reservation prices" in the form of interest rates below which they will not go in lending their savings. These reservation prices vary with the judgment of the lenders as to (1) the trouble and expense of making the loan; (2) the degree of risk; and (3) worthwhileness of waiting for higher rates of interest in the future. By examining Chart 17 we may readily understand how the existence of reservation prices on current savings affects the rate of interest and the extent to which current savings will be invested.

Chart 17 is based upon the purely arbitrary assumptions that (1) the current rate of saving is $100 million per day and is the only source of loan funds; and (2) the curve *s—s* is the supply curve

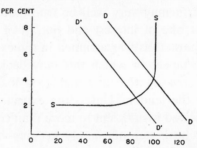

Chart 17. Loan Funds (in millions of dollars).

of funds offered in the market. It shows that so long as the interest rate is at least 4 per cent the whole $100 million of daily current savings will be released for investment. Below 4 per cent the liquidity preferences of savers begin to reduce their willingness to lend until, at 2 per cent, they refuse altogether to part with their cash in exchange for securities. With the investment demands for funds at *d—d* the rate of interest is above 4 per cent and all current savings are taken for investment. But when the investment demand falls, moving the demand curve to the left to *d'—d'*, the rate of interest falls to 2½ per cent and only $85 million out of the $100 million daily current savings are invested. With the demand for investment funds at *d'—d'* the market rate of interest would have to fall to about 1 per cent, obviously unacceptable to the savers, in order that the whole $100 million of daily current savings might find investment use. The moral of all this is simply that whenever profit prospects from new investment decline (the demand curve moves to the left) there may come a time when the rate of interest will not fall enough to induce business to invest an amount equal to current savings.

Investment, therefore, may sometimes be less than saving because falling interest rates may reach a level at which they no longer offset the disadvantages of investing in securities. Therefore, savers prefer to hold part of their savings in cash. For this reason the rate of interest cannot always be relied upon to insure that saving and investment will be equal.[2]

Other sources of investment funds. It will be recalled that we assumed at the beginning of this discussion that current saving was the sole source of investment funds. This, of course, is not necessarily true in real economic life. Actually there are two other sources of funds that may sometimes be drawn on for investment purposes. These are (1) past accumulations of uninvested savings in cash form; and (2) increases in the money supply. The first may become available for investment use as interest rates and business expectations rise. The second, an increase in the supply of money, may arise out of (1) gold imports; (2) an increase in Federal Reserve Bank credit; and (3) increases in commercial bank loans and investments based upon excess reserves.

The holders of uninvested accumulations of past savings and the holders of newly created money are like current savers in preferring to hold cash instead of investment securities whenever existing yields are too low to offset the trouble and risks of lending and the existing speculative motives for holding cash. If we turn again to our now

---

[2] The effect of "interest elastic" liquidity preferences upon the absorption of savings into cash hoards as interest rates fall may be seen in the familiar liquidity preference curve.

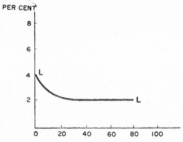

Chart 18. Savers' Demand for Cash (in millions of dollars per day, at varying rates of interest).

So long as interest rates are high enough to cover costs and risks of lending, and to prevent the appearance of speculative motives arising from expectations of higher rates, (*i.e.,* 4 per cent), all savings will be released for investment. But as interest rates fall, the demand for cash instead of securities increases until, at 2 per cent, savers prefer to hold all of their new assets in cash rather than in securities.

familiar supply and demand curves for investment funds, we can take into account the effect of the appearance of old cash savings and newly created money in the investment funds market. To do this we need a new curve showing the supply of investment funds. This new curve, located to the right of the supply of funds provided by current savers, may be seen in Chart 19. Here the curve *d—d*

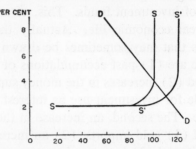

Chart 19. Quantity of Investment Funds Offered and Demanded (in millions of dollars per day, at varying rates of interest).

represents the demand for investment funds at varying rates of interest. The curve *s—s* represents the supply of funds made available out of current savings of $100 million per day at varying rates of interest. The new curve *s'—s'* is the supply of loan funds offered in the market at varying rates of interest from the combined sources of (1) current saving; (2) old cash hoards; and (3) new money. As a result of the additional funds provided out of old savings and new money the interest rate is 3 per cent and the daily rate of investment is $110 million. Thus we see how the appearance of additional loan funds may permit the interest rate to decline enough to cause investment to exceed current saving. The result is an increase in the level of income. Of course, one must note the possibility that investment demand (*d—d*) might decline (*d—d* moving to the left) to a point at which even the addition of added funds to the investment market cannot cause investment to equal or exceed saving.

Monetary Policy and the Rate of Investment

Control over the quantity of money is the core of monetary policy. Therefore, when monetary policy is used to influence the level of income and employment, it involves changing or controlling the quantity of money in such a way as to cause (1) an increase in the level of income if such an increase is needed; or (2) to maintain income at the desired level. As we already know, when the money supply is increased beyond current needs the holders of the new money seek to arrange their assets so that the money bears a satisfactory relationship to other assets. This they do by purchasing goods and securities. The purchase of securities tends to raise security prices and lower the rate of interest. Lower interest rates either attract new investment borrowing or the new money becomes absorbed by liquidity preferences arising from the falling rate of interest.

We can now apply our supply and demand analysis for investment funds more formally to changes in the supply of money, and trace the effects of such changes upon the rate of interest and the rate of investment, and through this the effect upon the level of income. We may best see the impact of monetary policy upon the level of income by examining two separate cases. The first is a situation in which a threat of inflation calls for such monetary restraint as to limit investment to the level of saving. The second is a situation that involves deflation and calls for sufficient monetary expansion to induce a rate of investment higher than the rate of saving so that the income may be pushed up to the full employment level.

Resistance to inflation. The threat of inflation requires a policy of corrective monetary restraint. Assuming that government revenues and expenditures are in balance, resistance to inflation requires that investment be held down to the level of saving. Or, if long-run growth of population and output calls for an annual money increase —4 per cent per year, for example—the supply of new money must be so regulated that investment will not exceed saving by more than the amount needed to provide the desired increase in income flow. Within the limits of human knowledge and foresight in monetary affairs, the Federal Reserve authorities are quite capable of limiting the creation of new money so as to head off excessive investment.

Expanding investment through monetary policy. Again assuming government revenues and expenditures to be in balance, any fall in investment below the rate of saving tends to reduce income and employment. In such a case monetary policy should be used to encourage investment. However, there is some question as to the effectiveness of monetary policy as a tool for increasing investment and income.

The experiences of the depression of the 1930's raised grave doubts about the powers of monetary policy to combat depression and unemployment. They led to a rather common conclusion that monetary policy was outmoded as a means for bringing about economic stability. It is important, therefore, to understand the conditions under which monetary policy is or is not likely to prove successful in inducing investment to rise above saving and generate a rise in the level of income and employment.

For monetary policy to be an effective tool for raising the level of income, an increase in the money supply must accomplish two things. First, it must effectively lower the rate of interest and increase the money actually available for investment purposes. Second, the decline in the rate of interest and the increased availability of funds must so encourage investment that it will exceed the current rate of saving. Should either of these two results fail to materialize, monetary policy cannot cause an increase in income.

As we know, within limits, an increase in the supply of money reduces the rate of interest. If a depression is relatively mild, precautionary motives for holding cash are not seriously stimulated. Therefore, an increase in the supply of money will result in a rise in security prices and a fall in interest rates. How great the decline in interest rates will be depends on the extent to which depression has generated new precautionary motives and the degree of speculative motives that arise among the holders of the new money. In the early stages of depression there is a very good chance that an increase in money will both depress the rate of interest and encourage investment. This situation is likely to exist in the case of a mild recession involving inventory reductions and readjustments, when longer-range investment prospects are still bright.

Once a depression has become severe, precautionary motives for holding money rise sharply. Consequently any increase in money may then merely be absorbed by the growing liquidity preferences of the holders, with little tendency to drive down the rate of interest. Even a modest drop in the interest rate will be sufficient to make the advantages of holding cash outweigh those of taking the risks inherent in lending and purchasing securities in time of severe depression.

The effect of a decline in the demand for investment funds that occurs during mild depression, and the possible effects of expanding the quantity of money at such a time, may readily be seen by examining Chart 20 below.

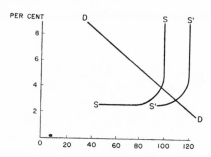

Chart 20. Supply and Demand for Investment Funds (in millions of dollars per day, at varying rates of interest.)

The line *d—d* represents the demand for investment funds at varying rates of interest under conditions of mild depression. The line *s—s* represents the supply of investment funds offered on the market from current savings at varying rates of interest. Without any additional investment funds in the form of new money created by the monetary authorities, the rate of investment is fixed at the point of intersection of the *d—d* and *s—s* curves at $95 million per day. Since this is less than the current saving of $100 million per day, income falls. Now, if as a result of newly created money the total supply of investment funds offered on the market at varying rates of interest becomes *s'—s'*, investment, shown by the intersection of *d—d* and *s'—s'*, will be $110 million per day, an amount greater than current saving of $100 million, and the increase in money will induce a rise in income.

The case is different, however, when depression has become severe enough to create a sharp increase in precautionary motives of money lenders and a serious fall in marginal profit expectations. In such circumstances not only must the interest rate be pushed to a very low level if investment is to equal current saving, but also the rise in precautionary and speculative motives among lenders makes it virtually impossible to drive interest rates down by increasing the supply of money. This possible situation in the market for investment funds is seen in Chart 21.

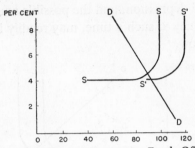

Chart 21. Quantity of Investment Funds Offered and Demanded for Investment (in millions of dollars per day, at varying rates of interest).

In Chart 21 the line *d—d* represents the demand for investment funds under the assumed depression conditions. The line *s—s* represents the supply of investment funds offered at varying rates of interest out of the current level of savings of $100 million. The line *s'—s'* represents the total supply of investment funds at varying rates of interest offered by current savers and the holders of newly created money.

Under circumstances illustrated in Chart 21, depression has so raised precautionary motives for holding money that owners of funds will not release them at less than 4 per cent interest. This is true irrespective of how far to the right the injection of new money may move the *s'—s'* curve. This being so, it becomes impossible for monetary policy to be effective in inducing the rate of investment to exceed the current rate of saving and thus bring about a rise in the level of income. Unless the public is content to wait for "natural" cyclical causes to restore investment incentives to a higher level and to reduce precautionary motives among holders of money, it will be necessary to invoke *fiscal policy*, with government expenditure above government revenue.

Monetary Policy, the Rate of Interest, and Investment

We have seen that in a severe depression monetary policy may prove unable to stimulate investment sufficiently to cause an expansion in income. In such a case it will be necessary to use fiscal policy to promote revival. With the rise in enthusiasm for the use of fiscal policy to counteract depression there developed a tendency to regard monetary policy as outmoded and inadequate for *all* control purposes. Thus, it was held that a tight money policy does not raise interest rates enough to be effective in restraining investment in times of boom. Consequently, only fiscal policy and, perhaps, selective controls over credit should be used during *both* depressions and booms to promote economic stability.

Does investment respond to changes in the rate of interest? The basis for the argument that monetary policy cannot be an effective means for controlling the rate of investment rests in the belief, supported both by testimony of businessmen and by analysis of investment practices, that the demand for investment funds shows little responsiveness to changes in the rate of interest. Two reasons may be given for this belief. First, changes in the rate of interest arising from changes in monetary policy are too small to be of significance. For example, during the second quarter of 1953, when the Federal Reserve tight money policy was in effect, the rate of interest on business loans in New York City averaged 3.52 per cent and in nineteen other cities of the country it averaged 3.74 per cent. A little over a year later, in 1954, during the Federal Reserve policy of "active ease," the interest rates on business loans in New York City and in the nineteen other cities had fallen only to 3.29 per cent and 3.56 per cent respectively. In the same interval, yields on corporate bonds declined from 3.61 per cent to 3.13 per cent. Second, in the light of such limited variations in interest rates that actually appear in the market, investment decisions cannot be expected to be seriously affected by interest rate changes brought about by monetary policy.

The belief that the demand for investment funds is unresponsive to changes in interest rates is supported by the following arguments:

1. Investment decisions of business firms depend upon such broad estimates of costs and expected returns that changes in the rate of interest paid for investment funds are insignificant. This view is supported by the well-known absence of business information about marginal costs and the resulting tendency to use some form of average costs as a basis for entrepreneurial decisions. Consequently, so long as *average* returns

promise to exceed *average* total costs by an acceptable margin, investment for expansion will take place.

2. Investment decisions relating to inventory accumulations depend mainly upon the accepted pattern of the relation of inventory to sales and upon changes in prices. Consequently, this substantial and variable item of investment is unlikely to be sensitive to changes in the rate of interest.[3]

3. Decisions to invest in new equipment are likewise often but little affected by changes in interest rates. The uncertainties of obsolescence and market changes often cause business firms to refuse to invest in new equipment unless it promises to pay for itself in a short space of time (three to five years). Interest costs obviously can have but a minor place in decisions of this kind. Moreover, when businessmen do attempt to relate profit expectations to a rate of interest, the rate of interest that new investment must earn to justify itself is some "standard" rate rather than the market rate of interest.[4]

4. The very large fraction of total investment that is made out of business gross savings, that is, depreciation allowances and undistributed earnings, introduces another important area in which the interest costs are unlikely to influence investment.

These arguments that interest rate changes can have but a modest influence upon investment are supported by the testimony of businessmen themselves and by records of their decisions.[5]

There remains one area in which investment is likely to respond to changes in the rate of interest. Investment in long-term capital such as housing and other construction, and transport and public utilities is doubtless sensitive to changes in interest costs. Since such long-term investments comprise only about a quarter of the

---

[3] R. G. Hawtrey has contended that traders are in fact influenced to modify the size of their inventory holdings by changes in the interest cost of borrowed funds. Cf. his *Currency and Credit*, New York, Longmans, Green & Co., 1928, 3rd ed., pp. 24–27, and *A Century of Bank Rate*, London, Longmans, Green & Co., 1938, pp. 189–195.

[4] Cf. Lutz, F. A., "The Interest Rate and Investment in a Dynamic Economy," *American Economic Review,* December 1945. Also see Hill, Horace G. Jr., *A New Method of Computing Rate of Return of Capital Expenditure,* Joel Dean Associates, New York, 1953, p. 4, where he says that a surprising number of companies had no system of evaluating or justifying a capital expenditure, but depended solely upon executive "judgment."

[5] Cf. *Oxford Studies in the Price Mechanism,* edited by T. E. Wilson and P. W. S. Andrews, London, Oxford University Press, 1951, pp. 27–30, 51–67. Also see Ebersole, J. Franklin, "The Influence of Interest Rates Upon Entrepreneurial Decisions," summarized in the *American Economic Review,* March 1938, Supplement, pp. 74–75.

gross investment of the country, their response to changes in the rate of interest does not provide a very strong case for the influence of interest rates over the general level of investment.[6]

The effect of interest rate changes on profit expectations. Even though, under given conditions of expectations, the demand for investment funds is not "interest elastic," it may still follow that the level of investment responds to interest changes. For example, a rise in money rates, known to have been induced by conscious central bank policy, increases the uncertainty as to both the future rate of interest and the future availability of funds. This growth of uncertainty must surely dim expectations and induce increased caution in the current investment thinking of businessmen. In such a case the demand curve for investment funds moves to the left.

Monetary Policy and Credit Availability

In spite of the arguments advanced to show that investment does not respond substantially to changes in interest rates, we should not summarily dismiss monetary policy as a useless tool. On the contrary, there is excellent reason to believe that monetary policy is not only useful but is often an indispensable device for promoting economic stability.

Credit availability affects the rate of investment. To understand the significance of monetary policy as a device for economic control let us examine the case of reasonable prosperity, with profit expectations high and with precautionary motives for holding cash at a low level. To avoid inflation under such conditions investment must be so restrained that the growth in money income matches the growth in output. Such restraint is made entirely possible by placing appropriate limits upon the rate of expansion in the supply of money. There can be no doubt that a restrictive monetary policy can prevent an expansion of money beyond the limits needed for economic stability. Even when the push-pull effect of rising wages and rising prices threatens to drive up the price level, the increase can be avoided by careful monetary restraint. For unless

---

[6] Lutz, *op. cit.,* p. 826.

business can obtain additional loan funds out of which to pay higher wages, wage increases will be held in check.[7]

What, we may ask, is the *manner* in which monetary restraint imposes limits upon investment? As we know, tighter money reduces the loan funds made available by commercial banks and tends to raise interest rates. But, as we also know, there are many areas of investment in which higher interest rates, in themselves, may not discourage investment demand. What actually happens is that the shortened supply of investment funds is rationed out among borrowers by some method other than by high interest rates. Lenders, confronted by a short supply of funds, do not auction those funds off to the highest bidder among the would-be borrowers. Why is this so? First, the loan market being what it is, speculative borrowers would tend to outbid the more conservative. Therefore, the auction of funds to the highest bidders would expose lenders to entirely unsatisfactory hazards. For this reason credit rationing must be and is used by lenders as a method for allocating a limited amount of loan funds in a market full of eager would-be borrowers.[8] Thus, when money is tight, lenders simply ration out the funds to whom they consider the best borrowers. Commercial banks, for example, when confronted by a shortage of reserves, higher central bank discount rates, and pressure to restrain credit expansions, simply devote their limited loan funds to satisfying the most pressing needs of their best customers. Each applicant's record with the bank is scrutinized. Does he repay loans promptly? Is he a genuinely good credit risk? Does he normally carry a balance on deposit with the bank that is "satisfactory" and appropriate in the light of his loan requirements? Applicants turned down are told, quite rightly, that loan funds are not now available.[9] At some later date, when money is more plentiful, they may reasonably expect to be accommodated. Thus the availability of funds de-

---

[7] Cf. Robertson, D. H., *Three Banks Review,* March 1949, as quoted by R. S. Sayers in *Oxford Studies in the Price Mechanism,* edited by T. Wilson and P. W. S. Andrews, p. 9.

[8] Cf. Ellis, Howard S., "The Rediscovery of Money," *Money, Trade, and Economic Growth,* New York, The Macmillan Company, 1951, p. 254–5.

[9] Cf. Adams, E. Sherman, *Monetary Policy and the Present Credit Situation,* American Bankers Association, 1955, for the reports by bankers that the Federal Reserve shift to a tighter money policy in 1955 had influenced them to be more selective in making loans.

termines the total amount of investment funds that can be borrowed at any given time. Credit rationing rather than the auctioning off of funds to the highest bidder is the established manner for determining who shall obtain funds and who shall be relegated to membership in the group sometimes referred to as the "fringe of unsatisfied borrowers." Thus we see that monetary restraint limits the rate of investment even though interest rates may not rise enough to cut off the borrower.

As a practical matter, central banks, mindful of their responsibilities as lenders of last resort to the money market, generally prefer to apply gradual pressure when imposing restraint. Thus they raise their discount rates and compel banks to go into debt in order to obtain funds to lend. As a result, rising interest rates reflect tighter money conditions and there arises restraint on investment both from higher costs of borrowing and from credit rationing by the bank. The effect of rising interest rates, however, appears in still another quarter. Nonbank lenders, both institutional and individual, become more reluctant to lend as interest rates begin to rise and security prices fall. Security underwriters or investment bankers shy away from handling new security issues at a time when falling security prices threaten their profit margin. Rising interest rates, therefore, may create an effective barrier to long-term business borrowing. In this case it is not so much that high interest rates discourage the borrower as that rising rates, by stimulating the speculation motives of money lenders, cut off the supply.[10]

Monetary ease and the rate of investment. If a monetary policy of restraint can be made effective by reducing the availability of funds and inducing credit rationing, can the reverse be said of credit ease? In the case of a mild recession in business a prompt policy of monetary ease makes possible the accommodation of borrowers who previously were unable to get funds. So long as the recession is mild, long-run profit expectations will remain relatively firm and investment will expand in response to the increased availability of funds. Therefore, monetary policy, quickly and positively shifted to meet the changes in business, can provide a ready means for encouragement of investment in time of slump.

---

[10] In support of this see Rosa, Robert V., "Interest Rates and the Central Bank" and Sproul, Allan, "Changing Concepts of Central Banking," both in *Money, Trade and Economic Growth,* New York, Macmillan Company, 1951.

Obviously emphasis is needed on the matter of proper timing of monetary policy. Mild restraint promptly applied before speculative aspects of a boom develop too far is a delicate yet powerful means of restraint. Likewise, when employment and income threaten to decline, monetary policy may be shifted to one of ease. Its greatest attractiveness rests in its flexibility and ready adaptability to changing conditions as they arise, and its freedom from many of the political handicaps that beset fiscal policy.

Questions for Study

1. Does the rate of saving change in response to short-run changes in the rate of interest?

2. What are the factors that influence businessmen's decisions to invest?

3. Does the demand curve for investment funds slope down and to the right as do the demand curves for commodities?

4. In the light of businessmen's testimony of the basis for their investment decisions, would you expect the investment funds demand curve to be steep or relatively flat? Why?

5. What happens to the investment funds demand curve when:
   a) New natural resources are discovered?
   b) Technological progress occurs?
   c) Business profit prospects decline?

6. If there were no cost attached to lending funds and no precautionary or speculative motives among savers, what would be the shape of the supply curve for investment funds at varying rates of interest?

7. Why do holders of loan funds have "reservation prices" for the use of their funds below which they will not lend?

8. What causes the loan fund supply curve to slope up and to the right? What changes occur in the loan fund supply curve when:
   a) Poor business prospects raise the precautionary motives of lenders?
   b) Banks' excess reserves are increased by open market security purchases by the Federal Reserve Banks?

9. Examine Chart 20 on page 413.
   a) Why is the curve $s'-s'$ to the right of the curve $s-s$? What are the sources of the added funds represented by the difference between the two curves?

b) Do you understand why, under conditions illustrated here, an increase in the available supply of loan funds from *s—s* to *s'—s'* will induce an expansion in income?

c) Do you see why a fall in profit prospects and a sharp movement of the demand curve *d—d* to the left would result in a fall in income?

10. Why is it possible to check an unwanted expansion in the supply of money by the use of monetary policy? How do you harmonize this with the often expressed view that in good times a tight money policy on the part of the central bank will not cause banks and other lenders to raise the rate of interest charged by an amount sufficient to discourage business borrowing? Why do interest rates move within such a limited range in response to changes in monetary policy?

11. Under what conditions can monetary policy be expected effectively to induce an expansion in the rate of investment above the level of saving and thus cause an increase in income?

12. When is it probably powerless to induce an expansion of income?

13. Why does effective monetary policy need to be prompt if it is to counteract a decline in business?

26

The Place of Fiscal Policy in Economic Stabilization

We are already familiar with the forces that govern the supply of money and their relation to the level of income, employment, and prices. In the light of these relationships we considered the place of monetary policy, as exercised through the Federal Reserve System, in the search for economic and price stability. We observed that while monetary policy is an effective and necessary tool for restraining the rate of expenditures during inflationary booms, it may prove ineffective as a stimulator of investment during depression. Consequently it is highly necessary that there be included in the arsenal of weapons for combatting economic instability the direct force of government expenditures. In other words, fiscal policy must be made a part of the equipment for controlling the level of income. Because it can be used to offset undesirable changes in expenditures that develop in the private sector of the economy, it is useful for moderating both booms and depressions.

Meaning of fiscal policy. Fiscal policy is concerned with revenues and expenditures of government. Quite understandably, state and local governments are in no position to adapt their own fiscal practices to the promotion of the general national welfare. Consequently, only Federal fiscal policy can be used in promoting stability and full employment.

Fiscal policy and economic stabilization. Unlike the credit policy of central banks, which is mainly limited to changing the cost and availability of loan funds in the money market, fiscal policy can be used more directly to vary the flow of money income. During booms, for example, an excess of taxes over governmental expenditures tends to absorb part of the excess money supply and dampen down the rate of spending. During depressions an excess of expenditures over taxes tends to expand the flow of money income.

Fiscal policy as a means for influencing the flow of income may involve (1) a change in the level of taxes; (2) a change in the level of government expenditures; or (3) a combination of the two. Whether the method of applying fiscal policy to the problem of economic stabilization takes the form of changing taxes or changing the level of government expenditures, the basic consequences are the same. To impose restraint, increased taxes or reduced expenditures tend to result in a surplus of tax revenues over expenditures. To encourage expansion, reduced taxes or expanded government spending tends to cause a deficit of revenue as compared to expenditures. Thus restraint through fiscal policy tends to operate through surpluses of tax receipts held by the Treasury. Expansion policy tends to operate through the appearance of a cash deficit.[1] It is important that we understand the stabilization effects of both methods of applying fiscal policy.

Stabilization through adjustment of taxes. Because the Federal budget is now of such enormous proportions, the use of fiscal policy as a stabilizer may be concentrated upon the adjustment of taxes rather than changes in the level of governmental expenditures. Thus, to combat depression, tax revenues should be reduced. With no reduction in government spending the reduction in taxes tends to create a deficit which must be made up by new bank credit and by borrowing uninvested savings. So long as employment and income are below the desired level, deficit financing should continue. On the other hand, during inflation tax revenue should be increased to provide a surplus and thus check expansion.

Increased taxes restrict spending by consumers, reduce profit ex-

---

[1] One should remember that an excess of *cash* receipts or of *cash* expenditures is of the essence of fiscal policy influence upon total expenditures and the flow of income. Because, for the purposes of the official "bookkeeping" budget, certain receipts, such as social security taxes, are considered as expended when transferred to trust accounts held by the Treasury, and because payments out of such accounts are not considered as budgetary expenditures, the bookkeeping budget may show a deficit at a time when cash receipts of the Treasury are in excess of expenditures. Similarly, at times, the expenditures of cash may exceed the bookkeeping expenditures if depression causes a drawing down of social security trust funds for unemployment insurance payments. Obviously it is the cash rather than the bookkeeping budget position of the Treasury that has significance for stabilization purposes.

pectations, and discourage investment spending. However, such tax increases, and the resulting Treasury surplus, may not be sufficient to outweigh other favorable factors, with the result that investment may not be checked after all. In this case monetary restraint must be called in to provide the necessary investment restraint. As an encouragement to business expansion and private investment a reduction of business taxes and taxes upon consumers tends to increase profit expectations.

In respect to the consumers, a change in taxes affects their disposable incomes. Higher taxes, for example, reduce disposable incomes and tend to reduce consumption expenditures, although to some extent savings may be reduced instead. Similarly, tax reductions increase disposable incomes and encourage consumption expenditure. Because the marginal propensity to consume is believed to be higher for small income receivers than for consumers with relatively large incomes, advocates of stabilization through adjustment of taxes often favor concentrating tax changes largely upon smaller income receivers. Thus, to counteract inflation, personal tax exemptions might be lowered. To combat depression, a rise in personal exemptions would be in order. The attractiveness of such a method of tax adjustments is lessened by the discrimination against the small income receiver that is involved. It is hard to justify singling out the small taxpayer for greater tax burdens during inflation merely because of his inability to draw upon his savings to absorb the tax, as can his more fortunate brethren with higher incomes.

The problem of introducing flexibility into Treasury revenues. To introduce appropriate counter-cyclical variations in Treasury tax receipts requires some dependable method of adjustment to current circumstances. Ideally, the adjustment of taxes should be automatic, or "built in." To a very considerable degree such built-in flexibility is provided by our social security taxes, personal income taxes, and corporate income taxes. Revenues provided by these types of taxes tend to rise and fall with changes in the national income. This is fortunate inasmuch as Congressional action in changing tax laws is slow and involves so many delays that many of the benefits of fiscal policy as a counter-cyclical force are nullified. Particularly is delay likely in the enactment of laws to raise taxes during booms. The effectiveness of fiscal policy would be strengthened if Congress could be persuaded to establish rules within which qualified administrative authorities would have the power to introduce desirable changes in taxes. Such delegation of power over taxes by Congress, however, appears a remote possibility. The inflationary bias of political decisions is closely related to the problem of tax flexibility. Consequently, brakes upon inflation in the form of higher tax rates will be applied reluctantly, if at all.

Flexible governmental expenditures as a counter-cyclical tool. The root of economic fluctuations appears to lie in variations in the rate of private spending. In the section above we examined the possibility of offsetting changes in such spending by changing the tax receipts of the Treasury. We saw that shrinkage in private investment, producing a decline in income and employment, may be partially offset by tax reduction. In spite of its attractive possibilities, tax reduction may be inadequate to offset income shrinkage. As we know, increases in disposable income resulting from lowered taxes on consumers may be salted away in cash hoards or savings to await more promising times. Also, reductions in business taxes, although happily received by business, may be of little real use in stimulating expenditure if profits are nonexistent or prospects of future profits look dim. Furthermore, tax reduction, by itself, cannot improve the income position and the consuming power of those unfortunate enough to be unemployed.

It is vital, therefore, that there be some positive means for restoring income to those who have lost it through unemployment. There are two standard ways to increase the incomes of the unemployed. The first, and most important as a source of immediate support to income, is an increase of "transfer payments" by the government.[2] The most significant counter-cyclical transfer payments are unemployment insurance benefits. These payments provide a partial substitute for income lost through unemployment and constitute a formidable prop to total income during depression. Unemployment insurance, like income tax variation, has the merit of being "built in" so that the results appear automatically without waiting for Congressional action.

Because of the limited time of coverage by unemployment insur-

---

[2] Transfer payments are money payments for which no actual productive service is currently rendered. They include, for example, unemployment insurance benefits, relief payments, veteran benefits, and the like.

ance, prolonged and severe depression may require other ways of expanding personal incomes through government expenditure. For example, should a prolonged depression use up unemployment insurance rights, an increased flow of relief payments would arise. Such payments, when dependent upon Federal assistance, would require Congressional action.

Public works expenditures. Should unemployment continue on such a scale as to require Federal expenditures over and above those involved in the unemployment insurance benefits, it becomes desirable that something tangible and useful should be produced in return for the payment. In other words, additional governmental expenditures should leave the realm of mere transfer payments and move into the area of public works. Here the payments are more defensible since there is no lack of worthwhile work that needs doing within the area of government responsibility. Roads, public buildings, and hospitals, to mention but a few, are chronically in short supply.

Public works have the advantage of providing useful employment in the construction trades and in the industries providing the necessary materials, both areas that are hard hit in times of serious depression. Although it is unrealistic to expect that public works will fill all the gaps of unemployment in the private sector of the economy, at least it provides some highly desirable relief.

To be genuinely effective in expanding investment during depression, public works require (1) proper timing; (2) proper financing; and (3) widespread approval in the business and investing community. The need for proper timing is obvious. Plans must be ready for rapid use if falling private investment is to be offset. At the same time, public works should be gradually terminated with the recovery of private investment. Such a program calls for long-range planning, as short-run improvisation is strewn with pitfalls.

Proper financing of public works requires measures that will be certain to provide a net increase in investment. But unless one visualizes a continually rising national debt, ultimate payment by the taxpayers cannot be avoided, and the proper timing of such taxes becomes an important question. The most promising procedure is to finance part of the expenditure for public works by expanding the government debt in the form of Treasury bills and notes. This policy encourages the banks to use their excess reserves as a basis for loan and deposit expansion. Government borrowing thus tends to replace private borrowing at the banks. In addition, the issue of government bonds will induce some investment by capitalists and institutional investors who otherwise would tend to hoard their cash accumulations because of investment uncertainties. The expansion of the government debt during depressions calls for its retirement during better times. Here, again, the timing problem may be a difficult one. As a partial alternative to borrowing, the government might impose heavier taxes upon large incomes from which arise heavy accumulations of idle savings during depressions. This action, however, might have undesirable psychological results.

Of quite a different sort is the problem that would attend the use of public works or government investment as a means of counteracting chronic depression. Some economists have believed that the approach of "economic maturity" of the capitalistic system inevitably leads to a condition of chronic depression owing to the continued lag in private investment. This view suggests that long-run economic prosperity and growth may eventually require a constant expansion of government investment to fill the gap left by the decline of private investment and the continued high propensity to save.

Finally, the success of public works in promoting recovery depends largely upon the approval of the business community. If businessmen believe that public works will be beneficial to business, they will respond favorably, and in turn will expand their own investments. On the other hand, private investment will not be stimulated if businessmen generally look upon public works as the height of folly. Indeed, under such circumstances, private investment may well fall below the level that would have been maintained in the absence of public works.

Fiscal policy and the size of the national debt. The use of fiscal policy to counteract cyclical fluctuations and unemployment raises some special problems concerning the national debt. To use fiscal policy to combat depression there is involved either a decrease in taxes, with a resulting budgetary deficit, or an increase in government expenditure. As we shall see later, under certain conditions some expansionary effect may be achieved by expanding government spending while increasing taxes so as to keep a balanced budget. Nevertheless, the effective use of fiscal policy to offset depression is almost certain to involve deficit financing. On the other hand, to offset inflationary tendencies taxes should be raised and, where politically feasible, expenditures lowered, with a resulting surplus in the budget. Fiscal policy, as a stabilizer over the cycle, is generally incompatible with an annually balanced budget of cash intake and outgo. Instead, counter-cyclical fiscal policy seems to require that the cash budget be balanced over the cycle rather than annually. The politically difficult task of establishing a sufficient surplus during good times to offset the deficits of bad times creates a serious barrier to the successful use of fiscal policy for stabilization purposes. Moreover, understandably enough, there is the opposition often raised to any deficits, even annual ones, made for the purpose of economic stabilization and promotion of full employment. Budgetary deficits are associated in the public mind with unsound monetary policies, and with good reason in many cases. Such opposition can be overcome only by demonstration that such a plan for fiscal policy use is soundly conceived and carefully and systematically operated without excessive political interference.

Fiscal policy and secular trends. Goals of policy must go beyond cyclical stability alone. The economy must be able to expand at a rate sufficient to absorb a growing population and provide a rising standard of living. At the same time it is important that this be accomplished without inflation. How, then, is fiscal policy to be related to the problem of long-run growth?

First, should private investment prospects become so rosy that a chronic or long-run expansion of an inflationary sort makes an appearance, fiscal policy should, on balance, be made restrictive. The most effective restraint involves cash revenues being kept above expenditures over the cycle, and long-run debt reduction. On the other hand, if, as some economists have feared, there is an approach of "economic maturity" of the capitalistic system, with full employment savings in excess of profitable private investment outlets, fiscal policy should move in the opposite direction. Government expenditure should exceed revenues, on balance, in order that government expenditure might fill the gap left by the deficiency of private investment. Such a situation would seem to require a long-run increase in the Federal debt and some kind of long-run program of public works as the price of full employment and economic growth.[3]

Balanced Budget Fiscal Policy and Economic Stabilization

The effects of government expenditures upon the level of aggregate spending and income flow are not entirely limited, as we have been so far assuming, to cases in which there are budget surpluses and deficits. Instead, any expansion of government spending may have a tendency to increase the income flow and any decline in government spending may tend to reduce it, even though the budget remains in balance. Consequently, in the search for stabilization by use of fiscal policy it is not enough to be solely concerned with the size of budgetary surpluses and deficits. In times of increased government expenditure an expansionary potential exists even though the increase is financed out of taxes.

There are two quite separate reasons for expecting a balanced-budget increase in government expenditures to be expansionary. First, increased expenditures often involve a considerable lag between the time that orders are placed and the time of delivery. During this period of lag, producers must spend funds obtained from borrowing (or from their own idle cash balances), with a resulting expansion in money incomes. Thus, before taxes are levied to make payment for the additional government purchases, an increase in the flow of income has already taken place. So long, then, as the new rising level of government expenditures is maintained, the effect of the initial outpouring of new income by the producers will continue, subject, of course, to the limitations of the multiplier effect. Conversely, a decline in government expenditure, evidenced by a decline in new orders to industry, may induce a shrinkage of business spending that precedes the decline in taxes. Tax reduction with a balanced budget must await the final delivery and payment for goods on order.

Second, disregarding the lag effect just considered, there is a

---

[3] Some expansionary effects may be achieved within a balanced budget by long-run increases in the level of government spending financed by taxes when the latter encroach more upon savings than upon consumption or business investment.

possibility that an increase in government taxes to match increased expenditures may not actually reduce the level of private spending by an equal amount. Increased taxes upon consumers may in part result in a decline in consumers' savings. If consumers' current savings were being hoarded because of unfavorable business conditions, their absorption by higher taxes for government spending would clearly add to the income flow. Or, if consumers' savings were currently being utilized for business investment, their absorption by taxes might well drive the businessman to the banks for new bank loans to finance his current investment needs. Only when savings are not hoarded and increased taxes, including the burden of the businessman's own share, are sufficiently discouraging to business prospects to cause a decline in private investment, will the balanced-budget increase in government expenditures be purely neutral and nonexpansionary in its ultimate effects. On the other hand, a reduction in government expenditures and taxes may have the effect of reducing the income flow if tax reduction should be followed by a rise in consumers' savings that is not offset by an increase in private investment incentives.

Monetary Policy vs. Fiscal Policy

Before the depression of the 1930's, monetary policy of central banks was looked upon as a proper and efficient instrument for the achievement of economic stability. The deliberate use of fiscal policy for that purpose had not yet achieved respectability. The eclipse of monetary policy as an important stabilizer grew out of the severe depression, when it seemed inadequate to revive business and employment. In its place fiscal policy took the limelight and became the fair-haired boy of the stabilizers. Monetary policy was considered old fashioned and obsolete. However, the inflation of the post-war period continued in spite of the fact that, for the most part, the cash budget of the Treasury showed a substantial surplus. Eventually the indispensable character of monetary restraint in an inflationary world began again to be recognized.

Monetary policy has two major advantages. First, it is impersonal and nondiscriminatory in nature (save for selective credit controls) and involves a minimum amount of direct governmental interference in economic affairs. Second, it is flexible in operation and can be applied quickly as situations in the economy develop or change. Easy money policies may be adopted and then modified or reversed in a short space of time without fanfare or public commotion. Unlike fiscal policy, it operates for the most part in an area free from political pressures. In this respect the power to apply economic restraint through monetary policy is especially important. On the other hand, the greatest weakness of monetary policy is its inability directly to expand income and investment. It can only improve the opportunity for private business to expand them.

In contrast to the weakness of monetary policy, fiscal policy is a powerful weapon for offsetting and checking depression and unemployment. The built-in changes in tax revenues and unemployment expenditures are both prompt and effective in counteracting moderate recessions. In the case of severe recessions, fiscal policy can be used to good account through public works expenditures. The weakness of fiscal policy as a stabilizing device lies in the difficulty of getting sufficient restraint in times of inflation to bring an expansion under control. Here it becomes imperative that monetary restraint be brought into the picture.

One must conclude, therefore, that neither monetary nor fiscal policy, taken alone, can provide the means for an adequate stabilization program. Instead, each is essential and must be used to supplement the other. Consequently, it is important that they be operated in complete harmony and not at cross purposes, and one should not be neglected in favor of the other. For most purposes fiscal policy operations should, so far as possible, be "built in" in such a way as to remove them from political pressures. This would leave to monetary policy of the central bank the initiative of voluntary actions of the discretionary type. Only when deflation and depression threatens to become excessive should Congressional action be required to fortify the automatic results of built-in fiscal policy and the central bank monetary policy. In such a case, special Congressional action to change tax rates and to embark on public works projects would be appropriate.

Debt Management and Economic Stabilization

The magnitude of the publicly held Federal debt and the continuous necessity of refunding maturing issues present a possibility of utilizing debt management for economic stabilization. Generally, debt management is concerned with the issue of new securities suited to current market conditions. In this way refinancing is accomplished at the lowest possible cost to the Treasury. In contrast, the use of debt management to promote cyclical stabilization requires that refunding security issues be tailored to *influence* the money market in some appropriate way.

To counteract depression, proper monetary policy should increase the money supply and increase the liquidity of banks and the general public. Treasury bills, with three-months' maturity, are highly liquid. Consequently, during depressions refunding issues might well take the form of Treasury bills. If taken by banks in exchange for maturing securities held by them, the Treasury bills put the banks in a more liquid position than if banks were compelled to accept securities of longer maturity. Moreover, when Treasury bills are issued to refund longer-maturity security holdings of non-bank investors, such investors find their liquidity increased. This is true whether they receive cash payment out of the proceeds of the sale of bills to the banks or accept the new bill issues themselves. In any event the result is some easing of the money market.

On the other hand, when monetary restraint is needed, the Treasury can issue long-term refunding securities, which compete for funds in the long-term capital market. The liquidity of banks and other investors is reduced and restraint is encouraged.

Counter-cyclical debt management of this kind is desirable if the Treasury is not to find its refunding operations in conflict with current monetary and fiscal policy.

Questions for Study

1. Why is fiscal policy an important part of the equipment for combatting economic instability? Why are its effects direct while those of monetary policy are indirect in nature?

2. Why is a cash deficit more significant than a bookkeeping deficit as a means for expanding money expenditures?

3. What are the "built-in" stabilizers that arise in connection with modern fiscal policy? Why are these features important to successful fiscal policy contributions to economic stability?

4. If a change in tax rates were to be made in order to influence the total rate of money expenditures, whose taxes should be changed the most to obtain the maximum results?

5. What are the advantages of using public works as a means for reducing unemployment? Under what circumstances are they most likely to be appropriate?

6. What does the use of fiscal policy to combat cyclical fluctuations require as to the balancing of the Federal budget? What would be the results of using it to combat secular stagnation?

7. Why may increased government expenditures, paid for out of current taxes, tend to result in a net increase in expenditures?

8. Why cannot fiscal policy provide a complete substitute for sound monetary policy?

9. In times of depression it is suggested that the Treasury's refunding of its debts should involve increased issues of short-maturing securities. Why is this so? Is the reverse policy advisable in times of inflation?

27

Goals of Monetary and Fiscal Policy

Monetary and fiscal policy, taken together, provide powerful tools for influencing the flow of money income and the level of output, employment, and prices. These tools can be properly used only after the ultimate policy goals are established and the paths leading to such goals are explored and identified.

In the search for optimum economic well-being more than one appropriate goal of policy emerges. Furthermore, attempts to achieve one goal may conflict with actions taken in the pursuit of others equally legitimate. For example, one commonly accepted goal of monetary policy is the insurance that funds shall be readily available for financing the normal seasonal and irregular needs of business. Without such availability of funds the operations of a free enterprise economy would be seriously handicapped. Another accepted goal of policy is the avoidance of employment and price level instability. These goals, each desirable in its own right, may lead to conflicting policy actions. To insure the availability of adequate funds for financing current trade and business may, inadvertently, lead to excessive monetary expansion. At the same time, a policy of price stability, rigidly adhered to, may sometimes impose undesirable restraint on business operations. A similar conflict may arise between policy actions directed at eliminating unemployment by monetary and income expansion and the equally valid goal of stability of price levels. It is apparent, therefore, that monetary and fiscal policy decisions require the exercise of judgment and care in order adequately to deal with policy goals that are individually desirable but capable of involving conflicting results.

434

Some Goals of Economic Policy

There are a number of basic goals of economic policy to be considered. First is the need to reduce cyclical instability and its attendant evils. Second is the necessity of insuring such a rate of income growth as will (1) absorb the growing population; and (2) embody the fruits of increased productivity arising out of technological improvements. Third is the need to protect individuals from disturbances in the distribution of income that arise from excessive changes in the price level. Each of these basic goals can lay claim to consideration by monetary and fiscal policy makers. The next problem is to discover objective guides to policy action that appear likely to advance the achievement of these goals. The remainder of this chapter will involve an exploration of proposed policy guides of this sort.

Monetary policy — financing trade and commerce. The use of monetary policy as a device for offsetting business booms and depressions is of relatively recent origin. Before 1920, when the gold standard was looked upon as the only proper monetary system, monetary policy of central banks was primarily concerned with the protection of gold reserves. An increase in the supply of gold was a signal for relaxation of credit, and a loss of gold was the signal for restraint in credit policy. Beyond this there was little room for policy affecting the quantity of money. Within the limits of gold standard restraints there was little opportunity to use monetary policy as a contra-cyclical or stabilizing device. There developed, therefore, a principle of credit policy embodying the view that the creation of money by bank credit expansion should be regulated by the simple rule that banks make only short-term self-liquidating loans to finance the current needs of business. This principle has sometimes been known as the "qualitative" standard of credit policy. Originally adopted by the Federal Reserve authorities, and incorporated in the Federal Reserve Act, this principle emerged naturally from long experience with the international gold standard. It represents that, within the limits set by the necessity of watching gold reserve ratios, the proper procedure of the central bank is one that will provide adequate credit to finance the legitimate short-term needs of commerce and industry. To accomplish this, it is necessary only to make sound loans to finance production and trade. Thus the solvency of the banking system is assured because such loans are self-liquidating and also have no tendency to result in inflation, since new credit money is created only to finance new production. On the other hand, loans of a speculative nature or loans to finance fixed capital expansion should be avoided, since they are not accompanied by a corresponding increase in goods during the life of the loan; in other words, they are not self-liquidating.[1] The theory that soundly made loans of a self-liquidating nature cannot become the basis for an undesirable inflation is now pretty thoroughly exploded. Yet, in spite of this, such a rule is wholesome from the standpoint of banking solvency under the gold standard, where quantitative control of credit is subject to little management in any particular country.[2]

A genuine merit of credit policy based upon the qualitative or self-liquidating commercial loan theory is that such a policy recognizes the important fact that the modern world imposes uncertainty and change upon the financial requirements of business firms. Short-run requirements of trade and commerce must indeed be "accommodated," to use the phraseology of the advocates of this theory. Moreover, emphasis upon short-term commercial credit recognizes the inflationary danger, verified by experience, inherent in the creation of money on the basis of speculative and long-term debts that are but remotely related to changes in current output.

Advocates of the qualitative or short-term self-liquidating commercial loan basis for credit policy have held that central banks should encourage commercial banks to limit themselves to making strictly self-liquidating loans. Speculative and capital loans based on securities, commodity trading, or fixed-capital expansion should be discouraged. Consequently, central banks should discount or lend upon self-liquidating commercial paper only, and should create cash reserve funds for commercial banks only in amounts required to finance current operations of trade and industry.

Weaknesses of monetary policy based upon the short-term commercial credit theory. One weakness in the application of

---

[1] The self-liquidating commercial paper theory of credit policy is sometimes referred to as the "banking principle" and sometimes as the "real bills" doctrine. For a good account of the application of the "banking principle," see Cannan, Edwin, *The Paper Pound of 1797–1821,* London, P. S. King and Son, 1925. Also see Viner, Jacob, *Studies in the Theory of International Trade,* New York, Harper & Bros., 1937, Chapters III and IV.

[2] For an extreme defense of this position, see Willis, H. Parker, *The Theory and Practice of Central Banking,* New York, Harper & Bros., 1936.

the short-term commercial credit theory arises from the difficulty, if not the impossibility, of any individual banker's being able to draw the line on bank loans before they become inflationary.[3] The banker should not be criticized for this. His is essentially a worm's eye view of the economic structure, and particularly is this true under the unit banking system. When business shows brisk improvement, borrowers' needs for "legitimate" loans expand. At the same time, loans appear to be sounder than ever, for improved profit prospects and rising prices constantly make for greater security for the lender. It is little wonder, therefore, that the banker sees a constantly expanding opportunity for the making of "sound commercial loans." Not until the evidence of disequilibrium becomes more obvious will the soundness of commercial loans be questioned. In the meantime, serious inflationary forces are unleashed. The situation is in no way remedied by the free discounting of self-liquidating commercial paper by the central bank.

The possibility of successful avoidance of inflationary credit expansion is somewhat better where the central bank undertakes to determine whether or not credit is being put to proper productive and nonspeculative uses, for the central bank has the very material advantage of being able to view the credit situation as a whole. Yet here, too, a serious limitation arises in the difficulty of devising adequate standards for measuring the legitimate credit needs of the business community. Essentially it is the problem of avoiding financing an expansion in business activity and investment that cannot be maintained—that is, an inflationary movement.

It is evident that attempts to formulate adequate standards of credit policy based upon qualitative considerations are beset with difficulties of great magnitude. In spite of its seeming automatic character, qualitative credit policy is by no means easy to apply. This was made abundantly clear by the struggle of the old Federal Reserve Board to establish satisfactory criteria for applying qualitative standards during the 1920's.

Quantitative standards of credit policy. In contrast to the view that proper and effective credit policy only involves faithful adherence to limiting bank credit to financing short-term business

---

[3] For a clear exposition of how bank credit created on the basis of commercial loans may easily become inflationary, see Robertson, D. H., *Money*, New York, Harcourt, Brace & Co., 1948, Chapter V.

and commercial needs, the present view is that credit policy ought to be directed at the maintenance of the correct *quantity* of money and credit. Support for quantitative standards is derived from the firm conviction of most economists that financing the needs of trade and industry is an inadequate means of meeting the needs of a modern world in search of economic stability. The enthusiasm for quantitative standards of credit control has been measurably heightened by the general abandonment of the restrictions of the gold standard and the consequent freedom to regulate currencies in the interest of domestic requirements.

The quantitative standards of credit policy, concerned with the maintenance of the right quantity of monetary purchasing power, involve but little interest in the nature of bank loans so long as they are well secured. Consequently, eligibility requirements for paper offered for advances at the central bank fade into relative insignificance. The expansion of stock market loans and bond investments becomes a matter of indifference so long as their quality is good and the resulting volume of money is correct.

Combining quantitative standards of credit policy with financing the needs of business. In spite of the recognized importance of control over the total quantity of money, there still remain the credit needs of businessmen. If the economy is to function properly, trade and commerce must be accommodated. Seasonal, irregular, and even cyclical changes in output must be financed. To meet these needs the banking system requires flexibility of the sort that only the central bank can provide. Consequently, central bank credit policy must necessarily meet the requirements stressed so strongly by those who advocated a standard based upon financing the needs of business. They must take into account such needs as well as the over-all quantity of money.

Clearly, then, the necessities of the workaday business world require attention to *both* qualitative and quantitative credit standards. One type cannot be completely subservient to the other. Exclusive concern with financing the needs of business leads to an abandonment of the goals of economic stabilization. Excessive attention to policy requirements of stabilization might well impose such monetary strait-jackets upon business as to defeat the basic quantitative goal.

This dual requirement placed upon central bank policy creates difficult problems. It requires central bankers constantly to be concerned with the state of the money market. They find it necessary to anticipate and offset day-by-day and seasonal variations in the supply of bank reserves. This necessity arises out of the central bank responsibility to provide credit accommodation to business. Otherwise the business and financial community would be abandoned to the haphazard credit stringencies and gluts arising from the typical short-run money market fluctuations. Wise central banking policy, therefore, requires the accommodation of commerce and industry from day to day and from season to season. At the same time such accommodation must be kept within the limits of a more broadly conceived monetary policy of the quantitative sort, aimed at achieving the longer-run goals of economic stabilization and growth. One may readily see the difficult task of the central banker in formulating practical policy.

Quantitative Standards of Control

Quantitative standards of credit policy apply also to fiscal policy. As we consider the criteria for applying quantitative monetary and credit policy we should remember that the results of fiscal policy are essentially quantitative in nature. Therefore, whatever we may conclude concerning proper quantitative credit policy standards will apply equally well to fiscal policy.

Price level stabilization as a policy goal. Before 1936, in what might be called the pre-Keynesian-stagnation era, the main purpose of advocates of quantitative credit and monetary policy was to combat cyclical fluctuations in business activity and employment. At that time unemployment was considered but an unfortunate and temporary deviation from the economic norm of full employment. The possibility of secular stagnation had not then reared its ugly head, at least not among the orthodox economic thinkers. Consequently, attention was naturally directed at curing, or at least offsetting, conditions that seemed to contribute to economic instability. By remedying the more important causes of such instability, it was believed that the demon business cycle might well be cut down to tolerable size. Mild fluctuations were considered inevitable; it was hoped that the more violent might be avoided.

An obvious characteristic of the more violent cyclical fluctuations has been the movement or change in the price level. Such price movements, once under way, greatly accentuate the economic fluctuations they accompany. For example, rising prices that often accompany the upswing provide windfall gains to a widening section of the business community. Such profits stimulate investment incentives and provide the basis for further expansion. Likewise, on the downswing, falling prices are the source of losses that depress the investment incentive. Quite naturally, therefore, students in search of cures for the business cycle have turned to the price level as a basis for quantitative credit and monetary policy.

One attractive feature of price stabilization as a basis of policy is the apparent ease with which it can be used. Statistics showing price changes are now available with fair promptness and in reasonably accurate form. The use of price level stabilization as a guide in the pursuit of a policy of economic stabilization has the additional merit of being easily comprehended and, possibly, easily accepted by the public as a desirable goal. Of even more importance, perhaps, is its definite, objective character. It fits well into the idea that what is highly necessary is an acceptable "rule" by which policy can be *guided* rather than being left to be determined by some "authority" exercising judgment.[4]

Attractive as is price stabilization as a guide for a policy of economic stabilization, it presents some rather obvious questions:

1. What price level should be selected for stabilization?
2. Is stabilization of prices at a given level a desirable thing? Or is a gradually rising or falling price level better?
3. Can any standard of price level control provide the stability and the high level employment so badly needed in the modern world?

The choice of price levels. It is well known that a substantial cyclical and secular divergence occurs among the several index

---

[4] Cf. Henry Simons' earnest effort in behalf of this idea in his "Rules *versus* Authorities in Monetary Policy," *Journal of Political Economy,* February 1936. Also see Mints, Lloyd W., *Monetary Policy for a Competitive Society,* New York, McGraw-Hill Book Co., 1950, Chapters 6 and 7, for support for the view that a nondiscretionary policy based upon price level stability would be preferable to discretionary action by the central bank.

numbers of prices. The index of wholesale prices responds more quickly to cyclical changes than do retail and cost of living index numbers. In turn, the price movements of certain "sensitive" commodities are much more rapid and violent than the price movements of wholesale commodities in general.

The choice of an index number to be used as a basis of stabilization efforts will depend largely upon what is considered the most urgent reason for attempting control. Thus, if the advocate of monetary stabilization is primarily concerned with the protection of the real wages of the consumer against price inflation, the consumers' goods index would seem to be the most desirable. On the other hand, if cyclical fluctuations are to be measured and guarded against, a price index sensitive to such changes is needed.

The advantage that can be claimed for using the consumers' goods index as a basis for stabilizing operations arises solely from the fact that a stable cost of living would insure the consumer against losses of real wages due to the lag of money wages behind price changes. Laudable as this motive undoubtedly is, it is overshadowed by the difficulties that would attend its use. First, to assemble an accurate and representative cost of living index for the average consumer presents a difficult statistical task. Second, stabilization of incomes and business activity is a much more significant goal of credit policy than stabilization of the cost of living. Cost of living indexes are too insensitive to short-run changes to be of much aid in anticipating cyclical movements. In contrast, wholesale prices do respond readily to cyclical changes. In any event, stabilization of wholesale prices would provide sufficient stability to retail prices to meet all practical requirements.

The wholesale price index. The wholesale price index as a criterion for stabilization operations has a number of distinct advantages:

1. It reflects promptly and clearly cyclical fluctuations in business activity.

2. It may be calculated quickly and on a sufficiently broad basis. This is essential to monetary control.

3. It reflects the movement of prices of internationally traded commodities. International cooperation for the purpose of stabilizing the

world price level would require the use of indexes heavily weighted with international goods.

Wholesale prices, to be sure, do not furnish an infallible guide to either domestic or international stabilization. Stable wholesale prices may be inflationary in a progressive economic society. As a guide to international efforts at stabilization, a wholesale price index such as that of the Bureau of Labor Statistics suffers from the weakness of including commodities that are purely domestic, and those commodities which do move in international trade are improperly weighted to provide a proper measure of the international price situation. Nevertheless, the wholesale price index more nearly covers the total range of commodities that are important in the profit calculations of businessmen than does any other index of prices yet available. For this reason, proposals for monetary stabilization commonly provide for the use of the index of wholesale prices as the basis or criterion for monetary control.

The case for stable prices is a fairly clear one. In a world of rigid costs, it is important that fluctuations in the price level be avoided if stable business is to be achieved. For, if prices rise, windfall profits encourage a rate of expansion of capital investment that cannot be maintained and that leads to an inevitable reaction. Falling prices, on the other hand, lead to losses, a falling off in economic activity, and unemployment. Thus, in a search for the basis of economic stability, a stable price level seems to hold the most promise. Moreover, from the standpoint of debtors and creditors, stable prices seem to offer substantial justice.

Some objections to stable wholesale prices. The primary criticism of the policy of wholesale price level stabilization rests in the technological improvements and reduction in real costs in a modern economy. A stable price level in the face of declining costs is objectionable on a number of grounds.

1. Stable prices permit debtors to appropriate the benefits of gains in economic efficiency at the expense of creditors.

2. Stable prices prevent the sharing in the benefits of economic improvements by those persons having relatively inflexible incomes. Such groups include annuitants, salaried people, and employees of government.

3. Stable prices in the face of rapidly falling costs may prove to be

inflationary and encourage overinvestment. This danger arises from the fact that widespread advances in technological efficiency have often not been reflected in proportionate increases in money wages and other costs. The result is more than normal business profits, an abnormal incentive to investment, and an overexpansion that leads to subsequent collapse. The experience in the United States in the 1920's has been cited as an example of such an experience. Table 30 presents some evidence to support this view.

TABLE 30

Indexes of Prices, Business Profits, Labor Costs, and Output
of Capital Equipment in the United States, 1922-1929 *
(1923-25 = 100)

	Wholesale Prices	Profits of 102 Corporations	Payrolls ÷ Production	Output of Capital Equipment
1922	96.0	81	95.4	81
1923	99.9	90	101.7	102
1924	97.4	109	101.4	91
1925	102.7	101	97.1	107
1926	99.3	128	96.7	120
1927	94.7	152	96.1	116
1928	96.0	186	91.9	118
1929	94.6	232	90.7	138

* Barger, Harold, "The Banks and the Stock Market," *Journal of Political Economy,* December 1935, p. 772. Quoted by permission of the University of Chicago Press.

Stable prices and the supply of money. A policy of price level stabilization presents a dual problem in the matter of the quantity of money. First, cyclical developments must be offset. Second, a gradual increase in the quantity of money must be provided to permit the production and sale of a rising quantity of output. Otherwise the increased output resulting from improved technology and a rising population could not be accommodated.

Rising and Falling Price Levels as Goals
of Monetary Policy

Slowly rising prices. Impressed by the obvious fact that rising prices give encouragement to business, some have advocated a policy of gently rising prices as a cure for unemployment and depression. The windfall profits that would be relied upon to provide the stimulus to business activity depend, of course, upon the tendency of wages and other costs to lag behind the rising prices. Yet this need not be objectionable to the wage earner, for he would gain in fuller employment more than he would lose by a lagging wage rate. Such a policy could hardly be expected to provide the economic millennium, for it would almost certainly be accompanied by an overexpansion in investment and inflation, which inevitably are followed by a collapse. Far from providing protection from business fluctuations and unemployment, a rising price policy would be certain to make matters worse.

Slowly falling prices. Because money costs of production are "sticky" and can be forced down only through depression, falling prices are quite generally viewed as the arch-enemy of economic stability and well-being. Nevertheless, some reasons can be given in favor of falling prices.

First, in contrast to rising prices, which reward the speculative businessman and shield the inefficient from the penalties of his errors, falling prices require high-grade managerial performance for business survival. From the standpoint of public welfare, this is a desirable result. Second, if prices do not fall so rapidly as to unduly depress business activity, the distribution of income is improved because of the increased share that tends to go to wage earners.[5] Third, slowly falling prices provide an escape from the inflationary effect of stable prices in an advancing economic society.

To some writers, the ideal money is one that in no way introduces any monetary influences into the economic situation. In other words, money should exercise neither an inflationary nor a deflationary influence on business activity. Such a money would be "neutral." The achievement of this ideal would eliminate one important cause of business fluctuations and bring the goal of economic stability that much nearer to attainment. This does not mean that a neutral money would entirely eliminate business fluctuations, for nonmonetary factors would remain.

The requirements for a neutral money may be stated very simply. In order for money to be neutral and not put monetary barriers in the way of economic stability and growth, its supply should

---

[5] Cf. Marshall, Alfred, *Official Papers,* London, Macmillan and Company, Ltd., 1926, p. 9.

increase in proportion to the increase in working population. Thus, output expansion resulting from improved technical efficiency of men and machines would be accompanied by an appropriate and proportional fall in prices, and all income receivers would share alike in the results of technical progress. On the other hand, the supply of money should rise with the size of the working population so that per capita money incomes would be stable. In addition, money would require both cyclical and long-run modifications in quantity to meet changes in liquidity requirements. Its management would be further complicated by the necessity of adjusting the quantity to meet the changing requirements arising out of structural changes in the productive processes and in business organization.

Objections to prices that fall with growing efficiency. Prices that fall as efficiency grows offer the advantage of an equitable sharing by all consumers in the benefits of technological improvements. In a world in which income differentials among occupations are slow in adjusting, this is no mean accomplishment. This advantage, coupled with the protection which it affords against the hidden inflationary results of falling costs and stable prices, would seem to make this an ideal goal.

In spite of its substantial advantages, to require a downward flexibility in prices in times of technological improvements may be difficult to achieve. As a result, strains may develop in the economy that may hinder its operation and growth. For example, money adjusted in quantity so as to offset changes in working population and income velocity only, requires that average prices fall as much as costs decline. Should technological gains result in economies of 2 per cent per year, prices, on the average, would have to decline by 2 per cent also. In a competitive economy, with all parts experiencing approximately the same rates of gains in efficiency, no undue strain would arise from expanding output at lower costs and prices. However, competition is obstructed by varying degrees of monopoly in many important areas. We can have no assurance that monopolists will increase output and lower prices in proportion to the decline in costs. To the extent, therefore, that monopolists maintain prices and refrain from output expansion, the full impact of output expansion and falling prices, including the absorption of any labor released by the monopolized industries, falls upon the competitive sector of the economy. This requires more severe wage and price adjustments than would be required of the competitive sector in case the money supply was permitted to rise enough to allow the average prices to be stable in the face of technological improvement.

A similar result would occur if, as is almost certain to happen, technical efficiency increases at unequal rates in different industries. Here, again, the imposition of a falling price level, corresponding to the average fall in costs, would unduly depress prices in industries that have enjoyed a less than average growth in efficiency. At the same time, industries whose efficiency is growing at a rate above the average would be somewhat inflated.

The Relative Merits of Stable Prices and Falling Prices

The choice of monetary policy directed at establishing control *over the price level* appears to lie between stable prices and a stable per capita money income. The theoretical requirements for economic stability appear to be most nearly satisfied by the latter. But as a practical matter it leaves much to be desired. In contrast, a stable price level policy has much to be said for it from a practical standpoint. In making a choice in such a matter, theoretical perfection must sometimes be sacrificed to practical considerations.

Practical objections to fixed per capita money incomes. The stabilization of per capita money incomes would surely meet with formidable objections in labor circles. It is difficult to persuade an individual of the advantages of receiving the benefits of industrial progress solely through the medium of lower prices. Labor, along with other recipients of money incomes, is much impressed with the importance of an expanding money income. It is not hard to see why this is so. The success of any individual or group of individuals in improving their relative position in the economic system normally requires some increase in money income. A monetary system that lessens the opportunity to strive for a higher money income is, therefore, certain to be viewed with suspicion if not with outright disfavor. Stable per capita incomes would require that trade union pressure for higher wages be stoutly resisted, for increased money wages would have to represent only increases in the proportion of the total national income that labor receives. The serious preoccupation of labor with the size of its money income furnishes a strong practical reason for a preference for stable prices, with wages rising with technical advance, rather than stable per capita money income. A stable price level not only permits a general rise in wages as efficiency of production is increased, but also it avoids the painful necessity of cutting piece rates with improvements in efficiency. Furthermore, stable prices with rising money wages avoids the need for absolute reductions in money wages of the less efficient workers.

Some Problems of Price Level Stabilization

The avoidance of inflation under stable prices. In spite of its shortcomings, a stable price policy would be a great improvement over highly unstable prices, for any resulting reduction in the amplitude of business fluctuations would be a substantial economic gain. The value of stable prices would be still further enhanced in case their inflationary tendencies in an advancing economic society could be avoided. What, we may ask, are the possibilities in this direction?

Because the inflationary effect of stable prices arises from the lag in the rewards of factors of production in the face of increasing productive efficiency, an obvious cure would involve an appropriate increase in such rewards. This question of lagging money costs with increased efficiency may now be less serious than it was in the 1920's. Active, vigorous labor organizations tend to reduce the lag between increased industrial efficiency and labor income. The inclusion of an annual production improvement factor in labor contracts also acts to reduce the lag in wage adjustments. Even so, these developments do not insure against the appearance of windfall profits out of stable prices and falling money costs. Furthermore, there seems to be no way, with a stable price level policy, to insure justice for consumers whose incomes fail to rise readily with increases in over-all economic efficiency.

The short-period aspect of price stabilization. In entering upon any general program of price stabilization, there arises the problem of the manner in which the monetary authorities are to exercise their powers. For example, should they maintain a somewhat loose type of control aimed at preventing the development of any dangerous cyclical price movements while allowing some short-run flexibility in the price level, or should they strive to impose a tight form of supervision with the aim of preserving, so far as possible, an absolutely stable level of short-run prices?

Practical attempts at price stabilization must involve the use of some selected index of prices. When this index shows signs of fluctuation, the monetary authority must take proper counteracting measures. But attempts to counteract every short-time change in the price level would be certain to prove both difficult and undesirable. In the first place, because of the inaccuracy of index numbers, it would be inappropriate to put the monetary controls into operation merely because of a small movement of the price index. Not until the movement reached some significant proportions should counteracting monetary operations be introduced. Nor are the instruments of control available to the monetary authority sufficiently precise to justify attempts to correct small price movements. Any price stabilization plan, therefore, seems to call for a margin of tolerance within which movements of the selected price index might be viewed with equanimity.

Furthermore, circumstances may easily arise that would make the rigid imposition of a stable price index a highly undesirable short-run policy. This may be illustrated by assuming that unfavorable grain weather has resulted in a short crop. The price of grain will rise, and with it the index of prices. If corrective action were to be taken to prevent or check such an increase in the price index, it would involve the deflation of other prices. Clearly, such action would be an outright injury to business stability, for it would impose a general business deflation upon the community in order that the precious stability of the price index might be preserved. Similarly, a bountiful crop would lead to lower grain prices and a fall in the price index. To introduce inflationary measures designed to raise other prices sufficiently to bring the average back up to the level agreed upon would also be highly undesirable. For this reason, it is important that price movements originating in such accidental and short-run occurrences be disregarded by a monetary authority bent upon price stabilization.

Finally, in spite of the best efforts of monetary and fiscal policy to counteract cyclical changes, we may be certain that some fluctuations will remain in a private enterprise economy. Whenever income rises during a recovery period, prices of products with short-run inelasticity of supply will tend to rise. To impose restraint upon expansion because of a resulting rise in the price index is obviously foolish. Similarly, a corrective recession, causing some prices to fall sharply, need not necessarily be a signal for all-out expansionary efforts in the interest of arresting a resulting decline in the price level.

Because of the need for a margin of tolerance in connection with price stabilization, it becomes all the more necessary that some effective means be available to the monetary authority by which it may judge the nature of economic developments. It must be in a position to judge, for example, whether or not a particular movement in the price index is due to an underlying inflationary or deflationary development. Promptness of action is essential, but it must be based upon sound knowledge. If neither a strictly fixed supply of money nor a strictly stable price level is desirable, there immediately arises the need for full knowledge of underlying conditions upon which judgments may be used. In such a case, a price index alone is no substitute for broad knowledge.

Full Employment as a Criterion for Monetary and Credit Policy

When John Maynard Keynes, in 1936, demonstrated the theoretical and practical possibility of an equilibrium at less than full employment,[6] he substantially modified the significance of earlier criteria of proper monetary and credit policy. No longer could one assume that reducing the violence of cyclical fluctuations in business would provide a certain and satisfactory answer to the problem of unemployment. For, according to Keynes, it is possible and perhaps even probable that secular stagnation may exist in a society devoid of cyclical fluctuations. Indeed, once one admits the possibility that the rate of saving at full employment may remain chronically above the rate of investment at acceptable rates of interest, the possibility of secular stagnation becomes a real threat. Consequently, a mere stabilization of the price level alone can no longer be accepted as an adequate goal of monetary and

---

[6] *The General Theory of Employment, Interest and Money.*

credit policy. Instead, *economic stability at full employment* becomes the proper goal.[7]

The meaning of full employment. Full employment does not require that every employable person be working the maximum possible number of hours per week. Rather, it requires only that the *normal* working force be employed for the customary hours per week. Persons past retirement age and young people still in school need not be drawn into the active labor force to satisfy the test of full employment. Moreover, full employment does not require the elimination of usual and normal seasonal unemployment or the so-called *frictional* unemployment arising out of labor turnover and shifts from one area to another and from one industry to another. It follows, of course, that the inclusion of full employment among the criteria for monetary and credit policy requires setting up a competent unemployment index for guidance.

Full employment policy and structural change. Frictional unemployment arises out of the peculiarities (seasonal factors, for instance) of particular industries and the desire or necessity of labor to change jobs and employers. Clearly, such types of unemployment are not amenable to correction by the over-all methods of monetary and fiscal policy. Instead they require steps to regularize seasonal industries and to improve the mobility of labor. The use of the expansionist methods of credit or fiscal policy in an attempt to cure frictional unemployment is worse than useless. Not only are such methods entirely unsuited for the task but they tend to generate a general inflation.

One especially troublesome problem in the application of a full employment policy is the difficulty in distinguishing between cyclical unemployment and that due to structural changes in the economy. Unlike seasonal factors, which may be readily identified, changes in the industrial structure which cause unemployment in declining industries are difficult to distinguish from a general cyclical decline. Full employment policy always involves difficult decisions in the

---

[7] We need not examine here the pros and cons of the theory of economic maturity and secular stagnation. For a competent analysis of the concept see Benjamin Higgins' "Concepts and Criteria of Secular Stagnation" in *Income, Employment, and Public Policy*, Essays in Honor of Alvin H. Hansen, New York, W. W. Norton and Co., 1948. For a criticism of the concept, see George Terborgh's *The Bogy of Economic Maturity*, Chicago, Machinery and Allied Products Institute, 1945.

matter of determining how far to press an expansionist program for the purpose of reducing unemployment. The decisions become even more difficult when complicated by the necessity of determining the extent of frictional unemployment arising from structural changes.[8] Sound policy requires that structural changes should be permitted to occur without interference from monetary and fiscal actions for promoting full employment.

Instruments of control. In general, the same monetary and credit controls appropriate for attempting to reach economic stability through price stabilization are likewise suitable for promoting stabilization at full employment. A fall in employment below the desired level, whether because of cyclical or other reasons, can be counteracted first with the usual easy-money policies of the central bank. Should the slackening of employment be mild, such steps, coupled with the built-in stabilizing effects provided by income taxes and unemployment insurance benefits, may be sufficient to reverse the downward trend. Particularly will this be true if the economy finds itself in the midst of a period of long-run expansion in which there is little threat of any major depression. But if the drop in employment proves severe, prompt fiscal policies can be brought into action. Taxes can be reduced, government spending on construction can be expanded, and other appropriate actions taken.

On the other hand, a threat of inflation can likewise be promptly and effectively dealt with by proper restrictive action by the central bank. Tighter money conditions can be enforced by open market sales of securities, higher discount rates, and increased reserve requirements. At the same time, selective credit controls may also be utilized to restrain expansion. The promptness with which central banks can act makes their part highly important in combatting inflation. Additional restraint is provided by the increase in tax revenues and the reduction in unemployment insurance benefits. Should serious inflationary pressures continue, positive steps to reduce government spending and to increase tax rates would be appropriate.

One of the prerequisites for successful anti-inflationary action is to establish reliable criteria for determining the timing and

---

[8] Cf. Roberston, D. H., *Essays in Monetary Theory*, New York, Staples Press, Inc., 1948, Chapter VIII.

strength of measures to be taken. Furthermore, there is need for a wider public acceptance of the idea that threatened inflation should be promptly dealt with if a program of economic stabilization is to be effectively established. Such public acceptance of prompt anti-inflationary steps will depend somewhat on confidence that deflation, in turn, can and will be effectively dealt with.

The threat of inflation. As the economy is pushed toward full employment, unequal pressure develops upon different parts of the economic structure. During periods of slack, some industries curtail their output while maintaining prices. Others, such as agriculture, maintain output but suffer from falling prices. A recovery and a rising income level tends to drive up the prices of commodities whose output cannot readily expand. In other words, cyclical bottlenecks, where supply cannot readily be increased, begin to appear and prices begin to rise. Clearly such price increases must be permitted if expansion and recovery are to continue into full employment.

A second inflationary force is found in the rise in labor costs that accompanies an expansion of output and employment. Less efficient members of the labor force will be attracted in, and old employees may slacken their efforts somewhat as unemployment declines and jobs become easier to hold. In addition, at such times union demands for higher money wages become more insistent. Such demands are fortified by the obvious rise in the cost of living, which responds to the increase in price of commodities having an inelastic supply. Furthermore, in good times, when profits are high and demand for their products is good, employers may readily accede to demands for higher wages. Thus there is a danger that an inflationary spiral based on wage increases may develop. When such increases in wages exceed the rate of improvement in labor efficiency, as they are likely to do at such times, the inflationary effects will be felt throughout the industries granting them. This process is facilitated by a banking system sympathetic to the "legitimate" needs of business for loan accommodation.

The pressure from the demands for higher wages need not inevitably lead to inflation. Comprehensive and adequate statistical data of prices, wages, and productivity, all properly publicized and utilized, combined with effective machinery for arbitration and mediation, may go far to induce restraint on labor's demands and to avoid excessive and inflationary wage increases. Moreover, employers' resistance to wage demands may be fortified by a realization that anti-inflationary credit policy reduces the opportunities to expand borrowing. Finally, a modification of full employment goals may be necessary if inflation is to be avoided. Clearly, it is undesirable to provide more vacant jobs than there are unemployed persons. A policy of full employment "no matter what" is not acceptable. Rather, whatever margin of unemployment that is necessary to prevent inflation and to permit adjustments arising from structural changes appears preferable to an all-out inflationary type of full employment. The critical questions raised by this conclusion are:

1. What minimum amount of unemployment may be expected to provide successful resistance to inflation arising from excessive wage increases?

2. Is that required degree of unemployment politically tolerable?

Estimates differ widely as to the degree of unemployment that is necessary to hold wage increases within the bounds of the growth of productivity. Some have held that inflationary pressures are generated whenever unemployment falls below 6 to 8 million. More conservative estimates are that from 3 to 5 per cent unemployment (about 3 million) is sufficient. Clearly there is still need for study of this important problem. There remains the further question of the political acceptability of an employment policy that is sufficiently restrained to make possible the avoidance of price-level inflation.[9]

Full employment and external disequilibrium. The experience of England and other European countries after the last war suggests yet another problem that can arise in the pursuit of full employment policy. As full employment is approached, the resulting higher level of consumer income tends to absorb into domestic consumption a growing fraction of the national output. This condition is brought about by a relative increase in domestic prices in comparison with prices in export markets. In addition, import demand rises with increases in industrial output and consumer income. The end result may very well be that successful efforts

---

[9] Cf. Ascheim, Joseph, "Price Level Stability at Full Employment; Recent American Experiences," *Oxford Economic Papers,* October 1955, Vol. 7, No. 3.

to promote full employment will cause a severe disequilibrium in a country's balance of payments. The consequent drain upon foreign exchange reserves creates a serious problem. Either currency devaluation may be required to correct overvaluation and induce the necessary rearrangement of industry, or the greater efficiencies and smaller money incomes associated with a somewhat lower level of employment must somehow be brought about. In such a case, the goal of full employment may have to be subordinated to the more urgent goal of equilibrium in the balance of payments. Fiscal and credit policy must then be used to restrict credit and business, even at the risk of some unemployment, if no other way can be found to restore equilibrium. The hope that full employment may be pursued without concern over the effect on the balance of payments explains the enthusiasm in some quarters for the retention of exchange controls.

Questions for Study

1. Why may proper goals of monetary policy sometimes be in conflict? Can you give examples?

2. What is meant by the policy aimed at "financing trade and commerce"? Why was it particularly suited to a gold standard world? Has it any validity as a basis for Federal Reserve Credit policy today? Why is it unlikely to provide a sufficient goal of credit policy today?

3. What is meant by "quantitative" policy standards? Do they apply to fiscal as well as to monetary policy?

4. Can you present reasons for favoring a stable price level as a policy? What can you say in favor of attempts to stabilize wholesale prices? Do stable wholesale prices insure that most groups in the economy are fairly treated? Why did the events of the 1920's seem to discredit stable wholesale prices as a policy goal?

5. Suppose the price level should fall to match the growth in industrial efficiency.
   a) What would this mean in respect to the necessary changes in the supply of money?
   b) What would be the effect upon per capita money incomes?
   c) What practical objections can you raise to such a policy goal?
   d) Why has such a goal been favored?

6. If some form of price-level stabilization becomes a goal of policy, what problems will be raised in respect to the limits of tolerance for the movements of the price index?

7. If full employment be chosen as a policy goal, what problem arises in respect to (a) unemployment found in declining industry areas? (b) the ability to avoid price-level inflation?

8. Why may a full-employment goal create a threat to a country's balance of payments?

28

The Development of Federal
Reserve Credit Policy

To conclude our study of monetary and fiscal policy we shall review some of the more significant events that accompanied the development and application of Federal Reserve policy. Before the depression years of the 1930's, formal efforts at economic stabilization were confined to the area of central bank credit policy. Since that time fiscal policy has entered the picture.

Federal Reserve policy before 1922. During the early years of the Federal Reserve System, credit policy was mainly passive. The Reserve Banks stood ready to lend to members when necessary, but the need for this was largely overcome by the importation of gold from the warring countries. Between 1915 and 1918 the net excess of our gold imports was over $1,000,000,000. In the absence of member bank discounting at the Federal Reserve Banks the latter purchased United States Government securities in the open market, not to influence the reserve position of the member banks but to provide themselves with earnings out of which to pay expenses and dividends.[1]

The entrance of the United States into the war in 1917 brought a tremendous demand for bank credit expansion to float government bond issues, and Federal Reserve Bank credit policy was shaped for the attainment of that end. Federal Reserve discount rates were maintained at relatively low levels during the war and early postwar period. Banks were encouraged to lend to customers who wished

---

[1] Reed, Harold L., *The Development of Federal Reserve Policy*, Boston, Houghton Mifflin Co., 1922, p. 250.

to buy government bonds beyond the capacity of their current incomes. Such customers' paper (known as war paper) was freely discounted by the Federal Reserve Banks. As a result the Government was able to float an enormous volume of bonds at low rates of interest.

The pressure to maintain low discount rates for the benefit of governmental fiscal needs continued until after January 1920. These easy money conditions fed the flames of the postwar boom, which collapsed so disastrously in the middle of 1920. At the peak of the boom, the reserve banks were compelled to give consideration to the adequacy of their reserves, which approached the legal minimum limits. In 1919, even, the Board warned member banks against a policy of constant expansion of loans based on discounting at the reserve banks. Such warnings were largely unheeded and the expansion continued. In January 1920, before the downturn in business started, the Federal Reserve Banks raised their discount rates. In June the rate on commercial and agricultural paper was increased to 7 per cent by the reserve banks of New York, Chicago, and Minneapolis. This increase in rates, accompanied by direct pressure on member banks to reduce their indebtedness to the Federal Reserve Banks, brought collapse to the already unstable, speculative commodity and land price boom. The collapse was accompanied by a sharp drop in prices and employment and a gradual shrinkage in the volume of bank credit. The reduction in credit resulted in an improvement in the legal reserve ratios of the Federal Reserve Banks. The pressures of high discount rates were continued throughout the period of decline in prices and business activity.

Judged by present standards the policy of the Federal Reserve System during the 1920–1921 depression seems most inappropriate. Having delayed the application of restraint in the earlier stages of the boom, out of deference to Treasury financing needs, the Federal Reserve Banks imposed severe restraint and pressure for credit liquidation during the later stages. Belatedly concerned about their gold reserve position, the Federal Reserve Banks adopted strong restrictive action. Because the restriction continued too long into the recession period, the severity of the depression was increased.

During the 1919–1921 period the Federal Reserve System failed to develop an appropriate policy of counter-cyclical action. On January 1, 1921, after six months of serious depression, five of the Federal Reserve Banks, including those of New York, Chicago, and Boston, still maintained at 7 per cent their discount rates on commercial, industrial, and agricultural paper. By the middle of 1921, although prices and business activity had been falling for a year, agricultural distress was acute, and severe unemployment had reduced many industrial workers to dependence upon soup kitchens, the Federal Reserve System steadfastly clung to a tight money policy. Not until business began a substantial improvement during the last half of 1921 did it relax its restraint upon credit. It was December 1921 before the average discount rates at the Federal Reserve Banks had been reduced to a little under 5 per cent. In the meantime the open market holdings of Government securities by the Banks, never very large, were reduced by about one-third during the period of depression. In general, the performance of the Federal Reserve System could hardly have been more inept.

The performance of the Federal Reserve System, however, must be judged in the light of the policy opinions applicable to central banks at the time. Under the gold standard, the first duty of central banks was to defend their gold reserve position. Second, central banks felt duty bound to provide accommodation to the money market in order to avoid collapse or general suspension, but such aid should be at a price or at a penalty rate to discourage unnecessary reliance of the money market upon the central bank.

The excessive restrictions imposed by Federal Reserve actions during 1920–1921 stirred up a hornets' nest of controversy. The severity of the depression, with a drop in wholesale prices of over 45 per cent in the course of 18 months, was especially difficult for agriculture. Farmers, heavily indebted for the purchase of land during the boom, found themselves faced with mortgage foreclosures and economic ruin. Quite understandably they blamed the severe deflationary action of the Federal Reserve for their plight. Complaints from agriculture resulted in legislative changes to insure a representation of agriculture in the Federal Reserve Board. Without doubt, the criticisms of policy during the depression also induced a new approach to the problem of credit policy and the significance of such policy in the determination of business conditions. In consequence, the Board came to recognize the importance of preventing the support of speculative booms in commodities and land by central bank credit.

Oddly enough, in spite of the severity of the depression of 1920–1921, its duration was mercifully short. After liquidation of speculative inventories had been accomplished, business recovered rapidly as the longer-run expansionary forces of the postwar period took hold. The quick recovery of 1921–1922 in some ways justified the tight money policy pursued by the Board during the liquidation period. It gave support to the view, then held by some, that a sharp depression has a salutary effect by purging the economy of inefficiency and speculative accumulations.

Policy development of 1923. The year 1923 saw a number of important developments in Federal Reserve policy. First, early in the year, the Board recognized the importance of open market transactions as an instrument of policy and ruled that the purchase and sale of securities should henceforth "be governed with a primary regard to the accommodation of commerce and business and the effect . . . on the general credit situation." [2]

The Board also set up certain rules of policy by which it chose to be governed. Briefly these rules were:

1. Reserve ratios were no longer serviceable as guides to credit policy since the United States was the only country on the gold standard. Gold movements, they wisely observed, no longer reflected the price level changes in the various countries nor did they induce corrective price changes.

2. The stabilization of prices as a guide to policy was rejected on the grounds that price changes result from basic developments in business rather than merely from changes in bank credit. Hence not only would it be impossible to control prices through credit policy but also attempts to do so would result in action too belated for the best interests of business.

3. Federal Reserve credit should be utilized for accommodating productive activities but not for financing speculative or investment operations. Not only should reserve bank credit be used exclusively for productive purposes, but its volume should be so restricted as to be commensurate with increases in national productivity.

4. Tests for determining whether or not reserve bank credit is being put to productive use should include:

---

[2] *Nineteenth Annual Report of the Federal Reserve Board,* 1923, p. 16.

(a) Is credit being used to hold goods for speculative increases in prices?

(b) Are goods moving smoothly from producer to ultimate consumer without speculative interference?

(c) Does consumption keep up with the volume of trade, production, and employment?

In respect to the application of its rules of policy, the Board said

"that good credit administration in times of active business expansion should not encourage or assist the excessive accumulation of forward commitments in business and banking which only later on will definitely reflect the rate at which they have been taking place in resulting changes of credit volume and changes of price levels; and in times of business reaction should discourage enforced liquidation of past commitments." In the same report it stated: "If industry and trade are in process of recovery after a period of reaction, they should be given support and encouragement of cheaper credit."

During the next five years the Board achieved an enviable record of success. Bringing into play the combined forces of the discount rate, open market operations, and moral suasion, it moved directly into the area of economic stabilization. In 1924 and again in 1927, the easy money policy adopted by the Federal Reserve System was quickly followed by recovery from the mild recessions of those years. The tide of monetary policy as an economic stabilizer was at its height. It remained for the stock market boom and the subsequent crash and depression to reveal the essential weakness of the guides to monetary policy being utilized by the Federal Reserve System.

The stock market boom and collapse. The stock market boom that developed in 1928–1929 was both a product of the basic prosperity that accompanied the major cyclical expansion of the 1920's and a contributor to that expansion. Business issued equity securities to finance expansion programs. The issues were quickly absorbed by the upsurge of the market financed by security loans of banks. Additional reserve funds, when needed, were acquired by member bank borrowing on Government securities and eligible paper.

The situation in 1929 proved puzzling to the Federal Reserve Board. It found, when applying its rules of 1923, that, unlike the boom of 1919–1920, speculative inventory accumulations were absent. Commodity prices were not rising, and goods seemed to be moving smoothly from producer to consumer without speculative interference. What the Board failed to see was (1) the increase in consumers' inventories made possible by the sharp rise in installment credit; and (2) an excessively rapid, hence unstable, expansion of investment that was taking place. The Board appeared not to have been aware of the general inflationary consequences of the stock market boom.[3] Therefore it was unwilling to impose general monetary restraint to slow down the expansion, since it believed that basic economic conditions were sound and stable. Instead it sought to induce the Wall Street banks to reduce their lending in the stock market. The reason given for such a request was the fear that the absorption of credit by the stock market might threaten the availability of credit for legitimate business operations. The voluntary restraint attempted by the Board was made ineffective by the inflow of funds from other cities and from nonbank lenders. It was the failure of this attempt that demonstrated the need for new legislation giving the Board power to control margin requirements on security loans. Unlike the Federal Reserve Board, officials of the Federal Reserve Banks believed that the stock market boom should be curbed by tighter credit policies. However, it was not until the middle of 1929 that the Board sanctioned a sharp increase in discount rates. By that time the stock market was so out of hand that the increase in rates had little effect.

The speculative excesses of the stock market collapsed in October 1929. The collapse shattered public confidence and, coupled with the slow-down in general business that had set in three months earlier, set off a major depression that was not entirely dispelled until World War II.

Federal Reserve policy of the 1930's. In keeping with its established rules of policy the Federal Reserve Board moved to offset the deflationary movement set off by the collapse of the stock market. The liquidation of brokers' loans in New York City was carried out in a reasonably orderly fashion with the aid of Federal Reserve Bank open market purchases and discounting for member banks.

After the collapse of the stock market in October 1929, the

---

[3] Cf. Mints, Lloyd W., *A History of Banking Theory,* University of Chicago Press, 1945, pp. 267-268.

Federal Reserve System moved moderately in the direction of easing money conditions. The New York discount rate was gradually lowered until it reached 2 per cent by December 1930. Also the System made some small increase in its Government security holdings. These had been increased by 292 million dollars by the end of January 1930, an entirely inadequate amount in view of the fact that member bank indebtedness to the Federal Reserve Banks still amounted to 800 million dollars. By the end of 1930, fourteen months after the stock market crash, the System's holdings of Government securities had been increased by a little less than one-half billion dollars. This still left member bank indebtedness at over 330 million dollars.

This gradual and inadequate process of easing the money market received a rude setback during the European banking crisis in the last half of 1931. To meet a gold drain of over one-half billion dollars, member banks sharply increased their borrowings at the Federal Reserve Banks and sold a substantial amount of bankers' acceptances. This increase in indebtedness and reduction in liquidity resulted in tighter money and increased interest rates. Discount rates on acceptances rose sharply and commercial loan rates increased. The New York Federal Reserve Bank raised its discount rate during October from 1½ per cent to 3½ per cent.

The record shows that at no time between the stock market crash of October 1929 and the bank holiday of March 1933 were Federal Reserve open market purchases of securities pushed far enough to enable member banks to get out of debt and to accumulate a sizable quantity of excess reserves. This means that there was a complete failure to develop a condition of genuine money market ease of the kind needed as an effective offset to serious depression. Genuine ease, with an abundance of excess reserves, did not appear until after the bank holiday of 1933. By that time depression had reached its worst and recovery had begun.

Two divergent conclusions have been reached, based on our monetary and credit experiences of the Great Depression. First, those who favor the use of fiscal policy alone as an anti-cyclical device find support for their views. They conclude that monetary policy failed utterly to check depression and restore prosperity, and thus its bankruptcy in depression stands clearly revealed. They neglect the fact that at no time before the depression had reached its worst was a really effective monetary policy achieved. No one should expect that easy money policy can reverse business expecta-tions and induce an expansion in investment once depression has reached the extreme stage where business solvency and confidence have been destroyed and economic life is completely demoralized. Consequently this much cited historical "proof" of the ineffectiveness of proper and prompt anti-deflationary monetary policy is largely groundless. There are good reasons to think that a prompt and effective increase in the liquidity position of banks and the money market early in 1930 might have warded off a good deal of the demoralization associated with the liquidity panic that led to the collapse of the banks. In such a case the severity of the depression might well have been greatly lessened. This is not to say that mone-tary policy makes fiscal policy unnecessary. Rather it should be a warning against discarding monetary policy entirely, as some have proposed, and substituting for it dependence on fiscal policy alone for economic stabilization.

A second conclusion based upon the depression experiences of 1929–1933 is that of some who confidently believe in the effective-ness of monetary policy. They hold that the halting, muddling progress of monetary policy in 1930–1932 is simply evidence of the ineptitude of central bank management. This experience, they hold, shows the urgency for fixing proper *rules* to guide monetary policy (price level stabilization, for example) so that policy will not be at the mercy of the errors of managerial discretion and judgment.

There are strong reasons for rejecting both of the conclusions just mentioned. As we have seen, those who have condemned monetary policy on the basis of the experience of the depression failed to note that in fact genuine anti-depression monetary policy came into being too late. On the other hand, the critics of the management and application of monetary policy are wrong in blam-ing the imperfections upon managerial errors alone and therefore holding that discretionary monetary policy is always doomed to failure. After all, a good deal has been learned about the applica-tion of central bank policy in the last quarter-century. The old shibboleth of "accommodation of trade and commerce" has been relegated to a secondary and more appropriate place in Federal

Reserve policy thinking. During the crisis years of 1930–1933 the primary reliance upon this old theory by the Federal Reserve System served to confuse and hamper the adoption of a genuine easy money policy that is essentially quantitative in nature. Furthermore, the faulty credit practices of 1930–1933 were not entirely a result of the application of outmoded monetary dogma. Of even greater importance were certain institutional restraints that hindered the development of genuine easy money market conditions.

Institutional restraints to easy money. In some instances member bank reluctance to borrow, in part related to earlier efforts on the part of the Federal Reserve to discourage continuous borrowing, and the eligible paper and Government security requirements for member bank borrowings constituted a barrier to the use of Federal Reserve credit by member banks. But even more restrictive was the outmoded rule that required the deposit of discounted eligible paper or gold and gold certificates as collateral for Federal Reserve notes. Whenever the Federal Reserve System purchased Government securities to expand member bank reserves and enable members to reduce their borrowings, the supply of discounted paper was reduced and the Federal Reserve Banks were compelled to substitute gold and gold certificates as collateral. This sharply reduced the Federal Reserve holdings of "free" gold available for export. Thus, whenever an actual or threatened export of gold appeared, the Federal Reserve Banks found it necessary to sell securities, and thus compel member banks to borrow again in order to obtain collateral for Federal Reserve notes and to release the gold. For example, before February 27, 1932, when Congress gave permission for the use of Government securities as collateral, the Federal Reserve Banks' supply of free gold (gold not tied up as reserve against deposits and as collateral against Federal Reserve notes) had dwindled to about $300 million. Had the Federal Reserve Banks at that time attempted to push their holdings of Government securities to the point at which member banks might have been able to get out of debt, the available free gold would have fallen far short of satisfying the collateral requirements for outstanding Federal Reserve notes. In all fairness, then, until the end of February 1932, the hands of the Federal Reserve authorities were effectively tied in any attempts to establish genuine money market ease.

Credit policy, 1933-1939. The return flow of hoarded currency to the reopened banks after the bank holiday relieved the pressure upon the banks' cash position and enabled them to reduce their borrowings. Excess reserves of substantial proportions appeared and the much needed ease in the money market became a reality. The devaluation of the dollar early in 1934 was the signal for the start of an unprecedented inflow of gold. Member bank excess reserves rose far above any conceivable needs. To hold this excess within manageable bounds the Board of Governors repeatedly raised reserve requirements. At the same time, to provide earnings, the System maintained its Government security holdings at about $2.5 billions. The increase in member bank reserves that resulted from the gold inflows of the 1930's, and the effects of these changes in reserve requirements in the 1936–1938 period, may be seen in Chart 22.

The "flexible open-market portfolio" policy. Before 1937, even though the main function of the Federal Reserve System's open

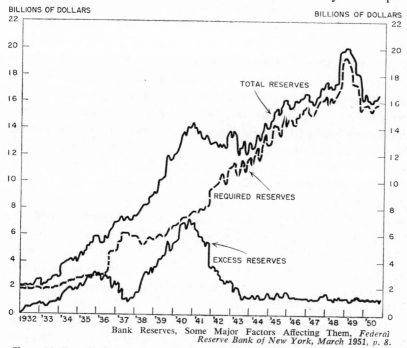

Bank Reserves, Some Major Factors Affecting Them, *Federal Reserve Bank of New York, March 1951, p. 8.*

Chart 22. Required Excess Reserves of Member Banks, 1932—October 1950 (monthly averages of daily figures).

market portfolio was to provide earnings, the fiction of influencing short-term interest rates was maintained. Consequently, the System held mainly Treasury bills of extremely low yields. However, in 1937, the Open Market Committee adopted a new policy of purchasing long-term Government securities for the purpose of checking a decline in their prices. This new action, referred to as the "flexible open market policy," enabled the Federal Reserve System directly to intervene in the long-term bond market instead of depending upon the influence of changes in short-term rates induced by changes in member bank reserve position. To understand the reason for this shift in policy, it should be remembered that during this period the high volume of excess reserves left the reserve banks out of contact with the money market and therefore helpless to exercise their traditional function of controlling short-term interest rates. When war broke out on September 1, 1939, high-grade bond prices fell sharply and the Federal Reserve System came to the rescue with heavy purchases of long-term Government securities. The avowed purpose of this action was to protect the market from "violent fluctuations of a speculative or panicky nature." Believing that its best contribution to public interest was to maintain orderly conditions in the market for Government securities, the Board of Governors, on September 1, 1939, announced a supplemental policy. All Federal Reserve Banks would lend on Government securities at par to both member and nonmember banks. This move was designed to encourage banks to borrow funds when in need rather than to sell bonds on the market.

War-finance credit policy, 1940-1945. The German invasion of the Low Countries in the spring of 1940 caused a quick expansion of the armament program, which later was merged into the all-out war effort in 1942. Between June 1940 and December 1945 the Federal Government spent about 380 billion dollars. Of this, 95 billions were provided by commercial and Federal Reserve Bank purchases of securities. There resulted a net increase of about $44 billion in checking accounts and $20 billion in currency in circulation.

The member bank supply of excess reserves was quickly exhausted by the increased circulation requirements and the banks had to turn to the Federal Reserve Banks for accommodation. Unlike World

War I, when banks were required to discount "war paper" to obtain reserves, the Federal Reserve System, in 1942, undertook to provide the banking system with ample reserves with a minimum amount of member bank borrowing. Although a preferential discount rate of one-half of 1 per cent on member bank borrowings on short-term Government securities was established, the main source of bank reserves was the open market purchases of securities by the Federal Reserve System. By posting a buying rate for Treasury bills at three-eights of 1 per cent, the Federal Reserve Banks opened the way for member banks to purchase such bills and convert them into cash reserves whenever needed. To make things even more attractive, banks were given a repurchase option on the bills that were sold.

Thus the "involuntary open market purchases" of Treasury bills became a principal avenue through which Federal Reserve Bank credit reached the money market. In addition, the Open Market Committee established the policy that open market purchases and sales of other types of Government securities should be made from time to time for the purpose of maintaining the desired level of prices and yields and to maintain an adequate supply of funds in the market. Under this policy the rate on twelve-month Treasury certificates was pegged at seven-eighths of 1 per cent. The reserve banks were limited in making direct purchases from the Treasury to the amount of five billion dollars. In the pursuit of this policy of providing member banks with ample reserves and maintaining low interest rates for government borrowing, the Federal Reserve Banks added more than 21 billion dollars to their open market portfolio of Government securities.

The dilemma of postwar credit policy. The low interest rate policy during the war assured the Government of adequate funds at minimum costs. Such a policy was entirely proper, for high interest rates on government borrowing during wars do not reduce significantly the need for credit expansion. Nevertheless, the tremendous size of the low-interest-bearing Government debt created serious problems of credit control after the war.

One means used to keep down the average interest charges on the debt was the issue of vast amounts of short-dated obligations, which were mainly absorbed by the banking system. The rate on these obligations was held down by the simple expedient of having the Federal Reserve Banks support the price by purchases in the open market. The bank holdings of this short-term debt at the end of 1945 were as follows:

	Total Outstanding	Held by the Federal Reserve Banks	Held by Commercial Banks
Treasury bills (3 months)	$17,037,000,000	$12,831,000,000	$2,476,000,000
Certificates of indebtedness (12 months) ...	38,155,000,000	8,364,000,000	18,091,000,000
Treasury notes (3 to 5 years)	22,967,000,000	2,120,000,000	15,701,000,000

To wind up wartime commitments the Treasury had to continue its borrowings after hostilities ceased. Furthermore, it was regularly compelled to sell new securities in order to refinance maturing issues. Therefore the Federal Reserve System continued its support of Government security prices and the wartime policy of low interest rates. But in the process of supporting the Treasury low-interest-rate policy, the Federal Reserve System necessarily was providing commercial banks with cheap sources of cash reserve. The banks could sell Treasury bills and other short-dated paper in the market and the reserve banks necessarily stood ready to purchase whenever a decline in price threatened to endanger the existing pattern of interest rates. In providing the market with funds required to keep interest rates low on short-term Government securities, the reserve banks were providing an abundant and never-ending supply of reserve funds for use by banks in any way they saw fit.

The situation would not have been so troublesome had the war been followed by a period of depression and serious unemployment. But the inflation that actually materialized created a dilemma for the Federal Reserve authorities. They wished to maintain a low market rate of interest on the Government debt. At the same time, they recognized an acute need to impose anti-inflationary credit restraint on business. But so long as the Federal Reserve Banks supported the easy money rates for Treasury borrowing they were unable to impose restraint on the expansion of bank credit for business. Furthermore, should the market rates of interest be allowed to rise, long-term Government bonds, floated at low rates of interest, would fall in price. A disorganization of the Government bond market was, of course, to be avoided.

The problem was pointed up by two developments. During the latter part of 1945 and early 1946, banks showed a tendency to sell some of their holdings of short-term Government obligations to the Federal Reserve Banks and use the proceeds to purchase long-term bonds. This "monetizing" of the long-term debt was profitable to the banks since they could dispose of Treasury bills yielding three-eighths of 1 per cent and purchase bonds that would yield something over 2 per cent. The possibility that this practice might reach large proportions constituted a serious additional inflationary threat, since sales of Treasury bills resulted in higher bank reserves. In the second place, the inflationary postwar expansion in business created a heavy demand for bank credit. Orthodox policy called for the imposition of restraint through tighter money and higher interest rates. The low interest rate policy on Government securities prevented the use of such restraint.

Attempts to deal with postwar inflation. The inflation of the postwar years was supported by the wartime monetary expansion and by a sharp increase in credit and money in the postwar years. During the war and the immediate period thereafter, price controls held down the velocity of money and largely prevented a rise in prices. Had the often-talked-of proposal to "get the debt out of the banks" been carried out before the removal of price controls, a reduction in the money supply would have reduced the inflationary potential. The postwar boom, however, rapidly got under way and so increased the private demand for loans that no absorption of bank-held debt by private investors took place.

The second source of postwar inflation was the rise in private borrowing to finance the reconversion to peacetime production. This expansion of credit was based upon reserves created by the Federal Reserve System in support of the Treasury's low interest rate policy and, consequently, had an unlimited inflationary potential. Two types of proposals were made for checking this inflation. The first was to continue the existing easy money policy but invoke certain other restraints upon inflation in the private sector of the economy. The second proposal was simply that the easy money policy be abandoned in favor of conventional monetary restraint.

Those favoring a continuation of an easy money policy were concerned with the effect of higher interest rates upon the cost of carrying the debt and the possibility of adverse effects of higher interest rates upon Government security prices, and, in some cases at least, feared that a tight money policy would result in depression, and possibly stagnation, that would impair the rate of future economic growth. The Treasury's desire for continued low interest rates was understandable in view of the necessity of issuing new securities in exchange for old in annual amounts of between $50 billion and $75 billion. In support for this desire for low interest rates one Treasury spokesman urged that higher interest rates would make inflation worse rather than less, since the Treasury would have to increase its borrowings to meet the additional interest charges. A second argument against higher interest rates, widely accepted for a time, was that the resulting decline in the prices of long-term Government securities would induce a violent dumping of these securities, a complete demoralization of the security markets, and the collapse of the Government's credit. In any event, some argued, higher interest rates arising from monetary restraint would not check inflation.

Efforts at restraint on commercial credit while maintaining low interest rates on the Government debt. The proposals and the actual attempts, during 1945–1951, to impose restraint while maintaining a low interest rate on Government borrowings took a number of forms. First, in 1945, the Board of Governors proposed that Congress might grant it authority to regulate the Government security holdings of commercial banks. Specifically, such authority would include authorization (1) to place a limit upon the amount of long-term Government securities each bank might hold in proportion to its demand deposits; and (2) to set a minimum percentage ratio of short-term Government securities to demand deposits which banks must hold. Such a requirement would have constituted a kind of compulsory secondary reserve and would have effectively locked into the commercial banks a large fraction of the Treasury short-term low-interest-bearing debt. Had this suggestion been granted the Board would have been in a position to prevent further monetization of the long-term debt and could have tightened money rates in the private sector without increasing the cost of short-term Treasury borrowing. Congress, however, failed to take any action on the Board's request.

Next the Board suggested that it be given authority to raise reserve requirements for member banks. This authority would have enabled the Board to absorb new reserves created by Federal Reserve purchase of securities in support of the Treasury's easy money policy. This request, too, fell upon deaf Congressional ears at the time.

In July 1947, the Board abandoned its published buying rate on Treasury bills of three-eighths of 1 per cent and allowed the rate on such bills to rise to more normal levels. The rise in the bill rate had but a modest restraining influence, for the Federal Reserve Banks continued to support the prices of Treasury securities in order to maintain an agreed-upon pattern of rates.

In the meantime inflation, unchecked by monetary restraints, moved ahead rapidly, with wholesale prices advancing 50 per cent between June of 1946 and August 1948. This increase in prices, incidentally, occurred during a period when the Federal budget was, on balance, showing an aggregate cash surplus of about 15 billion dollars. In August 1948, on the threshold of the recession of 1949, Congress authorized the Board of Governors to reinstate Regulation W controlling consumer credit, and to raise reserve requirements of member banks beyond the regular statutory limits. Both authorizations expired on June 30, 1949, after a short period of use.

When the slackening in industrial output and employment became noticeable early in 1949, the Federal Reserve System, already committed to an easy money policy, had little room for maneuver. Nevertheless, it did what it could by easing consumer credit terms and lowering margin requirements on security loans. In addition it made a series of reductions in reserve requirements that released altogether about 3.8 billions of dollars of reserves. The commercial banks followed their usual practice of using their excess reserves to purchase short-term Government securities. As interest rates fell under the impact of this buying the Federal Reserve Banks sold securities, both short and long-term, to meet market demands. At all times the System's open market operations were aimed at maintaining ample credit facilities for borrowers while holding to its objective of "maintaining orderly conditions" in the security markets. The continued ease in the money market was accompanied by a shift in the Government's fiscal position from a cash surplus of over

$8 billion in 1948 to a deficit of $1.3 billion in 1949. By the end of 1949 the cyclical upturn was well under way, and by the time of the outbreak of war in Korea in June 1950, business conditions were again at a high level.

Korea and monetary policy. The war in Korea began just as recovery from the 1949 recession was about completed. It brought with it a renewed expansion of military spending and a growing increase of speculative buying by business and consumers alike. When the Chinese intervened in December, and the unfavorable United Nations military position threatened a long and costly war, speculative buying became even more intense. In the face of a sharp increase in the demand for speculative credit, the Federal Reserve System, still a slave to the Treasury easy money policy, found itself without adequate weapons of restraint. Already recovered from the decline of 1949, wholesale prices rose about 17 per cent between June 1950 and February 1951. Banks and other investors disposed of Government securities at prices pegged by the Federal Reserve System to obtain funds to meet the demands of private borrows, increasing, as they did so, the supply of reserve funds available for multiple credit expansion.

In September 1950, under the authority of the Defense Production Act of that year, the Board of Governors reinstated Regulation W to restrain consumer credit. One month later, October 1950, the Board cooperated with the Federal agencies involved in regulating insured housing loans, to institute Regulation X, imposing limits upon mortgage financing of new residential construction. In January 1951, margin requirements on stock market loans were increased and the Board ordered reserve requirement increases amounting to $2 billion to absorb reserves arising from post-holiday currency returns and support purchases of Government securities. The inadequacy of these measures in resisting the strong inflationary pressure of the times is shown by an increase in wholesale prices of nearly 9 per cent in the four months November 1950 to February 1951.

The "accord" of March 1951. At the insistence of the Federal Reserve authorities the Treasury at last agreed to the Federal Reserve System's abandonment of its practice of supporting Government security prices at a fixed level of rates. A joint statement by the Treasury and the Board announced that a "full accord" had been reached and that debt management and monetary policies should have the common purpose to "assure successful financing of the Government's requirements and at the same time to minimize monetization of the public debt."

The Federal Reserve's gradual withdrawal of support in the Government security market led to a decline in price of long-term 2½'s from 100¾ to about 97 by May 1951. To avoid taking losses on the sale of bonds at a discount, banks turned to the Federal Reserve Banks to borrow when in need of additional reserves. During the remainder of 1951, however, the Federal Reserve assisted the Treasury's refinancing operations from time to time by purchasing maturing security issues.

The year 1951, therefore, marked the reassertion by the Federal Reserve System of its right to use its most potent weapons against inflation. It is worth noting that, though often prophesied, the restoration of tighter money and higher interest rates failed to result in a general dumping of Government securities and a demoralization of the security markets. Instead, owners of securities that had fallen in price because of higher interest rates held them in order to avoid taking losses on their sale. Thus was laid to rest one of the most popular monetary superstitions of the postwar world, and monetary policy was restored to its proper place as an indispensable tool of economic stabilization.

The withdrawal of Federal Reserve support to Government security prices in 1951 dried up the previously endless stream of loan funds derived, at the option of the market, by the sale of Government securities. The resulting restraint was felt both by banks which had to borrow at the Federal Reserve Banks and by insurance companies and other lenders that had been rearranging their portfolios by selling Government securities and substituting for them higher earning loans to business and real estate mortgage loans. The decline in bond prices abruptly reduced this hitherto profitable switch. New commitments for mortgage lending became hard to get, with the result that considerable restraint was felt in the construction field.

The tight money period of 1952-1953. The year 1952 was one of general wholesale price stability and sustained high level business activity. The Federal Reserve System assumed the responsibility for restricting credit and monetary expansion to the growth needs of the economy. Although the System relieved seasonal strains in the market, member banks were compelled to face the restraints of discounting at the Federal Reserve Banks to provide themselves with reserves wanted for expansion. At one time in December 1952, member bank discounting reached the $2 billion mark. In the atmosphere of quantitative restraint created by the restoration of credit policy, the Board suspended the operation of Regulation W in May, and that of Regulation X in September. During the year, with little change in velocity, the effective money supply (net demand deposits plus currency outside of banks) increased by about 4 per cent, an amount corresponding roughly to the rate of growth of the economy.

During the first part of 1953 the pressure upon credit was maintained. The Federal Reserve discount rates were increased from 1¾ per cent to 2 per cent, and member banks became more reluctant to lend borrowed money. By May, signs of excessive money market stringency began to appear, threatening to interfere with the meeting of normal credit needs. The Federal Reserve System therefore modified its restrictive policy and increased the supply of reserve funds by expanding its holdings of Government securities.

The depression of 1953-1954. By mid-1953, a mild recession in business had set in—the result of a slackening of defense demands as the Korean fighting stopped and a readjustment of overextended inventories. The Federal Reserve System further increased its open market security holdings and lowered reserve requirements. This quick reversal of policy to match changed conditions permitted member banks to reduce their borrowings and resulted in increased monetary ease.

As the recession of 1953-1954 became clearly evident, the Federal Reserve System adopted a policy that it chose to call one of "active ease." A further expansion of the System's open market purchases in the spring of 1954 and a mid-year additional reduction of reserve requirements provided banks with an abundance of reserves and enabled them to get out of debt at the Federal Reserve Banks and to increase their holdings of Treasury securities. As a further gesture, in February 1954, the discount rate was reduced from 2 per cent to 1¾ per cent, and in May it was further reduced to 1½ per cent.

The inventory liquidation of 1953-1954 was quickly accomplished. Residential construction, supported by a basic unsatisfied housing demand, expanded sharply as mortgage money became more available with the ease in the money market. By the end of 1954 the recovery was well under way. Not only was prompt monetary policy of help in stimulating the recovery but also fiscal policy had a part. Taxes paid by individuals were reduced, in part because of a decline in income and in part because of a lowering of rates. Unemployment insurance payments also expanded. As a result, in spite of a $7 billion decline in the gross national product in 1954, disposable personal income (after taxes) and consumer expenditures were larger in 1954 than in 1953.

The year 1955 was prosperous enough to justify the Federal Reserve authorities' adoption of a fairly neutral policy. The recession policy of "active ease" first gave way to one of "ease," to be followed by "mild restraint" by mid-year. Member banks found it necessary from time to time to borrow at the Federal Reserve Banks to meet losses of funds in particular areas. The aggregate level of excess reserves was in general approximately equal to aggregate member bank borrowing during the first six months of 1955.

During the latter half of 1955 and the early part of 1956, Federal Reserve credit policy became genuinely restrictive. The 1955 boom in housing construction and in durable goods sales financed on installment credit was reflected in increased pressure for expansion in commercial bank credit. To resist the inflationary pressure, Federal Reserve discount rates were raised, at intervals, from 1¾ per cent in April 1955 to 3 per cent in August 1956—the highest in over twenty years. Moreover, although making purchases of United States securities to meet seasonal pressure upon bank reserve positions, the System did not provide all of the funds needed to meet the demands for credit. Consequently, member banks found themselves compelled to borrow, and they were exposed to the pressure of higher discount rates. Such borrowing exceeded $1 billion in November 1955 and in April and May of 1956. As a supplement to the mild credit restraint of early 1955, the Board of Governors, in April, raised margin requirements for purchasing and carrying listed securities to 70 per cent.

For the year ending March 1956, the Federal Reserve monetary restraint limited the increase in the money supply to 1.2 per cent. This was considerably less than the 4 per cent average annual rate of growth of the economy. However, this limitation was clearly desirable in the face of the rise in the velocity of demand deposits. Corrected seasonally, this increase varied from 4 per cent for banks in 337 reporting cities to 6.5 per cent for banks in six other large cities and 13 per cent in New York City.

By mid-1956 considerable difference of opinion appeared as to the appropriateness of the continuation of the Federal Reserve's tight money policy. These differences arose out of the difficulty in evaluating the over-all significance of weaknesses in the automobile and residential construction fields against the continued inflationary developments in other areas. The Federal Reserve policy makers were prepared to ease the credit situation as soon as they were convinced that depression factors had begun to outweigh those of inflation.

Open market portfolio policy since 1951. Since the Federal Reserve System in 1951 withdrew its support of Government securities at fixed or pegged prices, policy emphasis has been concentrated upon the availability of reserves for the commercial banks. The tight money policy of 1952 and early 1953 involved compelling banks to pay for added reserves by borrowing at the discount window of the Federal Reserve Banks. The ease of 1954 was carried out by the lowering of reserve requirements and the purchase of short-term securities in the open market. With its interest shifted toward reserve availability and away from security prices, it became the policy of the Open Market Committee to trade only in short-dated obligations, preferably Treasury bills. In this way it could adequately adjust the size of bank reserves while scrupulously avoiding any hint of the old and distasteful policy of maintaining a fixed pattern of rates and prices on Government securities, a policy so happily put behind it by the "accord" of March 1951. Yet another reason lay behind the determination of the Open Market Committee normally to deal only in Treasury bills. This was the urging by the dealers in United States securities that they could perform their function of providing a continuous market in such securities only if the market was free from unpredictable interferences arising out of Federal Reserve policy. It was the dealers' contention that Federal

Reserve trading should be limited to short maturities only, thus leaving the prices of other securities of varying maturities to "find their own level" under the impact of the impersonal forces of the market. There has been some concern, both within and without the Federal Reserve System, about the Committee's stated policy of limiting its normal open market dealings to Treasury bills. Granting that it would be permissible under this policy to deal in long-term securities when necessary to correct "disorderly" conditions in the market, the opponents of the stated policy fear that the Committee may find itself committed by precedent *not* to deal in long-term securities in the exercise of normal policy functions. This would be an unfortunate barrier to policy action if conditions require a rapid lowering of long-term interest rates without waiting for the changes in short-term rates to filter down to the long-term market.

Present-Day Policy

Looking back on forty years of Federal Reserve history one can see two major and significant changes. First, the System is no longer a collection of twelve regional central banks loosely held together by the Federal Reserve Board. Second, it is no longer dedicated to the traditional theory that a central bank should be concerned solely with the adequacy of its gold reserves and the provision of reserves and currency needed by commercial banks to satisfy the short-term financial needs of business. Instead we find the System has gradually developed into a well-integrated, smooth-working central bank with highly centralized authority over significant policy decisions. Moreover, because of the absence of present concern over the adequacy of gold reserves, the System has been free to pursue an independent course of monetary management. Because of this freedom, and the experiences of the Great Depression and the inflation arising from World War II, the System has been able to incorporate into its aims or goals both a policy designed to insure the smooth accommodation of current business needs and the longer-run policy of economic stabilization and growth. Decisions on policy actions thought to be appropriate for the pursuit of these long-run aims are necessarily made from time to time in the councils of the Board of Governors and the Open Market Committee. These decisions are reached on the basis of analyses of business and employment conditions and their expected future developments. Thus is provided the basic blueprint for Federal Reserve policy action involving changes in discount rates, in reserve requirements, and in the direction and magnitude of open market operations.

Within the framework of general policy, the Open Market Committee instructs the manager of the System's trading account on measures to be taken to adjust current money market conditions to satisfy the general policy of "ease" or "restraint" as the case may be. Furthermore, in the day-to-day operations of the trading account its manager examines a constant flow of information bearing upon the current reserve position of the banks. In this way he tries to shield the market from alternate shortages and gluts of member bank reserves or "Federal funds." Here we have a modernized application of the traditional criterion of accommodating the needs of business. The discount windows of the Federal Reserve Banks supplement these offsetting open market operations.

Federal Reserve policy, then, in its present form, involves two quite separate but important goals. The first basic aim is to achieve, so far as wise monetary policy is able, economic stabilization, full employment, and growth. The second goal or aim is at all times to maintain a sufficient short-run balance in the supply of money market funds to insure, within the general stabilization goals, adequate funds to finance current business operations.

In spite of the increased skill and the improved methods now available for the administration of central bank policy, one ought not to expect full attainment of the established goals. This is true even with the added powers of fiscal policy. Fiscal policy can never be free from the compulsions of the budget necessities of the Treasury. Wars and threats of wars tend strongly to result in fiscal practices that are contrary to stabilization goals. Fiscal policy also suffers from the handicap of operating to a large extent in an atmosphere of political expediency. In spite of the greater sophistication of modern central bankers, monetary and credit policy is far from perfectly developed. It involves the combination of short-and long-range goals that may at any given moment be in conflict. When depression requires a monetary policy of expansion and ease, the day-to-day policy may sometimes require an absorption of reserves by open market operations to prevent a temporary market disturbance arising from excess funds. Or, when cyclical policy calls for general restraint, it may be necessary at the same time to put additional funds into the market to prevent a short-run stringency. The administration of Federal Reserve policy, therefore, requires constant study and search for insight into the problem of co-ordinating short- and long-range policy operations. In addition to the imperfections in the application of monetary and fiscal policies there are cyclical and other disturbances in a dynamic private enterprise society that may defy the best efforts of stabilization policy. Therefore administration of policy can be considered successful if it provides sufficient offsets to cyclical movements to prevent them from becoming disastrously cumulative, and if it provides sufficient funds to permit and encourage the long-run growth needed for full employment.

Questions for Study

1. What, in general, appears to have been the Federal Reserve credit policy of the years 1914-1921? How did credit policy during World War I resemble that of World War II? In what ways were the practices different?

2. Why were the Federal Reserve actions during 1919-1921 inappropriate for contracyclical policy? How can we explain those actions?

3. What was the policy developed and announced by the Federal Reserve Board in 1923? In what ways did it show the influence of the belief that financing trade and commerce should be the main concern of central banks? In what ways did this policy create difficulties for the Board in 1928-1929?

4. How adequate was the Federal Reserve Board's anti-depression policy of 1930-1933? How can this policy be explained? Does this explanation prove the weakness of monetary policy in times of depression?

5. What was the "flexible open-market portfolio" policy that developed after 1937?

6. How did the Federal Reserve Banks insure that the Government could borrow at low rates of interest during the war years of 1942-1945?

7. Why did the wartime low-interest rate pattern prove so difficult in the postwar years?

8. Can a low-interest rate policy during wars be justified?

9. After the war the banks sold Treasury bills to the Federal Reserve Banks to obtain funds to purchase higher-yield long-term bonds. Why was this action inflationary?

10. What was the special secondary reserve proposal designed to freeze short-term government obligations in bank portfolios? What dual advantages would have resulted from such a policy?

11. Why is Treasury fiscal policy unlikely to be an effective brake on inflation in times of high profit prospects? What does this mean as to the need for effective central bank credit policy?

12. What was the nature and effect of the "accord" of 1951? Why did it help restore to the Federal Reserve System its traditional authority to exercise control over the cost and availability of credit and over the money supply?

13. Why did the Federal Reserve follow a tight money policy in 1952 and the first part of 1953? Why and when was this policy reversed? Would you say that the Federal Reserve authorities showed ability to shift policy practices in the face of changing economic needs?

14. Why did the Open Market Committee, after 1951, generally confine its dealings in United States securities to those with short maturities? What reason was given by some people for their objection to this policy?

VIII____

INTERNATIONAL
MONETARY RELATIONSHIPS

29

Foreign Exchange

During periods of prosperity and peace, world trade has mainly been carried on by private enterprise on a relatively free basis. However, the great depression of the 1930's created serious balance-of-payment problems for many countries. The result was the erection of a multitude of tariff, quota, and exchange control barriers that in large measure disrupted normal trade patterns and mechanisms. World War II, which followed the years of depression, completed this disruption. Seeking foreign supplies on the most favorable terms, governments by-passed private importers and embarked upon a program of state trading. Furthermore, the war destroyed the normal trade relationships between belligerents. Pressure for scarce supplies led to strong measures of control over foreign exchange markets to insure that the limited supply of foreign exchange was used to satisfy most urgent military needs. Thus the war led to almost complete government control over foreign trade and foreign exchange markets.

The end of the war did not see a quick return to the use of normal peacetime international trade. Instead, because many countries preferred a rapid domestic rehabilitation that was believed to be incompatible with a restoration of free foreign exchange markets, state trading, exchange controls, and inter-governmental loans and grants-in-aid continued. Consequently, for almost a decade after the end of World War II, we saw a large fraction of world trade closely regulated by governments, and a by-passing of the normal private foreign exchange mechanism.

Gradually there has developed a loosening of governmental restraints on foreign trade. With this has come renewed emphasis upon the problem of restoring free foreign exchange markets and free convertibility among the free-world currencies. It is especially timely, therefore, that we acquaint ourselves with the mechanism of the foreign exchange markets and the basic principles upon which they operate. In this chapter we shall be examining the foreign exchange market and the manner in which foreign traders, both importers and exporters, are able to carry out the settlement of their monetary claims against each other.

The Problem of Financing Foreign Trade

Financing goods in transit. Regardless of whether or not the exporter of goods extends credit, he normally must arrange to finance the shipment while it is in transit. Only when the foreign buyer pays cash in advance can the seller escape this burden, and such cases are rare. When no credit is extended to the buyer, financing the shipment involves only the burden of waiting for payment until the goods arrive and remittance is received in return. If the exporter is in a strong enough financial position to wait during this interval, the foreign exchange banker's function is not one of financing but merely that of a collection agency. If the exporter is not willing or able to wait the time necessary to collect the funds, he can call upon his bank for aid. This aid may take the form of a loan secured by the draft drawn on the buyer and the documents of title to goods shipped, or it may involve the purchase (or discount) of the draft itself. In either event, the bank advances the funds before the collections are actually realized from the export.

Financing exports on credit. If the exporter agrees to sell on credit, in order to give the foreign buyer time to resell the goods before payment, his problem becomes more difficult. The time he must wait for payment is prolonged. Again he may resort to his bank for aid, either by borrowing or by discounting time drafts drawn on the foreign buyer. Exporting on credit is further complicated by the necessity for knowing the credit standing of the foreign buyer.

The exporter's protection. Whether the seller finances the export himself or relies upon the bank, he bears the risk, since he is legally liable as drawer of any drafts on the buyer which he discounts with his bank. Because of the difficulties involved in investigating the credit standing of foreign buyers, export credits are probably less generally extended upon open account than is the case in domestic trade. Exporters often keep control over their goods until they are paid (cash sales), or until drafts drawn on foreign buyers are accepted (credit sales). An exporter ships goods under an order bill of lading, which is a document of title, and the buyer cannot obtain his goods until he gets possession of the bill of lading. The exporter draws a draft or bill of exchange on the buyer, ordering him to pay on sight or on a certain date. To this bill of exchange he attaches the bill of lading and forwards both through his bank to a foreign bank, which in turn presents the bill of exchange to the importer for payment or acceptance. Or, the exporter may sell the bill of exchange to his bank, which then handles the transaction for itself. Instead of drawing directly on the buyer, an exporter may demand the right to draw a bill of exchange against a well-known bank that has previously authorized the drawing by the issuing of a letter of credit and has agreed to accept the bill and pay it upon maturity.

Foreign Bills of Exchange

Nature and origin of foreign bills of exchange. A foreign bill of exchange is simply a draft drawn by someone in one country on someone in a foreign country payable in the foreign country's currency. It may be payable at sight or after the expiration of a certain time. It may be drawn on an individual, a business firm, or a bank by an individual, a business firm, or a bank. Exporters of goods, who by their sales contract have agreed to receive payment in the currency of the buyer's country, draw foreign bills of exchange either against the foreign importer or against the importer's bank under a letter of credit. Bankers in the United States draw drafts or bills of exchange against their deposits in foreign banks and sell these drafts to American importers and others having remittances to make abroad.

Commercial bills of exchange. Drafts drawn by exporters (or by others to whom foreign funds are due) are known as *commercial bills of exchange,* because they arise directly out of commercial transactions. Commercial bills may be classified according to: (1) the time they are to run; (2) the security; and (3) if secured, the terms under which the documents are to be released to the buyer.

Commercial bills may be payable at sight or on time. If a bill is drawn in order to collect for services, there are no documents to attach, and the bill is therefore a clean bill. If it is drawn for the sale of goods and the documents are attached, it is known as a *documentary bill*. If the credit of the importer is good, the bill may be marked "documentary acceptance," meaning that he can get his documents entitling him to possession of the goods when he accepts the draft. Otherwise, the documents will be released only upon payment of the draft. Commercial bills drawn on banks under letters of credit are normally marked "documentary acceptance," and entitle the drawee banks to possession of the documents on acceptance of the bills.

Bankers' bills. Bills of exchange drawn by American banks on foreign banks are known as *bankers' bills*.[1] These bills are of several different types. Those payable on demand are either *sight drafts* or *cable transfers*. Those payable on time are divided into *short bills* and *long bills*.

Bankers' bills may be drawn against balances in foreign banks and sold to persons having obligations to pay abroad. They may also be drawn against foreign banks for the purpose of obtaining funds in the drawee bank's country. Such bills are known as *finance* or *loan* bills.

Use of bills of exchange in international settlements. We may, for convenience, think of foreign bills of exchange as having their origin in the transactions of American exporters who ship goods and draw drafts (on foreign buyers) ordering payment of the required amount in foreign currency. The exporters would like to exchange these orders for American dollars. On the other hand, American importers with remittances to make desire to exchange their dollars for drafts calling for payment in foreign currencies. There are, of course, difficulties that prevent the exporter from selling his foreign bills of exchange directly to the importer. In

---

[1] The term "bankers' bills" is sometimes used to include all bills drawn on bankers, whether by other banks or by individuals under letters of credit (which we have included under "commercial bills"). This usage applies particularly to the discount market.

addition to the physical difficulty of making contact, there is the question of size and maturities to consider. Foreign exchange merchants quite naturally developed as go-betweens for the buyers and sellers of foreign exchange.

The foreign exchange bank stands ready to purchase foreign bills from the exporters or other commercial drawers at the current rate of exchange. It buys both sight and time bills. These bills are collected, when due, through a foreign branch or foreign correspondent, which credits the proceeds to the account of the American bank. It is against these collected funds in foreign banks that the bank then draws the drafts or bankers' bills it sells to Americans wishing to remit abroad.

The Rates of Exchange

The meaning of foreign exchange rates. The rate of exchange on a foreign country is simply the price, in one's own currency, of bills of exchange payable abroad in the foreign currency. Thus the rate of exchange on London is the price, here, in dollars, of a pound sterling draft. The price of bankers' sight drafts formerly was considered the "basic rate" of exchange, and, ordinarily, published quotations were for sight drafts of this sort. Today, however, the basic rate is generally quoted as the price of a cable transfer, which is somewhat higher than that of a sight draft or bill.

Maturities of bills and the rate of exchange. The highest rate or price charged for a bill of exchange is for the cable transfer calling for immediate payment. The banker's sight draft costs somewhat less because the banker in America has a double use of the money received from the buyer during the interval elapsing from the time the draft is sent across to the time it is collected. In contrast to the sale of a cable transfer, the sale of a sight draft enables the banker to obtain interest, at the foreign rate, for the time the bill is uncollected. Time drafts or future exchange drafts bring a still lower price than the sight drafts, the difference being determined by the interest rate and the time between the date of sale and the payment of the bill.

Origin of the bill and the rate of exchange. Commercial bills, drawn by exporters, sell at a lower price than bankers' bills of similar maturities. The highest-priced commercial bills are sight bills drawn on well-known bankers under letters of credit. The price of such bills will be less than the price of bankers' sight bills by the amount of the commission or profit which the foreign exchange banker requires. Bills drawn on commercial firms instead of on banks sell for still lower prices, since the element of risk is somewhat greater.

Factors affecting the basic rates. The price of foreign bills, or the rate of exchange, depends fundamentally upon the forces of supply and demand. At any given time, the supply of commercial bills offered for sale in American foreign exchange centers depends upon the value of American exports (both visible and invisible). If the supply of such bills offered for sale is in excess of the demand for foreign bills on the part of Americans wishing to make remittances abroad, the price will fall. If the supply is relatively small, the price will rise. Thus, a favorable balance of indebtedness (an excess of export items) depresses the foreign exchange rate, whereas an unfavorable balance (an excess of import items) raises it. Whether the rates are high or low, the exchange banker endeavors to buy bills more cheaply than he sells them in order to preserve his margin of profit.

Limits to exchange rate fluctuations: Gold points under the gold standard. Before the general collapse of the world gold standard in 1931, foreign exchange rates were closely tied to the *mint par* gold value of the respective currencies. Mint par relationships between currencies is determined by comparing the amount of gold into which each currency may be converted or by comparing the price of gold in the countries involved.

Before England abandoned gold in 1931, the mint par of exchange with the United States was $4.8665 = £1. This meant that a banker owning a pound in England could, if necessary, convert it into gold and return the gold to the United States where it could be converted in turn into $4.8665. Therefore, at a time when United States exports (in the broad sense) exceeded imports, the resulting fall in the price of pound sterling bills of exchange could not exceed the cost involved in converting such bills into gold and the shipment of that gold to the United States. The cost of shipping (including packing, freight, insurance, loss of interest while in transit, etc.) was generally estimated at about two cents per pound. Hence bankers' bills drawn on London would not fall below $4.8465. This price was called the gold *import* point and marked the lowest point to which the price of pound drafts could fall. Likewise, when American imports (in the broad sense) tended to exceed exports, and the price of sterling bills rose, the maximum price of such bills would not exceed mint par ($4.8665) plus the cost (about two cents) of shipping $4.8665 worth of gold to London for conversion into pounds. Consequently, the maximum price of pound sterling bills would not exceed $4.8865, which was the gold *export* point.

Limits to exchange rate fluctuations: Inconvertible paper currencies. When a country's currency is not convertible into a fixed amount of gold, there is no gold export point to limit the drop in the price of bills payable in that currency. The value of bills of exchange drawn on a paper standard country is determined primarily by the buying power of that currency at home as compared with the buying power of other currencies in their respective countries. This is necessarily so because such bills cannot be converted into gold but must be utilized to buy commodities or services. If, for example, American exporters have bills of exchange drawn on English banks payable in paper pounds, they can be sold only to someone willing to purchase pounds with dollars. Fundamentally, the demand for pounds (barring speculative influences) arises from the desire to purchase British goods, services, and securities. For example, American importers will buy pounds only when, at the existing rate of exchange, British goods can be purchased and returned to America to be sold at a profit. The rate of exchange that permits trade between countries to proceed in a normal fashion is sometimes called "purchasing power parity." If bills of exchange drawn on the paper standard country are too high in price to make their use profitable for obtaining goods for export from that country (including services, travel, and so forth), they must become cheaper. Normally the rate of exchange on a paper standard country must be such as to maintain a balance between its import and export items.[2]

---

[2] "Import" and "export items" are used here to include both visible items (merchandise and specie) and invisible items, including shipping, insurance, security movements, interest on international indebtedness, foreign travel, and immigrant remittances.

Because paper currency exchange rates are not anchored to any gold parity, they are particularly exposed to speculative pressure. And since any breath of rumor is sufficient to start speculative movements, it is easy to see that financing of foreign trade under the circumstances becomes abnormally hazardous. To keep paper exchange rates free from speculative activities, it may be necessary for the central bank or the government to acquire sufficient foreign funds and credits to enable it to support the domestic exchange rates against bear raids of the speculators. This support is accomplished by the simple expedient of buying all domestic currency offered at what is considered a desirable rate, in exchange for bills on foreign countries. In this way exchange rates in paper standard countries may be given substantial stability.

Limits to exchange rate fluctuations: Controlled rates. During and since World War II, we have become accustomed to seeing a type of foreign exchange situation, made familiar by Germany in the 1930's, in which there are neither the gold shipping point limits nor flexible exchange rates that tend to move toward an equilibrium level. This system is known as *exchange control*. It is characterized by (1) a lack of free convertibility of the currency into gold; (2) the absence of exchange rate adjustment to provide equilibrium in the country's balance of payments; and (3) a rigid control over the price of foreign exchange bills by government interference in the market. Specifically, a certain "official rate" of exchange is established with another country by the government exchange control agency. All exporters are required to sell their foreign bills of exchange to the control agency. All importers must purchase foreign exchange from it. If, under the circumstances, the country's balance of payments is favorable (export items exceed imports) the control agency will tend to accumulate foreign exchange abroad. This tendency, in itself, is no immediate cause of concern save for the possibility that it represents a waste of resources. But it becomes much more serious whenever, at the official rate of exchange, a country's balance of payments is unfavorable (import items exceed exports). Under these circumstances the supply of foreign exchange is inadequate to meet the demand of the importers. Since gold cannot be freely exported to meet the deficit, and a rise in foreign exchange rates is not to be allowed, the control agency is compelled to ration the limited supply of avaliable foreign exchange according to some estimate of the worthwhileness of the various possible imports.

Arbitrage and Three-Cornered Exchange

Arbitrage. When foreign exchange markets are free, a perplexing problem often arises from the fact that foreign trade between two countries may be settled in terms of the currencies of either country (or, for that matter, of a third country). Americans exporting to England frequently draw drafts payable in sterling, and these create sterling exchange in New York. American importers purchase bankers' bills drawn against the proceeds of such commercial bills. There is no assurance, however, that these will be equal, that all American exporters will draw drafts payable in pounds, or that all American importers will purchase pound sterling drafts. Indeed, it is possible to imagine a case in which all exporters, regardless of which country they represent, sell only on terms permitting them to draw drafts on foreign buyers payable in the exporters' currency. Thus, American importers would be compelled to remit sterling drafts to pay for their imports, while English importers (to use the familiar New York-London illustration) would demand dollar drafts. Yet the English banks would receive no dollar commercial drafts with which to build up their dollar balances, and American banks would receive no sterling commercial drafts with which to establish sterling balances.

It is here that the arbitrage operations of the foreign exchange dealers come into play. Let us suppose that, because of the unwillingness of both English and American exporters to take payment in anything but their own currencies, foreign rates of exchange in both New York and London are high. If sterling drafts sell in New York for $2.81, and dollar drafts sell in London at the rate of $2.79 per pound sterling, there is a great opportunity for profit through arbitrage transactions. A New York dealer, in communication with his London correspondent, orders the London correspondent to sell cable transfers payable in dollars at $2.79 per pound and to credit the pound sterling to his account. The New York dealer is thus able to obtain a pound sterling in London by paying out $2.79 in New York. He then sells pound sterling cables in New York at $2.81 against his sterling account and realizes $.02 per pound, minus incidental costs, on each transaction. This arbitrage operation will continue until the New York price of sterling exchange is so near the London price of dollar exchange that no profit remains. Thus, regardless of the terms of settlement that foreign traders may use, the rate of exchange is substantially the same in either country.

Three-cornered exchange. To introduce a more realistic note into the foreign exchange discussion, it is necessary to consider the fact that international trade is not a simple two-sided matter between two countries but involves a multitude of transactions of different kinds among many countries. It is highly unlikely that the exchange of visible and invisible items between any pair of countries will be exactly equal. The United States may have an export excess to England, for example. England, however, may have export excesses to South American countries, while these countries in turn may have export excesses to the United States. Under these circumstances sterling bills will be cheap in New York, South American drafts will be cheap in London, while dollar drafts will be cheap in South America. In such a case the New York foreign exchange dealer would purchase cheap sterling drafts, utilize the proceeds to purchase cheap South American drafts in London, and use the South American funds to purchase cheap dollars. This procedure would continue until the rates of exchange became so adjusted as to yield no arbitrage profit. In other words, cross-rates would be equalized. The value of drafts on London would, therefore, reflect not only the net excess of our exports to England, but also our net excess of imports from South America.

If all international transactions were settled in terms of the currency of one country, the case would be simpler. Before World War I, the bulk of international trade was financed by the British banks. Exporters in the United States sold and drew drafts in terms of pound sterling. If South American countries bought from England, they agreed to pay in pound sterling. If Americans sold more to England than they bought, the excess of pound sterling exchange arising could always be used to pay for any imports from South America in excess of exports to it. Only when the United States showed a net excess in the value of exports to the whole world would the value of sterling exchange decline in New York.

Seasonal Exchange Rate Changes

Seasonal inequalities in trade: Short-term capital movements. Seasonal and irregular influences affect international as well as domestic trade. Consequently, even though the balance of payments is in equilibrium on an annual basis, there will almost certainly be times when temporary disequilibrium arises. For at one season imports will exceed the exports, and the reverse will be true at another. Therefore, there will be a strong tendency for foreign exchange rates to rise during the period when imports are greater and for a fall in rates during the period or season when exports exceed imports. Under the gold standard the rates might move to the gold shipping point causing gold to be transferred back and forth on the merely temporary mission of settling seasonal inequalities in trade. This uneconomic practice was largely avoided by the movement of "short-term capital" from the country having the favorable balance to the country with the unfavorable balance. This means simply that the bankers who purchased the foreign bills arising from excessive exports did not reduce the price of such bills to the gold import point. Instead, they temporarily lent the excess accumulations of foreign funds in the foreign money market. They were quite ready to do this because they were confident that in the near future the trade tide would turn and the resulting excess of *imports* would enable them to sell their bankers' bills drawn against their accumulated foreign funds at a profit. For example, when an excess of exports drove the old pound rate down to $4.85, the American banks that purchased pound bills at that price and held the proceeds invested in London, might later, when imports began to exceed exports, sell pound drafts for as much as $4.87 and thus realize an acceptable profit. In such a case the price of London bills remained within the gold points and no gold was shipped.

Banks were willing and able to operate on a narrow margin of profit in the situation just described because of the protection against risk of sizable losses afforded by the existence of the gold-standard gold shipping points. With the breakdown of the international gold standard, such short-term loans by banks in foreign money markets very largely disappeared. It is easy to see that with loss of convertibility into gold and the disappearance of the gold shipping points the risk attending the investment of short-term funds in foreign money markets was greatly increased. Consequently, seasonal fluctuations in foreign exchange rates between inconvertible currencies tend to be greater than they were under the gold standard. Only intervention into the exchange market by some government agency that is able to assume the risks of exchange fluctuations will adequately smooth out seasonal changes in rates and the speculative movements that may arise out of or accompany them.

Seasonal inequalities in trade: Forward exchange. With the disappearance of bankers' loans in foreign money markets to offset seasonal inequalities in trade, there has developed an increased use of "forward exchange" transactions. An American exporter may expect to ship goods abroad at some future time, say, a month hence. If he wishes to know definitely what he will realize on drafts which he expects to draw, he goes to the foreign exchange dealer and sells foreign exchange for future delivery; that is, when the time comes to ship the goods and draw drafts against the shipment, he will be able to sell the drafts at a fixed price already agreed upon. The bank is able to assume the risk of fluctuations in exchange because of its superior knowledge of trends in exchange rates and because of the possibility of hedging its purchase. It may hedge its purchase of future exchange by contracting to sell an equivalent amount of foreign exchange one month later to American importers. Similarly, a bank may contract to sell future exchange, at a given price, to importers needing it to pay for expected imports and may hedge or protect itself against loss from a rise in exchange rates by purchasing current (spot) or future foreign exchange bills from exporters. Dealings in forward or future exchange assist in the reduction of exchange rate fluctuations arising from seasonal inequalities in trade, since current excess supplies of foreign exchange may be bought and hedged against by sales of future exchange to importers in anticipation of the season when imports tend to exceed exports. Thus the foreign exchange dealer, by ridding himself of risk, can offer a better price for exchange during seasons of excess exports than would be otherwise possible.

Use of Letters of Credit and Bankers' Acceptances

Bank credit substituted for individual credit. Because of the superiority of drafts drawn by exporters on *banks* under letters of credit, such drafts have come to play an important part in the financing of foreign trade. This is particularly true of transactions in which the exporter grants credit to the foreign importer. The difficulty of obtaining credit information, as well as the longer credit terms often required, makes reliance upon the credit of a bank especially desirable.

Bank credit is introduced into international trade finance through the use of the letter of credit and the banker's acceptance. For example, if an American exporter wishes to sell to a foreign importer on six months' credit, he may request the importer to furnish a banker's letter of credit authorizing the drawing of drafts on the bank instead of upon the importer. Since the bank promises to accept any drafts properly drawn under the terms of the sales agreement, the exporter obtains a banker's acceptance instead of a draft on the importer.

Letter of credit. The foreign importer who must obtain a letter of credit makes application to a bank satisfactory to the exporter. If the importer is a customer of such a bank, his application can, of course, be made directly. If he is not a customer of such a bank, he will make his application through his own banker. The bank to which application is made may be located in another city or even in another country, including that of the exporter.

The application for a letter of credit is usually a formal document in which the importer (1) requests that the credit be issued or opened for a designated beneficiary; (2) describes the number, amount, and tenor of drafts to be drawn under the credit; (3) describes the bills of lading, insurance certificates, and other documents, such as commercial and consular invoices, certificates of inspection, weight, and health, and custom house declarations; (4) describes the origin and destination of the shipment; (5) describes the merchandise to be shipped; and (6) states the date of expiration of the credit. Further, the applicant must give the bank assurance that (1) he will provide funds to meet the draft when due; (2) he will pay all expenses and the bank's commission; (3) title to the goods will remain in the bank until it is reimbursed;

and (4) the bank may take any necessary steps to protect itself against loss.

If the bank is willing to issue the letter of credit, it proceeds to do so either by cable or by mail. If the credit is issued by cable, the bank instructs a certain correspondent bank in the exporter's country to notify the exporter (or beneficiary) of the credit and the terms on which he may draw drafts thereunder. If notification is by mail, the letter of credit may be given to the importer, who sends it directly to the exporter. The letter of credit may contain an agreement by the issuing bank to honor drafts only when accompanied by stated documents. This is known as a *documentary letter of credit*. If it contains no mention of such requirements, it is known as a "clean credit." If the issuing bank does not reserve the right to revoke the credit, the letter of credit is said to be *irrevocable* and cannot be canceled before the date of expiration. Such a credit can further be strengthened by being "confirmed" by the bank that notifies the beneficiary and undertakes to honor the drafts in case the issuing bank should fail to do so. So long as the terms of the credit are carried out, the importer cannot compel the issuing bank to cancel the credit on account of breaches in the sales contract by the beneficiary. If the letter of credit is revocable, the issuing bank may reserve the right to revoke the credit without notice to the beneficiary. Such credit is obviously of little value, is little used, and should not be classified as a letter of credit. In other cases revocable letters of credit may be revoked if the beneficiary is notified before he presents his drafts for negotiation.

Import and export letters of credit. When the issuing bank is located in the importer's country, it is said to issue an "import letter of credit." Sometimes the exporter may desire to avoid exchange fluctuations. In this case the agreement may call for the furnishing of a letter of credit by a bank in the exporter's own country, entitling the exporter to draw drafts on it payable in his own country's currency. The importer, through his bank, must arrange for a letter of credit by a satisfactory bank in the exporter's country. Such a letter is called an "export letter of credit."

Letters of credit for financing shipments between foreign countries. Sometimes the exporter desires a letter of credit issued by a bank in a third country. If so, the importer must make proper arrangements with such a bank. For many years, British banks have engaged in the practice of issuing letters of credit to finance shipments between foreign countries. Since World War I, American banks have also participated in such financing. The demand for this service arises out of the superiority of drafts drawn under such letters of credit over drafts drawn on banks in either the importing or the exporting country. The superiority of such drafts in the mind of the foreign traders may arise out of (1) the greater stability of exchange rates on the issuing country; or (2) the better price at which such bills may be sold. Thus, during the postwar period, New York banks have enjoyed the benefits of the undoubted prestige of the American dollar in a world of inconvertible and uncertain paper currencies. The British banks long enjoyed the advantages of a world demand for pound sterling drafts, arising not only out of the need for sterling funds to pay for British exports, but also from the fact that the highly developed discount market in London for the acceptances of British banks enabled foreign exporters to realize the highest possible amount through the discount of London drafts.

The banker's acceptance. The next step in the financing of foreign trade follows the receipt of the letter of credit by the exporter for whose benefit it was issued. First, the merchandise must be properly shipped to the importer under an order bill of lading. The various documents needed must be attached to the bill of lading as evidence of proper quality and other conformance with contractual obligations of the sale. The exporter is now ready to draw a bill of exchange against the bank which issued the letter of credit. This bill of exchange or draft, with documents attached, will then be sold to the exporter's bank. The latter sends it to a correspondent bank in the vicinity of the bank on which the bill of exchange is drawn. The correspondent bank then presents the bill for "acceptance," if a time bill, or for payment if it is payable on demand. The bank that first issued the letter of credit inspects the documents to see that everything is in order and then pays it if it is payable on demand, or accepts it if it is a time bill. The banker's acceptance resulting from the acceptance of a time bill may then be sold in the open market and the proceeds remitted back to the exporter's bank. The process involved in the use of the commercial letter of credit

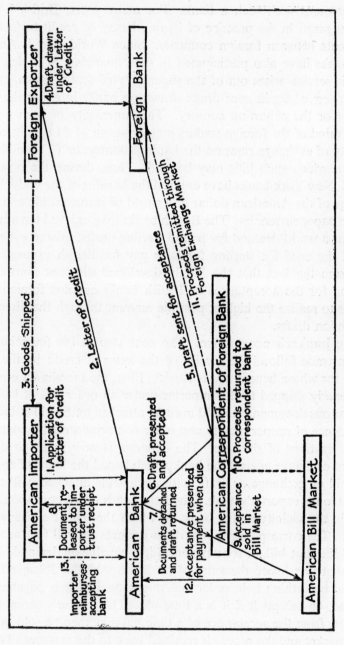

Chart 23. Financing an Import.

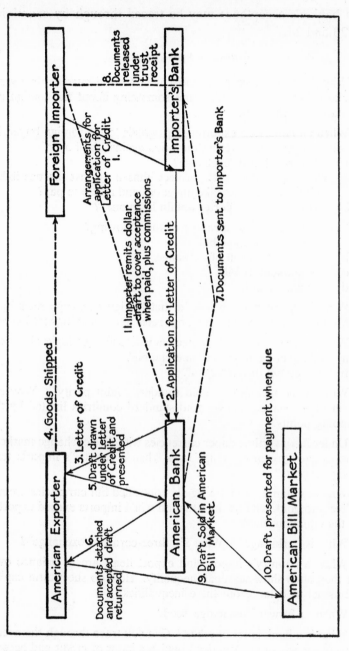

Chart 24. Financing an Export.

and the banker's acceptance may be traced through by examining Charts 23 and 24.

Questions for Study

1. Why does the present-day movement toward currency convertibility make it necessary to understand something about the foreign exchange market mechanism?

2. When an American exporter ships goods to the foreign buyer, he draws a bill of exchange covering the price against the buyer.
   a) What is a bill of exchange?
   b) How can the exporter protect himself against the possibility that the buyer may take the goods and refuse to pay?
   c) How does the exporter obtain his money?

3. Can you explain the meaning of the following?
   a) A foreign exchange bill.
   b) A commercial bill of exchange.
   c) A documentary bill.
   d) A banker's bill.

4. What is meant when it is said that foreign exchange rates have risen? What may cause foreign exchange rates to become higher? Lower?

5. Which type of foreign exchange bill will tend to be higher in price:
   a) A banker's bill or a commercial bill?
   b) A time bill or a sight bill?

6. What is the meaning of gold standard "mint parity"? Why are changes in the exchange rate on gold standard countries limited by the gold shipping points?

7. Under inconvertible paper currencies with free exchange markets, what happens to foreign exchange rates when a country's imports tend to outweigh exports?

8. When exchange rates are rigidly controlled but currencies are not convertible into gold, what is the situation when imports exceed exports? How is the situation met?

9. What is "arbitrage"? What is "three-cornered exchange"?

10. When a country's import and export items are in balance over the year they often show seasonal inequality. How do short-term capital movements act to balance out these inequalities?

11. When is forward exchange used?

12. What is a bank letter of credit? Can you trace through the necessary steps in the use of an American banker's letter of credit and acceptance to finance: (a) an American import; (b) an American export?

30

International Price Relationships Under the Gold Standard

Interregional Domestic Trade and Prices

The similarity between domestic and international trade. A decided similarity exists between interregional trade within a single country and international trade under the gold standard. Because of the familiar nature of the forces that operate in the domestic market, it will be of aid in studying the less familiar processes of international trade to examine first the interregional price relationships that exist within one country.

Interregional domestic price structure. The various specialists engaged in production are presumably located in areas best suited to their particular needs. Trade between these specialists, therefore, is interregional in nature. To the extent that monopoly does not interfere with the mobility of the factors of production, the prices of goods produced by these specialists tend roughly to correspond to their costs of production. The cost of production in any one industry is, of course, the market value of the services of the several factors of production that are used. This market value, or rate of reward to the factors of production, is simply the marginal product of these factors in their general use in other industries. In the long run, the factors of production enjoy a relatively high mobility between different industries within a given country. Factors of any given grade of efficiency, therefore, tend roughly to have the same marginal product and to receive the same reward regardless

501

of the industry in which they are employed.[1] One may conclude from this observation that goods produced and sold in the domestic market tend to be exchanged on a basis of substantial equality in respect to the quantity of the factors involved in their production. To be located in one industry rather than another tends to offer no particular advantage in the long run. To use a phrase common in discussions of international trade, the "terms of trade" are substantially equal. Exception must, of course, be made to industries operating under monopolistic control.[2]

The effects of a shift in demand for the product of a given area in the domestic market. Let us suppose that District *A* devotes its energies to making shoes. Under equilibrium conditions, the factors of production used in the manufacture of shoes receive the same income as similar factors in other areas engaged in other types of production. Let us now assume that the increased popularity of riding in motor cars, manufactured in District *B,* causes a decline in the demand for shoes. As a result, the price of shoes falls (unless monopolists in the shoe trade choose to maintain the price and sell fewer shoes), and the income of residents in District *A* is reduced. What adjustments will occur to meet this new development?

The lowered money incomes of the inhabitants of District *A* must cause them, sooner or later, to reduce the scale of their purchases of the products made in other areas. If we assume that the shoe-manufacturing trade is sufficiently competitive to lead to continued sales at lower prices, the "terms of trade" have turned against District *A,* for its shoemaking endeavors enable it to obtain smaller quantities than before of the goods produced in other districts. But the increased demand for motor cars produced in District *B* will increase the money incomes of its inhabitants. Eventually the more attractive rewards of the motor car industries will

---

[1] Obviously this is but a rough approximation to actual facts. Fixed capital frequently earns income much below the going rate of interest. Social and economic conditions often tie laborers to one industry or to one location where they earn less than the wages of similar grades of labor elsewhere.

[2] Whenever monopoly exists in a particular industry, it may enable the owners to trade with the rest of the economic world on somewhat better terms than can the owners of competitive industries. This advantage may be accomplished by restricting output and increasing the rewards going to owners' capital. Similar benefits in the terms of trade may accrue to groups of laborers that monopolize certain trades.

cause a transfer of an appropriate volume of the factors of production from shoemaking to the manufacture of automobiles. This transfer may involve an actual physical migration from one district to another or a movement of the automobile industry into District *A*. In any event, equilibrium tends to be restored, with prices in each district again reflecting the relative amounts of the factors involved in the production of their respective goods.[3]

Changes in interregional capital movements. Let us suppose that part of the savings of the inhabitants of District *B*, normally invested in the industries of that district, are suddenly diverted to investment in District *A*. This shift in the direction of capital investment from *B* to *A* immediately increases the supply of money available to *A* at the expense of *B*. If borrowers of capital in *A* wish to buy the same type of capital equipment as that previously purchased by the displaced borrowers of *B*, the resulting readjustment will be a simple one. The new borrowers in *A* will purchase the output of the capital goods industries of *B*, and the only disturbance will be a decline in the rate of growth of capital equipment in *B*. But if *A's* capital equipment requirements cannot be met by the producers in *B*, but instead must be produced by *A*, prices and incomes in the capital goods industries of *A* will rise while those of *B* will fall. In the last analysis, labor and capital either will shift from *B* to *A*, where they will aid in the production of capital goods, or, under the compulsion of low prices, will rearrange themselves so as to be in a position to produce in *B* the equipment wanted in *A*. Either or both of these adjustments may be made within an individual country. If neither adjustment were possible, District *B* would have to resign itself to lower incomes and a lower price structure that would enable it to develop a net excess of exports to *A* equal to the net capital investments made in *A* by the savers of *B*.

Shifts in the direction of investment within a single country may command little attention because of the ease with which lending districts can adjust themselves to meet the new capital goods

---

[3] A change in the foreign demand for the products of a country engaged in international trade will be unlikely to lead to such a restoration of the pre-existing "terms of trade" as is the case in purely domestic trade. The reason for this difference lies in the market immobility of the factors of production between countries. For this reason, a country that experiences a decline in the demand for its exportable goods will tend to have a decline in real income that may prove permanent unless new and more successful exports can be developed.

demands of the borrowing districts. Moreover, the ease with which the domestic banking system copes with the diversion of funds from one area to another helps to minimize the disturbance. When the domestic banking system is closely knit, a shift in the location of funds does not embarrass the banks in the lending areas or require credit restriction due to losses of reserves. This condition does not always prevail in the case of changes in international capital movements. During the interval between the time when the new lending occurs and the time when equilibrium is again established by the development of a favorable export balance by the lender, the heavy drain upon the gold reserves of the lending country's banks may cause serious difficulty.

International Trade and Price Relationships Under an International Gold Standard

The resemblance of international trade to domestic trade. Under the international gold standard, the relation between the price structures of the several countries closely resembles in one basic respect that between prices within a single country: both international and domestic prices are expressed in terms of gold. Just as disturbances to domestic trade equilibrium, which lead to an unequal balance of domestic payments, generate forces tending to re-establish equilibrium, so disturbances to the equilibrium of international balances of payments generate forces tending to restore equilibrium.

The restorative forces generated by disequilibria in the international balance of payments may meet with more resistance than do the corrective forces in domestic trade. For instance, under the gold standard a disequilibrium in the balance of payments requires a transfer of money from the country having an unfavorable debt balance, which we may call the debtor country, to the country having the favorable debt balance, which we may call the creditor country. This may require more than the mere shifting of book credits within the banking system, which suffices in the case of most domestic adjustments. The shipment of gold not only involves some expense in shipment and conversion into the currency of the creditor country but also may put strain upon the monetary and banking system of the debtor country. If the transfer of gold is promptly accompanied by a shrinkage of credit, prices, and imports of the debtor country and an increase in credit, prices, and imports of the creditor country, no disastrous consequences to the monetary structure of the debtor country will normally result. When disturbances to equilibrium in the balance of payments are of small magnitude, the corrections normally occur smoothly and easily. But if the causes underlying the debtor's unfavorable balance do not respond readily to gold movements and the resulting corrective price adjustments, the loss of gold continues and may become so serious as to compel the complete abandonment of the gold standard by the debtor country.

The Balance of Payments

All discussions of the problems of international trade revolve around the basic question of the balance of payments. Under the gold standard, payments arising out of international trade are primarily handled by the canceling of one debt against another, leaving a small residual amount to be paid in gold. If undue gold losses are to be avoided, a substantial equality of debits and credits is necessary. Under inconvertible paper currencies, when gold in fixed amounts may not be freely obtained in exchange for a country's currency, a balance may be struck between import and export items by the purchase and sale of gold, sometimes at varying prices, which acts as a balancing factor. Or, adverse balances may be settled by credit arrangements (capital movements) between the countries involved.

The nature of the balance of payments. The nature of the international balance of payments may be seen by examining the debit and credit items that enter into it. On the debit side should be listed all "import" items, such as (1) commodity imports; (2) imported or purchased services, including shipping, insurance, and financial, and the expenditures on foreign travel; (3) remittances of immigrants to relatives abroad and other private gifts (classed as "unilateral" items); (4) interest and principal owed to foreigners; (5) the import of long-term securities (including direct investment by American business firms in foreign properties) and the import

of short-term claims on foreign banks (known as "capital exports");
and (6) government unilateral transfers in the form of grants-in-aid
to foreign countries.

On the credit side of the balance of payments will appear: (1)
commodity exports; (2) exports of all kinds of services; (3) interest
and principal received on foreign investments; (4) expenditure of
foreign tourists here; and (5) the export of securities and other
monetary claims against American dollars to foreign investors (capital imports).

The United States balance of payments for the year 1955 appears
in Table 31.

One should note especially the four major sections in the balance
of payments as shown in Table 31. Section I includes "visible" items,
exports and imports of merchandise, and "invisible" items, consisting
of services of all kinds (travel, shipping, insurance, and financial)
and interest and principal payments on international investments.
Taken together, these items in Section I constitute what is known
as the "current account." Section II contains unilateral transfers
by the United States to foreign countries for which no direct return
is received. It includes immigrant remittances and other private
gifts, Government gifts, and grants-in-aid to foreign countries.
Section III contains the net capital movements, both capital exports
and capital imports. Section IV contains the balancing items of
gold movements, and errors and omissions. The combined results
of the items in Sections II, III, and IV must necessarily provide
sufficient negative or "import" items to offset the positive or net
"export" excess appearing in Section I on current account.

Temporary inequalities in the debit and credit sides of the balance of payments are sometimes corrected by offsetting short-term
capital movements. For example, an excess of debit items in a
country's balance of payments, tending to cause an export of gold,
may be offset instead by the import of foreign short-term capital
as foreign banks buy and hold bills of exchange payable in the
deficit country. Such short-term capital movements, however,
should not be relied upon to offset a more basic and permanent
disequilibrium should it develop. When a country's balance of
payments is in true equilibrium, its credit and debit items should
approximately equalize over a year's time (to eliminate seasonal

inequalities) without it being necessary for net gold or short-term capital movements to bring about a balance.

International price equilibrium. Like all concepts of equilibrium used in economic analysis, international price equilibrium is not an actually existing state. Rather, it is a relation between

TABLE 31
United States Balance of Payments, 1955 (Preliminary)*
(In millions of dollars)

I. Current account items:

Exports

Military transfers under aid programs	+ 2,146	
Other merchandise	+14,177	
Income on investments abroad	+ 2,453	
Other services sold abroad	+ 3,072	
Total exports		+21,848

Imports

Merchandise	−11,490	
Income from foreign investments in the U. S.	− 504	
Military expenditures	− 2,767	
Other services bought	− 2,895	
Total imports		−17,656
Balance on current account		+4.192

II. Unilateral transfers:

Private remittances and gifts	− 463	
Government grants-in-aid, etc.	− 4,113	
Total unilateral transfers	− 4,576	

III. Capital movements:

U. S. net imports of securities and other claims on foreign countries (capital exports)	− 1,241	
Net export of securities and other claims on domestic banks, etc. (capital imports)	+ 1,463	

IV. Gold sales by the U. S. .... + 40

Errors and omissions .... + 122

Net result of unilateral transfers, capital movements, gold sales, and errors and omissions		−4,192

* *Survey of Current Business,* March 1956, p. 6.

the price levels of the different countries that *tends* to result from powerful economic forces operating in the international markets. But certain forces are constantly appearing to disturb this equilibrium. Prices rise and fall, crops flourish and fail, the demand for commodities that move in international trade changes, the direction and magnitude of international capital movements shift. Only when the forces tending to maintain equilibrium in the balance of payments are sufficient to counteract these disturbing factors and promptly restore a substantial degree of equilibrium, can the international gold standard operate successfully.

Under the gold standard the price levels of the several countries are in equilibrium whenever, disregarding purely seasonal variations, claims arising from the exchange of goods, services, and titles to securities (including interest and principal payments but excluding short-term capital movements) cancel out. Under such circumstances, gold movements to pay for unfavorable debt balances are unnecessary. This state of international price equilibrium does not, of course, require an equality of values (of the items mentioned) in the exchanges between any two countries. Rather, it merely requires that the import items of each country and its export items to the rest of the world shall in the aggregate be equal. Thus, an excess of imports from one country may be offset by an excess of exports to other countries. If the full advantages of trade are to be realized, the various aptitudes of different countries for producing economic goods are almost certain to require a balance of this sort rather than an equality of imports from and exports to any single country. The propensity of the United States to produce large quantities of agricultural as well as manufactured products makes it inevitable that our exports of raw materials to England should exceed the value of our imports from her. But from countries able to supply some of our needs for materials (South America, for example) we buy more than we sell, and England in turn exports to them a net excess of manufactured goods. This three-cornered trade relation, commonly used to illustrate the multiple-sided character of foreign trade, is more typical of actual international trade than would be a simple two-way illustration. Actually, of course, the triangular trade example does not indicate the full complexity of the balancing operations in foreign trade that frequently involve transactions between a large number of nations.[4] Moreover, it must be remembered that international price equilibrium does not require that the prices of all commodities be equal in different countries. Nor does it mean that average money incomes are the same in the several countries. What, then, is involved in international price equilibrium?

The Relation Between Prices at Home and Abroad

Prices of goods that move in international trade. Whenever a competitively sold commodity moves freely in international trade, its price in terms of gold in the exporting country will differ from its price in the importing country only by the cost of transferring it between the two countries.[5] The gold prices of internationally traded commodities, in the absence of monopolistic dumping, therefore tend to move in parallel.

Home market or sheltered commodities. The basic factor that determines whether or not a commodity will move in international trade is the relative production costs in the different countries. Whenever the cost of production in Country *A* is below the cost of Country *B* by an amount in excess of the cost of transfer, the commodity will move from Country *A* to Country *B*. It follows, therefore, that the costs of transfer have a large bearing upon the international flow of commodities. Whenever a commodity's weight, bulk, or propensity to deteriorate makes transfer difficult, the possibilities of any sort of interregional trade are

---

[4] It is not appropriate here to examine the economic principles that determine what commodities will move in international trade under a free economy. Such a study belongs in the specialized field of international trade. For an analysis of these principles, see Ohlin, Bertil, *Interregional and International Trade,* Cambridge, Harvard University Press, 1933, Part III; Taussig, F. W., *International Trade,* New York, The Macmillan Co., 1927; Haberler, Gottfried von, *The Theory of International Trade,* New York, The Macmillan Co., 1937, Chapters IX-XII; and Viner, Jacob, *Studies in the Theory of International Trade,* New York, Harper & Bros., 1937. For an interesting analysis of some of the causes operating to determine when long-term capital movements will occur between countries, see Angell, James W., *Theory of International Prices,* Cambridge, Harvard University Press, 1926, pp. 381-382.

[5] This covers all costs, both customs duties and shipping costs, which must be incurred in the interregional movement of goods. The cost of transferring goods that commonly do not enter international trade but may do so if costs become sufficiently favorable includes the costs of making new trade contacts abroad. Cf. Angell, *op. cit.,* pp. 378-379.

limited. Such commodities may move short distances but are incapable of moving into distant markets. Tariffs that must be paid on many goods entering foreign markets constitute sizable barriers in the way of international trade. When pushed to its logical conclusion, a protective tariff may become so high as to prevent altogether certain goods from entering international markets. Personal services, which cannot be divorced from the individual producing them, provide another example of economic goods that cannot freely enter international trade, for the export of a service of this sort depends upon the ability of its producer to move into the foreign country long enough to perform it for the inhabitants of that country, or upon the ability of the foreigners to cross the boundary line and consume the service on the spot. To be sure, to a limited extent such exchange of personal services regularly takes place among the inhabitants who live near to the boundary. There also are times when the people of the United States purchase very sizable quantities of foreign services by travel abroad.

Those commodities that for all practical purposes are economically not transferable are called "home market" or "domestic" commodities, and as such they do not enter into international trade.[6] The home producers of such articles are protected from foreign competition and domestic prices are not directly influenced by the changes in prices of similar articles abroad. The producers of these articles are in a "sheltered" economic position, and the commodities themselves are sometimes known as "sheltered" commodities, to contrast them with "unsheltered" commodities that move freely in international trade.

Many commodities are more or less on the border line between home market or sheltered goods and international or unsheltered goods. Any change in the cost of production or in the price of such a commodity, or a change in the transfer costs, may shift it from the category of domestic to international goods, and vice versa. To the extent that the costs of transfer allow only a limited movement of such goods in international trade, they are partially sheltered.

---

[6] It should be noted that commodities may sometimes be exported to a near-by foreign country while transportation costs may prevent their sale in remote parts of the home market.

Gold Standard Equilibrium and International Prices

When the international balance of payments of one country in a gold standard world is in equilibrium, its price structure is such that, taking visible and invisible items into account, its exports are equal to its imports. Equilibrium is disturbed whenever the value of import and export items becomes unequal. Unless other forces promptly act to restore equilibrium in the balance of payments, gold must flow, and there must occur appropriate changes in the level of costs and prices at home and abroad.

When fundamental conditions have disturbed the balance of payments, price adjustments must take place if equilibrium is to be restored. But it is inadequate to show merely that the selling prices of internationally traded goods change and thus correct the trade balance. So long as there is any actual transfer of such goods in international trade, their prices at home and abroad tend constantly to be equalized, save for their transfer costs, regardless of whether the balance of payments is equal or unequal. The readjustments required for the basic equilibrium in the balance of payments must therefore go further than a change in *prices* of international goods. This eqilibrium involves changes in the *costs of production,* or in the prices of the factors of production involved in making these goods. For it is change in the cost of production that determines the extent to which commodities fall into the category of international goods capable of entering international trade. In the short run, when most factors of production have sticky prices, adjustments in the profits of entrepreneurs engaged in exporting, rather than changes in costs, may occur. But the willingness of producers to take losses rather than suffer a shrinkage of export markets must be supplemented eventually by readjustments in costs, if an unfavorable balance of payments is to be corrected.

The shift in relative costs, upward in a country having a favorable balance and downward in a country having an unfavorable balance, changes the degree of shelter afforded commodities by the transfer costs. Commodities previously just on the exportable margin can no longer be sold abroad when a favorable balance of payments results in rising costs. Falling costs in countries having an unfavorable balance of payments expand the list of exportable commodities by releasing some goods that were previously too costly for export. It is in this manner that a change in prices and price levels promotes a restoration of equilibrium in the balance of payments.

The effect of conditions of increasing cost. Because some domestic trades are industries of increasing cost, a country sometimes is able profitably to supplement its domestic production of a commodity with imports from abroad. The English wheat trade provides a familiar example of such industries. Some wheat may profitably be produced by English farmers for sale in the English market. But English farmers, having but a limited supply of available land, are unable to supply all of the wheat needed by the local population. Beyond a certain point, added production of domestic wheat incurs costs which exceed the cost of importing wheat from the great wheat-growing areas outside. Any change in the transfer cost involved in importing wheat and any change in the cost of growing wheat at home or abroad will change the relative proportions between the amount of wheat produced at home and the volume of imported wheat. For example, if an unfavorable balance of payments is tending to force down the English price level, a larger part of the wheat consumed in England will be produced at home and less will be imported. Thus, marginal quantities of wheat are shifted from the category of international to that of domestic goods.

The relation of domestic or sheltered goods to international price movements under the gold standard. As we have already observed, the prices of commodities that enter the international markets move in parallel, with prices in the export country below those of the importing country by an amount equal to the costs of transfer. Prices of goods of the semisheltered class are similarly, though not so rigidly, related, because any marked change in prices and costs may move them into the unsheltered category and lead to international shipments.

Prices of completely sheltered or purely domestic goods are in no direct way connected with prices of similar goods abroad. For example, there is no direct reason why the price of a given sort of stone house in England should resemble that of a similar house in Indiana, since price differences cannot be great enough to make it profitable to move either the house or the material of which it is made from one place to the other. Nor will the effects of any price differences be likely to affect materially the volume of tourists who might go to live in the low-cost houses.

Nevertheless, there is an indirect connection between the price levels of completely sheltered goods in different gold standard countries. This connection lies in the common origin of all economic goods produced in any given region or country. Basically, the same factors of production are involved in the production of both sheltered and unsheltered goods. Thus, when the price of factors of production used to make unsheltered goods are increased (because of international price movements), by the principle of opportunity costs the prices of factors used in making sheltered goods will tend to rise also. The degree of lag involved, of course, depends upon the degree of mobility of the factors of production between the sheltered and unsheltered goods industries. Furthermore, raw materials used in the production of sheltered goods may themselves be unsheltered and enter the international markets, whereas sheltered raw materials may be used in the manufacture of unsheltered goods. If domestic or sheltered goods have close substitutes that move freely in international trade, the prices of such domestic goods are exposed to the influences of international price movements.[7]

In spite of what we have been saying about the forces that tend to connect international price movements with the prices of purely domestic goods, it does not follow that there need be any exact equality of price for a domestic good in the different gold standard countries. The rewards of the factors of production involved in producing domestic commodities in a given country must be substantially the same as those producing goods that enter the export trade. The factors of production in one country may be more efficient than those of other countries. If so, their money rewards will be higher than the rewards of less efficient factors elsewhere. To illustrate, if Country *A*, using 1,000 units of factors of production, produces $1,000,000 worth of goods, which it sells to Country *B*, and Country *B* in turn uses 2,000 units of factors of production to produce $1,000,000 worth of goods for sale to Country *A*, the balance of payments between *A* and *B* will be in

---

[7] Cf. Ohlin, *Interregional and International Trade*, pp. 152-156.

equilibrium so far as their price and income structures are concerned. But the factors of production in Country *A* will be worth $1,000 per unit, and those in Country *B* will be worth but $500. Now, although the factors in either Country *A* or Country *B* must necessarily receive approximately the same rate of reward whether producing purely domestic goods or goods for export, the price of any given type of sheltered commodity in one country will correspond closely to the price in the other country only if the relative inefficiency of the factors in *B* is as great in the production of the sheltered commodity as in the production of goods for export. This is unlikely to be true. Let us suppose that in Country *A* 3 units of factors of production are required to build a house of a given type. Because the price of each unit of factors is $1,000, the house would cost $3,000 and would not be produced unless its value was at least $3,000. If factors of production required to build a similar house in Country *B* have the same absolute efficiency at house building as do the factors in Country *A*, then 3 units of factors in Country *B* would also provide a house. But because of the relative inefficiency of the factors of Country *B* in producing products for export, their money price is but $500, so that the cost of the house in Country *B* would be but $1,500. Under these assumed conditions, the price of the house in Country *A* would be $3,000 and in Country *B* $1,500, with no disturbance to the equilibrium in the balance of payments. Only if 6 units of factors were required in Country *B* to build the house would its price there be $3,000.

Methods of Settling Interregional Accounts

Settlements between different areas engaged in interregional trade involve, in one way or another, the clearing or offsetting of claims and the settlement of net differences by the transfer of some readily acceptable money. Domestic interregional trade is settled by the offsetting of checks through the collection arrangements maintained by the banks and the Federal Reserve System. Only net balances are paid by the transfer of ownership of member bank reserves deposited in the Federal Reserve Banks. The settlement, made in terms of the domestic currency, is readily accomplished so long as the banks of the debtor areas are in possession of or can readily obtain sufficient funds to meet their obligations. To ease the pressure arising from any substantial drains upon particular banks the Federal Reserve Banks lend additional reserve funds to member banks. Furthermore, banks suitably supplied with highly liquid secondary reserve assets, such as short-term Treasury obligations, dispose of such assets to other banks in order to acquire funds needed to make payments to other areas. The sale of such liquid assets comprises an "export" that helps to equalize the "balance of payments" of the area concerned. It follows, therefore, that present-day domestic arrangements permit settlements to be made readily and smoothly with a minimum of disturbance to the financial institutions concerned.

Settlement of international debt balances. The settlement of international balances also involves the offsetting, through the foreign exchange markets, of debit and credit claims arising in the balance of payments and the settlement of net differences only. As in domestic exchange, debtor-area banks borrow from foreign creditor banks to obtain temporary funds to meet seasonal and irregular balance-of-payments deficits. But more basic deficits must be met by paying out to creditor countries some form of internationally acceptable currency. Under the gold standard this payment is ultimately made by the shipment of gold. In the absence of a gold standard system, settlements are made in gold, United States dollars, or, among the Sterling Area countries, by the transfer of claims against British pounds.

In all cases it is necessary for a country to maintain its available supply of international currency reserves at such a level as to assure its ability to meet its international obligations. In doing this it is necessary that the basic elements in the balance of payments be maintained substantially in equilibrium and that departures from such equilibrium be promptly corrected. The various ways in which countries meet this problem under gold and inconvertible paper money systems will be examined in the next chapter.

Questions for Study

1. In what ways does interregional trade within a country resemble that between gold standard countries? How does it differ?

2. Examine the U.S. balance of payments for 1955 on page 507.
   a) What items are included under "current account"? What was the balance on current account? What does it mean?
   b) What are United States unilateral transfers abroad? Why are they offsets against the export surplus on current account?
   c) Did the United States lend more abroad than it borrowed?
   d) Do you understand why the plus and minus items are equal?

3. The statement is made that true equilibrium in a country's balance of payments requires that credit and debit items should balance over a year's time without needing gold shipments or offsets in the form of short-term capital movements.
   a) Why is the time period a year?
   b) Why should net short-term capital movements not be needed as a balancing factor?

4. Why is international price equilibrium not measured by equality of import and export items between two countries alone?

5. What are "sheltered" goods? What are "unsheltered" goods?

6. When competitively produced goods are exported from Country *A* to Country *B,* how much difference in price would you expect to find in the two countries? How can we *compute* the price differences in view of the differences in currencies?

7. Under a world gold standard, if one country's prices are too high:
   a) What will be the effect upon its trade?
   b) What will be the effect upon the price of foreign currencies (foreign exchange rates)?
   c) What correction will have to take place?

31

Maintenance of Equilibrium
in the Balance of Payments

We have already examined the nature and meaning of international price equilibrium and the relationship that must exist, under the gold standard, among prices in different countries or regions. Our next problem is to learn something of the mechanism by which disturbances to equilibrium in the balance of payments are offset and corrected.

Establishment of International Price Equilibrium
Under the International Gold Standard

The present-day significance of analyzing gold standard equilibrium. In a world in which national currencies rather than gold standard currencies are the rule, one may well inquire as to the significance of an analysis of the manner in which international equilibrium is maintained in a gold standard world. A justification for such an analysis may be found in that:

1. The problem of maintaining equilibrium in the balance of payments under the international gold standard is essentially the same as that confronting countries that now belong to the International Monetary Fund. Such countries agree to maintain the foreign exchange value of their currency at some fixed value in terms of gold or the United States dollar. The similarity exists even though free exchange markets are not permitted, and exchange control measures require special interferences with trade.

2. There is constant pressure for the abolition of exchange controls and for the general restoration of free exchange markets and currency

convertibility. Should this be attempted with a continued adherence to the present policy of fixed exchange rates, the effect would be a restoration of the world gold standard. The problem of equilibrium in the balance of payments would then be identical with what we shall examine here.

3. The case for independent, inconvertible paper currencies, in their various forms, is largely based upon the assumption that the balance-of-payments problems of an international gold standard are intolerably difficult in the modern world. This claim can only be adequately evaluated in the light of an understanding of how equilibrium is maintained under the gold standard.

Reasons for an adverse balance of payments.[1] A number of reasons may be given for the appearance of an adverse or unfavorable balance of payments for a given country. For convenience in examining them some of these reasons are listed below:

1. One important cause of disturbance may be a change in the foreign demand for a country's exports. This change may arise from changes in consumers' tastes abroad, from the development of cheaper or better supplies in other countries competing in the international export market, or from changes in transfer costs.

2. Another source of disturbance may appear in some catastrophe of nature which destroys the current supply of exportable goods.

3. A world depression may cause a sharp shrinkage in the demand for a country's exports, both raw materials and manufactured goods.

4. Cyclical fluctuations within the country itself, with the accompanying inflation of prices, tend to disturb the balance of payments.

5. Sizeable changes in the direction and volume of long-term capital movements or long-term lending and investing may prove embarrassing both to borrowers and lenders alike.

6. Abrupt and heavy movements of short-term capital—the result of flight from currencies suspected of weakness—sometimes prove disastrous because of their violent and cumulative nature.

7. Finally, war, so destructive of normal trade between nations, completely upsets existing equilibrium.

Corrective forces arising from international disequilibrium. It is clear that the gold standard can operate only if the drain of gold out of countries which develop adverse debt balances

---

[1] Conditions creating an adverse balance of payments obviously are of more concern than the appearance of a favorable balance. The adverse or unfavorable balance must be promptly corrected before an excessive loss of gold or other international currency reserves develops. On the other hand, the acquisition of gold by countries with a favorable balance need cause no immediate concern.

can be stopped before it goes so far as to jeopardize the safety of currency and banking systems of those countries. Long experience with the gold standard indicates that in the ordinary course of events the necessary corrections may actually take place smoothly and without too much disturbance. Since 1931, many writers have attacked the gold standard on the grounds that it cannot meet the strain put upon it. But these attacks, based largely upon the very real difficulties growing out of the depression of 1929-1939, must not cause us to lose sight of the fact that the gold standard did, in fact, operate with reasonable success over a long period of years.

The classical theory of international trade sought to explain the maintenance of equilibrium conditions between the price structures of the gold standard countries by resort to the quantity theory of money. According to this view, an unfavorable debt balance for one country causes foreign exchange rates to rise to the gold export point, and an outflow of gold results. Applying the quantity theory, the loss of gold reduces the volume of bank reserves, causes a shrinkage of credit, and leads to a fall in the price level. On the other hand, countries having a favorable debt balance gain gold. As a result, credit expands and prices rise. Thus, equilibrium is restored by a downward adjustment of prices in the country with an unfavorable balance of payments and a rise in prices in countries with favorable debt balances.[2]

The above line of reasoning that seeks to explain the maintenance of balance-of-payments equilibrium through the effects of gold movements upon internal price levels of the countries concerned is not entirely satisfactory or convincing. For example, we know that considerable lag may occur between the time when gold reserves are increased or decreased and the time when corresponding changes occur in the supply of money. A further lag tends to exist between changes in the supply of money and changes in the price level. Such lags in the appearance of corrective forces arising from gold movements would surely jeopardize the maintenance of gold convertibility. Because of the serious question of the effectiveness of gold movements in bringing about immediate price changes, at-

---

[2] Cf. Taussig, F. W., *International Trade,* New York, The Macmillan Co., 1927, pp. 198-199. For a detailed examination of the classical theory, see Viner, Jacob, *Studies in the Theory of International Trade,* New York, Harper & Bros., 1937, Chapter VI.

tempts have been made to develop more realistic explanations of
the method by which international price equilibrium is established
and maintained.[3]

**Spontaneous forces tending to restore international price
equilibrium.** What are sometimes called "spontaneous" causes
tending to restore and maintain international equilibrium rest primarily upon a shift or transference of purchasing power. According to this view, a country having an adverse or unfavorable
balance of payments loses purchasing power by an amount equal
to the deficiency. On the other hand, countries having a favorable balance of payments receive additional purchasing power.
Now this approach is not too dissimilar to the classical explanation
based upon gold movements, but there is this essential difference:
The theory based upon spontaneous causes attempts to show that
the corrective forces of shifting purchasing power may appear before gold movements occur. In such a case, the movements of gold
may be avoided altogether. But if some gold movements do occur,
the spontaneous forces fortify and supplement the corrective influences of the gold movements.

Let us examine the reasons for thinking that a shift in purchasing power will tend to occur from the country having an adverse
balance of payments to one having a favorable balance. So long
as a country's "import" and "export" items are in balance, there
will be no reason to expect any resulting change in its money
supply. But if for any reason its exports expand so as to exceed its
imports (or if its imports shrink) the drafts that exporters draw
against foreign buyers and offer for sale to the banks will exceed
the demands of importers for bankers' drafts drawn against foreign
balances held by the banks. Consequently, exporters, by selling
their foreign bills to the banks, receive domestic currency and bank
deposits in excess of that surrendered by importers. Thus the
banks of the country having a favorable balance of payments will
have expanded the domestic money supply in exchange for foreign

---

[3] For a discussion of the criticisms of the classical theory, see Haberler, Gottfried
von, *The Theory of International Trade,* New York, The Macmillan Co., 1937,
Chapter III. Also see Angell, James W., *The Theory of International Prices,*
Cambridge, Harvard University Press, 1926, Chapter XIV. Angell points out that
the majority of the Continental economists have never accepted the English
classical theory (pp. 365-368).

bills or claims against foreign currency. This occurs regardless of whether or not the banks continue to hold their expanding foreign balances or convert them into gold. On the other hand, the country having an unfavorable balance of payments will find its domestic money supply (currency and bank deposits in the public's hands) shrinking as importers' funds are transferred to the accounts of foreign banks.

The change in income levels generated in the countries with favorable and unfavorable balances will not be limited to the original shift in purchasing power or change in the money supply of the respective countries. The income of the favorable balance country, with the expanded supply of money arising out of its excess of export items, will be exposed to the same multiplier effect as that accompanying an expansion of domestic investment. Likewise, the country whose domestic supply of money is reduced because of its unfavorable balance of payments will find its income level reduced by some multiple of the reduction in the supply of money. In both cases the net effect upon income flow will be determined by the size of the multiplier in each. As we know, this cannot be accurately estimated in the short run because of the impossibility of correct anticipations as to the extent of the leakages that will occur. Nevertheless, shifts in the income flow in the right direction will occur because of these "spontaneous" forces that are set in motion. These corrective changes in income flow may of course be overbalanced by domestic developments that induce opposite changes in income. For example, domestic monetary expansion, whether arising from business or governmental borrowing, may be so great as to nullify the restraining influence of a balance-of-payments deficit. Consequently, domestic credit restraint, whether resulting from gold outflows or from central bank policy, may be needed if the corrective force of the spontaneous causes are to be felt. Similarly, the increase in purchasing power arising from an export excess may be offset by domestic deflationary developments. It follows, therefore, that a reasonably successful contracyclical domestic monetary and fiscal policy is compatible with the operation of the spontaneous forces.

These shifts in income arising spontaneously from disequilibrium in the balance of payments of the countries involved will normally be reflected in appropriate changes in the demand for commodities. Thus the rising demand for commodities in the country with the rising income will include a rise in the demand for imports. In contrast, the country that suffers a fall in income will experience a shrinkage in demand, including its demand for imports. It follows, therefore, that corrective adjustments in the movement of commodities may begin *without* price level adjustments or gold movements.

To be sure, one cannot assume that the income changes generated by the spontaneous forces will be sufficient to complete the restoration of equilibrium in the balance of payments. Disregarding the strength of other inflationary or deflationary factors in the domestic economy, the degree to which such income changes will succeed in such restoration depends upon (1) the size of the multiplier in the countries concerned; and (2) the extent to which changes in income levels in each affects the magnitude of their respective imports—that is, their marginal propensity to import. To the extent that the multiplier is large, thus generating relatively great changes in income, and the marginal propensity to import is also large (meaning that, for a given change in income, imports respond generously), the corrective effect upon the balance of payments will also be relatively large.[4]

It is unnecessary to demonstrate that spontaneous causes can provide a complete restoration of equilibrium without changes in internal prices. Indeed, the shifts in income levels from such causes are likely to result in some changes in prices and costs, which in turn have added corrective effects. A fall in prices, induced by the spontaneous forces, will provide additional incentives for the country with the unfavorable balance to reduce its imports and expand its exports. Furthermore, any gold movements that develop will further fortify the corrective developments.

Spontaneous correctives in connection with changes in international capital movements. Spontaneous correctives appear when changes in long-term capital movements threaten the balance of payments of the lending country. For example, if Country *L*

---

[4] If one were to make assumptions as to the size of the multiplier and the marginal propensity to import for each country, the extent of the correction of the spontaneous kind could be estimated. This we need not do here, for our purpose is only to understand the principle involved.

(lender) were to increase its loans to Country *B* (borrower) by purchasing more of Country *B*'s securities, sellers of securities—that is, borrowers—in Country *B* will draw bills of exchange upon lenders in Country *L*, which they will sell to banks in Country *B*. They receive in return checking accounts or other forms of bank credit money. On the other hand, the lenders in Country *L* honor the bills drawn on them by relinquishing deposits in banks in Country *L*. Should borrowers in Country *B* wish to spend their borrowed funds in Country *L*, the latter's exports would rise appropriately, with no change in the price or income levels of either country. Should borrowers in Country *B* require goods available in a third country, or goods produced at home, the adjustment becomes a little more complex. To generate appropriate adjustments, the income and price level of Country *L* must fall and at the same time income and prices of Country *B* must rise sufficiently to enable Country *L* to expand its exports and Country *B* to expand its imports.

It is entirely possible that the adjustment in price and income level may occur without any substantial shift of gold from the lending to the borrowing country. So long as the banks in Country *B* are amply supplied with excess reserves they can freely create money for the borrowers, taking in return foreign exchange bills. Moreover, if the banks are willing and able to expand domestic credit upon the basis of foreign exchange reserves, the need for gold shipments is even less.[5]

Gold Movements and International Price Equilibrium

To the extent that readjustments are not brought about promptly or completely by the spontaneous or automatic forces, gold movements must take place. Countries with favorable balances will gain gold at the expense of countries having adverse debt balances. Before gold movements will occur, however, foreign exchange rates

---

[5] For a detailed examination of this approach, see Ohlin, Bertil, *Interregional and International Trade*, Cambridge, Harvard University Press, 1933, Chapter XX. Also see Viner, Jacob, *Canada's Balance of International Indebtedness, 1900–1910*, Cambridge, Harvard University Press, 1924, for an account of the manner in which Canada's imports expanded to balance its long-term borrowings with a very modest inflow of gold. This successful adjustment occurred smoothly, even though Canada's borrowing was mainly from England while its excess of imports, representing the net capital inflow, came from the United States.

in a country having a favorable balance of payments must decline to the gold import point. A mild though not altogether negligible corrective factor appears in connection with this movement of exchange rates. The fall in foreign exchange rates encourages imports and discourages exports. Within the limits set by the gold import and export points, exchange rates will move in a manner which acts to restore equilibrium in the balance of payments.

Gold movements and the restoration of equilibrium. Gold movements between countries operate to affect the balance of payments in several ways. To the extent that gold moves from the debtor to the creditor country, this movement has no direct and immediate influence upon their money supply. The spontaneous factors will already have increased the money supply of the creditor country and decreased that of the debtor country by the amount of the balance of payments difference. In a sense, the gold movement in the first instance merely validates the transfer of purchasing power that has already occurred. However, the loss of gold out of the bank reserves of the debtor country puts deflationary pressure upon its banking system.[6] Money becomes tight and interest rates rise. The country acquiring gold will experience the opposite effects—easier money and lower discount rates.

The changes in discount rates, just referred to, set in motion two separate and distinct forces, each of which helps to check the outflow of gold. The first of these, which develops quickly and assists in dampening down the pressure upon the debtor country's gold supply, is the movement of short-term capital into the debtor country in response to the higher discount rate. The second operates more slowly to remedy the fundamental causes of disturbance in the balance of payments. It takes the form of stimulating business activity, prices, and imports when the discount rate falls because of gold imports, and of reducing business activity, prices, and imports when the discount rate is increased. Each of these will now be examined.

Short-term capital movements and the balance of payments. The gold standard, working properly, and commanding general

---

[6] Should all of the gold reserves be concentrated in the hands of a government agency the pressure would have to come from the monetary authority, which must protect the country's gold reserves by imposing a tighter money policy upon the banks by reducing available cash reserves.

confidence, provides the certainty that is required if short-term capital is to move freely between international money markets in response to differences in the discount rates. Short-term capital movements mainly take the form of the purchase of (1) bank balances; (2) bankers' and trade acceptances; (3) treasury bills; and (4) long-term internationally traded securities. The increase in the discount rate within the country having an adverse balance of payments induces the purchase of short-term claims against it by foreign bankers and other foreign investors. This action increases the credit side of the balance of payments and helps, temporarily, to restore equilibrium.

Some adverse debt balances arise from accidental or seasonal variations in trade. Given sufficient time, such variations will largely cancel out. In such cases the movement of short-term capital in response to differences in the discount rates quickly checks the movements of gold and minimizes them. Furthermore, some corrective short-term capital movements may occur without discount rate changes. For example, if the United States develops an unfavorable trade balance regularly each summer and a reversed situation during the winter months, foreign bills of exchange will be dear in summer and cheap in winter. If there were no speculative dealings in foreign exchange, rates would tend to move to the specie moving points, and gold would be shipped to meet the temporary disequilibrium in the international balance of payments. But, because of the predictable and regular seasonal nature of the movements of the balance of payments and the protection afforded by the gold points, American bankers are able to purchase foreign bills during the winter while they are cheap, collect the proceeds, and invest them abroad. Later, when foreign bills are dear, they will dispose of these foreign funds by offering drafts drawn against them in the foreign exchange markets. All this will occur *without* any gold movements and *without* discount rates being higher abroad than at home. This practice, common under the full international gold standard, involves excessive hazards under inconvertible paper, so that, without the gold standard, corrective movements of short-term capital are much less likely to take place.

Short-run capital movements that assist in the restoration and maintenance of equilibrium in the balance of payments may be described as "equilibrating" to differentiate them from the "disequilibrating" short-term capital movements that characterize "flights" from currencies under suspicion. The equilibrating type of short-term capital movements occur regularly, as we have just seen, in a well-established world gold standard, and largely depend upon confidence in the several currency systems. The disequilibrating type of short-term capital movements, on the other hand, occurs, in times of international financial panic and tends to upset the equilibrium in the balance of payments instead of helping restore it. The disequilibrating type of capital movements will be examined more fully later.

Even when disturbances in the balance of payments arise from causes other than regular seasonal developments, some short-term capital may move to the country which is temporarily experiencing an adverse balance, since bankers may anticipate that a reversal will shortly be forthcoming. In many cases, however, irregular and unpredictable adverse balances of any great size are unlikely to attract short-term capital in sufficient quantity to prevent altogether an outflow of gold.

Basic corrections in the balance of payments resulting from changes in discount rates. Long-term foreign borrowing and lending constitutes one important item in the balance of payments of many countries. The export of long-term capital, evidenced by a net inflow of foreign securities, is a debit item in a country's balance of payments. A change in the discount rate will cause some change in long-term interest rates, which in turn may affect the volume of such foreign lending. This may occur because of the effect of interest rate changes upon the absolute volume of capital that foreign borrowers will take, or because a change in interest rates relative to rates ruling in other international loan markets will cause a shift away from or to those other markets, as the case may be.

A second corrective result of a change in money market conditions and in discount rates arises from the effect of such changes on domestic business activity. Tighter money and a rise in the rates tend to retard, but easier money and a lowering of rates, tend to expand the rate of business operations. For example, if tighter money or a higher discount rate reduces business activity, two influences are put to work to correct an unfavorable balance of payments. The first and most immediate result is to cause a decline in imports. The second result, more remote and more basic, is the decline in prices and costs which the slackening of business brings about. On the other hand, if a favorable balance of payments leads to an import of gold and a drop in the discount rate, the resulting expansion in business activity will stimulate imports and lead to higher prices.

Gold movements without corrective effects on the balance of payments. The full corrective effect of gold movements appears only if changes in the gold supply cause equal changes in the reserve funds of the banking system. Furthermore, the change in reserves must lead to corresponding changes in the volume of bank credit if corrections are to appear that are of greater significance than the spontaneous ones discussed earlier. But neither of these results may actually be forthcoming. The extent to which the commercial banks make use of available reserves to support their credit structures varies with the state of business. In depression, excess reserves may pile up, as we so well know. During prosperous times, on the other hand, the banks are generally "loaned up." Still more important are the varying and unpredictable credit practices of central banks. To illustrate, the central bank may adopt any one of three policies following the receipt of newly imported gold. First, it may remain passive and allow the imported gold to increase the commercial bank reserves. Second, it may choose to offset the effect of the gold imports upon bank reserves by reducing its holdings of securities. Third, it may permit the newly acquired gold to become a base for new bank reserves in excess of those created directly by the gold imports. To accomplish this, it may lower the rediscount rate or purchase securities in the open market. Similarly, the central bank may ignore, nullify, or magnify the effect of gold exports.[7] Without doubt, central bank managers, in the formulation of their credit policies, believe that they are guided by the highest motives, the foremost of which is the desire to stabilize or improve internal business conditions. But

---

[7] It is difficult to discover a sufficiently well-defined pattern of central bank policy to permit any safe predictions as to the behavior of central banks. Cf. Viner, *Studies in the Theory of International Trade,* pp. 391-392.

the offsetting of gold movements in the interest of domestic stability, as practiced by central banks, reduces the corrective forces contributing to maintenance of equilibrium and therefore handicaps the operation of the gold standard. Furthermore, whenever an agency of the treasury or a stabilization fund operates to prevent gold movements from affecting bank reserves, the corrective effects are limited altogether to the spontaneous forces arising from the shift in purchasing power.

Finally, gold movements that arise between countries when international financial panic seizes the world's money markets cannot be thought of as assisting to maintain equilibrium in the balance of payments. Early in 1931, in certain countries, economic pressure due to the depression led to financial collapse followed swiftly by general panic. Deprived of the certain protection of the gold standard by the threat of a general abandonment of gold, short-term capital frantically began to seek security by moving rapidly away from money centers that were under suspicion to those believed to be safe. Under these circumstances, gold movements required to accommodate the shifts in short-term capital were in no way related to the requirements for basic equilibrium in the balance of payments.

The Time Involved in Restoring Equilibrium in the Balance of Payments

The ease of readjustment as related to types of commodities involved in foreign trade. The ease and rapidity with which a country's balance of payments may be restored to equilibrium depend to a great extent upon the type of commodities which make up its imports and exports. For example, if a country with an adverse debt balance normally imports high-priced consumption goods and durable goods, it will find it relatively simple to reduce the value of such imports because of the ease of postponing the purchase of durable goods and the possibility of switching from the purchase of high- to lower-priced consumption goods. The loss of income and purchasing power which results from the adverse balance of payments will tend to bring the shrinkage in imports just mentioned. In contrast, a country that imports foodstuffs and raw materials while exporting high-grade finished products may find it difficult to readjust its balance either by expanding its exports or by reducing its imports.[8]

Ease of restoration of equilibrium as related to the magnitude of the disturbances The restoration of equilibrium in the balance of payments may be easily and swiftly achieved when the disturbing forces are relatively small and temporary in nature. In the absence of wars and acute, prolonged depression, disturbances, though constantly appearing, are in fact small, and restoration of equilibrium occurs smoothly and successfully. In contrast, in the face of powerful and continuous disturbances of the sort arising from war debts, war indemnities, and severe depressions, the corrective forces that successfully restore equilibrium under ordinary circumstances are unequal to their task. This fact is well illustrated by the difficulties which arose in connection with the breakdown of the gold standard after 1929.

The significance of spontaneous factors in restoring and maintaining equilibrium. The significance of the action of spontaneous causes in restoring balance-of-payments equilibrium rests mainly upon the following considerations:

1. They operate promptly and positively to bring about appropriate changes in income in both the debtor and the creditor country.

2. They need not, although they are likely to, result in changes in the price levels of the two countries concerned.

3. They operate without the necessity for changes in the rate of interest arising from gold losses and gains. Thus, to the extent that they are effective in initiating corrective changes, the economy of the country with the unfavorable balance is not subjected to the shock and depressing consequences arising from a shrinkage of gold reserves and the forced liquidation of credit. In this respect it appears that the existence of powerful spontaneous correctives makes possible a justification of the steps of the central banks in offsetting the loss of bank reserves that result from gold movements.

---

[8] Cf. Paish, F. W., "Banking Policy and the Balance of International Payments," *Economica,* November 1936, pp. 413-422. He points out that countries whose imports are largely marginal or which have a "high marginal propensity to import" are likely to be producers of raw materials. Such countries tend to adjust their trade balance easily. Advanced industrial countries, on the other hand, have a "low marginal propensity to import" and do not adjust so easily. If the latter countries are also international banking centers, the strain on their monetary structure may be eased by an inflow of foreign-owned short-term balances. For a statement of the problem of adjusting merchandise movements to re-establish equilibrium in the balance of payments, see Viner, *Studies in the Theory of International Trade,* pp. 307-311.

The ability of spontaneous correctives to restore and maintain equilibrium in the face of normal and mild disturbances is indicated by the experience and practice of certain central banks before World War I. Both the National Bank of Belgium and the Bank of France appear to have paid little attention to gold movements in the determination of their discount policies.[9] This they were able to do because, unlike the Bank of England, they did not need to concern themselves with attracting and holding foreign bank deposits to protect their gold reserves. The Bank of England itself, which traditionally used the discount rate to protect its gold position against foreign bank withdrawals, at times adopted a stable discount rate policy and varied the price of gold as a means of controlling gold movements.[10] In the case of the National Bank of Belgium, the Bank of France, and, on occasion, the Bank of England, no balance-of-payments difficulties seemed to arise when, for internal purposes, a stable discount rate policy was put into effect. These experiences testify to the corrective power of the spontaneous factors that we have been considering. They also support the view that a return to an international gold standard need not prove so intolerable, given reasonably normal world conditions, as some critics would have us believe.

International Price Equilibrium Under Paper Currencies with Free Exchanges

As we have seen, when an international gold standard is in effective operation exchange rates are automatically held rigid within the narrow limits of the gold points. Disequilibrium in the balance of payments must, therefore, be corrected by adjustments in income levels and in internal price and cost structures.

The maintenance of equilibrium with pure paper currencies. When inconvertible paper currencies with flexible exchange rates are used, the equilibrium in the balance of payments may be restored and maintained by changes in foreign exchange rates, changes in prices, or both. Unlike the gold standard, pure paper currencies provide no gold points. Under pure paper cur-

[9] Cf. Whale, P. B., "The Working of the Pre-War Gold Standard," *Economica,* February 1937, p. 20.

[10] Cf. Sayers, R. S., *Bank of England Operations, 1890–1914,* London, P. S. King & Son, Ltd., 1936, p. 82.

rencies, therefore, the rates of exchange may vary widely in response to the changing forces of supply and demand. For example, if a country on a pure paper standard were to have an unfavorable debt balance, the price of foreign exchange would rise as it would under the gold standard. But whereas under the gold standard a limit to the increase in foreign exchange rates is set at the gold export point, under inconvertible paper no such limit exists. Instead, with flexible exchange rates, an unfavorable debt balance in a country using inconvertible paper currency must cause such a rise in foreign exchange rates that the supply of foreign bills will equal the demand for them.

The effect of seasonal inequalities. Before going further, it is necessary to recall that although an approximate equilibrium in a country's balance of payments for such a period as a year's time may easily come about, such an equilibrium cannot be expected for any given day or even for any single season. Obvious difficulties would accompany any attempt to equalize the basic debit and credit items in the balance of payments for a short period. For example, American exports of agricultural products have tended to be concentrated largely in the autumn and early winter. During this season the balance of payments is favorable, and it becomes unfavorable during other seasons when an excess of imports appears. Under the gold standard, no consequences attach to these seasonal disturbances to the balance of payments so long as they eventually cancel out. The day-by-day and the seasonal inequalities between debit and credit items are smoothly cared for by the movement of short-term capital. Such capital moves from the creditor to the debtor country in response to small changes in discount rates or, regardless of discount rate changes, to obtain a profit by buying foreign exchange cheap and selling it dear.

But with inconvertible paper currencies much less opportunity exists to offset short-term and seasonal inequalities in debits and credits in the balance of payments. Dealers in foreign exchange who would quickly transfer short-term capital to fill the gap under the gold standard are much more reluctant to take such a step under inconvertible paper currencies because of the risk of unpredictable fluctuations in the exchange rates. The purchase of foreign exchange, when a current favorable balance makes it cheap, involves vastly greater hazards when currencies are inconvertible paper than when the gold standard provides a point of certain reference in the form of gold parities.

Under pure paper currencies, therefore, an equality in the balance of payments during a season when exports normally exceed imports tends to induce a fall in the foreign exchange rate until one of two results occurs. First, the rate may decline to a point at which speculative purchases of foreign exchange will become numerous enough to take off the market the excess supply of foreign bills. Second, if speculative buyers do not appear in sufficient numbers to absorb the supply, the foreign exchange rate must fall until exports are reduced and imports increased to the point of equality. It follows, therefore, that regardless of the existence of equilibrium in the annual balance of payments, inconvertible paper currency requires marked seasonal and daily fluctuations in exchange rates to provide the necessary short-run equilibrium. This in part explains the need for stabilization fund operations by government agencies to provide short-run exchange stability for paper currencies.

Exchange rate adjustments to restore and maintain equilibrium. Over a period of time long enough to average out seasonal and irregular fluctuations, free market exchange rates between inconvertible paper standard countries and outside countries naturally tend toward a level that provides a basic fundamental equilibrium in their international balance of payments. An unfavorable or adverse balance of payments—brought about, for example, by an excess of import items—creates a domestic demand for foreign bills of exchange in excess of the supply provided by exports. Consequently, foreign exchange rates must rise. Such a rise in foreign exchange rates has a corrective effect, first by increasing the cost of foreign goods in terms of domestic currency and thus reducing the profitableness of importing, and second by cheapening domestic currency in terms of foreign currency. The result is a reduction in cost of domestic goods to foreign buyers and a stimulation of exports. Thus the rise in foreign exchange rates imposes corrective changes both by checking imports and by stimulating exports.[11]

---

[11] There are some who would minimize the corrective effects of changes in exchange rates (and changes in relative price levels under gold standard adjustments) by arguing that demands for internationally traded goods have a low price elasticity, and reducing their cost to foreign buyers cannot increase the total value of a country's exports. This view hardly seems warranted by the facts, but it has been used to support the "balance-of-payments" theory of exchange rates, which will be considered briefly at the end of this chapter.

An example may help us to understand the effects of changes in exchange rates on a country's exports and imports. In 1949, when the exchange value of the pound was $4, British goods, because of high domestic prices, were difficult to sell abroad and Britain's balance of payments tended strongly to be adverse. But after September of that year, when the pound was reduced to $2.80, British exports, in terms of current prices, were correspondingly cheaper for Americans. At the same time, British imports from the United States were correspondingly more costly. Consequently, the cheaper pound has tended to aid in the restoration of equilibrium in the British balance of payments by increasing exports to and reducing imports from the Western Hemisphere. Whether an expansion of exports or a fall in imports has the more influence cannot easily be determined. Nevertheless, the corrective force of the cheaper pound is undeniable.

When the exchange rate between paper standard countries is not one that provides equilibrium in the balance of payments, two results may occur. First, as we have already noted, the rate of exchange may shift to a point that satisfies the requirements of equilibrium. Second, internal prices within the countries concerned may move to levels that provide equilibrium at the ruling exchange rates. Because, under inconvertible paper standards, free market exchange rates are more flexible than are price levels, adjustments tending toward restoration of balance-of-payments equilibrium are more likely to occur in the form of changes in the rates of exchange than as changes in the price levels. Indeed, one of the advantages commonly advanced for inconvertible paper currencies and free exchange rates is the ease and rapidity with which exchange rates can adjust themselves to restore equilibrium in the balance of payments once it is disturbed. This is in sharp contrast to the slow and sometimes painful adjustments of cost and price levels required under the gold standard.

The equilibrium rate of exchange. The rate of exchange at which a country's balance of payments is in basic equilibrium is called the *equilibrium rate of exchange.* Under the international gold standard, gold parity exchange rates are fixed, and therefore the relative price and income levels must adjust so that the gold standard parity rate is the equilibrium rate of exchange. When *free* exchange rates, under inconvertible paper, adjust to provide basic equilibrium in the balance of payments, the resulting rate of exchange is the equilibrium rate.

Purchasing Power Parity Theory of Exchange Rates

We have already seen that under pure paper currencies there is some equilibrium rate of exchange that tends to maintain a balance of payments between the countries involved. From our analysis it clearly appeared that this rate is one that equalizes the various import and export transactions in the light of the ruling price levels. It naturally follows that some attempt should be made to explain this equilibrium rate of exchange in terms of the levels of prices. The *purchasing power parity* theory of exchange rates is an attempt specifically to relate the rate of exchange to the price level.[12]

The argument upon which the purchasing power parity theory rests is the very sensible one that people primarily want foreign money because of the purchasing power which it has in that foreign country over commodities, services, securities, and the like. When one offers his own money in exchange for foreign currencies, he is offering to give up buying power over commodities at home in exchange for buying power over things abroad. Therefore, one's valuation of foreign currencies in terms of one's own primarily rests upon the relative purchasing power of each currency in its own country.[13] This leads to the obvious conclusion that the rate of exchange depends upon the relative price levels and may be expected to vary with changes in these price levels.

The calculation of purchasing power parity exchange rates. The true normal or equilibrium exchange rate between countries cannot be calculated directly by comparing the buying power of a unit of domestic currency over a representative list of commodities and services with the buying power of a unit of foreign

---

[12] Professor Gustav Cassel is mainly responsible for the development and exposition of this theory in present-day economic literature. For a statement of his view, see his *Money and Foreign Exchange After 1914*, New York, The Macmillan Co., 1922, pp. 137-162.

[13] Cf. Cassel, *op. cit.*, pp. 138-139. For criticisms of the purchasing power parity theory, see Haberler, Gottfried von, *International Trade*, New York, The Macmillan Co., 1936, p. 32; Viner, Jacob, *Studies in the Theory of International Trade*, New York, Harper & Bros., 1937, pp. 379-387; and Ellis, Howard, *German Monetary Theory, 1905-1933*, Cambridge, Harvard University Press, 1934, Part III.

currency over a similar list. To calculate the importance or value of a unit of foreign currency for buying foreign goods to be brought back to one's own country, one must allow for all the costs of transferring the goods, such as import duties, freight, and other shipping expenses. These costs differ from commodity to commodity, and appropriate allowances for these costs would be next to impossible to make. Of still greater importance is the fact that most commodities move in but one direction, so that a comparison of prices of any given group in the two countries would have little significance. Prices of commodities exported from the United States to England must have a price in England, calculated at the ruling rate of exchange, sufficiently above the price here to pay the costs of transfer. The same rule applies to prices of goods moving from England to the United States. The purchasing power parity rate, if it be considered an equilibrium rate of exchange, is merely one at which the *total value* of everything bought from the rest of the world by the United States is equal to the *total value* of everything sold to the rest of the world. The money value of any particular bill of goods at home and abroad cannot possibly give a valuable clue to the equilibrium exchange rate.

Gustav Cassel, a leading proponent of the theory, attempted to calculate the purchasing power parity rate indirectly. He assumed that during some normal period, usually after the gold standard has been in operation for a time, the rate of exchange actually ruling is the purchasing power parity rate for the price levels that exist in the countries involved. For example, before World War I, mint par of exchange between England and the United States was £1 = $4.86, a rate which may be taken as the purchasing power parity for the ruling price levels at that time. After the gold standard was abandoned, if the price level in England had doubled and that of the United States had remained unchanged, the relative purchasing power of the pound would have declined by one-half, and the rate of exchange, purchasing power parity, would then stand at £1 = $2.43. To calculate purchasing power parity, therefore, the price levels for the normal period should be taken as a base (that is, 1913 = 100 in each country). The rate of exchange in this normal period is multiplied by the ratio of the price indexes for each country at the date for which the new equilibrium rate of exchange is to be calculated, and the result is the purchasing power parity rate. Thus, to use our previous example, if the old rate of exchange in 1913 was $\dfrac{£1}{\$4.86}$ and the ratio of prices in the two countries had shifted to $\dfrac{200}{100}$, purchasing power parity would have been

$$\frac{£1}{\$4.86} \times \frac{200}{100}, \text{ or } \frac{£1}{\$2.43}.$$

Limitations of calculated purchasing power parity. Cassel's method for calculating purchasing power parity has one outstanding merit. It provides an objective clue to the true equilibrium rate of exchange that should provide basic equilibrium in the balance of payments. As such it might well be utilized to provide a rough idea of the approximate level of the equilibrium rate after original rates have been made untenable because of the dislocations of wars, inflations, and other major disturbances. For example, when the International Monetary Fund, after World War II, provided for the establishment of fixed rates of exchange among its members, a calculation of purchasing power parity could have been used to indicate the approximate level at which rates should be fixed. Cassel himself used the calculation to explain the depreciation of exchange values of many currencies after World War I.

Although Cassel's method for estimating purchasing power parity is obviously a handy scheme for obtaining a general idea of the equilibrium rate, its accuracy may be seriously questioned. Objection to this method of calculation may be made on several grounds:

1. To be reasonably accurate, the calculation should be based upon price indexes that represent the production cost of goods capable of moving in international trade. Because such an index is not available, indexes of wholesale prices have been most commonly used. But the changes in the wholesale price index can but imperfectly represent the costs of goods that move in international trade. Consequently, calculations of purchasing power parity based upon such price indexes cannot be accepted as a reliable indication of the true equilibrium exchange rate.

2. Calculations of purchasing power parity are based upon some previous rate of exchange assumed to have been a normal equilibrium rate. But the appropriateness of this old rate depends upon the kind

and relative amounts of such commodities as moved in trade at that time. In the interval between the time when the base rate was in effect and the time of the calculation of purchasing power parity rates, types of commodities entering trade may change. Transfer costs, including tariffs, may vary and alter the conditions of trade. Furthermore, the equilibrium exchange rate for the base year was one that permitted capital-exporting countries to export an excess of merchandise. Likewise, the equilibrium rate of exchange for capital-importing countries was one that permitted an excess of merchandise imports. Consequently, any substantial change in international capital movements occurring between the base date and the time when purchasing power parity is calculated would invalidate the calculation.

3. Any event that impaired the level of invisible exports between the base date and the date of the calculation would destroy the reliability of the calculated purchasing power parity rate. This is well-illustrated in the case of England. During the last war she suffered a severe loss of invisible exports because of the loss of many of her foreign investments. It therefore became necessary for her to expand her commodity exports, as compared to commodity imports, in order to achieve an equilibrium in her balance of payments. This required the pound to be cheaper in the foreign exchange markets than was indicated by the calculation of the rate based upon price level movements.

Undervaluation and Overvaluation of Currencies

Under the international gold standard, exchange rates were controlled by gold parities. When disequilibrium in the balance of payments developed, necessary adjustments occurred in the income and price levels of the countries concerned until equilibrium was restored. These adjustments had the effect of making gold parities the true equilibrium rates of exchange. The general abandonment of gold during World War I led to fluctuating exchange rates when the wartime pegs were removed from the markets. Consequently, attention was inevitably drawn to the existing exchange rates determined in the market and the effectiveness of such rates in establishing equilibrium in the balance of payments. It was this interest that encouraged Cassel to calculate the purchasing power parity rate on the assumption that it would reveal the correct equilibrium rate of exchange.

Undervaluaton of a currency. Whenever, for some reason, the foreign exchange value of a currency is below its true equilibrium value, the currency is said to be *undervalued*. In such a case the country's exports tend to expand and its imports shrink, and a favorable balance of payments develops. Under the gold standard this development leads to the accumulation of foreign exchange claims against other countries and tends to set in motion the appropriate and familiar corrections.

With inconvertible paper currencies, and free exchange markets, undervaluation of a currency tends to be corrected by a rise in the currency's foreign exchange value. Such a rise toward the equilibrium value of the currency and the correction of undervaluation must inevitably occur unless some other development such as a flight of capital provides a sufficient supply of currency offered in the market to offset the normal collective force of expanding exports.

A currency may become undervalued for several reasons. First, the reduction of gold content or parity of a gold standard currency may result in undervaluation. Second, a rise in prices abroad without a similar increase at home will tend to make the pre-existing rate of exchange too low. Third, with inconvertible paper currencies, a flight of capital or the intentional dumping of the currency on the foreign exchange markets by the central bank will depress its exchange value and result in undervaluation. When adopted as a conscious policy, undervaluation is expected to stimulate domestic trade and prices by increasing exports, reducing imports, and thus expanding home employment.

Overvaluation of a currency. Overvaluation exists when the foreign exchange value of a currency is too high, or is above the equilibrium rate. Consequently, an overvalued currency attracts imports, makes exporting difficult, and causes an adverse or unfavorable balance of payments. If the rate of exchange is tied to gold parity, as is the case under the gold standard, the correctives must take the form of falling incomes and costs, under the impact of spontaneous forces and gold losses. An overvalued currency, then, means unemployment and depression until it is corrected. If downward adjustments in costs are difficult to achieve, the undesirable effects of overvaluation continue for a considerable time.

Under free exchange markets and inconvertible paper currencies, overvaluation tends to be corrected readily and relatively painlessly by a downward readjustment in the foreign exchange value of the currency.

Still a third situation may exist when currencies are overvalued. Governments of countries with overvalued currencies may be unwilling to permit either normal correctives, in the form of downward changes in prices, or a downward change in the foreign exchange value of its currency. In this case overvaluation persists and imports tend to exceed exports, and must be curbed by such restraints as tariffs, quotas, and exchange controls.

A currency may become overvalued in the foreign exchange markets in a number of ways:

1. The country having inconvertible paper may embark upon gold convertibility and choose a gold parity that is too high. In 1925, when England returned to the gold standard and the prewar pound, the result was some degree of overvaluation of the pound.

2. With fixed exchange rates, a relative rise in internal or domestic prices leads to overvaluation.

3. The flight of capital *to* a country with inconvertible paper currency may drive up its exchange value and cause it to be overvalued.

The Balance-of-Payments Theory of Exchange Rates

There is a school of thought, commonly accepted in German monetary theory, that holds that there is no natural equilibrium in the balance of payments in the sense that we have been considering it. It rejects the idea of the existence of corrective forces in the form of changes in income, prices, and exchange rates. Instead, the balance-of-payments theory holds that foreign exchange rates are determined by independent factors not directly related to internal price levels and the quantity of money. Such independent factors tending to cause a rise in foreign exchange rates would include requirements for debt payments, reparations, and an inelastic demand for raw materials needed from abroad. Because they deny that there is any real inter-currency parity corresponding to purchasing power parity, the adherents of this theory reason that causes of changes in exchange rates lie within the forces determining the balance of payments rather than in the internal price levels. They hold that exchange rates reflect rather than influence the balance of payments. Because they deny that there is anything automatic about the maintenance of equilibrium in the balance of payments, they find ample justification for tariffs, quotas, exchange regulations, and other forms of state interference designed to prevent an unfavorable debt balance. This is in sharp contrast to the classical view that equilibrium is automatically re-established either by an adjustment of price levels if under the gold standard, or by an adjustment of exchange rates if off the gold standard.[14]

A contemporary application of the balance of payments theory appeared in the discussions of the dollar shortage of England and Western Europe after World War II. The statement was frequently heard that the dollar shortage was something unique, arising out of profound technological and social change, and that it was in no way amenable to solution along the lines of exchange rate adjustment toward an equilibrium level. The devaluation of the pound, it was argued, could not possibly assist in the correction of the British adverse balance of payments because of the inelasticity of demand for both British exports and British imports. There seems to have been little justification for such an extreme position.

Questions for Study

1. Can you explain why, when most of the world is using inconvertible paper currencies, it is important to understand the manner in which international equilibrium is maintained in a gold standard world?

2. What would tend to be the effect of each of the following developments upon a country's balance of payments?
   a) Domestic price inflation.
   b) Increased borrowing from foreign countries.
   c) Depression of prices and employment abroad.
   d) A discovery of a cheap foreign source of a product that this country normally exports.

3. Under an international fixed-exchange-rate system such as that provided by a world gold standard, it is essential that a country promptly correct an adverse balance of payments.
   a) Why is promptness so essential?
   b) What is the classical explanation based upon the quantity theory of money? Why is it inadequate?
   c) What are "spontaneous" forces that tend to restore and maintain equilibrium?

---

[14] Cf. Angell, James W., *Theory of International Prices,* Cambridge, Harvard University Press, 1926, pp. 331-333 and Haberler, *International Trade,* p. 31. For a detailed examination of the "balance of payments" theories, see Ellis, *German Monetary Theory, 1905–1933,* Chapter XIV. Throughout the period of the 1920-1924 inflation in Germany, the Reichsbank, the government, the bankers, the industrialists, and the press insisted that the depreciation of the mark was caused by the state of the balance of payments. Cf. Costantino Bresciani-Turroni, *The Economics of Inflation,* London, G. Allen & Unwin, 1937, pp. 42-46.

4. Why does an excess of "exports" tend to result in an increase in the money supply even though gold has not flowed in? Why does an excess of "imports" tend to reduce the supply of money even though gold has not flowed out?

5. Do a country's imports decline as business activity slackens? Is it necessary that prices fall to bring this about?

6. Suppose that a gold standard country loses gold because of an unfavorable balance of payments.
   a) Will interest rates within the country tend to rise?
   b) What effect will a rise in interest rates have upon:
      1) The import of short-term capital?
      2) The level of business activity?
      3) The amount of lending to foreign countries?

7. What is the difference between equilibrating and disequilibrating short-term capital movements? Can you illustrate each?

8. What is the advantage of the existence of strong spontaneous factors working to restore and maintain equilibrium in the balance of payments?

9. What did the normal stable discount rate practices of the central banks of Belgium and France, and the occasional experiences of the Bank of England with stable discount rates, indicate in respect to the strength of the spontaneous correctives?

10. Why is equilibrium in the balance of payments more readily restored when flexible exchange rates and inconvertible currencies are in use?

11. What problems in respect to exchange rate instability arise out of seasonal and irregular factors in a country's balance of payments? How can such instability be handled?

12. What is the reasoning behind the calculation of purchasing power parity by using relative price level changes at home and abroad? Of what practical use is such a calculation? Why may it not be a true measure of the equilibrium rate of exchange?

13. What is an overvalued currency; how can it be recognized? What is an undervalued currency? What may cause a currency to become undervalued?

14. The "balance-of-payments theory" of exchange rates holds that an adverse balance of payments does not arise from too high a price level or an overvalued currency:
   a) What then, in this view, does cause an adverse balance?
   b) What is the proper remedy for an adverse balance in this case?
   c) How does that remedy differ from the two remedies we have studied in this chapter? Why is such a remedy objectionable?

Controlled Exchange Rates

Control under the gold standard. At first sight, foreign
exchange rates appear to be determined simply by the law of supply
and demand, without the use of artificial controls. Especially does
this appear to have been true in times when the international gold
standard was in operation. As a matter of fact, however, a considerable degree of control over exchange rates, or the forces
determining them, existed under the gold standard. For example,
one well-established principle of central bank management under
the gold standard was the control of credit and interest rates so
as to keep exchange rates within the gold points. By a change in
the discount rate the Bank of England was able to attract short-term
capital, to discourage long-term lending abroad, and to check
internal credit expansion at times when an unfavorable balance
of payments threatened the country's gold reserves. A spreading
of the gold points by modifying the terms upon which gold was
bought and sold was also used as a means to prevent gold movements.

An even more positive and conscious control over the forces
determining the exchange rates developed during the 1920's, when
European countries were re-establishing the gold standard. The
monetary uncertainty of the times made it inadvisable to rely too
heavily on the automatic action of the gold standard to protect
gold reserves. Special measures were therefore taken to guard
against contingencies that might lead to an unfavorable balance
of payments. Careful avoidance of budgetary deficiencies gave
assurance against internal inflation. Foreign credits were arranged
to meet any adverse balances. Home industry and exports were

encouraged, and central banks followed conservative credit policies.

The world-wide depression that began in 1929 and led to the financial collapse of 1931 saw the introduction of various types of intervention or controls over foreign exchange rates. The purpose of such intervention or control was to hold foreign exchange rates at some point different from the rates that would have existed in a completely free exchange market. Such control efforts included the stabilizing action of central banks and stabilization funds as well as the measures commonly referred to as *exchange control,* by which officially maintained rates of exchange are combined with restrictions on imports, blocked balances, clearing agreements, and the like.

The Purpose of Interference or Control in Foreign Exchange Markets

To understand the development of this movement toward control, we must first examine the motives responsible for it. These motives fall into three main categories:

1. Control (used in the broad sense of *any* interference in the exchange market) may be designed to offset seasonal, irregular, and speculative influences and to maintain a stable rate of exchange that approximates an equilibrium rate.

2. Control may be aimed at bringing about a depreciation or undervaluation of the domestic currency in order to stimulate exports and internal expansion.

3. Control may be intended to maintain the exchange value of a country's currency above the equilibrium rate for the purpose of avoiding internal inflation and to improve the "terms of trade" between that country and the outside world.

Maintenance of exchange stability. It is a well-recognized fact that stable exchange rates between countries engaged in trade are highly desirable. Without them the risks of trading become unnecessarily high if not prohibitive. This fact was recognized by the countries comprising the Sterling Area after England abandoned gold in 1931. At that time countries belonging to the Sterling Area wished to maintain fixed exchange rates on London. The degree to which this was accomplished may be clearly seen in the parallel movement of the value of their currencies in terms of gold, as shown in Chart 1 on page 47. The mechanism of control used by these countries was the familiar one used in connection with the gold exchange standards of the 1920's. In each country associated with the Sterling Area the central bank freely bought and sold sterling bills (bills of exchange payable in London) at the established rate. The appearance of an excess supply of sterling bills was a signal for more lenient internal credit conditions, and a shortage of sterling bills and a decline in sterling balances in London indicated a need for domestic credit restraint. The connection between sterling and the other currencies was a loose one. Nevertheless, the voluntary Sterling Area arrangements were maintained until superseded by more rigid exchange controls during World War II.

The need for control to provide exchange stability is especially great in the case of inconvertible paper currencies, which lack the automatic stability provided by the gold standard. Particularly are such currencies exposed to seasonal and speculative influences that must be held in check if wide exchange fluctuations are to be avoided. This need lay behind the establishment, in 1932, of the British Exchange Equalization Account, which bought and sold foreign exchange on gold standard countries for the purpose of maintaining short-run stability of rates.

Sometimes the existence of a powerful trading agency, whether the central bank or a government fund, is insufficient to counteract the effects of capital exports or flight. In such a case, more drastic measures are taken. The control agency then assumes control over all exchange transactions. Persons residing within the country are denied the privilege of buying foreign exchange unless they can prove that they will not use the proceeds to purchase foreign securities, foreign money or bank balances, or other foreign capital assets. Such control is commonly used to prevent or to minimize the flight of capital in the face of threatened domestic crisis. Frequently combined with this type of control is the "blocking" of accounts or claims of foreign creditors who are then denied the privilege of transferring out their claims for interest and debt payments. This blocking is done to remove the pressure of these claims from the balance of payments and to avoid the depressing effect of such claims upon the value of the country's currency in the foreign exchange markets.

Exchange depreciation to stimulate exports. At times, measures have been instituted to depress the foreign exchange value of the country's currency in order to improve the competitive position of its export trade. It was not until the 1930's that deliberate currency devaluation became common. The depreciation of the Japanese yen provided an early example of this type of action, which was later adopted in one form or other by a number of countries, including the United States.

Beneficial results from exchange depreciation may arise from two causes. First, it is obviously of benefit if it corrects a pre-existing overvaluation. Second, to the extent that it results in actual undervaluation, its benefits depend mainly upon the failure of other countries to take similar action. The gains in exports and in domestic employment resulting from undervaluation arise from the tendency for costs of production to lag and adjust slowly to the depreciation in the exchange value of the currency.

During the depression years of the 1930's, the purpose behind exchange depreciation was mainly to promote domestic employment and higher internal prices through the stimulating effect of expanding exports. In September 1949, the exchange value of the British pound was reduced from $4.03 to $2.80, a devaluation of 30.5 per cent. Twenty-nine other countries, including most of those in Western Europe and the Sterling Area, followed with devaluations that varied from 30.5 per cent downward. This wholesale devaluation was for reasons entirely different from those of the 1930's. Although the 1949 devaluations were designed to improve the balance of payments by expanding exports to the West, notably the United States, the purpose was not to stimulate domestic employment and prices. Employment in Britain, for example, stood at a high level, and high prices rather than low were the order of the day. The real purpose of the depreciation of the pound was to encourage a diversion of a larger fraction of British industrial output away from domestic consumption and export to other "soft currency" countries and toward the Western Hemisphere. Only thus could Britain hope to be able to pay her own way by expanding exports sufficiently to pay for her necessary imports, which at that time were partially paid for by United States economic assistance.

Control resulting in overvaluation. Control measures have been adopted for the purpose of maintaining an established or official rate of exchange in the face of a relative rise in domestic prices as compared with prices abroad. The resulting overvaluation of the domestic currency in the foreign exchange markets discourages exports, stimulates imports, and leads to the imposition of tariffs and quotas and the establishment of clearing and barter agreements as the natural trade channels break down.

Methods of Interference and Control: Stabilization Funds

Two methods, short of out-and-out exchange control, are available for influencing the foreign exchange rates by conscious action. The first, used in the 1930's by the non-British members of the Sterling Area, simply involves central bank regulation of the domestic money and credit supply for the purpose of maintaining a domestic price level compatible with the established rate of exchange on London. In this case, central bank monetary management is substituted for the so-called automatic regulation imposed by the gold standard. The second method of influencing the exchange market is through the operations of a trading agency or exchange stabilization fund. Such a fund is for the purpose of defending the exchange market from the effects of speculative inflows and outflows of short-term capital. The best example of this was the British Equalization Account, established in 1932, which functioned as a trader in the free foreign exchange market to maintain the pound at or near its equilibrium value. Unlike central banks that enter the foreign exchange market, the Equalization Account was not itself responsible for monetary policies bearing upon domestic conditions that determine the pound's true equilibrium value.

Capital flight. Capital flight is a general term applied to an attempt to withdraw assets from the country whose currency is under suspicion and acquire corresponding assets in more stable currency countries. Generally it involves converting securities into cash and going into the foreign exchange market to purchase drafts on stable currencies. The effect, of course, is to drive up the price of foreign exchange bills and to drive down correspondingly the foreign exchange value of the domestic currency. Capital flight is often cumulative, for the loss of confidence in the currency becomes worse as the fall in its value becomes a reality.

Capital flight may be carried on by domestic speculators seeking to profit by the purchase of foreign exchange at favorable prices and the later use of such foreign funds to repurchase domestic currency at lower prices. Also foreign holders of short-term claims, such as bankers' acceptances, Treasury bills, and bank deposits, may attempt to convert these claims into safer form by offering drafts against them for sale in the foreign exchange market. Clearly, when there develops a loss of confidence in the future exchange value of a currency, speculative capital flight, unless held in check, can result in an acute adverse balance of payments totally unrelated to the actual state of the country's current accounts.

The British Exchange Equalization Account. The primary purpose of establishing the British Exchange Equalization Account was to stabilize the exchange value of the pound and to prevent either excessive depreciation or excessive appreciation. The general panic that seized the financial world in 1931 brought waves of distrust upon first one currency and then another. As a result, short-term capital shifted rapidly from one money center to another, with consequent pressure upon exchange rates. Whenever a "flight" of capital *to* London occurred, the exchange value of the pound rose. But a dearer pound increased the difficulties of British exporters and could not be allowed to result from speculative movements of capital. The Account, therefore, stood ready to offset the effect of a flight of capital to London by freely selling pounds and taking foreign exchange instead. When the capital movement to London became pronounced, the Account came into possession of large amounts of foreign currencies, which were offset by an equal loss in pounds. On the other hand, when capital movements were away from London instead of toward it, the Account checked the fall in the exchange value of the pound by the purchase of pounds and the sale of the previously accumulated foreign exchange. Whenever the Account's foreign exchange supply became exhausted, it was necessary to export gold to replenish its foreign balances.

It was not the purpose of the Exchange Equalization Account to maintain the value of the pound at a level inconsistent with basic market conditions. In the face of changing price relationships between England and the outside world leading to a lower or higher equilibrium rate of exchange than that currently ruling, the market rate was permitted to adjust itself.

Exchange Control by Direct Pressure on the Balance of Payments

The reasons for direct control over balance-of-payment items. We have already learned how the British Exchange Equalization Account and foreign central banks were able to introduce short-run exchange rate stability by trading in the free exchange markets. So long as no powerful and sustained drive against a currency developed, such measures were effective. Furthermore, the supported rates were designed to correspond to the long-run equilibrium rates. So long as no fundamental disequilibrium arose, or there developed no severe capital flight, the methods of control used were adequate. But during the 1930's, two circumstances developed that spelled trouble for the balance-of-payments position of many countries. First, the great depression and the crisis of 1931 created severe exchange problems for numerous countries. Second, the threat of war, and its actual outbreak in September 1939, not only induced heavy flights of capital from troubled areas but created enormous distortions in the import-export relationships.

The choice between exchange depreciation and exchange controls. The financial crises of 1931 brought grave exchange difficulties. When a flight of capital accompanied these disturbances, it placed an almost unbearable burden upon the monetary systems of countries with inadequate gold supplies. Countries well fortified with gold, such as the United States and France, were able to weather the storm, but England, with its relatively small gold supply, was compelled to suspend gold payments in September. Especially difficult were the positions of weak debtor nations, which found that the depression had not only shut off the accustomed flow of foreign loans, but, by sharply reducing their export trade, had also made the servicing of old foreign debts extremely difficult.

The choices open to countries unable to draw upon an ample gold supply were limited. Because of panic conditions, an increase in the discount rates within the country losing gold was no longer effective in attracting foreign short-term capital. This was true even in London itself, where the discount rate had so long been successfully used for this purpose. At such a time, the effect tends to be just the opposite, for an increase in the rate is construed to be a sign of weakness. Smaller countries, of course, can make little use of the discount rate at any time to influence the flow of short-term capital. Nor was there any hope of relief, during such a period of general world depression, in embarking upon a program of internal price deflation. At best, success would be doubtful and could hardly be counted on to create such an immediate change in the balance of payments as to offset the effect of capital flight. Moreover, these countries were weary of depression, and any attempt to bring about a further deflation of prices and costs, with the accompanying aggravation of unemployment and bankruptcy, was not politically tolerable. The most natural policy to expect under such circumstances, therefore, was the abandonment of gold and a depreciation of the exchange value of the currencies. This was the policy successfully followed by England and the other members of the Sterling Area. It offered the advantage over deflation of being quickly accomplished, and at the same time it was free from the depressing effects of deflation upon the domestic economy. The depreciation of the exchange value of the currencies lowered the costs and prices of goods produced for export, increased the cost of imports, and encouraged domestic recovery. Through exchange depreciation, exchange rates were allowed to seek their equilibrium level, and the adverse balance of payments was largely corrected without imposing control or restraint over the items themselves that comprised the balance of payments.

But the idea of embarking upon a policy of exchange depreciation was repugnant in many countries that had not forgotten the ravages of acute inflation and the accompanying exchange depreciation of the years following World War I. The fact that exchange depreciation in the depths of world depression was quite different from the inflationary depreciation experiences of 1921-1925 did not alter popular distrust. Moreover, there was justifiable suspicion that depreciation of the foreign value of their currencies would be ineffective in halting the flight of capital induced by the general loss of confidence.

It is not surprising, therefore, that some countries rejected both deflation and exchange depreciation and sought relief for their troubles by bringing pressure to bear upon the transactions that were to blame for the adverse balance of payments. Such control naturally was aimed first at shutting off the flight of capital, which was such a powerful and demoralizing force in the exchange markets.

Control over capital exports. In order to prevent capital exports from a country two things must be accomplished. First, residents of the country must not be permitted to purchase foreign exchange for the purpose of acquiring and holding foreign securities or foreign funds not needed to pay for current imports. Second, foreign holders of domestic funds must not be allowed to withdraw them by selling drafts against them to others wishing to purchase goods from the exchange control country. To make the control effective, all dealings in foreign exchange must be brought under regulation. All exporters possessing foreign bills of exchange are required to sell these bills to the control agency at a set or official price, and the export of gold and currency is banned. Purchases of foreign exchange must be made from the official control agency and are restricted to noncapital transactions. To prevent the development of "black markets," where exporters dispose of their foreign bills at prices above the official rate to persons wishing to export capital, rigid controls are required, but even so some evasion is almost certain to occur.

To avoid the withdrawal of foreign-owned funds, it is necessary to "block" the bank deposit accounts of foreign ownership. The blocking of accounts simply means that funds within the control country belonging to persons living abroad may not be used to pay for exports from that country. If resort were not had to this policy, capital might leave the country in the guise of exported goods, and the proceeds from current exports would then be "unrequited," or not available to pay for the necessary imports. Moreover, to prevent pressure on the exchanges arising from the payment of interest and principle on foreign debts, such claims must also be placed in blocked accounts.

The goal sought in the establishment of blocked accounts includes the removal of the immediate threat to the rate of exchange arising from attempts to transfer such funds out of the country. The earliest outstanding example of blocked currencies was the German Standstill Agreements of 1931. The financial crises of that year swept over Europe and created great fear for the stability of currencies. Because, at that time, German banks and other debtors owed short-term debts to foreign creditors amounting to five billion marks (about 1½ billion dollars), it became necessary for the German Government to declare a debt moratorium and to impose control over foreign exchange transactions. It was these debts which were first blocked under the Standstill Agreements.

A number of other countries followed Germany's example in blocking foreign-owned funds within their borders. But it was not until the outbreak of war in 1939 that exchange control and blocked accounts became commonplace. The end of the war saw no relaxation of exchange controls. Instead, blocking of old debts became even more urgent, for huge additional debts were accumulated because of the war. Only by continuing to block foreign-owned balances could countries be certain that the proceeds from current exports would be available to pay for current needed imports.

Exchange Controls with Overvalued Currencies

The blocking of foreign-held balances and a strict avoidance of capital export should, on the face of things, greatly simplify the balance-of-payments problems of a country. With the threat of capital movements out of the way, it should be relatively easy for the country to achieve a balance between current imports and exports. Unfortunately this does not necessarily prove true. First, the suspension of service on foreign debts places an almost insurmountable barrier in the way of new loans from abroad. This closes the door to one possible source of relief from the original difficulties of the adverse balance of payments. Second, exchange control of this sort necessarily involves the maintenance of an official rate at which foreign bills of exchange may be bought and sold. So long as the official rate is the same as the equilibrium rate of exchange, which permits a balance between current noncapital import and export items, no trouble need arise. But even though the official rate of exchange is the equilibrium rate when first established, it is unlikely to remain so for any very long period. There are a number of reasons for this condition. First, for example, during the depression of the 1930's the fixed exchange value (in terms of gold) of the German mark came to be overvalued because German prices and employment were stimulated by domestic expansion measures, whereas in the gold currency countries prices continued to fall. Thus German prices became relatively too high to justify the official foreign exchange value of the mark. The mark also became overvalued in relation to the Sterling Area currencies and later the United States dollar as those currencies were depreciated. The currencies of the European Gold Bloc countries suffered a similar fate previous to their eventual devaluation.

Second, and even more significant today, is the fact that established official exchange rates often become overvalued rates as a result of the upheavals of war. These upheavals cause unequal degrees of price and cost inflation in the different countries of the world. Those countries whose price and cost levels have increased substantially more than those of other areas find that the old official rates of exchange tend to overvalue their currencies. Furthermore, war not only causes unequal changes in price levels of the countries involved. Also, to a varying degree, it destroys markets, dissipates foreign investments, creates new debts, and exhausts natural resources. After such changes a rate of exchange that would provide an equilibrium in a country's balance of payments would almost certainly differ substantially from the prewar rate. It was the dislocations arising out of the war that made the postwar official exchange value of the British pound and other European currencies too high in terms of the United States dollar and ultimately resulted in an adjustment downward through devaluation.

It follows, therefore, that an official rate of exchange, though correct at the start, may often overvalue the domestic currency at a later date. Then exports languish while imports are stimulated, and the balance of payments is again upset. It then becomes necessary to extend control to the items of current trade. "Unnecessary" imports must be discouraged by quotas, tariffs, or by refusing to sell foreign exchange to unlicensed importers. Bureaucratic interference with normal trade becomes burdensome and uneconomical, with undesirable results on the domestic economy.[1]

---

[1] For an able discussion of the problem of exchange control, see Ellis, Howard S., *Exchange Control in Central Europe*, Cambridge, Harvard University Press, 1941.

Bilateral clearing agreements. Whenever officially established exchange rates result in overvaluation of a currency, imports tend to exceed exports and an adverse balance of payments results. Difficulties arise in finding sufficient foreign exchange to pay for imported food and raw materials necessary for the country's existence. At the same time other countries that normally depend upon the exchange-control country as a market for their exports are loath to see the market disappear. A partial solution to this problem is often sought in the making of bilateral trade and clearing agreements.

Under the bilateral trade agreement the exchange-control country agrees to purchase from the other countries provided they will accept payment in blocked currency accounts or credits. These blocked funds may be used only for the purchase of certain materials that the exchange-control country is prepared to export. As more and more countries established exchange-control mechanisms during and after the war, such bilateral agreements were commonly made between each separate pair of countries and came to dominate world trade.

Each country entering such a bilateral agreement eventually possesses a limited captive market. Proceeds from sales in these markets accumulate as credits in the clearing accounts. So long as trade between any given pair of countries is in balance, claims in the clearing accounts are set off against each other.

When settlement between these two accounts is made in foreign exchange, the arrangement is known as a *payment agreement*. When settlement is made solely by offsetting claims in one account against those in the other, it is known as a *clearing agreement*. Sometimes foreign exchange is not available for settlements, nor are balances permitted to accumulate on open book accounts to await periodic balancing of the totals. In such a case, each individual import must be offset by an export of equal value. Such barter arrangements are called *compensation*. The use of the compensation method of settlement limits the choices of importers and exporters, since their trade involves the difficulty of the "double coincidence of wants." The advantage consists, however, in the fact that compensation settlements allow some trade to continue at times when an unliquidated clearing balance makes further use of clearings impossible.

Trade Discrimination Through Controlled Exchanges

Trade discrimination is not a new thing in international economic relations. Trade agreements as well as unilateral action may be the basis for discrimination. Trade discrimination commonly involves giving preference to imports originating in one country over those from other countries. The preference may arise out of political ties or out of the economic necessity of favoring imports from countries which in turn provide a vital export market.

The devices by which discrimination is shown include (1) establishment of quotas on imports from countries discriminated against; (2) discriminatory tariffs against imports from such countries; and (3) use of exchange control. Our interest here lies in the use of exchange control as a method of diverting trade into approved channels.

The power of discrimination through exchange control. Exchange control involves the purchase by the control authority of all or part of the foreign exchange arising from export transactions. Importers, wishing to buy foreign goods, must purchase from the control authority the foreign exchange necessary for payment. The control agency must then decide not only the appropriateness of the import of particular commodities but also the further question of the appropriateness of the origin of the goods. If it wishes to discriminate against the imports from a particular country (1) it may refuse altogether to sell exchange for the payment for such imports; (2) it may limit the amount of foreign exchange it will sell for purchases from the country discriminated against; and (3) it may charge a discriminatory price for exchange, higher than that charged for exchange used to pay for imports from more favored countries. An example of this discrimination is found in the practices of Argentina, which has sold foreign exchange at low, favorable prices for payment for imports from England, with which she has an export surplus. In contrast, imports from the United States have had to be paid for with exchange bought at a higher price in the free market or at less favorable official rates.

Multiple exchange rates. Exchange-control countries have frequently found it desirable both for purposes of discrimination and for other reasons to maintain different foreign exchange rates for different commodities and for trade with different countries. The "official" rate is generally set to give a high foreign exchange value for the domestic currency, a value that frequently results in overvaluation. Such a rate, of course, tends to discourage exports and to encourage imports. Exporters of commodities enjoying a strong foreign demand are required to sell their foreign exchange receipts to the central control authority at the official rate. This restriction is somewhat unfavorable to the exporters save for the possibility that they may require a higher price of the foreign buyer. It is of advantage to the control authority in that it is thus able to acquire foreign exchange at a relatively low price in terms of domestic currency. For example, Argentinian exporters of grains and meats were required to sell their foreign exchange receipts at the official rate. Importers of approved goods or goods originating in favored countries were allowed to purchase foreign exchange at the official and, to them, favorable rate. On the other hand, exporters of commodities having a weak foreign demand were allowed to sell their foreign exchange bills in the free market or at a controlled rate more favorable to exporters. Importers of less favored commodities or from less favored countries, in turn, were required to buy foreign exchange in the more costly free market or at a higher and less favorable official rate.[2]

The official rate of exchange sometimes intentionally is set so as to overvalue the domestic currency in the belief that the control country may thus be able to improve the "terms of trade" with at least part of the outside world. This means simply that a larger quantity of necessary imports may be obtained in exchange for available exports. The possibility of gain from this source rests in the ability of the control country to continue to sell its exports

---

[2] Cf. Wiley, Jay W., *Some Problems of Foreign Exchange Control in Argentina* (Abstract of Thesis, University of Illinois), 1948, pp. 2-3. Also League of Nations' *International Currency Experience*, 1944, p. 174. A similar multiple-exchange-rate system exists in Brazil. There, in 1956, the foreign exchange value of the cruzeiro was reduced from 50 to 55 cruzeiros per U.S. dollar for exports of such things as fruit, timber, wax, tea, manganese, iron ore, and vegetable oils; from 43 to 55 cruzeiros per dollar for exports of soya beans and leaf tobacco; from 20 to 67 cruzeiros per dollar for the export of manufactured goods. At the same time the rate remained 27 cruzeiros per dollar for coffee exports and 43 cruzeiros per dollar for exports of cotton, cocoa, and hides. In this manner the export of those goods that are weakest competitors in world markets was encouraged. *International Financial News Survey,* International Monetary Fund, June 8, 1956, p. 387.

in spite of the higher cost to the importing country arising from the overvaluation of the control country's currency. The possibility of achieving this beneficial result may arise out of economic duress imposed by a stronger control country upon its weaker satellites or because of a sellers' market for exports such as existed in the world following World War II. But in the less favorable markets it is necessary to allow the exchange value of the currency to depreciate in order that exporting may be carried on. The practice of maintaining multiple exchange rates can be explained, therefore, both by the desire to engage in discrimination and by the hope of improving the terms of trade.

The Effects of Exchange Controls

One of the frequent consequences of direct exchange control during depression is the establishing of an official rate that tends to be higher than the equilibrium foreign exchange rate. Thus, exports languish, imports are stimulated, and the problem of an adverse balance of payments reappears in the form of an inability to bring current export and import items into balance. This situation calls for remedial action, which may take the form of surcharges on imports from which export bounties may be granted. Moreover, the shortage of foreign exchange makes it imperative that unnecessary imports be held in check in order that needed imports may be had in the desired amounts. This, in turn, requires the allocation of foreign exchange to those importers whose claims seem most impressive to the ears of the exchange-control authorities. Thus, the interference with the internal economic functions, through the subsidizing of exports and the restraints upon imports, becomes more and more disturbing.

The use of clearing agreements places yet more interferences in the natural channels of international trade. Under such agreements, trade tends more and more to become strictly bilateral, since purchases from countries with which such agreements exist tend directly to promote exports. Purchases from countries with which no agreements exist must be kept at a minimum to husband the scarce supply of free foreign exchange required for such necessities as must be purchased abroad in free exchange markets.

This tendency decreases the normal trade between the control country and third countries, to their mutual disadvantage. It is not surprising, therefore, that most of the nations of the free world look upon the restoration of free foreign exchange markets as a desirable ultimate goal.

Exchange Depreciation

Exchange depreciation during depression. During periods of serious depression two outstanding reasons arise for the practice of currency depreciation. First, the decline in price and income levels in the outside world disturbs international trade in such a way as to result in the overvaluation of certain currencies. For example, in the 1930's, depression in industrial countries caused a severe fall in the value and quantity of exports of raw-material-producing countries. Furthermore, such countries were generally capital importers (borrowers) from the industrialized areas of the world and the depression tended abruptly to shut off the inflow of capital. Consequently these raw material countries found it undesirable and even impossible to bring their balance of payments into equilibrium through internal price deflation. In the face of shrinking international currency reserves (gold and foreign exchange), they felt compelled to abandon the existing exchange rates and to permit their currencies to depreciate. In addition, they frequently found it necessary to supplement the effects of depreciation by tariffs and quotas on imports.

A second reason for the adoption of exchange depreciation in the 1930's was the desire to embark upon an anti-deflationary program by monetary and fiscal expansion. To accomplish this in a depressed world necessarily required the abandonment of the old gold parities and sufficient depreciation of the currency to correct any overvaluation that such expansionary efforts might cause by the relative increase in domestic income and prices. In other words, depreciation of a country's currency permitted internal recovery measures. Both of these two reasons are legitimate and have a salutary effect upon the world economy. The avoidance of overvaluation enables countries to proceed with their internal expansion programs to the benefit of both the countries involved and their neighbors as well. A good example of this result is found in the experience of England and the rest of the Sterling Area after the abandonment of gold in September 1931. The abandonment of gold was involuntary rather than the result of conscious policy. Its results, however, in releasing the Sterling Area countries from the depressing effects of gold drains proved generally beneficial. Trade, particularly among the countries of the Sterling Area themselves, increased substantially and provided a bright, cheerful, and promising outlook in an otherwise badly depressed world.[3]

A third and much less laudable motive for exchange depreciation was the desire, in the face of acute depression, to undervalue the currency to a point at which exports would expand and imports shrink sufficiently to create a *favorable* balance of payments. The reason for this desire stems from the well-recognized fact that a favorable balance of payments stimulates domestic employment. It is obvious that if exports can be increased and imports reduced, there will be more employment at home. Or, to use a somewhat more sophisticated analysis, a favorable balance, if achieved, injects into the domestic income flow an amount of funds equal to the favorable excess. This occurs whether gold and other acceptable forms of funds are "shipped in" in payment or the excess is financed by the extension of credit. The increase in income so generated is subject to the well-known "multiplier" effect. It is not surprising, then, that individual countries have frequently sought to benefit themselves by undervaluing their currencies. To be sure, *under*valuation by one country tends to make other countries' currencies *over*valued, so that the policy of undervaluation through exchange depreciation came to be known as a "beggar-my-neighbor" policy, or "exporting unemployment." Little wonder that exchange depreciation invited retaliation, and that in the 1930's competitive exchange depreciation became commonplace.

The Results of Currency Depreciation During Depression

We have seen that the reasons for currency or exchange depreciation fall into two main categories: (1) to correct for or prevent overvaluation and thus restore or maintain equilibrium in the balance of payments; and (2) to undervalue the currency and thus

---

[3] Cf. Harris, S. E., *Exchange Depreciation*, Cambridge, Harvard University Press, 1936, pp. xxii-xxiii.

promote domestic employment. To assess the results of depreciation, one must both explore the probable and possible results by
theoretical analysis, and, so far as possible, study the actual historical
consequences.

**Results on employment to be expected from undervalua-
tion.** One can readily appreciate the very real advantages that
follow the depreciation of a currency that previously has been
overvalued in the foreign exchange markets. Identical advantages
tend to appear in the country that intentionally forces down the
foreign exchange value of its currency *below* the true equilibrium
rate. The cheapening of the domestic currency in the foreign exchange markets makes exports cheaper for foreigners to buy and at
the same time makes importing more costly. We are already familiar
with the way in which the economic forces operate to restore the
equilibrium rate of exchange once it is disturbed. If exchange
rates are free to move, adjustments appear quickly through appropriate changes in the rate. If, as is the case with intentional exchange depreciation, the exchange rate is stoutly held below the
equilibrium point, a slower adjustment tends to take place through
appropriate movements in the level of prices. It is clear that so long
as prices are not sufficiently adjusted to make the new low exchange
rate the equilibrium rate, exports are stimulated, imports are re-
tarded, and domestic industry is encouraged.[4] Thus, a lag in the
adjustment of prices may be considered beneficial in promoting
employment. The prices of goods that move freely in international
trade can be expected to make an almost immediate adjustment to
the change in the exchange rate. Prices of such commodities must
necessarily become adjusted so that the difference in price at home
and abroad, when calculated at the ruling rate of exchange, is no
more than the cost of transfer from one country to the other. Even
so, the costs of producing such commodities will lag behind their
prices substantially. Though export prices rise, the stimulating
effects of exchange depreciation do not disappear so long as the
lag in costs persists, since exporters retain a relative, competitive
advantage over producers in countries with overvalued currencies.

---

[4] Even after prices have risen within the country practicing exchange depreciation, the beneficial effects are not entirely lost. The initial impetus to business
recovery may be followed by a general cyclical improvement. A genuine advantage
from higher prices is found in the improved cost-debt-price relationship.

If retaliatory action is immediately taken by other countries, the realized benefits from exchange depreciation may not be so great as anticipated. Such retaliation may take the form of (1) exchange depreciation; or (2) tariffs and quotas on imports from the country practicing depreciation.

The gains in domestic employment arising directly from undervaluation of the currency continue so long as changes in cost levels—downward in countries whose currencies have become overvalued and upward in those whose currencies have become undervalued—have not adjusted enough to make the new exchange rate the equilibrium rate. Fundamental factor costs, such as wages, tend to adjust slowly so long as the productive factors are not fully employed. Therefore, if the country that undervalues its currency is plentifully supplied with idle factors of production, the changes in prices of exportable goods will have but little immediate effect upon costs, and the improvement in employment will continue. Since countries that tried voluntary exchange depreciation in the 1930's were in the throes of depression, a considerable lag in cost adjustment was to be expected.[5]

Effect of undervaluation upon domestic prices. In addition to attempts to increase employment by exchange depreciation in the 1930's, attempts were also made to raise the domestic price level by the same method. The outstanding example of the latter was the devaluation of the United States dollar early in 1934.[6] The administration believed that cheapening the dollar in terms of gold would raise the United States price level.

The appropriateness of the devaluation of the dollar was the subject of much controversy. Although such undervaluation is likely to induce some changes in import and export prices, there is little reason to expect anything like a proportional change in the fundamental price structure of a country that devalues its currency. In a small country, where imports and exports play a large part in the

---

[5] For evidence that costs showed a very slow adjustment to exchange depreciation during the 1930's, see Harris, *op. cit.*, p. 69.

[6] The bullionist point of view (that the value of money depends upon the value of the gold in the monetary unit and that the level of prices can be changed by changes in the amount of gold in that unit) prevailed among some of the Presidential advisors at that time and provided a good deal of the drive behind the devaluation movement. However, the actual effect upon domestic prices, if any, must have resulted from the undervaluation of the dollar in terms of the remaining European Gold Bloc currencies.

total economy, the adjustments in import and export prices tend to cause substantial adjustments in the total price level. On the other hand, in a large country like the United States, where foreign trade is relatively small as compared with domestic trade, the effect on the general level of prices is unlikely to be of any great immediate importance.

The effect of devaluation on a country's price level depends also on whether price adjustments take place in the *domestic* market or in *foreign* markets. Obviously, one cannot forecast accurately whether equilibrium will be restored by an increase in prices and costs within the country practicing exchange depreciation or by a fall in prices in the outside world. Nevertheless, there are certain conditions under which one effect is more probable than the other.

Exchange depreciation results mainly in a rise of domestic prices rather than a fall in prices abroad when: [7]

1. The country's exports constitute but a small fraction of the total world trade in such commodities. Thus, if the country is small and if the product is produced by many other countries, the expansion of exports from the depreciated country will be unlikely to depress world prices. Foreign demand for the country's exports is elastic.

2. The country's supply of exports is inelastic, that is, it does not expand readily in response to a higher price.

3. The domestic demand for the exportable products is inelastic. Thus a rise in the price of exportable goods will not cause the domestic market to release goods for export.

4. But a few countries, preferably small ones, are attempting to expand exports by undervaluation.

5. Foreign trade commodities make up a large part of those entering domestic markets. In such a case the internal price level should respond relatively quickly to changes in export and import prices resulting from undervaluation.

On the other hand, exchange depreciation should tend to depress foreign prices rather than raise domestic prices when:

1. Domestic supplies of export goods are elastic.

2. Foreign demand for such goods is inelastic because of few alternate sources of supply.

3. The number and size of countries engaging in currency depreciation are large compared with the importance of countries not indulging in the practice.

[7] Harris, S. E., *Exchange Depreciation*, Cambridge, Harvard University Press, 1936, Chapter II.

One may, therefore, expect that exchange depreciation practiced by a small country whose exports consist of widely produced staples and whose imports consist of goods having an elastic supply would be very effective in raising import and export prices within that country. As a recovery measure, it might be recommended for such a country. Moreover, the imports and exports of a small country directly affect domestic trade and the whole domestic economy to a much greater degree than is the case with large countries. Being small, such a country might safely engage in exchange depreciation without stirring up opposition abroad in the form of tariffs and quotas against exchange dumping. This policy practiced by a small country is more likely, therefore, to raise internal prices than to depress world prices.

But when a large country engages in exchange depreciation, there is less likelihood that domestic prices will rise and more likelihood that prices abroad will fall. The imports and exports of a large country have relatively greater weight in the world markets and, therefore, are more likely to cause a shift in foreign prices. Exchange dumping by a large country will invite retaliatory action on the part of other countries. Furthermore, the greater the number of countries involved in exchange depreciation, the less will be the likelihood of domestic price increases. If all countries were to make the attempt to depreciate their currencies at the same time and to the same extent, all advantage would disappear.

The merits of undervaluation as a remedy for domestic depression. There is some reason to believe that successful attempts at undervaluating a currency will, for a time at least, bring some benefits in employment to a depressed country. The benefits derive from exporting one country's unemployment to its unfortunate neighbors. Also, undervaluation may result in some rise of the domestic price level, with whatever gains an improvement in the cost-price relationship will bring.

However, as a remedy for unemployment and depression, undervaluation of a currency must be rated as objectionable. Its effectiveness is at best questionable, due to the defenses that will be raised by alert neighboring countries. Such defenses reduce world trade and tend to aggravate world depression. Unless a country is so small that it finds its economy dominated by its neighbors, other

measures to promote recovery from depression are vastly to be preferred. Monetary and fiscal policy can be used to increase domestic
employment much more effectively than currency depreciation.
Coupled with flexible exchange rates to prevent internal expansion
from resulting in overvaluation, the latter measures not only benefit
the country itself, but also the world at large.

Devaluation in Time of Full Employment
to Correct an Adverse Balance of Payments

Unlike the devaluations of the 1930's, those of 1949 were not
designed for combatting unemployment and depression. Rather, the
critical need was for closing the gap betwen purchases from and
sales to the dollar area. Therefore, the urgent question was the extent to which devaluation could contribute to the elimination of the
dollar shortage.

Pushed far enough, currency depreciation could hardly avoid
bringing about a correction of the dollar shortage. It encouraged
exports to the dollar area both by making it profitable for exporters
to switch exports from existing markets in the soft-currency areas to
the United States, and, with adequate domestic restraints against
inflation, by diverting a larger fraction of the domestic output from
domestic consumption. At the same time, depreciation in terms of
the dollar reduced imports from the dollar area. This change was
brought about both by diverting import demand away from the more
expensive dollar market into other possible sources of supply in
soft-currency areas and by a general over-all shrinkage of imports.
This is not to say that depreciation provided a palatable and satisfactory cure for the dollar shortage. At a time of full employment,
exchange depreciation, by limiting imports, may well cause a reduction in employment and a considerable degree of economic
dislocation. Consequently, it is not hard to see why Britain adopted
devaluation of the pound in 1949 reluctantly and with reservations
as to the outcome.

There is little doubt that the devaluations of 1949 contributed to
the reversal of the decline in dollar and gold reserves of the Sterling
Area and Western Europe. United States imports rose substantially
from both the dollar area (Canada and part of Latin America) and

the nondollar areas. At the same time, exports to nondollar areas declined from the 1949 level. The gold and dollar reserves of Western Europe and the Sterling Area have greatly improved since the low point of 1948-1949. It would be inaccurate to say, however, that devaluation alone eliminated the dollar shortage. During the period a number of other favorable developments occurred. Quotas and exchange controls were tightened to reduce imports from the dollar areas. The United States greatly expanded its purchases of raw materials during the early part of the Korean War and continued substantial grants and gifts to other countries, including Western Europe. All of these things played a part in helping to correct the dollar shortage. One can only say that devaluation had some part in the improvement.

Questions for Study

1. When the British Exchange Equalization Account was operating in the 1930's, what was its primary purpose? Why was it needed?

2. What is meant by capital flight? What is its effect on a country's balance of payments? Can it be readily offset by an increase in a country's merchandise exports?

3. Contrast the difference in the method of checking capital flight used in the 1930's by the British Exchange Equilization Account and that used in Germany.

4. Why, in 1931-1939, were some countries faced with a choice between exchange depreciation and exchange controls? Why were the traditional gold standard remedies not acceptable?

5. Why did control over capital exports appear to be a necessity for countries like Germany in 1931? What are "blocked currencies"? Why do they prevent capital export?

6. Can you explain why currencies of countries with exchange controls often tend to become overvalued? What corrections for an adverse balance of payments is likely to be adopted by a country having officially fixed rates of exchange and inconvertible currency?

7. Why do bilateral trade agreements frequently accompany exchange controls? What do such agreements do to the normal patterns of world trade?

8. How can exchange control be used to discriminate against purchases from a particular country?

9. Why do countries sometimes adopt systems of multiple exchange rates?

10. Why have countries deliberately depreciated the foreign exchange value of their own currencies? When is their purpose right and proper?

11. Why have countries used exchange-rate depreciation as a remedy for unemployment and low prices during depressions?

12. Under what circumstances will the undervaluation of a currency tend to be successful in stimulating domestic employment? Why will it be a better practice for a small country than for a large one?

13. When will undervaluation be more likely to raise domestic prices than to force down prices abroad?

14. How long do stimulating effects on employment last in the case of currency depreciation?

15. Why did the British devalue the pound in 1949? How did their reasons differ from the reasons for the devaluation of the 1930's?

IX____

POSTWAR
MONETARY PROBLEMS

33

The Monetary Consequences
of War

Without question the greatest monetary and price level up-heavals of modern society have their origin in the disturbances of war. Not only do wars themselves directly induce inflation but their secondary consequences in the shape of post war dislocations pose equally serious problems. In this chapter, therefore, we shall trace briefly the inflation-generating events of war and examine the monetary problems, both national and international, that appear in the wake of actual hostilities. We shall also try to learn something of the solution of these postwar problems that have been tried or have been proposed.

The wartime increase in governmental expenditures. The outbreak of war normally brings an almost immediate increase in the expenditure of the central government. Mobilization expenses must be met; troops and supplies must be transported; payrolls mount as increasing numbers of men are put under arms. Old training camps must be enlarged and new ones built; guns, munitions, airplanes, uniforms, food, and other equipment must be swiftly obtained; the navy must be strengthened. Strong nations frequently find it necessary not only to equip their own armed forces but also to assist in supplying the sinews of war to weaker allies. Only when the war is small in scale and of short duration can it be carried on without a marked increase in governmental spending.

The volume of governmental spending involved in a serious and prolonged war, therefore, creates difficult problems of public finance. This is true whether the government purchases its supplies in open competition with private individuals or whether it commandeers the operations of industry. One may visualize the seriousness of the problem of financing a war by observing the magnitude of the money expenditures of the United States during the four war years, 1942-1945. During that period the Federal government spent approximately 310 billion dollars, 280 billions of which was for war purposes.

To finance its war expenditures the government increased both its tax levies and its borrowing. During the years of World War II, government borrowing amounted to about two-thirds of the total government expenditures.

The Korean war and our subsequent attempt to insure that the free world should not again be caught unprepared, have required continued high levels of military expenditure. The resulting difficulty in balancing the Federal budget is, of course, well recognized.

Why Borrowing Is Inevitable During Wars

There are a number of reasons why financing modern wars involves heavy borrowing. These reasons include:

1. Taxation is too slow to enable the treasury to obtain necessary funds to meet the immediate needs. The levying and collection of new taxes involves a considerable amount of time, and war requirements cannot wait. Borrowing must therefore be used to bridge the gap between the time when funds are needed and the time when new taxes can be collected.

2. Actual fiscal requirements cannot be estimated accurately in time of war. War budgets commonly turn out to be too small. Therefore, in spite of a well-worked-out taxation plan, some resort to borrowing is generally necessary to supplement tax income in order to meet unforeseen requirements. Furthermore, borrowing the current money savings of the public is almost certain to prove too slow to meet the urgent requirements, and resort to an expansion in bank credit can hardly be avoided. To tie down expenditures during a war to the limits set by the government's ability to levy and collect taxes and to sell bonds to investors would be definitely undesirable. The cost of delay in a program of appropriate military action may easily be so great as to outweigh entirely the inflationary consequence.

3. Psychologically and politically, it is more expedient for the government to borrow funds than to extract them by taxation while the war is in progress.

4. Closely related to reason 3 is the desire to postpone the final allocation of the costs of the war until the actual hostilities are over. This does not mean that domestic borrowing actually postpones the costs of war. Obviously, this cannot be so. More funds can be extracted from the community, however, with less complaint by borrowing than by taxation.

5. There is a definite advantage in expanding the quantity of money by inflationary borrowing during the time when an expansion of physical output is being sought.

Why Is Government Borrowing Inflationary?

Governmental borrowing need not be inflationary in all cases. At times, when private savings outrun private investment demands, government borrowing may merely help to close the gap between savings and investment and thus prevent deflation. However, under the impact of the needs of war, private plus governmental borrowing tend strongly to outrun private savings. Consequently, part of the necessary funds must be provided by the expansion of bank credit and an increase in the money supply.

Because war effort requires an expansion in total output and total hours of employment, some monetary expansion is desirable and needed. For instance, at the beginning of World War II the American economy was far from a full employment level. It became most important, therefore, to expand employment and output to the maximum. This necessitated a sharp increase in the income flow, since an expanding employment level could hardly be achieved otherwise. This increase, of course, required some monetary expansion. Thus an expansion of bank credit based upon government borrowing provided the required monetary supply needed for a rising flow of money income. This rise in money income made possible the wage and price incentives required to expand employment and output.

But wartime monetary expansion is by no means an unmixed blessing. Gradually, as the war economy gets fully under way, the peacetime slack is taken up and output approaches a maximum level. But deficit financing of war expenditures continues to create an expanding supply of money that can no longer be matched by an increased flow of goods. The resulting "inflationary gap" between the income flow and the value of current output at *existing prices* puts heavy pressure on the price level. Under normal conditions, this gap is quickly closed by rising prices as the increasing money income is spent. Avoidance of an inflationary price spiral built upon this expanding money supply thus becomes a major wartime problem.

Avoidance of Price Inflation

The objectionable features of price inflation make it highly desirable that the inflationary results of war finance be minimized as far as possible. There are three avenues of approach to this problem. The first is by avoiding an expansion of the means of payment. The second is by expanding output of goods wherever possible. The third is by outright control of prices.

Prevention of an expansion in the quantity of money. The most obvious way to escape monetary inflation is to avoid budgetary deficits by a prompt and drastic program of taxation. This, however, is the counsel of perfection, which can hardly be followed by a government confronted by the gigantic task of marshalling its full resources for war. Assuming, then, that a government at war is almost certain to depend upon borrowing part of the funds its needs, are there any ways to prevent such borrowing from becoming inflationary? It is possible to resort to some form of compulsory saving that will enable the government to borrow out of the current incomes of its citizens. One method is a drastic rationing of consumers' goods, which frees a large part of the consumers' incomes for investment in government securities. Government loans that are subscribed entirely out of income thus saved are not in themselves inflationary. The same result may be accomplished in another way without dependence upon rationing of consumers' goods. Income payments might be diverted at the source; that is, part of an individual's income would not be paid in cash, but instead would be transferred directly to the government in exchange for government bonds, which would go to the individual in lieu of part of his cash income. In this manner, consumption would be curtailed and the remainder of the national income would pass directly into the hands of the government. The income receiver would receive a claim against future taxes in his government bonds.

Wartime interest rates. In the absence of some such methods as those just described, government deficits are almost certain to lead directly to some credit expansion. Even so, it is still possible and highly desirable to minimize the inflationary consequence by placing barriers in the way of private business inflation. One method of holding business investment in check is to maintain interest rates at a high level. Thus, new and speculative investment borrowing might be kept within due bounds, and some of the extreme, inflationary results of war finance be avoided. But there are serious obstacles in the way of a high discount rate policy at such a time. First, the Treasury desires to float a large volume of government securities at as low a rate of interest as possible. Its influence, therefore, inevitably is thrown on the side of low rather than high interest rates. Second, there arises the question of the effect of high rates of interest upon the expansion of those industries necessary for the prosecution of the war. Any slowing down of necessary industrial effort is clearly undesirable. Therefore, however salutary the probable effect of high interest rates upon the nonessential industries, there is scant possibility of their adoption as a part of wartime policy. Inflation in the nonessential industries must therefore be held in check by other methods. Such methods include the rationing of capital and of materials. So long as the nonessential industries are not permitted to have access to the capital market or to purchase scarce materials needed for essential industry, they are not in a position to contribute greatly to an inflationary movement. Finally, the most important source of wartime inflation is unlikely to be seriously affected by a high interest policy. Whether interest costs are high or low, the government demands for borrowed funds to prosecute the war must be met. There is little reason to believe that voluntary saving will show any very marked response to higher rates of interest. Therefore, the net result of a tight money policy is likely to be an increased money cost of financing the war with little restraint upon the expansion of money incomes.

Although expediency appears to dictate that wars be financed at low interest rates maintained for the Treasury's benefit by appropriate discount and open market central bank policies, the "easy money" policy of the war period may create serious problems after the war has ended. Inflationary developments in the postwar period may require monetary restraint. The Treasury, however, desires a continuation of low interest rates both to keep down the interest cost of refinanced short-term debt and to prevent a fall in long-term government security prices. This was the situation that provided the background for the celebrated postwar policy conflict between the Board of Governors of the Federal Reserve System and the Treasury.

Output expansion as a brake on inflation. So long as output is increased in response to government spending of new money, the inflationary consequences of wartime monetary expansion are held in check. The labor force may expand under the impact of increased demand and a longer working week may ensue. Imports may be encouraged and output restrictions reduced. All of these tend to occur in wartime and constitute an anti-inflationary effect.

The Use of Rationing and Price Controls During Wars

There are two main reasons for the use of price controls in time of war. First, some critical commodities are made relatively scarce because of war requirements. Without control over such commodities, prices would rise sharply. Such price increases are undesirable for a number of reasons: (1) They encourage commodity speculation and hoarding and thus tend to withhold badly needed supplies from the market; (2) they unnecessarily increase the cost of the war; and (3) they cause large windfall profits to accrue to those fortunate enough to possess stocks of the scarce goods or facilities for producing them. Moreover, although high prices are useful in stimulating an expansion of output of scarce and needed commodities in the long run, they are inadequate to induce the rapid and wholesale conversion of industry to war production in the time required by the emergency of war. Instead, recourse must be had to compulsion in some form. This may take the form of priorities and allocations of scarce materials and even the threat of outright commandeering of industry for war purposes. It is the need for price control over scarce commodities that is the basis for the belief, advanced and acted on at the beginning of World War II, that "selective" price controls were all that were needed.

The second need for price controls arises out of the "inflationary gap." The constantly rising flow of money income, resulting from continuing deficit financing, can be absorbed in only two ways. First, prices in general may rise, creating all the evils and disturbances that accompany general price inflation. Under these conditions the price spiral tends to become higher and higher and lagging taxes account for a smaller fraction of increasing government expenditures. This means that a greater volume of government borrowing and hence a greater monetary expansion would occur than would be necessary if prices were held in check. The second and more desirable way of absorbing the excessive money income flow is to hold prices down and compel income receivers to accumulate the excess as cash savings. This method has the further advantage of making it easier for the Treasury to sell noninflationary savings bonds to the public.

In order to minimize the over-all inflationary effects of the constantly rising money supply it is necessary to impose rigid over-all ceilings on prices and to accompany them with strict rationing or allocation of goods in short supply. Wartime price controls present a multitude of problems that we need not consider here. It is sufficient to note that so long as there exists a general public acceptance of controls as a war necessity, price controls achieve their main purpose. For example, the wholesale commodity price index stood at 98.8 during 1942 and had risen only to 105.8 for the year 1945. Similarly consumers' goods prices were 116.5 in 1942 and rose to 128.4 for 1945. To be sure, these figures cannot be taken entirely at face value. They do not allow fully for quality deterioration that occurred, nor for the dealings in the black markets. Nevertheless, price controls did accomplish their main purpose of holding prices in check and minimized the inflationary spiral.

The benefits of price control. The use of price control during war has a threshold benefit. First, it avoids, in large measure, the distortion of real income distribution likely to result from general price inflation. Rationing of consumers' goods assures low income receivers of their fair share. At the same time, price controls help to avoid excessive windfall profits arising from lagging costs. Furthermore, they minimize work stoppages arising from strikes. In the second place, price controls help minimize the money cost of the war. As a result, the postwar debt burden is much less than it would otherwise have been. Third, the postwar inflation problem is eased by price control. Price control over goods purchased by the government obviously reduces the need for inflationary borrowing while the war is in progress and therefore reduces by that much the inflationary potential of cash hoards. Therefore, the country enters the postwar period with a very much smaller supply of money than would have been the case without controls. Consequently, in spite of the rise in prices certain to follow the termination of price controls, the magnitude of the rise is still much less than that which would have occurred had there been no price control during the war.

Price Movements After Wars

There are good reasons, both in theory and experience, to expect some price inflation to follow war. In fact, such an inflation occurred throughout the world after World War I. Moreover, in spite of dire predictions of serious postwar unemployment, World War II was followed by a serious inflation of prices. The reasons for this are not difficult to see. First, the inflationary potential existing in the form of wartime cash savings is released with the relaxation of controls. This flood of cash, coupled with an accumulated shortage of durable consumers' goods, puts heavy price pressure upon the limited output. Encouraged by the high level of consumer spending, businessmen seek additional funds for expansion by borrowing at the banks. This borrowing adds still more to the money income stream and puts further pressure upon the price structure. Moreover, in many countries, governments find difficulty in bringing budgets into balance, and this causes added inflationary borrowing. Under such conditions it is fruitless to argue that rising production will provide an effective brake to inflation. Rather, unless price controls are continued for a substantial period after the war, it seems inevitable that a boom of substantial proportions will develop, to be followed by a cyclical collapse.

Basically, the reason for war and postwar inflation lies in the unwillingness or inability of governments to raise most of their necessary funds by taxation and noninflationary borrowing once a high level of wartime output has been achieved. Added to this is the fact that the burden of debt inherited from the war itself causes government treasuries to desire a continuation of a policy of low interest rates in the postwar period. Such a policy, when adopted by the central banks, encourages additional credit and monetary expansion that further contributes to postwar inflation.

Something of the magnitude of the monetary expansion and its relation to the changes in output and price level that took place during and after World War II may be seen in the experiences of the United States as shown in Table 32.

TABLE 32

War and Postwar Changes in Money, Output, and Prices in the United States, 1940-1953 (1940 = 100)

Year	Index of Supply of Money[a] (end of year)	Index of Annual Output[b]	Index of Prices[c] Annual Averages	
			Wholesale	Consumer
1940	100	100	100	100
1941	114	115	111	105
1942	148	130	125	116
1943	188	145	131	123
1944	214	156	131	125
1945	242	153	134	128
1946	258	136	154	139
1947	269	135	188	159
1948	264	142	204	171
1949	263	140	194	170
1950	278	154	201	171
1951	295	164	224	185
1952	305	171	218	189
1953	309	178	215	191

a. Adjusted demand deposits plus currency outside of banks, compiled from the *Federal Reserve Bulletin*.
b. Computed from the figures for the gross national product at constant dollars, *National Income Supplement, Survey of Current Business,* 1954 ed., p. 216.
c. Computed from price index data appearing in the *Federal Reserve Bulletin*.

Between the year-ends of 1940 and 1945, the money supply increased by a little over 140 per cent while the output was increasing only 53 per cent. The fact that prices rose only 30 per cent is evidence of the restraining influence of price controls that were in force during the period.

Between the end of 1945 and the end of 1951 the supply of money increased by a little over 20 per cent and output increased by a little less than 8 per cent. In the meantime, with controls largely abandoned, prices at wholesale rose 67 per cent and consumer prices rose 44 per cent. Altogether, between the end of 1940 and the end of 1953, the money supply increased by 209 per cent, output by 78 per cent, and prices at wholesale by 115 per cent.

Questions for Study

1. Why is it inevitable that governments borrow during wars?

2. Why, in practice, is wartime borrowing generally inflationary? What do you think of the proposal for compulsory savings through payroll deductions?

3. To what extent was monetary expansion useful during the early months of World War II?

4. Why is it easy to justify a low-interest-rate policy during wars? Under such a policy, what steps are required to prevent undue private investment? Why does this policy create credit policy problems in the postwar period?

5. What reasons can be given to justify selective price controls? Why did they prove inadequate? What is the "inflationary gap"?

6. In general, how successful were efforts to control prices during World War II? What sound reasons can you give for the attempt?

7. It is sometimes argued that wartime price control only postponed and did not reduce the ultimate magnitude of price inflation. Is this true?

8. Why are postwar periods so often characterized by inflation?

_34_

Monetary Problems
Following World War II

Dual nature of postwar monetary problems. Monetary problems following a war involve two main questions. The first is how to deal effectively with domestic inflation. The second involves the establishment of satisfactory relationships between the domestic and foreign currencies so that trade with other nations may be carried on effectively. The second question, obviously, cannot be entirely divorced from the first, for stabilization of the foreign exchange values of a country's currency requires first the introduction of a reasonable degree of stabilization of the currency's home value.

Restoration and Collapse of Currencies After World War I

After the inflation and collapse of prices that followed World War I, a gradual movement toward monetary and exchange stability was undertaken. Budgets were brought into balance, belatedly in some cases, and a general restoration of the gold standard was accomplished. But the financial crises and collapse of the 1930's proved too severe to be handled by the automatic workings of the gold standard. Especially troublesome were the international war debts and the short-term international interbank balances that lent themselves to the devastating capital flight that grew out of the crises and general loss of confidence. The results were: (1) the suspension of gold payments by England and the other Sterling Area countries and the depreciation of their currencies in terms of gold; (2) the abandonment of gold convertibility, the adoption of exchange controls, and the appearance of overvalued currencies in Germany and certain other central European countries; and (3) the devaluation of the United States dollar and a determined though futile attempt on the part of France, Belgium, Italy, the Netherlands, Luxemburg, and Switzerland (the European Gold Bloc) to maintain gold convertibility at the old parities. The Gold Bloc collapsed in 1936.

Therefore, by the end of the 1930's, before the outbreak of World War II, the world's monetary systems fell into three main patterns. The first included the countries, both within and outside of the Sterling Area, that had abandoned the gold standard in favor of the freedom offered by independent paper currencies and flexible exchange rates. These countries imposed little direct control over foreign exchange dealings, being mainly content to maintain stability in a relatively free exchange market.

The second pattern involved currencies that were no longer convertible into gold but whose foreign exchange value was maintained at a fixed level in terms of gold. Countries with this type of currency system commonly pursued a policy of economic expansion. Inevitably such a policy tended to make the currency "overvalued" in the foreign exchange markets. The consequent shrinkage of exports created such difficulties in the balance of payments as to require the imposition of strict exchange controls. Germany provided the outstanding example of this type.

Finally, there was the gold standard currency of the United States. Although the fixed gold parity of the dollar had been reduced, the free import and export of gold was permitted. Because it stood practically alone, the United States was free to adopt such price and credit policies as seemed best suited to its purposes.

Domestic Currency Problems Arising Out of World War II

The inflation of prices, 1939-1948. During World War II, currency inflation followed the usual wartime pattern. Because of the difficulty involved in making revenues rise as fast as expenditures, governments were compelled to borrow vast sums. Part of the borrowing was from the commercial and the central banks and resulted in a rising quantity of bank deposit and note currency. The currencies of countries that were occupied by enemy forces were further disorganized by the addition of occupation currencies, whose issue bore little relation to the currency needs of the country concerned. The rigid price controls commonly used during the war aided in preventing prices from rising as they would have risen had controls been absent, yet black market prices rose to fantastic heights, reflecting both a scarcity of goods in the legal markets and the superabundance of currency.

Some measure of the inflation during World War II can be obtained from the official wholesale price indexes of various countries shown below in Table 33. These index numbers fail to indicate accurately the true extent of the increases in prices since they represent the "official" prices and do not allow for black market price changes.

Postwar inflation. Many of the monetary problems that plagued

TABLE 33
Official Wholesale Prices in Warring Countries *

	U.S.	Canada	United Kingdom	France	Japan	The Netherlands
1939........	100	100	100	100	100	100
1940........	102	110	133	132	111	124
1941........	113	120	148	162	118	142
1942........	128	128	154	191	127	149
1943........	133	133	158	222	134	152
1944........	135	137	161	252	150	156
1945........	137	138	164	357	198	172
1946........	157	145	170	617	1,031	239
1947........	197	172	186	941	3,292	258
1948........	214	204	212	1,630	8,973	267
1949........	203	208	226	1,825	14,626	277
1950........	211	222	254	1,972	17,228	312
1951........	236	253	309	2,526	24,047	382
1952........	230	236	315	2,640	24,406	373
1953........	224	232	315	2,526	24,585	357
1954........	224	228	318	2,477	24,406	363

* Yearly averages of prices computed from data appearing in the *Federal Reserve Bulletin.*

the world after World War I reappeared after World War II. Again, many governments seemed unable to bring their budgets into balance, and the resulting deficits brought continued inflationary pressure on the price levels. With the gradual breakdown or removal of rationing and price controls, the currency expansion of the war years burst from the restraints that had held it in check. It was little wonder, then, that acute inflation reappeared in the war-torn countries of Europe. Even the United States, which brought its budget into balance and reduced its government debt, did not escape the inflation movement. Private spending of wartime savings and new bank borrowings by business and consumers swelled the spending stream faster than output could be increased.

The evil consequences of "hyperinflation," as it has sometimes been called, are of course well known. Speculation becomes a more absorbing interest than production. Important groups within the economy are impoverished and others are unfairly enriched. Moreover, the inflation, when once under way, tends to become self-perpetuating because of the mounting difficulties of achieving a balanced governmental budget through adequate taxation.

The nature of the problem of internal stabilization. After World War II, the problem of internal price and currency stabilization was acute. The problem was made worse by the prolonged occupation of many countries and the accompanying expansion of the currency. Furthermore, there arose a wide discrepancy between controlled official prices and prices in the black market. Controlled wages, tied to a level in harmony with controlled commodity prices, failed miserably to provide adequate incentives for work when fantastically high black market prices diverted much of the available supply of goods away from the legal markets. In Germany, barter transactions took the place of trade involving the use of reichmarks and, by the spring of 1947, one-half of all commerce in the Anglo-American zone was reported to be on a barter basis.[1]

Steps toward monetary reform. The attempts to reform the currencies after World War II generally involved two steps. First came the blocking of existing cash and deposits of the public so as to take them from the actual or potential spending stream. The

---

[1] Cf. Klopstock, Fred H., "Monetary Reform in Western Germany," *Journal of Political Economy,* August 1949.

second step involved the disposition of the blocked funds. The second step was more difficult than the first, for it involved the determination of how much cash should be released to care for legitimate business requirements at the level of prices sought to be maintained. The release of too much purchasing power would nullify the anti-inflationary effects; too little would create economic deflation and unemployment.

The blocking process involved: (1) fixing a date before which all currencies to be blocked were to be deposited; (2) invalidating all currency not deposited by the stated deadline; and (3) blocking all bank deposits. After the blocking operation was completed, limited amounts of new currency and a fraction of the blocked deposits were released. Generally, in Western Europe, holders of old currency and deposits received in exchange claims upon an equal amount of the new. However, only a part of the new currency was made immediately available. The remainder was withheld in order to reduce the supply of outstanding purchasing power to the desired level. The release of blocked funds was carried out gradually, but generally a part was blocked permanently and earmarked for some form of special taxation or conversion into government securities. For example, under the "Plan Gutt," the coins, bank notes, and bank deposits blocked in Belgium after its liberation in 1944 amounted to 155 billion francs. Of this amount, 57.4 billions were released at once, 39.1 billions were temporarily blocked but earmarked for gradual release, and 58.8 billions were permanently withdrawn and earmarked for absorption by taxation or conversion into government securities.[2]

In France, a somewhat different pattern was followed. In June 1945, it was announced that notes of all denominations of 50 francs or over were exchangeable, franc for franc, for a new issue. Neither the currency nor the bank deposits were blocked. Certain types of government bonds were required to be stamped or exchanged for new instruments. This "photographing" of the public's holdings of currency and state bonds facilitated an expected program of capital taxation.[3] In this act of conversion the customary attempt to reduce

---

[2] Bareau, Paul, "Reconstruction in the Low Countries," *Lloyds Bank Review,* January 1947. Also cf. Gurley, J. G., "Excess Liquidity and Monetary Reforms," *American Economic Review,* March 1953.

[3] Snider, D. A., "French Monetary and Fiscal Policies," *American Economic Review,* June 1948, pp. 314-315.

the volume of currency was absent; therefore it could hardly have been expected to have any direct anti-inflationary consequences.

Monetary reform in Western Germany. Among the many currency reforms, that instituted by the Military Governments in Western Germany deserves special notice. The purpose of this reform was to shrink the currency supply to proportions appropriate for the productivity of the region. Specifically, as of June 21, 1948, all the old money, except that of a denomination up to one mark, was declared invalid. Deposits in banks were blocked for the time being. To provide an immediate supply of valid money, 40 new marks per capita were paid out to individuals in exchange for an equal amount of the old invalidated marks on presentation of food ration and identity cards. Two months later, an additional 20 marks per capita were released. Business enterprises received advances of new marks for old in amounts of not over sixty marks per employee. All remaining old marks both in currency and bank deposits were required to be registered by June 26.[4] On June 26, the Allied Military Governors of the American, French, and British Zones announced that old marks were convertible at the rate of ten old for one new deutsche mark. One half of the new deutsche marks were credited to a "free account," which could be withdrawn at once. The other half of the new marks were placed in blocked accounts for later release from time to time as economic conditions justified. Seventy per cent of these blocked marks were wiped out by cancellation in the following October. Steps were also taken to prevent the conversion of funds arising from illegal earnings. Debts unpaid on June 21 could be settled by paying the creditor one new deutsch mark for every ten old marks due.[5]

The purposes behind the German currency reform were (1) to eliminate the black market profit; and (2) to reduce the volume of currency to a level at which controlled prices would match existing purchasing power. The effects upon the economy of Western Germany were gratifying. Production for sale in regular markets

[4] *New York Times,* June 19, 1948.

[5] *New York Times,* June 27, 1948. Although each individual received 60 new deutsche marks in exchange for old, out of any additional holdings of old reichmarks he could convert at the 10:1 ratio only such amounts as exceeded 540 reichmarks. In other words, the 60-mark advance was charged against his conversion privilege. Cf. Klopstock, *op. cit.*

again became profitable, and incentives to productive effort were markedly increased.

The Problem of Restoring Multilateral Trade

The breakdown of normal international trade which began during the depression years of the 1930's was accentuated by the outbreak of war, for the war not only caused a breach in the trade relations with enemy countries but also caused trade among allies to assume new forms and to take new directions. Consequently, the postwar period found international trade in a state of unparalleled confusion and dislocation. This situation was most unfortunate. Political reconstruction and stability depended largely upon the economic recovery of war-devastated countries. Economic recovery, in turn, called for both internal currency stability and a revival of a healthy international trade.

In general, countries obtain the maximum benefit from trade that is multilateral in nature, since only through such trade can the advantages of international specialization be best realized.[6] Multilateral trade, unlike narrow bilateralism, enables a country to sell in the best (highest-priced) foreign markets and buy in the best (cheapest) markets. It does not require trade between each pair of countries to be equal. Instead, multilateral trade, functioning properly, merely requires that combined exports of one country to the outside world shall equal its combined imports. The advantages of multilateral trade of this sort can be readily appreciated if one looks at the trade of individuals in the domestic market. Normally an individual need not concern himself about attempting to equalize the amount of his purchases from and sales to another individual. Such action, indeed, would constitute an abandonment of the benefits of the use of money and a retreat to simple barter. So great are the gains from the use of money that

---

[6] Some deny that general multilateral trade is necessary in order to obtain the greatest advantages from international specialization. See Bernstein, E. M., "British Policy and World Recovery," *American Economic Review,* December 1945, pp. 892-893, for an examination of this view. Also see Balogh, T., "The Dollar Crisis Revisited," *Oxford Economic Papers,* September 1954, for a reiteration of his position that Britain's dollar shortage is due to dynamic progress in the United States that has outstripped the rest of the world. This, he holds, requires a British commercial policy of quantitative discriminatory control along with a continuation of exchange controls. He concludes that for Britain the best policy is one in which a dollar shortage is consciously induced.

barter will be used only when (1) the money system has collapsed (perhaps because of extreme inflation); or (2) economic dislocations prevent the individual from finding for his products purchasers able to offer adequate money payments.

The requirements for multilateralism. In both domestic and international trade, multilateral exchange requires an adequate supply of generally acceptable currency. Domestic trade requires enough domestic currency to enable the public to withstand the irregularities of incomes and expenditures and to carry on normal economic operations. Foreign trade requires an ample supply of *internationally* acceptable currency. Each country must have access to such currency in amounts adequate to meet the seasonal and cyclical irregularities in its balance of payments. Such currency may be called *international currency reserves.* These reserves consist of internationally acceptable currencies of which a country may freely dispose to meet an adverse balance of payments. They include excess gold reserves of central banks, gold held by stabilization funds, and foreign currencies that are acceptable in other countries in settlement of foreign trade balances. Under the gold standard, settlements for multilateral trade could be made by shipping gold or by drafts on balances carried in gold standard countries. After 1931, the Sterling Area countries accepted pound sterling from each other in settlement of trade balances. Today, countries able to acquire adequate amounts of gold or American dollars possess a highly acceptable form of international currency reserves.

The breakdown of multilateral trade. In the 1930's, multilateral trade broke down because of balance-of-payments difficulties arising from the depression. To solve the problem of adverse trade balances, some countries attempted to obtain necessary imports by barter or bilateral trade. After World War II, similar difficulties stood in the way of a restoration of multilateral trade. Many countries found it impossible to produce and sell abroad, for internationally acceptable currencies, enough goods to pay for their desired imports. In other words, they were unable to acquire adequate amounts of international currency reserves to enable them to restore unrestricted multilateral trade. This difficulty was especially apparent in connection with the shortage of dollars and other "hard currencies." [7] Actually, hard currencies, especially dollars and gold convertible into dollars, constitute the only generally acceptable international currency of the postwar period. The continuation of bilateral trading during this period largely reflects this dollar shortage.

Much attention has been given to the problem of restoring multilateral trade. The prerequisites for multilateralism include (1) a solution of the balance-of-payments problem of individual countries; and (2) the provision of adequate supplies of international currency reserves.

The consequences of war on the balance of payments. Countries at war, anxious to muster their maximum economic forces, tend to restrict their commercial exports and expand their imports. Belligerents must pay for their excess of imports by exporting gold, liquidating readily saleable foreign securities, and borrowing abroad. Because the United States entered the war with ample unused resources and high excess gold reserves, it was able to meet its needs with but a modest adverse balance of payments and gold losses. Most belligerents, however, ended the war enmeshed in exchange controls, with their international currency reserves depleted, and with serious problems in respect to their balance of payments. There were a number of reasons for the appearance of adverse balances of payments after the war. The shift to a war economy often involved loss of old export markets, and the devastation of the war and its wastage reduced the capacity to produce for export. In addition, foreign investments that provided a source of income before the war were partially dissipated.

The British balance-of-payments problem. A good example of the postwar balance-of-payments problem is provided by Britain. During the war, Lend-Lease arrangements enabled her to acquire supplies from the United States without the necessity of providing equivalent exports. Thus she was able to divert a maximum part of her resources and effort directly to war purposes. This policy caused such a decline in exports that by 1944 their volume had fallen to 30 per cent of the 1938 level. The sudden end of the

---

[7] Hard currencies are those which are "hard to get" or for which the demand exceeds the supply. They include currencies convertible into gold and currencies of countries, mainly in the Western Hemisphere and Switzerland, whose exports are in great demand.

war in 1945, and with it the termination of Lend-Lease, found
Britain with current exports greatly reduced from their prewar
level at a time when she had an urgent need for normal imports
of raw materials and food. The situation was made worse by the
sharp reduction in earnings from overseas investments, from shipping, and from other services normally sold to foreign countries
in the prewar period.

The change in Britain's balance-of-payments position is clearly
revealed by the comparison between the years 1938 and 1947,
which is given in Table 34.

TABLE 34
British Balance Of Payments On Current Account *
(In millions of pounds)

	1938	1947
Trade:		
Imports (f.o.b.)	835	1,574
Exports and re-exports (f.o.b.)	533	1,125
Adverse trade balance	302	449
"Invisibles":		
Government expenditure overseas	16	211
Net income from investments	175	51
Net income from shipping	20	17
Net income from other items	53	− 83
Income or loss (−) on invisibles	232	− 226
Over-all deficit	70	675

* *Labor and Industry in Britain, A Quarterly Review,* March 1948, British Information Services.

The 1947 deficit of 675 million pounds was entirely owed to
the Western Hemisphere and was payable in hard currencies, mainly
United States and Canadian dollars. Expressed in dollars, it
amounted to $2.7 billion. Additional drain was put upon the
British dollar supply by other members of the Sterling Area,[8] who
were permitted to draw against the dollar pool to finance their
current imports requiring payment in dollars. Furthermore, under
the Anglo-American Loan Agreement of 1946, Britain undertook,

---

[8] The Sterling Area includes all the independent countries of the British Com-
monwealth (except Canada), the United Kingdom colonies and dependencies, and
six non-Commonwealth countries: Burma, Iceland, Iraq, the Irish Republic, Jor-
dan, and Libya.

with misgivings, the obligation to convert into dollars all pound sterling currently earned by foreign countries after July 15, 1947. As a result of Britain's commitments to other Sterling Area countries, and under the provisions of the Anglo-American loan, she was called upon to pay out $1.4 billion above her own deficit of $2.7 billion. Altogether, in 1947, Britain lost about $4.0 billion. These losses were met by (1) reducing the existing holdings of gold and dollars; (2) drawing on American and Canadian credits; and (3) drawing on the International Monetary Fund. Clearly, such payments were essentially "stop-gap" in nature and could not be relied upon as a continuous policy.

Possible Solutions to the Postwar Balance-of-Payments Problems

The balance-of-payments problem of Britain, and other countries as well, had to be solved before necessary economic expansion and recovery could be properly realized. In some manner or other, debit and credit items had to be brought into balance. There were a number of ways of attacking the problem.

Curtailment of imports. One possible solution involved a rigid curtailment of imports until they no longer exceeded exports. This might have been accomplished by tariffs, import quotas, or exchange controls. But such a method was highly objectionable as an immediate solution because it sharply reduced the chances of a future rise in productivity and an expansion of exports based thereon, for imports are largely foodstuffs and industrial raw materials. Without reasonably adequate amounts of both, economic reconstruction would be hamstrung. Clearly, then, unless a sizable quantity of *unnecessary* imports could be pruned away, there was little promise in this approach.

Monetary restraint. One obvious method of approach to the problem of correcting an adverse balance of payments is through a monetary policy of credit restraint. In fact, so long as exchange rates are fixed, this is the only way for restoring equilibrium in the balance of payments without resort to tariffs or the use of arbitrary quota and exchange rationing limitations on imports. But during the immediate postwar period, when economic reconstruction and expansion was imperative, a shrinkage of imports through internal deflation was intolerable. However, after 1952, with economic rehabilitation and recovery achieved, Britain and the Western European countries have applied gradual monetary restraint to check the rising internal inflation that was threatening their balance-of-payments position with the United States, Canada, and other dollar area countries of the Western Hemisphere. Evidence of this application of monetary restraint appeared in the rise in the Bank of England discount rate from 2 per cent at the end of 1949 to 4 per cent early in 1952 and to 5½ per cent in 1956. Similarly the Bank of France and the West German central banks raised their rates and imposed restraint upon their money supply.

Bilateral trade agreements. The crux of the postwar balance-of-payments problem lay in the adverse balance of Britain and other Sterling Area countries with the Western Hemisphere. The United States, Canada, and Latin America could provide an abundant supply of goods badly wanted by the rest of the industrialized world, but they were unable or unwilling to import amounts sufficient to provide adequate amounts of dollars and other hard currencies. Consequently there developed a chronic shortage of dollars. In other words, the balance-of-payments problem was to a very considerable degree one of dollar scarcity. One solution was to seek imports from countries that do not require payment in dollars. To accomplish this Britain negotiated numerous bilateral trade agreements with countries both inside and outside the Sterling Area, whereby certain amounts of raw materials and foodstuffs would be provided in return for certain British exports. Britain's power to make such agreements on favorable terms lay in the importance of British markets for the exporters of many raw material countries. Such a solution to the balance-of-payments problem was, of course, a step away from international multilateral trade and was doubtless inferior to a working system of multilateralism. But it was justified on the grounds that it provided trade that would not otherwise have existed at all.[9] American traders, of course, object

---

[9] For a good treatment of the purpose and nature of postwar bilateralism, see Judd Polk and Gardner Patterson, "The Emerging Pattern of Bilateralism," *Quarterly Journal of Economics,* November 1947. See also *A Survey of the Economic Situation and Prospects of Europe,* United Nations, Department of Economic Affairs, Geneva, 1948.

to such bilateral trading agreements because they tend to reduce foreign purchases from United States sources.

Exchange depreciation. Another available solution is exchange depreciation. This device may be used to check imports and to expand exports. But so long as the limiting factors on exports were lack of raw materials and inadequate productive facilities rather than high prices, such a corrective could offer no real gain. So long as the sellers' market continued in the postwar world, exchange depreciation was an undesirable tool for correcting an adverse balance of payments. Instead of being a benefit it would have unnecessarily worsened the "terms of trade" with the outside world by raising the cost of imported goods and raw materials while reducing the returns from exports at a time when all exports could be easily sold without devaluation if they could be produced.[10] But in September 1949 Britain, the other Sterling Area countries, and the countries of Western Europe succumbed to the pressure and devalued their currencies. This step was taken reluctantly and

---

[10] This conclusion of course assumes that the internal problem of diverting current output from the high-priced domestic market into export channels could be accomplished without exchange depreciation.

For a strong denial that exchange depreciation is a useful and acceptable method of attacking the adverse balance-of-payments problem of postwar England and Western Europe, see Balogh, Thomas, "Exchange Depreciation and Economic Readjustment," *The Review of Economics and Statistics,* November 1948. He holds that neither of the two most important probable causes of adverse balances of England and Western Europe with the Western Hemisphere can properly be overcome by exchange depreciation. First, the "structural changes" in the productive facilities of the various parts of the world, which occurred during the war, have put the United States far ahead in efficiency and competitive advantage in world markets. Exchange depreciation, he holds, would merely permanently depress the income levels of the less fortunate countries. Only protective devices such as discrimination and bilateral trade will enable such countries to re-establish their productivity through improved techniques and new industries so as to be able, ultimately, to compete in outside markets. Second, there is the danger that an economic slump in the United States will so check American imports as to impose an adverse balance upon other countries, which cannot successfully be met by exchange depreciation. The elasticity of demand for United States imports, in such a case, is likely to be too small to enable outside countries to expand the value of their sales to America by exchange depreciation. Moreover, exchange depreciation practiced by individual countries in an attempt to improve the balance of payments is likely to set off either competitive depreciation or a round of deflation in other countries. He quotes, with approval, the argument that devaluation, being a blunt and indiscriminate instrument, is less desirable as a method for correcting adverse balances than selective policies (*i.e.,* discrimination). Cf. also Balogh, Thomas, "The Dollar Crises Revisited," *Oxford Economic Papers,* September 1954.

under considerable pressure from the United States as a means of reducing the dollar shortage.

Loans and grants. Finally, there is the method of meeting the postwar problem of international disequilibrium that was actually used. This involved introducing loans and grants-in-aid on the credit side of the balance of payments of the countries concerned. Clearly, loans and unilateral transfers (grants) by the United States Government provided a timely and most fortunate short-run solution to the postwar problems of countries unable, through exports, to earn enough dollars to purchase the imports needed for their economic rehabilitation and recovery. This aid enabled the receivers to obtain a vast quantity of American goods with which to repair the ravages of war. As a result, productive and export capacity has been so restored as to lift income far above prewar standards and justify serious consideration of the abandonment of controls and the restoration of multilateral trade on a free exchange basis. Such action, of course, requires that any necessary steps be taken to assure the existence of fundamental balance-of-payments equilibrium. The problems, and their possible solutions, arising from a gradual movement in the direction of free multilateral trade with currency convertibility are explored in the next chapter.

Questions for Study

1. After World War I, what was the major step taken to reform the currencies of the world? What was the final outcome of this attempt at reform and stabilization?

2. What were the three types of currency systems found in the world before the outbreak of World War II?

3. Examine Table 33 on page 581. Can you see the results of price controls during the war period? Why the sharp upswing in U. S. prices after 1945? How did our postwar price level behavior compare with that of Canada? France?

4. After World War II some countries reformed their currencies by blocking and cancelling off a large fraction of the total supply. What did this do to the black market prices? How did it affect workers' incentives?

5. What is multilateral trade? Why is it superior to the bilateral trading of the postwar years?

6. What are the basic prerequisites for restoration of multilateral trade? Why did the war complete its breakdown in the world at large?

7. Examine Table 34 on page 588. Can you explain why the British balance of payments with the hard currency or dollar areas was so adverse in the postwar period? Why did its position as banker for the Sterling Area complicate its position? How did it meet its deficits of 1947?

8. A number of methods could have been used to bring the balance of payments of England and Western European countries into equilibrium with the dollar area in the early postwar period.

   a) What various methods might have been used?
   b) What valid objections could be made to many of them?
   c) What did the countries themselves do to bring their import-export position into balance?
   d) What did the aid granted by the U. S. Government accomplish? Why did it make a fundamental contribution to the basic improvement to the balance-of-payments position of the countries that received it?

between — and Western European countries into equilibrium with the dollar area in the early postwar period.

—————35

Steps Toward Multilateralism and Currency Convertibility

In Chapter 34 we examined a number of alternatives that
were available for the solution of the postwar balance-of-payments
problem and that might contribute to the restoration of international
economic equilibrium and the expansion of trade. In this chapter
we shall examine some of the actual developments of the postwar
years and their contributions.

The Devaluation of Currencies in 1949

In an earlier chapter dealing with exchange depreciation we
studied the results that might be expected from devaluation, and the
reasons behind its use. It will be helpful to examine again the 1949
experience as a contribution to the solution of the postwar problems.

Although currency devaluation seemed inappropriate in the early
postwar years, when shortage of exportable goods rather than overvaluation seemed responsible for the dollar shortage, later conditions made it inevitable. In September 1949, Britain reduced the
exchange value of the pound from approximately $4.00 to $2.80.
Other Sterling Area countries and the countries of Western Europe
also devalued their currencies in terms of dollars. As production
expanded in the postwar world and brought an end to the sellers'
market, it became increasingly difficult for the soft (overvalued)
currency countries to sell their products in the dollar area markets.
American loans and grants-in-aid enabled them to obtain vast
quantities of imports, highly necessary for postwar rehabilitation,

that could not have been purchased and paid for with exports alone. In spite of this aid the deficit of the Sterling Area and Western Europe caused continued drains upon their dollar and gold reserves. Overvalued currencies, therefore, required correction both to check international currency losses and to strengthen their foreign exchange position against the time when foreign aid would end.

Objections to the devaluation of 1949. The effectiveness of the devaluation of 1949 in restoring equilibrium in the balance of payments of the countries practicing it has been much disputed. At least four objections have been raised. First, it is argued that foreign demand for British goods is inelastic in relation to price changes, while the British demand for imports, largely foodstuffs and industrial raw materials, is likewise inelastic. Therefore it is hopeless to attempt to improve the balance of payments by exchange depreciation which cheapens exports and increases the cost of imports. Exchange depreciation with inelastic demand, it is assumed, would result in a fall in the total value of exports and a rise in the total value of imports. Statistical studies of the response of United States imports to relative price level changes have sometimes tended to support the contention that our imports respond mainly to changes in U. S. industrial production and little, if any, to changes in the foreign prices of importable goods in relation to United States prices. Later studies, however, indicate that although changes in industrial production explain changes in the aggregate quantity of United States imports of *crude* and *semi-manufactured* goods, mainly of the sort not domestically produced, changes in relative prices of *manufactured* goods substantially affect imports of such commodities. Consequently, the devaluation of the pound and other Western European currencies should be credited with contributing genuine improvement in the exports, mainly finished manufactures, of Britain and Western Europe to the United States.[1]

Second, against devaluation it is argued that the increased cost of raw materials and of imported foodstuffs will certainly generate

---

[1] For a useful study of the question, see John H. Alder, Eugene R. Schlesinger, and Evelyn Van Westerborg's *The Pattern of United States Import Trade Since 1925, Some New Index Series and Their Application,* Federal Reserve Bank of New York, 1952. Also, in support of the effectiveness of exchange depreciation as a corrective of adverse balances of payments, see Orcutt, Guy H., "Exchange Rate Adjustment and Relative Size of the Depreciating Bloc," *Review of Economics and Statistics,* February 1955.

such increases in industrial costs, including wages, as to defeat whatever corrective results might appear. As to this point, one can only say that this argument rests upon the assumption that labor will refuse to accept the reduction of living standards that are necessary if the country is to live within its income. In actual fact, weekly wages in England failed to rise in proportion to the devaluation of the pound during the first three years after the devaluation of 1949. It seems likely, therefore, that the costs of British exports and of domestic import substitutes did not rise enough to prevent some favorable results on the British balance of payments.

Third, the objection is made that even though devaluation should restore equilibrium in the balance of payments, a subsequent depression in the United States, long expected in some circles abroad, would again result in the overvaluation of the pound and other soft currencies and require still further devaluation. The decline in business activity in the United States in 1949 did indeed prove embarrassing to the balance-of-payments situation of Britain and Western Europe. Nevertheless, because of the well-balanced economic growth and the economic strength of those areas since 1949, they were able to weather the United States recession of 1953-1954 without trouble.[2]

Finally, it is contended by the more enthusiastic advocates of government planning of economic affairs that a balance of payments brought into equilibrium by exchange depreciation is intolerable because it involves a worsening of the terms of trade against countries trading with the United States. Therefore discriminatory controls to direct British trade toward less efficient areas would bring more favorable results.[3]

---

[2] Cf. *Annual Report*, 1954, The Federal Reserve Bank of New York, pp. 9-12.

[3] The difficulties confronting European countries whose technical improvements lag behind those of the United States are well illustrated by the analogy used by D. H. Robertson when he likened them to the cook who prepared meals for the gifted scientist, to the advantage of both. When the scientist invented a completely automatic cooker the erstwhile cook found himself relegated to the position of bootblack with obvious reduction in status. When the scientist invented a "dust-repelling shoe," the shoeblack is further demoted to the job of emptying trash cans. Each time, the new technology of the scientist reduced the importance and the value of the services of the man who originally had a reasonable livelihood from his job as cook. Consequently, the terms of trade had turned more and more against him. It might be better, therefore, for him to give up altogether the idea of trading with the scientist and cultivate trade with others who are technically less sophisticated. *Britain in the World Economy*, London, George Allen and Unwin, Ltd., 1954, pp. 58-59.

Favorable results of devaluation. Such evidence as we have suggests that devaluation did in fact help to reduce the pressure upon the balance of payments with the dollar area. Certainly it offered a bonus to British and Western European traders to cultivate and invade the American markets. Certainly it offered a real incentive to search for satisfactory imports from other soft-currency areas to replace the more costly imports from the Western Hemisphere. In fact, since the devaluation in 1949, the Sterling Area gold and dollar reserves have shown a substantial improvement despite a sharp reduction in the receipts of foreign aid. To be sure, the improvement cannot be entirely credited to devaluation alone. The Korean War raised, for a time, the prices of many raw materials supplied by members of the Sterling Area. Also, imports from the dollar area were put under more severe quantitative restriction, and later, central bank credit policies were tightened with salutary effects upon the internal inflationary conditions within the soft-currency countries.

Even though the combined effects of devaluation, import restraints, and tighter money have substantially improved the position of the Sterling Area and Western Europe, it is by no means certain that the world is yet ready for a restoration of free exchange and multilateral trade.

Postwar International Loans and Grants

Since the end of World War II a vast amount of foreign aid has been extended in the form of credits and outright grants. The United States has provided the largest part of this aid. Canada is the second largest lender by virtue of having extended over two billion dollars in postwar credits. Other important contributors to the supply of foreign loans are Sweden, the United Kingdom, Argentina, and Switzerland.[4]

Up to December 31, 1955, United States postwar assistance to foreign countries amounted to about 53 billion. Roughly half of this was for nonmilitary aid and was extended before the outbreak of war in Korea. Table 35 below gives a general picture of the

---

[4] Cf. Kriz, M. A., "Postwar International Lending," *Essays in International Finance*, No. 8, Princeton University, Spring 1948.

magnitude and nature of the foreign assistance program of the
United States through 1955.

TABLE 35

United States Credits and Grants-in-aid to Foreign Countries, July 1, 1945–December 31, 1955 *

Net credits—nonmilitary		$10,973,000,000
Net grants-in-aid:		
Nonmilitary	$26,240,000,000	
Military	15,744,000,000	
Total net grants		41,984,000,000
Total Net Credits and Grants		$52,957,000,000

* Source: *Survey of Current Business,* U.S. Department of Commerce, October
1954, p. 9, April 1955, p. 10, and April 1956, pp. 11-12. These figures do not
include the capital investment of $3.4 billion made by the Government in the
International Bank for Reconstruction and Development and in the International
Monetary Fund.

Except for the military aid, our assistance program was established to provide humanitarian relief and to promote improvement
in foreign economic and political conditions. Starving, impoverished populations have required assistance to remain alive. In
addition, enlightened self-interest has dictated the granting of aid
for the economic recovery of Europe and the assisting in the economic development of other areas of the world. Not only has the
United States stood to gain from trade with a world restored to
economic health, but also such a world promises to be a stouter
bulwark against expanding Communism. The basic soundness and
effectiveness of our contribution of economic and military aid to
the free world has been demonstrated by the recovery of economic
health and independence in Western Europe and the emergence
of NATO as a genuine barrier to aggression in that area.

Long-term International Capital Movements and Multilateral Trade: The World Bank

A successful solution of the balance-of-payments problem of the
postwar world does not necessarily require that the imports and
exports of individual countries be equal. On the contrary, international multilateral trade has always been carried on with the

aid of long-term capital movements between countries. Capital-hungry areas borrow as a matter of course from countries blessed with an abundance of productive and lending power. In the past the bulk of the peacetime capital transfers have been carried out by private financial agencies. But the restoration of an adequate level of international investment through private channels appears to be unlikely in the face of present-day conditions. Credit risks of loans to foreign firms and governments in many instances are impossibly high for private lenders to assume. These risks grow out of the uncertainties of economic prospects of foreign borrowers in the postwar world and the added threat that balance-of-payments difficulties in the borrowing country may lead to the imposition of exchange controls and the blocking of both principal and interest payments.

The International Bank for Reconstruction and Development. In anticipation of the probabilities that private international investment would prove inadequate for the needs of the postwar world, provision was made under the Bretton Woods Agreements of 1944 for the establishment of the International Bank for Reconstruction and Development. The purposes of the Bank are to promote the international flow of long-term capital, to encourage an expansion of world trade, and to assist in the maintenance of equilibrium in the balance of payments of member countries. Unlike the postwar intergovernmental grants and loans, which are based upon the necessities of current circumstances rather than on the prospects of repayment, the loans of the International Bank are intended to be made on a sound basis with reasonable certainty of repayment. In each case the Bank must be satisfied that the over-all effect of a loan, combined with the resources and efforts of the borrowing country, will be to improve the economic position of the country sufficiently to give reasonable assurance that the money needed for repayment will be available.

In 1956, fifty-eight countries were members of the Bank. To become members countries must (1) belong to the International Monetary Fund; and (2) subscribe to a certain minimum number of shares of the Bank's capital stock. The Bank's authorized capital was set at $10 billion and actual subscriptions by the fifty-eight members amounted to $9 billion in 1955. Of their total subscriptions member governments must pay in 2 per cent in gold and 18 per cent in their own currencies. The remaining subscription of 80 per cent is subject to call by the Bank should additional funds be required to meet the obligations of the Bank for funds borrowed by it or on loans which it has guaranteed.

The Bank's loan funds are derived from the following sources:

1. The paid-in capital of $1.8 billion.
2. Currencies borrowed by the Bank in the money markets of member countries whose funds are wanted by borrowing members.
3. Accumulated net profits of the Bank.

The Bank may assist members needing loans of foreign currencies in three ways: (1) it may lend the currency needed by the borrower directly out of the loan fund described above; (2) it may issue the Bank's own bonds in the money markets of the country whose currency is desired and lend the proceeds; or (3) it may assist by guaranteeing the borrower's note or promise to pay in order to enable it to borrow through private investment channels of the country whose currency is wanted. In addition, private investors may actively purchase loans previously made by the Bank, without the additional security of the Bank's guarantee.

The total loans and guarantees made by the Bank cannot exceed the amount of its unimpaired *subscribed* capital, or about $9.1 billion. Therefore, buyers of the Bank's bond issues (or issues guaranteed by the Bank) are given the double protection of the borrowing member's obligation, plus the claim against all members for their unpaid stock subscription. In addition, the Bank accumulates a reserve fund out of commissions of 1 per cent per annum charged on all loans and guarantees.

Whenever the Bank proposes to lend or aid in the lending of any member's currency, it must first obtain the member's permission. Furthermore, all loans made or guaranteed by the Bank must be made directly to a member country's government or must be fully guaranteed by that government, its central bank, or some comparable and acceptable agency.

During the postwar years the operations of the Bank have been overshadowed by the magnitude of intergovernmental credits and grants described earlier. Nevertheless, it has played a significant part in promoting sound international investment of a self-sustaining sort. By June 30, 1956, the Bank had granted loans of $2,667 million, of which nearly $2 billion had been actually disbursed. Of this, $526 million had been repaid or sold by the Bank to private investors. Of the total loans, $1,635 million were in U.S. dollars.[5]

In 1956, to expand the scope of its international cooperative investment program, the World Bank sponsored the creation of an affiliate, the International Finance Corporation. This organization, with thirty-one member countries and subscribed capital of $78,000,000 payable in gold or dollars, will supply venture capital to undeveloped areas. Unlike the loans of the World Bank, investments by the Corporation will not require government guarantees. It is hoped that contributions by the Corporation will encourage the flow of private funds into productive enterprises.

The Scarcity of International Currency Reserves

In the preceding sections we have studied the problems involved in the search for methods by which the "soft-currency" countries might achieve an equilibrium in their balance of payments without jeopardizing economic recovery. Until the balance-of-payments problem is successfully solved, there is little merit in seeking to promote international trade by attempting to impose general convertibility of currencies. The necessary first step toward a restoration of multilateral trade must be the development of conditions under which the tendency toward chronic adverse balances of important countries is corrected. Only then will a system of interconvertibility, based upon an adequate supply of international currency reserves, have a chance of success.

Regardless of the difficulties that have delayed the solution of the balance-of-payments problem, it is essential that progress toward multilateralism should not be hampered by lack of an adequate mechanism through which developing multilateral trade can be cleared. This goal requires provision for an adequate supply of some form of generally acceptable international currency reserves. Furthermore, it calls for a means of expanding the volume of such reserves available to individual countries to meet adverse

---

[5] *International Financial Statistics,* International Monetary Fund, December 1955, pp. 11-12.

payments balances arising from irregular, seasonal, and even cyclical changes. The old gold standard provided such flexibility in ordinary times through gold shipments and "equilibrating" movements of short-term capital. The British pound has provided a limited form of international currency reserves, permitting multilateral trading within the Sterling Area.

Bilateral trade. In the absence of adequate stocks of generally acceptable international currency reserves after the war, the countries of Western Europe and the United Kingdom managed to develop a sizable volume of trade through the use of bilateral trading agreements. Such agreements generally called for periodic settlements of accumulated adverse balances by payment in gold or by credits extended by the country having an export excess. At first, before the exhaustion of gold and established credits, trade developed along normal lines with little tendency to require equality of imports and exports between pairs of countries. Later, as the credits and gold supplies of debtor countries became exhausted, trade took on a more rigid and restrictive pattern. Because debtor countries could no longer settle for their imports, commodity surpluses accumulated in some countries.[6]

Steps toward multilateral European trade: The European Payments Union. The establishment of the European Payments Union (EPU) on July 1, 1950, was a positive and effective step in the direction of restoring free multilateral trade among the countries of Western Europe. As early as 1948 the newly formed Organization for European Economic Cooperation took tentative steps to develop multilateral arrangements for offsetting among European countries the accumulation of inconvertible bilateral balances. It was not until 1950 that the formal organization of the European Payments Union was completed. The Bank for International Settlements of Basel, Switzerland, was made the agent to administer the clearing operations.[7]

As we have seen, bilateral trade agreements governing most intra-European trade after the war were unable to equalize trade between each pair of countries. Consequently the credit allowances

---

[6] Cf. *A Survey of the Economic Situation and Prospects of Europe,* United Nations, Department of Economic Affairs, 1948, Geneva, pp. 99–100.

[7] Cf. Auboin, Roger, "The Bank for International Settlements, 1930–1955," *Essays in International Finance,* No. 22, Princeton University, May 1955.

included in these agreements were quickly exhausted and surplus countries (those with excessive exports to their bilateral partners) found themselves compelled to reduce exports, and as a result normal trade relations tended to break down. This shrinkage of trade arose even though the *net* imports and exports of a country with the whole European community might have shown an approximate balance in the absence of trade restraints. The EPU provided a way to clear debt and credit claims for the whole European community and, essentially, to re-establish multilateral trade relationships and reduce trade barriers required by strictly bilateral trading.

The EPU agreement established a quota for each member based on the size of its aggregate "visible" and "invisible" current transactions. Each country was given a top limit to the credit it could be required to *extend* to the EPU in case of an export surplus, and also a top limit to the credit it might receive from the EPU in case of an import surplus. At the end of each month the Bank for International Settlements, as clearing agent for the EPU, receives from each member country reports of its bilateral debt and credit balances with each of the other member countries. Thereupon the Bank calculates the net surplus or net deficit of each member with the *whole* of the EPU. Net deficits owed to the EPU are settled by the payment of 75 per cent in gold (or U.S. dollars) and 25 per cent by credit extended by the EPU. For net surpluses a member receives payment of 75 per cent in gold and 25 per cent in book credit with the EPU.[8] Whenever a deficit member country reaches its established limit of credit at the EPU, additional deficits must be paid entirely in gold unless private arrangements are made on the side. To give the EPU a capital fund the United States Government, as a part of its European aid program, undertook to make available to the Union as much as $350 million.

The EPU proved to be a most valuable aid to European recovery. By avoiding the necessity of matching imports and exports

---

[8] At the outset in 1950, deficit countries' maximum required gold payments to the EPU were put on a variable scale beginning at zero for the first 20 per cent of the quota and increasing to a point at which most gold payments were 40 per cent. The 75 per cent requirements of the agreement of 1955, which extended the life of the EPU, was thus a further step in the direction of full gold convertibility.

between each pair of countries under bilateral trade agreements, the Union's clearing activities permitted the reduction of trade barriers among its members and the reopening of the natural flow of goods.[9] Even so, not all discriminatory restraints upon trade were removed, for, so long as bilateral trade agreements continued, the appearance of a deficit with one partner that threatens the over-all position of a given country tends to invite restraint on trade with that partner as a ready means for correcting the trade balance. When and if complete multilateralism is restored through general convertibility, over-all measures such as restrictive monetary policy or exchange depreciation are more likely to be utilized as a means for maintaining balance-of-payment equilibrium.

The EPU was conceived as a temporary expedient to help break down the barriers to intra-European trade by introducing a system providing for a limited form of currency convertibility. From time to time the agreement under which it operates has been amended and renewed. Emphasis has been put upon the removal of restraints upon trade within the European community and with the dollar area. Efforts in this direction have resulted in a significant degree of cooperation among the member countries. Eventually the EPU's limited convertibility function should be replaced by general convertibility. In such a case there has been proposed the establishment of a European Fund able to extend short-term credits to Western European countries to enable them to maintain convertibility without resort to trade restrictions.

Multilateral Trade, Convertibility, and the International Monetary Fund

Clearly the abandonment of trade restrictions, the restoration of multilateral trade, and free currency convertibility are inseparable parts in the restoration of the world economy and its continued economic health and growth. We have examined some of the developments in the postwar world that have constituted progress in this direction. Let us now look at the prospects for complete multilateralism and currency convertibility in the free world. Our

---

9 Some evidence of the contribution of the EPU is the doubling of the volume of intra-European trade since 1948. Cf. *Monthly Review,* Federal Reserve Bank of New York, September, 1954, p. 121.

first step requires some acquaintance with the important international institution created in 1947 for the express purpose of encouraging the relaxation of trade restraints and the expansion of multilateral trade. This institution is the International Monetary Fund.

The International Monetary Fund. A product of the United Nations Conference at Bretton Woods in 1944, the International Monetary Fund was established on March 1, 1947. Just as the World Bank proved to be too modest a device to deal effectively with the postwar international loan situation, so the International Monetary Fund found itself confronted by economic dislocations, trade barriers, and exchange problems with which it was unable to cope. It has been criticized as being (1) too grandoise a plan for practical use in the real world; and (2) too moderate and tolerant an instrument to meet the necessities of the times. Nevertheless, its establishment was an important milestone on the road to international economic cooperation.

The purpose of the Fund is to permit stabilization of exchange rates on a freely convertible, multilateral basis while avoiding deflation and unemployment as a means of correcting an adverse balance of payments. Deficits in a country's balance of payments may be of two kinds. First, there are those which arise out of seasonal and irregular needs, such as the failure of a principal export crop. Similar, though more persisting, are adverse balances arising from cyclical fluctuations at home and abroad. Assuming that a country wishes to avoid deflation and follow a policy of full employment, it is necessary that it be sufficiently fortified with disposable international currency reserves to meet the adverse balances as they arise. If gold standard countries and countries committed to maintaining fixed exchange rates possess large gold reserves in excess of minimum requirements, they will have little trouble in meeting either seasonal or irregular adverse balances. Even gold losses arising from depression can be met successfully, except when the depression becomes prolonged and the adverse balance becomes very great. But countries that lack sizable amounts of surplus gold or other forms of international currency reserves must rely upon outside help. The International Monetary Fund can provide such help. In the second place, an adverse balance of payments may arise when a "fundamental disequilibrium has developed that will not be corrected by a normal reversal of seasonal and even cyclical conditions. In other words, the existing exchange rate "overvalues" the currency and thus promotes a *chronic* adverse balance. Two corrections for this condition are available. The correction necessary if exchange rates are to be held rigidly to the existing level is a fall in prices and internal depression. But such "disinflation," as it is sometimes called, was looked upon as objectionable in a world that was able vividly to recall the devastating depression of the 1930's and was anxious to restore economic health. Consequently, a second and more attractive method for correcting overvaluation, or "fundamental disequilibrium," was provided in the provision for exchange depreciation under rules and conditions designed to prevent competitive undervaluation or depreciation.

The composition of the International Monetary Fund. There were fifty-eight member countries in the Fund by 1956. To each member is assigned a "quota." This quota is important for a number of reasons. First, it determines the contributions that each member country must make to the common currency pool comprising the Fund. Second, it determines the amount that any member can draw from the Fund, since such withdrawals are limited to a certain fraction of a member's quota. Third, it determines the voting power of the member.

The total quotas of all members amount to $8.7 billion. Each original member was required to pay in gold an amount equal to 25 per cent of its quota or to 10 per cent of its official holdings of gold and United States dollars, whichever was the smaller. The remainder of its quota was paid in its own currency. Minimum gold subscriptions for new members are now determined by the Board of Governors of the Fund. The Fund's holdings of member currencies are carried on deposit with the central bank or other depositary in the respective member country. Members may substitute non-negotiable, noninterest-bearing demand securities for currency held by the Fund in excess of current requirements. Other assets of the Fund, including gold, are held in selected depositaries. Initially, one-half of such assets was held in the United States and at least 40 per cent in depositaries chosen by the four member countries having the next highest quotas.

The purchase of currencies from the Fund. Membership in the Fund entitles a country to "purchase" from the Fund the currencies of other members by transferring to the fund an equivalent amount of its own currency at the ruling par value. Thus members may increase their supply of foreign currencies needed to meet an adverse balance of payments of a temporary nature arising out of *current* foreign trade transactions. This means that within the limits governing purchases of other currencies, a country is protected from the necessity of paying out minimum gold reserves or of shrinking current imports down to the current export level to meet short-time inequalities in the balance of payments. Thus a buffer supply of international currency reserves is provided to members of the Fund to care for current fluctuations in the balance of payments arising from causes *other than fundamental disequilibrium*.

During any 12-month period, a member country may normally purchase foreign currencies in exchange for its own currency to an amount of not over 25 per cent of its quota. In addition, its total purchases are limited by the rule that, without special permission from the Fund, the Fund's holdings of a given country's currency cannot exceed 200 per cent of its quota. Therefore, if a country has paid 25 per cent of its quota in gold and 75 per cent in its own currency, it can offer its own currency in exchange for foreign currencies to the amount of 25 per cent in any one year and to the total amount of 125 per cent of its quota.

Because the privilege of purchasing foreign currencies from the Fund is meant to answer only the *current* needs of members, pressure is exercised to induce members to buy back as promptly as possible their currencies offered to the Fund in exchange for foreign funds. Two regulations are designed to accomplish this purpose. First, in addition to a service charge of one-half of 1 per cent made at the time of the purchase of a foreign currency, the Fund levies a charge on its holdings of a currency in excess of 100 per cent of the member's quota. Thus, should a member that has paid 75 per cent of its quota in its own currency wish to purchase other currencies from the Fund, no charge save the initial service charge would be levied except on purchases in excess of 25 per cent of the member's quota. The charge, when made, rises with the size and duration of the member's drawings against the

Fund, and is normally paid in gold. Second, not only are members *permitted* at any time to repurchase for gold any part of the Fund's holdings of their currencies in excess of their quotas, but also they are *required* to repurchase such excess holdings under certain stated conditions relating to their supplies of gold and foreign exchange reserves.

The choice of par values. Each member of the Fund is expected to adopt a par value for its currency in terms of gold or the United States dollar. This initial par is reviewed by the Fund and approved by it. Generally speaking, the par values originally adopted corresponded to the dollar exchange rate previously in use and were accepted by the Fund as an appropriate starting point. Future modifications of initial par exchange rates, under the rules of the Fund, were anticipated as the more permanent postwar pattern of trade became clear.

The ultimate or long-run aim of the Fund has been to adopt par rates of exchange that will enable the countries concerned to restore a tolerable balance of payments after economic reconstruction, currency convertibility, and sound, prosperous economic conditions have been restored in the main trading nations of the world. The Fund quite properly admitted that the choice of such a par exchange rate was quite impossible by mere inspection of the economic conditions of the immediate postwar years. Therefore it adopted the policy of approving original exchange parities so long as they promised not to interfere with expansion of postwar exports. In the long run it expected that modifications of existing parities would be required to avoid the adverse effects of currency overvaluation. The Fund concluded that up to the autumn of 1947, initial parities did not hamper exports. During 1948 and 1949, however, the varying rates of price inflation and deflation threatened to hamper exports to the dollar area countries. The devaluations of September 1949 were made after consultation with the Fund and with its approval, as a means of correcting overvaluations in terms of the dollar.

Changes in exchange rate parities. One of the aims of postwar economic plans is to avoid the necessity of a country's deflating and reducing employment as a means of achieving equilibrium in its balance of payments. In the absence of adequate amounts of international currency reserves, individual countries may now purchase foreign currencies from the Fund to meet temporary adverse balances arising out of current transactions. But should an adverse balance of payments of a *chronic* nature develop, it would indicate that the existing par of exchange is too high or that the currency is "overvalued." In such a case, either the par value of the currency must be reduced if domestic deflation and unemployment are to be avoided, or monetary and fiscal restraint must be applied to "disinflate" the domestic economy. Overvaluation of the currency may arise out of domestic inflation, falling prices abroad, or shifts in the international demand away from a country's exports. In any event, the circumstances might warrant a reduction in par value of the currency.

The rules of the Fund provide for a reduction of parities whenever a "fundamental disequilibrium" develops in a country's balance of payments. This has been interpreted to include the appearance of unemployment of a chronic or persistent character arising from pressure on the balance of payments. Changes in par value may be made only on the request of the member country. In order to avoid the danger of competitive exchange depreciation by countries seeking to undervalue their currencies to promote employment at home by "exporting unemployment," a member must first consult the Fund before changing par values. The Fund has no veto power over changes not exceeding 10 per cent of the initial par values. But the Fund has the right to approve or disapprove of greater changes. Incidentally, whenever the exchange value or parity of a currency is lowered or raised, the gold value of that currency held by the Fund cannot be allowed to change. Therefore appropriate adjustments, up or down as the case may be, are made in the amount of currency in the hands of the Fund.

In spite of the Fund's basic policy of fixed gold parities and single exchange rates, it has been compelled as a matter of expediency to accede to requests to violate such policies. Since September 1950, Canada has abandoned gold parity and has allowed the foreign exchange rate of the Canadian dollar to be established by free market forces. Moreover, a number of member countries have, in one way or another, established multiple exchange rates within their exchange-control systems.

Capital transfers. The International Monetary Fund in itself does not provide protection against flight of capital or heavy unilateral capital transfers that may press heavily on a country's balance of payments. To be sure, the introduction of stable exchanges in itself tends to eliminate speculative capital transfers, which proved so burdensome in the unstable currency days of the early 1920's and the 1930's. But the right to reduce the exchange value of a currency to correct fundamental disequilibrium may encourage the speculative sale of a currency in anticipation of devaluation. It would be disastrous to the Fund, however, if its resources were exposed to drains arising from capital transfers and flight. Hence there is a provision that "a member may not make net use of the Fund's resources to meet a large or sustained outflow of capital, and the Fund may request a member to exercise controls to prevent such use of the resources of the Fund."

The reduction of exchange controls. A fundamental aim of the Fund is to introduce freedom of payments and transfers for current international transactions. Therefore members of the Fund agree to impose no restrictions on international payments on current transactions without the approval of the Fund. Moreover, they agree to refrain from any discriminatory currency arrangements or multiple currency practices except as authorized by the rules or approved by the Fund. In spite of the intention that such practices be reduced, the Fund has found it necessary to approve or acquiesce to their continuance in a number of cases. The Fund recognizes that the reconstruction period has presented difficulties in the balance of payments that justify temporary retention of exchange controls which are undesirable in the long run.

The sale of currencies by the Fund. The sale of currencies by the Fund to meet member countries' temporary needs have been of modest proportions. The postwar requirements, growing out of economic dislocations of the times, were cared for by intergovernmental grants and loans, which we have discussed earlier. Nevertheless, some drawings have been made against the Fund. In 1955 twenty-six of the fifty-eight members of the International Monetary Fund were reported as having purchased currencies from the Fund during the eight years of its existence. Altogether, the total purchases, measured in U.S. dollars, amounted to $1.2 billion. After repayments the net outstanding drawings upon the Fund were $350 million, mainly in U.S. dollars.

The United States assistance program of the postwar period prevented any serious drain upon the dollar supply of the Fund. Consequently, by carefully limiting its sales of currencies to meeting only short-term needs of member countries, the Fund has not been compelled to resort to rationing of scarce currencies.

Currency Convertibility

Free interconvertibility of currencies provides a necessary environment for obtaining the greatest benefit from multilateral trade. Only when such convertibility exists can traders sell freely in one country and buy in another without concern about the transferability of funds. Consequently the problem of restoring free convertibility of currencies is of vital importance.

Two concepts of currency convertibility. To most people currency convertibility means the restoration of the gold standard with the right to convert currency into gold at a fixed price and to export the gold to other countries. Thus, when the Continental members of the EPU talk about the possibility of general convertibility they mean convertibility into gold at a fixed price corresponding to parity exchange rates established by members of the International Monetary Fund. The gradual movement of the EPU in this direction may be seen in the increased proportion of settlements among its members that are made in gold.

However, free gold convertibility is not the only type of convertibility that may be used to promote a return to multilateral trade. For example, the British pound, from September 1931 down to the beginning of World War II, was freely convertible into other currencies in the exchange market. Although sterling was not convertible into gold, its holders were free to sell pounds at any time and at any price in exchange for other currencies. This privilege applied both to foreign owners of pound balances and to the British public at home. This type of convertibility, permitting sale at varying prices in terms of other currencies, eliminates official rates of exchange and exchange controls, and restores free market convertibility at flexible rates. A current example of this form of free market convertibility without gold parity is the Canadian dollar. British preferences also lean heavily in the direction of flexible, non-gold convertibility.

The indivisibility of currency convertibility. We already know the essential meaning of these two forms of convertibility. The first, convertibility into gold at fixed rates, is essentially a restoration of the gold standard. Should one country alone attempt to restore free gold convertibility, on the grounds that its over-all foreign position was in balance, it would find itself committed to pay out gold to foreign holders of its currency but at the same time would be unable to collect its current claims against other countries in gold. The result might well be such loss of gold reserves as to lead to the failure of the convertibility attempt. This possibility is the basis for the position of the Continental members of the EPU that a restoration of gold convertibility must be general and not piecemeal. It lies at the root of their belief that should Britain establish flexible exchange rate convertibility without gold payments, gold payments by the rest of the EPU countries would become impossible.

The preference of the Continental EPU members for fixed gold convertibility arises out of their experiences in the interwar period when the absence of gold convertibility was accompanied by violent exchange depreciation and internal inflation, as was the case in Germany and France in the 1920's, and competitive exchange depreciation that occurred in the depression years of the 1930's. Because these countries prefer gold convertibility and fixed exchange rates over flexible exchange rates, they are deeply opposed to Britain's preference for the latter.

Britain, on the other hand, with its responsibility for the convertibility of the pound for the whole Sterling Area, believes that its gold and dollar reserves are inadequate to enable it to embark upon gold convertibility while reducing discriminatory restrictions on imports from the dollar areas. To make the attempt and fail would constitute a major set-back to the efforts to liberate world trade. Furthermore, Britain is unwilling to abandon its freedom in independent management of its domestic monetary affairs. Such freedom, provided by flexible exchange rates, would be seriously limited by the return to full gold convertibility.

The problem presented by the opposing views on convertibility is a serious one. Should the British position that world trade conditions are not yet sufficiently flexible and sound to allow the restoration of freedom of trade without the protection of flexible exchange rates prove correct, attempts at general gold convertibility might fail, and such failure might jeopardize later attempts when conditions are even more favorable. However, full gold convertibility of the pound, coupled with similar convertibility of other European currencies, would aid in the restoration of London's position as an international money market and increase its ability to attract and hold equilibrating short-term capital that provides an important protection against gold losses. Second, under the rules of the IMF, orderly reductions of gold parities to correct "fundamental disequilibrium" is still possible. This privilege of reducing gold parities to correct for overvaluation of a more fundamental nature is somewhat less than a perfect instrument. It necessarily involves occasional and periodic changes of a substantial nature once "fundamental disequilibrium" is clearly evident. Therefore, when a change in gold parity appears imminent, it becomes difficult to avoid speculative behavior on the part of traders and the general public. For example, should a reduction of the gold parity of the pound appear reasonably certain, British exports would tend to be postponed until the higher value of foreign currencies in terms of the pound becomes a reality. At the same time, British imports would increase sharply in anticipation of the devaluation of the pound. Furthermore, if the exchange market were to be free, in the sense that short-term capital movements were permitted to obtain the benefit of their normal gold-standard *equilibrating* action, expectations of devaluation would set in motion a *speculative* transfer of funds (flight) out of London into nondevaluating currencies. It is not surprising that monetary authorities find themselves in the awkward and unenviable position of stoutly denying all intentions of devaluating the currency up to the moment when such action is actually announced.

In contrast to periodic, abrupt, and disturbing devaluations of the sort permitted under the International Monetary Fund, the gradual changes allowed to take place with flexible exchange rates, without fixed gold parities, operate in such a way as to permit corrections in a country's balance of payments with a minimum of disturbance to trade and the foreign exchange markets. But, as we learned from the British experience in the 1930's, flexible exchange rates require the short-run stabilizing action of some official agency able to absorb the risks of short-run balance-of-payment inequalities.

Is a convertibility compromise possible? It would be most unfortunate if the progress in the direction of freer trade and currency convertibility were checked by the conflict between supporters of fixed gold convertibility and flexible exchange rates convertibility. Is some compromise or some middle ground possible?

One basis of concern about convertibility, regardless of the type, is the questionable adequacy of existing international currency reserves available for meeting convertibility requirements.[10] Pressure on such reserves arises from seasonal, accidental, and cyclical developments. Without adequate supplies of such internationally acceptable currency a country will be unable to maintain convertibility during the period of time required to bring into play appropriate corrective measures. It is understandable that the British should hold that the ready corrective of exchange rate flexibility is more compatible with limited supplies of international currency reserves than is the monetary restraint required under gold convertibility. In any event, access to such reserves should be eased as much as possible if convertibility is to be successful. This might involve an increase in the existing supply of reserves by a general reduction of all gold parities by action through the International Monetary Fund. Objections in the United States to further reduction of the gold content of the dollar appears to be a barrier to such action. Another possibility is an increase in the lending powers of the International Monetary Fund and by the provision for other supplementary sources of credit for countries experiencing short-term deficits.

However, the conflict between the two schools of thought on convertibility runs deeper than the question of adequacy of international currency reserves. On the one side is the desire of the Western European members of the EPU for the protection against inflation and for the advantage of fixed exchange rates associated

---

[10] The gold reserves of the Sterling Area and Western European countries, though about as great as before World War II, are now considerably smaller than prewar reserves, when compared with the increased nominal amounts of international trade. *Midland Bank Review*, London, February 1955, p. 2.

with gold convertibility. On the other hand is the deep-seated fear of the British of becoming involved in deflation and depression originating in the outside world without adequate methods for taking counteraction. If Britain could be confident that the outside world, especially the United States, would successfully resist serious cyclical declines, it might more willingly agree to fixed gold convertibility. On the other hand, could the continental countries be convinced that a "floating pound" of flexible exchange value would be managed in such a way as to avoid both short-run cyclical and long-run undervaluation, they might be reconciled to flexible pound convertibility while maintaining their own fixed gold convertibility. This would require that the British Equalization Account scrupulously avoid temptation to fatten its international currency reserves of gold and dollars at the expense of its European neighbors. Regardless of the manner of its accomplishment a satisfactory solution to this difficult problem is urgently needed.

Convertibility and international capital movements. Yet another thorny problem arises in respect to currency convertibility: Shall the privilege of free market convertibility be extended to all currency holders or shall it be limited only to those needing foreign exchange to settle the current account items in the country's balance of payments? If complete convertibility is adopted, the residents of a given country would be free to purchase foreign exchange not only to pay for current imports but also to purchase securities and other capital assets abroad. Likewise foreign holders of funds would be permitted freely to withdraw such funds by selling drafts against them in the foreign exchange market.

On the other hand, convertibility might be limited merely to current account transactions. In such a case, residents of a country could freely purchase foreign exchange to pay for current commodity and service imports but could not purchase foreign securities and other assets for foreign investment (in other words, could not lend or otherwise export capital to foreign countries) without special permission of some agency concerned with avoiding possible unstabilizing effects of capital exports. Similarly, foreign holders of money claims against this country could not draw against these claims without special permission. In other words, foreign-owned balances would be blocked.

One may readily understand the reluctance to permit free capital exports by a country whose international currency reserves are precariously small. Especially is there danger in the withdrawal of foreign-owned balances that were previously blocked. It is likely, therefore, that the approach to convertibility will often be cautious and that in many cases it will be limited at first to transactions on current account. However, unless convertibility is extended to capital transactions as well, many of the advantages of convertible currencies are lost. Equilibrating short-term capital movements become difficult if not impossible. Long-term capital movements, so necessary if the world economy is to thrive and expand, are stifled by the threat of blocked funds. Consequently the benefits of convertibility will not be fully realized until it includes freedom to transfer capital funds as well as funds needed for current purposes. Therefore it will be necessary to devise some satisfactory way to minimize the threat of capital flight which has at times proved so unstabilizing. Under the gold standard type of convertibility such protection requires (1) the careful maintenance of conditions conducive to the avoidance of basic disequilibrium in the balance of payments; and (2) an adequate supply of available international currency reserves. Under inconvertible paper currencies with flexible exchange rates there is required a foreign exchange trading agency similar to the British Exchange Equalization Account of the 1930's, sufficiently powerful to offset and check speculative movements before they get out of control.

Questions for Study

1. Immediately after the end of World War II in 1945, attempts to expand the value of British and Western European exports by currency devaluation would doubtless have been difficult if not impossible. Why was this so? Why, by 1949, was devaluation needed?

2. In case the demand for a country's exports were inelastic, it appears impossible to expand the value of total exports by lowering their prices either by devaluation or by deflation. Why is this so? Is there reason to think that the U. S. demand for British and Western European exports is elastic?

3. If a country's imports are mainly food and raw materials:
   a) What would you expect to be the nature of its demand for such imports?
   b) Might the elasticity of demand be greater for such imports from a particular country than from the world in general?

    c) Why is it useless to devalue a currency to improve its balance-of-payments position and then allow wage increases to match the resulting increase in the cost of living?

4. Devaluation of a country's currency in order to cheapen its exports tends to worsen the terms of trade for that country. Why?

5. Why have the British sometimes felt that devaluation of the pound to increase exports to the U. S. was less advantageous than bilateral trade with countries showing slower technological progress?

6. The $53 billion of U. S. credits and grants made since 1945 have made possible the purchase of that amount of goods by other countries without having to pay for them with current exports.

    a) Should such aid be terminated by Congress, would we find the receivers of this aid in a better balance-of-payments position than they were before the assistance was given?

    b) What evidence is there that the assistance program was successful?

7. What is the primary purpose of the International Bank? How does one account for the modest size of its operations?

8. What are international currency reserves? Why does their scarcity tend to drive a country into bilateral trading?

9. How has the European Payments Union contributed to the development of multilateral trade and currency convertibility?

10. What privileges go with membership in the International Monetary Fund? What is the quota assigned to each member? Why is it important?

11. On what occasions may a member of the IMF (a) apply for the "purchase" of a foreign currency? (b) apply for the privilege of changing its exchange parity?

12. Currency convertibility may mean (1) a return to gold with fixed exchange rates; or (2) the free purchase and sale of currencies in the foreign exchange markets at varying prices.

    a) In what way do these two differ?

    b) Why would gold convertibility by some countries be incompatible with fluctuating exchange rate convertibility by others?

13. Why does the IMF privilege of reducing gold parity of a currency to correct a fundamental disequilibrium in the balance of payments seem to invite exchange speculation?

14. Currency convertibility might be limited only to current account. What would this involve? Why would it serve but a limited purpose?

15. What steps would be needed to avoid capital flight in case full convertibility should be adopted?

Independent Currencies vs. International Monetary Standards

The restoration of unrestricted multilateral trade in the present-day world requires currency convertibility. Such convertibility, as we already know, requires that the holders of a given currency shall be free to exchange it for other currencies by selling it in the foreign exchange market. Furthermore, currency convertibility may be associated with a restoration of some form of gold standard, with the right to buy and sell gold at a fixed price in terms of the various currencies, and with the right freely to import and export gold. Or, convertibility may merely involve the right to sell a currency in the foreign exchange markets for whatever price it may bring without the stabilizing influence of gold convertibility. In other words, currency convertibility may involve either a restoration of a world gold standard or a restoration of free exchange markets with fluctuating rates of exchange. Each type of convertibility has some advantages and some disadvantages. In this chapter we shall consider the relative merits of each.

It is the modern view that central governments have a duty to provide general economic and price level stability and such full employment conditions as are conducive to economic growth. Monetary and fiscal policy, the tools available for government use, are closely associated with control over the supply and the spending of money. Therefore there is strong support for the view that money should be the servant of government economic policy rather than the master, and that the maintenance of conditions suited for monetary management should be of primary concern.

The incompatibility of monetary management with an international gold standard. We already know how the international gold standard works by inducing price changes in one country that parallel those in the outside world. This occurs through the influence of fixed exchange rates on the prices of internationally traded goods and through the effect of spontaneous forces and gold movements. Any attempt by a single country to maintain a price level either above or below that ruling in the outside world tends to be defeated by the inexorable operation of the international gold standard. Consequently, a single country that attempts to pursue a policy of price level and general economic stabilization within the framework of the international gold standard is likely to find its efforts frustrated.

The case for fixed exchange rates provided by the international gold standard. The nineteenth century saw the flowering of modern *laissez faire* capitalism. The foundations of this development were to be found in a tremendous growth of international trade accompanied by the rapid expansion of international lending. The whole structure was tied together and articulated by a common international standard of value, namely gold.

There can be no doubt of the contribution to that development made by the fixed exchange rates provided by the free convertibility of currencies into gold. But fixed or rigid exchange rates alone are not enough. Our experience with the elaborate mechanism of trade restraints, exchange rationing, and other exchange controls indicates clearly that exchange-rate stability maintained by such controls is an entirely inadequate substitute for stable rates based upon free gold convertibility.

The advantage of rigid exchange rates fixed by gold convertibility had their price. Price levels throughout the world had to move together in harmony. The general world movement of prices, to which the price level of individual countries had to conform, was determined in the short run by cyclical developments in different parts of the world economy. In the long run it reflected the relation of changes in the supply of monetary gold to changes in the world's monetary requirements. Therefore, gold, though working well as an international standard at least part of the time, was subject to two serious defects. First, it was exposed to long, sweeping changes in world price levels arising from a failure of gold to expand at a rate corresponding to monetary requirements. Second, the gold standard not only failed to give protection against cyclical price fluctuations but in some instances it tended to accentuate them. This was especially true in periods of acute deflation, when a general loss of credit confidence led to money panics and forced credit liquidation. The results of such a liquidating movement were seen in the collapse of the gold standard after 1929.

The Case for Monetary Nationalism

The case for monetary nationalism (or independent paper currencies) rests primarily upon the belief that unemployment and cyclical fluctuations of the modern business world can be satisfactorily met only by a controlled and independent currency system. The gold standard, as is well known, requires that prices within the individual countries adjust themselves to harmonize with world prices. This result requires reasonable flexibility of the whole internal price structure if the strains and disturbances associated with wide dispersion of individual price movements are to be avoided. The more readily the internal price structure adjusts itself to necessary changes, the greater the success of an international monetary standard such as gold. But there is reason to believe that prices may not be sufficiently flexible in the modern economic world to make the international gold standard tolerable. To support this view, one may refer to the experiences of the decade that began in 1929, when in fact the gold standard suffered a complete collapse. In addition, there is evidence tending to show that price rigidity is increasing.

The question of increased rigidity of prices. Several reasons may be cited for believing that the price structure of the modern world is becoming more rigid. First, there is undeniably a marked trend toward increased governmental interference in economic affairs. This trend takes the form both of price-fixing and of an expansion of direct governmental action in economic fields. At best, prices controlled by the government are but tardily adjusted to general price movements. Farm price support policies, for example, tend to prevent downward revision of prices in the agricultural sector. Moreover, the expansion of the scope of government services furnished to the public tends to saddle upon the business community a rigid tax burden that cannot be adjusted to commodity price changes.

Second, the growing power of unions, with their emphasis upon the maintenance of existing wage rates in the face of falling prices, adds a powerful influence to other forces leading to rigidity of costs. When such rates are supported by unemployment benefits paid by the government, the tendency toward rigidity is further strengthened.

Third, in modern economic society, large-scale business enterprise is the inevitable result of modern technology. The growth of large-scale business units reduces the potential number of competitors operating within any given market, and encourages the formation of price-fixing agreements and the adoption of other methods of avoiding competition. In industries dominated by a few large-scale firms, a decline in demand is likely to be met with a fall of output rather than by a lowering of prices. "Administered" prices, in which the seller fixes his price and sells what he can at that price, are common both in fields dominated by large firms and among all products bearing a brand or other distinguishing mark. Although "administered" prices do fluctuate, they tend to move more slowly and through a narrower range than do prices fixed in markets where numerous traders deal in standardized, non-differentiated goods.

Independent currencies and the influence of foreign cyclical movements. One important advantage claimed for the use of independent currencies is that it permits the freeing of the domestic economy from cyclical price movements originating abroad. Is there good reason to believe that this assumption is true? In answering this question, one must take into account the fact that an individual nation is by no means a closed economy dealing only with itself. Instead, all nations must deal with others, and are parts of the larger world economy. Regardless of whether or not a country adopts an independent currency with flexible exchanges, a depression abroad will adversely affect the export market. Conversely, boom conditions abroad stimulate exports and domestic business. Monetary management, with or without an independent currency system, can prevent a foreign-generated boom from spreading to the domestic economy. It is unlikely, however, that it can prevent entirely the disturbing consequences arising from a severe depression abroad. Nevertheless, an independent domestic currency with flexible exchange rates provides a country confronted by world depression with two major advantages.

First, granting that foreign depression will reduce the demand for a country's exports and thus tend to reduce employment, flexible exchange rates permit the use of depreciation in the exchange value of the domestic currency in order to avoid the deflation of domestic prices to match falling prices abroad. This benefit is of especial importance in countries where domestic trade is closely tied to imports and exports. This opportunity to avoid domestic price deflation provides a pleasant contrast to the results of gold-standard fixed exchange rates which tie together the movements of domestic and foreign prices of internationally traded commodities. The domestic economy may therefore be spared the depressing effects of falling prices generated by foreign depressions.

Second, an independent currency not tied to gold permits a country to take positive steps to promote domestic expansion to relieve the unemployment and to fill the gaps left by a decline of exports caused by depression abroad. This action can be taken without fear that an adverse trade balance may arise and cause serious gold losses. Such an opportunity to resist depressions of foreign origin is often denied the individual country under the international gold standard. Here we find a most potent argument in favor of convertibility with flexible exchange rates as opposed to gold standard convertibility.

Some Objections to Independent Currencies

The inflationary bias of independent currencies. Stressing cost and wage rigidities as the essential reason for the need for an independent currency, the advocates of such a currency are primarily concerned with the desirability of avoiding the depressing effects of price deflation. Because of this, the pursuit of a national policy of stabilization may lead to the development of an inflationary movement in domestic prices.

The source of inflationary bias in independent currencies is not hard to see. Monetary authorities, charged with the responsibility for control of the money supply, cannot pursue a policy opposed to or in conflict with that of the government. For monetary authorities —normally central banks—by their very nature must be subservient to the governments that establish them, and inevitably must support rather than hinder the established policies of their creators. But the pressures upon government, whether for defense expenditures or for assistance to special groups, tend to increase government expenditures and lead to deficit financing. Furthermore, in the understandable concern for maintenance of labor peace and full employment, governments sometimes encourage wage settlements that involve increases unwarranted by the growth in productivity. These increases tend to set off inflationary spirals. Confronted by inflationary policies and practices of government, the central bank is handicapped in the adoption of a policy of restraint based upon the principle that resistance to inflation is more important than national defense and expanding employment.[1] Especially is this true when more compelling reasons for restraint do not exist in the form of a responsibility to maintain gold-standard or fixed-exchange-rate convertibility.

Independent currencies and long-term lending. Perhaps the gravest criticism of independent currencies with flexible exchange rates concerns their effect upon international lending and invest-ment. Both long- and short-term capital movements are affected by the abandonment of the gold standard anchor for the world's cur-rencies. Fixed exchange rates without convertibility create risks of loss of earnings on foreign investments because of difficulties in transfer. Independent currencies that are convertible freely in

---

[1] This problem is well put by D. H. Robertson when he says, "We must remem-ber the enormous impetus to which any banking system is subject both from within and without, towards increasing continually the volume of its loans, and the formidable difficulty of so regulating the supply of money as really to meet the legitimate needs of trade. We must remember, too, the pressure exerted upon Governments in the name of the consumer to provide this and that—coal or railway-transport or house-room—by some means or other below its economic cost. It is not surprising if both bankers and Governments in their more respon-sible moments desire to have some charm more potent than a mere metaphysical index-number both to elevate before the people and to contemplate in the privacy of their own cells." *Money*, New York, Pitman Publishing Corporation, 1948, p. 147, quoted with permission of the publisher.

unregulated foreign exchange markets inevitably involve flexible and fluctuating exchange rates. When the hazards of uncertainties connected with the transfer of earnings and unstable exchange rates are added to the ordinary risks of foreign long-term lending, it may well be that such lending will be sharply curtailed. If so, this is a serious basis for criticism of independent standards. Modern capitalism has reached its high level of effectiveness through international division of labor supported by generous movements of capital from the older areas to newer and undeveloped areas. The stagnation in world economic life during the 1930's was undoubtedly made worse by the drying up of international lending. The absence of an international monetary standard, such as gold, provides an added barrier to such lending.

Advocates of independent currencies do not always admit the validity of our assumption that long-term lending must necessarily languish in the absence of an international gold standard. They see as causes of the decline in foreign investment of the 1930's such things as the depression itself, trade barriers, former losses on foreign loans, and, to a lesser extent, fear of fluctuating currencies. Foreign loans are customarily expressed in terms of the lender's currency. Since this is so, it matters little to the purchaser of foreign securities of this type whether or not the lending country or the borrowing country is using an independent currency so long as general convertibility is available. The lender can rest content in the promise that he will be repaid in his own currency. The borrower, though exposed to the danger of fluctuating exchange rates, still need not be concerned if exchange rates on the lending country rise, if the cause is a rise in prices in his own country; for the rise in prices will increase the borrower's income along with the rise in the burden of servicing his foreign loans. In any event, foreign investment need not take the form of fixed income-bearing securities. Investment in foreign stocks and property is becoming increasingly common. On such investments there seems to be no reason to expect prohibitive hazards arising out of fluctuating exchange rates.

Independent currencies and seasonal factors. International trade is not something that moves smoothly and regularly, with a constant balance between imports and exports. Instead, it is irregular in nature, conforming to seasonal forces that influence both demand and supply. Consequently, there is no daily, weekly, or even monthly balance between imports and export items. Under the gold standard it is sufficient for trade and long-term capital items entering the balance of payments to be equalized over a fairly long period of time. This is true because bankers, protected by the gold shipping points in the foreign exchange markets, readily allow seasonal excess claims to accumulate in foreign money markets— that is, they "export" short-term capital against a later date when the demand for foreign exchange exceeds the supply.

Independent currencies, with freely fluctuating exchange rates, discourage bankers' accumulations of foreign exchange so that the gold standard "equilibrating" short-term capital movements will not readily occur. Hence, some form of stabilization fund must be provided in order to avoid widely fluctuating exchange rates from season to season.

Domestic Stabilization Under an International Standard

The advocates of monetary nationalism believe that an independent currency is a prerequisite to successful monetary management. This opinion is based on the belief that international monetary stabilization is impossible, and that independent action by one country alone requires the freedom that can be provided only by an independent currency. Before accepting this claim at full face value, one must inquire more fully into the possibilities of (1) domestic control while operating within an international monetary system; and (2) international cooperation.

Secular price trends and domestic stabilization. Any attempt under the gold standard, or other international currency system, to regulate the price level of a single country so that it will run counter to the secular trend of world prices must sooner or later fail. If world prices are rising, stable domestic prices would eventually tend to impose an intolerable supply of gold upon the domestic banking system. On the other hand, if world prices are falling, stable domestic prices must sooner or later cause such a loss of gold, or other international currency reserves, by the domestic banking system that it will require the abandonment of the standard. But this is not of such vital importance as might appear at first thought, for the primary problem of stabilization has to do with relatively short-run cyclical price movements.

**Domestic cyclical stablization and an international mone-
tary standard such as gold.** Contrary to the common assumption
of those advocating an independent currency system, a considerable
measure of control over cyclical fluctuations remains in a domestic
monetary authority in spite of an adherence to an international
monetary system. First, booms that originate either within or without a country can be as effectively counteracted under the gold
standard as on inconvertible paper. Similarly, recessions originating at home can be met with the full battery of monetary weapons
regardless of whether gold or paper standards are in use. But,
one may ask, what becomes of stabilizing efforts when depressions
develop in the outside world? At such a time, a decline in domestic
prices and business activity will be inevitable under the gold standard. The degree to which the domestic economy will suffer depends,
of course, upon the relative importance of foreign trade. But even
under the gold standard, monetary authorities are not entirely helpless in the face of world-wide depression. Monetary and fiscal policy
can be used to stimulate the domestic economy. Inconvertible paper
would, of course, offer two advantages over gold in this connection.
First, it offers the rather questionable opportunity to stimulate exports by resort to exchange depreciation. Second, it would avoid
the deflationary consequences of a loss of gold arising from an excess
of imports due to a revival of business and a rise in domestic prices.
But gold losses due to business revival need not be serious, for rising
security prices and improved profit prospects at home will attract
rather than repel foreign investments. Even though some gold losses
do occur, they need not prove detrimental to recovery so long as
they do not exceed the power of the central bank to meet them out
of excess reserves. For this reason, a proper distribution of the
world's gold reserves is a desirable thing if cyclical stabilization is
to be sought. One can hardly concur with the statement that cyclical
stabilization by monetary means is entirely impossible under an
international standard. Nevertheless, the advantage in this regard
clearly rests with inconvertible paper.

Monetary Management Through International Cooperation

Some difficulties of international cooperation. The case for
independent currencies rests largely upon the proposition that inter-

national cooperation is unable to produce a satisfactory international currency. Some reasons for lack of faith in such cooperation are:

1. Nationalism presents a powerful barrier to anything like effective cooperation among nations on matters of monetary policy Jealousy, fear that the interests of foreign countries do not coincide with one's own, and popular distrust of "foreign theories," all complicate the problem of cooperation.

2. Even if an international monetary agreement could be reached, the gold standard itself is not entirely amenable to management. Gold output rises and falls without regard to monetary requirements. Hoarding and industrial demands for gold cannot be controlled.

3. Genuine differences in the economic situation in the several countries may require different monetary policies in order to achieve full employment and stability in each. An example of this is the problem raised in respect to countries that enjoy different rates of economic progress. A monetary policy suited to a country in which economic efficiency is advancing rapidly might be objectionable in a country in which improvements are appearing more slowly.

Even though all of these objections are serious ones, they do not rule out entirely the possibility of international monetary cooperation. Nor should the fact that current circumstances make the prospects of such cooperation at the moment somewhat dim prevent serious consideration of the problem. If any genuine improvement in economic affairs is to be accomplished through rational methods, long-run aims cannot be dismissed merely because they are momentarily impracticable. Little of genuine value is likely to come out of temporization on the basis of short-run situations alone.

International cooperation to promote stable currency relationships. Whether difficult or not, some degree of international cooperation to promote more stable relations among currencies is urgently needed. This is especially true as the world moves in the direction of general currency convertibility. A first step might well involve agreements among important trading nations to resist economic instability within their own boundaries, and to follow a program designed to promote long-run growth. If such a cooperative program were followed the prospects for successful currency convertibility would be greatly improved. This would be true whether convertibility takes the form of flexible rates in free markets or of fixed-exchange-rate convertibility into gold. In either event relative stability of prices and economic activity would be of great benefit. Fluctuations of flexible free-market exchange rates could then be readily held within tolerable limits. Or, if gold convertibility were established, price and economic stability would provide freedom from violent balance-of-payment disturbances that have destroyed the gold standard in the past. International cooperation in the use of monetary and fiscal policy for economic stabilization might come about without formal agreement but by mere tacit understanding, or even by independent actions in pursuit of desired and well-recognized policy goals.

Increasing the supply of available international currency reserves. Successful convertibility of currencies is dependent upon an adequate supply of international currency reserves out of which to meet adverse balances when they arise. The purpose of the establishment of the International Monetary Fund was in part to provide a pool of currencies upon which debtor member countries might call to meet temporary adverse balances without exhausting their gold and other reserves. The adequacy of this source of funds would be enhanced if the Fund itself were allowed to act as a kind of central bank for central banks, with the privilege of creating obligations of its own that might be lent, under careful restriction, to debtor countries. Such a privilege would be especially valuable to raw material countries that experience cyclical difficulties with their balance of payments.

Yet another method of increasing the available supply of international currency might involve a general reduction in the gold parities of currencies through action within the International Monetary Fund. Such reduction, without disturbing the inter-currency parities, would expand the nominal amount of available gold reserves.

Changing exchange rate parity to correct fundamental disequilibrium. As we already learned, under the International Monetary Fund individual countries may obtain permission to reduce (or increase) the par value of their currencies in order to correct for fundamental disequilibrium in their balance-of-payments position. This privilege permits a country that undertakes to maintain stable exchange rates, such as those arising from the gold standard, to correct an overvaluation should it threaten to impose deflation, depression, and an undue loss of international reserves. This clearly improves the possibility of the successful adoption of a fixed-exchange-rate type of convertibility for world currencies.

Conclusion. With the approach of the time when free foreign exchange markets may be restored, the world is again confronted with the choice between independent currencies freely convertible into each other at fluctuating exchange rates, and currencies tied together through fixed gold convertibility. Each type, as we have seen, has its advantages. The independent fluctuating-exchange-rate type of currency is clearly more subject to internal monetary management. However, its very flexibility at home creates difficulties in dealing with foreign countries. On the other hand, gold convertibility provides a very useful stability of foreign exchange rates as well as an automatic check or limit to monetary expansion. The latter may be useful as a means of warding off inflationary political pressures that endanger internal management. We have seen that gold convertibility is made more tolerable by the existence of the International Monetary Fund and the privilege of changes in gold parities to correct for fundamental disequilibrium.

Questions for Study

1. What are the two alternate types of currency convertibility?

2. In the choice between independent currencies and an international standard such as gold, the concern over monetary management must play an important part. Why is this so?

3. Why does the international gold standard create serious difficulties for monetary management?

4. What are the main advantages of the international gold standard from the standpoint of (a) convenience in foreign trade? (b) the possibility of inflation arising out of political pressures and the desire to maintain full employment? What price is exacted for the benefits of the gold standard?

5. Why is an independent paper currency with flexible exchange rates preferable from the standpoint of (a) domestic monetary management in the pursuit of price level and economic stability? (b) corrections for an adverse balance of payments?

6. Why is it thought that present-day prices are more rigid than in earlier times? To the extent that the increased rigidity is real, how does this affect the case for gold vs. national independent currencies?

7. Can the use of an independent paper currency prevent the decline in business activity abroad from adversely affecting domestic business? Why, then, does an independent paper currency provide a better chance for a successful fight against domestic deflation and unemployment?

8. Why are independent currencies said to have an inflationary bias? Does this mean that they are inevitably inflationary?

9. Independent currencies are criticized as interfering with international lending. Why is this so? How is this objection met by those who advocate such currencies? Does the position of Canada as a heavy capital importer provide an answer?

10. What do you think of the possibility, under the gold standard, of resisting (a) inflation? (b) deflation originating abroad?

11. If effective international cooperation in the area of monetary policy could be achieved, how would the case for gold be affected?

12. How have the following developments affected the case for fixed-exchange-rate convertibility?

    a) The establishment of the International Monetary Fund with its lending powers.

    b) The provision for changing gold parities to correct fundamental disequilibrium.

    c) The world-wide policy of promoting full employment and economic growth.

Index

DATE DUE

MAY 1 '64	NOV 29 '67		
MAY 15 '64	DEC 13 '67		
MAY 15 '64	JAN 3 '68		
DEC 7 '64	JAN 18 '68		
JAN 4 '65	NOV 16 '70		
APR 15 '65	NOV 30 '70		
MAY 4 '65	MAY 6 '71		
DEC 3 '65	NOV 18 '71		
DEC 17 '65			
JAN 14 '66			
MAY 23 '66			
JUL 12 '66			
DEC 15 '66			
JAN 3 '67			
APR 3 '67			
APR 19 '67			
MAY 18 '67			
MAY 23 '67			
GAYLORD			PRINTED IN U.S.A.